GERMANY, TURKEY, AND ZIONISM
1897—1918

GERMANY, TURKEY, AND ZIONISM

1897—1918

ISAIAH FRIEDMAN

OXFORD
AT THE CLARENDON PRESS
1977

Oxford University Press, Walton Street, Oxford OX2 6DP

OXFORD LONDON GLASGOW
NEW YORK TORONTO MELBOURNE WELLINGTON
IBADAN NAIROBI DAR ES SALAAM LUSAKA CAPE TOWN
KUALA LUMPUR SINGAPORE JAKARTA HONG KONG TOKYO
DELHI BOMBAY CALCUTTA MADRAS KARACHI

© *Oxford University Press 1977*

Published with the assistance of the Alexander Kohut Memorial Foundation of the American Academy for Jewish Research

British Library Cataloguing in Publication Data
Friedman, Isaiah
    Germany, Turkey, and Zionism, 1897–1918
    1. Jews in Palestine   2. Zionism—Germany
    3. Germany—Foreign relations—1888–1918
    I. Title
    956.94 004 924
    ISBN 0–19–822528–8

*Printed in Great Britain
at the University Press, Oxford
by Vivian Ridler
Printer to the University*

12-04-78

TO
BARBARA AND JONAH

Preface

THIS work is an expansion of my doctoral dissertation, 'Germany and Zionism, 1897–1917', presented to the University of London in 1964. Although urged to publish it in its original form, I felt, rightly or wrongly, that not until I had exhausted all the material available should the work appear in print. My ambition was to present a comprehensive and definitive study, but I was not aware of the price I would have to pay. The difficulty was compounded further when, in the course of writing, I became involved in another study which subsequently appeared under the title *The Question of Palestine, 1914–1918: British–Jewish–Arab Relations* (London, New York, 1973). Thus for a number of years I was pregnant with twins, unable to forecast which of the two would be born first, if at all. According to the rules, *Germany, Turkey, and Zionism* should have been the first-born, but *The Question of Palestine* usurped the right of primogeniture. The reception accorded it by scholars and critics in all parts of the world reassured me that the child did not come into the world unwanted, but to all those who were eagerly awaiting the appearance of *Germany, Turkey, and Zionism* I owe an apology.

The two books are complementary. To appreciate the phenomenal rise of Zionism as a factor on the international scene during the First World War, one should study simultaneously the political processes taking place on both sides of the fence. It was the competition of the belligerent powers to win the goodwill of world Jewry that put Zionism on the map. Inevitably a comparative study invites a reassessment of accepted views and stereotyped notions. Heretofore the spotlight in history books was directed on to the British Zionists, and on Weizmann and Sokolow in particular. Having studied the archival material, I felt that a correction of this imbalance was long overdue and that the German Zionists deserved to be rescued from the obscurity into which they had fallen. Had it not been for their skilful diplomacy and persistent efforts in rallying the support of the American, but primarily of the German, Government, the Yishuv would not have survived the war. In a *judenrein* Palestine the Balfour Declaration would have been of little consequence.

That the Germans should have emerged as the saviours of the Jews and the Zionists' chief protectors may startle the reader as it startled me. Yet the frequency of communications—literally tens of thousands of dispatches and cables were exchanged between Berlin, Constantinople, and Jerusalem—is sufficient proof that this was no casual aspect of German policy. The German Government had a stake in the Yishuv's survival. Propaganda apart, they discovered in Zionism an instrument for the solution of the Jewish problem in Eastern Europe in the aftermath of the war, and a means to advance their own interests in the Orient.

When writing *The Question of Palestine* I had the benefit of Leonard Stein's masterful *The Balfour Declaration*, though the documents I used were new and my conclusions different. But with *Germany, Turkey, and Zionism* I had no similar advantage. I had no predecessors and the material on which I was working was virgin soil for research. It was an exacting and time-consuming task to read well over 20,000 microfilmed frames, but many fine gems were discovered. The official German records, when collated and corroborated with documents from the Zionist archives as well as with contemporary diaries and memoirs, offered a wealth of data, with the help of which it was possible to construct a comprehensive story. Among the published sources I am particularly indebted to Richard Lichtheim's memoirs *She'ar Yashuv* (Tel Aviv, 1953) in Hebrew, and *Rückkehr* (Stuttgart, 1970) in German. Verification and comparison with the German and Zionist documents proved them to be most accurate. The numerous original letters reproduced there add particular weight to Lichtheim's book. The same qualities of reliability characterize the Herzl *Diaries*. Their spontaneous nature, compelling frankness, and the fact that Herzl had no opportunity to re-edit or correct them substantiate our credence.

I have limited myself specifically to the diplomatic history of German–Zionist relations in the given period and have brought other Powers into the picture only when I thought it was necessary. Turkey figures prominently in my book and this was why I finally decided to mention her in the title. I regret that I was unable to study the Ottoman archives, an omission for which, I hope, the readers will forgive me. It would have made the book too long and postponed its publication *ad infinitum*. The Ottoman documents require a special study which, I understand, is currently being carried out by a scholar at the Hebrew University, Jerusalem.

In the method of handling the material I have followed the well-trodden path of other scholars, especially of my distinguished teachers at the London School of Economics. The documents have been meticulously tested, collated, corroborated, and only then was the whole body of evidence integrated and narrated. I had no preconceived opinions. My approach was pragmatic and my views were formed in the course of the study; facts alone determined my conclusions. Whenever there was no conflicting evidence I considered it more appropriate to pass judgement, rather than to remain non-committal. I do not claim infallibility, and the reader is at liberty to accept or ignore my opinions, but the last thing of which I can be accused is omission or conscious suppression of any data which do not fit into my thesis or seem to me unpalatable. With the horrors of the holocaust under the Nazi regime still fresh in our minds, it is practically impossible for our generation to approach any subject dealing with German–Jewish relations with the required composure and detachment. But passions were never a good guide in historiography. As a humble student of history I acknowledge the wisdom of my Alma Mater's motto: *Rerum Cognoscere Causas.*

Acknowledgements

ONE of the happiest moments for an author comes when he can thank publicly all those who have helped to make possible his final achievement. I should like to express my gratitude to my former supervisor, Professor Elie Kedourie, Professor of Politics at the London School of Economics and Political Science, for his scholarly advice and criticism. I am also deeply indebted to Professor W. N. Medlicott, M.A., D.Litt., F.R.Hist.S., Emeritus Stevenson Professor of International History at the London School of Economics, and to his successor, Professor James Joll, who during and after my post-graduate studies at the School gave unstintingly of their time and knowledge whenever I turned to them for advice.

I am very fortunate to have the goodwill of Professor Sir Isaiah Berlin, O.M., President of Wolfson College, Oxford. His interest in my welfare and faith in my work have been a constant source of encouragement at difficult times and have left an indelible impression on me.

It would be unjust here not to pay tribute to my first supervisor at the L.S.E., the late Dr. W. W. Gottlieb, whose stimulating instruction remained vivid in my memory. No less lamentable to me was the death of Richard Lichtheim, the only living authority in German Zionism and German–Zionist relations of this period. He read and criticized the first draft of my earlier chapters when my research was still an adventure into the unknown. Correspondence with him was as illuminating as it was instructive. I missed him greatly in the later stages of my study.

I had also many enlightening discussions with Dr. Robert Weltsch, at that time Director of the Leo Baeck Institute, London, who gave me generously of his time and offered many vital insights. I felt privileged that personalities like Dr. Nahum Goldmann, President of the World Jewish Congress, Dr. S. Levenberg, Representative of the Jewish Agency for Israel in London, the late Moshe Sharett, then Chairman of the Jewish Agency, formerly Prime Minister and Foreign Minister of the State of Israel, Viscount Edwin Samuel, and Ambassador Max Nurock showed interest in my work. For all their help I should like to express my warm thanks. Nor can I omit to mention Mrs. Joyce Maxwell and the late Mrs. C. A. Marks, whose assistance I valued.

I should like to record my indebtedness to the staff of many libraries and archives who have been so courteous and helpful. I am particularly grateful to Dr. Michael Heymann, Director of the Central Zionist Archives in Jerusalem, to the late Dr. Johannes Ullrich, Director of the Politisches Archiv of the Auswärtiges Amt, Bonn, and to his successor Dr. Weinandy; to Dr. Wilhelm Momsen, Director of the Bundesarchiv, Koblenz; to Dr. Enders of the Deutsches Zentralarchiv, Potsdam, and to Dr. Richard Blaas, Director of the Österreichisches Staatsarchiv in Vienna. The Public Record Office, London, the British Museum, London University Library, the Library of the London School of Economics and Political Science, the Institute of Historical Research, the Wiener Library, the Bayerische Staatsbibliothek in Munich, and the Jewish National and University Library in Jerusalem—all gave me ready access to the materials at their disposal.

Financial difficulties retarded greatly the completion of this book. Therefore, I gladly acknowledge grants from the Memorial Foundation for Jewish Culture and the Leo Baeck Institute, London. It was, however, primarily the generous Fellowship grants from the Deutsche Forschungsgemeinschaft, Bonn, that enabled me to expand on my doctoral dissertation and bring the book to its present form. To Professor Walter Laqueur and to the Institute of Contemporary History and Wiener Library, through which the D.F. funds were channelled and administered, I owe a great debt of gratitude. A grant from the Lucius Littauer Foundation, New York, was very helpful in the final stages of my work. To Mr. Harry Starr, the Foundation's Chairman, and to the Members of the Board, I am deeply beholden. Purchase of microfilms when preparing my doctoral dissertation was made possible through grants from the Central Research Fund at the University of London.

My debt to my wife remains the greatest of all. The countless pages she typed, the encouragement and impetus she provided at difficult times—these have been the labours of love. Our son, too, suffered from my attachement to this work; like my wife, he showed sympathetic understanding during the long hours I remained locked in my study. I have the greatest pleasure in dedicating this book to them.

Contents

Abbreviations

A.A.	Auswärtiges Amt
A.A.A.	*Auswärtiges Amt Akten*
B.C.	*The British Consulate in Jerusalem in relation to the Jews of Palestine, 1838–1914.* Documents ed. by A. M. Hyamson (London, 1941), 2 vols.
C.Z.A.	Central Zionist Archives, Jerusalem
D.Z.	Deutsches Zentralarchiv, Potsdam, East Germany
E.A.C.	Engeres Aktions-Comitee
E.G.	*Europa Generalia (A.A.A.)*
F.O.	Foreign Office
F.R.U.S.	*Papers relating to the Foreign Relations of the United States*
G.A.C.	Grosses Aktions-Comitee
I.C.A.	Jewish Colonization Association
J.N.F.	Jewish National Fund
K.f.d.O.	Komitee für den Osten
N.E.	*Nachlass Eulenburg*
P.E.C.	Provisional Executive Committee for General Zionist Affairs (New York)
P.R.O.	Public Record Office, London
S.T.H.	*Sefer Toldoth ha-Hagana* [*History of Self-Defence*] ed. Ben-Zion Dinur (Tel Aviv, 1955)
V.J.O.D.	Vereinigung jüdischer Organisationen Deutschlands zur Wahrung der Rechte der Juden des Osten
Wk.	*Weltkrieg*
W.O.	War Office

PART I

The Background
1517–1897

1

The Birth of Zionism
in Germany

HELMUTH VON MOLTKE was the first German to recognize the importance of Palestine for German interests. During his extensive travels as a young officer in the East in the 1840s he deplored the complete absence of German influence in Palestine and suggested that the control 'ought to be handed over to a sovereign prince of the German nation and of genuine tolerance'. Although not a maritime power, Germany had the advantage of commanding the shortest commercial route to the East via the Danube and the Austrian ports of the Adriatic. She should therefore 'seize the opportunity of extending her civilization . . . energy and industry . . . beyond the German frontier'. Palestine was the gateway to the East. Situated on the direct route of communication between India and Europe, its ports and highways, Moltke predicted, 'would be filled with the treasures of the two continents', while, strategically, it would be 'a wall of protection for Syria against Egypt . . . if the latter should be governed by any hereditary dynasty, other than Ottoman'.[1]

Moltke's analysis seems analogous to that of Lord Palmerston, his contemporary. But whereas the British statesman thought that any expansionist designs of Mehemet Ali might best be checked by the settlement of Jews in Palestine under the Sultan's protection,[2] Moltke advocated direct control of Palestine by Germany, without any reference to the Jews. Again, in contrast to Palmerston's

---

[1] Field-Marshal Count Helmuth von Moltke, *Essays, Speeches and Memoirs* (Engl. trans. London, 1893), i, pp. 274–96. Published originally in the *Augsburger Allgemeine Zeitung* (1841) under the title 'Germany and Palestine'. It is worth noting that when Moltke wrote his article Austria was still a member of the German Federation.

[2] Isaiah Friedman, 'Lord Palmerston and the Protection of Jews in Palestine, 1839–1851', *Jewish Social Studies*, xxx, no. 1 (Jan. 1968), 31, 33, 35.

conviction that 'it was essential for British interests to preserve the Ottoman Empire',[3] Moltke placed no great faith in its viability. The Empire was 'rushing . . . rapidly down the steep road to ruin'. It was a body devoid of life, as Islam permitted 'neither progress, nor change'.[4]

Moltke's suggestion for the foundation of a German principality in Palestine fitted into his scheme of *Mitteleuropa* and of German expansion towards the highlands of Anatolia and Mesopotamia.[5] Some years later, when a field-marshal, he modified his views to comply with the official line. His statement, made on 24 April 1877, that Germany should not 'be so foolish as to weaken [herself] by the extension of her territory',[6] might well be taken as echoing the views of his Chancellor, Otto von Bismarck. Yet it was the ideas of von Moltke the young officer that foreshadowed German ambitions in the East, rather than those of the Field-Marshal. It would not be wrong, therefore, to consider him as one of the principal forerunners of a number of German thinkers, economists, and strategists, who propounded the idea of *Drang nach Osten*.[7]

Whatever had been written about the future of Germany in the Near East, Bismarck could see no German interests there. The region, he was quoted as saying, was 'not worth the bones of a single Pomeranian Grenadier'. His policy was shaped by the necessity of maintaining friendly relations with both Austria and Russia, who were at odds with each other over the Near East. To avoid any suspicion or unnecessary complications, he declared Germany's disinterestedness in that region. Under these circumstances any association with Palestine had to be discounted. The foundation of four German colonies in the late 1860s and early 1870s was inspired by religious rather than by political motives. If members of the Society of

---

[3] Charles K. Webster, *The Foreign Policy of Palmerston* (London, 1951), i, p. 87.

[4] Moltke, op. cit., pp. 272, 287; see also p. 246.

[5] Henry C. Meyer in his *Mitteleuropa in German Thought and Action, 1815–1945* (The Hague, 1955) credits Friedrich List as 'the oldest prophet of *Mitteleuropa*' (p. 11) and makes no mention of Moltke. The publication of Moltke's articles coincided with that of List's *The National System of Political Economy* (1841).

[6] Speech in the Imperial Diet, reproduced in *German Opinion on National Policy prior to July 1914*, Handbook prepared under the Direction of the Historical Section of the Foreign Office, No. 155, H.M.S.O., 1920 (hereafter cited as F.O. Handbook, No. 155).

[7] For a critical list of authors and publications which advocated this idea see Meyer, op. cit., pp. 57–8, 95–102; G. W. Prothero, *German Policy before the War* (London, 1916), p. 39; Percy Evans Lewin, *The German Road to the East* (London, 1916), pp. 26–32; J. E. Barker, 'The Future of Asiatic Turkey', *XIX Century and After* (June 1916), no. 472; Vladimir Jabotinsky, *Turkey and the War* (London, 1917), p. 56.

Knights (Tempelgesellschaft) managed to carry out their scheme in the Holy Land, it was in spite of the opposition of the Prussian Government. The number of German colonists remained, however, insignificant.[8] During the Congress of Berlin in 1878 a memorandum suggesting the establishment of a Jewish state in Palestine was submitted to Bismarck, only to be dismissed by the Chancellor as 'a crazy idea'.[9] Not until the New Course era of Wilhelm II, when the hypothetical value of the bones of a Pomeranian Grenadier in relation to German interests in the Orient became an anachronism, did the interest in Jewish settlement in Palestine revive.

There is abundant literature on Germany's penetration of the Orient, but its connection with the Jews is less well known. The more pronounced the drive to the East, the more emphatic became the protection afforded to German Jews and protégés in Palestine. 'It was Germany's merit', Paul von Tischendorf, the Consul-General in Jerusalem, reported, 'to be the only European Power to advocate in 1893 the cancellation of the [Ottoman] decree prohibiting Jews from purchasing land.'[10] But it was not until the eve of Wilhelm II's departure for the East in the autumn of 1898 that it looked for a while as if the Emperor intended to declare his

---

[8] On German colonies in Palestine see Claude Reignier Conder, *Tent Work in Palestine*, Palestine Exploration Fund (London, 1878), ii, pp. 301–5; Paulus Christoph, 'Die Tempel Colonien in Palästina', *Zeitschrift des Deutschen Palästina Vereins* (1883), vi, 31; Fritz Lorch, 'Die deutschen Tempelkolonien in Palästina', *Mitteilungen und Nachrichten des Deutschen Palästina-Vereins* (1909), 44–55, 65–74; J. Hoffman, 'Die wirtschaftliche Arbeit der Templer in Palästina', *Deutsches Orientjahrbuch* (1913), 46; Arthur Ruppin, *Syrien als Wirtschaftsgebiet* (Berlin, 1920), 2nd edn., pp. 104–6; Lewin op. cit., pp. 100–1; Foreign Office Handbook, *Syria and Palestine*, x, No. 60 (London, 1920), p. 45. In 1883 the Templars throughout Palestine numbered one thousand. By 1913 the figure had risen to slightly over 2,000 (1,400 in Haifa, Jerusalem, and Jaffa, and the remainder in the villages of Sarona, Wilhelmina, Beer-Salim in the south, and Waldheim and Bethlehem near Nazareth).

[9] Richard Lichtheim, *Die Geschichte des deutschen Zionismus* (Jerusalem, 1954), p. 37 (cited hereafter as *Geschichte*). The Hebrew edition *Toldoth Haziyonoot B'Germania* (Jerusalem, 1951), p. 29 (hereafter *Toldoth*); Nathan M. Gelber, 'The Palestine Question and the Congress of Berlin', *Historia Judaica*, ii (New York) (Apr. 1940) see esp. 44, 47.

For Disraeli's attitude to the project and the comments of the *Spectator* see Nahum Sokolow, *History of Zionism* (London, 1919), ii, p. 208, and Headlam-Morley, *Studies in Diplomatic History* (London, 1930), pp. 206–7. The Palestine question was only lightly touched on by the Congress and no reference made to the Jewish aspect. For the text of Article 62 of the Treaty see W. N. Medlicott, *The Congress of Berlin and After* (London, 1938), pp. 418–19.

[10] *Auswärtiges Amt Akten, Türkei*, Nr. 195, *Die Juden in Türkei*, K 692/K 175847–64 (hereafter *Türkei* 195), Tischendorf to Auswärtiges Amt (referred to hereafter as A.A.), 19 June 1897.

protection of Jewish immigration and colonization in Palestine in earnest. Guided by his friend and mentor, Count zu Eulenburg, the Kaiser arrived at the conclusion that Turkey would benefit economically from Jewish settlement in Palestine, while Germany would gain a firm foothold in the Orient, simultaneously easing the solution of the Jewish problem.[11]

Such a combination of foreign policy with domestic considerations relating to Jews was unprecedented in German thinking. Until the turn of the nineteenth century references to Jews and Palestine in German literature were made only in an anti-Semitic context. Fichte, warning his countrymen against the emancipation of the Jews, saw no better solution than to send them off to the Land of their Fathers.[12] Constantin Frantz was no solitary voice among the philosophers and historians to follow Fichte in suggesting two solutions for the Jews: either 'behead[ing] the lot of them and giv[ing] them fresh heads . . . or let Europe reconquer the Holy Land . . . and let them be packed off to their Palestine'.[13] Paul de Lagarde, the Orientalist and Fichte's disciple, stated that even if the two million Polish and Austrian Jews were prepared to germanize themselves, they would not be accepted, as 'it is impossible to tolerate a nation within a nation; and the Jews *are* a nation, not a community of co-religionists'. The Germans, he feared, were 'too soft a material to be able to resist the impact of the Jews and their Talmudic discipline'; and it was 'impossible to tolerate a nation within a nation'.[14]

Fichte's thesis that Judaism constituted a separatist state in permanent conflict with other states had a perceptible effect on a number of German thinkers and politicians. Bruno Bauer, who followed in Fichte's footsteps, wrote that if the Jews wished to assimilate with the German people they must first discard their 'chimerical' peculiarities and sacrifice their 'baseless nationality'.[15] Christian Friedrich Rühs, his predecessor, went even further by

---

[11] Below, pp. 65–8.

[12] J. Levy, *Fichte und die Juden* (Berlin, 1935), p. 2; Simon M. Dubnow, *Die neueste Geschichte des jüdischen Volkes, 1789–1914* (Berlin, 1923), i, pp. 203–4.

[13] Louis Sauzin, 'The Political Thought of Constantin Frantz', *The Third Reich* (London, 1955), 145. On Frantz see also Hans Kohn, *The Mind of Germany. The Education of a Nation* (New York, 1960), p. 276.

[14] Paul de Lagarde, *Deutsche Schriften* (Göttingen, 1903), p. 34. The relevant article was published first in 1874 but delivered as a lecture in 1853. For Lagarde's ideas see Jean-Jacques Anstett's article in *The Third Reich*, 148–202; Hans Kohn, op. cit., pp. 270–2; Joseph Becker, *Paul de Lagarde* (Lübeck, 1935).

[15] Bruno Bauer, *Die Judenfrage* (Brunswick, 1843), p. 60.

rejecting completely the idea of assimilation as 'incompatible with German nationalism, for the Jews . . . were a nation apart'.[16] On similar grounds, the Conservative deputies in the Prussian Parliament objected to Jewish emancipation. Judaism was not merely a faith; it was inseparable from their nationality. 'Zion is their Fatherland.' The Jews could at best be obedient citizens but never Prussians 'from the bottom of their heart'.[17] Even the liberal-minded Paulus, a Professor of Theology at the University of Heidelberg, could not reconcile himself to the thought that the Jews could be accepted as ordinary *Staatsbürger* (subjects of a state). They were a distinct people and could be tolerated only as *Schutzbürger* (protégés).[18]

To dismiss this attitude merely as the product of prejudice would be an oversimplification. Several decades before the concept was tinged with emotion by Fichte and his disciples, Immanuel Kant, probing the peculiarities of the phenomenon, concluded that Judaism was a national religion. The Jews formed a political community (*staatlichpolitische Gemeinschaft*), not a religious sect. As such they constituted 'a state within a state'.[19] Kant had no ulterior motives. His views were formulated in the age of rationalism, and he was regarded as a friend of the Jews.[20] He stated what was axiomatic to the Jews themselves during the pre-emancipation period, and admitted readily by the Zionist ideologists a century later. But the fact that the concept was used by some propagandists as a political weapon to bar Jewish enfranchisement vitiated its objective quality. It had a far-reaching effect on German Jewry. They realized that their emancipation could be won only at the expense of a voluntary denial of their identity as a distinct people among the nations.

Moses Mendelssohn, the celebrated philosopher, pioneered this new orientation but it was the Great Sanhedrin, convened by Napoleon in 1807, that gave it an official imprimatur. The Sanhedrin, in which delegates from territories of southern Germany occupied by the French troops also participated, made the momentous decision of differentiating between the religious and political provisions of Mosaic Law. It proclaimed that, since the destruction of their

---

[16] Dubnow, op. cit. ii, pp. 12–13.

[17] Cited in Gustav Meyer, 'Early German Socialism and Jewish Emancipation', *Jewish Social Studies* (New York, 1939), i, no. 4, p. 41.

[18] Dubnow, op. cit. ii, pp. 15–16.

[19] See Heinz Moshe Graupe, 'Kant und das Judentum', *Zeitschrift für Religions- und Geistesgeschichte* (Cologne, 1961), 4, pp. 308–33.

[20] Adolph Kohut, *Judenfreunde* (Berlin, 1913), pp. 93–118.

state by the Romans, the Jews had ceased to be a body politic and no longer constituted a national entity. Thenceforth they were 'neither a nation within a nation, nor cosmopolitan'; they were an integral part of the nations among which they lived, differing only in religion and therefore entitled to claim equality of rights.[21] This doctrine, which subsequently became a hallowed credo of Western Jewry, found its most receptive response in Germany. It was finally confirmed by the Conference of Reform Rabbis in 1845.

In Germany, where the battle for emancipation was harder than in any other country in the West, the Jews were forced to adopt more radical measures to win the acceptance of Gentile society. Rituals, other than those directly connected with the worship of God, were reformed and age-old beliefs in the Return to Zion were revised. Hope in the Messianic Redemption was condemned to oblivion as an irrelevant anachronism and the relevant prayers were expunged from the liturgy. The aspirations for the Ingathering of Exiles and Restoration to Zion were superseded by 'the Mission of Israel', a strange doctrine aimed at justifying the dispersion of Jews in the lands of the Diaspora in order to propagate universal monotheism among the Gentiles. Judaism was thus stripped completely of its national element and reduced to a Church. This was the gospel of Reform Judaism.[22] But orthodox Jewry also avidly embraced the new identity of Germans of the Mosaic faith. So ingrained did this concept become that any references to Jewish nationhood aired by Gentiles were dismissed as expressions of anti-Semitism and as dangerous heresy when made by daring individual Jews. Anti-Zionism was thus in being long before the Zionist movement appeared on the scene.

---

[21] Diogène Tama, *Collection des actes du Grand Sanhédrin* (Paris, 1807), pp. 65–73, 83, 90–1; *idem, Collection des procès-verbaux et décisions du Grand Sanhédrin* (Paris, 1807), pp. 47–9; Heinrich Graetz, *History of the Jews* (Philadelphia, 1895), v, pp. 481–99; Dubnow, op. cit. i, pp. 125–53; Sokolow, op. cit. i, pp. 82–3; R. Anchel, *Napoléon et les Juifs* (Paris, 1928), pp. 128–225.

[22] On which see Simon Dubnow, *Die Weltgeschichte des jüdischen Volkes* (Berlin, 1929), ix, pp. 84–102; Samuel Holdheim, *Geschichte der Entstehung und Entwickelung der jüdischen Reformgemeinde in Berlin* (Berlin, 1857); *Abraham Geigers' Leben in Briefen*, ed. Ludwig Geiger (Berlin, 1878); Emanuel Schreiber, *Abraham Geiger als Reformator des Judentums* (Loebau, 1879); Frederick Neilsen, *Das moderne Judentum, seine Emanzipation und Reform* (Flensburg, 1880); Max Wiener, *Abraham Geiger and Liberal Judaism* (Engl. trans. Philadelphia, 1962); Alexander Altmann, *Studies in Nineteenth Century Jewish Intellectual History* (Harvard University Press, 1964); Caesar Seligmann, *Geschichte der jüdischen Reformbewegung von Mendelssohn bis zur Gegenwart* (Frankfurt-on-Main, 1922); David Philipson, *The Reform Movement in Judaism* (London, 1931).

The emancipation of Jews in 1869, extended in 1871 to the entire German Empire, seemed to open a new era; liberalism had triumphed over old prejudices. This was also the logical corollary of the recognition, gaining ground, that religion must be separated from the state. In the Reichstag Bismarck extolled the Jews and even advocated intermarriage between them and the German nobility.[23] Like many liberal-minded personalities he hoped to solve the problem through intermarriage and a gradual fusion.[24] This proved a misjudgement. The Jews were not as quick to assimilate and the Germans were slow to absorb them. The German intellect, as Nietzsche remarked, suffered from indigestion; 'it can assimilate nothing'.[25] So long as the idea of Jews as inferior beings persisted among broad sections of the population,[26] real equality and integration between Gentiles and Jews (as distinct from de-judaized individuals), were unlikely. In the final analysis, the success of emancipation depended not so much on the nature of legislation as on its social application. In Germany a favourable climate of opinion for this was lacking. German nationalism developed as an antithesis to Western enlightenment and liberalism. It was exclusive by nature and aimed at achieving racial and cultural homogeneity. With this ideal dominating its thinking, toleration of different ethnic groups had little chance. Not only the Jews but also the Poles, Danes, and Alsace-Lorrainers had to be germanized.[27] The Jews in particular, despite their protestations to the contrary, were considered alien, and, unless ready to disappear voluntarily as a distinct group by complete assimilation, could not be regarded as equals. As Professor

[23] Louis L. Snyder, *From Bismarck to Hitler* (University of Pennsylvania Press, 1935), p. 142.

[24] Kohn, op. cit., p. 207. That Bismarck was not anti-Jewish was demonstrated by Otto Jöhlinger in his *Bismarck und die Juden* (Berlin, 1921); also Veit Valentin: *The German People*, trans. (New York, 1946), p. 495. However, see also Ismar Elbogen, *A Century of Jewish Life* (Philadelphia, 1946), p. 8; Snyder, op. cit., p. 142 and Dubnow, *Die neueste Geschichte*, iii, p. 26. For Bismarck's powerful intercession during the Congress of Berlin and after in favour of the emancipation of Jews in Rumania and Serbia see Medlicott, op. cit., pp. 31–2, 83, 91, 141, 358.

[25] Cited by L. B. Namier, 'Introduction to Arthur Ruppin', *The Jews in the Modern World* (London, 1934), p. 31; see also *The Third Reich*, p. 60; Snyder, op. cit., pp. 44–6.

[26] Eva G. Reichmann, *Hostages of Civilization. A Study of the Social Courses of Anti-Semitism* (London, 1950), p. 23.

[27] This was one of the leitmotivs of the Pan-German League. Snyder, op. cit., pp. 113–14; Mildred S. Wertheimer, *The Pan-German League, 1880–1914* (New York, 1924). On the League's attitude to the Jews see Reichmann, op. cit., pp. 154–5, and below, p. 252.

Eduard Hartmann put it: Jewish *Stammesgefühl* (pride in racial ancestry, origin, or roots) must be sacrificed on the altar of *National-gefühl* (patriotic feelings).[28]

It was in intellectual circles that modern 'scientific' anti-Semitism[29] crystallized. Thus Robert von Mohl, Professor of Civil Law and a liberal, in his *Staatsrecht, Völkerrecht und Politik* (1869), criticized the emancipation as a 'precipitate, imprudent and immature' edict. The Jews possessed 'dual nationality', which in his opinion disqualified them from natural equality with other citizens.[30] Johannes Scherr, the historian, claimed that the Jews were certainly entitled to a nationhood of their own, but in that case they should settle in Palestine or elsewhere: 'to be simultaneously a German and a Jew is impossible'.[31] Paul de Lagarde, Wilhelm Marr, and Constantin Frantz accused Bismarck of judaizing the Reich.[32] Frantz referred to emancipation as a 'most hateful folly'. He maintained that the Jews formed a nation apart and that all Jews should leave Europe for Palestine.[33] Richard Wagner was appalled by Bismarck's 'frivolity'. The Germans were doomed if they did not 'purify their bloodstream by ridding themselves of the Jews'.[34] Heinrich von Treitschke, the 'professor prophet' and idol of the intellectual patriots, declared that 'on German soil there is no room for double nationality', and that if the Jews wished to be considered a nation, 'they had better emigrate and establish a Jewish state elsewhere'.[35] What was espoused with cool objectivity by Treitschke was echoed in vulgar demagoguery by Adolph Stöcker, a Court Chaplain: 'Judaism is a foreign drop of blood in the German body . . . Semitism stands

[28] Cited in Dubnow, op. cit. iii, p. 32; Lichtheim, *Geschichte*, pp. 85–6; Marvin Löwenthal, *The Jews of Germany* (Philadelphia, 1944), pp. 307–8.

[29] The literature on this question is rich. In addition to Dr. Reichmann's book it is worth while mentioning Peter C. J. Pulzer: *The Rise of Political Anti-Semitism in Germany and Austria* (London, New York, 1964) and its bibliography.

[30] Lichtheim, op. cit., pp. 81–4.

[31] Dubnow, op. cit. iii, p. 23.

[32] Edmund Vermeil, 'The origin, Nature and Development of German Nationalist Ideology in the 19th and 20th Centuries', *The Third Reich*, p. 61.

[33] Sauzin, 'The Political Thought of Constantin Frantz', 145–6.

[34] Kohn, op. cit., p. 207. On Wagner's views see also Snyder, op. cit., pp. 47–55, and Leo Stein, *The Racial Thinking of Richard Wagner* (New York, 1950).

[35] Dubnow, op. cit. iii, p. 13. The Treitschke–Graetz controversy is reproduced in the Hebrew edition only, iii, Appendix, pp. 381–2; see also Lichtheim, op. cit., pp. 50–1, 86; Snyder, op. cit., pp. 25–35; Löwenthal, op. cit., pp. 308–9; Arthur Rosenberg, 'Treitschke und die Juden', *Die Gesellschaft* (Berlin, 1930), 78–83; Raymond J. Sontag, *Germany and England. Background to Conflict, 1848–1894* (New York, London, 1938), pp. 332–42.

in direct contrast to the German spirit.'[36] Stöcker's solution of the Jewish problem was equally simple: 'Back with the Jews to Palestine.' Not until the Christian communities were rid of them would they be able to live a Christian life.[37]

German Jews rejected these charges but in the long run they were fighting a losing battle. Material prosperity provided some comfort but was no answer to their difficulties. In 1893 the Central Union of German Citizens of Jewish Faith (Zentralverein deutscher Staatsbürger jüdischen Glaubens),[38] covering all sections of German Jewry, was established to combat anti-Semitism. Its name was its programme, and its argument was that, as the Jews no longer constituted a nation, neither their history nor their ethnic peculiarities should prejudice their civic status. They sincerely believed that living as Germans and thinking as Germans would make them *ipso facto* Germans. But this was an illusion—'Germans of Jewish Faith', a formula introduced to suit a political convenience, provided dubious protection. What mattered was not what the Jews considered themselves to be but what their environment thought of them. It was, as Herzl concluded, 'the majority who may decide who are the strangers'.[39] By denying their identity they deprived themselves of their inner pride and the strength to resist anti-Semitism. Escapism and a distorted sense of values also took their toll. The rosy optimism of the 1870s gave way at the turn of the century to cool opportunism or to a frivolous and cynical fatalism. To the dangers inherent in hostile theories, German Jewry for the most part turned a blind eye.[40]

Admittedly, in spite of some ominous portents, the prospects did not look gloomy. Anti-Jewish doctrines did not proceed from theory to practice, and the majority of Germans shied away from them. Theodor Mommsen, replying to Treitschke, labelled anti-Semitism 'an abortion of nationalism'. Gustav Freytag, the novelist, described it as 'a disease of the popular mind', and the Crown Prince, later

[36] Cited in Löwenthal, op. cit., p. 304. On Stöcker see also Snyder, op. cit., pp. 13–24; Kohn, op. cit., p. 281; Valentin, op. cit., p. 495.
[37] Cited by Wickham Steed in *Chaim Weizmann*, ed. Paul Goodman (London, 1945), p. 70. Steed commented, 'his hatred of Jews did not strike me as a persuasive expression of the Christian doctrine of love'. (Ibid.)
[38] See Dubnow, op. cit. iii, pp. 47–8; Lichtheim, op. cit., p. 97. Löwenthal, op. cit., p. 269.
[39] Theodor Herzl, *The Jewish State* (New York, 1946), p. 76 (cited hereafter as *The Jewish State*).   [40] Lichtheim, op. cit., pp. 87–8.

Frederick III, denounced it as 'the shame of the nineteenth century'. Seventy-six distinguished German scholars, officials, artists, and industrialists, in a counter-appeal to the Stöcker–Marr mass petition, called on all to wipe out 'this national disgrace', whilst Heinrich Ricket, a leader of the Union To Combat Anti-Semitism, declared confidently in the Reichstag that 'three-quarters of the German nation were on his side'.[41] Anti-Jewish theories had little bearing on daily life. If admission to certain clubs or bathing resorts was restricted, this was a minor evil compared with the material wealth and progress which the Jews enjoyed as a result of emancipation. The remarkable development of German industry and trade between 1870 and 1900 opened up unprecedented opportunities for the middle classes in general and for the Jews in particular. Anti-Semitism was not taken seriously.[42] Paul Nathan, editor of the liberal *Nation* and a prominent leader of the Zentralverein, dismissed it as 'an artificial product' and a means of 'keeping reaction alive'. However, what to Nathan was artificial and transient was to Treitschke 'a natural reaction of the German folk-feeling'.[43] Treitschke's following among his students was considerable, as was the impact that Stöcker made on the masses. Bismarck rejected Stöcker's political anti-Semitism, as did Wilhelm II, but anti-Jewish feelings spread and became respectable.[44] 'Actually, every decent person is an anti-Semite', stated one of the Conservative party leaders. Discrimination against the Jews remained common and, when members of the opposition in the Reichstag complained of breaches of the Constitution, they were told that 'this is how it should be, since a Jew is not equal to a Christian'.[45]

When German nationalism became infected with racialism it embarked on a course which proved dangerous both for the Jews and for the Germans themselves. The belief that people's qualities depended on blood and race undermined any argument in favour of assimilation. The notion of *Volk* or *Volkstum*, a romantic association with the Middle Ages, now gaining ground, was not applicable

---

[41] Löwenthal, op. cit., pp. 313–14.   [42] Lichtheim, op. cit., pp. 87–8.

[43] Cited in Löwenthal, op. cit., pp. 346, 355. On Nathan see Ernest Feder, 'Paul Nathan: The Man and his Work', *The Leo Baeck Institute Year Book*, iii (London, 1958), 66–80.

[44] Snyder, op. cit., pp. 13–24, 25–38; Sontag, op. cit., p. 327; *The Third Reich*, pp. 61–2; Kohn, op. cit., p. 281; Löwenthal, op. cit., p. 309; Valentin, op. cit., p. 495; Valentine Chirol, *Fifty Years in a Changing World* (London, 1927), p. 268.

[45] Dubnow, op. cit. iii, pp. 458–60.

to the Jews. The ghost of mass expulsion, if not the brutal remedy of the 'Assyrian method' aired by Lagarde and Frantz,[46] seemed to be materializing.

Moses Hess[47] was the first Jewish thinker in Western Europe to take anti-Semitism seriously. The Germans, he proclaimed in his *Rom und Jerusalem* (1862),[48] were anti-Jewish racially. It was therefore futile to expect that reform or emancipation would by some magic render the German Jews socially acceptable. Judaism formed a unique synthesis between the national and the universal. An antinational universalism as preached by the German Jewish reformers 'is just as unfruitful as the anti-universal nationalism of mediaeval reaction'. Assimilation was no solution. The Jews were a separate nation, not a religious group. Denial of one's identity was self-deception and could not command respect. Self-effacement was no recipe for harmonious co-existence between individuals or groups of different ethnic origins.

A year earlier (1861) a booklet under the title *Drishat Zion* had been published by Rabbi Zevi Kalisher of Poznań in German-occupied Poland. Like Rabbi Yehuda Alkalai, his counterpart in Serbia, Kalisher, by the standards of his time, propounded the revolutionary concept that Israel's redemption could not be brought about by a sudden miracle of divine grace. It depended primarily on the efforts of the Jews themselves. It was their duty to initiate the practical steps in anticipation of the Almighty's blessing. An active resettlement of Palestine fully accorded with the commandments of Judaism.[49] Twenty-two years later Rabbi Isaac Rülf reiterated this idea in *Aruchat Bath-Ami* (1883). None of the Rabbis, however, made any impact on their contemporaries, whilst Moses Hess remained, as Sir Isaiah Berlin put it, 'a prophet without much honour in his own generation, certainly not in his own country'.[50]

[46] *The Third Reich*, pp. 173; see also p. 146.

[47] On whom see Theodor Zlocisti, *Moses Hess* (Berlin, 1921); Adolf Böhm, *Die zionistische Bewegung*, 2nd edn. (Tel Aviv, 1935), i, pp. 81–8; Getzel Kressel, *Moses Hess* (Hebrew), Tel Aviv, 1961; and particularly Isaiah Berlin, *The Life and Opinions of Moses Hess* (Cambridge University Press, 1959); also Edmund Sibner, *Moses Hess* (Leiden, 1966).

[48] Translated into English by M. Waxman (New York, 1945).

[49] *Mivhar Ktavim* (Selected Writings) (Tel Aviv, 1943); Arthur Herzberg, *The Zionist Idea. A Historical Analysis and Reader* (New York, 1959), pp. 125–7, 111–14.

[50] *The Life and Opinions of Moses Hess*, p. 2.

The awakening of Jewish nationalism in Germany was slow and confined to academic youth. In 1886 a students' society, Viadrina, was founded in Breslau. It set itself the task of combating anti-Semitism and instilling national consciousness in its members. They publicly admitted their Jewishness and announced that they would suffer neither insult nor injustice. This was a new phenomenon in Jewish life,[51] though by no means an isolated one. The Jung-Israel society in Berlin followed a similar pattern. It was established by Heinrich Löwe, a talented student, subsequently a professor. Löwe came of an assimilated German-Jewish family. Of a fiery temperament and proud by nature, he felt offended by the anti-Jewish prejudices endemic in German academic circles. The purpose of his society was to educate a new type of Jewish intellectual: ready to defend his honour, attached to Jewish historical values, and sensitive to the plight of his people in eastern Europe. Löwe was also a co-founder of the Russian-Jewish students' society in Berlin, the Russisch-jüdisch wissenschaftlicher Verein, which proved a breeding ground for some prominent Zionist leaders and thinkers such as Leo Motzkin, Nachman Syrkin, Shmarya Levin, and Victor Jacobson.[52] Student societies sprouted in various universities, unobtrusively because the Zionist idea was still anathema to the German-Jewish public. How cautious the students had to be can be gauged from the innocuous names (Humanitätsgesellschaft, Spervia, etc.) which they adopted to conceal their real aim. By 1892 the societies were strong and numerous enough to confederate into the Verein jüdischer Studenten in Deutschland. These were modest beginnings though not unimportant. The societies provided the milieu in which the debating faculties of their members were sharpened, their thoughts crystallized, and political experience matured. The values implanted gave them a sense of dignity and reassurance *vis-à-vis* an unfriendly environment.[53]

One of the young intellectuals, a lawyer by profession, who was to make a particular mark on Zionism in Germany was Max Bodenheimer. He was completely unaware of the students' societies. His awakening to the Zionist idea had a peculiar individual stamp. It came, as he testified in his memoirs, from a 'sudden inspiration':

---

[51] Elbogen, op. cit., pp. 194; Lichtheim, op. cit., pp. 95–6.
[52] Lichtheim, op. cit., pp. 112–18; see also p. 103.
[53] Ibid., pp. 118–22; Walter Gross, 'The Zionist Students' Movement' *Leo Baeck Institute Year Book*, iv (London, 1959), 143–64.

It was like a light that suddenly broke forth within me. The remarkable character of this phenomenon shook my whole being. I felt like a slave for whom the road to liberty suddenly opens, like a prisoner who by a miracle finds the tool to break his chains. The state of mind into which this thought transported me can hardly be described. Whereas shortly before I had wrestled with the decision to abandon Judaism and seek refuge from Jew-hatred in new surroundings where my origin was unknown, I was now filled with a holy zeal to serve the cause of my people. Perhaps it came from the fact that I suddenly recognized the futility of such an assimilation for the people as a whole, perhaps also because my feeling of honor resisted such a flight from the community into which I had been born . . . the change was inexplicable.[54]

Perhaps not altogether inexplicable. Childhood memories of how the teaching of the New Testament turned Christian children against the Jews had left deep scars. At the Gymnasium belief in the brotherhood of man had revived, and though he personally was held in high esteem by his Gentile colleagues, their opinions often made him ponder the origins of so deeply rooted a hatred. His faith in progress remained unshaken, as did his attachment to all that was German. But the growth of anti-Semitism continued to concern him. The pogrom of Konitz in East Prussia horrified him. The persecution of Jews in Russia made him bitter, but the most traumatic experience was a public meeting in Berlin where Adolf Stöcker spoke. 'Lies and libels were advanced with eloquent sophistry . . . Germany for the Germans was the slogan.' Bodenheimer was most depressed by the thunderous applause which greeted Stöcker's call to fight the Jews.[55]

The transformation in his outlook was now complete. This and similar incidents opened his eyes to the fate of his people. It was their homelessness, their minority status among the nations, cut off from the soil, that lay at the root of their misfortune. Everywhere they were considered an alien body. This he attributed partly to the Jews' own habit of segregation, but pinned the primary blame on the Gentiles. Their hostility to Jews had remained a constant factor throughout history; only the arguments had changed. During the Middle Ages religious dissimilarity provided the excuse, whereas in modern times it assumed a political character. Bodenheimer reasoned

---

[54] *The Memoirs of Max I. Bodenheimer: Prelude to Israel*, ed. H. H. Bodenheimer, transl. (New York, London, 1963), p. 60; the first German edition *So wurde Israel. Erinnerungen von Dr. Max I. Bodenheimer* (Frankfurt-on-Main, 1958) was preceded by a Hebrew one: *Darki L'Zion* (Jerusalem, 1953).   [55] *Memoirs*, pp. 35–6, 42–3, 61–2.

that, if the underlying cause of the problem was Jewish dispersion, the remedy should be sought in the ingathering of a substantial number of Jews in a country of their own. It was only in the land of their ancestors that a Jewish nation could revive in a normal social environment, that they would acquire a new image and status in the world. The mere existence of a Jewish state would prove the most effective antidote to anti-Semitism. Bodenheimer believed that his ideas were original and unique. Their strangeness frightened him. A friend to whom he turned for comfort dismissed them as 'childish fantasy' and harmful. Should the Jews aspire to territorial concentration as a nation, they would be accused of narrow-mindedness and would forfeit their role among the nations. Anti-Semitism was but a passing phenomenon. Other friends considered him a crank or insane. Nor did he find encouragement in Cologne, where he moved in 1890. For the head of the Teachers' Seminary the redemption of the Jewish people was a divine prerogative. Nothing should be done to expedite it until the coming of the Messiah.[56]

News of the establishment of the first Jewish colonies in Palestine in the 1880s tended to dispel some of Bodenheimer's bewilderment. It was not true, he felt, that his ideas were a childish fantasy. But it was not until a new outburst of persecution in Russia in 1891 that he decided to come out into the open. To avoid unnecessary controversy he clothed his views in a philanthropic garment, but his pamphlet *Wohin mit den russischen Juden?* (*Whither Russian Jews?*) attracted little attention; through it, however, he discovered the Zionist student societies and established contact with Nathan Birnbaum in Vienna, the author of *Selbst-Emanzipation* and the first to use the term Zionism, and with Leo Pinsker, leader of the Hibbat Zion movement in Russia and the author of *Auto-Emancipation*. Of greater practical significance was his acquaintance with David Wolffsohn, who had come to Cologne from Russia. A man of engaging manner and deeply learned in Jewish matters, Wolffsohn was also a successful businessman. Bodenheimer's idea of the creation of a Jewish state in Palestine fired his imagination and a lifelong friendship was formed. In 1893 they established the Cologne Association for the Promotion of Agriculture and Industry in Palestine (Kölner Verein zur Förderung von Ackerbau und Handwerk in Palästina), which may justly be regarded as the beginning of the Zionist movement in Germany.[57]

[56] Op. cit., pp. 61–71.　　　[57] Op. cit., pp. 71–9; Lichtheim, op. cit., pp. 111–12.

A campaign to win new converts was soon launched and contact with the 'Lovers of Zion' in England was established. But it was the appearance of Theodor Herzl's book *Der Judenstaat* in 1896 that gave the most powerful uplift to the morale of the Cologne society. 'For us', Bodenheimer recorded, 'the book signalized a new epoch. Herzl had spoken out openly on what moved us. We had the feeling that behind this man there was more than a mere utopian visionary. We surmised that in him was the genius for statesmanship, which hitherto had been lacking in our circle.' Wolffsohn went to meet Herzl and returned captivated by his personality.[58] Herzl breathed new life into the Zionist societies, liberating them from their parochialism and later fusing them into an international movement.

Greatly encouraged, the Cologne society adopted a more ambitious name: National-jüdische Vereinigung Köln. Early in 1897 it published its programme, called also 'Theses'. It consisted of three points:

(i)   Jews all over the world are united by a mutual bond of common origin and historical past. They therefore constitute a national entity [*nationale Gemeinschaft*]. This is not inconsistent with their patriotism, nor does it impede the fulfilment of their civic obligations towards their countries of domicile in general and towards Germany in particular.

(ii) Experience has shown that civic emancipation has fallen short of securing the social and cultural future of the Jewish people. The final solution of the Jewish question lies therefore in the establishment of the Jewish State. Only a state of their own will be able to represent the Jews within the framework of international law and provide a refuge for those individuals who are unwilling or unable to remain in their countries of domicile. The state ought to be founded legally and its natural place is the Land of Israel, sanctified by Jewish history.

(iii) The indispensable steps towards the achievement of this goal are the reawakening of Jewish consciousness and practical work in Palestine.[59]

Save for the term 'practical work' in Palestine, Herzl was reported to be in agreement with the Cologne programme. To Herzl, endorsement by international law was an indispensable prerequisite to any

[58] Bodenheimer, op. cit., pp. 80–2, 84. On Bodenheimer's impression of Herzl see ibid., p. 100.
[59] Reproduced in Lichtheim, op. cit., pp. 134–5; in an abbreviated form in Bodenheimer, op. cit., pp. 85–6.

scheme of colonization and immigration. But with the exception of several other individuals, German Jewry rose in a fury of protest. The Rhineland Lodge of the B'nai B'rith, followed closely by other lodges in Germany, regarded the Zionist programme as 'treason to the Fatherland'. It was, they stated, 'a hopeless, utopian' piece of literature composed by men unacquainted with the world. It played directly into the hands of anti-Semites.[60] Herzl's *Der Judenstaat* thus came under strong attack.[61] The Association of Rabbis in Germany issued a manifesto protesting against this distortion of the meaning of Judaism. 'The efforts of the so-called Zionists', the Rabbis maintained, 'contradicted the Messianic promise to Jewry . . . Judaism obliges its adherents to devote all their strength to the Fatherland to which they belong.' However noble colonization of Palestine might be, the idea of a Jewish national state was harmful.[62] The powerful Zentralverein deutscher Staatsbürger jüdischen Glaubens shared this view.

The Zionists disregarded the mounting opposition and on 11 July 1897 called a conference at Bingen at which the Zionist Federation of Germany (Zionistische Vereinigung für Deutschland) was founded. The conference endorsed the Theses and repudiated the Rabbis' manifesto. The Zionist idea, it affirmed, was neither an affront to Judaism, nor was it incompatible with the patriotic sentiments of its adherents.[63] Herzl, on his own accord, published a strong reply in *Die Welt* (16 July 1897),[64] the newly established Zionist organ. Rebuffed by the Jewish community of Munich, which declined to act as host to the First Zionist Congress, he found Basle more hospitable. The Congress convened there on 29–31 August 1897 and proved an event of historical significance. Two months later a second conference of the Zionist Federation of Germany met at Frankfurt-on-Main to elect an Executive, of which Max Bodenheimer was chosen chairman and David Wolffsohn treasurer.[65]

[60] Bodenheimer, op. cit., pp. 85–6, 91.

[61] Lichtheim, op. cit., pp. 127–8; Alex Bein: *Theodor Herzl. A Biography* (London, 1957), pp. 179–80.

[62] Published originally in the *Allgemeine Zeitung des Judentums* of June 1897. Cited in Lichtheim, op. cit., pp. 133–4; Bein, op. cit., pp. 221–2; reproduced in full in Ludwig Lewinsohn, *Theodor Herzl. A Portrait for this Age* (New York, 1955), pp. 304–5.

[63] Lichtheim, op. cit., pp. 135–6, 147–8; Bodenheimer, op. cit., pp. 96–7.

[64] 'Protestrabbiner', *Gesammelte Zionistische Werke* (Berlin, 1934), i. 169–74.

[65] Lichtheim, op. cit., p. 137; Bodenheimer, op. cit., p. 96. Others elected to the Executive were Rabbi Isaak Rülf, Professor Hermann Schapira, and Lipman Prins. Henriette Hannah Bodenheimer, *The History of the Basle Program* (Hebrew) (Jerusalem,

Like all revolutionaries, the Zionists were inspired by an ideal and considered themselves the *avant-garde* of their people; although a tiny minority, they were enthusiastic and stout-hearted, qualities which enabled them to weather all opposition. They made a particular appeal to the youth and the intelligentsia, and, while immersed in ideological disputes, they were not mere dreamers. Practical achievements always told strongly in their favour among their co-religionists. Nor were the advantages of Jewish colonization in Palestine lost on the German Government. Yet politically the Wilhelmstrasse had to avoid any useful compact with Zionism. The opposition of German Jewry had some bearing, but this was a relatively minor consideration among officials when compared to the regard that Germany had to pay to Turkey's susceptibilities. Since the latter factor exercised so powerful an influence on German policy, we must first examine the reasons for the Sublime Porte's[66] hostility to Jewish settlement in Palestine and to the Zionist enterprise in particular.

1947), pp. v, ix, xii, xvi, xxix–xxx, xxxiii–xxxiv; Werner J. Cahnman, 'Munich and the First Zionist Congress', *Historia Judaica*, iii (1941), 7–23; and on the anti-Zionist reactions in Western Europe in general See Ben Halpern, *The Idea of the Jewish State* (Cambridge, Mass., 1961), pp. 131–76.

[66] Sublime Porte, in Turkish 'High Gate', was derived from the palace gate at which justice was administered. The term designated the central office of the Empire and was commonly used as a synonym for the Ottoman Government.

2

The Jews in Palestine under Ottoman Rule 1517–1856

FOR over four centuries Turkey had been regarded as a friend of the Jews. Her warm hospitality, extended to the refugees from Spain at the end of the fifteenth and the beginning of the sixteenth centuries, left an indelible impression. The Spanish Jews found in Turkey not only a haven but freedom and prosperity.[1] Some, such as Don Joseph Nasi and Solomon Ashkenazi,[2] rose to the highest positions in the state hierarchy. Under the *millet* system[3] Ottoman Jewry enjoyed a wide measure of autonomy and the Chief Rabbi, the *Chacham Bashi*, was entitled to exercise authority in both religious and civil matters. His decrees were sanctioned by the government and became law.[4] Ali Pasha, the Turkish Foreign Minister (subsequently Grand Vizier), did not exaggerate when he pointed out to his ambassador in London in 1865 that the Jews in Turkey enjoyed rights 'which they would be happy to possess in most Christian countries in Europe'.[5] Nor was his successor, Safret Pasha, wrong

[1] Graetz, *History of the Jews* (Philadelphia, 1894), iv, pp. 400–7; Moïse Franco, *Essai sur l'histoire des Israélites de l'Empire ottoman* (Paris, 1897); Dubnow, *Die Weltgeschichte*, iv, pp. 18–75; Abraham Galante, *Documents officiels turcs concernant les Juifs de la Turquie* (Stamboul, 1931), idem, *Turcs et Juifs* (Stamboul, 1932), *Histoire des Juifs d'Istamboul* (Stamboul, 1941); Shlomo A. Rozanes, *Divre-Y'me Israel b'Turgma* [*History of Jews in Turkey*] (Tel Aviv, 1930; Sofia, 1938), 5 vols.; Cecil Roth, *A Short History of the Jewish People* (London, 1948), pp. 274–9.

[2] Cecil Roth, *The House of Nasi. The Duke of Naxos* (Philadelphia, 1948); Graetz, op. cit. iv, pp. 593–628; Franco, op. cit., pp. 35–71; Dubnow, op. cit. vi, pp. 26–35.

[3] For the position of non-Muslims under the *millet* system see Nasim Sousa, *The Capitulatory Regime of Turkey* (London, Baltimore, 1933), pp. 89–93.

[4] Galante, *Documents officiels*, pp. 32–5; Dubnow, op. cit. ix, p. 273.

[5] *United States Foreign Affairs* (1864–5), Pt. 3, p. 282, Ali Pasha to Musurus, 30 Nov. 1865.

when assuring Horace Maynard, the United States Minister to Constantinople, that 'the Israelites have enjoyed every privilege and immunity accorded by the laws to Ottoman subjects'.[6]

In Palestine[7] the Ottoman rulers treated the Jews as tolerantly and benevolently as elsewhere. Selim I's conquest of Syria and Palestine in 1517 marked a new era in the history of the country, which was to remain under Ottoman rule for four hundred years. The native Jews hailed Selim's victory enthusiastically. They had long been dissatisfied with the inefficient Mameluk regime and had good reason to believe that incorporation into the Ottoman Empire and direct contact with its Jewish inhabitants, the most influential and numerous at that time in the world, would open new vistas. They were not disappointed. Following the example set by Selim I, Suleiman the Magnificent (1520–66) and Selim II (1566–74) allowed the Jews to move freely into the Holy Land and settle wherever they liked. The Jewish population, which in past centuries had been severely decimated by recurrent political and natural catastrophes,[8] was now augmented by successive waves of immigration, mainly of the *Sephardi*[9] extraction. At the beginning of the sixteenth century the total Jewish population in Palestine was estimated at no more than 5,000 to 6,000; fifty years later the community in Safad alone had risen to 10,000.[10]

During the sixteenth century Safad witnessed a period of unprecedented cultural and economic growth. Not all the immigrants chose to crowd into the town; many settled in the adjacent villages and engaged in farming, horticulture, or fishing around the lake of Genessareth. The magnificent scenery and the ancient belief that deliverance was bound to come from Galilee attracted many

---

[6] Ibid. (1877), p. 594, Maynard (Constantinople) to Evarts (Washington), 26 June 1877.

[7] On Palestine under Ottoman rule see Jacob de Haas, *History of Palestine* (New York, London, 1934), pp. 324–437; James Parkes, *A History of Palestine from 135 A.D. to Modern Times* (London, 1949), pp. 152–293; Itzhak Ben-Zvi, *Eretz-Israel Ve' Yeshuva* [*Palestine under Ottoman Rule. Four Centuries of History*] (Jerusalem, 1955); Dov Weinryb, 'Problems of Research on the History of the Jews in Palestine and their Economic Life since the Turkish Conquest', *Zion* (Hebrew) (Jerusalem; July, Oct. 1937).

[8] It is estimated that in A.D. 637, during the Arab conquest of Palestine, the Jewish community numbered between 300,000 and 400,000. After the Crusaders, who practically annihilated the non-Christian population, the number of Jews was reduced to a few thousands.

[9] The Sephardim are the descendants of Spanish Jews. *Sepharad* means Spain in Hebrew.

[10] Ben-Zvi, op. cit., p. 150; *Encyclopædia Ivrit*, vi (Jerusalem, 1957), p. 490.

Cabbalists who were eager to hasten the arrival of the Messiah. They made Safad their citadel, and it also became a venerated centre of rabbinical learning. Here the authoritative and practical religious code, the *Shulchan Aruch*, was composed, and in 1578 the first Hebrew book was printed.[11] But the most intriguing episode is perhaps the abortive attempt of Don Joseph Nasi, Duke of Naxos, to rebuild Tiberias as a Jewish centre.[12]

Don Joseph stood in high favour with Prince Selim and Sultan Suleiman, and in 1561 managed to procure a concession for Tiberias and seven neighbouring villages. There is not enough evidence to determine whether Nasi intended to found the 'kernel of a Jewish state', as some historians think,[13] or whether he was less ambitious and planned to create merely a refuge for Spanish Jews and Marranos. What is certain is that the enterprise was practical. A protective wall and houses were built, and mulberry trees were planted with a view to maintaining silk-worms. Wool was imported for weaving cloth. There are reasons to believe that it was not only the financial aspect (the lease yielded an annual income of 1,000 ducats) that induced the Ottoman Government to grant the concession. A loyal and industrious population in a desolate part of the Empire could well have fortified a region of strategic importance without involving the state in extra expenditure. Yet for all the official blessings the project failed to live up to expectations.

That the Ottoman Government remained favourably disposed towards the idea even after Don Joseph's death in 1579 is evident from the fact that several years later the lease was renewed to another Marrano magnate, Alvaro Mendes, alias Solomon Ben Yaish. Ben Yaish played an important role in shaping Turkey's foreign policy and had honours bestowed upon him, but his cherished dream was the rebuilding of Tiberias and the seven villages. The lease was granted to him and his son but again, in the absence of evidence, the whole episode remains obscure.[14]

[11] Ben-Zvi, op. cit., pp. 169–96; Dubnow, op. cit. vi, pp. 26–35, 52–75; *Sefer Tsfat* [*Safad Volume. Studies and Texts on the History of the Jewish Community in Safad*], ed. I. Ben-Zvi and M. Benayahu (Jerusalem, 1962).

[12] Cf. Roth, *The House of Nasi*, pp. 97–135; Graetz, op. cit. iv, pp. 593–628; Dubnow, op. cit. vi, pp. 35–46; Ben-Zvi, op. cit., pp. 196–202; Joseph Braslawski, 'Jewish Settlement in Tiberias from Don Joseph Nasi to Ibn Yaish', *Zion* (Hebrew) (Oct. 1939), pp. 45–72. Braslavski names Gracia Mendes, Don Joseph's mother-in-law, as the initiator of the project.   [13] Graetz, op. cit. iv, p. 611; Roth, op. cit., p. 110.

[14] The documents discovered by Abraham Galante, *Don Solomon Aben Jaech* (Stamboul, 1936), do not add substantially to our knowledge.

The Ottoman Empire reached its zenith during the sixteenth century. Thereafter a steady decline followed. Endemic revolts of the Janissaries (the backbone of its military strength), the continuous loss of vast territories in Europe, exorbitant taxation—these were only a few of the symptoms of the *malaise* that infected the Empire. Bribery, the notorious *baksheesh*, crept into Ottoman politics and corrupted the government. When the Porte finally managed to quell the unruly Janissaries it found that it had amputated its own military arm. Mobilization of armed forces was henceforth delegated to provincial governors who used the opportunity to the full to buttress their own position. They maintained private armies and, save for nominal acknowledgement of the Sultan's sovereignty, ruled almost independently. Feudalism struck root and became the dominant feature of the social system.[15] The Empire, a rotten tree, seemed ready to collapse under its own weight. If it did not disintegrate sooner, this was mainly due to the counterbalancing jealousies of the European Powers who allowed the Sick Man of Europe neither to die nor to recover.

Inevitably, Turkey's eclipse affected Syria and Palestine. Moreover, the discovery of an alternative route to India around the African coast robbed these provinces of much of their former international importance, and the opening-up of the New World moved the centre of gravity away from the Mediterranean. For more than two centuries Syria and Palestine remained half forgotten. Commerce and industry stagnated and agriculture sank to a primitive level. The local pashas were autocratic and often corrupt. Their exorbitant taxation and arbitrary extortions, of citizens and tourists, coupled with inefficient administration, ruined the economy. Assaults from the bedouins, endless feuds among Arab families, and highway robbery made life and property insecure . The country became notorious for its backwardness, whilst epidemics, due chiefly to poor sanitary conditions and ignorance, decimated the population.

The Jewish inhabitants were deeply affected by this state of affairs. With the weakening of the central administration their fate became subject to the authority of the local pashas whose attitude varied according to temperament and personality. At the end of the sixteenth century the Jews were hit by a succession of natural disasters coupled with sporadic raids by Muslim fanatics. Safad

[15] The feudal system goes back to the Mameluk period, on which see: A. N. Poliak, *Feudalism in Egypt, Syria, Palestine and the Lebanon, 1250–1900* (London, 1939).

and its environs, in particular, became a prey to these evils. Its economy crumbled and in the absence of a fresh inflow of students the centres of Talmudic learning declined rapidly. In 1613, when the Druse Emir Fakhr ad-Din (1583–1635)[16] became the *de facto* ruler of the Syrian coast and of the interior of Galilee, it was already too late for the native Jews to benefit from his benign, though short, rule.

Fakhr ad-Din, for all his adventurous career, was known as a constructive and imaginative ruler. 'Small in stature but great in courage', he was not slow to take advantage of Turkey's involvement in the war with Persia to establish his supremacy in western Syria and Galilee. He managed to enlist the support of the Arab peasantry, came to terms with the Christians both in the Lebanon and in Nazareth, and was said to be friendly also with the Jews. He made use of their commercial connections and linguistic qualifications, employing them in the public service. Fakhr was known to have nourished an ambition to develop trade on an international scale. But the more powerful he became and the greater independence he displayed, the more angry was Sultan Murad III. The downfall of the Fakhr family was only a question of time. Their deposition, however, did not make the province any happier; anarchy and internal strife superseded a relatively orderly administration. In the circumstances it was only the collective protection of a clan or tribe that could provide the individual with some security. The Jews possessed none.

In 1656 both Safad and Tiberias were sacked by Druses and bedouins. This was their death-blow. For nearly a century these hitherto flourishing centres remained depopulated and desolate.[17] The panic-stricken inhabitants found refuge in the southern cities of Gaza, Hebron, and, particularly, Jerusalem. Henceforth, Jewish immigrants from Italy, North Africa, and Eastern Europe bypassed Galilee and turned southwards, and Jerusalem recovered some of its former pre-eminence. But here, too, conditions were far from attractive.[18] In 1625, when Muhammad Ibn Farukh, an Arab sheikh from Nablus, appropriated the office of pasha of Jerusalem,

[16] The story of Fakhr and his family was extensively recorded by contemporary travellers and biographers. Ben-Zvi, op. cit., pp. 17–23; de Haas, op. cit., pp. 339–42.

[17] Ben-Zvi, op. cit., pp. 206–14.

[18] Ibid., p. 218; *idem*, 'Palestine Settlement in the Seventeenth Century', *Zion* (Apr.–July 1942), 156–71; Cecil Roth, 'The Jews of Jerusalem in the Seventeenth Century', *Miscellanies of the Jewish Historical Society of England* (1935).

it became evident that his sole intention was to use his position for personal gain. His term of office was described by contemporary chronicles as 'the darkest Jerusalem had ever experienced'. His avarice and despotism were proverbial. The Jewish community was terror-stricken on suddenly learning that all their property and funds had been confiscated. Notables and wealthy individuals were imprisoned and not released until a heavy ransom was paid. To free the detainees the impoverished community was forced to borrow money at high interest rates. But Farukh's malevolence eventually boomeranged; Jewish leaders in Constantinople prevailed upon the Sultan to dismiss him. Ibn Farukh defied the Porte and refused to vacate his post. When he was finally forced out, the Jews could breathe more freely. But their sorrows were not over. Heavily mortgaged to their Muslim neighbours, they and the rest of the population suffered in the following years one of the most devastating plagues, accompanied by a famine which afflicted the whole country. By 1806 the Jewish community in Jerusalem had sunk to 1,000, out of a total city population of 8,774. Formerly more or less self-supporting, they were now condemned to live as wretched paupers. In such depressing conditions it is astonishing that they survived at all. It was sheer sentiment and the unquenched hope of supernatural deliverance that made them cling so tenaciously to their dwellings.[19]

Nor were they forgotten. Jews all over the world had always considered it their pious duty to assist their brethren in Palestine. In synagogues and in private homes special collecting-boxes invited contributions. This was no mere charity: it symbolized a bond, expressed sympathy and self-identification with those who chose to spend their lives in the Holy Land in study and devotion. The funds were allocated for general communal necessities and disbursed among the needy. Hence the name of the system—*Haluka*, which in Hebrew stands for division or dole. It was useful and did not humiliate recipients; but there were serious drawbacks. Reliance on charity killed initiative and encouraged an unproductive way of life.

During the eighteenth century the Jews seemed to have fared better in Galilee. This was particularly the case under the rule of Dahr al-Omar (1735–75), a sheikh of the bedouin tribe of the Beni

---

[19] Ben-Zvi, op. cit., pp. 220–34; for the position after Farukh see A. Shochet, 'The Jews in Jerusalem in the XVIIIth Century', *Zion*, i, no. 4 (1936), 377–410.

Zaidan. Despite his turbulent career Omar proved one of the most tolerant and efficient of local rulers; justice was meted out equally to Muslim, Jew, and Christian. Bedouin raids were stopped and security of life and property was assured. Acre was fortified and made into a capital. Christian and Jewish merchants were encouraged to settle to revive commerce and industry, Haim Abulafia, the Rabbi of Smyrna, was invited to take over the concession to develop Tiberias. When the Rabbi arrived in Palestine in 1740, Omar received him with full honours. Soon the ruined town of Tiberias rose again. An impressive synagogue was built and roads were constructed. Jewish agricultural settlements were founded at Pekiin, Shefa Amr, and Kefar Yasif. The more they prospered the warmer became the friendship between the Rabbi and the Sheikh. But Omar, like Fakhr ad-Din his predecessor, had to pay dearly for his independence. The Treaty of Kutchuk Kainardji, concluded with Russia on 21 July 1774, gave Abdul Hamid I the opportunity to turn against him. When the Sultan's fleet anchored off the coast of Acre, Omar's troops revolted against their master and assassinated him.[20]

Ahmad Al-Jezzar, Omar's successor, was cast in a different mould. For twenty-nine years (1775–1804) he ruled his province with an iron rod. His cruelty and avarice were extraordinary. As if determined to live up to his name Jezzar, which means 'butcher', he did not limit himself to the role of judge, but is said to have himself amputated selected limbs or executed condemned prisoners. Yet no maltreatment of his Jewish subjects is recorded. It was during his rule that the first group of 300 Russian Hassidim arrived in 1777, followed by others, and Safad was revived. Jezzar's leniency towards the Jews may be attributed in part to the influence of his Minister of Finance and adviser, Chaim Farhi. Chaim was a descendant of an illustrious Jewish family in Syria renowned for its valuable services to the Ottoman cause. Contemporary travellers described the Farhis as the 'true rulers of Syria', and Chaim himself won Lady Hester Stanhope's admiration. In a key position, he never shrank from interceding on behalf of his co-religionists. Jezzar's restraint was repaid. His Jewish subjects proved their loyalty when, on 20 April 1799, Napoleon issued a proclamation to Asiatic and African Jews promising 'to give them the Holy Land' if they came over to his side.

[20] Ben-Zvi, op. cit., pp. 25–31, 51, 299–319; Parkes, op. cit., pp. 159–61; de Haas, op. cit., pp. 350–65.

However attractive the promise, the Ottoman Jews did not revolt against their own government. Farhi was entrusted by Jezzar with the defence of Acre, and contemporary chronicles give much credit to his contribution in withstanding Napoleon's siege.[21]

Between 1804 and 1832 Farhi served all Jezzar's successors well. Abdullah (1824–32), in particular, owed much of his education to the Jewish Minister. Nevertheless, shortly after his accession, in a moment of anger, Abdullah executed Farhi and confiscated all his property (1820). Farhi's brothers tried to avenge him and, after securing approval from the Porte, besieged Abdullah's fortress of Acre. However, Abdullah managed to bribe the Syrian pashas who were helping the Farhis to withdraw, and then took revenge on the Jews of Acre, Safad, and Tiberias. So heavy were the fines and taxes imposed that a saying was current that the Jews had to pay for 'the very air they breathed'.[22] Abdullah's rule came to an ignominious end in 1832 when Ibrahim Pasha, Mehemet Ali's stepson, conquered the country.

Ibrahim's administration lasted eight years (1832–40). Like his stepfather, the founder of Egyptian independence, he was a great innovator and reformer. He maintained law and order, and travellers could move freely in relative safety. Syria and Palestine were thrown open to Western influence and it was during his rule that European schools, hospitals, and biblical and missionary societies were established. Christian and Jewish representatives were admitted to the Municipal and Provincial Councils (*Majlis Ummumi*).[23] When Sir Moses Montefiore, accompanied by the British Consul-General, Colonel Patrick Campbell, called on Mehemet Ali in Alexandria on

---

[21] Ben-Zvi, op. cit., pp. 31–3, 320–3, 339–40; Graetz, op. cit. v, p. 488; Sokolow, *History of Zionism*, i, pp. 63–4, 69–72, and Appendix II, p. xl; de Haas, op. cit., pp. 365–84; G. Roloff, *Die Orientpolitik Napoleons* (Weimar, 1916); C. M. Walson, 'Bonaparte's Expedition to Palestine in 1799', *Palestine Exploration Fund* (Jan. 1917), 17–35; F. Kobler, 'Napoleon and the Restoration of the Jews to Palestine: Discovery of an Historic Document', *New Judea*, xvi, no. 12, xvii, nos. 1–2, 3, 5; N. M. Gelber, *Napoleon* (Jerusalem, 1950), pp. 263–88; Parkes, op. cit., pp. 210–13; François Pietri, *Napoléon et les Israélites* (Paris, 1966). The original text of Napoleon's proclamation in French and Hebrew was lost. The one discovered is in a German translation, retranslated later into English.

[22] Ben-Zvi, op. cit., pp. 340–4; de Haas, op. cit., pp. 380–7.

[23] Ben-Zvi, op. cit., pp. 344–8; de Haas, op. cit., pp. 388–99; Poliak, op. cit., pp. 75–84; H. D. V. Temperley, *England and the Near East: The Crimea* (London, 1936), pp. 91, 179. *Cambridge Modern History*, x, pp. 545, 571; Asad Jibrail Rustum, *Materials for a corpus of Arab Documents relating to the History of Syria under Mehemet Ali Pasha* (Beirut, 1930–4), 5 vols.

13 July 1839, they were assured that although on religious grounds Jews and Christians were not permitted to give evidence against Muslims, they were none the less treated on an equal footing.[24]

Economically, however, the Jews were no better off. A contemporary German traveller estimated that only 20 to 30 per cent of the Jewish population was able to earn its living; the remainder depended on funds collected abroad.[25] This description tallies with that of William Young, the first British Vice-Consul in Jerusalem.[26] Sir Moses Montefiore, when visiting Safad in 1839, was deeply depressed by the 'awful spectacle' of its destruction and the poverty of its Jewish inhabitants. Hunger, plundering by Muslim neighbours, the devastating earthquake of 1837, coupled with a deadly raid by the Druses, filled the cup of their misfortune. But their spirit, Montefiore was comforted to note, was not crushed. They were anxious to be employed, preferably in agriculture. Montefiore had been informed that the land in Galilee was fertile. It 'could produce almost everything . . . I am sure that if the plan I have . . . would succeed, it will bring happiness and plenty to the Holy Land.' He hoped to establish a company to cultivate land in Palestine, and that at least one to two hundred villages could be built.[27]

Mehemet Ali did not reject the plan. His eyes 'sparkled with delight' when Montefiore proposed the establishment of a bank with a capital of £1,000,000, with branches in Beirut, Damascus, Jerusalem, Alexandria, and Cairo as a quid pro quo.[28] However, nothing came of it. The Damascus affair[29] so shocked liberal opinion that the

[24] *Diaries of Sir Moses and Lady Montefiore*, ed. L. Loewe (London, 1890), i, pp. 198–200 (cited hereafter as *Diaries of Montefiore*). There is a biography of Sir Moses by Lucien Wolf, *The Life of Sir Moses Montefiore* (London, 1884); see also Sokolow, op. cit. i, pp. 115–20.

[25] U. J. Seetzen, *Reisen durch Syrien, Palästina* . . . (Berlin, 1854), ii, p. 23; Ben-Zion Gath, *Ha-Yishuv ha-Yehudi b'Eretz-Israel b'Shnot: 1840–1881* [*The Jewish Settlement in Palestine: 1840–1881*], (Jerusalem, 1963), pp. 17, 93; Abraham Yaari, 'The Vicissitudes of the Ashkenazi Jews in Jerusalem at the Beginning of the Nineteenth Century' (Hebrew, reprint from *Sinai*) (Jerusalem, 1940).

[26] *The British Consulate in Palestine in relation to the Jews of Palestine, 1838–1914*, ed. A. M. Hyamson (London, 1939), i, p. 5, Young to Palmerston, 25 May 1839 (cited hereafter as *B.C.*).

[27] *Diaries of Montefiore*, i, pp. 165–8.

[28] Ibid. i, pp. 198–200.

[29] This was a notorious blood libel. On 5 Feb. 1840 Thomas, a Capuchin friar, together with his Muslim servant disappeared and soon after the Capuchin Order spread the news that they had been murdered by the Jews in order to use their blood for the Passover. The French Consul, under whose protection the Catholics in Syria were, instead of investigating the matter, allied himself with the accusers. The affair, and particularly

question of colonization was pushed into the background and, on 4 August 1840, when Montefiore next met Mehemet Ali, there were more pressing matters to discuss.[30] A year later Ali no longer ruled that region.

The idea of the Jewish colonization of Palestine attracted Lord Palmerston but, misrepresented to the Porte by Viscount Ponsonby, the British Ambassador, the scheme fizzled out.[31] Perhaps the Jews themselves were not yet ready for so ambitious a project. Those in the West were fully immersed in their struggle for emancipation, while those in Eastern Europe pinned their hopes on redemption by a Messiah. In this respect Hassidic thought represented a turning-point.[32] The insistence on an actual presence in the Holy Land constituted a link between the passive expectation of divine deliverance and Zionist activism. The immediate emotives which precipitated Hassidic immigration to Palestine were yet factional. At loggerheads with their opponents, the Mitnaggedim,[33] they hoped that if some of their members were to settle in Palestine their movement would gain immensely in prestige and their message carry greater weight. But the Mitnaggedim were not slow to appropriate their rivals' tactics. One positive result of this competition was that it reinforced the bond between the Diaspora and Palestine and stimulated immigration. During the eighteenth and nineteenth centuries the trickle broadened into a stream. This was the first massive and

the barbarous manner in which the investigation was carried out by the Muslim authorities, outraged Jews and non-Jews in Western Europe. A Jewish delegation led by Sir Moses Montefiore and Adolphe Crémieux appeared before Mehemet Ali who on 28 August 1840 ordered the release of the Jewish prisoners in Damascus. (Dubnow, op. cit. ix, pp. 308–16; Sokolow, op. cit. i, pp. 110–11; S. Posener, *Adolphe Crémieux* (Paris, 1933), i, pp. 197–247; Galante, *Documents* . . . pp. 157–61; Zosa Szajkowski, 'The Damascus Affair' (Hebrew), *Zion* (1954), 167–70). At Montefiore's request Sultan Abdul Mejid issued a *firman* (6 November 1840) attesting the innocence of the Jews. '. . . We cannot permit the Jewish nation . . . to be vexed and tormented upon accusations, which have not the least foundation in truth . . .' (see Friedman, 'Lord Palmerston and the Protection of Jews', 27–8 n. 35).

[30] *Diaries of Montefiore*, i, pp. 225–8.

[31] I. Friedman, 'Lord Palmerston and the Protection of Jews in Palestine', 28–36.

[32] See Shlomo A. Horodetzki: *Ha-Chasidut Ve'Hachasidim [Hassidism and the Hassidim]* (Jerusalem, 1923), iv, p. 61; Dubnow, 'The First Hassidim in Palestine', *Pardess*, ii (Odessa, 1893); D. Weinryb, op. cit., p. 64; Ben-Zion Dinaburg, 'Ideological Background of Palestine Immigration: 1740–1840', *Zion* (Apr. 1937), 93–105; *idem*, 'The Beginnings of Hassidism and its Social and Messianic Elements', *Zion* (Apr.–July 1945), 149–96.

[33] The meaning in Hebrew is opponents. They were concentrated mostly in Lithuania and northern Russia. In Palestine the Mitnaggedim were called *Perushim*, which means separatists.

consistent immigration, composed predominantly of Ashkenazim.[34] It was they who laid the foundation of the old Yishuv.[35] Jerusalem and Hebron were invigorated, whilst Safad and Tiberias, heretofore lying waste, were rebuilt.[36] But the new immigrants had no desire to become craftsmen or tillers of the land. Their object was to spend the rest of their days in prayer and learning. Devotion to religious practices overrode any mundane consideration. Living on charity and in social isolation, their outlook became fossilized. Gradually they grew more bigoted and impervious to any modern ideas. It was amongst them that, in subsequent decades, the Zionist pioneers found their most implacable enemies.

The advent of the Ashkenazim introduced a new element on to the Palestinian scene. Unlike the veteran Sephardic community the Ashkenazim were reluctant to become Ottoman subjects and preferred foreign protection.[37] They acknowledged that the Turkish Government in Palestine was 'one of the most tolerant in the world in matters of religion',[38] but felt too insecure to submit to Ottoman jurisdiction. The laws, although just and humane, became in the hands of local officials 'a dead letter'. The pashas were known to be incompetent and corrupt, and in the prevailing conditions a foreigner could desire nothing better than protection from his consul. The treaty rights accorded to foreign Powers an extraordinary status. They could use force whenever their subjects or protégés were maltreated, but in most cases a mere warning from a consul had a sobering effect on the local authorities. Consular protection proved an invaluable instrument for securing Christian lives. It was also a source of succour to Jewish protégés.[39] The Ashkenazim were not the only minority to solicit the protection of foreign Powers. The Samaritans and the Copts, though

---

[34] *Ashkenaz* in Hebrew means Germany, whence during the Middle Ages Jews migrated to Eastern Europe. The term *Ashkenazim* denotes the Central and East European Jewry and their offshoots in Western Europe and the United States, in contrast to the Sephardi and the Oriental Jewish communities.

[35] The 'Old Settlement', in contrast to the new Yishuv founded in the 1880s by the Hibbat Zion colonists, on which see below, pp. 37–9, 46–7.

[36] Ben-Zvi, op. cit., pp. 299–306; Israel Halpern, *Ha-Aliyot Ha-Rishonot shel ha-Hassidim b'Eretz-Israel* [*The First Waves of Immigration of the Hassidim to Palestine*] (Jerusalem, 1940), pp. 20–37.   [37] *B.C.* i, p. 95.

[38] Ibid., p. 191, Finn to Earl of Malmesbury, 29 Apr. 1852; James Finn, *Stirring Times or Records from Jerusalem Consular Chronicles* (London, 1878), i, p. 223.

[39] Finn, op. cit. i, pp. 128, 181, 185, 187, 269, 341; ii, pp. 144, 190, 281. On the Sultanic laws (the Edicts of Toleration), ibid. i, pp. 223; ii, p. 446.

Ottoman subjects, were also eager for a similar privilege.[40] Even Muslim Arabs were reported to be 'prepossessed by one idea . . . —the hope of deliverance from the rapacious rule of the Turkish Pashas'.[41] But the Ashkenazim had additional reasons for sheltering under foreign protection: it noticeably enhanced their status *vis-à-vis* the Sephardim.[42] Since the sixteenth century the latter had been the leading element in the Jewish community in Palestine. The Sephardi Chief Rabbi enjoyed considerable executive powers and his verdicts were sanctioned, and often even implemented, by the Ottoman Government. A special guard enhanced his prestige, whilst his title, 'the First in Zion', was one of peculiar dignity. But the Ashkenazim, with their numbers steadily increasing,[43] challenged the Sephardic supremacy. They resented the demands of the Sephardim to pay a tax for the privilege of living in the Holy Cities, and, with their different religious customs, were reluctant to place themselves under Sephardic rabbinical jurisdiction.[44] This, by implication, was tantamount to rejection of the Ottoman jurisdiction. The Ashkenazim were disinclined to assimilate to the Oriental way of life and, as Consul Finn rightly observed, the majority of them were, and probably would always be, Europeans.[45] In the Ottoman State they remained an alien element. This had profound implications: the Turkish Government considered only the Sephardim as 'Jews *par excellence*';[46] the Ashkenazic community was never officially recognized. But it was not until the end of the 1850s that the Porte realized that foreign protection of the Ashkenazim was harmful to Ottoman interests.

[40] *B.C.* i, p. 185, Finn to Palmerston, 29 Dec. 1851.   [41] Finn, op. cit. i, p. 226.

[42] On 1 Jan. 1858 James Finn reported: 'Forty years ago [before the establishment of the Consulates, the Ashkenazim] were not recognized in Jerusalem . . . but now they are rising into importance, under the patronage of their respective Consuls—their political status is greatly improved and their number has been augmented.' (*B.C.* i, p. 257.)

[43] For a description of the Jewish community see ibid., and by contemporary travellers: Conder, *Tent Work in Palestine*, i, pp. 293–7; W. H. Bartlett, *Jerusalem Revisited* (London, 1855), pp. 77–83; Gath, op. cit., pp. 10–11, 15, 22–32; Frank Manuel, *The Realities of American—Palestine Relations* (Washington, 1949), pp. 16–19. Until 1872 the Sephardim were in a majority, but by 1877 the Ashkenazim outstripped them and constituted about 60 per cent of the total Jewish population. The Hibbat Zion immigration in the eighties was composed predominantly of Ashkenazim (Gath, op. cit., pp. 21–2). Shochet's statistics (op. cit., p. 81) differ slightly from those of Gath. In addition to the Sephardim and Ashkenazim there was also a number of Jews from Morocco (20 per cent), from Georgia, Central Asia, the Caucasus, and Yemen.

[44] *B.C.* i, p. 127, Finn to Moore, 27 June 1849; Manuel, op. cit., p. 18.

[45] *B.C.* ii, p. 298, Finn to Bulwer, 22 May 1862.   [46] Finn, op. cit. i, p. 102.

3

The System of Capitulations and its Effects on Turco-Jewish Relations in Palestine 1856–97

THE eagerness of the Ashkenazim to shelter under foreign protection suited admirably the interests of the Powers. The consuls vied with each other to protect as many Jews as possible. Even the Spanish Consulate, notwithstanding the exclusion of Jews from Spain itself, was said to be glad to have a few under its protection.[1] In the early 1850s, out of 5,000 Ashkenazim, 3,000 enjoyed Austrian protection, 1,000 were registered with the British Consulate, and the remainder with the Prussian, American, Dutch, and Russian consulates.[2] Following the decision of the Russian Government to withdraw jurisdiction from its Jewish subjects in Palestine, the great majority of these turned to the British Consulate. This arrangement lasted until 1890, when its usefulness had evidently spent itself and when the Russian Government decided to reverse its decision, reclaiming the right of protection.[3]

[1] *B.C.* i, p. 259, James Finn (Jerusalem) to Earl of Clarendon (London), 1 Jan. 1858; also Finn, *Stirring Times . . .* , ii, p. 281. The British Vice-Consulate was established in 1839 and in 1841 was upgraded to the status of Consulate. In 1843 the Prussian, Sardinian, and French consulates were established, in 1844 the American, in 1849 the Austrian, and in 1854 the Spanish. Palestine lay also within the jurisdiction of the Russian Consul-General at Beirut. He had an agent representing him in Jerusalem, a rabbi, and a Vice-Consul in Jaffa.

[2] Bernhard Neumann, *Die Heilige Stadt* (Hamburg, 1877), p. 376; Elizabeth Anne McCaul-Finn: *Reminiscences of . . .* (London, 1929), p. 81. The total number of Jews in Palestine in the mid nineteenth century was approximately 11,000.

[3] I. Friedman, 'Lord Palmerston and the Protection of Jews in Palestine', 25, 39; below, p. 48.

The Sublime Porte tolerated this long-standing system with remarkable equanimity. It was known as the Capitulations (the treaty was divided into chapters—*Capituli*), and was based on the idea of extraterritoriality. In contrast with the modern concept which relates sovereignty to territory, earlier ideas linked it to persons. A monarch or a state exercised jurisdiction over his or its own nationals and not over aliens, who were subject to the exclusive jurisdiction of their respective mother countries, from which, in case of need, they sought protection. This was particularly the case in circumstances where law was inextricably interwoven with religion, and where there existed no equality between believers and unbelievers. In Muslim countries jurisdiction could hardly be applied to non-Muslims and even less so to aliens, who were practically outlaws. During the sixteenth century, to resolve the difficulty, France, followed by other Powers, concluded a series of treaties with the Turkish sultans which gave the Powers the right to safeguard the interests of their respective subjects who were visiting or living in the Ottoman Empire.

Originally, the system proved a blessing to all concerned. It spared the Ottoman Government the complicated task of administering the affairs of foreign visitors; on the other hand it increased their security and stimulated trade. But with Turkey's decline, particularly during the nineteenth century, the system degenerated into blatant abuse. The privilege of extraterritoriality was extended to a sizeable non-Muslim population who misused it, flouted local regulations, and did not hesitate to make capital out of their legal security. Foreign banks, post offices, and commercial houses mushroomed on Turkish soil and took full advantage of the country's feebleness, while the Consuls grew more insolent as they grew more powerful. Protégés of foreign Powers, claiming partial immunity from the laws and exemption from local taxation, became a scourge to the country. But it was not until the late 1850s that Turkey, becoming more conscious of her own sovereign rights, began to regard the Capitulations as a humiliating encroachment. The turning-point came in 1856 when Turkey first raised the question of abrogating the capitulatory rights, holding them to be both harmful and obsolescent. The system had been suitable in earlier times under different conditions, when law was personal and not related to territorial sovereignty.[4]

---

[4] See Sousa, *The Capitulatory Regime of Turkey*, pp. 93–101 and bibliography quoted therein; G. B. Ravdal, 'Capitulations', *Modern Turkey*, ed. E. G. Mears (New York,

On 26 January 1856, when the Government published the *Hatti-Humayun* (the Edict of Toleration), it was confident that the edict would eliminate the need for the European Powers to protect their subjects and protégés and would facilitate Turkey's admission to the comity of European nations on an equal footing.[5] Realities, however, fell short of expectations. Article XXXII of the Treaty of Paris of 30 March 1856 provided that all treaties and conventions which had existed heretofore 'were to continue to operate' and that 'no change was to be effected without the consent of the Powers concerned'. The London Conference of 7 January 1871 reaffirmed and extended this principle and the Treaty of Berlin of 1878 put a final seal on it.[6] The Capitulations thus assumed a binding character and acquired a valid international status. The non-intervention guarantee was a dead letter. Turkey remained, in fact, outside the pale of international law.

Whatever the rights or wrongs of this policy, it had a profound effect on Turkey. It determined her attitude towards the European Powers and foreigners in general. For decades Turkish diplomacy strove, albeit unsuccessfully, to nullify, or at least to restrict, their excessive prerogatives. The process started in 1856. After the Crimean War James Finn, the British Consul in Jerusalem, recorded that the pashas found out that revenge could after all be wreaked on the consuls, and the old tactic of playing off one consul against the other reasserted itself.[7] Yet however experienced the Turks were in this particular art, they were powerless to effect any change in the legal position; the most that they could expect was to reduce drastically the number of protégés. These became a permanent target of

1924), 430–47; Ben-Zvi, *Eretz-Israel Ve' Yeshuva*, pp. 123–36 and bibliography quoted therein; A. J. Toynbee and K. P. Kirkwood, *Turkey* (London, 1926), pp. 137–40; Finn, op. cit. i, p. 91. On the doctrine of exterritoriality see William Edward Hall, *A Treatise on International Law*, 8th edn. (Oxford, 1924), pp. 217–20; *Encyclopædia Britannica* (London, 1963), iv, pp. 813–14, 851–2.

5 Finn, op. cit. i, pp. 91, 222–3; ii, pp. 445–6; Bernard Lewis, *The Emergence o, Modern Turkey* (London, 1961), p. 114; A. L. Tibawi, *British Interests in Palestine: 1800–1901* (London, 1961), pp. 115, 130, 180; Roderic H. Davison, *Reform in the Ottoman Empire, 1856–1876* (Princeton University Press, 1963), pp. 52–80; William Miller, *The Ottoman Empire and its Successors, 1801–1927* (Cambridge University Press, 1934), pp. 288–9; and for the effect of the *Hatti-Humayun* on the Jews see Franco: *Essai sur l'histoire des Israélites de l'Empire ottoman*, pp. 143–51; Dubnow, *Weltgeschichte*, ix, p. 493; Sokolow, *History of Zionism*, i, pp. 152–3; ii, p. 412.

6 Sousa, op. cit., pp. 167–70; Hall, op. cit., p. 60 n. 1; Davison, op. cit., pp. 413–14. The protocol is cited in full in *Modern Turkey*, ed. Mears, p. 442.

7 Finn, op. cit. i, p. 187.

suspicion as conscious or unconscious tools against Ottoman sovereignty.

The first move was made on 17 July 1869, when a law of nationality was introduced. Coinciding with the general upsurge of xenophobia, it ordained that every resident of the Ottoman dominions was an Ottoman subject until he proved the contrary.[8] The Ottoman Government, not without reason, suspected the expanding activities of the Christian Powers in the Holy Land. The colonies of German Templars, the large caravans of French, Austrian, and Russian pilgrims, the influx of Russian Jews into Jerusalem and Safad were thought to be politically motivated.[9] As a countermeasure the Ottoman Government encouraged the annual *Nabi Musa* procession, to overlap with Easter.[10] Muslims from Algeria, the Caucasus, and the Balkans were given every facility to settle in Palestine and the adjacent territories; non-Muslims were discouraged, and so strict did the prohibitions against their acquiring land and immovable property become that the Consuls wondered whether the Sultan's promises, embodied in the 1856 Edict, to allow Europeans to purchase land would be fulfilled at all.[11] A typical instance occurred in 1866, when forty American families arrived in Jaffa to establish a colony in that neighbourhood. So serious were the objections raised by the Porte that a *démarche* by the American Minister in Constantinople proved of little avail.

The policy of the Turkish Government does not favour the acquisition of real estate by foreigners . . . If the Porte were to give its consent to the establishment of the colony in question, it would sanction a violation of the standard policy and legislation of the empire and would establish a precedent for the creation of similar settlements by subjects of other countries also.[12]

[8] *Papers relating to Foreign Relations of the United States* (1886), pp. 862–4, Cox (Constantinople) to Bayard (Washington), 5 Jan. 1886 (cited hereafter as *F.R.U.S.*). The Law of Nationality of 1869 had no retrospective effect; H. H. Jessup, *Fifty-three Years in Syria* (New York, 1910), ii, p. 438; also *F.R.U.S.* (1879), p. 993, Maynard (Constantinople) to Evarts (Washington), 15 Oct. 1879; Finn, op. cit. i, pp. 253–4, 263, 344; ii, pp. 443–9.

[9] Conder, *Tent Work in Palestine*, ii, pp. 310–11; *B.C.* i, p. 268, Finn to Lord Russell, 21 Jan. 1860. [10] Ben-Zvi, op. cit., p. 337.

[11] Public Record Office, London, F.O. 195/604, no. 2, Finn to Bulwer, 24 Aug. 1859. According to Muslim law foreigners were not allowed to hold real estate, except on lease for a short period. However, before 1859 this principle had been 'frequently relaxed'. (Ibid.)

[12] *F.R.U.S.* (1865–6), Pt. ii, p. 258, Ali Pasha to Morris (Constantinople), 28 Nov. 1866; ibid. (1866), pp. 257–8, Morris to Seward, 30 Nov. 1866.

Turkey's resentment at the system of Capitulations affected its attitude towards Jewish settlement. In 1855, when Sir Moses and Lady Montefiore arrived on their fourth visit to Palestine, they were received by the local authorities 'amiably and respectfully'. Furnished with a *firman* from the Sultan to rebuild an ancient synagogue in Jerusalem, Sir Moses also purchased a tract of land to the west of the Holy City, outside its walls; the first Englishman to whom such permission was granted. In 1859, however, the building of the projected almshouses (the *Mishkenot Shaananim*) was suspended, for the Turks were no longer willing to classify the project as 'business or trade', or even to consider it as philanthropy: it had become a matter of principle. It took a year of considerable efforts to make Fuad Pasha, the Foreign Minister, grant Sir Moses 'exceptional permission' to proceed with his project.[13] But this was an exception: in general, the authorities were as obdurate as ever. Even those individual Jews who were born in the country and inherited their properties were told that unless they renounced consular protection their title-deeds would be invalidated.[14]

The twin objects of Turkish policy were to impress upon foreign Jews the necessity of adopting Ottoman nationality and to deny the Powers the right of protection. On 12 May 1874 Rashid Pasha, the Foreign Minister, requested the British Embassy in Constantinople to renounce its protection of a certain number of Jews in Syria and Palestine. 'Times have changed,' he insisted, 'protection has become an obsolescent institution' and constituted a 'fruitful source of trouble and dispute.'[12] Soon after, the Governor-General in Damascus made it clear that he would treat all persons of 'doubtful nationality' as Ottoman subjects. But with the consuls remaining unco-operative the Turkish authorities had to resort to the unprecedented step of advising the Jewish protégés of the foreign Powers directly that their certificates of registration with the foreign consulates, ominously referred to as *permis de séjour*, must be countersigned by the local authorities. Failing this, their certificates would become invalid. Despite the ambassadors' protests against the innovation of the term *permis de séjour* as a limitation on the freedom of movement of their respective nationals and protégés,

[13] *B.C.* i, pp. 233–5, 238, Finn to Lord Stratford, 24 July, 30 Aug. 1855; same to Bulwer, 15 Aug. 1859; same to same, 12 Feb., 14 Apr., 15 Aug., 17 Nov. 1859 (pp. 261–7); *Diaries of Montefiore*, ii, pp. 44–6, 51, 109–10.

[14] *B.C.* i, p. 266, Finn to Bulwer, 24 Aug. 1859.

[15] Ibid. i, p. 393, Locock to Earl of Derby, 12 May 1874.

the Porte remained adamant.[16] In its view the promulgation of the Ottoman Law of Nationality in 1869 *ipso facto* terminated the right of Russian Jews to foreign protection, after their original nationality had been renounced. That an entire population was subject to alien jurisdiction on the territory of the Empire without the sanction of the Porte and for the 'sole object of enjoying immunities which limited the sovereign rights of the Ottoman authorities, was utterly inadmissible'.[17]

It is necessary to sketch this background in order to explain why the 'back to Palestine' movement of the Hibbat Zion societies, and subsequently of the Zionist Organization, from the first encountered determined opposition from the Turkish Government. With the French intervention in the Lebanon in 1860 and the Bulgarian question still fresh in Turkish memory, the Sultan, as an informed agent of Baron de Hirsch testified, was reluctant to burden himself with a Jewish question.[18] Thirty years later this view was confirmed by Rabbi Nahoum Effendi, the Chief Rabbi of Turkey and an intimate friend of Talaat Pasha, the Grand Vizier, who thought that the many bitter experiences in other provinces made the Turks fear that the existence of large and coherent Jewish colonies in Palestine might lead to diplomatic interference by foreign Powers, to the detriment of their sovereign rights in that important region.[19]

The Hibbat Zion (Love of Zion)[20] movement originated in Russia in the wake of anti-Jewish pogroms in 1881-2. So traumatic was the experience that it shattered irreparably the dream of

[16] Ibid., p. 394, Elliot to Aurifi Pasha, 4 Aug. 1874; pp. 431-2, Eyres to White, 27 Dec. 1886, encl. in White to Salisbury, 4 Apr. 1887; pp. 432-3, White to Sublime Porte, 6 Jan. 1887; p. 434, Porte to White, 2 Apr. 1887.

[17] Ibid., p. 438, Said (Turkish Foreign Minister) to White, 11 Aug. 1887.

[18] 'weil der Sultan sich keine "jüdische Frage" auf den Hals ziehen wolle.' Veneziani to (?), 7 Jan. 1883, in A. Druyanov (ed.): *Ktavim L'Toledoth Hibbath Zion V'Yishuv Eretz-Israel* [*Letters regarding the History of Hibbat Zion and the Settlement in Palestine*] (Odessa, 1919), i, p. 77 (cited hereafter as Dryuanov).

[19] Below, pp. 292-3.

[20] Among the voluminous literature on Hibbat Zion and its colonization in Palestine see Dubnow, op. cit. ix, pp. 293-302; Sokolow, op. cit. i, pp. 213-27; Böhm, *Die zionistische Bewegung*, i, pp. 96-115; Leonard Stein, *Zionism* (London, 1932), pp. 35-6; Israel Cohen, *The Zionist Movement* (London, 1945), pp. 18-19, 54-66; *idem*, *A Short History of Zionism* (London, 1951), pp. 28-39; Rufus Learski, *Fulfilment* (New York, 1951), pp. 41-58; Alex Bein, *The Return to the Soil* (Jerusalem, 1952), pp. 4-10; Shmuel Yavnieli, *Tkufat Hibbah Zion* [*The Period of Hibbat Zion*] (Jerusalem, 1961), 2 vols.; Israel Klausner, *B'Ithorer Am* [*Awakening of a People*] (Jerusalem, 1962); *Encyclopædia Ivrit*, pp. 508-12.

enlightenment and russification in which some Jewish youth and intelligentsia indulged. Disillusioned and rejected, they sought compensation in a rediscovery of their national identity. The revival of the Hebrew language and literature was given a new fillip, and restoration of the national life in Palestine became the central theme in the new thinking. Aspirations for emancipation gave way to self-emancipation.

Bilu,[21] a group of Jewish students from Russian universities, was one of the most notable societies to give substance to this ideal. Imbued with the will to build a model society on social justice, they set a personal example and a number of them made their way to Palestine, founding two colonies south of Jaffa: Rishon-le-Zion (1882) and Gedera (1884). Other Russian Jews in 1882 restored the settlement of Petah-Tikva, north of Jaffa (founded in 1878 by some Jerusalemite Jews and abandoned following an outbreak of malaria). In the same year a group of pioneers from Romania established two colonies: Samarin (renamed later Zichron Yaakov) on the way to Haifa, and Rosh-Pina, near Safad, whilst immigrants from Poland founded Yesod Haamale near Lake Hula in Upper Galilee. The following year saw the establishment of Nes-Tsiyona in Judaea. In addition there existed Mikve-Israel, an agricultural school near Jaffa, established in 1870 by Carl Netter on behalf of the Alliance Israélite Universelle, and Motza, a tiny settlement near Jerusalem. By 1889 there were twenty-two Jewish rural settlements in Palestine on a land area of 76,000 acres, with a total population of about 5,000.[22] The settlements were widely dispersed but they served as a pointer to the districts in which the next colonies were to be founded.

Although enthusiastic, the pioneers were ill equipped for their venture. The difficulties were more formidable than they had anticipated. They were exposed to the dangers of malaria, an unpleasant climate, and raids by bedouins; they were ignorant of the country and of Arabic and had little or no experience in agriculture; they were unused to hard physical labour and suffered from lack of funds. Had it not been for the generous financial support afforded by Baron Edmond de Rothschild of Paris,[23] the infant

---

[21] The name was taken from the Book of Isaiah 2: 5, *Beth Jacob lechu ve-helcha* ('O house of Jacob, come ye and let us go forth') and also formed their motto.

[22] Bein, op. cit., pp. 4–6; Abraham Revusky: *Jews in Palestine* (London, 1938), pp. 10–12.

[23] See David Druck, *Baron Edmund Rothschild. The Story of Practical Idealism* London, 1928); Israel Margalith, *Le Baron Edmond de Rothschild et la colonisation juive*

settlements would soon have foundered. But what seemed an almost insuperable obstacle was the positive discouragement of the Ottoman authorities. Such an unfriendly attitude seemed at first incomprehensible to the colonists. It was certainly inconsistent with the image of Turkey projected by Jews throughout the centuries, as one of the most hospitable and tolerant countries in the world.

A Bilu delegation which arrived in Constantinople in 1881 with the intention of winning over the Turkish Government to its project was greatly surprised when its application for the purchase of land in Palestine was rejected.[24] Equally unsuccessful was Jacob Rosenfeld, the editor of the Russian-Jewish paper *Razsviet*, when he met Daud Effendi, the Jewish assistant to the Ottoman Foreign Minister. For a while it looked as if Romanian Jews might be more fortunate in their negotiations with the Porte, since de Castro, a Sephardic Jew and an adviser to the Sultan, acted as their mediator. Their plea that Turkey could not remain indifferent to the plight of Jews in Romania, because provinces of that country had formerly belonged to the Ottoman Empire, carried some weight, and negotiations seemed at first to make headway. But the news of the annexation of Egypt by the British had such a devastating effect in Constantinople that any overtures were doomed.[25] Laurence Oliphant, writing from Constantinople, listed the annexation of Egypt by the British as one of the reasons for Turkey's objection to Jewish immigration; the others he attributed to the Sultan's reluctance to allow non-Muslims to settle in Palestine and to the adverse influence of anti-Jewish (Catholic?) circles.[26]

The Porte soon resorted to action. In June 1882 entry to the country was forbidden, purchase of real property was made impossible, and even building of houses was strictly prohibited; those

---

en Palestine: 1882–1899 (Paris, 1957). The total amount invested by Rothschild in the Jewish settlement in Palestine is estimated at £5·6 millions, of which £1·6 million was spent between 1883 and 1889. It is worth while to compare this sum to that invested by the Hovevé Zion societies, which did not exceed £87,000 (Bein, op. cit., p. 6 n.; *Encyclopædia Ivrit*, p. 510).

[24] Sokolow, op. cit. i, pp. 206–9; ii, pp. 267–9.

[25] Klausner, op. cit., pp. 227–34; *idem, Hibbat Zion b'Rumania* (Hebrew), (Jerusalem, 1958), p. 110.

[26] Druyanov, i, p. 37, Oliphant to David Gordon, 24 June 1882. On Oliphant see Sokolow, op. cit. i, pp. 207–9, 250, 267–9, 306–7; Albert Hyamson, *British Projects for the Restoration of the Jews* (London, 1917), pp. 31 ff.; Philip Henderson, *The Life of Laurence Oliphant* (London, 1956).

built without permission were liable to be demolished.[27] This did not necessarily mean that Turkey threw its traditional hospitality overboard. In the following month a Council of Ministers affirmed that Jews from any country were to be allowed to settle in any part of the Empire, though not in Palestine, and in groups no bigger than 100 to 150 families. The immigrants had to become Ottoman subjects, to take an oath of allegiance to the Sultan, and to comply with Ottoman law. In return the Porte offered every facility: the settlers would be given government lands free of charge, would be granted exemption from taxation and from military service for a certain period, and would enjoy the same religious freedom as other subjects of the Empire.[28] These guide-lines were to remain a constant feature in Turkish policy. Jews were to be treated as benevolently and tolerantly as before but Palestine was to remain out of bounds. No new nationality problem was to be created.

Nelidow, the Russian Ambassador in Constantinople, was the first to protest, in 1882, against the prohibition of Jewish immigration to Palestine. Criticism was aired in *Novoe Vremya*, a leading Russian paper, and in August of the following year Giers, the Russian Foreign Minister, was reported to have assured a Hovevé Zion (Lovers of Zion) leader of his interest and support.[29] But with Turkey's sensitivity reaching a new pitch, any interference from a foreign Power was bound to have an adverse effect. Russia, with her black record of pogroms, could only be suspect in Turkish eyes of nourishing ulterior motives when interceding for Russian Jews in Palestine. A characteristic argument was that the European governments were deliberately inducing the Jews to emigrate to Palestine 'in order to provide themselves with a pretext to annex it'.[30] In February 1884, when M. Fernandez, a leader of the Jewish community in Constantinople and head of the Alliance Israélite Universelle Bureau in the Orient, approached the Ottoman Minister of Interior

---

[27] Druyanov, i, *passim*; Moshe Smilansky: *Prakim B'Toledoth Ha-Yishuv* [*Chapters in the History of the Jewish Settlement in Palestine*], (Tel Aviv, 1945), i, pp. 33–4, 38–9, 53, 60, 67–8; Klausner, op. cit., pp. 200, 342–3; Frank Manuel, *The Realities of American-Palestine Relations*, pp. 55, 56; also Neville Mandel, 'Turks, Arabs and Jewish Immigration into Palestine, 1882–1914', *St. Antony's Papers*, no. 17, *Middle Eastern Affairs*, no. 4, ed. A. Hourani (Oxford, 1965), pp. 79–83.

[28] *F.R.U.S.* (1882), pp. 516–17, Wallace (Constantinople) to Frelinghüsen (Washington), 11 July 1882; Manuel, op. cit., pp. 52–3.

[29] Klausner, op. cit., pp. 340–1.

[30] *Mevaseret Zion*, no. 3 (Jerusalem, 1884); *Kol Kitvey Eliezer Ben-Yehuda* [*Works of . . .*] (Jerusalem, 1941), i, p. 165; Klausner, op. cit., pp. 346–7.

on Baron Rothschild's behalf, he was told forthrightly that fear lest the Jews create a 'second Bulgarian question in Palestine' precluded the Porte from taking a sympathetic interest in his plea. A similar reply was given to Emanuel Veneziani, a representative of Baron de Hirsch.[31]

In Turkey the gap between principle and practice was always wide. Whatever orders might have been issued at Constantinople 'it was always possible', as a Zionist report put it, 'to get round the individual official with a little artifice'.[32] Rauf Pasha, the *Mutassarif* (Governor) of the Sanjak of Jerusalem (1876–88), was a resolute and incorruptible administrator, but he was a notable exception, who himself used to complain that 'almost every official' was taking *baksheesh*.[33] 'Turkish officials to a man are open to bribery', wrote a contemporary settler. 'Money is *the oil that turns the wheels . . .* and blinds everybody.' Local judges and administrators were a law unto themselves, and Jewish immigrants came reluctantly to realize that graft was an effective means of circumventing prohibitive orders.[34] The settlers of Rosh-Pina managed to prevent the destruction of their houses, built illegally, through the intercession of influential Jewish personalities in Damascus and Constantinople, but those in Samarin found it more convenient to 'soften the heart' of the gendarmes by pecuniary means.[35] Even Baron Rothschild was forced to conclude that better results could be obtained locally by resorting to 'good words and some napoleons' than by raising the issue at a diplomatic level in Constantinople.[36] Jewish immigrants infiltrated the country via Syria or Egypt (obvious loopholes in the law); others chose to acquire false passports which were sold freely by Turkish officials or intermediaries on board ship.[37] Once an individual possessed an American, Austrian, British, or German passport he was sure of protection.

[31] Druyanov, i, pp. 147–8, Gordon to Rabinowicz, 25 Feb. 1884; pp. 522–3, Veneziani to Pinsker, 26 May 1885; cited also in David Gordon: *Ktavim*, i, p. 76; Klausner, op. cit., p. 343; Manuel, op. cit., p. 58.

[32] Report to the Twelfth Zionist Congress, *Palestine during the War* (Zionist Organization, London, 1921), p. 7.

[33] Druyanov, pp. 191, 319; Smilansky, op. cit. i, p. 26; Klausner, op. cit., p. 339; *Sefer Toldoth Ha'agana [History of Self-Defence]*, ed. Ben-Zion Dinur (Tel Aviv, 1955), i, p. 58 (cited hereafter as *S.T.H.*); Manuel, op. cit., p. 15.

[34] Druyanov, i, p. 747, Hirsch to Pinsker, (?) Apr. 1886; iii, p. 690, Altschuller to Mohliver, (?) Feb. 1885; Manuel, op. cit., p. 36.

[35] Smilansky, op. cit. i, pp. 33–9.   [36] Margalith, op. cit., p. 100.

[37] Klausner, op. cit., p. 340.

A typical instance occurred in Petah-Tikva in 1882. After having registered part of their land in the name of Yoel Moses Salomon, a German protégé, the settlers took the risk of building their houses without an official permit. Rauf Pasha promptly instructed the court to order the demolition of the houses and Salomon's punishment. When Salomon solicited the support of the German Consul in Jerusalem, Dr. Reitz lost no time in lodging a strong protest, to which Rauf replied that Petah-Tikva was not 'a German quarter' but 'a Russian colony', and that the treaty rights gave the foreign Powers no title to interfere in matters of real estate. Reitz still demanded the cancellation of the order, saying that he would summon German colonists from the neighbouring village of Sarona to defend Petah-Tikva, if necessary by force. Unwilling to create international complications, Rauf eventually gave way. The feeling among Jewish settlers was that 'without . . . protection they would not have been able to survive'.[38]

Beneficial as the consuls' protection was, in the long run it proved a double-edged weapon. It confirmed Turkey's belief that the Jewish settlers were being used as pawns by the Powers to the detriment of Turkish sovereignty. Thoughtful individuals soon sensed the risks. A letter of Eliezer Rokeah, a pioneer in Zichron-Yaakov, dated April 1888, is illuminating:

The Ottoman administration is impotent and ineffective . . . Even a minor official is free to act on his own accord, regardless of authority and law. Witnessing how harshly and arbitrarily the native Mohammedans were treated, our people desired to escape a similar fate. Protection of the foreign Consuls seemed, hence, preferable. But one can visualize that the Ottoman Government would not tolerate such a situation for long . . . [Exterritoriality] is a running sore in the Ottoman body and undermines its very existence. The Government, quite justifiably, loathes the foreigners, and the Jewish newcomers, who enjoy the protection of the European Powers, are viewed unfavourably.[39]

Eliezer Ben-Yehuda, an early immigrant to Palestine and father of the revival of spoken Hebrew, was one of the first to give a personal example by embracing Ottoman nationality. Thereafter he untiringly propagated this idea in his periodical *Haor*. Leaders of the Hovevé Zion societies were fully alive to the importance of the

---

[38] *Sefer Hayovel shel Petach Tikva* [*The Jubliee Book of Petach-Tikva*], ed. Yaari Poleskin (Tel Aviv, 1929), pp. 227–43.
[39] Druyanov, i, p. 740, Rokeah to Pinsker, (?) Apr. 1886.

question[40] and their first conference, held in Katowic on 7 November 1884, expressed unanimously its unreserved loyalty to the Sultan. 'Our people', the resolution read, 'wish to settle in the Promised Land as honest and loyal subjects, imbued with sincere love and obedience to the government of the country . . . and without any ulterior motives.'[41] Baron Edmond de Rothschild also endeavoured to prevail upon the colonists to adopt Ottoman nationality.[42] However, harsh realities discouraged this process. The failure of the local authorities to administer justice and provide security of life and property[43] made the newcomers think twice about the wisdom of surrendering to Ottoman jurisdiction. Moreover, the advantages accruing from consular protection were too tangible to forgo. The protégés felt relatively secure, they were exempt from local taxation, and enjoyed other privileges stemming from their extraterritorial status.

The Porte could not remain indifferent. To show that loyalty paid, the Minister of the Interior instructed the local authorities to be more forthcoming towards those individuals who embraced Ottoman nationality. It soon became evident that the new nationals were favoured whenever they applied for permission to build houses or plant vineyards and orchards.[44] The Caimakam of Safad specifically declared that he would not interfere with the colonists if they agreed to adopt Ottoman nationality. 'We all know', wrote a Hovevé Zion leader, 'that the Government raises no obstacles to the settlement of naturalized persons, particularly in Galilee, where the land is more fertile and the population is scarce; and on political and religious grounds there are fewer objections there than in the Sanjak of Jerusalem.'[45]

However, when the inducements failed to persuade more than a section of the immigrants to adopt Ottoman nationality,[46] the stick

[40] Ibid. i, pp. 215, 492, David Gordon to Rabinowicz (1885), and Pinsker to Fein (1885).

[41] Ibid. i, pp. 283, 305, where the full text of the resolutions is reproduced.

[42] Ibid. ii, p. 1, Scheid to Pinsker, 25 Sept. 1886.

[43] *F.R.U.S.* (1881), pp. 1184–5, Blaine to Wallace, 29 June, 8 Aug. 1881; also Frelinghüsen to Wallace, 7 Jan. 1882 (ibid., 1882, p. 498).

[44] Druyanov, ii, p. 385, Scheid to Pinsker, 25 Sept. 1887; p. 400, Erlanger to Pinsker, 9 Dec. 1887; p. 488, Pines to Pinsker, (?) Feb. 1888; p. 437, Erlanger to Pinsker, 3 Jan. 1888.

[45] Ibid. ii, p. 1, Scheid to Pinsker, 25 Sept. 1886; i, p. 414, Pinsker to Fein, (?) Feb. 1885; iii, pp. 251–2, Plaskov to Lilienblum (no date).

[46] No exact statistics are available. However, it is estimated that by 1893 about 50 per

was applied with greater vigour. By the end of 1885 a Bureau of Nationality was established and those who failed to prove the validity of their claim to foreign protection were liable to expulsion. Oscar Straus, the American Minister to Constantinople, managed to frustrate Rauf Pasha's order to deport 400 imprisoned immigrants.[47] But early in 1887 the Porte issued new instructions prohibiting foreign Jews from residing in Jerusalem or in Palestine 'generally'; only pilgrims were allowed to stay for a short period.[48] Permission to sell property was consistently refused, and obstructions to colonization became more frequent.[49] Officially these rigorous measures were explained on sanitary and economic grounds, but privately Kiamil Pasha, the Grand Vizier, told Oscar Straus that the recrudescence of religious fanaticism among both Muslims and Christians impeded protection of the Jewish minority. In addition, rumours had reached the Porte that the Jews throughout the world wished to re-establish their ancient kingdom in Jerusalem. Straus dismissed these arguments out of hand,[50] but what primarily concerned the Turks, though they could not admit it officially, was the violation of their prerogatives. On 6 October 1887 new orders were issued that foreign visitors must be furnished with proper passports visaed by Ottoman consular authorities abroad affirming that the bearer intended to go on a pilgrimage to the Holy Land but not to engage in commerce or to take up residence. On disemarkation the passport was to be exchanged for a *permis de séjour*, entitling the bearer to stay in the country for three months. These instructions were enforced throughout Palestine as well as at certain ports along the Syrian coast.[51] So

cent of the colonists under the patronage of Baron Rothschild had adopted Ottoman nationality. In contrast to those in agricultural settlements those in towns remained predominantly foreign subjects (*S.T.H.* i, p. 117).

[47] *F.R.U.S.* (1885), pp. 862–8, 878; Oscar S. Straus, *Under Four Administrations* (New York, 1923), pp. 80–4; Druyanov, ii, pp. 350–2; Margalith, op. cit., p. 188.

[48] *B.C.* ii, p. 429, Moore (Jerusalem) to White (Constantinople), 5 Mar. 1887; Druyanov, ii, pp. 312, 418–21, 438; Margalith, op. cit., pp. 190–1, de Guillois (Jerusalem) to Flourens (Paris), 17 Sept. 1887.

[49] Druyanov, ii, pp. 24, 90, 99, 258–60, 334–5 (where the relevant documents are reproduced).

[50] *B.C.* ii, p. 429, Moore (Jerusalem) to White, 5 Mar. 1887; *F.R.U.S.* (1888), Pt. ii, pp. 1559–60, Straus to Bayard, 28 Jan. 1888; Straus, op. cit., pp. 80–1; Manuel, op. cit., pp. 61–2; Moshe Medzini; *Hamediniyuth Hatziyonitd* [*The Zionist Policy*] (Jerusalem, 1936), p. 59.

[51] *F.R.U.S.* (1888), Pt. ii, p. 1627, Mavroyeni Bey to Bayard (Washington), 2 Mar. 1888; p. 1588, Straus to Bayard, 19 May 1888; *B.C.* ii, pp. 440–1, Raouf to Moore, 24 Sept./6 Oct. 1887; Manuel, op. cit., p. 64.

strict was their application that not only Russian but even British and American subjects of Jewish faith, who had failed to obtain visas, were prevented from landing.[52]

This greatly annoyed the foreign missions, which regarded it as a breach of treaty rights.[53] In justification the Foreign Minister pointed out that, whenever in the past Jews had been expelled from other parts of Europe, 'in Turkey they had always found peace, security and complete liberty of conscience'.

Today even more, a great number of Jews seek refuge on Ottoman soil. Their religion is not considered a reason for their exclusion. With the exception of Palestine, they are free to establish themselves in the Empire at large and to exercise their professions without interference. If the Imperial Government had to impose restrictions on mass immigration it was chiefly for reasons of public order and certain economic considerations . . . especially as the actual resources of Palestine could not meet the needs of a very numerous population.[54]

Eventually, a formula was agreed that only in cases of immigration *en masse* would the Porte apply restrictions.[55]

The appointment of Rashid Bey as Rauf's successor signalled a change of policy. There were no serious clashes with the consuls and it seemed that the former restrictions were being dropped. Rashid paid frequent visits to Jewish colonies, granting permits to build houses, plant orchards, and purchase land. The initiative, it was thought, came from Constantinople.[56] In September 1890 several hundred Jews landed without any interference.[57] By July of the following year the influx of Jews, especially from Russia, was estimated to be 'very considerable'.[58] Selah Merril, the American

---

[52] *B.C.* ii, pp. 442, 444–5, Moore to White, 3 Mar., 29 May, 31 Aug. 1888.

[53] Ibid. ii, p. 441, White to Moore, 19 Oct. 1887; *F.R.U.S.* (1888), Pt. ii, pp. 1560–1, 1589–91, Straus to Bayard, 19, 26 May 1888; Margalith, op. cit., p. 200; Manuel, op. cit., p. 62.

[54] Margalith, op. cit., pp. 200–1, where the note, dated 23 Feb. 1888, is reproduced in full.

[55] *B.C.* ii, p. 446, White to Moore, 6 Oct. 1888; *F.R.U.S.* (1888), Pt. ii, p. 1619, Porte to U.S. Legation, 4 Oct. 1888; also pp. 1619, 1628; Straus, op. cit., p. 86; Manuel, op. cit., p. 66; Margalith, op. cit., p. 202; Druyanov, op. cit. ii, pp. 419–20.

[56] Druyanov, iii, p. 260, Dizengoff to Lilienblum, 20 Apr. 1890; *S.T.H.* i, pp. 58, 60.

[57] Druyanov, iii, p. 238; Manuel, op. cit., p. 67.

[58] *B.C.* ii, p. 462, Dickson to Fane, 16 July 1891. Dickson thought that during the first six months of 1891 about 1600 Jews came from Russia alone of whom '400 quitted

Consul in Jerusalem, predicted that Palestine was passing into 'the control of the Hebrew race'.[59]

The steep rise in immigration coincided with the expulsion of Jews from Moscow in 1891 and the reintroduction of discriminatory legislation by the Tsarist Government.[60] In the course of several months thousands of immigrants from all social strata—industrialists, merchants, artisans, and labourers—made their way to Palestine. Jaffa gave the impression of a boom city, and in Haifa the nucleus of modern urban settlement was formed. In 1891 two new large colonies were founded: Rehovot in the south, and Hadera, midway between Jaffa and Haifa. Of the two, Hadera had far greater obstacles to overcome. Situated in a marshy area infected by malaria, its early settlers faced immense difficulties. In 1890 Mishmar Ha-Yarden was founded in north Galilee, and in the following year Ein-Zeytim, near Safad, was added to the map. The year 1896 saw the establishment of two workers' settlements: Beer Tuvia in southern Judaea, founded by Hovevé Zion, and Metulla, in northern Galilee, founded by Baron Rothschild.

Yet for all the enthusiasm and energy of the new settlers their achievements rested on flimsy foundations; only a few of the ambitious schemes announced by Zeev Tiomkin, the Hovevé Zion representative in Palestine, materialized. Baron Rothschild's munificence earned him the accolade of the Father of the Yishuv, but philanthropy brought its own evils. The administrators lacked the Baron's sympathy for, and understanding of, the colonists who, when treated arbitrarily, lost much of their initial pioneering spirit. They fell back on the employment of cheap Arab labour, thus making nonsense of their original objectives. The produce of their vineyards was bought, through Rothschild's generosity, at inflated prices, and therefore the colonists enjoyed a relative, though largely artificial, prosperity. The heart of the trouble was that the subsidies

... leaving about 1,200 as permanent settlers'. Dickson's figures of the Jewish population in Jerusalem, 35,000 to 40,000 out of the total 60,000 inhabitants, are higher than those of Selah Merril, the American Consul, who calculated that there were only 25,322 Jews in Jerusalem and 42,000 to 43,000 in the whole of Palestine (Manuel, op. cit., pp. 70–1). Merril's figures are lower than those quoted by Luntz (i.e. 28,112 cited in Ben-Zvi, op. cit., p. 414). According to Arthur Ruppin between 1880 and 1895 the Jewish population in Palestine rose by immigration and natural increase from 20,000 to 50,000, of whom 3,000 lived in agricultural settlements (Cohen, op. cit., p. 66).

59 Manuel, op. cit., p. 71.   60 Dubnow, op. cit. x, pp. 183–99.

were ill planned. They failed to make the economy more viable, nor did the mixture of patronage and bureaucracy stimulate self-reliance and initiative. It was only after the administration of the Rothschild colonies was transferred to the Jewish Colonization Association (I.C.A.) in 1900 that the colonists regained their autonomy and earlier mistakes were rectified.[61]

The deficiencies of these experiments during the first *aliya*[62] were mercilessly exposed by Ahad Ha'am, the foremost thinker of the Hovevé Zion. In a series of articles, 'The Truth from Palestine',[63] written in 1891 and 1893 following his visits there, he showed how unhealthy was its body politic, mainly because it lacked a legal foundation. The method of getting round the local officials led nowhere. Nor did he consider consular protection a safe prop: in the long run it was self-defeating. Ahad Ha'am did not say how the Sultan's official blessing, which he regarded as an essential prerequisite to the progress of the colonization, could be secured, but on the whole his gloomy prognostications proved right.

The liberal policy pursued under Rashid Bey was soon reversed. Jewish immigrants had been offered hospitality on condition that they acquired Ottoman nationality but instead they elected to register with foreign consuls, and this, in the words of Said, the Turkish Foreign Minister, was an abuse which could not be tolerated. The Porte did not confine itself to words and henceforth made every effort to prevent the Jews from establishing themselves permanently in the country. In July 1891 a group of 5,000 and later one of 120 immigrants were not permitted to disembark, but subsequently both groups were allowed to stay for a limited period as visitors. Settlement of the Jews in the Sanjak of Jerusalem was forbidden, on strict instructions from the Grand Vizier. Acquisition of land was prohibited, even for Ottoman Jewish subjects, since the newcomers were circumventing the law by registering immovable property in the name of their Ottoman co-religionists.[64] The reason

---

[61] The Jewish Colonization Association (I.C.A.) was founded in 1891 by Baron Maurice de Hirsch. A special agency for Palestine was created under the name Palestine Jewish Colonization Association (P.I.C.A.).

[62] In Hebrew *aliya* means wave of immigration. The first *aliya* extended over the period 1882–1903.

[63] Ahad Ha'am: 'Emeth me'Eretz-Israel', *Al Parashat Derachim [At the Crossroads]* (Berlin, 1924), i, pp. 28, 36. There is an admirable biography on Ahad Ha'am by Leon Simon (London, 1960).

[64] *B.C.* ii, pp. 472–3, Said to White, 7 Sept. 1891; p. 461, Ibrahim Hakki to Dickson, 24 June/6 July 1891; p. 481, Dickson to Clare-Ford, 30 Dec. 1892; p. 485, Dickson to

for the exceptional stringency of the new regulations—the implementation of which the Porte controlled with greater efficiency after the Sanjak of Jerusalem had been subordinated to Constantinople in 1887—was[65] the government's fear that its interests would be prejudiced by large numbers of settlers in Palestine claiming foreign protection.[66] The Russians, steadily expanding their influence in Palestine, had discovered in the Jews useful pawns for meddling in Ottoman affairs and in 1890 withdrew their tacit approval of British protection of their former subjects.[67] From the Turkish point of view the change was disconcerting since, unlike the British, Russia's claim to protect her Jewish nationals was based on solid juridical grounds and her designs posed a far greater threat to Ottoman sovereignty.

How determined the Turks were is evident from the fact that, in defiance of treaty rights and protests from governments concerned, they requested all foreign shipowners to refuse Jews passage to Turkey.[68] But what seems even more surprising is that the July 1891 regulations were strictly applied with regard not only to Russian Jews but also to nationals from Britain and the United States, although there was no imminent risk of mass immigration from those countries.[69] But this was no mere obsession. Through official British channels the 'Lovers of Zion' Society in England submitted a petition to the Sultan asking him for a *firman* for colonization of the territory east of the River Jordan.[70] In the spring of 1897 some prominent British Jews, delegates of the Maccabean

Clare-Ford, 29 Apr. 1893; *F.R.U.S.* (1893) p. 651, Terrel to Gresham, 29 July 1893; *S.T.H.* i, pp. 55, 155; Druyanov, iii, p. 691, Altschuller to Mohliver, (?) Feb. 1885.

[65] Finn, op. cit. i, pp. 159–60; de Haas, *History of Palestine*, pp. 430–1; Harry C. Luke and Edward Keith-Roach, *The Handbook of Palestine and Transjordan* (London, 1930), p. 208. Under the Turkish regime Palestine was neither a separate country nor did it constitute a single administrative unit. In addition to the independent Sanjak of Jerusalem there were two other sanjaks: that of Acre, which included the sub-districts of Acre, Haifa, Safad, Nazareth, and Tiberias, and the Sanjak of Nablus, which included the sub-districts of Nablus, Jenin, and Tulkarm. Both were subordinate to the vilayet of Beirut. Sanjak in Turkish means district, and vilayet province.

[66] *B.C.* ii, p. 484, Clare-Ford to Roseberg, 24 Apr. 1893; p. 489, Porte to Italian Embassy, 3 Apr. 1893, encl. in Nicolson to Dickson, 23 July 1893; p. 472, White to Salisbury, 10 Sept. 1891; *F.R.U.S.* (1898), pp. 1106, 1103–8, Porte to Angell, 27 Mar. 1894.

[67] F.O. Handbook, *Syria and Palestine*, p. 44.

[68] *B.C.* ii, pp. 474–5, Salisbury to White, 9 Nov. 1891.

[69] Ibid. ii, pp. 490–1, Dickson to Nicolson, 25 Aug. 1893; *F.R.U.S.* (1894), pp. 750–1, Wallace to Short, 3 Oct. 1894; ibid. (1898), pp. 1089–90.

[70] Sokolow, op. cit. ii, p. 279, where the document is reproduced in full.

Society, toured Palestine. There were rumours about a forthcoming world Zionist Congress. All this, coupled with the resolution adopted by a mass meeting in New York on 4 May 1897 in favour of creating a Jewish state in Palestine, intensified the Porte's suspicion that Palestine had become the focus of national aspirations not only of the Jews in Eastern Europe but also of a sizeable section of those in the West. Considered in this light, immigration became a 'political danger'.[71] A year later, when Oscar Straus interceded on behalf of forty-five American Jews who had been prevented from landing, Tewfik Pasha, the Ottoman Foreign Minister, reassured him that Turkey had no intention of discriminating against American citizens. Turkey's only object was to prevent the further colonization of Palestine by Jews, since this might lead to political complications. Straus gained the impression that stricter enforcement of the regulations had followed the foundation of the Zionist movement.[72] But it is clear that Turkey's attitude towards Jewish settlement in Palestine had been determined earlier than that. At the root of the problem lay the system of Capitulations and the refusal of foreign Jews to adopt Ottoman nationality. As Paul Weitz, the correspondent of the *Frankfurter Zeitung* in Constantinople and a well-informed student of Turkish affairs, attested:

So long as the Capitulations were in force, the Ottoman Government was bound to view Jewish immigration with mixed feelings; this in spite of the economic benefits to be gained. The Jewish immigrants from Russia persisted in clinging to their foreign nationality after settling in the country. In any conflict with Ottoman law and the Ottoman authorities, they sought protection from their consuls, who gave it eagerly because increased immigration magnified their powers at the expense of the Ottoman Government's prerogatives. It went so far that the Sublime Porte ceased sometimes to be master in its own country. How then could the Turks have sympathized with an immigration that constantly created increasingly an additional source of friction?[73]

When Herzl appeared in Constantinople at the turn of the century he was woefully ignorant of how remote were the chances of making his scheme acceptable at the Golden Horn.

[71] *Türkei* 195, Tischendorf to A.A., 19 June 1897, dis. no. 49, K 692/K 175859–62.
[72] *F.R.U.S.* (1898), pp. 1086–8, 1092–3, Porte to Riddle (Constantinople), 27 Aug. 1898; Riddle to Day, 3 Sept. 1898; Straus to Hay, 22 Nov. 1898. John Dickson, the British Consul in Jerusalem, shared this assumption (*B.C.* ii, pp. 542–3, Dickson to O'Conor, 9 Feb. 1899). [73] *Frankfurter Zeitung*, 2 Apr. 1918.

PART II

Before the War
1897–1914

4

The First Encounter with Zionism[1]

IT was anti-Semitism that made Herzl and Max Nordau, his close collaborator, conscious Jews.[2] Both were steeped in European culture, but the resurgence of modern anti-Semitism wounded their dignity. Herzl was particularly stirred by Eugen Dühring's book *Die Judenfrage als Frage des Rassencharakters und seiner Schädlichkeit für Existenz und Kultur des Volkes* (*The Jewish Problem as a Problem of Race, Morals and Culture*). As the years went by, the feeling grew stronger, but it was not until the Dreyfus trial in 1894–5 that his hopes of emancipation were irreparably shattered. He realized that the civilized nations could not cope with the Jewish question, which was a legacy from the Middle Ages. 'They have tried it through emancipation but it came too late.' The belief of the doctrinaire libertarians that 'men can be made equal by publishing an edict . . . was erroneous'. The Jews themselves were not yet accustomed to freedom, and the people around them had 'neither magnanimity nor patience'. They saw in those liberated only their bad characteristics. Lacking historical perspective, they failed to realize that some of the anti-social qualities attributed to Jews were the product of oppression in earlier times.[3] In vain did the Jews endeavour to show their loyalty, sometimes even exaggerated patriotism, towards their

---

[1] The following four chapters are chiefly concerned with the diplomatic aspect of Herzl's activities. For writings by and on Herzl see Alex Bein, *Theodore Herzl. A Biography*, pp. 529–34. A more comprehensive list is given in the paperback edition (New York, 1962) pp. 531–42. To this should be added Böhm, *Die zionistiche Bewegung*, i, pp. 151–287, which gives a general account of the development of the Zionist movement until Herzl's death. For an appreciation of Herzl's personality see *Theodor Herzl— A Memorial*, ed. M. W. W. Weisgal (New York, 1929); Bein, op. cit., pp. 504–26.

[2] *The Complete Diaries of Theodor Herzl*, ed. Raphael Patai, English trans. (New York, London, 1960), i, p. 196 (hereafter *Diaries*); Anna and Maxa Nordau, *Max Nordau, A Biography* (New York, 1943), pp. 114–23.

[3] *Diaries*, i, pp. 4–5, 9–10, 120.

countries of domicile. In vain were their sacrifices, their achievements in science, and their contributions to commerce. In the
'fatherlands' in which they had lived for centuries, they were denounced as 'strangers'.[4]

Herzl appreciated that anti-Semitism was a complex phenomenon.
In some countries it did occasionally reveal a religious bias, but its
virulent character was primarily a consequence of emancipation.
Contrary to the general belief that hostility to the Jews would
disappear, he feared that it would worsen. Hence it was futile to
combat anti-Semitism. Assimilation had failed, since in any genuine
sense it could be effected only by intermarriage and the nations would
not tolerate members of an unassimilable group becoming their
leaders. Perhaps they were 'fully within their rights'. In Russia and
in Romania persecution would be inspired officially; in Germany
discrimination would be legalized and in Austria people would allow
themselves to be intimidated by the mob into initiating a 'new St.
Bartholomew's Night'. Hungary, Herzl's country of birth, would be
no exception. The calamity would come in a 'most brutal form; the
longer it is postponed, the more severe it will be; the more powerful
the Jews will become the fiercer the retribution. There is no escape
from it.'[5]

He hoped that in the long run anti-Semitism would not harm the
Jews and that educationally it might even prove useful. 'It forces
us', he concluded, 'to close ranks, unites us through pressure, and
through our unity will make us free.' It was this feeling of freedom
that made Herzl declare: 'We are a people, one people. We recognize
ourselves as a nation by our faith.' Henceforth he no longer regarded
the Jewish question as a social or religious problem but as a national
one, which should be solved politically by the council of the civilized
nations. Sovereignty over a portion of land 'large enough to justify
the rightful requirements of a nation', to which the Jewish masses
would emigrate, would provide the right solution. Pondering the
choice between the Argentine and Palestine, the 'ever memorable
historic home' seemed preferable. Its very name would attract the
people 'with a force of marvellous potency'.[6]

    [4] *The Jewish State*, pp. 76–7.
    [5] Ibid., pp. 75–7, 89; *Diaries*, i, pp. 6, 9, 46, 71, 83, 131–2, 180, 190, Herzl to Albert
Rothschild, 28 June 1895, pp. 343–4; Theodor Herzl, *Michtavim* [*Letters*] (Tel Aviv,
1937), p. 266, Herzl to Ernst Metzie, 10 Mar. 1903.
    [6] *Diaries*, i, pp. 10, 56, 92, 96, 231, 276; *The Jewish State*, p. 76. In asserting that Jews
are a nation, Herzl was preceded by Moses Hess in *Rom und Jerusalem* (Leipzig,

Herzl wanted to give the Jews 'a corner . . . where they can live in peace, no longer hounded, outcast, and despised . . . a country that will be their own', to rid them of the faults which centuries of persecution and ostracism had fostered in them and to allow their intellectual and moral gifts free play, so that finally they might no longer be 'the dirty Jews, but the people of light'. There they would regain self-esteem and dignity, and 'the derisive cry of "Jews!" may become an honourable appellation, like "German! Englishman! Frenchman!"'[7]

The solution of the problem, however, should not be left to Jews alone. 'The Jewish State is a world necessity!' Those civilized nations who were trying 'to exorcise a ghost out of their past', must also shoulder responsibility. He believed that a potential community of interests did exist between the anti-Semites and the Zionists. 'The antisemites will become our most dependable friends, the antisemitic countries our allies. We want to emigrate as respected people', parting as 'friends from our foes . . . The solution of the Jewish Question must be a mighty final chord of reconciliation.' Eventually it would place relationships between Jew and Gentile on a normal footing. If the Powers, with the concurrence of the Sultan, recognize Jewish sovereignty over Palestine, the Jews in return could undertake to regulate Turkish finances; they would form there 'a portion of . . . Europe . . . an outpost of civilization'. The Jewish State will become 'something remarkable . . . a model country for social experiments and a treasure-house for works of art . . . a destination for the civilized world'.[8]

Herzl was primarily a man of action who wished to translate his ideas into reality. His basic premiss, that Zionism constituted an effective antidote to anti-Semitism, led him to the conviction that the countries most plagued by this problem were his potential allies. As early as 9 June 1895 he jotted down in his diary: 'First I shall negotiate with the Tsar . . . regarding permission for the Russian Jews to leave the country . . . Then I shall negotiate with the German Kaiser, then with Austria, then with France regarding the Algerian Jews, then as need dictates.' That Herzl should have expected

---

1862) and Leon Pinsker *Auto-Emancipation* (reprinted in *The Road to Freedom, Writings and Addresses* (New York, 1944)). When Herzl wrote *The Jewish State* he was unaware of this literature.

[7] *Diaries*, iii, p. 873; i, pp. 97, 101, 103, 181.
[8] Ibid. i, pp. 41, 45, 84, 103–6, 171–2, 303; *The Jewish State*, pp. 95–6.

Germany to support him is not surprising, since it was there that modern anti-Semitism originated. In an interview with Baron de Hirsch in 1895 he exclaimed: 'I shall go to the Kaiser, he will understand me . . . I shall say: "Let our people go! We are strangers here; we are not permitted to assimilate with the people, nor are we able to do so. Let us go!"' He was confident that one day the Kaiser would be grateful to him for leading the 'unassimilable people out'.[9]

In this assumption Herzl was basically correct, but it was rather the philo-Semites who first gave him support. When a long-awaited reply from ex-Chancellor Bismarck was not forthcoming and the German Press appeared to be critical of his *Judenstaat*,[10] a saviour from an unexpected quarter called on him. It was the Reverend William Hechler, Chaplain to the British Embassy in Vienna. Hechler impressed Herzl as a likeable, sensitive, and enthusiastic man. He believed that in 1897–8, the years of 'prophetic crisis', Palestine would be returned to the Jews, a prediction that was backed by abstruse computations. Having read the *Judenstaat*, he no longer doubted that the 'foreordained movement' had come into being. In Herzl's quizzical eyes Hechler appeared 'a naïve visionary', but it is undeniable that it was he who raised Herzl's cause to the diplomatic plane by introducing him to the Grand Duke of Baden, at whose court Hechler had been a tutor. Hechler also knew the Kaiser and thought it possible to arrange an audience for Herzl.[11]

On 26 March 1896 Hechler wrote to the Duke about Herzl's project, noting with satisfaction that the anti-Semitic movement had made the Jews see that they were 'Jews first and [only] secondly Germans, Englishmen etc.' It reawakened in them a longing to return 'as a nation to the Land of Promise . . . Palestine belongs to them by right.' Should Germany and England give their support and take the Jewish State, declared neutral, under their protection, the Return of the Jews would be a great blessing and would put an end to anti-Semitism, which was detrimental to the welfare of European nations. He also suggested that the issue be laid before the Kaiser, the Duke's nephew.[12]

[9] *Diaries*, i, pp. 42–3, 52, 189–90.

[10] Ibid. i, pp. 117–22, 187–8; Bein, op. cit., pp. 179–80; Richard Lichtheim, *Die Geschichte des deutschen Zionismus*, p. 126.

[11] *Diaries*, i, pp. 310–13, 319–23. In 1882 Hechler published a leaflet 'The Restoration of the Jews to Palestine according to the Prophets'.

[12] Hechler to the Grand Duke of Baden, 26 Mar. 1896, reproduced in Hermann and Bessie Ellern, *Herzl, Hechler, the Grand Duke of Baden and the German Emperor, 1896–*

The Duke took the opportunity of the Kaiser's visit to Karlsruhe to brief him on the subject. Hechler was invited to the reception and, to the amusement of the court assembly, the Kaiser addressed him in a jocular way: 'Hechler, I hear you want to become a minister of the Jewish State.'[13] The Kaiser was not fully acquainted with the matter and did not take it seriously. Nor, it appears, was Grand Duke Frederick truly convinced of Herzl's cause. He agreed with Hechler that its realization would be a blessing for many, but feared that his support might be misinterpreted as a disingenuous stratagem to drive his Jewish subjects out of his country. Their departure would also entail an enormous loss of money; in any case, since the number of Jews in Germany was not excessive, the matter was only of marginal interest.[14]

Herzl did his best to dispel the Duke's misgivings. On 22 April 1898, when they first met in Karlsruhe, he explained that establishment of the Jewish State would be an act of goodwill, not a consequence of persecution, that emigration would be voluntary, and that it concerned chiefly the Jews of Austria, Russia, and Romania. German Jews would welcome it; it would divert the migration of their East European co-religionists away from Germany. Moreover, it would reduce the number of Jewish proletarians and, by the same token, the number of revolutionaries. Nor was the Duke's fear of the loss of capital justified. In the industrial age capital was mobile and the Jews of Baden were not likely to leave their country. Moreover, Herzl argued, Jewish enterprise would restore to health 'the plague-spot of the Orient'.

We would build railroads to Asia, the highway of the civilized peoples. . . . If Turkey were partitioned in the foreseeable future, an *état tampon* could be created in Palestine. However, we could contribute a great deal toward the preservation of Turkey. We could straighten out the Sultan's

1904 (Tel Aviv, 1962), pp. 1–8 (hereafter Ellern). Mr. Ellern, an Israeli banker born in Karlsruhe, Germany, discovered forty-eight documents in the Grossherzogliches Familienarchiv, Karlsruhe, and the Deutsches Zentralarchiv, Abt. Merseburg, East Germany. They were Herzl's and Hechler's letters to the Grand Duke, correspondence between the last-named with Wilhelm II and Tsar Nicolas II, and an *aide-mémoire* of the Foreign Ministry, dated 26 Jan. 1904. All the documents are reproduced in facsimile.

[13] *Diaries*, i, p. 329. Hechler replied (letter to Grand Duke, 18 Apr. 1896) that he was 'a mixture of pure Schwarzwald and Great Britain' and had no personal interest in the Jewish State. Ellern, p. 9.

[14] *Diaries*, i, pp. 329–40. On the liberal regime of the Grand Duchy of Baden see Arthur Rosenberg, *The Birth of the German Republic, 1871–1918* (London, 1931), p. 48.

finances once and for all, in return for this territory which is not of great value to him.

Yet the Duke wondered whether it would not be better, first to send a few hundred thousand Jews to Palestine, and only then to raise the question at diplomatic level. These cautious tactics, which later were adopted by the Zionists, were firmly rejected by Herzl. Under no circumstances would he persuade immigrants to sneak into the country. He wished to do 'everything open and above-board, fully within the law'.[15] Honest as Herzl's intention was, it proved to be a major error of policy.

The Grand Duke was won over and remained Herzl's staunch supporter. Verdy du Vernois, the former Prussian Minister of War and an expert on the Orient, was also convinced that the Zionist project would benefit Turkey,[16] while Hechler continued untiringly to win new converts, particularly in British and German clerical circles. He was grieved to note that opposition was loudest in Jewish circles. They 'care but little for the glorious history of their ancestors . . . and still less for Jehovah and the prophets', but the results of the First Zionist Congress reassured him that its leaders were 'unconsciously fulfilling the Scriptures'. Their honesty of purpose was manifest and Herzl, he believed, 'may become God's worthy and humble instrument'.[17]

The First Zionist Congress, held in Basle from 29 to 31 August 1897,[18] was an unusual event which attracted the attention of the international Press and of diplomatic circles. Von Tattenbach, the German Minister to Berne, was one of the many diplomats to be attracted by its novelty. He briefed Berlin extensively on its proceedings and sent a report on the lecture given by Johannes Lepsius, who forecast that, with the dismemberment of the Ottoman Empire, the Jews would gain possession of Palestine. A national renaissance of the Jewish people would follow which, however, would precipitate an internal *Kulturkampf*.[19] The Kaiser read Tattenbach's

[15] *Diaries*, i, pp. 334–8, 343.   [16] Ibid. ii, pp. 452, 503–4.
[17] Ellern, pp. 22–5, 27, 43–4, Hechler to the Grand Duke, 3 Sept. 1896, 21 Aug. 1897, 26 Sept. 1898.
[18] On which see *Diaries*, ii, pp. 580–6; Bein, op. cit., pp. 226–48; Böhm, op. cit. i, pp. 180–4; below, p. 95.
[19] *Auswärtiges Amt Akten, Europa Generalia*, Nr. 84, K 694/K 181250–60 (hereafter E.G. and the coding K 694 is omitted). A copy of this report is in the files *Türkei*, Nr. 195, *Juden in Türkei*, K 692/K 175903–10. During and after the First World War Dr. Lepsius made his name as a philo-Armenian and historian. For the reaction of the

report and commented: 'Let the *Mauschels* go to Palestine, the sooner they move off the better. I shall not put obstacles in their way.'[20] But the Emperor did not intend to render any practical assistance to the Zionist movement and a year later Hechler tried in vain to secure an audience for Herzl. However, the ever-sympathetic Grand Duke Frederick came to Hechler's assistance. He advised him to win over Count Philipp zu Eulenburg, the German Ambassador in Vienna, a gifted politician, whose influence upon the Kaiser was profound. Hechler was instructed to tell the Ambassador that in the Duke's opinion 'something was involved that might prove to be important for German policy in the Orient'.[21]

Briefed by Hechler, Herzl was now confident that his movement would receive help. He hoped to persuade the Grand Duke that settlement by a neutral national element along the shortest route to Asia could be of value to Germany. He also prepared a draft letter to the Kaiser, explaining that the Jews were the only people who could colonize Palestine; the land was too poor to attract others. For the Jews it was rich in memories and hopes. Settlement by other European nationals would engender jealousy amongst the Powers, while settlement by the Jews, as a neutral element, would create fewer complications. Should Germany support the Zionist aspirations, 'the new Imperial journey to Zion may leave lasting traces in history'.[22]

On Hechler's advice the letters were not dispatched, but they reflect the working of Herzl's mind. He attempted to strike a balance between the principle of neutrality, embodied in the Basle Programme, and an endeavour to solicit the support of a European Power—in this case Germany—for his cause. The two elements were complementary. The Zionists, he hoped, would be regarded as the lesser evil, since no Power would let any other have Palestine.[23]

During the summer and autumn of 1898 everything seemed, at least superficially, to be going well for Herzl. When Hechler failed

Austro-Hungarian Minister at Berne see Isaiah Friedman, 'The Austro-Hungarian Government and Zionism, 1897–1918', *Jewish Social Studies* (July, Oct. 1965), 147.

[20] Marginal note on *E.G.*, K 181260; copy in *Türkei* 195, K 175910.

[21] *Diaries*, ii, pp. 638–9. On Eulenburg's friendship with the Kaiser see the touching biography of Johannes Haller; *Philipp Eulenburg. The Kaiser's Friend*, English trans. (London, 1930); Ralph Flenley, *Modern German History* (London, 1959), p. 309.

[22] *Diaries*, ii, pp. 639–43.

[23] Ibid., p. 645. For the text of the Basle Programme (in English translation) see Sokolow, *History of Zionism*, i, p. xxiv.

to meet Count Eulenburg in Vienna, the Duke wrote directly to the Kaiser. Earlier he had hesitated to introduce Herzl to Wilhelm, but now that the Zionist movement had made substantial progress, it warranted a certain amount of attention, especially on the eve of the imperial visit to Palestine. Jewish colonization had proved successful and consistent efforts were being made to lay the foundations of a Jewish state. The Duke revealed Hechler's intention of undertaking scientific research for the excavation of the Ark of the Covenant which, if rediscovered, would have 'worldwide historical importance'. He asked the Kaiser to approach the Sultan with a request to cede the territory in question, advising that 'the Sultan should be told that only an archaeological research is intended . . . as otherwise he would not be very much disposed to meet "our wishes".' He enclosed material on the Zionist movement for Count Eulenburg to study.[24]

Hechler, with whom the idea of the Search for the Ark originated, suggested that the whole district east of the River Jordan and the area of the Dead Sea be granted to the Emperor, to facilitate the search for the tablets of the Ten Commandments given to Moses on Mount Sinai. The vision stirred his imagination, and he fervently believed that the Jews were unconsciously fulfilling the biblical prophecies; the prayer 'Next Year in Jerusalem' would be transformed into a living reality. He thought that Wilhelm II should become the protector of both Protestants and Jews in the East.[25]

It took Wilhelm a month to reply to his uncle's letter. The Zionist aspirations appealed to him, and he instructed Eulenburg to examine the material, but he doubted whether the movement was ripe enough to justify official support. He noted also that Zionism was meeting with strong opposition from influential sections of Jewry,[26] but the Duke remained optimistic. On 2 September 1898 he received Herzl in Mainau Castle and, as if to demonstrate his confidence, discussed secret political matters with him. Originally the Kaiser's trip was to be strictly religious, but subsequently it was decided to give it

[24] Ellern, Grand Duke to Wilhelm II, 28 July 1899, pp. 32–5.

[25] Ibid., Hechler to the Grand Duke, 26 Sept. 1898, pp. 38–47.

[26] *Nachlass Eulenburg* (Eulenburg Papers), Wilhelm to the Grand Duke, 28 Aug. 1898, Nr. 52, p. 298; Friedrich von Lucanus (head of the Kaiser's Zivilkabinett) to Eulenburg, 29 Aug. 1898, Nr. 52, p. 298h. The original papers of Count Eulenburg were destroyed during the Second World War. However, copies of some of them made by Eulenburg were later discovered and re-edited. The *Nachlass Eulenburg*, consisting of nine volumes, is deposited in the Bundesarchiv, Koblenz.

a political character. *En route* to Palestine the Emperor would pay an official visit to the Sultan. Through Ambassador Marschall the German Government had made inquiries in Constantinople and learned that the Sultan viewed the Zionist cause with favour. Since the Cretan affair the Kaiser had been on excellent terms with the Sultan and the Duke was confident that the Kaiser's word would certainly be heeded by his host. This was important because legal security was necessary for the foundation of a state; he thought a formula could be found preserving Ottoman overlordship on the pattern of the former Danube principalities. His main misgiving was that certain groups of Jews would see something anti-Semitic in the move, but Herzl reassured him: the German Jews, once made aware of the official attitude, would not risk disfavour by opposing Zionism. 'An exodus of all Jews was not intended anyway. Assimilation [of the reluctant ones] would start in earnest then', thus easing the solution of the problem. With the migration of the Jews '*a German* cultural element would come to the Orient', which might be not disadvantageous to Germany. The overwhelming majority of the Jews had closer links with German culture than with any other; the leadership of the Zionist movement was in German hands; German was also the official language of their Congress. If and when a protectorate became feasible, Jews would prefer it to be German. The Duke welcomed these statements and wished to make public the fact that Herzl had had an audience with him, but Herzl preferred complete secrecy.[27]

Shortly after, on 16 September, Herzl was invited to meet Count Eulenburg in Vienna. The Ambassador was not yet fully acquainted with the project and nourished some misgivings: the soil of Palestine was poor and the Turks would view the immigration of 'two million people' with disfavour and suspicion; the Sultan was obsessed by fear. However, after listening to Herzl, the Ambassador grew 'perceptibly warmer'. The project was new and visibly fascinated him. But the strongest impression made on him was Herzl's statement that since Zionism existed, one Power or another would sooner or later espouse it. 'Originally, I thought that it would be England. It lay in the nature of things'; but now Germany would be even more welcome. The mention of England, as Herzl observed, was conclusive for Eulenburg. He promised Herzl to try to persuade the

---

[27] *Diaries*, ii, pp. 655–60. On the Cretan question see William L. Langer, *The Diplomacy of Imperialism, 1890–1902* (N.Y., London, 1935), i, pp. 315–35, 355–7.

Emperor to intercede with the Sultan in order to obtain the country for the Zionists on 'the basis of autonomy'. He also suggested that Herzl should meet the Foreign Minister, Bernhard von Bülow.[28]

Herzl impressed Eulenburg as 'an unusually gifted man' of striking appearance: 'a tall gentleman, with a head like that of King David, the type of valiant leading Jews from the time of the Jewish Kingdom, without any trace of a *Handelsjude*.'[29] This reaction was typical of Eulenburg's romantic nature. His deeper reasons for so fervently supporting Herzl can only be surmised, for there is little documentary evidence. In December 1896 Eulenburg had complained to Bülow that he was persistently attacked by the *Neue Freie Presse*; it made his position in Vienna untenable. Bülow replied that he should get in touch with somebody on that paper.[30] One of the most gifted journalists on the *Neue Freie Presse* was Herzl. In fact, in his second conversation with Herzl, the Count hinted: 'perhaps the moment will come when I shall claim favours from you'.[31] Years later, when the Count, attacked by Maximilian Harden in *Die Zukunft*,[32] was in great distress and needed help badly, Herzl was no longer alive.

It would, however, be unjust to ascribe Eulenburg's interest solely to personal motives. A man of his character would hardly have supported Zionism unless in his view it coincided with the political interests of his country. He believed that Herzl could collect 'absolutely unlimited sums' to offer the Sultan as a quid pro quo for the concession of Palestine.[33] Since Eulenburg was the first German statesman to commit himself, at least by implication, to the maintenance of the Ottoman Empire,[34] it is possible that Herzl's offer to straighten out the Sultan's finances made a strong appeal to him.

[28] *Diaries*, ii, pp. 661–4. That Herzl meant England seriously and did not use it merely as an argument is evident from his remark in the *Diaries* that though so far he had been mistaken in expecting England's help she 'might still come through after all'. Earlier, in the summer of 1897, in a message to a Jewish conference in London, he declared: 'From the first moment I entered the Movement my eyes were directed towards England.' For the full text see Paul Goodman, *Zionism in England* (London, 1949), pp. 18–19.

[29] *Nachlass Eulenburg*, Nr. 52, p. 298a, *Die Zionisten*, initialled by the editor September 1898, but from the text it seems that the note was written several years later.

[30] Haller, op. cit. i, pp. 361, 364. Haller makes no mention of Herzl.

[31] *Diaries*, ii, pp. 698–90. Herzl racked his brains in vain later to discover what Eulenburg could have meant by 'favours' (ibid., pp. 693–4).

[32] Haller, op. cit. ii, pp. 169–268.   [33] As note 29.

[34] He was reported to have stated to Goluchowski, the Austrian Foreign Minister, in Nov. 1895: 'As long as I am in office, I shall not allow Russia to get Constantinople.

Von Bülow had other ideas. He received Herzl with 'captivating kindness', impressing him as a gentleman of the *vieux jeu* of diplomacy rather than the iron type of the Bismarck era. He complimented Herzl profusely on his writing, but his conversation was more in the nature of a chat than a serious political discussion. Bülow was already informed about the Second Zionist Congress and asked why the *Neue Freie Presse* had remained silent, and the *Frankfurter Zeitung* had reported it in an unfriendly way. He doubted whether many German Jews would emigrate; in any case their departure seemed to him undesirable. He was pleased to learn from Herzl that at Vienna the Zionists had won students away from socialism. Herzl's projected state, however, he dismissed as a '*polis* of Plato'. He expected that the main difficulty would be to convince the Sultan to enter into negotiations with the Zionists, adding ironically that 'it would make a big impression on him should the Kaiser give him such advice'. Yet Herzl felt intuitively that Bülow was not in favour of the Kaiser granting him an audience.[35]

Bülow was a cultured and subtle diplomat and an expert in manipulating people. 'He liked to play with ideas and with human beings [but] had no taste for pathos or for lofty strains of thoughts', but 'beneath the charming façade was a narrowness of vision'. That the anti-Socialist aspect of Zionism should have attracted his attention is hardly surprising, since 'the most important domestic question for him was the fight against the Socialists'.[36] His biographer notes that, while recognizing Herzl's great literary talents, he was unable to work up any enthusiasm for his political ideas. Bülow was well aware of the hardships which the Jews in Eastern Europe had to endure, but was not convinced that mass emigration to Palestine would improve their lot. He also doubted whether Herzl's project could be applied to German Jews, who were strongly attached to Germany and felt no need 'to rush into an unpromising and

On this point H.M. the Emperor is in full agreement with me.' (*Die Grosse Politik der europäischen Kabinette* (Berlin, 1922–7), x, Nr. 2497, p. 158.)

[35] *Diaries*, ii, pp. 665–9. Nordau was sceptical about Bülow (ibid., p. 773). For a report by the German Minister at Berne to Berlin on the Second Zionist Congress (29 Aug. 1898), see *Türkei* 195, K 175921–4.

[36] Marshall Dill, *Germany: A Modern History* (University of Michigan, 1961), p. 199; Veit Valentin, *The German People*, trans. (New York, 1946), p. 526; Koppel Pinson, *Modern Germany. Its History and Civilization* (London, 1954), pp. 281, 286; L. Snyder, *From Bismarck to Hitler*, p. 13; Rosenberg, op. cit., p. 35. As early as June 1895 Herzl recorded in his *Diaries*, 'our entire youth . . . will abandon their vague socialistic leanings and turn to me' (i, p. 102). See also ii, pp. 657–8; iii, pp. 783, 888–9; iv, p. 1530.

undefined venture in Palestine'. Zionism, in Bülow's opinion, could at best attract the destitute, not the prosperous and educated among the Jews of Europe; but beggars were not capable of founding a state or even of colonizing it.[37]

Bülow was largely influenced by Justizrat Silberstein, and particularly by Professor Ludwig Stein. In a memorandum prepared at Bülow's request Stein dismissed the Zionist project as 'not worthy of consideration',[38] a conclusion he had reached during a fact-finding mission to Palestine in 1895 on behalf of the Esra Verein. The Verein was investigating the possibilities of Jewish migration from Russia to Palestine, but Stein, though impressed by the existing colonies, discounted them as 'mere oases in the desert. . . . The stony soil, the lack of humus, the dearth of fauna and the scanty flora' were 'insurmountable obstacles to any considerable colonization.' Moreover, in his opinion, Abdul Hamid's opposition to the settlement of aliens made the Verein's project impracticable. On the eve of the Kaiser's visit to the East, when discussing with Bülow the entire complex of the Jewish question, Stein proposed the acquisition of stretches of land along the projected Baghdad Railway as an alternative outlet for the settlement of Russian-Jewish emigrants. He claimed that both the German-Jewish leadership and the Baron de Hirsch Fund Committee (the Jewish Colonization Association, the I.C.A.) supported the idea.

In 1929 Stein admitted that he had been mistaken:

> In justice to the memory of Herzl, I must confess that in his visionary ecstasy he foresaw many things which logical rationalism considered Utopian. Herzl and Nordau have prevailed. They brought to life a movement that . . . grew far beyond the limits of my wildest dreams. . . . Had I possessed prophetic vision . . . then my judgement as recorded in my diary [memorandum ?] would have been different. But being a philosopher by profession, I could not assume the role of seer.[39]

Bülow, too, in October 1914 (by then no longer a Minister) admitted to Bodenheimer that reports from Jewish quarters had misled him

---

[37] Sigmund Münz, *Prince Bülow: The Statesman and Man*, English trans. (London, 1935), pp. 102–3. On Bülow's opinion of Herzl see his *Memoirs*, English trans. (London, 1931), ii, pp. 249–50.

[38] Max Bodenheimer, *So Wurde Israel. Erinnerungen von . . .* , pp. 83, 199.

[39] Ludwig Stein, 'They have Prevailed. A Tribute to Herzl and Nordau', *Theodor Herzl—A Memorial*, pp. 30–2 (cited hereafter Stein). The Esra Verein was a Zionist religious philanthropic but non-political organization (Lichtheim, *Geschichte*, pp. 101–3, 117–18).

into adopting a negative attitude towards Zionism. Bodenheimer agreed that 'to implement the idea of a Jewish state in Palestine in 1898 would have been too adventurous'.[40] And Bülow, by nature, was not adventurous.

Unable to rely on Bülow, Herzl wrote to Eulenburg to request an audience of the Emperor before the latter's departure for Constantinople. He made five points:

1. In various countries Zionism might lessen the danger of socialism, since it was often dissatisfied Jews who provided the revolutionary parties with leaders and ideas.
2. A reduction in Jewish numbers would weaken anti-Semitism.
3. Turkey stood to gain from the influx of an intelligent and energetic element into Palestine. Large sums of money injected into her economy and the increase in trade would improve her finances.
4. The Jews would bring civilization and order back to a neglected corner of the Orient.
5. A railroad from the Mediterranean to the Persian Gulf was a European necessity. 'The Jews could and must build this great road of the nations which, if undertaken otherwise, might call forth the most serious rivalries.'[41]

This memorandum had a remarkable success. In less than a week the Kaiser, in consultation with Eulenburg, whose counsel he valued, made up his mind to give full support to Herzl's cause. In a letter to his uncle, the Grand Duke, thanking him for providing the stimulus and guidance in a matter of which hitherto he had had only a superficial knowledge, the Kaiser wrote:

The fundamental idea of Zionism has always interested me and even aroused my sympathy. I have come to the conclusion that here we have to deal with a question of the most far-reaching importance. Therefore I have requested that cautious contact should be made with the promoters of this idea. I am willing to grant an audience to a Zionist deputation in Jerusalem on the occasion of our presence there.

---

[40] Bodenheimer, op. cit., p. 199.
[41] *Diaries*, ii, pp. 669–71 (21 Sept. 1898). On the diplomatic rivalry concerning the Baghdad Railway see Edward Mead Earle, *Turkey, the Great Powers and the Bagdad Railway. A Study in Imperialism* (London, 1923); John B. Wolf, 'The Diplomatic History of the Bagdad Railroad', *University of Missouri Studies*, xi, no. 2 (Apr. 1936) (Columbia); Langer, op. cit. ii, pp. 629–47.

I am convinced that the settlement of the Holy Land by the wealthy and industrious people of Israel [*Volk Israel*] will bring unexampled prosperity and blessings to the Holy Land, which may do much to revive and develop Asia Minor. Such a settlement would bring millions into the purse of the Turks and of the upper class and effendis and so gradually help to save the 'Sick Man' from bankruptcy. In this way the disagreeable Eastern question would be imperceptibly separated from the Mediterranean. . . . The Turk will recover, getting his money without borrowing, and will be able to build his own highways and railways without foreign companies and then it would not be so easy to dismember Turkey.

In addition, the energy and the creative powers and abilities of the tribe of Shem would be directed to more dignified purposes than the exploitation of Christians, and many Semites of the Social Democratic party, who are stirring up opposition, will move eastwards, where more rewarding work will present itself . . . I know very well that nine-tenths of all Germans will be deeply shocked when they hear, at a later time, that I sympathize with the Zionists or even that I place them under my protection when they appeal to me.

Wilhelm then alluded to the story that 'the Jews killed the Redeemer', but thought it was up to God himself to punish them, as He had done. However, he added, 'neither the anti-Semites nor others including myself, were ordered or empowered to maltreat these people to the greater glory of God. He that is without sin among you, let him cast the first stone', and 'thou shalt love thine enemy.' These moral arguments the Kaiser reinforced with those of expediency.

From the point of view of secular *Realpolitik*, the question cannot be ignored. In view of the gigantic power (very dangerous in a way) of international Jewish capital, would it not be an immense achievement for Germany, if the world of the Hebrews looked to her with gratitude? Everywhere the hydra of the most awful anti-Semitism raises its terrible and brutal head, and the Jews, full of anxiety, are ready to leave the countries where they are threatened to return to the Holy Land and look for protection and security. I shall intercede with the Sultan, for the Scripture says, 'Make friends even with unjust Mammon' and 'Be ye wise as serpents and harmless as doves'.[42]

This extraordinary document sheds an interesting light on the Emperor's character and ideas. He was certainly not free from the

---

[42] Ellern, pp. 48–53, Wilhelm II to the Grand Duke, 29 Sept. 1898. The letter was handwritten. Its contents were passed on confidentially to Herzl by Count Eulenburg and also by the Grand Duke of Baden (*Diaries*, ii, pp. 675, 678).

religious prejudices which Stöcker and his Calvinist tutor G. E. Hinzpeter had implanted in him;[43] but here his reaction to anti-Semitism was unusual. By proposing a constructive solution to the Jewish problem he seemed to stand out from most of his contemporaries, though obviously, without the impact of Herzl's memorandum (re-echoed partly in his letter), it is doubtful whether his conclusions would have been so far-reaching.

The idea that the Turkish Government would gain from Jewish immigration into Palestine had been expressed a year earlier by Paul von Tischendorf, the German Consul-General in Jerusalem, in a conversation with the Turkish Governor, Ibrahim Hakki Pasha. The Consul endeavoured to convince the Pasha that there was ample space in the country for Jewish colonization, which would become an ever increasing source of revenue for the Turkish Government. Tischendorf had his own reasons for welcoming emigration from Europe, where the inclination of the Jews to concentrate in the great cities constituted a 'real political danger', as many of them turned to the Social Democratic party, feeding it with men and ideas. Hence the attraction of Zionism as a safety-valve. Equally important to Tischendorf was the fact that the Jewish merchants in Palestine were good importers of German goods, thereby creating promising opportunities for the future.[44]

It is not clear whether the Kaiser had read Tischendorf's report, but the similarity between their reasoning is striking. However that may be, it is evident that it was Eulenburg who had kindled his interest. The Count understood the Emperor and in serious matters knew how to make his counsel effective. 'Only by *consistently* rational and timely advice was it possible to confine the . . . temperamentally exuberant . . . Emperor within limits.'[45] The Kaiser 'has to be greatly interested in a matter', Eulenburg told Herzl during his second interview on 8 October, as 'otherwise he soon loses sight of it. My standing with the Kaiser is such that I am able to speak to him differently from, and more than, many others. Very few people can

---

[43] Bodenheimer, op. cit., p. 94; Pinson, op. cit., p. 278; Rosenberg, op. cit., p. 35. Wilhelm was essentially a deeply religious man. See Sydner, op. cit., p. 60.

[44] *Türkei* 195, K 175847–64, Tischendorf to Prince Hohenlohe-Shillingsfuerst, 19 June 1897 (contains also an extensive report on Jewish colonization in Palestine). It was customary for embassy and consular dispatches, intended primarily for the Foreign Ministry, to be addressed to the Chancellor. By contrast, cables were sent direct to the Ministry.

[45] Haller, op. cit. ii, p. 40, Eulenburg to Bülow, 3 Feb. 1898.

go as far as I . . . I have been able to bring the matter up again and again and I have succeeded.'[46]

It was at Rominten during a royal hunting-party that Eulenburg managed eventually to inculcate into the Emperor's mind his ideas on Zionism. From Rominten on 27 September Eulenburg wrote to Herzl:

I have only *good* news for you . . . His Majesty has shown complete and deep understanding of the movement headed by you. Convinced of its righteousness, I was a zealous exponent of your cause; my friend Bülow is of the same mind and this might be of great significance for your cause.

Following my exposition, His Majesty has declared himself ready to intervene with the Sultan and as far as possible to present your case urgently and *vigorously*. In this, the Kaiser will be supported by State Secretary von Bülow, who will accompany him. As I was in a position to inform the Kaiser of the Sultan's willingness to meet [Zionist wishes] half-way, as suggested by Herr von Marschall, the Kaiser, on his part, saw no obstacle in making a further step. I have no doubt that, with his lively mind, he will prove an able exponent.

Then Eulenburg advised Herzl that the Kaiser would be pleased to receive a Zionist deputation in Palestine, which would give Herzl an excellent opportunity to present his case.

On the next day, 28 September, Eulenburg sent Herzl a highly confidential postscript.

I have just had another thorough conversation with His Majesty regarding your letter. His Majesty has instructed me to inform you that your confidence in H.M.'s interest to further your cause and to protect the poor and oppressed Jews, is not misplaced. His Majesty would discuss the matter with the Sultan in a most emphatic manner and will be pleased to hear more from you in Jerusalem. The Kaiser has already issued orders to the effect that no obstacle is to be placed in the way of the [Zionist] delegation.

In conclusion, H.M. wishes to tell you that he is very much *prepared* to undertake the protectorate in question. His Majesty, naturally, counts on your discretion in conveying this information.[47]

[46] *Diaries*, ii, p. 689.

[47] These letters of Eulenburg, as well as that of the Grand Duke of Baden of 5 Oct. 1898, mentioned in the *Diaries* (pp. 675, 677, 678, 685), were missing from Herzl's private collection and were not found until 1954, when Dr. Alex Bein, Director of the Central Zionist Archives in Jerusalem, discovered them in a safe-deposit at the Anglo-Palestine Bank, London among the papers of Mr. Joseph Cowen. They were published by Dr. Bein in the Herzl Centenary Supplement of the *Jerusalem Post*, 6 May 1960, and in *Davar* (Hebrew daily) on the same date. On 17 Dec. 1962 I was fortunate to discover

The Duke assured Herzl of the Emperor's 'warm . . . and lively interest'; he would suggest his protection of the Zionist project when he met the Sultan; thereafter he would receive a Zionist deputation in Jerusalem in order to demonstrate his sympathy.[48]

The meeting with Eulenburg on 8 October was even more encouraging and made Herzl confident that Germany's intervention and protection were a foregone conclusion. But Eulenburg advised caution. No matter how desirable the object was, its implementation was uncertain. 'Germany will not go to war for the sake of the Zionists.'

Eulenburg did not share Herzl's fear that Russia might cause difficulties. The Holy Places, the only concern of Russia, might be given extraterritorial status and in the last resort the Kaiser could write to the Tsar and win him over. Since Russia had no objection to the departure of Jews, any obstacles could be discounted. Eulenburg anticipated difficulties only from England and France, but Herzl was quick to point out that France was undergoing a severe internal crisis and was too weak to take any action. Eulenburg pondered Herzl's suggestion that it might be wiser to receive the Zionist deputation secretly in Berlin or Constantinople but concluded that, since a protectorate could not remain concealed for very long, the best way was 'to come right out with it, immediately and demonstratively. The world would then have to come to terms with it.' Herzl commented: 'Here I recognize the Prussian . . . This is the forthright grand old style. Open and above-board.'

Although elated, he still had some qualms about the reaction to a German protectorate, but soon reconvinced himself that, since it had been offered, the only correct course to follow was to accept it gratefully.

To live under the protection of this strong, great, moral, splendidly governed, tightly organized Germany can only have the most salutary effect on the Jewish national character. Also, at one stroke we would obtain a completely ordered internal and external legal status. The suzerainty of the Porte and the protectorate of Germany would certainly be sufficient legal pillars.[49]

A subsequent conversation with the Grand Duke in Potsdam

a copy of the letters in the *Nachlass Eulenburg* in the Bundesarchiv, Koblenz (Nr. 52, pp. 298 e–g). They are reproduced in full in Appendix A.

[48] Grand Duke to Herzl, 5 Oct. 1898, on which see n. 47 above.

[49] Ibid. ii, pp. 689–93. Herzl had raised the idea of exterritorial status for the Holy Places earlier in *The Jewish State* (p. 96).

on 9 October fortified Herzl's conviction. 'The Kaiser has been thoroughly informed . . . and is full of enthusiasm. That word is not too strong. He has taken to your idea quite warmly. He speaks of it in the liveliest terms. He would also have received you by now, for he has confidence in you: but it is now deemed better to receive you at Constantinople and Jerusalem.' He added that a good report had come from Marschall and that the Kaiser believed that the Sultan would consider his advice favourably. The Duke was so optimistic about a successful outcome that he was already considering the form of its presentation to the public: 'With the consent of the Sultan, the Kaiser will take the migration of the Jews under his protection.'[50]

Both the Duke and Count Eulenburg thought it desirable for Herzl to meet Bülow again; Eulenburg described the Foreign Minister as 'his best friend and a most outstanding statesman', whom he had been fortunate to win over to the Zionist cause. But he was mistaken. When Herzl called on the Foreign Secretary, he found him in the company of Prince Hohenlohe, the Imperial Chancellor. Herzl immediately grasped what an ordeal awaited him. Throughout the interview the two statesmen remained cold and aloof. 'Do you think that the Jews are going to desert the Stock Exchange and follow you? —the Jews who are comfortably installed here in Berlin?', Hohenlohe asked acidly. Never at a loss, Herzl replied that it would be the poor Jews who would go with him. When questioned on the attitude of the Porte, Herzl quoted Marschall's favourable report, about which he had learned from the Grand Duke and Eulenburg. But Bülow denied any knowledge of it. Now and again he supported the sceptical Hohenlohe, interjecting ironic remarks such as Money might do the trick [with the Turk]. With it one can swing 'the matter', and if the Israelites were willing to emigrate, 'it would be their first eastward migration . . . until now they have always moved westward'. Herzl remarked that the 'Jews have already encircled the globe', hence 'East is West again'.

The Zionist leader had reason to feel gratified that even the Imperial Chancellor was obliged to enter into discussion with him, whereas three years before Bismarck had not even bothered to reply to his letter. However, the conversation was, on the whole, frustrating. Herzl tried to explain away the indifference of his hosts as part of the diplomatic game, but it was a poor consolation. He

[50] *Diaries*, ii, pp. 697–700.

presumed that perhaps the Chancellor and the Foreign Minister were themselves 'at odds with their Imperial master, but do not dare to stand up to him. So for the present they treat the matter with dilatory coldness in order to trip it up at the proper moment and bring the whole thing to the ground.'[51]

Herzl's intuition was not at fault. Neither Hohenlohe nor Bülow had been consulted on the Zionist question. Unofficial court diplomacy, as practised in this case, must have annoyed them. There was nothing unusual in this. Prince Hohenlohe used to complain about his 'peculiar relations' with the sovereign, whose 'acts of thoughtlessness and want of consideration' led him to conclude that the Emperor purposely avoided him.[52] Indeed, Wilhelm believed that he could conduct policy more ably than his Ministers. This had resulted earlier in a breach with Bismarck and the Foreign Minister, von Marschall. With the advent of the New Course era major decisions were made by the Emperor himself, whilst the position of Chancellor declined further. Caprivi was quick to adjust himself and under Hohenlohe 'the usurpation by the Sovereign of his Chief Minister's functions made further progress'.[53]

However, unlike the Chancellor, who was too old to curb the impulsiveness of the Emperor, Bülow was in the prime of his career and would not be ignored. He endeavoured to keep the Emperor entirely dependent upon him; in fact, as his biographer wrote, 'he did not tolerate near him anyone who had any claim to distinction'.[54] In this he was most unscrupulous. Although he owed his career to his friendship with Eulenburg, his conduct to his friend was treacherous.[55] Even later, at the zenith of his power as Chancellor, he found it intolerable that Eulenburg's influence on the Kaiser was

---

[51] Ibid., pp. 689, 700–5.

[52] *Memoirs of Prince Chlodwig of Hohenlohe-Schillingsfuerst*, ed. Friedrich Curtius (London, 1907), ii, p. 470. No mention is made of Herzl in these *Memoirs*.

[53] Flenley, op. cit., p. 312; Pinson, op. cit., p. 286; Dawson, *The German Empire, 1867–1914*, ii, pp. 325–6.

[54] Dill, op. cit., p. 198; Pinson, op. cit., 286; Münz, op. cit., pp. 217, 241. For Bülow's relations with the Kaiser see Münz, op. cit., pp. 70, 211 and Spectator, *Prince Bülow and the Kaiser* (London, n.d.), pp. 29–45.

[55] Spectator, p. 61. Eulenburg's biographer wrote: 'We know how the friendship between Eulenburg and Bülow began and who most profited by it.' (Haller, op. cit. ii, p. 3.) The Eulenburg–Bülow alliance was a counterweight to Holstein's intrigues, which were dangerous to both of them but subsequently Bülow fell under Holstein's spell (ibid., pp. 8–9, 306). Eulenburg recommended Bülow to become Chancellor (*Nachlass Eulenburg*, Eulenburg to Wilhelm II, 22 Oct. 1900) but greatly underestimated Bülow's loyalty to him.

perhaps stronger than his own.[56] He must have been even more sensitive on the eve of the Near Eastern tour,[57] when Eulenburg had the Emperor's ear on Zionism, if not on Turkish policy as a whole. This element of jealousy may have reinforced Bülow's objections to the Zionist policy.

Eulenburg's contention that Turkey might be strengthened by Zionism failed to convince him, since he did not believe in the viability of the Ottoman Empire at all. His conversations in Constantinople with Marschall and Testa, the first dragoman of the Embassy, led him to a pessimistic assessment of Turkey; Turkey was a dying Empire, no longer the 'sick man' but 'an *old* man' who could not stand any drastic cure. Hence he found it his duty to moderate the Kaiser's excessive enthusiasm for everything Turkish[58] and Zionist.

Marschall did not share Bülow's pessimistic view of Turkey. He had made his name as a diplomat by initiating the era of German–Turkish friendship which became one of the chief leitmotivs of Germany's foreign policy.[59] There is hardly any evidence about his attitude to Zionism; the 'favourable report' to which both Eulenburg and the Grand Duke of Baden referred has not so far come to light. It is not among the documents of the German Foreign Ministry,[60]

[56] Spectator, p. 62. A few years later Bülow 'signed the order for his friend's arrest' (ibid., p. 63). The anonymous writer, 'Spectator', who appears to have had an intimate knowledge of Foreign Ministry affairs, stated: 'the tragedy of Phillip Eulenburg will probably remain a mysterious episode in Bülow's career' (ibid., p. 61). Reproducing the Zedlitz Report, he reiterated emphatically that 'on Bülow's shoulders rests the whole guilt of the Eulenburg scandal, because he had personal motives to desire it' (ibid., p. 63). Bülow himself discounted Holstein's accusations against Eulenburg as unfounded, but remained silent on his complicity in the affair (see *Memoirs*, iii, pp. 281–4; cf. below, p. 89 n. 39).

[57] Bülow was invited by the Kaiser to join the tour but it does not seem that he was consulted in policy. In fact, he disliked the Kaiser's pro-Turkish zeal and criticized his 'predilection for the Sultan' (see *Memoirs*, ii, pp. 237, 246–7).

[58] Bülow, *Memoirs*, ii, pp. 245–8. Bülow's assessment differed from the one widely held at that time. The Cretan crisis and the defeat of Greece by Turkey made a considerable impression in European capitals. It was realized that 'even if [the Ottoman Empire] could not reform it could at least resist. It was not so near the point of dissolution as had been generally supposed. The final collapse was still pretty far off.' (Langer, op. cit. i, p. 378.)

[59] *The Memoirs of Count Bernstorff*, trans. (London, 1936), p. 20; Richard von Kühlmann, *Die Diplomaten* (Berlin, 1939), p. 43; J. B. Wolf, op. cit., pp. 19–20, 45; Erich Eyck, *Das persönliche Regiment Wilhelm II.* (Zürich, 1948), p. 239; Valentin, op. cit., p. 523; Earle, op. cit., p. 43; Lord Eversley, *The Turkish Empire* (London, 1923), p. 273; Dill, op. cit., p. 208.

[60] On 2 Sept. 1898 Marschall had an audience with the Sultan but the question of Zionism was not discussed (Marschall to Hohenlohe, 2 Sept. 1898, dis. no. 366, A.A. 37, Nr. 1, Bd. 2).

nor can it be traced in the *Nachlass Eulenburg*, or among the Emperor's papers.[61] We can only surmise why it was too risky for him to support such a venture.

His first objective was to cement relations with Turkey; the second, to facilitate Germany's peaceful penetration of the Ottoman Empire without arousing suspicion. This was not an easy task since the Russian Press was giving much prominence to the alleged German plans to colonize Asia Minor, and even Petersburg made known its displeasure with Berlin's *Drang nach Osten*. Zinoviev, the Russian Foreign Minister, was incredulous when Tewfik Pasha, his opposite number, denied any knowledge of talks, let alone any agreement, with the German Government on the settlement of German colonists in Asia Minor. It was the French who were responsible for feeding the Russians with this kind of information, which Marschall dismissed as 'terrible nonsense, such as only Frenchmen, when speaking about Germans, are able to produce'.[62] But German protection of Jewish colonization would have substantiated the Russian and French allegations, and in the given circumstances caution was imperative.

Moreover, Marschall was aware that the Sultan's objection to foreign colonization was based on religious grounds and that the Muslim clergy were particularly sensitive on this issue. For this reason, von Siemens, the Director of the Deutsche Bank, wanted to give the Anatolian and Baghdad Railways project a purely economic character and avoid any association with political factors.[63] The Embassy shared his view and in 1905 Marschall asked a representative of the Hilfsverein der deutschen Juden to advise the Zionists to moderate their political aspirations.[64] Yet the question still arises: why, if Marschall was aware of the pitfalls entailed in support of Zionism, did he not warn the Emperor in the autumn of 1898?[65]

[61] The Zivilkabinettarchiv deposited in the Deutsches Zentralarchiv, Abt. Merseburg, East Germany (letter from the D.Z. to the author, 16 Apr. 1963).

[62] *Türkei*, Nr. 189, *Plan deutscher Ansiedlungen in Kleinasien, 1891–1913* (cited hereafter as *Türkei* 189), Marschall to Hohenlohe-Schillingsfuerst, 10 June 1898, dis. no. 137. Tewfik Pasha served as Foreign Minister from 1895 to 1909; he had been Ambassador in Berlin from 1885 to 1895.

[63] Ibid., Marschall to A.A., 5 Dec. 1899, tel. no. 358; Oppenheim to A.A., 25 Sept. 1905, dis. no. 243.

[64] Ephraim Cohn-Reiss: *M'Zichronoth Ish Yerushalaim* [*Memoirs*] (Jerusalem, 1933), 1, p. 261; *Türkei* 195, K 176902, Cohn-Reiss to James Simon, 20 Jan. 1915.

[65] Wilhelm disliked Marschall 'partly because he was a South German' (Flenley, op. cit., p. 312). The strained relations between Marschall and Eulenburg were a matter

Soon after the Zionist delegation arrived in Constantinople it experienced a bitter foretaste of its future disappointments; Marschall declined to grant Herzl an audience on the pretext that he did not know him. Bodenheimer's explanation that Dr. Herzl was the Zionist leader who had been in touch with Count Eulenburg and that the matter concerned 'the reception of a deputation by His Majesty the Kaiser', had no effect.[66] To the Zionists' regret, Eulenburg did not join the Near Eastern tour and his cousin, August zu Eulenburg, who accompanied the Emperor as Court Marshal, had no political standing. Bülow was unreliable and Marschall enigmatic. To bring matters to a head, Herzl wrote to Wilhelm requesting a confidential audience. He assured the Kaiser that France, weakened internally, would not be able to make a move, that 'to Russia, the Zionist solution of the Jewish question meant an enormous relief', and that no effective objection was to be feared from England, since the English Church was known to favour the Zionist cause. 'Everything depends on the form of the *fait accompli.*' As for the Sultan, even if he did not immediately realize what aid the Zionists would bring to his impoverished state, it was unlikely that he would decline to accept the Kaiser's advice. Once personal contact between the two sovereigns was established, they could ignore the intrigues of other Powers. Herzl's request boiled down to a concession for a 'Jewish Land Company for Syria and Palestine' under German protection.[67]

of common knowledge (Bodenheimer, op. cit., p. 98; also Bodenheimer, 'Theodor Herzl', *Theodor Herzl—A Memorial*, p. 75, hereafter Bodenheimer, 'Theodor Herzl').

[66] *Diaries*, ii, pp. 712–13. Bodenheimer was a member of the Zionist deputation which, with David Wolffsohn and Moses Schnirer, accompanied Herzl to Constantinople and Jerusalem.

[67] Ibid., pp. 716–17, Herzl to the Kaiser, 18 Oct. 1898. The original is reproduced in Ellern, pp. 54–7. Herzl's references to Syria pertain to the sanjaks of Acre and Belqua in the vilayet of Beirut. The former included the north-western part of Galilee and the latter Samaria, the central part of western Palestine.

5

The Fiasco

THE long-awaited audience with the Emperor took place on 18 October in Bülow's presence.[1] The Kaiser listened attentively to Herzl's exposition and expressed confidence that the Zionists, with the financial and human resources at their disposal, would be successful in their venture. That the word 'Zionism' was used by the German Emperor as an accepted term was a source of pride to Herzl, but other utterances were less pleasant. 'There are elements among your people whom it would be quite a good thing to settle in Palestine', the Kaiser stated. 'I am thinking of Hesse,[2] for example, where there are usurers at work among the rural population. If these people took their possessions and went to settle in the colonies, they could be more useful.' Herzl was taken by surprise because earlier he had been assured by both Eulenburg and Bülow that Wilhelm II was by no means anti-Semitic. Herzl soon regained his confidence and launched an attack on anti-Semitism, only to be parried by Bülow who commented that the Jews, by flocking to the opposition and even to the anti-monarchical parties, showed their ingratitude to the House of Hohenzollern. Herzl replied that Zionism would take the Jews away from the revolutionary parties. Bülow stuck to his

[1] What follows is based on Herzl's *Diaries*, ii, pp. 726–34, 737, unless otherwise stated. In his memoirs (written presumably in the early 1920s) Wilhelm attested that Herzl's account of his meeting in Constantinople was 'absolutely correct, reliable and praiseworthy'. Herzl impressed him as 'a clever and a highly intelligent figure with expressive eyes . . . an enthusiastic idealist', who communicated his ideas in 'a captivating manner'. Wilhelm recalled that he agreed to recommend Herzl's plan to the Sultan. The latter, though not enthusiastic, assured the Kaiser that he would instruct his Ministers to inquire into the matter and report. (Excerpt from *Memoirs* of Wilhelm II published by Dr. Alex Bein (in German) in the *Festschrift* in honour of Dr. N. M. Gelber (Tel Aviv, 1963), p. 17.)

[2] At the turn of the century about 25,000 Jews lived in Hessen, many of them engaged in small-scale farming. Hessen was known to be a stronghold of German anti-Semitism.

guns and, when Wilhelm expressed confidence that the Jews would support the colonization of Palestine once they knew it was under his protection, the Foreign Minister interjected that the rich Jews were not in favour of it, nor were the big newspapers. At every opportunity he contradicted the Emperor, only stopping short of using 'the little word NO . . . since the *voluntas regis* [was] YES'. On one occasion the Kaiser had laid it down that '*suprema lex regis voluntas est*'.[3]

However, the Emperor, who often allowed himself to be guided by his Minister, in this case supported Herzl and agreed that Zionism was a 'completely natural' solution. Bülow again raised a doubt as to the attitude of the Porte, although individual Turkish Ministers might prove more amenable if offered sufficient bribes. But the Kaiser brushed aside Bülow's misgivings, confident that it would make an impression if he showed interest. 'After all, I am the only one who still sticks by the Sultan.' Throughout the conversation the Kaiser looked at Herzl directly. Only when the latter spoke of the new overland route to Asia and the Persian Gulf did he stare into space, and his thoughtful expression revealed that Herzl's words had made an impact. The interview was concluded by the Kaiser's undertaking to ask the Sultan for a 'chartered company under German protection'. He shook Herzl's hand vigorously, promising to work the details out with Bülow. Events showed that he gravely misjudged the attitude of the Porte and his own Minister.

Though flattering his Sovereign as 'a monarch of genius!', Bülow remained unconvinced. He told Herzl (after the Kaiser had left) that in his opinion the Turks were unfavourably disposed and advised him to see Marschall, who possessed 'exact information'. Soon after Herzl drove to the German Embassy, only to find that Marschall had left to attend the dinner in the Kaiser's honour. It was there that the Emperor made his diplomatic overture to the Sultan and failed.

Wilhelm's account of his encounter with Abdul Hamid, quoted already, is too sketchy to enlighten us. In 1902 the Grand Duke of Baden told Dr. Bodenheimer that at the dinner the Kaiser twice attempted to discuss the matter of Palestine with the Sultan, but the latter displayed a 'complete and ostentatious lack of understanding'. Earlier, in 1901 Herzl was told by Count Eulenburg that he had been unable to discover what the difficulty had been. The

---

[3] Quoted in Pinson, *Modern Germany*, p. 278.

Sultan rejected the Kaiser's suggestion so brusquely that it was not possible to pursue the matter further; 'we are anxious to remain on good terms with him. As a guest the Kaiser could not, of course, press the subject.' But it was Newlinski's version which was the most detailed. According to his information the Kaiser had told the Sultan that the Zionists were 'not dangerous to Turkey, but everywhere the Jews are a nuisance', of whom one 'should like to get rid'. To which the Sultan was reported to have replied that he was quite satisfied with his Jewish subjects.[4]

Turkey was the worst place to air anti-Semitic sentiments; anti-Semitism had never struck root there and an astute politician like Abdul Hamid could hardly be expected to offer refuge to elements which appeared undesirable to a German Emperor. If the circumstantial evidence adduced above is correct, the Kaiser's diplomatic venture was clumsy. Wilhelm II has been described as quick, versatile, and responsive to ideas, but also as a man without depth; impulsive by nature, he scarcely penetrated the problems which he studied. In personal relations he was benevolent and amiable, yet on some occasions he was inclined to act in a most erratic and tactless manner. Despite his intellectual gifts, there was much of the irresponsible dilettante in him. He undoubtedly had an instinct for politics, but he was no master of diplomacy. 'What he needed most—and never had—was someone in authority over him.'[5]

Not only Eulenburg, the Emperor's most trustworthy friend, but also Bülow were aware of these shortcomings. It was unfortunate that Eulenburg was not present, because Bülow's reliability was still to be tested. Shortly after taking office, he wrote to Eulenburg that personally the Kaiser was 'charming', but as a ruler, owing to his temperament, he would stand in the greatest danger unless he was surrounded by 'entirely *loyal and trustworthy* servants'.[6] A few

---

[4] Bodenheimer, 'Theodor Herzl', p. 75; *Diaries*, iii, p. 75; ii, p. 770. Philip Michael de Newlinski was a Polish-Austrian political agent and journalist. Following the accession of Abdul Hamid II (1876) he gained the new Sultan's friendship, which enabled him to be helpful to Herzl; also Bein, *Theodore Herzl*, pp. 192–4; Josef Fraenkel, 'Lucien Wolf and Theodor Herzl' (London, 1960), pp. 8–10; and for Herzl's appreciation, *Diaries*, i, pp. 370, 390, 403; ii, 438, 528–9, 817, 823–4; below, pp. 92–3, 96.

[5] Frank P. Chambers, *The War behind the War, 1914–1918* (London, 1939), p. 131; Snyder, *From Bismarck to Hitler*, pp. 58–9; Pinson, op. cit., pp. 277–8; Valentin, *The German People*, pp. 512–13.

[6] Haller, *Philipp Eulenburg*, ii, p. 35, Bülow to Eulenburg, 22 Aug. 1897. A year earlier Bülow had assured Eulenburg that he would carry out the Kaiser's wishes loyally (*Nachlass Eulenburg*, Nr. 42, p. 524, Bülow to Eulenburg, 23 July 1896), but in fact his

months later Bülow protested his unswerving loyalty to both Wilhelm and Eulenburg. The Near Eastern tour provided Bülow with an opportunity to prove it. As a diplomat he possessed great skill and a ready wit, which helped him to improvise and to extricate himself from embarrassing situations.[7] But it does not seem that he placed these qualities at the disposal of Wilhelm in Constantinople. He had opinions of his own on the 'chartered company under German protection', but the question which needs to be answered is this: if Bülow was aware that the Turks were unfavourably disposed, why did he not think fit to warn the Kaiser, or prepare him better for negotiations with the Sultan, or alternatively to postpone them for a more propitious moment? Did he think Wilhelm so enthusiastic about the Zionist project that it was useless to argue with him, or did he deliberately keep silent in order to wreck a plan of which he disapproved?

Unaware of the Emperor's failure, Herzl drafted the official address he was to deliver in Jerusalem:

We are bound to this sacred soil through no valid title of ownership. Many generations have come and gone since this earth was Jewish. If we talk about it, it is only about a dream of very ancient days. But the dream is still alive, lives in many hundreds of thousands of hearts; it was and is a wonderful comfort in many an hour of pain for our poor people. Whenever foes oppressed us with accusations and persecutions, whenever we are begrudged the little bit of right to live, whenever we are excluded from the society of our fellow citizens—whose destinies we have been ready to share loyally—the thought of Zion arose in our oppressed hearts.

There is something eternal about that thought, whose form, to be sure, has undergone multifarious changes with people, institutions and times.

Zionism was the political expression of an old idea. It aimed at solving the Jewish question by modern means, but its essence was to realize the centuries-old craving to return to Zion.

This is the land of our fathers, a land suitable for colonization and cultivation. It cries out for the people to work it. And we have among our

---

objective was to undermine Wilhelm's personal regime (Friedrich Thimme, 'Fürst Bülow und Kaiser Wilhelm II.', *Front wider Bülow. Staatsmänner, Diplomaten und Forscher zu seinen Denkwürdigkeiten* (Munich, 1931), 1–22. In 1899 Eulenburg jotted: 'So, Bernhard . . . is reluctant to speak *openly* and frankly to His Majesty! He talks so cunningly that His Majesty is satisfied.' *Nachlass Eulenburg*, Nr. 49, pp. 622–3.)

[7] Pinson, op. cit., p. 286.

brethren a frightful [*sic*] proletariat. These people cry out for a land to cultivate.

It was the task of the Zionist movement to effect a union of the two, a cause so worthy of sympathy that it would fully justify the Emperor's protection. The Sultan, too, should be persuaded of the usefulness of the Jewish Land Company.

We are honestly convinced that the implementation of the Zionist plan must mean welfare for Turkey . . . Energies and material resources will be brought to the country; a magnificent fructification of desolate areas may easily be foreseen; and from all this there will arise more happiness and more culture for many human beings. . . . Our idea offends no-one's rights or religious feelings; it breathes long-desired reconciliation. We understand and respect the devotion of all faiths to the soil on which, after all, the faith of our fathers, too, arose.

Jewish aspirations transcended their purely national context. They were part of the human endeavour.

This is the fatherland of ideas which do not belong to one people or to one creed alone. The farther men advance in their morality, the more clearly do they recognize the common elements in these ideas. And thus the actual city of Jerusalem, with its fateful walls, has long since become a symbolic city sacred to all civilized men.[8]

The exalted note echoed the Messianic hope of the Hebrew prophets, who believed that redemption of the Jewish people would coincide with the redemption of mankind. Lofty as its content was, it brought no definite result. Circumstances were against Herzl; it does not require much imagination to realize why 'German protection of a Jewish chartered company' could not commend itself to the Sultan. For years Turkey had been struggling against the system of Capitulations, which provided the European Powers with an instrument for meddling in her internal affairs. 'The spectre of a second Franco-Lebanon [in the form of a Judeo-] German Palestine',[9] was alarming. Ahmed Tewfik, the Turkish Foreign Minister, who accompanied the Kaiser on his tour in Palestine, made it clear that 'the Sultan would have nothing to do with Zionism and an independent Jewish kingdom'. As a result Wilhelm lost his enthusiasm for Zionism.[10]

---

[8] *Diaries*, ii, pp. 719–21, 741, drafted on 18, 29 Oct. 1898.

[9] F.O. Handbook, *Syria and Palestine*, p. 45.

[10] Bülow, *Memoirs*, ii, p. 250. However, Bülow erred in recording that Wilhelm refused to receive 'the advocates of Zion' in Jerusalem.

Tewfik was also reported to have declared at the time that the Turks had settled their accounts with the Armenians in three days; with the Zionists it would take only three hours. Moses Halevi, the Chief Rabbi in Constantinople, warned the Chief Rabbi of Jerusalem, Elyashar, to keep clear of Herzl. Ottoman Jewry should not get mixed up with a movement to which the Sultan objected. Elyashar, determined not to incur the Government's displeasure, avoided meeting Herzl.[11]

Herzl may have been flattered when the Kaiser stopped for a while and chatted with him at the gates of Mikve-Israel, to the astonishment of the spectators watching the imperial procession on its way to Jerusalem. 'Water is what it needs, a lot of water. . . . It is a land of the future', the Kaiser told Herzl, but the interview which Herzl had with the Legation Counsellor Klehmet, whom Bülow had brought with him from Berlin as his secretary, was discouraging. He objected to a number of passages in Herzl's draft address and insisted on the deletion of the passages requesting the Emperor to take the Land Company under his protection. It was noticeable, Bodenheimer observed, that the Foreign Ministry took great care to ensure that the Kaiser would not, in a moment of enthusiasm, announce his protection of Zionist colonization. Hechler was also present but his influence seems to have waned.[12]

The official audience with the Emperor took place on 2 November 1898, in Jerusalem, again in Bülow's presence. The Emperor welcomed Herzl affably and displayed interest in his address, but then stated that the matter required 'thorough study and further discussion'. The German and Jewish colonies had impressed him and served as an indication of 'what could be done. . . . The country has room for everyone'; the work of the Jewish colonists 'will also serve as a stimulating example to the native population. Your movement, with which I am thoroughly acquainted, contains a sound idea.' He assured the deputation of his continued interest, but the conclusive statement which Herzl was so eagerly awaiting was not forthcoming, and the political aspect of the scheme was passed over. The Kaiser said 'neither yes nor no', and Herzl inferred that his

---

[11] Cohn-Reiss, *M'Zichronoth Ish Yerushalaim*, pp. 256–7, 260; *Diaries*, ii, pp. 710, 745–6, 757.

[12] *Diaries*, ii, pp. 743–4, 748–9, 751–2; Bodenheimer, *Memoirs*, pp. 101–2; Bülow, op. cit. ii, p. 239.

stock had depreciated. On the day itself he still clung to the belief that the reception might have some 'historic consequences', but disillusion was soon to follow. The colourless official communiqué issued by the German news agency (of which Herzl learned on his return journey) dispelled earlier hopes. It read:

Kaiser Wilhelm has received a Jewish deputation . . . Replying to an address by its leader, Kaiser Wilhelm said that all those efforts which aimed at the improvement of agriculture in Palestine, and which furthered the welfare of the Ottoman Empire, commanded his benevolent interest, with due respect for the sovereignty of the Sultan.[13]

The substitution of 'Jewish' for 'Zionist' was significant. Moreover, two days earlier, on 31 October, at the consecration of the Church of the Redeemer, the Lutheran church in the old city of Jerusalem, the Kaiser had declared his intention of protecting the German Christians in Turkey,[14] but no similar assurances were given to the Zionists. This is understandable, for the Emperor was fully entitled under treaty rights to protect his own subjects, but protection of the Zionist movement, which was international and had distinct political aspirations, was a much more complicated undertaking. The emphasis on respect for Ottoman sovereignty also reflected the caution employed by German officials, but such an emasculated formula was hardly what Herzl expected. A month earlier he had asked Eulenburg whether it would not be wiser for the Kaiser to receive the Zionist deputation privately. Unaware of the fiasco in Constantinople, he felt he had been misled. However, unlike his colleagues, he remained undaunted; the protectorate was not an end in itself, but only a means to achieve his objective. The fact that the Kaiser did not assume the protectorate appeared to him, on further reflection, even an advantage. It would have had a clear and immediate benefit, but not so in the long run. 'We would subsequently have had to pay the most usurious interest for this protectorate.' A few months later, when the Grand Duke of Baden reverted to his original plan and advised Herzl to concentrate on

---

[13] *Diaries*, ii, pp. 754–7, 767; the author has translated this communiqué from Herzl's *Tagebücher*; Bodenheimer, op. cit., pp. 103–4.

[14] *Grosse Politik*, xii, ch. lxxxiii; Lewin, *The German Road to the East*, p. 105; Earle, *Turkey, the Great Powers and the Bagdad Railway*, p. 43, who in notes 26, 27, p. 54 gives a list of contemporary accounts and other literature on Wilhelm's visit to Palestine; Langer, *The Diplomacy of Imperialism*, ii, pp. 638–9; Dawson, *The German Empire, 1867–1914*, ii, pp. 393–5; *The Annual Register* (1898), p. 257.

acquisition of land and settlers' privileges and then to work for the protectorate, Herzl recorded: 'One can't be any more cautious and prudent than that. The only thing to be said against it is that once we have got that far, we shall no longer need the onerous German protectorate.'[15]

Herzl was probably not entirely wrong in attributing the text of the communiqué to Legation Counsellor Klehmet, if not to Bülow himself, since it was Bülow who attempted to censor the Kaiser's speech in Damascus two days later, only to find that Marschall had forestalled him in allowing the transcript of the speech to be telegraphed verbatim by the Wolff Agency. Bülow feared lest exaggerated expressions of sympathy might give rise to misconceptions in Constantinople and even provoke suspicions in Paris, London, and St. Petersburg, since each of these governments ruled over millions of Muslim subjects.[16] To dispel any Turkish suspicions Bülow declared in the Reichstag that 'Germany sought no special political influence in Constantinople, such as one or other Power had exercised in past times', and that she made no claim to protect all Christians, only German nationals. He ridiculed the accusation that the Kaiser intended to follow in the Crusaders' footsteps and to annex Syria and Palestine; Germany stood for 'the maintenance and integrity of Turkey'. In the Wilhelmstrasse it became clear that only by showing disinterested sympathy with Turkey and by avoiding policies which could be objectionable to the Sultan was peaceful German economic penetration of the East possible.[17]

The Sultan's objection was the decisive, though not the only, reason that made Berlin write off its support of the Zionists. Neither Paris nor St. Petersburg could view the proposal of a Jewish state under German protection with equanimity. As Tischendorf reported, both the Russians and the French were encouraging their respective Christian nationals to acquire as much land as possible in Palestine in order to check the expansion of the Jewish colonists whom they regarded as 'disagreeable competitors'. Their efforts, however, were of little avail because Jewish immigrants managed to circumvent

---

[15] *Diaries*, ii, pp. 692–3, 767, 788.
[16] Bülow, op. cit. ii, pp. 254, 248.
[17] G. P. Gooch, *Before the War. Studies in Diplomacy* (London, 1936), i, p. 791; *The Annual Register*, pp. 260–1; Cohn-Reiss, op. cit., p. 261; J. B. Wolf, 'The Diplomatic History of the Bagdad Railroad', p. 10.

Ottoman regulations and make their economic influence felt.[18] Had
the Kaiser proclaimed his protection over the Jews, as he did over
the German Catholics, the balance would have undoubtedly been
tilted against the Russian and French positions in Palestine.

In Paris the Kaiser's Near Eastern tour was viewed with profound
distrust. Wild rumours were circulating that the Germans were
planning to colonize Palestine and Syria and develop a harbour in
Haifa or Acre.[19] 'It was clear to us', Bodenheimer recorded, 'that
Paris watched suspiciously over the events in Palestine. Any incautious declaration of a protectorate of a Jewish state would have led
to dangerous European complications. Should the French Fleet,
alerted at Toulon, have anchored off the Syrian coast, trouble
would certainly have ensued.'[20] As early as August 1896 King Milan
of Serbia warned Herzl that 'France wanted her Syrian protectorate and an Arabian Empire'. The Rothschild administrators were
uneasy about Herzl's encounter with the Kaiser at the gates of
Mikve-Israel and soon afterwards Niego, the school's Director,
expressly requested Herzl not to pay a second visit there. As the
Grand Duke of Baden later confided to Hechler, one of the main
reasons which prevented the Kaiser from carrying out his plan was
that too many of the Jews in Palestine were under the protection of
France. A year later Oscar Straus, the American Ambassador in
Constantinople, told Herzl in confidence that neither the Greek
Orthodox nor the Roman Catholic Churches would let the Zionists
have Palestine; Mesopotamia, in Straus's opinion, was more at-
tainable.[21] Bodenheimer admitted that the German Ministers who
opposed the Kaiser's wishes reasoned 'quite correctly that the
attempt to establish a German protectorate over Herzl's Jewish
state would lead to dangerous complications'.[22]

The Russians too seemed perturbed. On 25 April 1899 Count
Osten-Sacken, the Russian Ambassador in Berlin, made the unusual
move of requesting the German Government to carry out a full
investigation into the nature of Zionism in Germany. According to
the information of the Russian Ministry of the Interior, a large
number of Jews had joined the Zionist movement not out of belief
in its ideals but solely with the object of propagating Socialist

[18] *Türkei* 195, K 175851–2, Tischendorf to Hohenlohe-Schillingsfuerst, 19 June
1897, dis. no. 49.
[19] Langer, op. cit. ii, p. 638.   [20] Bodenheimer, op. cit., pp. 101–2.
[21] *Diaries*, ii, pp. 450, 744, 759, 773; iii, p. 899.
[22] Bodenheimer, op. cit., p. 199; *Idem*, 'Theodor Herzl', p. 76.

doctrines within its ranks. The Ambassador insisted that the movement, which originally had entertained 'purely national and religious
aspirations, might in due course assume a dangerous political
character'.[23] Obsessed by the fear of Socialism, the Russian Government apparently confused the Zionist movement with the Russian
Jewish Labour party, the Bund,[24] which was founded in the same
year.

The German Prefect of Police dismissed Russian suspicions as unfounded. 'The principle of the creation of a national and autonomous
state in Palestine stands in sharpest contrast to the international
aspirations of Social Democracy.' Moreover, he added, the Kaiser's
reception of the Zionist delegation in Palestine and the latter's
assurances of loyalty served as additional proof that Zionism was far
removed from the Social Democratic movement. Herr Roete, the
Minister of the Interior, was also of the opinion that, save for individual Zionist labourers and craftsmen domiciled in Russia and
Galicia, the movement as a whole stood aloof from Socialism. He was
informed that the suggestion made at the Second Zionist Congress
to establish a Socialist-Zionist party was met with disfavour.[25]

Berlin's assurances, however, failed to convince the Russian
Government. In January 1900 Professor Max Mandelstamm, a Rus-
sian Zionist leader, informed Herzl that the Russian Chief of Police
had threatened 'to close the Zionist shop'.[26] As Elmershaus von
Haxthausen, the German Consul-General in Warsaw, explained, the
Jewish people constituted 'a very insecure element' for the Russian
Government, since they supplied the Socialist party with a propor-
tionately greater number of adherents than any other section of the

---

[23] *E.G.*, Nr. 84, K 181277–80 and K 181300–1, Osten-Sacken to Bülow, 25 Apr. 1899.
The dispatch is in French. Copies were forwarded to Eulenburg and the Kaiser. Neither
made any special comment.

[24] Allgemeiner jüdischer Arbeiterbund in Russland und Polen (on which see Dub-
now, *Die neueste Geschichte*, iii, p. 383; Michael T. Florinsky, *Russia. A History and an
Interpretation* (London, 1960), ii, p. 1202; Louis Greenberg, *The Jews in Russia: The
Struggle for Emancipation, 1881–1917* (Yale University Press, 1951), ii, pp. 147–9, 152–7;
Bernard J. Johnpoll, *The Politics of Futility: The General Jewish Workers Bund of Poland,
1917–43* (Oxford University Press, 1961). On the Bund's antagonism to Herzl see
Diaries, iv, p. 154.

[25] *E.G.*, Nr. 84, K 181281–2, A.A. to Ministry of the Interior; K 181285, note by
Roete (Minister of the Interior); K 181286–8, Windheim to Roete, 23 June 1899;
K 181284–5, Roete to A.A., 12 July 1899; K 181289–90, A.A. to Osten-Sacken, 22
July 1899.

[26] *Diaries*, iii, p. 901. Mandelstamm was one of the Russian Zionist leaders and
a staunch follower of Herzl.

community. This was one of the reasons impelling the Russian police to prohibit Zionist activities.[27]

In these circumstances St. Petersburg was even less likely to credit any denials of alleged German protection of Jewish settlement in Palestine. In 1899 the Russians were particularly mistrustful of German policy in the Orient. Neither Count Muraviev, the Russian Foreign Minister, nor Osten-Sacken believed the protestations of their opposite numbers that Germany's interests in Turkey were exclusively commercial. The ambitions of the two Powers collided. As Sir Cecil Spring-Rice, the British Ambassador in Constantinople, observed, 'Russia like a vulture was watching dying Turkey, intending to eat it when it was dead and rotten. . . . But Germany has come in with an antiseptic process and . . . Turkey is no longer an edible object.'[28] Russia never abandoned her efforts to gain control of Constantinople, but another interest of vital importance was the Holy Places in Palestine. The influential Imperial Russian Palestine Society took great pains to extend its influence in the Orthodox Church. It also organized pilgrimages on a large scale, maintained schools for missionaries, erected churches, and acquired land and property in Palestine. Here, too, suspicions were deep. On 7 March 1900 Friedrich Rosen, the German Consul-General in Jerusalem, reported:

From occasional remarks of my Russian and French colleagues I gathered that the non-German foreigners in Palestine believe that Germany is planning an all-embracing colonization covering not only Palestine but also, if possible, those regions which will be opened up by the Baghdad Railway. . . . This idea is being used by the French and Russians in particular in their dealings with local Turkish authorities, and is also brought in tendentiously in connection with the bogy of the Zionist Jewish State, and the view is aired that the Kaiser is willing to accept the protectorate of the Jews in Palestine.[29]

Thus it seems that neither the official communiqué, following Wilhelm's reception of the Zionist deputation in Jerusalem, nor Bülow's soothing statements in the Reichstag, dispelled French and Russian apprehensions. France remained touchy over Syria, and Russia was

---

[27] *E.G.*, Nr. 84, K 181322, Haxthausen to A.A., 24 Feb. 1902.
[28] *The Letters and Friendships of Sir Cecil Spring-Rice* (London, 1929), v, p. 259.
[29] *Türkei* 195, K 175961, Rosen to Hohenlohe-Schillingsfuerst, 7 Mar. 1900, dis. no. 30/517.

the untiring opponent of the Baghdad Railway scheme. However, unable to prevent its construction, the Russians restricted themselves to general protests and intrigues, about which Marschall complained bitterly, as he did about the French for spreading malicious rumours. Afraid that his rivals might obstruct the ratification of the Baghdad Railway concession, he assured the Sultan that the Reich Government definitely dissociated itself from any statements made by the Deutsches kolonial-wirtschaftliches Komitee about German colonization in Turkey (which the French and Russians quoted). The Auswärtiges Amt lost no time in advising the DkwK that their propaganda was undesirable, and the Consul in Smyrna was instructed not to afford to any of its members the protection normally granted to German nationals.[30]

Against this background it is clear why Jewish colonization under German protection had to be written off. It was imprudent and risky for the Government to allow its rivals to use the Zionist stick to beat Germany with at the Porte.

Herzl was trying to make the best of the circumstances. If Germany was unable to undertake the protectorate, he reasoned, perhaps a combination of Powers would resolve the difficulty; a German-British joint protectorate seemed to him the most desirable. Under this scheme the Zionist Land Company and its financial institutions would have their seat in England, whilst political activities would be centred in Germany and Austria-Hungary. Herzl presented this new proposal to the Grand Duke, Count Eulenburg, and the Kaiser.[31]

There was an element of soundness in this calculation. Since the winter of 1897 Anglo-German relations had undergone a marked change for the better. The British Press viewed Wilhelm's Near Eastern tour with favour. Following his visit to Germany in the spring of 1899, Cecil Rhodes declared that 'Asiatic Turkey ought to be turned over to Germany, since England could not rule the whole world and needed a buffer area between herself and Russia', an opinion which Joseph Chamberlain, the Colonial Secretary,

---

[30] *Türkei* 189, Marschall to A.A., 5 Dec. 1899, tel. no. 358; Bülow to Marschall (undated), tel. no. 161; Bülow to Valois (Chairman of the Komitee), 22 July 1900; A.A. to Consul in Smyrna, 31 Mar. 1900.

[31] *Diaries*, ii, pp. 774–8, 792–5; *Türkei* 195, K 175936–42, Herzl to the Kaiser, 3 Mar. 1899.

apparently shared. In November 1899, during Wilhelm's private visit to England, Chamberlain made known his desire for an Anglo-German entente, in the Near East in particular. German proposals for the internationalization of the Baghdad Railway were on the whole received favourably in Britain.[32]

This was how the picture appeared on the surface but in fact both in Britain and in Germany there was a strong undercurrent against Chamberlain's suggestion. It was pointed out that an alliance with Germany would be too costly and would undermine Britain's freedom of action. Nor was there any popular enthusiasm on the German side. Germany at that time was not seriously menaced by the Franco-Russian Alliance and her position as a mediator was very strong. 'We must remain independent,' Bülow declared, 'we must be the tongue [*sic*] of the balance, not the restlessly swinging pendulum'. But it was primarily the bitter hostility aroused by the Boer War, the ill effect of the mutual recriminations in the Press, the rejection of Chamberlain's proposal, and lastly the introduction of the Navy Bills in the Reichstag that made an Anglo-German *rapprochement* impossible. Consequently, British public opinion came to look upon the Baghdad Railway and German expansion in the East as a threat to British interests in Egypt and the Persian Gulf.[33]

An Anglo-German alliance proving illusory, the idea of a co-protectorate became a mirage. Count Eulenburg, when sounded out by Herzl, took the opportunity to express his satisfaction with the attitude of the *Neue Freie Presse*, and to leak information on German-Austrian relations, but remained silent about an Anglo-German co-protectorate.[34] He regretted not having accompanied the Kaiser

---

[32] Langer, op. cit. ii, pp. 492–8; Earle, op. cit., p. 67, 148, 178; Gooch, op. cit. i, p. 28; *Diaries*, iii, p. 1169; M. K. Chapman, 'Great Britain and the Bagdad Railway, 1888–1914', *Smith College, Studies in History*, xxxi (1948), 36–7.

[33] Earle, op. cit., thinks that the Balfour Government's failure to effect the internationalization of the Baghdad Railway was 'a colossal diplomatic blunder'. He quotes Sir Harry Johnson, a former British consular official, who thought it reasonable to acknowledge the *Drang nach Osten* as 'legitimate'. Johnson believed that, with the dismemberment of the Ottoman Empire, Germany would become the predominant Power in Asia Minor, Syria would fall under French protection, while 'Judea might be offered to the Jews under international guarantee'. Sinai and Egypt would pass under British protection and Arabia would be recognized as a federation of independent Arab states. The remainder of Asiatic Turkey, minus Armenia, might be handed over to Russia. This would provide a splendid outlet for the energies of all parties, keeping them busy and happy for at least a century ahead (ibid., pp. 180, 188, 205–7).

[34] *Diaries*, ii, pp. 777–8.

on his Near Eastern tour. 'I was sorry for Herzl and for the Zionists and am still sorry today', he noted in his diary. 'How strong the cards were which we held in our hands! . . . I fear that the unfortunate turning-point caused "out of deference for politics" will paralyse the Zionists' noble and worthy aspirations for an immeasurable time to come.'[35] He confirmed the Grand Duke's information that the Orthodox Jews of Jerusalem had made an unfavourable impression on the Kaiser. Whether this was only an excuse, as Herzl presumed, for the German leaders to back out of the protectorate, is a matter for conjecture,[36] but their volte-face seems to have been almost complete. Bülow told Arthur von Huhn, the Berlin correspondent of the *Kölnische Zeitung*, that the Kaiser had cooled off towards Zionism as quickly as he had become enthusiastic about it. The question mark that he inserted in the margin of Herzl's letter of 15 December 1898 to the Duke (which the latter had forwarded to him) speaks louder than words. He declined to receive Herzl and advised him to see Bülow. Herzl was completely discouraged but on the Duke's advice he wrote to the Kaiser saying that should the Emperor refuse to receive him he would take it as a sign that German support could not be expected. This was what happened. The Kaiser regretted not being able to see Herzl and left it to his discretion whether or not to see Bülow.[37]

Herzl was aware of Bülow's hostility, but to avoid the impression that he ignored the Emperor's advice, he swallowed his pride and submitted a memorandum to Bülow.[38] Its effect on the Foreign Minister was nil. Two months earlier Count Eulenburg had also

[35] *Nachlass Eulenburg*, Nr. 52, *Die Zionisten*, pp. 298, a, b.

[36] *Diaries*, ii, pp. 774, 777–9, 793. Before his trip to the East the Kaiser informed the Chief Rabbis of Jerusalem that he would be delighted to accept their welcoming address. Indeed, at the entrance to the city, he lingered at the Jews' arch longer than at the Turkish one and expressed joy at being privileged to follow in his late father's footsteps—Friedrich III, a philo-Semite, who had visited Jerusalem thirty years earlier. (Cohn-Reiss, op. cit. i, pp. 246–7, 9; *Diaries*, ii, p. 745.)

[37] *Diaries*, ii, pp. 789, 791–2, 811; *Türkei* 195, K 175934, Herzl to Lucanus (Chief of the Imperial Privy Council), 27 Feb. 1899; K 175932, Lucanus to Bülow, 28 Feb. 1899; K 175936–42, Herzl to the Kaiser, memorandum, 3 Mar. 1899 (draft in *Diaries*, ii, pp. 792–5); Ellern, *Herzl, Hechler, the Grand Duke of Baden and the German Emperor*, p. 66, Lucanus to Babo (Head of the Privy Council of the Grand Duchy of Baden). On 11 Mar. 1899 Ernst Rohmer, a missionary to the Holy Land, appealed to Wilhelm II to follow the example of the Persian King Cyrus and proclaim an Edict of Deliverance to the people of Israel, which would earn him 'the eternal gratitude of the whole Christian world'. (*E.G.*, Nr. 84, K 181271–3.)

[38] *Türkei* 195, K 175944–52, Herzl to Bülow, 18 Mar. 1899 (draft in *Diaries*, ii, pp. 797–801).

sounded out Bülow, but without any positive result. 'Since the
"ocular inspection" in Jerusalem . . . and the unfavourable results
. . . I have seen little of Herzl and avoided talking with him on
Zionist plans.' Nevertheless, Eulenburg wanted to inform the
Minister that the Zionist leaders were still working indefatigably
and were soon to decide whether to establish their centre in London
or Berlin; it was natural that they would depend on the state whose
capital they chose. 'The decision is in our hands.'[39]

But the decision rested solely in Bülow's hands, and from his
attitude neither Eulenburg nor Herzl could draw any comfort. At
the end of March 1899 the Foreign Minister was reported to have
told von Huhn that although Herzl had made a very good impression
on him, he did not believe in his project. The Zionists 'have no
money, the rich Jews won't have any part in it, and there is nothing
to be done with the Polish "*Lausejuden*"'. During his tour in the
East he had detected yet another 'serious weakness in the Zionist
dream . . . I don't think I have ever seen such a barren country as
Palestine', Bülow told his biographer. In his opinion the Eastern
Jews were more likely to improve their lot by emigration to the
Argentine than by a 'return to the shores of the Dead Sea'.[40]

Not only Stein but also the Chief of Police told Bülow that
the influence of the Zionist movement in Germany was limited,
since leading Jewish personalities in Germany, the Rabbis, and
the German-Jewish Press strongly opposed it. Moreover, nothing
occurred at the Third Zionist Congress that might have impelled
the Foreign Minister to change his mind. His son Alfred, who was
Minister in Berne, was impressed with the steady growth of the
Zionist movement and the quality of its leaders, but the realization
of their aspirations, he thought, was still a matter of the distant
future. The funds at their disposal (£250,000) were inadequate for
colonization and were negligible as a guarantee for the solvency of
Ottoman finances. The Zionists had replaced the term 'The Jewish
State' by the innocuous phrase 'a charter under the Sovereignty of
H.M. the Sultan', but in Alfred von Bülow's opinion it was unlikely
that the Porte would agree to 'the hoisting of the Jewish banner in

[39] *Nachlass Eulenburg*, no. 53, pp. 14–15, Eulenburg to Bülow, 13 Jan. 1899. Bülow
seemed to be deliberately withholding information from Eulenburg in order to weaken
his position with the Emperor (ibid., no. 54, pp. 242–5, Bülow to Eulenburg, 6 Dec.
1899; cf. Bülow, op. cit. i, 411–12). Following Bülow's appointment as Chancellor,
Eulenburg's influence came practically to an end.
[40] *Diaries*, ii, p. 811; Münz, op. cit., pp. 102–3.

Palestine, or to a concession for the charter'. The Turks feared that in the wake of increased Jewish immigration there was a danger of the establishment of the 'old Kingdom of Judaea'.[41] In Jerusalem Friedrich Rosen (apparently unaware that the Zionists had, in the meantime, modified their terminology) warned that the much-publicized Herzl–Nordau plan for the settlement of 'seven million Jews in Palestine with a view to establishing a Jewish state under the Sultan's suzerainty', was bound to arouse Turkish suspicions and result in the tightening-up of the prohibition on further immigration.[42]

The South African crisis at the turn of the century provided Herzl with an opening for making yet another overture. With attention diverted from the Orient, he thought the moment opportune for Germany to undertake the protectorate. 'The *fait accompli* may be managed without arousing much opposition', he wrote to the Grand Duke. In the Porte he had succeeded in gaining supporters for his cause and, in view of his forthcoming audience with the Sultan, the Kaiser's personal support would be most useful. A German protectorate could then be created 'without any risk'.

The Duke was willing to help and Count Eulenburg invited Herzl to meet him, but the attitude in Berlin remained negative. The Duke told Herzl frankly that it was precisely because of the British set-backs in the South African War that German security, if not the peace of the world, was in jeopardy. Should Britain be unable to overcome the Boers, she might take revenge upon Germany. Berlin had therefore to avoid any commitment that might give Britain an excuse for retaliation.

Herzl gained the impression that his letter of 5 March had been examined by the German diplomats and that the Duke was expressing official German policy. The kindness was the Duke's, but the thinking was that of the Wilhelmstrasse. The Duke admired Herzl's perseverance and suggested that since Germany was in no position to recommend the Zionists in Constantinople, Austria might well be able to do so. Eulenburg also explained why it was impossible for Germany to sponsor Herzl's cause, but encouraged him and

[41] *E.G.*, Nr. 84, K 181286–8, Windheim to Roete, 23 June 1899; K 181306–14, Alfred von Bülow to A.A., 28 Aug. 1899 (copy in *Türkei* 195 K 175954–9).

[42] *Türkei* 195, K 175962–3, Rosen to Hohenlohe-Schillingsfuerst, 16 May 1900, dis. no. 59/763.

thought that the support of the British Parliament, where Herzl had managed to enlist forty sympathizers, was 'very important'.[43]

When Herzl left to seek support in other countries, Bodenheimer took over. Of German nationality, he was an esteemed Justizrat in Cologne and a staunch patriot. He had personal connections with the Foreign Ministry, and on 23 February 1902, in a long memorandum, he endeavoured to show that German and Zionist interests coincided. First, Zionism would divert the migration of East European Jews away from Germany to Palestine and thereby relieve the Reich Government of an embarrassing problem, for on humanitarian grounds it was unable to shut its borders. Second, because of the linguistic affinity of Yiddish (a language which originated from the High German of the Middle Ages), those East European Jews who settled in Palestine would be more responsive to German influence, both cultural and commercial, than to any other. The official language of the Zionist Congress was German and Zionist aspirations were 'compatible with the progress of German *Kultur* in the Orient'.

Bodenheimer's arguments fell on sterile ground. Von Richthofen, the Under-Secretary of State, was sceptical of the colonizing abilities of the Jews and of their leaning towards German *Kultur*. 'We shall not expose ourselves to political complications for the sake of the Russian Jewish colonies.' He showed greater interest in Bodenheimer's subsequent letter informing him that Herzl had been most graciously received by the Sultan. Marschall confirmed this; he was unaware of the substance of the negotiations, but from the comments made by Ibrahim Bey, the Ottoman Chief Master of Ceremonies, he inferred that there was little likelihood of the Porte agreeing to the implementation of the Zionist plan. When asked about Dr. Herzl's requests, Ibrahim Bey gave the laconic reply: 'des choses impossibles'.[44]

[43] *Diaries*, iii, pp. 909–11, Herzl to the Grand Duke, 5 Mar. 1900; pp. 915–17, 928–34, 1020–2. The meeting with the Grand Duke took place on 18 April 1900, and with Eulenburg on 3 January 1901. No correspondence on this matter between the Grand Duke and the Auswärtiges Amt has been found in the A.A. files. Dr. Alex Bein, Director of the Central Zionist Archives, searched in the Grossherzogliches Familienarchiv, Karlsruhe, but no material additional to that already discovered by Mr. and Mrs. Ellern was found. (Letter to the author, 12 Oct. 1962.)

[44] *Türkei* 195, K 176030–48, Bodenheimer to Richthofen, 23 Feb. 1902, which bears the latter's marginal annotations; K 176051–3, Richthofen to Marschall, 4 Mar. 1902, dis. no. 161; K 176054–5, Marschall to Prince Bülow, Chancellor, 19 Mar. 1902, dis. no. 42.

6

Negotiations with the Porte

TURKEY was Herzl's main stumbling-block; to win her over was one of his main objectives.[1] As early as 1895 (the year of his Zionist awakening), when the Eastern question had gained renewed prominence in diplomatic circles, he hoped that a favourable opportunity might arise for the Jews to claim Palestine as a 'neutral land'. But when prospects of Turkey's dismemberment faded, he veered in the opposite direction: 'We shall bestow enormous benefits upon Turkey.' If Palestine were ceded as 'an independent country', the Jews would undertake to straighten out Turkish finances. If Jewish capital could be raised for the most exotic undertakings, would none be found for 'the most immediate, the direst need of the Jews themselves?', he wrote to Baron Hirsch in 1895.

Briefed by Moritz Reichenfeld, Director of the Union Bank of Vienna, he calculated that a sum of eighteen million Turkish pounds would suffice to relieve the Porte of foreign debt; this he hoped to supplement with an additional two million. These calculations were, however, based on a misconception. The Turks were disinclined to grant even minor concessions, while the rich Jews were in no mood to raise the money. Dionys Rosenfeld, editor of the *Osmanische Post* in Constantinople, told Herzl on 3 May 1896 that, despite her financial straits and diplomatic weakness, Turkey would not relinquish sovereignty over any of her provinces, an opinion that Philip de Newlinski confirmed: the Sultan would never part with Jerusalem.

[1] Herzl's negotiations with the Porte can be followed in his *Diaries*, where his correspondence with leading Turkish politicians and officials, as well as with Abdul Hamid, is reproduced: i, pp. 80, 366–7, 374–94, 403, 412, 419–22, 427; ii, pp. 435, 439–46, 457, 467–71, 479–85, 496, 581, 588, 609–11, 813, 827; iii, pp. 847–8, 866–7, 899–900, 961–3, 967–73, 979, 997, 1006, 1016–18, 1079, 1086, 1092–3, 1112–17, 1121–36, 1144, 1150–66, 1187–93, 1216–30; iv, pp. 1274–1310, 1314–23.

Herzl's first encounter with Turkish diplomats was not encouraging. Ziya Pasha, the Ottoman Ambassador in Paris, to whom he was introduced by Newlinski, observed that, however useful the financial offer and the support of the Press might be, it was against Turkish principles to sell any territory. 'Under no circumstances will you get Palestine as an independent country; maybe as a vassal state.' Karatheodory Pasha, a member of the Council of State, and Tewfik Pasha, who were present, nodded approvingly. In Constantinople, Izzet Bey, Second Secretary to the Sultan, adopted a negative attitude; Khair Eddin Bey, Secretary-General to the Grand Vizier, was distrustful, and Nuri Bey, the Chief Secretary of the Foreign Ministry, let Herzl know that the suggestion was impracticable. But the news conveyed by Newlinski was the greatest blow: the Sultan had declared that he could not sell even a foot of land; it did not belong to him but to his people. 'Let the Jews save their billions. When my Empire is partitioned they may get Palestine for nothing. But only [when] our corpse will be divided. I will not agree to [voluntary] vivisection.'

To Newlinski's astonishment, Herzl did not betray any sign of despair. His instinct told him that not every statement should be taken at face value. Indeed, Izzet soon after advised him that should the Jews acquire any other territory in the Ottoman Empire, they might perhaps be able to exchange it for Palestine at a later date. Nuri Bey also suddenly appeared to favour Herzl's plan. He received him cordially and suggested that the Jews should buy up Turkish bonds and appoint directors to the Public Debt Commission. Daoud Effendi, Nuri's assistant, who was a Jew, dropped a broad hint that, when Turkey was completely bankrupt, Herzl might reach his goal provided he knew how to sugar-coat the pill. Herzl's sympathetic presentation of Turkey's problems in the formerly hostile *Neue Freie Presse* earned him the Sultan's goodwill. Although Palestine remained out of the question, Herzl inferred from Newlinski that the Ottoman Sovereign might accept some kind of arrangement. The only opponent was the Grand Vizier. He received Herzl in his capacity as a journalist and discussed current affairs, but Palestine was not mentioned. Herzl still hoped that once the benefits became more tangible opposition at the Yildiz Kiosk would melt away. Moreover, to dispel any lingering suspicions he modified his terminology. 'Independent Jewish State' and 'republic' were replaced by 'autonomous vassal state . . . under the suzerainty of the

Sultan'; Jewish immigrants were to embrace Ottoman nationality and settle in Palestine at the express invitation of the Sultan; they were to pay a tribute of one hundred thousand pounds, a sum which would rise to one million annually, *pari passu* with the increase in immigration. In return they would be granted autonomy and be allowed to maintain an army.

On his return from Constantinople (July 1896) Herzl's first priority was to raise the necessary funds. In London the idea of a Jewish state had an electrifying effect on the poor Jews of the East End, but the rich Jews remained aloof. A notable exception was Sir Samuel Montagu, M.P. (later the first Lord Swaythling), a prominent banker and a Hovevé Zion leader. Even so Montagu made his support conditional on that of Baron de Hirsch and Baron Edmond de Rothschild of Paris, but, as neither was moved by Herzl's appeal, Sir Samuel's sympathy had little practical value. Rothschild had no faith in Turkish promises and doubted the feasibility of the project. Warm as his patronage of the Jewish colonies in Palestine was, he was not prepared to accept the risk of having to maintain hundreds of thousands of immigrants. Moreover, his experience convinced him that a politically motivated project would not be favoured in Constantinople. Rothschild's rejection was a bitter blow to Herzl, but despair was a luxury he could not afford. A year earlier he had written to Zadoc Kahn: 'I believe that we are at a great turning point of our history.' If the big capitalists refused, perhaps the little Jews would band together and raise the money. A national movement had to be shouldered by the people themselves, not by single individuals. It was this reasoning, among others, that prompted him to convene a world Zionist Congress.

The Turks were apparently unaware of Herzl's financial set-back. Themselves in a state of near bankruptcy, they adopted a friendly tone. In August 1896 Izzet Bey advised Newlinski that if the Jews were in earnest, the Porte would be willing to propose a 'modified plan', and on 14 October Mahmud Nedim Pasha, the Ottoman Ambassador in Vienna, bestowed the Mejidiye order upon Herzl, on the Sultan's behalf. Nedim made no attempt to conceal the grave financial conditions of his country and seems to have agreed with Herzl that for Turkey the only way of salvation was 'an agreement with the Jews regarding Palestine'. He made it clear, however, that only those who adopted Ottoman nationality would be permitted to enter. In Constantinople Ahmed Midhat Effendi, a leading Turkish writer, advised moderation; the term 'autonomy' should not be used; it conjured up disagreeable associations. Herzl learned also that his plan was under review in Yildiz Kiosk.

It was in deference to Turkish susceptibilities that references to the idea of Jewish statehood were dropped. In the June 1897 issue of *Die Welt*, the Zionist organ, Herzl introduced for the first time the term *Heimstätte*, which means homestead, and prevailed upon the First Zionist Congress to incorporate it in its official programme: 'Der Zionismus erstrebt für das jüdische Volk die Schaffung einer öffentlich-rechtlich gesicherten Heimstätte in Palästina.' He insisted on the wording 'öffentlich-rechtlich' (under public law) as against one of the alternative suggestions 'völker-rechtlich' (under international law) which implied intervention by the foreign Powers in the internal affairs of a sovereign state. He dismissed the term 'rechtlich' (under private law) since in the given context it was too weak. By contrast, 'öffentlich-rechtlich gesicherte Heimstätte' (secured by public law) was flexible enough to be interpreted in Constantinople as meaning by public Ottoman law, whereas, in London, Paris, and Berlin it could be read as international law, enabling the European Powers to guarantee the Jewish home.[2] Like the Delphic utterances, it could be interpreted either way, but to Herzl it could have had only one meaning:

At Basel I founded the Jewish State. If I said this out loud today, I would be answered by universal laughter. Perhaps in five years, and certainly in fifty, everyone will know it. The foundation of a State lies in the will of the people. . . . Territory is only the material basis; the State, even when it possesses territory, is always something abstract . . . At Basel I created this abstraction . . . I gradually worked the people into the mood for a State and made them feel that they were its National Assembly.

The Turks, however, were not deceived, and on 4 February 1898 Tewfik told Herzl that he welcomed Jewish immigrants to Turkey but would not grant them any specific territory or autonomy. To Herzl such a solution, tantamount to a 'settlement of new Armenians in Turkey', was totally unacceptable. Nor did Wilhelm II prove to be Herzl's saviour; as it turned out, the Kaiser's *démarche* with

---

[2] Nathan Feinberg, 'The Basle Programme—its Legal Meaning' (Hebrew), *Shivat Zion. Year-Book of Research in Zionism and the State of Israel* (Jerusalem, 1950), i, 131–7.

Abdul Hamid did more harm than good. Strangely, it never occurred to Herzl that the intervention of a foreign Power would prejudice his case with the Ottoman ruler. Newlinski's sudden death was an additional misfortune. Rejected by the German Government and aware of the poor state of Zionist finances, Herzl almost reached breaking-point. The big question mark inserted on 17 April 1899 in his diary reflected his state of mind.

An accidental meeting with Nuri Bey in June 1899, at the Peace Conference in The Hague, seemed to give Herzl a renewed opportunity. Nuri went straight to the point. An indirect strategy might prove more advantageous. He advised Herzl to get Aleppo first, buy land around Beirut, and, when difficult times came for the Turks, ask for Palestine. Such devious tactics were not to Herzl's liking, but, when Nuri suggested buying public opinion in the Ottoman capital, he sensed what Nuri was after. Yet if only to procure an audience with the Sultan, the sum of 40,000 francs as *baksheesh* (of which 10,000 francs were to be paid in advance) was still worth while.

The extensive correspondence between Herzl, Nuri, and Eduard Crespi, Nuri's secret agent, was a sort of cat-and-mouse game, with the Turks trying to ascertain the extent of Herzl's finances, attempting from time to time to extract lavish personal gratuities, and Herzl pretending to command considerable resources. Oscar Straus confirmed Herzl's assumption that all power was concentrated in the Sultan's hand; the Ministers were cowardly and corrupt; conversations or negotiations with them were worthless. Nor did Straus consider the task of winning over the Sultan to be insuperable. 'If he could see money or benefits of another kind, he might perhaps be won over.'[3]

However, it was not Nuri Bey, but Arminius Vámbéry, a Hungarian-Jewish orientalist and traveller, who procured an audience with the Sultan for Herzl. Vámbéry was fluent in twelve languages and changed his religion as lightly as his coat. As a young man in Constantinople he had embraced Islam and later, when appointed Professor of Oriental Languages at the University of Budapest, had adopted Protestantism. A personal friend of Abdul

---

[3] For Straus's opinion of Herzl see *Under Four Administrations*, pp. 156–8. Herzl and Nuri had met in Constantinople three years earlier. Correspondence between them, as well as with Crespi, is reproduced extensively in the third volume of *Diaries*. At the Central Zionist Archives there are also a considerable number of unpublished letters.

Hamid II and of King Edward VII, and an authority on Central Asia, he had carried out several diplomatic missions for both the British and Turkish governments. When Herzl met him on 16 June 1900 he was seventy years old, not clear about his own identity, whether a Turk or an Englishman, but his study of religions had made him an atheist. Herzl's personality attracted him strongly, and, as events showed, his help to the Zionists was genuine. Beneath his cosmopolitan veneer lurked Jewish sentiments, and Herzl played on them well. 'You and I belong to a race who can do everything but fail', and on 23 December 1900 Herzl urged him on: 'Your true mission is to help your people.'

Vámbéry kept his word. On 8 May 1901, on his return from Constantinople, he brought good news: the Sultan would receive Herzl as a Jewish leader and an influential journalist, though not as a Zionist. 'You must not talk to him about Zionism. That is a phantasmagoria. Jerusalem is as holy to these people as Mecca is.'

However weighty the religious motives, what made the Turks so obdurate was the fear of intervention by the Powers. Should the Jews be allowed to immigrate freely, the Powers would seize an early excuse to occupy Palestine by military force. Ahmed Tewfik made little effort to conceal from David Wolffsohn how annoyed his Government was with Herzl's *The Jewish State* and reiterated the standard Turkish position. Earlier, on 21 November 1900, new regulations were introduced permitting foreign visitors to stay in the country no longer than three months. Immigration was illegal and transgressors were liable to be deported. The consuls were requested to assist the Ottoman police, should individuals refuse to comply.[4]

That the Sultan none the less did receive Herzl warmly is not surprising since with Zionism deliberately excluded there was nothing to sour the occasion. The meeting took place on 17 May 1901. Before the audience Herzl was presented with the Grand Cordon of the Order of Mejidiye, the highest Turkish decoration, and after they had met, the Sultan gave him a diamond tie-pin as a token of personal friendship. For Herzl the gifts had only a symbolic value. His impression of Abdul Hamid was of 'a weak, cowardly, but thoroughly good-natured man', neither crafty nor cruel, but

---

[4] *F.R.U.S.* (1901), p. 517, Merril (Jerusalem) to Griscom (Constantinople), 14 Jan. 1901; *B.C.* ii, p. 559, Dickson (Jerusalem) to de Bunsen (Constantinople), 29 Dec. 1901, and encl. to O'Connor, pp. 561–2, where the text of the Ottoman regulations is reproduced in full; *Wiener politische Korrespondenz* (27 Dec. 1900), cutting in *Türkei* 195, K 176015.

'a profoundly unhappy prisoner in whose name a rapacious, infamous, seedy camarilla perpetuates the vilest abominations'. In contrast, Herzl impressed his host as 'a leader' and 'a prophet'. The audience lasted for two hours. Herzl thanked Abdul Hamid for his benevolence towards the Jews, which the latter accepted as confirmation of an established fact: his Empire was wide open to Jewish refugees and, among the non-Muslims, they were the most reliable subjects. This gave Herzl an opening to proffer certain services, quoting the story of Androcles and the lion. 'His Majesty is the lion, perhaps I am Androcles, and maybe there is a thorn that has to be pulled out.' The thorn, Herzl disclosed, was the Public Debt; if eliminated, Turkey would be given a new lease of life. Herzl put his finger on the sorest spot of Turkey's body politic and, noting how amused his host was by the parable, asked for permission to make the Sultan's pro-Jewish sentiments public from whatever platform and on whatever occasion he deemed fit. Abdul Hamid, unaware that Herzl had in mind the Zionist Congress, agreed, and said that what Turkey needed most was the industrial skill of the Jewish people. He asked Herzl to recommend a financial adviser and promised 'permanent protection' to those Jews who sought refuge in his lands.[5]

In contrast to Abdul Hamid, for whom he had some sympathy, Herzl found the Sultan's entourage a 'troupe de malfaiteurs'. Both Nuri and Crespi demanded their pound of flesh for what Vámbéry had accomplished. To pacify them Herzl paid the agreed sum of 40,000 francs. But the most trying encounter was with Izzet Bey, who quoted the figure of thirty million pounds as the sum necessary for the consolidation of the Public Debt. Herzl, suspecting a fraud or a deliberate attempt to discourage him, wrote to the Sultan, and Izzet soon after lowered his demand to four million pounds. He insisted, however, that the immigrants would have to adopt Ottoman nationality, to which Herzl replied that he would be only too delighted should they come under the 'glorious sceptre of Abdul Hamid'. Nor was Herzl thrown off balance when Izzet further stipulated that there must not be a mass Jewish immigration, and that the colonists should not be concentrated geographically; 'five

[5] Herzl's impression of Abdul Hamid is confirmed by Professor William Langer and Professor Bernard Lewis. They rejected as 'historical legend' the reputation pinned on him of 'bloody assassin' and 'uncompromising reactionary' (Langer, *The Diplomacy of Imperialism*, i, p. 159; Lewis, *The Emergence of Modern Turkey*, p. 174).

families here and five there—scattered, without connection'. Herzl's contention that was it pointless to encourage haphazard immigration, that scattered settlements would lack the necessary economic foundation, and that their capacity to pay the annual tribute to the Sultan would be affected, left Izzet silent.

Vámbéry, whom Herzl met on his return journey, thought that his achievement in Constantinople was 'tremendous' and hoped that the concession for the charter company would be granted within a year. The Press, too, presented the audience in rosy colours. The *Kölnische Zeitung* (29 October 1901) saw in it a proof that the Turkish Government was not at all averse to Jewish national aspirations. Elated, Herzl hoped to be more successful with Jewish financiers, but was again disappointed. Benno Reitlinger, a relative who was a banker, despaired of influencing rich Jews; nor did renewed negotiations with the Jewish Colonization Association (I.C.A.) and with Baron Edmond de Rothschild prove any more fruitful. London showed itself friendlier than Paris. Socially, Herzl scored an unquestionable success; his address to the Maccabean Club was well received; the Press gave him favourable coverage; but Jews in high finance were indifferent. The Rothschilds remained unconvinced. Herzl complained to a friend that had it not been for this 'miserable money' he would have been 'almost through with . . . the Sultan'.

But of course we cannot make a display of our rage and pain, because then the Sultan would become aware of our weakness, and I must do my best to hold him off, to gain time, trying meanwhile to squeeze water out of stones and scrape gold from the mud. Yes, it would be the easiest thing for me now to drop the whole business and to issue a proclamation: 'Thus it is, Jewish people; in five years, I, a poor, helpless journalist, have reached the point where I could conduct these negotiations with the Sultan himself. But you've left me in the lurch. . . .' This *beau geste*, which should be so easy and comfortable, is forbidden me. I must continue to drag the burden.[6]

Determined not to declare a state of bankruptcy, Herzl kept reassuring the Sultan; the flow of Jewish capital for economic development of Asia Minor, Palestine, and Syria would eventually remove the 'lion's thorn'. But the sands were running out. Whatever confidence the Turks might have placed in his promises, with financial

[6] Herzl to Mandelstamm, 18 Aug. 1901, quoted in Bein, *Herzl*, pp. 369–70.

difficulties becoming acute, they would not rely on him exclusively. A loan from Maurice Rouvier, a French financier, being negotiated at the same time, was more attractive, and Herzl rightly feared that in a battle against such a powerful competitor, he was armed only with 'a wooden sword'.[7]

Herzl consistently underestimated the French and their resourcefulness. Their influence at the Golden Horn was still strong, and Jean-Ernest Constans, the newly appointed Ambassador in Constantinople, described by Herzl as 'the craftiest and most brutal of French politicians', was an able enough diplomat to realize that reconciliation with Germany, rather than rivalry, was more likely to restore French influence in the Orient.[8] Thus Franco-German *rapprochement* isolated Herzl still further and narrowed his field of manœuvre.

On the eve of the Fifth Zionist Congress he managed to elicit from the Sultan a telegram of good wishes, but though it reassured the delegates, it displeased Ahmed Tewfik. On 5 February 1902 Herzl was summoned to Yildiz Kiosk and during the meeting (15 February) Ibrahim Bey pointedly complained of his indiscretion. Herzl replied that the Sultan had permitted him to make a statement whenever the occasion warranted; but when Izzet reminded him about the 'moral and material aid' which he had promised, whereas all he did was to make declarations, he pointed out that this was necessary in order to create a favourable climate of opinion. Izzet repeated the stereotyped formula that the immigrants would have to become Ottoman subjects, fulfil all civic duties, including military service; they would be permitted to establish themselves in any part of the Ottoman Empire except Palestine. In return, the Jews would set up a syndicate for the consolidation of the Public Debt and undertake a concession for the exploitation of the natural resources in the Empire.

The exclusion of Palestine was more than a cold douche for Herzl, but, never at a loss at critical moments, he replied: 'I can do a lot for Turkey but in return I must be given something tangible for my

---

[7] The Quai d'Orsay supported Rouvier's negotiations with the Porte. At that time he was a member of the Chamber of Deputies. In 1887 and in 1905–6 he was Prime Minister.

[8] *Diaries*, ii, p. 781. For the general background see Langer, op. cit. ii, p. 640; Earle, *Turkey, the Great Powers and the Bagdad Railway*, pp. 165–71; Chapman, 'Great Britain and the Bagdad Railway', pp. 35–6.

Jews.' He dismissed Izzet's proposition and suggested that, unless the Porte offered to form an Ottoman-Jewish Colonization Company, Jewish financiers would hardly be attracted. On the following day, at Izzet's request, Herzl elucidated: the Jews were looking to the Sultan not for personal but for national protection. They wanted immigration to be unrestricted and controlled by themselves. After consulting the Sultan, Izzet delivered the final decision: with the exception of Palestine, the Empire was to be open to all Jews willing to become Ottoman subjects, but only in regions determined before-hand by the Government; the Ottoman-Jewish Company would not be allowed to operate in Palestine. Herzl refused at once. A charter without Palestine was a contradiction in terms. But Izzet was not willing to forgo Jewish money so easily. 'Enter this country as financiers, make friends, and later you will do whatever you want . . . Take our finances in hand and you will be the boss.' Herzl pretended that the idea was 'brilliant', but officially he advised the Sultan that the conditions were unacceptable. He preferred to leave and wait for more reasonable proposals. These never came. On 14 March he learned that the Sultan had apparently approved Rouvier's loan. He now realized that his presence had merely been used to extract better terms from the French.

Herzl did not give in. On 3 May 1902 he offered to found a Jewish university in Jerusalem 'of the very first rank'; it would obviate the need for Ottoman students to go abroad and would render a service to scholarship. Izzet was not impressed. Jewish loyalty was 'incontestable', but more important was provision of income for the Ottoman Treasury. On 9 July Costaki Anthopulos Pasha, the Turkish Ambassador in London, advised Herzl that the Sultan wished to see him urgently; that his conditions for consolidation of the Public Debt were more attractive than those proposed by the French; and that the Sultan was eager to demonstrate his sympathy for the Jews. Herzl was sceptical and tried to play for time, but, as the Sultan insisted, he decided to accept the invitation.

Accompanied by Wolffsohn, he called at the Yildiz Kiosk for the fifth and last time. Believing the moment propitious, he asked that the Porte should reject Rouvier's offer and grant a concession for the Jewish colonization of Mesopotamia and Haifa and its environs. Mesopotamia was merely camouflage for his real ambitions, and Haifa was only a stepping-stone. He was careful not to disclose the identity of his 'friends' in the world of high finance, and warned that the consolidation of the Ottoman Public Debt would be a 'slow and complicated' process. The fees paid by the Company would be proportionate to the number of the immigrants allowed to enter the regions concerned. Should the Sultan make a special declaration, a favourable response throughout the world would follow. It would attract intelligence, capital, and enterprise from which the Ottoman Empire as a whole would benefit.

Mehmed Said Pasha, the Grand Vizier, complimenting Herzl on his 'humanitarian and commendable' aspirations, assured him that in principle the Sultan was prepared to negotiate. But when it came to the point, Said was decidedly negative: Turkey feared complications with the Great Powers, and even Haifa could not be conceded since it was strategically important. Moreover, the Jewish offer fell short of outbidding the French. Herzl realized once again that he had been used merely to scare his rivals. Before leaving he obtained a warm letter from Abdul Hamid ('Le Sionisme est très noble'), but on matters of substance, the deadlock was still unresolved.

In Search of International Support

HERZL did not lose hope. Some day, when the Turks were in dire need, they would become more amenable. In the meantime he shifted his efforts to Britain in the expectation that she would allow him to establish a Jewish colony under her protection somewhere in the neighbourhood of Palestine. His eyes had been turned to England since 1895. Initial reactions to his ideas reinforced his belief that London should be one of his main bases. Gladstone, the former Prime Minister, liked *The Jewish State*, Bishop Wilkinson thought that Zionism was a practical proposition, while the Press reported sympathetically on the First Zionist Congress; the Conservative *Pall Mall Gazette* and the radical *Daily Chronicle* advocated a European conference for the settlement of the Jewish question. The Fourth Zionist Congress, which met in London (13–16 August 1900), also attracted favourable comment, and friendly sentiments were expressed at Westminster and elsewhere. Yet, for all the sympathy that Herzl gained no practical results ensued. Salisbury, the Prime Minister, declined to receive him, and the idea that a railroad from Palestine to the Persian Gulf, constructed by a Jewish company, would benefit Britain struck no chord.[1]

It was not until 1902 that negotiations with the British Government began in earnest. With Palestine barred, Herzl hoped to

---

[1] *Diaries*, iv, p. 1344; i, pp. 144, 360, 363–4; ii, pp. 500–1. Herzl to Hechler for Salisbury, 1 Dec. 1896 (it is not certain whether Salisbury received the message), ii, pp. 595–96; iii, pp. 871, 940, 976, 1165–6; Goodman, *Zionism in England*, pp. 18–19; Sokolow, *History of Zionism*, ii, pp. 389–91; Oscar K. Rabinowicz, *Herzl, Architect of the Balfour Declaration* (New York, 1958), pp. 6, 8.

On 24 Mar. 1897 Mustafa Kamil, a leader of the Egyptian national movement, solicited Herzl's support for the idea of freeing his country from 'British domination'. Despite the historic irony, it made Herzl reflect that should the British be forced to leave Egypt, they might fall upon a modern Jewish Palestine as an alternative base on the road to the Persian Gulf and India (*Diaries*, ii, pp. 527).

acquire at least a staging post in its neighbourhood; a foothold in Cyprus, in the Sinai Peninsula, or in the El Arish area. Joseph Chamberlain, who met him on 22 October and again on 23 October 1902, thought Cyprus impracticable, but agreed that in the El Arish area, or in Sinai, which was uninhabited, a self-governing Jewish colony could be founded, provided Lord Cromer, the British Agent in Cairo, approved. To Herzl this was no mean achievement, and two days later he told Rothschild enthusiastically that, should the plan materialize, 'a refuge' and a 'home for the hard-pressed Jews' would be created, while England would increase her influence in the south-eastern corner of the Mediterranean and rally 'ten million' friends to her side.[2]

The plan did not materialize. The Sultan, who exercised at least nominal sovereignty over Sinai, objected; so did the Egyptian Government. The difficulty of providing irrigation was another factor weighing heavily against the plan in official calculations, and Cromer, by no means personally hostile, gave it the *coup de grâce*. In the spring of 1903 Chamberlain offered instead the Guas Ngishu plateau near Nairobi in East Africa for a Jewish settlement under the British flag. Herzl, pressed by the need to provide a refuge, even temporary, for the persecuted Russian and Romanian Jews, thought it politically imprudent to reject the offer. Moreover, the very fact that a Great Power was negotiating with him amounted to *de facto* recognition of his movement; rather than impede, it might bring the realization of his ultimate goal nearer. As his close assistant, Leopold Greenberg, editor of the *Jewish Chronicle* and the *Jewish World*, put it: 'From the political point of view it would be no mean thing to say that the British Government offered us a Refuge and I think it could be used in the nature of a Drill Ground for our National forces.' In a subsequent letter, on 7 June 1903, Greenberg was more precise:

It seems to me that intrinsically there is no great value in East Africa. It will not form a great attraction to our people for it has no moral or historical claim. But the value of the proposal of Chamberlain is politic-ally immense *if we use it to its full*. An essential of this is, I submit, that the Agreement we get from the British Government should be as well a definite declaration of its desire to assist our people—something in the form I prepared for the Sinai scheme. That will be of infinite value to you, both within our Movement and outside . . . It matters not if East Africa is afterwards refused by us—we shall have obtained from the British Government a recognition that it cannot ever go back of [*sic*] and which no other British Government will ever be able to upset. Everything after that will have to start from that point—the point of recognition of us as a Nation. It also follows naturally that . . . if it is found that East Africa is no good they will have to make a further suggestion and this it is possible will gradually and surely lead us to Palestine.[3]

This was fully in line with Herzl's thinking. 'This British East African beginning', he wrote to Nordau, 'is politically a Rishon le Zion.' If the Zionists gratefully acknowledged Chamberlain's offer, it would enhance his sympathy and commit him to do something for them, should a Zionist fact-finding mission disqualify East Africa as a suitable place for settlement. At no time did Herzl lose sight of Palestine. At the Sixth Zionist Congress he assured the delegates who had suspected him that he would in no way deviate from the Basle Programme. He ended his closing speech to the Congress with the ancient oath: 'If I forget thee, O Jerusalem, may my right hand wither.'[4]

In negotiating with St. Petersburg Herzl acted with an even greater sense of realism. The prospect of shaking hands with Ministers who were responsible for the pogrom in Kishinev (1903) was abhorrent, but it was unavoidable if he wished to induce the Russian Government to support him diplomatically *vis-à-vis* the Porte, to allow Russian Jews to emigrate to Palestine, and to lift the legal restrictions imposed on the Zionist Organization in Russia. Since June 1896 he had tried to obtain an audience with the Tsar, Nicholas II; a number of distinguished personalities had interceded on his behalf, including the Grand Duke Constantine, but all efforts were fruitless. Constantine was Inspector of Military Training and a person of some consequence, but when he approached the Tsar on the Zionist question he was curtly rebuffed. Herzl's requests to meet Vyacheslav Plehve, Minister of the Interior, and Constantine Pobedonostsev, went equally unheeded.[5]

St. Petersburg strongly suspected the Zionists of maintaining

---

[3] Cited in Rabinowicz, op. cit., pp. 50–1. For Herzl's negotiations with the British Government see ibid., pp. 5–66; idem, 'Herzl and England', *Jewish Social Studies*, xiii (Jan. 1951), 25–46; 'New Light on the East Africa Scheme', *The Rebirth of Israel*, ed. Israel Cohen (London, 1952), 77–97; Bein, *Herzl*, pp. 417–47, 467–70, 483–6; Stein, *The Balfour Declaration*, pp. 23–34.   [4] Bein, op. cit., pp. 445–6, 453–64.

[5] *Diaries*, i, pp. 52, 322, 373–4, 399; ii, pp. 471, 691, 782–4; iii, pp. 842–9, 857–60, 878–81, 910, 1148–9, 1167; iv, pp. 1493–7.

clandestine links with the Socialist and Liberal parties, and the stimulus that they gave to Jewish nationalism ran counter to the official policy of assimilation. But it was particularly the conference in Minsk in September 1902 that aroused the Government's ire. There the political objectives of Zionism, primarily the idea of mass emigration to the Jewish State, took second place to the cultural aspect. Plehve regarded this tendency as 'hostile to the policy of assimilation of Jews with other races'; it was against the 'fundamental principles of state', and could not be tolerated. He instructed all the governors, city prefects, and chiefs of police to prohibit Zionist propaganda and ban Zionist public meetings and fund-raising.[6] Sergei Witte, the Minister of Finance, and Vladimir Lamsdorf, the Foreign Minister, soon endorsed these measures.[7] It was not until Herzl requested Plehve's help for 'organised emigration without re-entry',[8] that the doors to official Russian circles were opened to him.

Plehve received Herzl on 8 August 1903. 'The Jewish Question is not a vital question for us, but still a rather important one', he stated. 'We used to be sympathetic to your Zionist movement, as long as it worked towards emigration. You don't have to justify the movement to me. *Vous prêchez à un converti.* But ever since the Minsk conference, we have noticed *un changement des gros bonnets.* There is less talk now of Palestinian Zionism than there is about culture, organization, and Jewish nationalism. This doesn't suit us. We have noticed in particular that your leaders in Russia . . . do not really obey your Vienna Committee.' Russia desired homogeneity of its population, but he admitted that a massive assimilation of Jews was impractical. The answer was emigration. This conclusion played

---

[6] *The Times*, 11 Sept. 1903, where Plehve's secret circular is reproduced; cutting in *E.G.*, Nr. 84, K 81341. The Minsk Conference (1902) was the first convention of Russian Zionists. The debate centred on organization and revival of Hebrew culture and education. This annoyed the Tsarist Government, which had permitted this Conference to convene. Consequently, in June 1903 all Zionist activity was prohibited on the grounds that the Russian Zionists had gone back on the original aim of their movement, i.e. promotion of emigration to Palestine, and had concentrated instead on strengthening Jewish nationalism in Russia. On this Conference see Böhm, *Die zionistische Bewegung*, ii, pp. 296–7, 517; Bein, op. cit., pp. 405, 449; Greenberg, *The Jews in Russia*, ii, p. 180. Ahad Ha'am's influence on this Conference was decisive. He was the father of 'cultural Zionism' as opposed to Herzl's political Zionism; see Leon Simon, *Ahad Ha'am. A Biography* (London, 1960). On the impact that Herzl made on Russian Jewry see Greenberg, op. cit. ii, pp. 176–80.

[7] *E.G.*, Nr. 84, K 181318, Romberg (St. Petersburg) to Bülow, 4 Oct. 1903, dis. no. 727.

[8] *Diaries*, iv, pp. 1509–10, Herzl to Mme von Korvin-Piatrovska, 8 July 1903, a Polish lady who interceded on Herzl's behalf with the Russian Government.

straight into Herzl's hands, and he tried to give it a practical content: 'Help me to reach land sooner, and the revolt [at the Minsk conference] will end. And so will the defection to the Socialists.' Surprisingly, Plehve agreed to all Herzl's requests. They consisted of an 'effective intervention' with the Sultan in order to obtain a charter for the colonization of Palestine, a financial subsidy by the Russian Government for Jewish emigration, and facilities for the Russian Zionist societies to act in conformity with the Basle Programme.[9]

The second conversation with Plehve on 13 August was of even greater consequence. He conceded that the 'creation of an independent Jewish State, capable of absorbing several million Jews', suited the Russian Government best. This did not mean that he wanted to lose all the Jews. 'Les fortes intelligences — et vous même êtes le meilleur exemple qu'il y en a — nous voudrions les garder.' Herzl replied that everything depended on the outcome of the intercession with the Sultan and on the legalization of the Zionist societies in Russia. Earlier, Plehve had intended to recommend to the Cabinet the complete suppression of Zionism, but now he told Herzl that he would take up the matter again with the Emperor and press it energetically, though the final decision would be taken after the Sixth Zionist Congress.[10] The postponement of the decision was apparently designed to ward off criticism. Some time before Herzl's arrival Plehve had asked two Russian Zionist leaders to see that the events in Kishinev were not mentioned at the Congress; the two men gave an evasive reply.[11] Plehve's fear that the events might be discussed influenced his discussions with Herzl, who observed correctly that Witte would not hesitate to exploit his colleague's embarrassment, and even to cause his downfall.[12]

Witte was Plehve's rival and an unsparing critic of his responsibility for the Kishinev pogrom. In outlook they were poles apart. Witte thought it more prudent to grant a large measure of autonomy to non-Russian races, and regarded the anti-Jewish laws as degrading and harmful to Russia's reputation.[13] He did not exaggerate when

[9] Ibid., pp. 1520–8. The following day Plehve told Mme Korvin-Piatrovska that he could have employed a person of Herzl's calibre as director of one of his departments (ibid., p. 1527). [10] Ibid., pp. 1534–40.
[11] *E.G.*, Nr. 84, K 181330–32, Hauthausen to Bülow, (?) Aug. 1903, dis. no. 72/201.
[12] *Diaries*, iv, pp. 1524, 1533.
[13] Ibid., p. 1526; *The Memoirs of Count S. Witte*, ed. A. Yarmolinsky (New York, 1921), pp. 381–4; Greenberg, op. cit., pp. 105–6; E. J. Dillon, *The Eclipse of Russia* (London, 1918), pp. 42–3, 145.

he told Herzl at their meeting on 9 August that whenever he could he stood up for the Jews; none the less their participation in the revolutionary parties worried him. This was why he found Herzl's proposal so attractive. Satisfied that the Holy Places in Palestine would remain inviolable, he eventually agreed that the Zionist solution would be a 'good one, if it could be carried out', and promised to lift the restrictions on the financial activities of the Jewish Colonial Trust.[14]

Witte's influence on Russia's foreign relations was far greater than that of the foreign ministers of his time,[15] but Herzl did not rest until he had succeeded in committing the Ministry of Foreign Affairs too. It was with this object in mind that he appealed to General Alexander Kireyev, the Tsar's aide-de-camp. The General, who had met Herzl earlier, introduced him to Nikolas de Hartwig, Head of the Asiatic Department in the Ministry and President of the Imperial Palestine Society. Like Plehve, Hartwig was well acquainted with the subject and told Herzl that his cause found favour with his Ministry. So long as 'no one pushed it, it didn't get anywhere', but now he intended to consult Zinoviev, the Ambassador at Constantinople, to ascertain what could be done. On 23 November/ 6 December 1903 Plehve wrote to Herzl that Count Lamsdorf had agreed to inform the Sublime Porte that the Russian Government viewed the Zionist project of resettlement of Jews in Palestine favourably, and that a friendly response from the Porte to the Zionist request would attest to the 'bond of friendship that exists between the two Empires'.[16]

Although the Tsarist archives have not been examined, Herzl's success is indisputable. Of outstanding importance was Plehve's letter to him of 30 July/12 August 1903. It read:

So long as Zionism consisted of wanting to create an independent state in Palestine and undertook to organize the emigration from Russia of

[14] *Diaries*, iv, pp. 1528–32. Herzl found Witte coarse and his manners repugnant. This is reminiscent of Theodor Roosevelt's impression of Witte during the 1905 Portsmouth Conference (Florinsky, *Russia. A History and an Interpretation*, ii, pp. 1260–1). Herzl, however, erred in considering Witte a rabid anti-Semite (*Diaries*, iv, pp. 1530–3), although this was the general opinion among Jews (Dillon, op. cit., p. 7); Baron Rosen, *Forty Years of Diplomacy* (London, 1922), i, pp. 289–91.

[15] Florinsky, op. cit. ii, p. 1260.

[16] *Diaries*, iv, pp. 1521–4, 1541–2, 1582–3. The original letter of Plehve to Herzl of 23 Nov./6 Dec. 1903 is found in C.Z.A., H/VI/E. (I give both dates, first that of the Julian Calendar, which was in use in Tsarist Russia until the Bolshevik Revolution, and second that of the Gregorian Calendar (New Style), which is widely used today.)

a certain number of its Jewish subjects, the Russian Government could be completely favourable to it. But once this principal Zionist objective is abandoned, to be replaced by straight propaganda for a Jewish national entity in Russia, it is obvious that the Government can in no way tolerate this new direction taken by Zionism. It would only create groups of individuals quite alien and even hostile to the patriotic sentiments which are the strength of every state.

That is why confidence can be placed in Zionism only on condition that it returns to its former programme of action. If it did so, it would be able to count on moral and material support from the day when certain of its practical measures would help to reduce the size of the Jewish population in Russia. This support could take the form of protecting the Zionist emissaries to the Ottoman Government, of facilitating the work of the emigration societies, and even of providing for the needs of these societies, obviously from sources other than the state budget, by means of a tax levied on the Jews.

Plehve concluded by stating that in its treatment of the Jewish question the Russian Government 'had never abandoned the . . . accepted principles of morality and humanity', and hoped that as emigration increased, the position of the remaining Jews would improve.[17]

According to what Herzl told Hartwig, Plehve's undertaking was given in the name of the Emperor and the Russian Government.[18] The importance of this document has so far been overlooked in Zionist historiography. It preceded the British Government's letter[19] by two days, but in its phrasing and in its implications it was of far greater moment. Sir Clement Hill referred to 'the establishment of a Jewish colony' in East Africa, which would enable the settlers to observe 'their National customs'. Plehve favoured the creation of 'an independent state in Palestine', a term which Herzl himself was reluctant to use. The British document is tentative and guarded in its language, while the Russian one refers clearly to 'moral and

---

[17] *Türkei* 195, K 176071. Herzl gave copies of this letter, as well as that of Sir Clement Hill, to the Grand Duke of Baden for the Foreign Ministry. The original (in French), at the C.Z.A., is mentioned briefly in Bein, op. cit., p. 449. It has never been published in full before.

[18] *Diaries*, iv, p. 1542; p. 1558, Herzl to Eulenburg, 11 Sept. 1903; p. 1561, to the Grand Duke, 12 Sept. 1903; pp. 1609–11 to Tittoni, 4 Feb. 1904.

[19] Dated 14 Aug. 1903 and signed by Sir Clement Hill, Chief of the Protectorate Department in the Foreign Office. It is published in full in Rabinowicz's 'New Light on the East Africa Scheme', 94–5. Dr. Rabinowicz, however, makes too much of this letter by implying that recognition of national autonomy (*imperium in imperio*) meant 'Jewish Statehood' (ibid., p. 97).

material support' on practical issues. The motives are also different. That of the British Government was primarily humanitarian, while that of the Russian Government was shaped by domestic considerations. References to Russia's interests in the Near East were not spelled out in the document, but the silence over the Sultan's sovereignty, which had been specifically mentioned by Herzl, and the emphasis on an 'independent state', were significant and reflected the general line of Russian policy aimed at the dismemberment of the Ottoman Empire. By fostering the separatist aspirations of the non-Turkish nationalities, Russia hoped not only to weaken Turkey from within, but also to emerge as the champion of those struggling for liberation. However, this policy did not crystallize before 1906, when Izvolsky was appointed Foreign Minister. In 1903 it was still in its infancy.

Plehve's letter served as the corner-stone of Herzl's diplomacy. He thought that some of the major diplomatic difficulties had already been surmounted. Since Russia declared herself in favour of an 'independent Jewish state', by implication she renounced any claim to Palestine, and France would therefore have no grounds for protest. No objections could be expected from England either. Moreover, Plehve's letter opened the possibility of regaining German support. 'I will gladly let Wilhelm II have the glory of placing himself at the head' of the Concert of Powers on the Zionist question. Although Sir Clement Hill's letter was 'as generous as it [was] wise . . . we stubborn Jews are more attached to the sand and chalk of Palestine' than to East Africa, Herzl confessed to Eulenburg. Plehve's solution was therefore preferable. Now, should the Kaiser win over the Triple Alliance, 'we shall be all set'. He also urged the Grand Duke of Baden to persuade the Kaiser to raise the matter with the Austrian Emperor, Franz Josef, during their forthcoming meeting in Vienna, when presumably the Eastern question would be discussed.[20]

This line of reasoning dispels any lingering suspicion that Herzl had abandoned Palestine in favour of East Africa, for it appears that his main purpose was not necessarily to obtain the East Africa concession, but to ease Germany's task in gaining Palestine for the Zionists. East Africa was only the diplomatic stepping-stone to the

[20] *Diaries*, iv, pp. 1557-9, Herzl to Eulenburg, 11 Sept. 1903; pp. 1560-1, to Grand Duke of Baden, 12 Sept. 1903; Ellern, pp. 92-5.

main goal. This is how the term *Nachtasyl* coined by Nordau must be understood. That there was no substitute for Palestine is also clear from Herzl's letter to Izzet Bey, which was his last contact with the Porte. He wrote:

> A territory we can find elsewhere. We have found it. You have un-doubtedly read in the papers that the English Government has offered me a territory of 60,000–90,000 square leagues in Africa, a rich, fertile country, excellent for our colonization. But nevertheless, I come back once more to my plan for finding the salvation of the Jewish people among the brothers of our race and our coreligionists who live under the sceptre of the Caliph, bringing to them what we have . . . the spirit of enterprise, industry, economic progress.[21]

With no satisfactory response from Constantinople forthcoming, Herzl continued to consolidate his position among the Powers in the hope that they would exert concerted pressure on Turkey. His achievements in the Italian and Austrian capitals were noteworthy. He never turned to France.

Victor Emmanuel III of Italy received Herzl graciously on 23 January 1904. He was proud that in his kingdom there was no racial discrimination; Jews held posts in the Diplomatic Service and almost every government included a Jew. Italy had no Jewish prob-lem but Zionism had its positive attractions. Palestine 'will and must get into your hands', the King told Herzl. 'It is only a question of time. Wait until you have half a million Jews there!' He thought that the partition of Turkey was inevitable but that the Zionists in the meantime should refrain from using the term 'autonomy'; the Sultan disliked this word. Plehve's letter, in the King's opinion, represented 'a great success'. Herzl was able to witness the effect of the royal goodwill when he met Tommaso Tittoni, the Foreign Minister. The conversation was short but productive. The Minister promised Herzl that he would write to the Italian Ambassador at Constantinople and ask him to proceed jointly with the Russians.[22]

Herzl could not claim any comparable success with the Vatican. He had long been aware of the Holy See's animosity towards his

---

[21] *Diaries*, iv, pp. 1574–5, Herzl to Izzet, 12 Dec. 1903. One square league is equi-valent to three square miles.

[22] Ibid., pp. 1595–1600, 1606–7. The original of Herzl's letter to Tittoni of 13 Feb. 1904 (ibid., pp. 1609–11) is with archives of the Italian Foreign Ministry (microfilm copy in the possession of the author).

movement. But, if the task of winning the Papacy over was beyond him, he could at least attempt to neutralize its opposition. Giving the Holy Places extraterritorial status would, he hoped, remove the main stumbling-block, but the differences went much deeper than he presumed. Cardinal Merry del Val, the Papal Secretary of State, was reluctant to do anything for the Jews. 'We certainly cannot make a declaration in their favour', he stated. 'Not that we have any ill will towards them . . . But they deny the divine nature of Christ. How then can we, without abandoning our own highest principles, agree to their being given possession of the Holy Land again?' He admitted that the Christian heritage was derived from the history of Israel, but the Jewish people 'would first have to be converted' before he could back Herzl in the way that he desired. Pope Pius X expressed himself in similar vein: 'We cannot give approval to this movement. We cannot prevent the Jews from going to Jerusalem —but we could never sanction it . . . The Jews have not recognized our Lord, therefore we cannot recognize the Jewish people . . . *Gerusalemme* must not get into the hands of the Jews.' To all of Herzl's arguments the Pope had one formal reply: 'Non possumus'.[23]

Herzl was an Austro-Hungarian citizen and enjoyed the confidence of successive Prime Ministers, Count Kazimierz Badeni (1895–7) and Ernst von Koerber (1900–4), but it was not before the autumn of 1903 that he could rely on his own Government's support. Koerber was impressed by Herzl's achievements in Russia and assured him of his interest.[24] On 30 April 1904 Herzl met Count Agenor von Goluchowski, the Foreign Minister. Initially the latter was sceptical, but Plehve's letter made all the difference. Since Russia was in favour, he too could reach agreement with Herzl. Though strongly critical of anti-Semitism, he thought Herzl's project so praiseworthy that every government should support it financially. When the question was discussed on an international plane, 'there must be no petty or half-way measures. If it were a question of only one or two hundred thousand Jews, the Great Powers could not be stirred into action. But they could if [they] asked Turkey for land and legal rights for 5–6 million Jews.'

[23] *Diaries*, i, pp. 332, 353–4; ii, pp. 587, 589, 590–2; iv, pp. 1593–5, 1601–5. The meeting with Cardinal del Val took place on 22 Jan. 1904, and that with the Pope on 25 Jan.
[24] C.Z.A., H VI E I, Koerber to Herzl, 28 Sept. 1903. For fuller details see I. Friedman, 'The Austro-Hungarian Government and Zionism: 1897–1918', 148–51.

This was more than Herzl had dared to hope. However, Goluchow-ski declined Herzl's suggestion to take the lead in the matter; the moment was inopportune. It would be better if England took the initiative and if Herzl secured the support of members of the Hungarian Government, and especially of Count Tisza.[25]

The Foreign Minister's reluctance to take the initiative arose from the need to keep in step with Russia. Since 1897 the two countries had had a secret agreement under which they undertook to maintain the *status quo* in the Balkans. This was qualified by Article III which specified that should circumstances change, the contracting parties would act together.[26] The Turkish provinces in Asia were not mentioned in the text but it could be assumed that the principle in Article III applied there as well. This explains the change in Austria's attitude to Herzl following the revelation of Plehve's letter. Thus, whilst intending to overcome Russian objections in order to regain German support, Herzl had unwittingly won that of Goluchowski.

But in spite of the professed *status quo* principle, the long-term policy of the two Powers aimed at the gradual dismemberment of the Ottoman Empire. Count Goluchowski's goal was 'to create in the future a large Greece . . . a big Romania . . . and an independent Albania—at the cost of Turkish domination'. A Jewish Palestine, with a population of five to six million, could have fitted well within this pattern. The Sultan's suzerainty over Palestine (a formula advanced by Herzl) did not matter, since it was meant to be only nominal. Moreover, Goluchowski hoped that if London committed itself to the Zionist cause (as the Italians had already done) this might revive the 1887 tripartite Mediterranean Agreement, but there is no documentary evidence on this point.[27]

[25] *Diaries*, iv, pp. 1623–7. Hungarian influence on the foreign policy of the Dual Monarchy started with Kalnoky and persisted under Goluchowski (Luigi Albertini, *The Origins of the War of 1914* (Oxford University Press, 1952), i, p. 90).

[26] For the text of the Goluchowski–Muraviev Agreements of 8 and 17 May 1897 see A. F. Pribram, *The Secret Treaties of Austria-Hungary, 1897–1914* (London, 1920), i, pp. 184–91; *Grosse Politik*, xii, no. 3126. For its interpretation see Albertini, op. cit. i, p. 93; Sidney Fay, *The Origins of the World War* (New York, 1934), i, p. 365; and Florinsky, op. cit. ii, p. 1284.

[27] On the diplomatic background, particularly on the Macedonian question, see Albertini, op. cit. i, pp. 92, 132–6; Langer, *The Diplomacy of Imperialism*, i, pp. 196–202, 208–10; Pribram, op. cit. i, pp. 94–103. Constantin Dumba, *Memoirs of a Diplomat* (London, 1933), pp. 92–4, 101, 131, 138, 144, 152–4. On Article XXIII of the Treaty of Berlin 1878, dealing with reforms in Macedonia, see Medlicott, *The Congress of Berlin and After*, App. 11.

At the beginning of 1904 it looked as if Herzl's plan to rally European support for his cause was promising, but in fact the diplomatic edifice which he was laboriously constructing was beginning to disintegrate. The Russian intercession with the Porte was not forthcoming as early as Herzl had hoped, and so the other Powers could not follow suit. On the British front the prospects of the East African project vanished altogether, but the greatest blow came from the Wilhelmstrasse. On the very day that Herzl wrote to the Grand Duke of Baden about his success in Rome, the Foreign Minister, Baron Oswald von Richthofen, was completing the final draft of his memorandum on Zionism. It was the outcome of prolonged study, drafted originally in November 1903 as a reply to the Grand Duke's letter of 29 September 1903. The final draft, dated 26 January 1904,[28] reads:

As a matter of principle the Imperial Government has always welcomed any humanitarian endeavour. If such an endeavour originates in Germany, or serves German interests, the active support of the Auswärtiges Amt is assured. However, upon a close examination of Zionist aims, it was found that no German interest is involved. Herzl is not a German citizen and the movement he has created has only a few adherents among the Jews in Germany . . . Hence there is no justification for German intervention in favour of Zionism. In addition, important political considerations make it very difficult for the German Foreign Ministry to back Dr. Herzl's plans. For years Turkey has been in conflict with the Great Powers in order to prevent the establishment of national autonomy, or even of a nucleus of such autonomy, in Macedonia. She is also strongly opposed to the introduction of reforms under European supervision. There is, therefore, a danger of international complications and even a threat to world peace.

Herzl is asking for something that, up to the present, the Powers have tried in vain to secure from the Sultan. Whilst Macedonia is populated mainly by Christians, in Palestine there is only a small number of Jews. Their numbers have grown as a result of the philanthropic settlements of Baron Rothschild and Baron Hirsch, and Turkey, concerned about the political future of Palestine, has restricted the immigration of Jews. These restrictions are ascribed generally to the appearance of Herzl and the publication of his book, *The Jewish State*. Should a foreign state, such as

---

[28] *Diaries*, iv, pp. 1600–1, Herzl to the Grand Duke, 25 Jan. 1904, also Ellern, pp. 98–100; *Türkei* 195, K 176065–8, Duke of Baden to Richthofen, 29 Sept. 1903, encls. copies of Plehve's and Sir Clement Hill's letters; K 176090–9, memorandum by Richthofen, 26 Jan. 1904. A copy is found in the *Grossherzogliches Familienarchiv*, and reproduced in Ellern, pp. 101–3.

Germany, extend its protection to the Zionist movement, there is no doubt that the Sultan's apprehensions will be intensified and the position of Jews in the Ottoman Empire will be worsened. Ottoman Jewry, who now enjoy a reasonable status and prosperity, might face the fate of the Armenians, who were treated well until the Sultan became aware that their political aspirations were supported by foreign Powers. It is the agreed opinion of competent experts and Foreign Ministry advisers on Turkish affairs that the time is not ripe for political intervention on behalf of Zionism. Such intervention can only do harm to Zionism and diminish the prospects of the realization of Dr. Herzl's ideals. It would also damage other German interests in Turkey . . .

This memorandum confirms previous evidence that it was not from ill will or indifference that the German Government did not intervene on Herzl's behalf. The question of the Macedonian reforms introduces a new factor. Apparently, it served as a test case for Richthofen and explains the delay in the completion of his memorandum. The Porte, as Marschall advised Berlin, was very much annoyed over the Mürzsteg demands, which would have given both Austria and Russia a privileged position in Macedonia's administration. It was a blow to the Triple Alliance,[29] and damaged Austro-German relations. In these circumstances to act in concert with the two Powers in a joint intervention with the Porte, as Herzl wished, was unthinkable for Berlin.

Herzl's position seemed hopeless, but this word was not in his vocabulary. Although he persevered zealously in his course, the quick solution which he expected was not forthcoming. He was aiming at a goal which during his own lifetime was unattainable. His desire to reach it by the shortest route weakened his sense of reality, blurring the distinction between the desirable and the possible; and politics is the art of the possible. The fiasco in Jerusalem demonstrated the drawbacks of the short-cut method and on his return journey he admitted the wisdom of the Grand Duke's words that 'such world-historic matters required great patience'.[30] But Herzl remained impatient. The Duke's earlier advice, that it might be better for a start to send a few hundred thousand Jews to Palestine and raise the question at the diplomatic level later, remained unheeded. For Herzl, legal security and political agreements remained the indispensable prerequisite to any colonization. Sound

---

[29] Albertini, op. cit. i, pp. 132, 136–7.
[30] *Diaries*, ii, pp. 765–7, Herzl to the Grand Duke, 18 Nov. 1898; above, p. 58.

as this principle was, its implementation depended on the co-operation of all the Powers concerned, but this, at the turn of the century, was unobtainable. Following the Sixth Zionist Congress, Herzl himself confessed that if Palestine was not won in his next diplomatic round, 'the ultimate goal . . . will not be reached within the foreseeable future'. He doubted whether he would live to see it.[31]

Herzl's sense of urgency was dictated by his conviction that anti-Semitism was incurable and that unless a mass exodus of Jews took place they would be overwhelmed by catastrophe. This nightmarish spectre called for an immediate and radical solution. He believed that it lay in the interests of anti-Semites themselves to find an answer to the problem. Hence rather than denounce the evils of anti-Semitism he hoped to harness it for his own purposes. However, the premiss that the anti-Semitic countries would be helpful was borne out only in the case of Russia. It was Plehve who gave Herzl his unqualified support for a Jewish state and, together with Lamsdorf, decided to intervene with the Porte; the Russian ministers discovered in Zionism a safety-valve against Jewish revolutionaries. What Herzl's fortunes would have been had he remained alive is a matter for speculation. The outbreak of the Russo-Japanese War on 8/9 February 1904 diverted St. Petersburg's attention from Turkey, a fact that explains the delay in Zinoviev's intervention. But in 1906, with the emphasis of Russian ambitions shifting from the Far to the Near East, Herzl's chances would have been incomparably better. Moreover, it is reasonable to assume that had Russia taken the initiative, Austria and Italy would have followed, while England would either have joined them or assumed an attitude of benevolent neutrality. Herzl was bound sooner or later to realize his mistake in overlooking France which, if won over, would have completed the concert of Powers. What position Germany would have taken in that case is difficult to surmise. Assuming that the other Powers would have exerted pressure on Turkey, Berlin, bent on demonstrating its friendship for the Sultan, would have endeavoured to ensure that Palestine remained under Ottoman sovereignty. This was not inconsistent with Herzl's ambition, provided he was granted a charter for a Jewish Colonization Company guaranteed by the European Powers.

The European conferences following the Balkan Wars in 1912–13 might have given an opportunity to the Powers to intervene with

[31] *Diaries*, iv, p. 1547.

Turkey, but at the turn of the century the moment for an international debate, let alone action, was not yet ripe. And only united action held out promise of success. So great was the fear of war, and so great the respect for the *status quo*, that no isolated move by a single Power could have been contemplated. It was therefore an illusion to expect that friendly advice by the Kaiser to the Sultan would be sufficient to put Herzl's chartered company into operation.

Herzl's policy towards Turkey was based on give and take but this principle proved unworkable since the funds with which he hoped to restore Turkish solvency were denied him, and the Sultan refused to issue a declaration which could have stirred the Jewish masses and warmed the hearts of Jewish financiers. Nor was it likely that Herzl would have been more successful had the necessary resources been placed at his disposal. The Sultan was not in the habit of selling his land and limiting his sovereignty voluntarily. Fear of political complications, real and imaginary, should the Jews be allowed to establish themselves in Palestine, weighed far more heavily with the Turks than financial benefits, however alluring. In the circumstances, it was only the combined pressure of the Powers that could have forced Turkey to make certain concessions, and more than the talents of a Herzl was needed to bring that about.

Herzl failed to carry the majority of the Jewish people with him. In a moment of despair he noted: 'We shall have to sink still lower . . . to be even more insulted, spat upon, mocked, whipped, plundered, and slain before we are ripe for this idea.' He thought that the centuries-old oppression had demoralized the Jews and distorted their character; although emancipated, spiritually they still remained ghetto-minded, refusing to become free. So enraged was he with the rich Jews, on whom initially he had pinned all his hopes, that he called the house of Rothschild 'a national misfortune'. Yet, despite repeated frustrations, he never despaired of his eventual triumph. 'To-day I am isolated and a lonely man, tomorrow perhaps the intellectual leader of hundreds of thousands—in any case, the discoverer of and proclaimer of a mighty idea.' Later he realized that the Zionist idea had not originated with himself and that his contribution was only the way in which it was propounded and the method of its implementation.[32] It is here that his main achievement lay.

[32] Ibid. i, pp. 9, 80, 103, 116, 132, 279, 442. Herzl to Zadoc Kahn, 26 July 1896.

Herzl was the founder of political Zionism. He turned a mystique, a dream, into a political factor. The movement which he brought into being became the most dynamic force in modern Jewish history. He founded its organ, *Die Welt*, its financial arm, the Jewish Colonial Trust, and the Congress, which became the embodiment of Zionist parliamentarianism. Like any great man of history, he foresaw what was going to happen. His prediction of a Jewish catastrophe was fulfilled during the Nazi holocaust and, exactly fifty years and eight months after he had recorded it in his diary, the State of Israel was proclaimed.

But prophets do not always command the respect even of their own followers. A series of disagreements soured the mutual relationship. The Zionists of the 'practical' school of thought preferred the method of peaceful 'infiltration' of Palestine to diplomacy. Herzl recoiled from this idea, regarding it as both hazardous and dishonest. He wanted the chartered company to act within the law and to be based on a sound foundation. Infiltration, in any case, fell short of providing an answer to the problem; certainly it could not match its magnitude. More serious was the clash at the Sixth Zionist Congress, following the British offer of land for Jewish colonization in East Africa. The Russian Zionists, in particular, fearing that Herzl might abandon Palestine, were in a state of open rebellion. Their suspicion, as the records adduced above show, was totally unfounded.

The air of mystery with which Herzl surrounded himself gave additional ammunition to his critics, but he insisted that diplomacy must remain strictly his own preserve. Always walking the tightrope, he was aware that the slightest false step could ruin his efforts, and as a rule he preferred to keep secrets to himself and to his closest advisers. Again, the shifts of emphasis in his diplomatic activity from one capital to another gave the impression at the time that his policy was inconsistent, if not contradictory; but this was not so. His strategy was multilateral, though evolving in response to opportunities rather than by design. His basic principle was that the Jewish question was an international one and should therefore be tackled within the framework of international law. He strove to gain recognition and support from all the Powers concerned; which one was to take the lead was of secondary importance. As Israel Zangwill stated, Herzl was neither German, English, nor Turkish, but the 'first Jewish statesman since the destruction of Jerusalem'.[33]

[33] Quoted in Böhm, op. cit. i, p. 258.

He was a statesman without a state, a leader without a people to support him. If he impressed monarchs, Ministers, and intellectuals, it was thanks to his own qualities. He aroused both admiration and opposition, but nobody could ignore the magnetism of his personality, his intelligence, his sincerity, and his idealism. A visionary, who sometimes naïvely believed that because an idea was good and just it must necessarily prevail, he was also a shrewd and down-to-earth politician, with no illusions about human nature. A liberal and a great European, he became the foremost exponent of Jewish nationalism, which was neither chauvinist nor escapist, but an endeavour to restore Jewish honour within a normal national environment. 'We shall enter the Promised Land . . . under the banner of labour . . . We must be a people of inventors, warriors, artists, scholars, honest merchants . . . workmen.' Though the *Judennot* was the primordial force which fired Herzl, he never lost sight of the universal aspect of the Jewish renaissance. 'God would not have preserved our people for so long if we did not have another role to play in the history of mankind.'[34] And in a speech in London on 26 June 1899 he declared that, following their return, the ideal for which the Jews would strive would be 'the ennoblement of humanity'.

There are people who misunderstand us, and think that the goal of our efforts is to return to our land. Our ideal goes beyond that; our ideal is the great eternal truth; it is an ideal that is always advancing; it is an unattainable ideal as with each step forward our horizon advances, and in perspective we see before us an even greater and nobler end which we shall endeavour to approach.

We are different from the Crusaders . . . we Jews shall return to the East with visions of Western culture ever present in our minds . . . We shall return the soul to the Jewish people; for the ideal which is ever before us, is to impart the highest culture to our people. We shall lift up the Jewish soul to its greatest heights; if I am spared, I would wish to be there.[35]

[34] *Diaries*, i, pp. 53, 101, 103.
[35] *The Messenger of Zion*, suppl. to *Young Israel*, 30 June 1899, reprinted by Dr. A. Bein in the *Jerusalem Post, Herzl Centenary Supplement*, 6 May 1960.

8

In the Political Wilderness

THE premature death of Herzl on 3 July 1904, at the age of 44, robbed the movement of a leader of international calibre. He had become a legendary figure in Jewish history, even in his own lifetime; what he accomplished did not make Zionism poorer but Jewry richer. Both friend and foe were shocked by his sudden passing. Ephraim Cohn-Reiss, a notorious opponent of the Zionists, described the deep grief that enveloped the Orthodox Jewish community in Palestine. Everybody appreciated that Herzl's ideas emanated from love of his people. Prominent rabbis saw in his activities 'an indication of the forthcoming Messianic Age and acceleration of the Redemption'.[1] Stefan Zweig in his autobiography gave a similar testimony of the effect that Herzl's death had on Jews all over the world:

> . . . it was this gigantic outpouring of grief from the depths of millions of souls that made me realize for the first time how much passion and hope this lone and lonesome man had borne into the world through the power of a single thought . . . by his prophetic instinct he had foreseen the entire tragedy of his race at a time when it had not appeared to be an inevitable fate.[2]

Herzl was the soul and fountain-head of the Zionist movement and without him it looked as if Zionism was approaching the end of the road. One of those who reached such a pessimistic conclusion was Alfred von Bülow, the German Minister at Berne. He thought that the proceedings at the Seventh Zionist Congress (Basle, 27 July–2 August 1905) gave 'clear proof' that the Zionist movement was approaching its dissolution at a gigantic pace.

[1] Cohn-Reiss, *M'Zichronoth Ish Yerushalaim*, i, p. 307.
[2] Stefan Zweig, *The World of Yesterday. An Autobiography* (New York, 1943), p. 102; also p. 109.

There was such an upheaval and such a sharpness of controversy that Max Nordau, the President, was almost on the point of giving up the whole matter . . . The realization of Zionism (at least in its 'pure' form) is a Utopia, as the idea no longer appeals to the majority of the Jews. Preservation of their national entity and customs does not concern them . . . their main wish is to gain power, influence, and wealth amidst other civilized peoples. The old Jewish Temple will not be resurrected with a new brightness, but the power of modern international capitalism on the one hand and Jewish Socialism on the other, will blossom still more fruitfully.[3]

This prophecy of doom was ill founded. Zionism was too firmly rooted to wither. The Uganda controversy left deep scars and over-shadowed the Seventh Congress but, although the debate was acrimonious, it helped to clarify the direction of the movement. At the final session the Congress declared its undivided loyalty to the Basle Programme; the Uganda project or any alternative territorial solution was rejected. The price, however, had to be paid. Offended by the intolerant attitude of the Zion loyalists (Zione Zion), Israel Zangwill, the celebrated Anglo-Jewish writer, and Nahman Syrkin, the Zionist Socialist leader, seceded from the movement and founded a separate body called the Jewish Territorial Organization (I.T.O.), which aimed at establishing an autonomous Jewish settlement in some part of the world. The exodus was a blow to the Zionists but on balance it was the programme of the I.T.O. adherents that proved to be Utopian. Their negotiations with various governments led to nothing; nor could any territory be found to attract interest among would-be immigrants. Twenty years later the Organization went into self-liquidation.[4] The Zionists, on the other hand, felt that they were on the right side of history. They emerged from the crisis strengthened in their belief and more determined than ever to pursue their original goal.

Another question of primary importance which confronted the

---

[3] *E.G.*, Nr. 84, K 181351–6, Bülow to A.A., 20 Aug. 1905. On this Congress see Böhm, *Die zionistische Bewegung*, i, pp. 307–22.

[4] See D. I. Marmor, 'The Diplomatic Negotiations of the Jewish Territorial Association and the Reasons for their Failure' (Hebrew), *Zion* (Jerusalem, Sept. 1945–Apr. 1946, and July 1946); Robert G. Weisbord, 'Israel Zangwill's Jewish Territorial Organization and the East African Zion', *Jewish Social Studies* (Apr. 1968), 89–108. Following the Balfour Declaration the I.T.O. declared its readiness to co-operate with the Zionists. See Isaiah Friedman, *The Question of Palestine, 1914–1918: British–Jewish–Arab Relations* (London, 1973), p. 306. Syrkin and his Socialist party rejoined the Zionist movement following the Young Turk Revolution of 24 July 1908.

Congress was that of orientation. Herzl gave his movement a distinct political complexion. He did not necessarily discourage individual Jews or groups of Jews from going to settle in Palestine; and the institutions which he founded such as the Jewish Colonial Trust and the Jewish Colonial Fund made practical work possible. None the less, his guiding principle was that not until a minimum of guarantees was granted by the sovereign government should a large-scale immigration and colonization be embarked upon.[5] But, when Herzl's diplomatic *tour de force* proved abortive, there was a demand to change the order of priorities: practical work should be the forerunner of diplomacy, not its consequence. There were no short-cut solutions; only concrete achievements could form the basis for negotiations; creation of facts should precede the political struggle. The 'politicals', loyal to Herzl's precepts, did not give in so easily. Bodenheimer, their leading protagonist, was on firm ground when he pointed out that the country was not an empty one; piecemeal and unsystematic colonization would inevitably strengthen the native non-Jewish inhabitants and would make their opposition to the Zionist project carry greater weight with the Turks. Hence the answer was a massive immigration within the framework of international agreements. Bodenheimer's critics replied that to wait for the charter was tantamount to deferring the matter to the Greek Calends. But in principle the 'practicals' were not opposed to diplomacy. Otto Warburg, a leading exponent, called for the creation of a Jewish cultural centre in Palestine, increased economic development, and attainment of a charter on the basis of administrative autonomy.[6] Eight years later, when addressing the Eleventh Zionist Congress, then as Chairman of the Executive, he stated: 'Our Palestine work is not merely a factor of equal rank with our political work but is the necessary forerunner of our political efforts.'[7]

The two schools of thought were not mutually exclusive. The difference was only that of method; the aim remained very much the same. Although the debate raged for years, a compromise formula was worked out by the Seventh Zionist Congress which read that 'parallel to the political-diplomatic activity, systematic development work should be undertaken in Palestine; it would provide the former

[5] Böhm, op. cit. i, pp. 3, 35; above, pp. 58, 118.
[6] *Stenographisches Protokoll der Verhandlungen des VII. Zionisten Kongresses*, Cologne, 27 July–2 Aug. 1905, pp. 150, 204, and *passim*; Böhm, op. cit. ii, pp. 307–19.
[7] *Protokoll, XI. Kongress*, p. 9.

with a realistic basis'. Any philanthropic or unplanned colonization was rejected.[8]

The Congress also had to elect a new leadership, a hard task, since there was no personality to equal Herzl. Moreover, Nordau, Wolff-sohn, and Bodenheimer, his closest collaborators, were more advisers than co-makers of policy. Nordau would have been the most natural choice but he rejected the invitation and proposed Wolffsohn instead. And it was only under great pressure that the latter agreed to become the second president of the Zionist movement. He acted simultaneously as head of the Inner Actions Committee,[9] the Executive. Other members who were elected to this body represented the two schools of thought equally. Leopold Greenberg (London), Jacobus Kann (The Hague), and Alexander Marmorek (Paris), were 'politicals', whereas Menahem Ussishkin (Yekaterinoslav), Kogan-Bernstein (Odessa), and Otto Warburg (Berlin) adhered to the 'practical' school of thought. But they were so widely scattered over Europe that the Executive could not function effectively as a body. The Eighth Congress (1907) therefore decided to limit the Executive membership to three: Wolffsohn, Kann, and Warburg, an arrangement that was confirmed by the Ninth Congress (1909).

After the initial stormy period the Wolffsohn era (1905–11) was bound to be prosaic. Zionism no longer enjoyed the aura of novelty and entered now a more down-to-earth stage. It was essential to weld the shattered movement together and to begin practical work in Palestine. Wolffsohn was widely believed to be the right man for the job. He was born in Lithuania and had a good grounding in Jewish tradition; a former adherent of Hoveve Zion, he was co-founder of the Zionist Federation in Germany and Herzl's confidant. His organizational skill and business acumen were strong assets, as was his probity of character. He was a warm-hearted and an extremely dedicated man, though he had some limitations. Intellectually he was inferior to his colleagues and he lacked originality of ideas. He was not a skilful politician and did not know how to delegate responsibility. When he attempted to emulate his hero and adopt autocratic techniques he brought about his own undoing. His critics accused him of being too domineering, devoid of 'personality

---

[8] *Protokoll, VII. Kongress*, p. 316.
[9] In German, Engeres Aktions-Comitee, the E.A.C. The English equivalent to the Grosses Aktions-Comitee (G.A.C.) is Council.

or vision', a man 'without ability . . . who did not understand the Herzlian ideal of which he professed to be a disciple'.[10]

However, this criticism was exaggerated and it would be wrong to dismiss Wolffsohn as a failure. His relationship with Edmond de Rothschild, which he was at pains to cultivate, was more fruitful than that of his predecessor and the enthusiastic welcome accorded to him by the Jewish communities in South Africa and Palestine, during his visits in the autumn of 1906, was a lively expression of confidence. He met Andrassy, the Austro-Hungarian statesman, and in June 1908 was received cordially by Stolypin, the Russian Premier, as well as by Izvolsky, the Foreign Minister, and Makarov, the Deputy Minister of the Interior. The Russian Ministers followed the pattern set by Plehve during his meeting with Herzl in 1903; they were willing to lift the ban on the Zionist movement provided it ceased to be active in Russian domestic affairs and concentrated on emigration instead. Wolffsohn's encounter bore no immediate results but in principle St. Petersburg continued to be sympathetic towards the idea of Jewish settlement in Palestine.

A year earlier it seemed that he might have had some luck with the Turkish Government but except for permission to establish a Zionist agency in Constantinople (under the guise of a bank) nothing came of the negotiations. Diplomatically isolated, attacked by almost all sections of Jewry, and with meagre financial resources (the annual budget of the Executive did not exceed the figure of £4,000), the Zionist movement was too weak to be taken seriously. In the given circumstances it is hard to envisage how any other leader could have fared better; Wolffsohn had the courage to take over an organization on the verge of collapse. As Harry Sacher said:

> The tug master who brings the storm-battered ship home to port does a notable service. That service Wolfsohn rendered to Zionism, and no other could in the time and the circumstances have done it as well.[11]

With Wolffsohn's resignation at the Tenth Congress (Basle, 9–15 August 1911) the road was at last open for the 'practicals'. They

[10] On Wolffsohn see E. B. Cohn, *David Wolffsohn: Herzls Nachfolger* (Amsterdam, 1939); Itzhak Gruenbaum, *Hatnua Hatziyonit* [*The Zionist Movement*], (Jerusalem, 1949), iii, pp. 74–5, 146–58, 164–73; Böhm, op. cit. ii, pp. 485–503; Lichtheim, *Geschichte*, pp. 185–92; *idem, She'ar Yashuv* [*A Remnant will Return*], (Tel Aviv, 1954), pp. 119–21, and the German edition *Rückkehr* (Stuttgart, 1970), pp. 117–19.

[11] Louis Lipsky, *A Gallery of Zionist Profiles* (New York, 1966), pp. 23–30; Harry Sacher, *Zionist Portraits and other Essays* (London, 1959), p. 35; above p. 16; below, pp. 139–41, 146–7.

captured all the seats on the Executive and took over the leadership. The presidency remained vacant and Warburg willingly confined himself to the role of a chairman. Dr. Arthur Hantke was the second German member on the Executive, while Victor Jacobson, Shmarya Levin, and Nahum Sokolow were all veteran Russian Zionists. The headquarters were transferred from Cologne to Berlin and it seemed that a new era had been ushered in. But the 'practicals' did not have it all their own way. The old guard accused the new leadership of embarking on risky and unprofitable economic ventures, of reducing the movement to a colonizing agency, and of throwing diplomacy to the winds. However, there was more rhetoric than substance in these charges. Pioneering experiments could not be measured by a business yardstick and, as events showed, it was colonization that saved Zionism from stagnation. It was also ironic that during the pre-war period Zionist diplomacy was reintroduced by such 'practicals' as Sokolow, Jacobson, and Lichtheim.

The newly founded Russo-German Zionist coalition was sound and enjoyed a wide measure of support. Relations within the Executive were harmonious. This was largely due to ideological identity but even more to the absence of personal rivalries. Warburg was a true gentleman to whom ambition, let alone intrigue, was alien. He shunned politics and left ideological squabbles to others. His passion was practical work in Palestine. He stood firmly by his convictions but his innate modesty and understanding made him an ideal chairman. He was a member of the well-known Hamburg banking family, a professor at the University of Berlin, and a botanist of world repute. He was the co-founder of numerous companies, notably of the Kolonial-Wirtschaftliches Komitee, and very much respected in German academic and official circles. It seemed therefore unusual for a man of his standing to turn to Zionism. What attracted him particularly was the socio-economic experiment in Palestine and the pressing need to ameliorate the position of his people in Eastern Europe. His enthusiasm for colonization was tempered by the rigorous thinking of a scientist.

Unlike Warburg, Hantke came from a traditional background, but in outlook and temperament they suited each other admirably. Self-controlled and of unquestionable integrity, he too was free of any personal ambition. His fine sense of humour and amiability made his companionship pleasant, while his gift for conciliation calmed many storms. He was patient, orderly, punctilious, and had a good analytical mind. These qualities were well tested within the German Zionist Federation, of which he was chairman from 1910. There were far better orators or writers than he, but few excelled his administrative skill. Without it the Executive would have accomplished little.

Politics were left to the Russians. Sokolow was an old hand. In 1905 he had accepted Wolffsohn's invitation to serve as the Secretary-General of the Organization and edit its German and Hebrew organs: *Die Welt* and *Ha-Olam*. Following the defeat of the 'practicals' at the Ninth Congress (1909) he resigned but after his election to the Executive in 1911 he re-entered full-time service of the movement. His reputation as a leading littérateur and speaker had been made much earlier when editor of the Hebrew daily *Hatzefirah* in Warsaw. His linguistic ability was prodigious. He knew half a dozen languages and wrote and spoke fluently in all of them. His writings did not amount to a comprehensive and orderly philosophy, for he was self-taught and his mind was not too methodical. However, if his encyclopedic knowledge did not overwhelm any of his interlocutors it was because of the warmth of his personality and his humility. His versatility, coupled with exemplary manners, stood him in good stead when he became, in subsequent years, the foremost Zionist diplomat.

Jacobson, too, was a promising diplomat. He was the son-in-law of Menahem Ussishkin, the influential Russian Zionist leader. Steeped in Russian and Western culture, Jacobson's manners were refined. Poise and good sense helped him to win converts to Zionism and disarm his critics. By 1911 he already had two years of experience as the Zionist agent in Constantinople, where he was successful in establishing useful contacts with Turkish statesmen and the Press. His campaign did not materially affect Turkish policy towards Zionism but, an optimist by nature and a sincere Turcophil, he never despaired of reaching a *modus vivendi* with Constantinople.

In sharp contrast to his colleagues, Shmarya Levin was a human volcano. Kurt Blumenfeld described him as 'the most colourful personality in the Executive'. He was the Zionist emissary *par excellence* and a splendid orator. His audiences in all parts of the world were swept off their feet by his electrifying addresses. He was angry at Jewish indifference: 'Emancipation would drive the Jews into assimilation and extinction.' His happiest moments were when he spoke about the work of the pioneers in Palestine and the Hebrew renaissance. Levin was more than a propagandist: he was an inspiring teacher of a whole generation of Jewish educators and Zionist youth.[12]

The Eleventh Congress (Vienna, 2–9 Sept. 1913) reconfirmed all the members of the Executive, and in addition elected Dr. Yehiel Tschlenow, a Moscow physician, who thereafter sacrificed his professional career in order to give full-time service to the Zionist cause. He too was an adherent of the 'practical' school and a disciple of Ahad Ha'am. He was not a forceful personality but was highly esteemed in the movement for his sound judgement and tact.[13]

When Congress took stock of the position it had no reason to be dissatisfied. The machinery was running smoothly and the ideological differences were largely reconciled. Settlement in Palestine had passed the experimental stage and the movement was steadily expanding. It was still a minority group within Jewry; its membership did not exceed the figure of 130,000 but this did not reflect the number of sympathizers.[14] Following the February/March 1917 Revolution in Russia, when legal disabilities imposed on the Russian Zionists were lifted, the number of *shekel* payers all over the world rose to 250,000.[15] The budget of the Executive doubled, from 123,000 marks in 1905 to 244,000 marks (equivalent to £12,000) in 1911. The total amount collected by the Jewish National Fund up to mid-1914 was 340,000 marks (£170,000).[16]

Russian Zionists were the most numerous with 36,000 active members; but it was the Germans who provided the movement with organization and ideas. Though opposition to Zionism was strongest among German Jews, the Zionist Federation made impressive progress. From the handful of individuals who founded it in July 1897 it grew by 1912 to 10,000 members, which was a sixth of the number of the Centralverein, the largest Jewish organization in Germany. The budget of the Federation also increased markedly: from 350

[12] These profiles are based on Lichtheim: *Geschichte*, pp. 154–6, 197–201; *idem, She'ar Yashuv*, pp. 129–30; *Rückkehr*, pp. 124–5; Kurt Blumenfeld, *Erlebte Judenfrage* (Stuttgart, 1962), pp. 65–84; Lipsky, op. cit., pp. 65–72, 78–85.

[13] For a biographical sketch see Sokolow, *History of Zionism*, ii, pp. 281–2; an obituary in *Zionist Review* (Mar. 1918); Yechiel Tschlenow, *Pirkey Hayav U' Peulato . . .* [*His Life, Activities . . .*] ed. S. Eisenstadt (Tel Aviv, 1937).

[14] For statistics see *Protokoll, XI. Kongress*, p. 113.

[15] *Türkei* 195, K 692/K 179614–27, K 180216–24; E.A.C. to A.A., 18 Oct. 1917, 19 Feb. 1918. The *shekel* was a nominal membership fee which entitled the contributor to vote in elections to Zionist congresses. Its name was taken from the biblical coin and tax (Exod. 30: 13). See Josef Fraenkel, *The History of the Shekel* (London, 1952).

[16] Gruenbaum, op. cit. iii, pp. 36, 234; Israel Cohen, *The Zionist Movement* (London, 1945), p. 95, note.

marks in 1897 to 240,000 marks in 1912. Within the World Zionist Organization the German *shekel* payers occupied the third place, trailing only behind their Russian and American colleagues, but *per capita* their contributions to the general Zionist cause and its institutions were the highest. This was not because they were wealthier. The ordinary members of the Federation were drawn from the lower middle class, academics, and students; they surpassed their counterparts in their organizational skill, discipline, and a strong sense of duty. They were articulate and ideologically oriented. From October 1911 to May 1912 alone they held over 500 meetings throughout the country. Publications appeared regularly and the *Jüdische Rundschau*, the Federation's organ, made its view known to a wider public.[17] Purchased in 1902 from the *Israelitische Rundschau*, it had within two years doubled its size to sixteen pages or more, and its circulation was the third largest of any Jewish paper in Germany.[18]

German Zionism grew in response to assimilation rather than to anti-Semitism as it did in Eastern Europe. Thus conflict with other sections of Jewry was inevitable. Those who professed to be a religious community rejected nationalism as a dangerous heresy and a sacrilege of their hard-won emancipation; Jewish separatism played into the hands of anti-Semites.[19] The Zionists, on the other hand, pointed out the danger of Jews assimilating themselves out of existence. They called upon their co-religionists to take pride in their national heritage. The self-effacing Jew who concealed his identity, they claimed, earned the contempt of his Gentile neighbour; the proud Jew was respected. Jewish nationalism was not incompatible with German patriotism; nor did it conflict with the ethics of Judaism.

The most outspoken advocates of this thinking were Richard Lichtheim and Kurt Blumenfeld. Deeply assimilated, they turned against the very world they came from. In Lichtheim's family all members were either completely de-judaized or had even been converted to Christianity. They seemed to be unperturbed by anti-

[17] Lichtheim, *Geschichte*, pp. 141–2, 150–3, 164, 175–84; *She'ar Yashuv*, pp. 136–7; *Rückkehr*, pp. 131–2. On Zionism in Germany in the pre-war period see also: Robert Weltsch, 'Deutscher Zionismus in der Rückschau', *In Zwei Welten*, ed. Hans Tramer (Tel Aviv, 1962), pp. 27–42.

[18] *Jüdische Rundschau*, 17 June, pp. 254–5; *Zionistisches A–B–C Buch* (Berlin, 1908), pp. 85–6.

[19] Eugen Fuchs, *Um Deutschtum und Judentum*, ed. L. Hirschfeld (Frankfurt-on-Main, 1919), pp. 22–7, 230–46.

Semitism, but Lichtheim, from his early youth, sensed their insincerity, which bordered on self-delusion. He realized that the Jew was different. An invisible wall separated him and the Gentile. However advanced economically and assimilated culturally he was, he could not be accepted as an equal. Conversion was an easy solution but this Lichtheim discarded as sheer deception. He found his way back to Judaism through Zionism.

Kurt Blumenfeld had an identical career. His father was a liberal and respected judge in East Prussia and his mother a talented pianist; German culture monopolized his parents' interests and they mixed solely with Christian friends. Yet, like Lichtheim, Blumenfeld was quick to note the perpetual alienation that engulfed his fellow co-religionists within the Gentile society. Zionism offered him a release from an intolerable strain and a vehicle through which he could rehabilitate himself as a Jew. He called it 'post-assimilationist Zionism'.

Blumenfeld, Lichtheim, and Pinchas Rosenblüth (later Rosen, Minister of Justice in Israel) were in their twenties when they joined the Zionist movement. They represented the younger generation which challenged the old guard, led by Bodenheimer, for their exclusive concern was with the plight of East European Jewry and its solution. Zionism, they claimed, was applicable to the German scene too; it should restore the true image of the Jew and his identity. This strong nationalist ideology was characteristic of the 'practicals' who, besides colonization of Palestine, became seriously concerned with the spiritual survival of the emancipated Jew in the West. Their moment came in 1910 when Hantke replaced Bodenheimer as chairman of the Zionist Federation. Blumenfeld was elected secretary (from 1911 he was simultaneously Secretary of the Zionist Executive) and Lichtheim was appointed editor of *Die Welt*. Lichtheim's brochure *Das Programm des Zionismus* (*The Zionist Programme*) appeared late in 1911 and, judging from its distribution (20,000 copies), it scored an extraordinary success. Two years later a second edition was printed and it was translated into several languages.[20]

Lichtheim described the moral plight of the German Jews, who in their battle for civic rights had sacrificed their individuality and,

[20] The above is based on Lichtheim, *She'ar Yashuv*, pp. 9–55, 69, 132–4, 151; *Rückkehr*, pp. 17–64, 75–6, 127–9, 142; *idem, Geschichte*, pp. 147–8, 154–6, 169–71. Blumenfeld, op. cit., pp. 27–64.

although they zealously emulated their Gentile fellow citizens, were scorned, hated, and derided. Self-imposed acculturation removed their traditional background but did not make them any more socially acceptable. Rejection in turn bred frustration which bordered on self-hatred and nihilism. Many embraced Christianity but, guided by opportunism, few found happiness and security. At all events, Lichtheim argued, conversion was not a course that Jewish masses were likely to follow. German Jews adopted a middle course, professing themselves to be Germans of Jewish persuasion. But this formula, Lichtheim maintained, was a deliberate distortion of Jewish identity to suit a political convenience. It was artificial, since Judaism was not a set of dogmas or articles of faith which could be categorized like Christian denominations. Jewish festivals and customs bore a national character and were rooted in age-old traditions; so was the perennial hope of a return to Zion. The national and religious components in Judaism were inseparable and the suppression of either of them undermined its very essence. An emasculated and distorted form of religion could not ensure the survival of Jewry.

It was here that Zionism became relevant. For though Palestine could only accommodate a fraction of Jewry, a settlement of between several hundred thousands and one million people there could provide a source of inspiration for those who would remain behind. A model society and centre for Hebrew culture would be built in Palestine. Its influence would radiate through world Jewry and lend it a sense of dignity and inner freedom. With the revival of ancient values Jewish lives would take on a different meaning and purpose. Jews would become better equipped to find their place in the world. Lichtheim rejected the notion that Jewish nationalism was incompatible with patriotism; nor was it 'a return to the ghetto'; it was a bid for the emancipation of the Jews as a people as distinct from the emancipation of individuals; an endeavour towards their spiritual and cultural regeneration.[21]

If Lichtheim made his name as a perceptive writer, Blumenfeld showed his talents as an organizer and orator. Of a methodical mind, he was highly cultured and particularly adept at making contact with the intelligentsia and youth. He steadfastly emphasized the

[21] Richard Lichtheim, *Das Programm des Zionismus* (Berlin, 1911), pp. 25–42. On the Reform, see Seligmann, *Geschichte der jüdischen Reformbewegung;* Philipson, *The Reform Movement in Judaism*; Plant W. Gunter, *The Rise of Reform Judaism* (New York, 1963).

national character of Zionism and called for the transformation of its ideology. Jews should cease to regard themselves foremost as Germans and ought to reassert boldly their own uniqueness. Their 'Jewish personality' would develop freely only when they identified themselves fully with their own past and common future. They should take advantage of the best that European culture could offer, without being totally submerged by it.

Blumenfeld's call for a national renaissance was only a prelude to the more radical concept of a physical return to Palestine. At the Federation's biennial convention, which took place in Posen in 1912, he declared that every Zionist should incorporate settlement in Palestine into his life's programme. Only by self-realization (*persönliche Verwirklichung*) could one ultimately achieve one's own fulfilment. Every Zionist should consider himself a potential citizen of a future Jewish state.

Such an ideology was too radical even for certain Zionists, particularly of the old guard, like Bodenheimer, Franz Oppenheimer, Adolf Friedemann, and Hermann Struck. For them Zionism, though a political movement, was essentially philanthropic in nature, aiming at alleviating the plight of their persecuted brethren in Eastern Europe, while they assumed the role of mentors. A passionate debate engulfed German Zionism during the following two years, and during the Leipzig Convention in 1914 Blumenfeld's concept came under strong fire. Oppenheimer and his supporters deprecated the notion of 'Jewish uprootedness'; he considered himself both a Jew and a German but whose fatherland was Germany. Blumenfeld replied that he merely acknowledged a phenomenon that existed. Jews were uprooted and there was no substitute for the idea of building a Jewish home in the land of their ancestors. An overwhelming majority of the delegates supported him by voting in favour of a 'Palestine-oriented Zionism'. The resolution reflected the mood of disillusionment with the fruits of emancipation (in Prussia, one hundred years old) and the growing sense of alienation. Yet it was not until the thirties, following the Nazi rise to power, that Blumenfeld's ideology became a reality. In 1914 the debate was still academic. Emigration was rare and there were no more than twenty German Zionists living at that time in Palestine.[22]

[22] Lichtheim, *Geschichte*, pp. 142–4, 166–9; *idem*, *She'ar Yashuv*, pp. 132–5; *Rückkehr*, pp. 127–30; Blumenfeld, op. cit., pp. 59–60, 69, 89–92, 113–16; *Jüdische Rundschau*, 14 July 1912, p. 222; ibid. (19 June 1914), pp. 269–70; Weltsch, loc. cit.,

One of the few who did go was Arthur Ruppin. He was a lawyer, an economist, and a social scientist. A promising academic career awaited him in Germany or he could have returned to the family business. What motivated him to settle in such a distant and undeveloped country? As he revealed in his memoirs,

> I had a feeling that no matter how much I would achieve, I would continue to encounter hostility and be regarded as an outsider. I was hoping that in Palestine I would be able to work without friction as a member of the [Jewish] community . . . The possibilities of the country attracted me.[23]

He was born in eastern Germany and despite depressing poverty managed to work his way up and graduate from the universities of Berlin and Halle. A realist to the core, he grew sceptical of emancipation and developed an interest in the contemporary life of his people. In 1904 his book *Die Juden der Gegenwart*[24] appeared, which became the standard work on this subject. The following year he founded the Bureau for Jewish Statistics and began publication of the periodical *Zeitschrift für Demographie und Statistik der Juden*. The Jewish problem and its solution were to preoccupy him for the rest of his life. In 1904, by then a member of the Zionist Organization, he was invited by Wolffsohn and Warburg to go to Palestine on an exploratory mission and in the following year he was asked to found an office there: he was then 32 years old. No better man could have been chosen. A keen observer, he had an unusual gift for diagnosing the sources of maladies and prescribing the necessary remedies. He revealed himself to be a man who could envisage great results from small beginnings. The new social experiment in Palestine excited him and released in him an enormous fund of energy and initiative. Although not an adventurer, he could undertake tremendous risks and make the dream a reality. His arguments were always convincing; they were cool, rational, and analytical.

His first report on his mission in 1907 was a remarkable document. He was heartened by the contribution made by the Jewish settlers to the improvement of Palestinian agriculture; their plantations

---

pp. 31-5; Saul Esh, 'Kurt Blumenfeld on the Modern Jew and Zionism', *Jewish Journal of Sociology*, vi (1964), 232-42; Ismar Schorsch, *Jewish Reactions to German Anti-Semitism, 1870-1914* (New York, 1972), pp. 188-95.

23 Arthur Ruppin, *Memoirs, Diaries, Letters*, ed. Alex Bein (New York, 1971), p. 86.
24 English translation *The Jews of Today* (London, 1913).

were a model of good farming and their colonies looked like 'veritable oases of culture'. Yet their economic foundation was not sound. They limited their cultivation to monoculture such as grapes, oranges, or grain, which made them vulnerable to market uncertainties and, still worse, dependent on cheap hired Arab labour. Under the Rothschild administration they were brought up in a spirit of complete dependence and whenever something went wrong they expected assistance, with the result that they lost their initiative and idealism. Rothschild's enterprise was that of 'a rich man who wanted to indulge in the luxury of seeing a piece of work completed in less time than it should have taken by a process of organic growth'.

What could be done? With regard to the cities, his answer was simple: 'We must liquitate the Chalukka system' and introduce light industry and a variety of crafts. This applied particularly to Jerusalem, which economically was a dead city. But his prime concern was settlement on the land. If the existing colonies were to be rescued from premature ageing, some new blood should be injected. Young and enthusiastic people should be brought in from Europe but not until they were adequately trained would their rejuvenating influence be fully brought to bear. They should be transformed from city dwellers into landworkers. Six years later, in a speech at the Eleventh Zionist Congress, he explained why this principle was so important:

> Only if we create 'a work of our own hands' in Palestine and not by the exploitation of alien labour will we earn for ourselves a moral right to the land which we have legally acquired . . .
> Employment of Jewish workers does not in any way indicate hostility towards the Arabs, but is . . . [an] endeavour to train ourselves to work and fertilize our land with our own sweat.

Some of the newcomers, he insisted, would have to settle on land and engage in mixed farming; the pattern set in the old colonies proved risky, both economically and socially. He proposed to establish a central land purchasing company with a capital of at least one million marks. However, on his return to Palestine in the spring of 1908, when the P.L.D.C. (Palestine Land Development Company) was founded, its capital consisted of 100,000 marks (£5,000), exactly one-tenth of the proposed sum. In addition, he had at his disposal 200,000 marks (£10,000) from the Olive Tree Donation Fund for the creation of a Herzl forest and 100,000 marks from the Palestine Industry Syndicate. The three land reservations of the Jewish National Fund (J.N.F.) proved to be more of a burden than a help. They were isolated, with no water-supply, and therefore unfit for any sort af agricultural enterprise. To sell them was impossible, nor could he let them lie idle, if only because it was forbidden by Turkish law. There was no way out of the dilemma but to take the risk. With such meagre means, as compared to the fifty million marks invested by Baron Rothschild, it seemed foolhardy for Ruppin to embark on a colonization scheme.

But [he noted] optimism triumphed in the end. I said to myself: In the beginning was the deed. The name of that deed was: Kinnereth. I decided to make use of the funds of the PLDC in order to found a Farming colony in the National Fund area.

During the first five years of Ben Shemen and Hulda a considerable number of workers were trained who subsequently were able to make their living from manual labour. Without them the colonies would have withered. But of more momentous import was the success of the experiment in Kinnereth. Dissatisfaction with an autocratic manager, followed by a strike, prompted the workers to suggest that the farm be cultivated on their own responsibility with profits distributed equally amongst themselves. This was a most unorthodox, even a revolutionary, concept. But Ruppin, though not a Socialist or a Communist, was very much impressed by the seriousness with which the workers stated their case. He was a practical man who looked for the best and cheapest way of making young Jews familiar with Palestinian agriculture and believed that this system offered the solution. Thus the first collective farm, the *kevutzah*, was founded. Ruppin modestly admitted later in his memoirs that at that time he did not fully realize the importance of this event for the future development of the country.[25]

The labourers at Kinnereth had come to Palestine with the second *aliya* (1904–14).[26] No other wave of immigration had such high

[25] Arthur Ruppin, *Building Israel. Selected Essays: 1907–1935* (New York, 1949), pp. 1–12, 35–51, 89, 103, 106; *idem, Memoirs*, pp. 86–7, 146–8; Lichtheim, *She'ar Yashuv*, pp. 164–71, 174, *Rückkehr*, pp. 153–60, 163; Bein, *The Return to the Soil*, pp. 45–50.

[26] On which see *Sefer Ha'aliya Hashniya*, ed. E. Schochat (Tel Aviv, 1947); *Sefer Hashomer*, ed. I. Ben-Zvi, I. Schochat, and others (Tel Aviv, 1957); *Moshe Braslavsky, Tnuat Hapoalim Ha'eretz-israelit* (Tel Aviv, 1955), i, pp. 67–134; Berl Katznelson, *Prakim l'Toldoth Tnuat Hapoalim, Kitvei . . .* (Tel Aviv, 1949), xi, pp. 15–31; Ruppin,

quality in human material or was so rich in idealism and originality of thought. Most of the immigrants came from White Russia,
Eastern Poland, and Lithuania. They were craftsmen, clerks, lower-
middle-class people, and graduates of universities and rabbinical
colleges. The 1903 pogroms had had a traumatic effect on them.
They felt particularly affronted by the indifference of the Russian
Socialists, whose ideals they had earlier shared. The Russian Socialists not only refrained from protesting, but cynically commented
that Jewish blood was oil on the wheels of the Socialist revolution.
This convinced the young Jews that it was futile to expect the Jewish
problem to be solved in a socialist regime in Russia. They founded
their own Socialist-Zionist parties, the Poale Zion and the Hapoel
Hatzair, which aimed at the creation of a Jewish labour class in
Palestine. Their adherents were not abstract theoreticians; by
a personal example they hoped to demonstrate how the anomalous
socio-economic structure of their people could be remedied. They
were also impressed by the argument (advanced in Ussishkin's pamphlet *Our Programme*) that unless a Jewish worker was substituted
for the Arab labourer 'the whole Yishuv will be built on sand, or
rather on the edge of a volcano'. Following an appeal by Joseph
Vitkin, a teacher at Kfar Tabor in Lower Galilee and an ideologist,
they made their way to Palestine. Between the beginning of 1904
and the outbreak of the First World War some 35,000 to 40,000
people arrived. Not all stayed; those who did were made of superior
pioneering stuff, without personal or materialistic motives. Their
only ambition was to rebuild their own homeland and form the
nucleus of a new Jewish society based on social justice.

The reality which they encountered in Palestine was discouraging.
Adjustment to manual work was not easy, but the most bitter
disappointment was when they found that they were not wanted.
Most of the Jewish farmers in Judaea and Samaria were content to
employ cheap Arab labour. The pioneers endeavoured to prove that
their own work was of better quality and that they were more reliable
than the Arabs. This was the essence of *Kibbush Ha-Avoda* ('conquest of labour') which became the motto of the second *aliya* in
general. The idea of Jewish labour, however, transcended its economic connotation. It was tinged with ideology and became elevated
to the plane of near-religious mysticism. A. D. Gordon, a man

Memoirs, p. 110; Bein, op. cit., pp. 36–45, 57–71, 76–7, 118–21; Walter Laqueur,
A History of Zionism (London, 1972), pp. 277–95.

of fifty, who had no prior experience in manual work, was a living example of the doctrine that he was preaching. He became its apostle; labour, he maintained, was the basic instrument of Jewish renaissance.

All the same, the Jewish farmers were not impressed. The workers found themselves frequently unemployed. In the summer of 1908 Vitkin conceived a new idea of *Kibbush Ha-Adama* ('conquest of the soil'). The establishment of workers' settlements was to achieve a twofold purpose, of cultivating the J.N.F. lands, which if left unoccupied could be forfeited, and of providing employment. The workers were eager to cultivate the farms on their own responsibility and to pool their earnings. This was the origin of the co-operative system of farming, a unique feature of Jewish labour colonization. The first agricultural commune was founded in Sejera, in Lower Galilee, on the I.C.A. farm. The idea was original. It was born on native Palestinian soil and developed not from a pre-conceived doctrinal concept but as a result of trial and error dictated by local conditions. Sejera was the prototype of Kinnereth, mentioned earlier, and of Degania which became known as the Mother of the *kevutzot*. Of no less significance was the introduction of modern methods in irrigation and mixed farming; it became the pattern for future settlements. The pioneers, who at first seemed to be romantic idealists, showed that Zionism was no Utopia and that the land was cultivable.

The second *aliya* was also concerned with problems of Jewish self-defence, though the idea had germinated earlier in Russia during the 1903 pogroms. Palestine was notorious for its insecurity and the colonists were in the habit of appointing a sheikh as a guardian of their property or of employing Arab watchmen. This arrangement was not satisfactory since the watchmen were often working hand in glove with the robbers. The leaders of the second *aliya* considered it an insult to Jewish dignity and a risk to the very existence of the Yishuv. In 1907 they founded their own organization of watchmen, which in the following year became known as *Ha-Shomer* (the Watchman). It soon proved its worth. Like the workers, the *shomrim* (watchmen) were idealists. Courage and skill in weapon-handling and in horse-riding were essential; so was a command of Arabic. They were familiar with the local customs and took great pains to cultivate friendly relations with the Arab neighbours; their object was not only to repel assaults but to prevent them. It was largely due to this combination of vigilance and diplomacy that no major clashes between Jews and Arabs took place during that period.

Workers' communes in the cities and emancipation of women were further contributions by the second *aliya* to Jewish life in Palestine. In 1910 Shmuel Yavnieli, one of its leaders, went at Ruppin's request as an emissary to the Yemen with the object of furthering emigration to Palestine. Yemenite Jews were steeped in Jewish tradition and throughout their long history had clung tenaciously to the idea of a return to Zion. So great was the enthusiasm that he aroused that he had difficulty in persuading them that he was not the Messiah, and that redemption could be brought about only by their own efforts. As a result, about 2,000 Yemenite Jews emigrated to Palestine prior to the outbreak of the First World War. Most of them became agricultural labourers, others found employment as stonemasons or worked as independent craftsmen. Contingents of immigrants arrived also from Salonica, Bokhara in Central Asia, and other parts of the world.

Ruppin realized that the time element was crucial and made the best use of the funds at his disposal, however limited. 'We do not have time to pursue a money-box policy', he told the Eleventh Zionist Congress,

our work is too urgent. Palestine is being developed and even if we collect millions, they will not suffice to make up later for opportunities missed now. What we can now do with hundreds of thousands, we may later no longer be able to do with millions.[27]

Between 1908 and 1913 some 50,000 dunams (12,500 acres) of land were bought in various parts of the country. In March 1914 Ruppin purchased a large and magnificently situated property on Mount Scopus, designated for a Jewish university in Jerusalem. On the day that the First World War broke out the Palestine Office was on the point of buying 140,000 dunams in the Jezreel Valley. Private investment, both in rural and urban enterprises, was also encouraged. One of the most pressing needs was to provide better housing; conditions in Arab quarters of Jaffa and Jerusalem were unsatisfactory. In 1907 Ruppin, then still a visitor, was approached by a society of middle-class Jews who wished to establish a Jewish suburb near Jaffa. Their capital, however, was short of the required investment, and Ruppin prevailed upon the J.N.F. headquarters to grant

[27] Ruppin, *Memoirs*, p. 147.

a loan in order to make up the balance. On 21 July 1907 he wrote to Cologne:

> I consider it extremely important that there be a Jewish quarter both in Jaffa and Jerusalem . . . The narrow streets, the dirt and the monstrous style of architecture in the present Jewish quarters are a downright disgrace to the Jews and discourages many worth-while people from settling in the country.

Two years later, with Turkish opposition finally overcome, a new suburb was founded and named Tel Aviv. By 1914 its total population had reached the figure of 1,420. It became a bustling centre of trade and culture. Its example inspired urban development in other parts of Palestine, and it was largely at Ruppin's instigation that a modern suburb in Haifa on the slopes of Mount Carmel (later named Hadar Ha-Carmel) was built. Haifa was chosen as the site for a technical college and plans were afoot to found a university in Jerusalem. There was already the beginning of a national library, a theatre, publishing houses, and two Hebrew dailies. Revival of Hebrew was a major achievement. It was used as a language of instruction in schools from kindergartens to the Teachers Seminaries and in public life in general.[28]

In 1912 when Ahad Ha'am, a confirmed pessimist, revisited Palestine he admitted that a miracle had taken place. What had been a vision thirty years earlier had become a reality. 'The Jew can become a capable farmer . . . who understands agriculture . . . and makes a living out of it.' Relations between the colonists and the workers improved substantially; the colonists began to realize that it was not only their duty but also in their interest to patronize Jewish labour. But what delighted Ahad Ha'am most was the refreshing atmosphere of Hebrew national life. A national spiritual centre was in the making, 'a centre of study and learning, of language and literature, of bodily work and spiritual purification'.[29]

In contrast to their achievements in Palestine, diplomatically the Zionists remained in the wilderness. There was not even one capital

---

[28] Ruppin, *Memoirs*, pp. 119–26, 149; *Bericht des Aktion-Komitees der Zionistischen Organisation an den XI. Zionisten Kongress* (Berlin, 1913), p. 111; H. Sacher (ed.) *Zionism and the Jewish Future* (London, 1916), pp. 156–9, 171–95; Bein, op. cit., pp. 122–7; below, pp. 158–60. A dunam equals 1,000 square metres or roughly one-fourth of an acre. The term is derived from the Turkish *dönüm*.

[29] 'Summa Summarum' in *Ten Essays on Zionism and Judaism*, trans. Leon Simon (London, 1922), pp. 143, 148, 154–6.

in Europe to which they could confidently look for support. In Germany the principles laid down by Baron von Richthofen, in his memorandum dated 26 January 1904, remained valid.[30] In March 1907 Baron von Mirbach, Master of Ceremonies and an acquaintance of Bodenheimer, tried in vain to secure an audience for David Wolffsohn with von Tschirschky, the Foreign Minister. 'In view of our relations with Turkey', the latter explained, 'official support of the Zionist aspirations . . . should be weighed with considerable misgivings.'[31] Equally unsuccessful in his endeavour was Jacobus Kann, a member of the Zionist Executive and the private banker of Queen Wilhelmina of the Netherlands. He told Karl von Schlözer, the German Minister in The Hague, that the Zionists had recently won the support of the Rothschilds and were in a position to offer the Sultan the sum of £12,000,000 as a reward for concessions in Palestine; they were also willing to pay an annual tribute of £500,000. Kann wondered whether the Kaiser would receive Wolffsohn and mediate with the Sultan, but von Schlözer thought that the Zionists were likely to find 'safer channels' elsewhere to present their case to the Sultan than through the Kaiser. Berlin's reaction was unequivocal:

That the support of the Zionist wishes would be risky for us—goes without saying. It is therefore recommended to refrain absolutely from giving any committing answer.[32]

Like Herzl, Wolffsohn realized that not until Turkey's attitude changed would the chancelleries of Europe be more forthcoming. Vámbéry specifically advised him not to invoke the Powers' intervention with the Porte; it could do more harm than good. It was also Vámbéry who revealed that Turkey was in the grip of a severe financial crisis and that the moment was 'most propitious' for the Zionists to start a new round of negotiations.[33] Independently, Wolffsohn heard that Dr. Wellisch, a Zionist and the Director of the Health Department at the Turkish Ministry of the Interior, had been advised by Behor Effendi, a Jew and a member of the Parliament, that, should the Zionist Organization render unspecified

---

[30] Above, pp. 114–15.

[31] *E.G.*, Nr. 84, K 181380–5, Mirbach to Tschirschky, 2 Mar. 1907; Tschirschky to Mirbach, 3 Mar. 1907.

[32] Ibid. K 181391, von Schlözer to A.A., 10 Dec. 1907, and A.A.'s marginal annotation.

[33] C.Z.A. W 61 II, Vámbéry to Wolffsohn, 5 Apr., 4 July 1907.

financial services, the Government might prove more amenable to its long-standing request to lift the ban on Jewish immigration to Palestine.[34] Encouraged by the new prospects, Wolffsohn arrived at Constantinople on 25 October 1907 and, after some *pourparlers* with Ottoman officials, submitted a detailed plan. According to this, 50,000 Jewish families were to settle in Palestine (excluding Jerusalem) and adjacent territories. They were to become Ottoman nationals, be subject to Ottoman law, and serve in the army but be exempt from taxation for a period of twenty-five years. The Government would allocate tracts of land which would be registered in the name of the Zionist Organization and thereafter be transferred to the settlers. In return Wolffsohn offered the sum of £2 million. The Turks wanted £26 million but remained silent about the concessions. With so wide a divergence negotiations were deadlocked; the only concession that the Porte granted was permission to establish a bank in Constantinople, named the Anglo-Levantine Banking Co. It served as a cover for a political agency, an arrangement that the Turks apparently did not mind.[35] The man chosen as its head was Dr. Victor Jacobson, a prominent Russian Zionist and director of the Anglo-Palestine Bank branch in Beirut. By merit of his qualities and familiarity with Turkish affairs he was well equipped for his assignment[36] which assumed an even greater importance after the Young Turk Revolution on 24 July 1908.

The overthrow of the Hamidean absolutism and proclamations of liberty and equality were widely interpreted as the beginning of a new era. It evoked tremendous enthusiasm among all the peoples of the Empire.[37] Many Zionists too were optimistic. At a meeting in Paris Nordau stated that had Herzl remained alive, 'he would have been overjoyed and said: "This is my Charter!"'[38] But Wolffsohn was cautious. Yet, with the new regime still not consolidated in Constantinople, he advised Jacobson to maintain the utmost reserve towards Turkish party politics. His task was to gather information and establish contact with competent Turkish persona-

---

[34] C.Z.A. W 61 II; W 8, notes, dated Sept. 1907.

[35] Ibid. W 35/3, p. 26; W 10, pp. 18–25, Wolffsohn's diary (unpublished) and report on his visit to Turkey, 25 Oct.–13 Nov. 1907.

[36] Ibid., file Z 2/6; above, p. 126.

[37] *British Documents on the Origins of the War, 1898–1914*, ed. by G. P. Gooch and H. W. V. Temperley, *The Near East*, v (London, 1934), p. 253; Henry Morgenthau, *Secrets of the Bosphorus, Constantinople, 1913–1916* (London, 1928), p. 7.

[38] Cited in Laqueur, *A History of Zionism*, p. 140.

lities, but not to get involved prematurely in negotiations. 'Explain our point of view in a general way . . . Show that Zionism is compatible with the laws and interests of the country and its people.'[39]

When Jacobson took over his job he found that the climate of opinion was not too unfavourable. Early in September both Ahmed Riza, a prominent Young Turk leader and editor of *Mechveret* (later President of the Chamber), and Tewfik Pasha, the Foreign Minister, in an interview with a correspondent of *Ryetch*, a Russian paper, made some exceptionally friendly statements about Zionism; they were willing to lift former restrictions on Jewish immigration to Palestine. Haim Nahoum, the Deputy Chief Rabbi of Turkey, confirmed that the new regime viewed Jewish settlement in Palestine with favour, though they would not allow Palestine to become politically autonomous. The Turks needed 'an alliance with the Jews in order to counter the influence of the Greeks and the Armenians'. Nahoum was ready to support the Zionists provided they adhered to a moderate programme. Behor Effendi also was of the opinion that the moment was more auspicious than at any time in the past. Yet caution was imperative. He advised Jacobson that it would be more politic to concentrate on specific projects of colonization, which could be met on the administrative plane, rather than present demands which required major decisions of policy and legislation by the Parliament. Vitali Faradji, a leading solicitor and politician, also thought that the Zionists should avoid claiming 'special privileges', and should never mention the word 'autonomy'. This would play directly into the hands of their enemies, who were still quite numerous. Thus Ekrem Bey, the former Governor of Jerusalem, in an official memorandum depicted the Russian Jews as a 'dangerous element' and 'detrimental to the Empire', whose influx should be checked. Ekrem's memorandum had an impact. A few days later Ibrahim Hakki Pasha, the Minister of the Interior, told Vladimir Jabotinsky, the Constantinople correspondent of the Russian paper *Razsvyet*, that the Government was disinclined to allow further Jewish immigration to Palestine. By 21 October Jacobson had reached the conclusion that the Young Turk Revolution was by no means synonymous with a change of attitude towards Zionism.[40]

In fact, the policy had not crystallized; various pronouncements reflected the views of their authors rather than the view of the Porte

[39] C.Z.A. Z 2/7, Wolffsohn to Jacobson, 31 Aug., 15 Sept. 1908.
[40] Ibid., Jacobson to Wolffsohn, 3, 9, 10, 16 Sept., 8, 21 Oct. 1907.

as a whole. Subhi Bey, who had been appointed to replace Ekrem as the Governor of Jerusalem, told Jacobson that no decision had been taken and that he was still awaiting instructions. Jacobson thereupon intensified his lobbying of individual Turkish politicians. He also met two Jerusalemite Arab deputies to the Ottoman Parliament, Said Effendi and Rohdi Bey el-Khalidi. He noted: 'We should do everything in our power to be on good terms with Arab [Palestinian] leaders. The Turks will not antagonize them for our sake. Their protests . . . may cause us a great deal of damage.'[41]

Ottoman Jewry too commanded Jacobson's attention. 'If won over', he wrote to Wolffsohn on 8 February 1909, 'they could be the best intermediaries between ourselves and the Turks, while if inimical, they might harm us.' A great deal of education was still needed since, as Nahoum told him, Ottoman Jewry was largely materialistic and indifferent. Some individuals were actively opposed to Zionism, fearing that it would invite the Government's wrath on Ottoman Jews as a whole. Jacobson took great pains to dispel the notion that Zionism entertained separatist aspirations and ran counter to Ottoman interests. He also endeavoured to cultivate friendly relations with representatives of non-Zionist Jewish organizations, such as the Alliance Israélite Universelle and the I.C.A.[42] His efforts, as well as those of Jabotinsky who assisted him, bore fruit, since there was much latent sentiment for the idea of settlement in the Holy Land; the Jewish community of Salonica in particular proved a tower of strength.

There were approximately 80,000 Jews in Salonica, out of a total population of 173,000. Jews could be found in almost every profession; Jewish stevedores were famous and on the Sabbath the town and port came to a standstill. Salonica Jews were predominantly liberal.[43] They were also acutely aware of their ethnic peculiarities. Jacob Meir, their Chief Rabbi (later Sephardic Chief Rabbi of Palestine), was very sympathetic to Zionism; so was Saadia Levi, the editor of *L'Epoca*, the local Jewish paper, and Joseph Naor, the respected Mayor of Salonica. But the greatest gain was Emmanuel Carasso, a prominent figure in the Young Turk movement and a deputy for Salonica in the Ottoman Parliament. He thought that the

[41] C.Z.A. Z 2/7, same to same, 23 Sept., 24 Oct., 5 Dec. 1907.
[42] Ibid., same to same, 30 Nov., 21, 31 Dec. 1908, 19 Jan. 1909.
[43] *Encyclopaedia Judaica*, 14 (Berlin, 1928), p. 703; P.R.O., F.O. 800/79, *Private Papers of Sir Edward Grey* (1911), Fitzmaurice to Tyrrel, n.d. (received in London on 9 Mar. 1911).

leadership of the Committee of Union and Progress (C.U.P.) was not as hostile to Zionism as was generally assumed, though Zionist aims should be made more palatable to it. Of equal importance was the conversion of Nissim Matzliach Effendi and Nissim Russo, both of whom were deputies to the Ottoman Parliament, the former for Smyrna and the latter for Ismir(?). They were members of the small group that founded the C.U.P. and, despite their youth, were exceedingly influential. Matzliach was secretary of the C.U.P. and thereafter also of the Parliament.[44]

Like Carasso, Russo and Matzliach saw no incompatibility between patriotism and interest in Palestine. They were eager to convince Turkish politicians that opposition to Zionism was based on a misconception. In a meeting which took place on 31 December 1908 in the presence of Jacobson and Jabotinsky they declared that they had decided to join the Zionist Organization and found an Ottoman branch, provided it would disclaim any separatist political aims. 'We agree to the Zionist idea and it is merely a question of finding the right way to proceed.' They suggested that the C.U.P. should first be won over and through it the Parliament and consequently also the Government. Hilmi Pasha was singled out in particular. He was the most influential statesman in the Parliament and Minister of the Interior, the 'man of the future'. Russo was his former secretary and hoped to sway him. Jointly with Matzliach he considered submitting a memorandum to the C.U.P. and the Ministry of the Interior and, in order to keep the public in Constantinople better informed, they thought it absolutely essential that the Zionists establish a paper.[45]

Behor Effendi, who in the meantime was elected Senator (the only Jew to attain that eminence), became appreciably friendlier. This was also true of Faradji who thought that the development of an intellectual centre in Palestine was of crucial importance to world Jewry; the absence of anti-Semitism in Turkey made the idea realizable. This coincided with the proposal made by Carasso early in February 1909 to found an Ottoman Immigration Company for Palestine and Turkey in general. The phrase 'Turkey in general' was

[44] C.Z.A. Z 2/7, Jacobson to Wolffsohn, 25 Nov., 10, 18, 22, 29 Dec. 1907. On Carasso see Dubnow, *Die neueste Geschichte*, iii, pp. 540–4; obituary notice in *The Times* (8 June 1934), p. 19; Abraham Galante, *Turcs et Juifs*, pp. 86–90, where there is a description of Russo, Matzliach, and other leaders.

[45] C.Z.A. Z 2/7 Jacobson to Wolffsohn, 1, 11 Jan. 1909 and App. 'Minute of the meeting . . . 31 December 1908', 4, 8 Feb. 1909.

apparently meant to dispel the suspicion that Jews were bent on concentrating in a single territory as the first step towards their objective of political autonomy. Moreover, a number of Turkish non-Jewish personalities were to be invited to join the Board. Jacobson did not object to Carasso's ideas. His instinct told him that such phrasing might break the ice with the Porte and that, should the Zionists reach an accord with the Alliance, I.T.O., I.C.A., and the Hilfsverein, a division of spheres in colonization could be charted out, the Zionists concentrating in Palestine and the others in the neighbouring countries. Indicative of the improved atmosphere was a congratulatory cable sent by Nahoum, shortly after his election as Chief Rabbi of Turkey, to a Zionist meeting in Odessa; the names of Russo and Matzliach were appended to the telegram. Jacobson commented that three or four months ago 'this would have been impossible. That [any Jewish leader] should demonstrate here his sympathy with Zionism so openly is a real victory.'[46]

Wolffsohn welcomed this development and readily assured Russo and Matzliach of his movement's loyalty to Turkey. The charge that it constituted a 'danger' was 'a monstrous folly. Zionism had nothing in common with the tendencies directed against the integrity of the Ottoman Empire ... Its realization is in full harmony with the interests of your homeland.' The immigrants would embrace Ottoman nationality and contribute to the country's progress in agriculture and industry. 'We demand for our unhappy people a small corner on earth where, under the protection of the new and liberal Turkey . . . they could fully develop according to their national characteristics.'[47] Several days later Sokolow, the General Secretary of the Zionist Organization, denied in a leading article in *Die Welt* (22 January 1909) the allegation that Zionism aimed at the establishment of an independent Jewish state; there was no word of it in the Basle Programme.

Russo and Matzliach soon approached a number of prominent C.U.P. leaders such as Ahmed Riza, Enver Bey, and Talaat Bey, and found them quite sympathetic; the most explicit statement was made by Niazim Bey, a leading member of the Unionist Central Committee. He would like to have six to eight million Jews in Tur-

[46] C.Z.A. Z 2/7, same to same, 18 Dec. 1908, 19 Jan., 4, 8 Feb. 1909. On the Hilfsverein der deutschen Juden see Ch. 9.

[47] Ibid., Wolffsohn to Matzliach and Russo, 24 Jan. 1908. The draft was prepared by Jacobson (letter dated 14 Jan.).

key; they were the 'most reliable element'. He approved of Carasso's plan and was willing to join the board of the proposed Immigration Company but with regard to Palestine he would allow no more than two to four million Jews to come; settlement in excess of this number would constitute 'a danger'.[48]

Jacobson kept in touch also with the Decentralization party of Prince Sabaheddin. Statements made by Fazli Bey, one of its leaders, sounded even more encouraging but, realizing that its fortunes in Ottoman politics were declining, Jacobson, unlike Wolffsohn and Nordau, decided to stick to the pro-C.U.P. line. However, his optimism was tempered by apprehension lest the newly formed Arab party in the Ottoman Parliament would become a focus of opposition. But Niazim reassured him that the very fact that Arab deputies, particularly those from Syria, were opposed to C.U.P. would weigh strongly in the Zionists' favour.[49]

Jacobson had hardly taken stock of the situation when the Young Turks staged their second *coup* in April 1909. It brought in its wake a radical change in direction. Promises of equality to all Ottoman subjects without distinction of religion and race became invalid and slogans like Freedom and Liberty were discarded. Ottomanism gave way to Turkism and the dream of a free association of peoples in a multinational and multidenominational Empire vanished for ever. Turkey became a centralized state. For the non-Turkish nationalities this was a crippling blow. But the Young Turks also had grievances. Their principal concern was how to save the Empire. Like the Young Ottomans of the 1860s and 1870s they curbed the power of the Sultan and tried to satisfy the aspirations of the minorities in the hope that constitutional government and equality of rights would give greater stability to the Empire.[50] However, neither policy lived up to their expectations. Abdul Hamid was plotting against the Young Turks, while the non-Turkish elements were set on a course leading towards autonomy and secession. On 5 October 1908 Bulgaria declared her complete independence. The next day Crete announced her decision to unite with Greece and on the same day Austria-Hungary annexed Bosnia and Hercegovina. These crises, coming in quick succession, had a traumatic effect on the Young

---

[48] Ibid., Jacobson to Wolffsohn 8, 12 Feb. 1909.

[49] Ibid., same to same, 8, 11, 12, 15 Feb. 1909. On Sabaheddin's attitude see same to same, 5 Dec. 1908.

[50] Feroz Ahmad, *The Young Turks* (Oxford University Press, 1969), p. 16; Bernard Lewis, *The Emergence of Modern Turkey*, pp. 208-9.

Turks. They were also disappointed by the voting pattern of the non-Turkish deputies in the Ottoman Parliament; the Arabs, the Greeks, and the Armenians consistently opposed them.[51] With the fear of losing the Empire uppermost in their minds, a *modus vivendi* with the non-Turkish nationalities after the April 1909 *coup* was doomed.

The recrudescence of Turkish nationalism blighted the Zionists' prospects. The absence of co-ordination between Jewish organizations was another factor which adversely affected their standing. The Alliance Israélite Universelle especially, bent on furthering its own and French interests in the East, became progressively more vociferous in criticizing Zionist ideology. It culminated in a speech made by Narcisse Levene, the Alliance's President, during a reception given to an Ottoman parliamentary delegation in Paris in the summer of 1909. The Turkish Press picked up the theme, and consequently some of the Ottoman Jewish leaders damped down their earlier enthusiasm. Those involved were closely linked with the Alliance, like Chief Rabbi Nahoum. Arab opposition likewise became more vocal. It was manifest among the landowners who, unlike the *fellahin*, feared that increased Jewish immigration would undermine their privileged social and economic position.[52]

In June 1909, when Wolffsohn, accompanied by Sokolow, arrived in Constantinople for renewed negotiations, the atmosphere was not conductive to a mutual understanding. Wolffsohn met Husain Hilmi Pasha, the Grand Vizier, Ahmed Riza, the President of the Chamber, and a number of ministers and parliamentarians. Carasso's project served as a basis for negotiations, but it soon became apparent that the two parties were at cross-purposes. Wolffsohn maintained that Palestine and the neighbouring countries should be designated as the territory for Jewish immigration, whereas the Turks insisted on the phrase 'all' Turkish provinces without making any specific reference to Palestine. Hilmi's refusal to abrogate the prohibition laws[53] meant that legally Palestine remained out of bounds.

---

[51] Abraham Elmaliyach, *Palestine and Syria during the First World War* (Hebrew) (Jerusalem, 1928–9), i, p. 255. In 1908 out of the total of 288 there were 147 Turkish, 60 Arab, 27 Albanians, 26 Greek, 14 Armenians, 10 Slavs, and 4 Jewish deputies in the Ottoman Parliament (Ahmad, op. cit., pp. 4, 155).

[52] C.Z.A. Z 2/247, Jacobson's statement at the meeting of the E.A.C., 27 Apr. 1911; Z 2/8, Jacobson to Wolffsohn, 7, 8 Nov. 1909; Z 2/31, circular dated 8 May 1911 (secret).

[53] Ibid. W 16, Wolffsohn to Jacobus Kann, 13 July, 10 Aug. 1909; Z 2/8, Jacobson to E.A.C., 9 Sept. 1909.

Following Wolffsohn's departure Jacobson made another effort to convince the Porte. On 20 September he met Djavid Bey, the Minister of Finance, and two weeks later Hamada Pasha, the Minister of the Waqf properties, and separately Talaat Bey, the Minister of the Interior. At the latter's request Wolffsohn forwarded a memorandum in which he explained the historical and religious attachment of the Jews to Palestine and reiterated the points made during his meeting with Hilmi Pasha.[54] It elicited no response. None the less, the Zionists continued to protest their loyalty. In his opening address at the Ninth Congress on 26 December 1909 Wolffsohn declared:

> We can find no incompatibility between Ottoman interests and Zionist ambitions . . . The integrity of the Turkish State, its position as a world Power, its welfare and prosperous development fully accord with the very postulates of our work . . . We consider its new liberal Constitution an adequate guarantee for our personal and national security.

Wolffsohn thus implicitly revoked the idea of the charter. Nordau pointed out that the charter was Herzl's personal idea which had outlived its usefulness; it was a means to an end. In the absolutist regime the Zionists were bound to ask for guarantees but under the new constitution special privileges were unnecessary. 'We respectfully deposit the charter idea in the archives of modern political Zionism and speak of it no more. The Charter has nothing to do with the Basle Programme.' He dismissed the notion that the phrase *öffentlich-rechtlich gesicherte Heimstätte* (secured by public law) implied intervention by foreign Powers; it meant 'secured by public Ottoman law'. Personally, when participating in the drafting of the Basle Programme at the First Zionist Congress, he favoured the shorter version *rechtlich gesicherte Heimstätte*, but in order to reach a consensus, Herzl prefixed the word *öffentlich*, which should, however, not be misread. The allegation that the Zionists nourished separatist aspirations and wished to found a state of their own was 'ridiculous'.

> We aspire to build within the framework of the Ottoman Empire a nationality like other nationalities in the Ottoman realm. Our ambition is to earn the reputation of being the most loyal, trustworthy, and useful nation among the national groups, but as a Jewish nation.

---

[54] Ibid. Z 2/8, Jacobson to Wolffsohn, 20 Sept., 8 Nov. 1909; Z 2/9 Wolffsohn to Jacobson, 2 Dec. 1909 and Appendix.

Nordau was prepared to waive the idea of the charter but not of Jewish nationalism. And in an oblique reference to the Porte he stated that the proposal that the Zionists should immigrate to Palestine, or still worse to Asia Minor or Macedonia, as Ottoman Jews, was inadmissable. 'If we wish to assimilate we have a closer and easier way of doing it at home.'[55]

The Zionists' declarations, though motivated by political expediency, were sincere. Loyalty to Turkey became the corner-stone of their policy, almost an article of faith. All the same the Turks were not impressed. With their bitter experience in the Balkans fresh in their minds, they would not risk creating a new nationality, however trustworthy. With the regime of Capitulations still in force and the majority of Jewish settlers in Palestine reluctant to adopt Ottoman nationality, the Porte had reason to be suspicious.

On his return to Constantinople early in 1910 Jacobson found no friends in official circles. Niazim Bey, the Young Turk leader, told him that he still favoured Jewish immigration to Turkey but evinced no sympathy towards Zionist aspirations, which, he implied, were 'separatist'; they could undermine the hitherto harmonious relations with the Jewish community. This he would regret since the Jews were 'a very valuable element'. Moheidin Bey, the Prefect of Pera, and Chief Rabbi Nahoum confirmed that in the ruling circles in Constantinople hostility towards Zionism was increasing.[56] In consequence Ottoman Jewish leaders became reserved. Jacobson could hardly rely on Ezechiel Sasson, the Baghdad Jewish Deputy to Parliament, whom he termed 'an Arab patriot',[57] but even Carasso, Matzliach, and Russo remained aloof. David Fresco, the editor of *El Tiempo*, the Judaeo-Spanish periodical, with whom Jacobson planned in 1908 to co-edit a paper, turned against the Zionists and in a series of articles from December 1910 till February 1911 accused them of disloyalty to Turkey.

Jacobson did his best to parry Fresco's assaults and to neutralize his influence over Chief Rabbi Nahoum; this was not easy since Nahoum was at that time being attacked by the Ashkenazi Jewish community in Constantinople, who incidentally were also Zionist-oriented. The Ashkenazim challenged the Sepharadi pre-eminence and managed almost to unseat Nahoum but, thanks to Jacobson's

[55] *Protokoll, IX. Kongress*, pp. 6–8, 21–5; cf. above, p. 95.
[56] C.Z.A. Z 2/9, Jacobson to Kann, 7 Sept. 1910.
[57] Ibid. Z 2/7, Jacobson to Wolffsohn, 22 Feb. 1909.

good sense, his relations with Nahoum remained friendly despite the controversy.[58] He noted that a basic undercurrent of sympathy with the Zionist ideal still existed among Ottoman Jewry, though it was subdued and inarticulate. To create a more favourable climate of opinion he founded three papers: *Ha-Mevasser* in Hebrew, *L'Aurore* in French, and *El-Judeo* in the Judaeo-Spanish dialect, for which he had been pressing since the autumn of 1908. Their editor-in-chief was Vladimir Jabotinsky, a brilliant orator, writer, and linguist, whose pen and political insight made them informative organs as well as attractive to the growing readership among Jewish youth and intelligentsia. A subsidy of £1,000 which had been approved by the Ninth Zionist Congress made the papers financially sound.

Of a different order was the Zionist's co-operation with Jalal Nuri Bey, a young Turkish writer in the publication of the daily *Le Jeune Turc*, formerly known as *Courier d'Orient*. Here, too, full use was made of Jabotinsky's talents and in consequence the paper grew both in stature and circulation. It was directed primarily towards the educated élite of Turkish society, and its editorials were often quoted in Parliament and by foreign embassies. Its premises were thrown open to writers and politicians who used to meet there informally. This gave Jacobson an opportunity to broaden his circle of acquaintances. *Le Jeune Turc* was a Turkish paper, but against an annual subsidy of £1,000 Nuri agreed to advocate a liberal policy towards non-Turkish nationalities and rebut anti-Zionist articles or statements whenever they were made. The agreement did not cover matters of foreign policy and this was a flaw which did the Zionists no good.[59]

Le Jeune Turc soon became noted for its unfriendly tone towards Britain; the articles which appeared early in February 1911 were notorious. They were written by Ahmed Agayeff, an extreme Turkish nationalist writer, and by the editor himself. Embarrassed, Wolffsohn protested to Jacobson:

The Jews generally, and especially the Zionists, have more to thank England for than all the other Powers put together . . . I implore you to

---

[58] Ibid., same to same, 4 Sept., 3 Nov. 1908; P. A. Alsberg, 'The Political Orientation of the Zionist Executive on the Eve of the First World War' (Hebrew), *Zion* (1951), nos. 2-3, pp. 153-4.

[59] C.Z.A. Z 2/12, Jacobson to E.A.C., 8 June 1911; Z 2/245, Jacobson's statement at the E.A.C.'s meeting, 23 Nov. 1910; Z 2/10, Z 2/11, Jacobson's letters to E.A.C., Jan. 1910–Feb. 1911; Lichtheim, *Shear Yashuv*, pp. 200-1; *Rückkehr*, p. 187; J. B. Schechtman, *The Jabotinsky Story, 1880-1923* (New York, 1956), i, pp. 156-7.

take care that the ultrapatriotic pronouncements of our friend Jalal and his assistants do not land us in trouble. I fear that *Le Jeune Turc* has already caused us irreparable damage.

Jacobson agreed with Wolffsohn but was in no position to dictate the paper's policy on foreign affairs; nor did he deem it wise to intervene when its popularity in the Ottoman capital was on the ascendant for its vigorous defence of Turkish national interests.[60]

Wolffsohn's intuition was not at fault. In the British Embassy in Constantinople it became 'an *idée fixe* that powerful Jewish forces closely linked with Germany were working to undermine the British position in the East, and that among these must be counted the Zionists.'[61] Sir Gerard Lowther, the Ambassador, forwarded to London copies of articles in *Le Jeune Turc* which, he maintained, was 'financed and directed by Jews'.[62] He reasoned that

the Turk, devoid of real business instincts, has come under the almost exclusive economic and financial domination of the Jew . . . and [that] as Turkey happens to contain the places sacred to Israel, it is natural that the Jew should strive to maintain a position of exclusive influence and utilize it for the furtherance of his ideals, viz. the ultimate creation of an autonomous Jewish state in Palestine or Babylonia . . . In return for 'unrestricted immigration' of foreign Jews he has offered the Young Turk . . . to take over the whole of the Turkish National Debt.

Moreover,

The Jew hates Russia and its Government, and the fact that England is now friendly with Russia has the effect of making the Jews to a certain extent anti-British in Turkey and Persia—a consideration to which the Germans are . . . alive. The Jew can help the Young Turk with brains, business enterprise, his enormous influence in the press of Europe, and money in return for economic advantages and the realisation of the ideals of Israel, while the Young Turk wants to regain and assert his national independence and get rid of the tutelage of Europe, as part of a general Asiatic revival.[63]

---

[60] C.Z.A. Z 2/11, Wolffsohn to Jacobson, 15 Feb. 1911; Jacobson to Wolffsohn, 16 Feb. 1911; Lichtheim, *She'ar Yashuv*, pp. 201–2; *Rückkehr*, pp. 187–8.

[61] Leonard Stein, *The Balfour Declaration* (London, 1961), p. 34 et seq.

[62] *British Documents on the Origins of the War, 1898–1914*, x, Pt. II, no. 1, Lowther to F.O., 22 Aug. 1910.

[63] Elie Kedourie, 'Young Turks, Freemasons and Jews', *Middle Eastern Studies* (January 1971), see App. Lowther to Hardinge, 29 May 1910, pp. 99, 100.

This was a gross exaggeration. The Zionists were isolated at that time and the Ottoman Jews were quite unable to influence their Government's policy. The notion that international Jewry, jointly with the Freemasons and the C.U.P., was bent on eliminating British positions in Egypt and Mesopotamia was fantasy.

Yet it was this very misconception that dictated British policy. With their fortunes in the Ottoman capital on the decline, they were determined to bring about the downfall of the Young Turks; those singled out were Talaat Bey, Minister of the Interior, and Djavid Bey, the Minister of Finance, the first 'of Gypsy descent' and the latter 'a crypto-Jew . . . the only members of the Cabinet who really count . . . the apex of Freemasonry in Turkey'.[64] This was why London (as well as Paris) tried to impose such humiliating conditions on Djavid during his negotiations for a loan. His fall, and that of the committee, were averted because at the crucial moment the Germans stepped in and offered the Turks generous financial help on terms that in no way offended their dignity.[65] This was also why the British so assiduously encouraged the Opposition party.[66] Ambassador Marschall was quick to note how anti-Jewish sentiment was whipped up and directed also against Dönmeh,[67] Djavid in particular.

There is no doubt that anti-Semitism is being encouraged by the English in order to bring about the downfall of Djavid Bey and Hakki Pasha [the Grand Vizier]. Fitzmaurice, the First Dragoman of the British Embassy, is said to be extremely active in this respect.[68]

[64] Ibid., p. 98. On the decline of British standing in Turkey see ibid., pp. 89–90; W. W. Gottlieb, *Studies in Secret Diplomacy during the First World War* (London, 1957), pp. 21–4. [65] Ahmad, op. cit., pp. 79–81.

[66] The Opposition, founded in Apr. 1909 as the Society of Muhammed, was crushed in the summer of 1910 but reappeared early in 1911 under the name of the 'New Party'. It resented the C.U.P.'s westernizing reform and aspired at the restoration of the Muslim ideals of state (ibid., pp. 40–3, 86–90).

[67] Dönmeh is the Turkish for 'Apostates'. It is the name of a Judaeo-Muslim sect founded by those adherents of Shabbetai Tzevi who followed his example in adopting in 1666 the Islamic faith. Though ostensibly Muslim, the sect maintains many Jewish practices in secret, believes in Shabbetai Tzevi as the Messiah, and in certain antinomian doctrines. Some of the Dönmeh, notably Djavid Bey, took a leading part in the Young Turk Revolution of 1908.

[68] *Türkei* 195, K 176294–5, Marschall to Bethmann-Hollweg, 3 Mar. 1911, dis. no. 57. Fitzmaurice was a 'rabid Catholic' who hated the Freemasons and Jews with 'a religious hatred', sincerely believing that they dominated the Young Turk movement. (*T. E. Lawrence to his Biographers, Liddel Hart and Robert Graves* (London, 1938), p. 88.) Fitzmaurice later showed some friendly interest in Zionism (Stein, op. cit., p. 34 n. 121; Friedman, *The Question of Palestine*, p. 54). For Fitzmaurice's intrigues against the Porte see Djemal Pasha, *Memoirs of a Turkish Statesman, 1913–1919* (London, 1922), pp. 30, 33–4, 45, 48.

Matters came to a head during the debate in Parliament on 1 March 1911. Cosimidi Effendi, an Opposition leader, accused Djavid Bey of subordinating state interests to those of the Jews, while Ismail Bey, his colleague, saw in Djavid's negotiations with Sir Ernest Cassel of London, as well as with the Dreyfus Bank and the Mobiller Co. of Paris, 'a finger of Zionism'. Zionism was an 'evil creed. Its aim was to bring to Palestine a great number of foreign Jews, purchase land and erect a Jewish state there.' Despite strong protests from deputies Carasso and Matzliach, Ismail accused the Government of failing to check the Zionists, who counted upon co-operation of highly placed Jews in Turkey and aspired to extend their influence 'from Palestine to Mesopotamia'.

Talaat replied that the Zionists' overtures had been rejected and accused Ismail of slandering the faithful Jewish community. Hakki Pasha, the Grand Vizier, added that Ottoman Jews were 'realistic and practical people' who would not let themselves be misled by Zionist dreams. During the reign of Abdul Aziz colonization of Palestine by Jews and non-Jews was permitted but, following the Crimean War, when the Government had realized how injurious the system of Capitulations was, particularly as the newcomers declined to surrender their original nationality, all foreign immigration was prohibited. This policy, Hakki maintained, was still in force. The charge that negotiations for a loan with the British and French firms were inspired by the Zionists was 'ridiculous'. In fact, it was the Deutsche Bank that showed understanding of Turkey's needs.[69]

However, the Opposition, reinforced by a splinter group from the C.U.P., became progressively more clamorous. They capitalized on the slogan 'Islam is in danger', and used a chance theft in the Mosque of Omar in Jerusalem to accuse the Young Turks, Freemasons, Djavid Bey, and his co-religionists of selling religious treasures to the infidel. Djavid was also charged with nepotism and of furthering the aims of Zionism. Marschall saw in these tactics a determined effort to unseat the Government and ensure Islamic predominance.[70] But what infuriated him most was the discovery of British involvement in this campaign in order to discredit Germany. Hans von Miquel, the Embassy's Counsellor, wrote:

[69] *Türkei* 195, K 176296–8, *La Turquie* (2 Mar. 1911); C.Z.A. Z 2/11, Jacobson to Wolffsohn, 2 Mar. 1911.

[70] *Türkei* 195, K 176310–17, Marschall to Bethmann Hollweg, 22 Apr. 1911, tel. no. 81.

When the intrigues of Mr. Fitzmaurice . . . and his close association with the Members of Parliament were more closely examined, it became evident that it was he who was arousing feelings against us by claiming that Zionism and the placing of [Ottoman] Jews in positions of power, is our work . . . Fitzmaurice's insinuations that Germany is the protecting power of Zionism are ridiculous . . . since it is well known that we are opposed to the founding of any foreign political milieu within the Ottoman Empire.

Von Miquel presumed that the holding of the recent Zionist Congress in Germany, the use of German as the language of communication, and the German names of many of the Zionist leaders served Fitzmaurice as a pretext for his argument, though perhaps Germany herself had 'unconsciously played a part' in creating that impression. He was critical also of the Zionists for their lack of caution which unnecessarily irritated the Turks and the Arabs. He recommended:

Just as the *Alldeutschen* have become much more cautious with their plans for founding German colonies along the Baghdad Railway, so it will be a good thing if the Zionists dilute their wine too. Otherwise they will harm other Jews in Turkey and will hinder the German Government from intervening on behalf of those German-Jewish undertakings, which, in principle, it is often glad to help.[71]

[71] Ibid. K 176325–9, von Miquel to Bethmann Hollweg, 26 July 1911, dis. no. 202. The idea of the colonization of Asia Minor by means of large societies established along the Anatolian and Baghdad railways was propounded by Dr. Kaerger in the *Alldeutsche Blätter* (Lewin, *The German Road to the East*, p. 31). The *Blätter* was the chief organ of the Pan-Germans, who preached vigorously the idea of political absorption of Turkey. On the Pan-German League and its aims see Snyder, *From Bismarck to Hitler*, p. 112.

9

Peaceful Penetration

WHATEVER the motives compelling German diplomacy to dissociate itself from the support of Zionism, interest in Jewish colonization in Palestine persisted. 'If we are willing to see a Jewish settlement in Palestine,' wrote Dr. von Miquel in his report of 26 July 1911, 'we are concerned with those Jews who refuse to participate in the Zionist movement and who can be useful to us because of their knowledge of the German language.' Like the French, the Germans were quick to grasp the importance of their language as a medium which could ease peaceful economic and cultural penetration, and in the process the Jews were singled out as the most suitable agents for its dissemination.

Assurances of respect for the integrity of the Ottoman Empire did not prevent Germany from pursuing her policy of winning paramount influence in this part of the world. Between 1891 and 1913 the Reich's trade was doubled, and by the outbreak of war one-tenth of the 24 billion marks invested abroad was in Turkey. There was also a notable increase in German trade with Palestine and Syria. In 1899 the Deutsche Palästina Bank was founded with branches all over the country. Religious activities too were intensified. Following the Kaiser's visit the Jerusalem-Verein erected the Church of the Redeemer under the patronage of Augusta Victoria, the Kaiserin, and the famous Stiftung on the Mount of Olives, built in 1910, was also dedicated to her. The Palästina-Verein, a society for the promotion of Catholic missions in the Holy Land, established and maintained schools, hospitals, dormitories, as well as churches, which were instrumental in the propagation of *Deutschtum*. The Jerusalem Verein alone maintained in 1902 eight schools with more than 430 pupils.[1]

[1] Paul Rohrbach, *Deutschland unter den Weltvölkern* (Berlin, 1908), p. 323; Gottlieb, *Studies in Secret Diplomacy*, pp. 21–4; Earle, *Turkey, the Great Powers and the Bagdad*

The German drive to the East had, however, one inherent weakness: the flow of capital was not backed by a stream of immigrants. Thus there was a lack of security for the tremendous investments, which only a planned colonization could have provided. As Dr. Curt Nawratzki pointed out, the difficulties in the way of European settlement in Asiatic Turkey were almost insurmountable. The inhospitable climate ruled out any possibility of large-scale colonization by Europeans,[2] and political difficulties were also discouraging. After the Crimean War the Ottoman Government put every possible obstacle in the way of foreign colonization. So deep rooted was its opposition that General von der Goltz had to advise his countrymen 'not to migrate to the Near East if friendly relations with the Ottoman Empire were to be maintained', an opinion shared by Dr. Paul Rohrbach, a noted German writer on Eastern affairs. A secret clause to the Baghdad Railway concession of 1903 stipulated that the Deutsche Bank should discourage German or other foreign immigration into Turkey, the only exception being individuals wanting to settle in the Holy Land for religious reasons.[3] No wonder that in these circumstances the German colonies in Palestine failed to expand; until 1914 their total population did not exceed 2,500. Politically and economically they were only a minor asset.[4]

This helps to explain why Jewish colonization, expanding steadily in spite of Turkish opposition, attracted the attention of German diplomats. In 1911, when Dr. von Miquel visited Palestine, he found the Jewish colonies 'good and prosperous', but it was not until the following year that the Consulate and some economists in Germany discovered that the Jewish settlement in Palestine might be useful for German interests. This discovery placed Berlin in a dilemma as to the expediency of reaching an accommodation with the Zionists, since it was they who were the driving force behind the colonization schemes. Until that time the Wilhelmstrasse had dealt exclusively with non-Zionist German Jews. It was not only that their patriotism

Railway, pp. 37, 89–9, 132–6. Earle makes a number of errors: the majority of Jewish immigrants at this period originated in Russia and Romania, not Germany; the Hilfsverein was not 'the German section' of the Alliance Israélite Universelle, and the latter was not a Zionist organization. Jewish settlers in Palestine, even those from Germany, did not consider themselves 'an integral part of the German community in the Holy Land'.

[2] Curt Nawratzki, *Die jüdische Kolonisation Palästinas* (Munich, 1914), pp. 37–44, 51–3.   [3] Earle, op. cit., pp. 124–5.
[4] *Türkei* 195, K 176040–1, Bodenheimer to Richthofen, 23 Feb. 1902.

seemed to be unquestionable, but intervention on their behalf did not entail any political complications; their protection provided an excuse for asserting Germany's rights under the system of Capitulations. 'If we take care to see that the German Jews [and protégés] are not discriminated against . . . in the acquisition of land,' von Miquel wrote in his memorandum, 'this is solely due to our intention to retain our Treaty rights. . . . Strong control over the Sublime Porte is needed because so far as Palestine is concerned, the Porte is reluctant to carry out her legal obligation with regard to the acquisition of land by foreigners.'[5]

Von Miquel had particularly in mind the Hilfsverein der deutschen Juden, which had been founded in 1901 by the cotton magnate, James Simon, and Dr. Paul Nathan, the undisputed leaders of German Jewry; the first acted as President and the latter as Director. Simon, a distinguished philanthropist and a personal friend of the Kaiser, added weight to the Association, but it was its Director, far better versed in Jewish affairs, who was recognized as its 'guiding genius'. He was for over twenty years (1884–1907) editor of the *Nation*, the most influential liberal organ, and played a conspicuous role in the Radical-Liberal party of Friedrich Naumann; on retirement he devoted his energies to Jewish social and philanthropic activities. The Hilfsverein played a role in the relief and betterment of the Jews in Eastern Europe and developed an admirable system of education in the Ottoman Empire,[6] but though ostensibly a counterpart of the Alliance Israélite Universelle,[7] in practice it proved to be its undeclared rival and a willing instrument in furthering German cultural penetration in Eastern Europe and the Near East.

Its programme had been foreshadowed on 21 September 1898 when Nathan, on the eve of the Kaiser's departure for the East, approached the Foreign Ministry requesting its approval for Der deutsche Schulverein für die Juden des Orients. Nathan maintained firstly that hitherto education had been monopolized by the Alliance Israélite, which was linked with French cultural policy, but, since German industry and trade had acquired a strong foothold in Turkey,

[5] For Miquel's memorandum see above, pp. 152–3.

[6] Lichtheim: *Geschichte*, pp. 93–4, 171–2; idem, *She'ar Yashuv*, pp. 138, 181; *Rückkehr*, pp. 133, 170.

[7] Cohn-Reiss, *M'Zichronoth Ish Yerushalaim*, ii, p. 2; Stein, *The Balfour Declaration*, p. 22 n. 77.

the Alliance's predominance was no longer justifiable. Second, unlike their Spanish co-religionists, Polish and Russian Jews, whose
immigration to Turkey was increasing, showed a marked preference
for the German language and commerce rather than the French.
This would give the Schulverein a good opportunity to further
German influence.[8]

The project was referred to Marschall, who consulted Dr. Rosen,
the Consul-General in Jerusalem. The latter doubted whether the
Schulverein's activities would yield any direct political advantage
to Germany, because the majority of the orthodox Jews in Palestine
were concerned primarily with religious affairs, whereas the liberal
ones were mainly Zionists. None the less, he thought that the introduction of German would check the spread of French and the
population in the East would realize that European learning was
not necessarily synonymous with French. Marschall accepted the
argument, and Richthofen, the Foreign Minister, thereafter assured
Dr. Nathan that the German Consulate in Palestine would support
the Schulverein establishments 'so long as they were managed by
Germans, or bore decisive German features'. The Minister was,
however, less responsive to Nathan's plea to intercede with the
Porte in order to lift the restrictions on Jewish immigration and
land purchase.[9]

Subsequently the Association changed its name to Hilfsverein der
deutschen Juden and embarked upon the organization of a network
of Jewish schools in Turkey. Von Kiderlen-Wächter, the new
Foreign Minister, held Nathan in high esteem and regarded him as
'a man of tested German convictions'. Before his trip to the East in
August 1907 Nathan was warmly recommended to the Embassy in
Constantinople and the consular authorities. His stay in Constantinople coincided with the Young Turk Revolution of July 1908 which
took the Wilhelmstrasse entirely by surprise. Nathan was now presented with an unexpected opportunity to render a service to his
country. He approached prominent Jewish personalities in Constantinople and elsewhere, urging them to influence their people to join
the moderate Muslims who favoured reform but rejected revolutionary and 'Utopian experiments'. He was confident that Turkish
Jews would follow a line 'compatible with the Auswärtiges Amt

---

[8] *Türkei* 195, K 175925–7, Nathan to A.A., 21 Sept. 1898.
[9] Ibid. K 176006–13, Marschall to A.A., 30 Aug. 1900, dis. no. 123, citing also Rosen;
K 176019–22, A.A. note, 5 May 1901.

intentions', but the opposite happened. They welcomed the Revolution and remained loyal to the new regime.[10]

Although Nathan's attempt to intervene in Turkish politics proved unsuccessful, his educational enterprise was of lasting importance. He laid the foundation of an extensive network of schools in Palestine, from kindergartens to a Teachers Training College which, unlike the Alliance Israélite schools, employed modern pedagogic methods. Instructors were competent and the Hilfsverein's educational director, Ephraim Cohn-Reiss, was known as an efficient administrator. Nathan was also responsible for the introduction of Hebrew as a medium of instruction, in the belief that it would serve as a unifying factor for the polyglot composition of the Yishuv. Scientific subjects, however, were taught in German. From its inception until the outbreak of war the total investment in the Hilfsverein's schools amounted to 106,500 francs, and during the war an additional sum of 70,000 francs was spent on maintenance.

Though the motives for introducing Hebrew as a language of instruction were pedagogical rather than national, the Zionists fully appreciated the Hilfsverein's activities. Being short of financial resources sufficient to maintain an independent schools' system, they willingly co-operated. This harmonious relationship paved the way for a partnership in a more ambitious project, the foundation of a Technical College (Technikum) in Haifa, Nathan's brainchild. With Dr. Shmarya Levin, a member of the Zionist Executive, he managed to prevail upon Kalman Wissotzky, a Russian tea magnate, to make a large financial contribution; while Levin himself interested Jacob Schiff, the celebrated Jewish financier and philanthropist in New York, in the project and received a sizeable donation from him. Both Wissotzky and Schiff were represented on the board of the preparatory committee over which James Simon presided; the Hilfsverein members were in a majority. Three Zionists: Ahad Ha'am, Dr. Yehiel Tschlenow, and Shmarya Levin also joined the board, though strictly in their private capacity. It was understood that the language of instruction for scientific subjects in the College would be German,[11] but Simon went further in assuring the Foreign

---

[10] *Türkei* 195, K 176144–5, Kiderlen-Wächter to Marschall, and to Consulates, 5 Aug. 1907, dis. nos. 682, 243, and marginal annotation; Nathan to A.A., 6 Aug. 1908. The episode is related in my forthcoming article 'The *Hilfsverein der deutschen Juden* and the German Foreign Ministry, 1901–1918'.

[11] The above is based on the following sources: *Im Kampf um die hebräische Sprache*, herausgegeben vom Zionistischen Actions-Comité (Berlin, 1914), pp. 9–15; Jacob

Ministry that it would help to promote *Deutschtum* in the East. He made it clear, however, that the College would be exclusively an educational and non-political institution; it would be open to both Jewish and non-Jewish students and render valuable service to Turkey,[12]

The foundation of a Technical College in Turkey had been mooted in the Wilhelmstrasse for some time and the Hilfsverein's proposal was therefore well received. Marschall was instructed to obtain the required concession from the Porte. On 18 April 1912, when the foundation-stone of the College was laid, Loytved-Hardegg, the Vice-Consul in Haifa, attended the ceremony, and this was taken as a hint that it was under German protection.[13] He thought that it would play a significant role in meeting the need for engineers and technicians in Turkey, which was likely to increase as soon as various projects for the construction of roads, railways, ports, power-houses, and for irrigation systems got under way.

The event gave the Vice-Consul an opportunity to reappraise Germany's attitude towards Zionism. 'Is it not natural that the Jews, influenced by the awakening of national movements and stimulated by the general drive of colonization, have become more conscious of their own racial and religious distinctiveness? . . . This reawakened consciousness manifested itself first in a variety of philanthropic endeavours among Eastern Jews . . . and in the nostalgia for their ancient homeland.' But it was not until Herzl's appearance that the idea of building a Jewish national home in Palestine gained momentum. Judging from its achievements in colonization and its strong idealist motivation, Zionism in all

Thon, 'Jewish Schools in Palestine', *Zionist Work in Palestine*, ed. Israel Cohen (New York, 1912), pp. 87–8; Selig Brodetsky, 'Cultural Work in Palestine', *Zionism and the Jewish Future*, ed. Harry Sacher (London, 1916), pp. 171–89; Israel Cohen, *The German Attack on the Hebrew Schools in Palestine* (London, 1918), pp. 6–7; *Palestine during the War*, p. 8; Lichtheim, *She'ar Yashuv*, pp. 137, 181; *Rückkehr*, pp. 132, 170; Cohn-Reiss, op. cit. ii, pp. 282–3. It appears that Cohn-Reiss was the first teacher to introduce Hebrew as the language of instruction in Palestine. The experiment was made in the Boys School founded by von Lämel, subsequently taken over by the Hilfsverein (ibid. pp. 145–8).

[12] *Türkei* 195, K 176225–8, Simon to Kiderlen-Wächter, 21 Sept. 1909; K 176234–5, same to Zimmermann, 25 Oct. 1909; K 176213–6, same and Nathan to A.A., 25 Jan. 1911.

[13] Ibid. K 176230–302, correspondence between A.A. and the Embassy, Sept. 1909–Mar. 1911. This confirms the statement made by Dr. Chaim Weizmann in his *Trial and Error*, p. 143, which invalidates Dr. O. K. Rabinowicz's criticism of Weizmann in *Fifty Years of Zionism* (London, 1952), p. 90.

likelihood 'would bring about the solution of the Jewish problem and the cultural renaissance of the Jewish people'.

Loytved-Hardegg did not accept the Zionists unreservedly. He thought that politically they still had 'to learn a lot . . . above all their frequently manifested arrogance will have to be replaced by more tactful conduct', but as 'proponents of "preservation of race"', they deserved more respect than the assimilationists. He believed that the Zionists, because of their idealism, were likely to gain greater influence over Jewry in general, and in the Technical College in particular. As a result of their efforts Hebrew had been transformed from a written to a spoken language and eventually would become 'the living national language of all Jews'. It is worth noting that, unlike subsequent developments, the revival of Hebrew did not worry the Vice-Consul unduly. So long as Yiddish remained the dominant medium of communication among Jews, and so long as they showed a marked preference for German *Kultur* and merchandise, he thought that German interests would not be impaired. Moreover, the Zionist Organization, its organ, *Die Welt*, and the Jewish National Fund all had their headquarters in Berlin, while the Technical College in Haifa was to adopt the German educational pattern. Considering the prevalent mood among Palestinian Jews, the Hilfsverein leaders would be well advised to pay more attention to Zionist wishes and take heed of Jewish national aspirations.[14]

To Dr. Nathan (who received a copy of Loytved-Hardegg's report) this advice was unacceptable. Ideologically, he insisted, the Hilfsverein and the Zionists were worlds apart and, in view of Turkish hostility to the Zionists, too close an identification with them might bring the Hilfsverein as well into disfavour with the Turkish Government.

Loytved-Hardegg replied that in this case ideological differences were of little consequence since the consensus of the Muslim and Christian population in Palestine was that all Jewish enterprises in Palestine served the cause of Zionism anyhow. He was aware of his duty to protect the Technikum but if he thought it desirable for the Hilfsverein to come closer to the Zionist point of view, it was because of his conviction that one day Zionism, growing in importance and influence, was likely to capture the allegiance of the majority of Jews. The Technikum too would be conquered for the Zionists

[14] *Türkei* 195, K 176334–9, Loytved-Hardegg to A.A., 18 Apr. 1912, dis. J. no. 1063/no. 54.

from within by Jewish students coming from Russia, where their admission to universities was restricted. As for *Deutschtum*, the Technikum was important only in so far as it served to spread knowledge of the German language and science, but personally he regarded this institution primarily as 'a purely Jewish undertaking'.[15]

This exposé, and particularly the last statement, which elicited no objection from the Foreign Ministry, shows that Zionist apprehensions from 1913 to 1914 that the Technikum 'was to become a German institution' were greatly exaggerated.[16] Equally there was no proof that 'secret pressure [was] exercised by the German Government with a view to making the Jewish schools nurseries of Prussian *Kultur*'.[17] More likely it was the Hilfsverein representatives themselves who, 'repeatedly pointing to the Jews as a link between Germany and the Orient, praising the projected Technikum in Haifa as a stronghold of *Deutschtum* in the Holy Land . . . fed the Zionists' suspicions that Jewish colonization was to be subordinated to German political aspirations.' This was the conclusion of Dr. Heinrich Brode, the Consul in Jaffa, when reviewing the episode about two years later.[18] At the time the Palestinian Zionists took the Hilfsverein's pronouncements as the thin end of the wedge, assuming them to have been inspired by the Wilhelmstrasse, but documentary evidence shows that this impression was mistaken. Neither Berlin nor the Consulate in Palestine nourished any intention of pushing German *Kultur* at the expense of Hebrew education.

Quite the contrary. In his annual trade report for 1912 Dr. Brode described Zionist colonization in most glowing terms.[19] The German colonists in Palestine looked upon their Jewish compatriots as undesirable competitors, but this opinion was not shared by the

---

[15] Ibid. K 176343–51, Nathan to Simon, 18 June 1912 (a copy was sent to Loytved-Hardegg); K 176357–62, Loytved-Hardegg to A.A., 10 July 1912, dis. J. no. 1707/no. 89.

[16] In his article 'The Political Orientation of the Zionist Executive's Policy on the Eve of the First World War' Dr. P. A. Alsberg concludes: 'There is no doubt that the German Foreign Ministry hoped that the Technikum would become a German institution', and that the German Vice-Consul in Haifa 'exerted his influence in favour of its adopting a German character' (p. 166). On the other hand he assumes that 'no secret negotiations' between the German Foreign Ministry and the Hilfsverein took place. The article is a chapter of an unpublished doctoral dissertation (Hebrew University, 1957), based on Zionist material.

[17] Israel Cohen, *The German Attack* . . ., pp. 18–19; *idem*, *Travels in Jewry* (London, 1952), p. 27; F.O. Handbook, *Zionism*, x, No. 162 (London, 1920), p. 44.

[18] For Brode's memorandum see below, pp. 256–8.

[19] *Deutsches Handelsarchiv* (Oct. 1913).

Consulate, or by the Embassy in Constantinople.[20] Celebrated agricultural experts like Dr. H. Auhagen, Dr. Lothar, and Dr. R. Eckhardt, when visiting Palestine, expressed admiration for the Jewish settlements, and Dr. Alfons Paquet, who in 1913 studied the region, became convinced that in Palestine 'a new Jewish agricultural people was developing'.[21]

In the Wilhelmstrasse, too, the climate seemed to become more favourable. By then Bülow's Chancellorship had come to an inglorious end. Zionism was not so important as to command the attention of his successor, Bethmann Hollweg, but the new Foreign Minister, Alfred von Kiderlen-Wächter, displayed some interest.[22] Palestine affairs were handled by Dr. Alfred Zimmerman. Although not of noble extraction, he was in 1911 appointed Under-Secretary of State because of his industry and a good deal of special knowledge. He was also one of the few persons in the Foreign Ministry who took part in policy decision-making. His pleasant personality and dignified bearing impressed his contemporaries, and even Bülow, usually critical of the Foreign Ministry's staff, singled him out as 'a man of honour and a patriot'.[23] Zimmerman's industry can be seen in his meticulous annotations on ambassadorial and consular dispatches. Before the war his sympathy with Zionism was not much in evidence, but the fact that he did not object to Loytved-Hardegg's ideas is suggestive. But it was not so much the change of staff at the Wilhelmstrasse as the substantial improvement in Germany's diplomatic position in the Near East[24] that allowed her to take a more relaxed attitude towards Zionism. It was easier for Germany to consider some sort of association with the Zionists particularly when they themselves suppressed their political ambitions in Palestine in favour of practical work. Such an accommodation became more pressing as soon as it was apparent that the French were determined to capture Ottoman Jewry.

[20] *Türkei* 195, K 176324–8, Miquel to A.A., 26 July 1911, dis. no. 202.

[21] Cited in Kurt Blumenfeld, 'Der Zionismus, eine Frage der deutschen Orientpolitik', *Preussische Jahrbücher* (Berlin, 1915), 19–20.

[22] Bodenheimer, *Memoirs*, pp. 178–9.

[23] Theodor Wolff, *The Eve of 1914*, trans. (London, 1935), p. 308; Henry Morgenthau, *Secrets of the Bosphorus*, p. 265; Bülow, *Memoirs*, iv, p. 263.

[24] On the diplomatic background and particularly on Franco-German relations in the East see: J. B. Wolf, 'The Diplomatic History of the Bagdad Railroad', pp. 55–6, 87–8, 96–9; Fay, *The Origins of the World War*, pp. 500–1; Stein, *The Balfour Declaration*, pp. 51–4; *British Documents on the Origins of the War, 1898–1914*, x, Pt. II, nos. 122, 134, 135, 143, 201.

French interests in the East were of long standing. Early in the twentieth century France suffered some setbacks but with Poincaré's accession to power a determined effort was made to regain the lost ground. In his budget speech on 21 December 1912 Poincaré told both Houses that in Lebanon and Syria the French had 'special and long seated interests, which must be respected'.[25] For the French Syria included Palestine, the distinction between the two countries never being explicitly admitted. One well-tried means of penetration was dissemination of the French language and culture which, apart from prestige, also yielded handsome political and economic dividends.

French influence was particularly strong among Ottoman Jewry. The schools of the Alliance Israélite Universelle preceded those of the Hilfsverein by at least two decades, and the election of Haim Nahoum Effendi in 1908 to the position of Chief Rabbi of Turkey, despite opposition from the Hilfsverein and the German Embassy, was a considerable triumph for the Francophiles.[26] In April 1911, at the instigation of the French Embassy in Constantinople, all the foreign missions requested the Porte to rescind restrictions on land purchase in Syria and Palestine by foreign Jews,[27] and in December 1912 the French Ambassador made an unprecedented move by telling the Chief Rabbi that France was ready to watch over the interests of Jews in the East and to meet their requests.

This news astonished Freiherr von Wangenheim, the newly appointed German Ambassador in Constantinople. He suspected that France aspired to assume an over-all protectorate of Jews in the East and advised Berlin to do everything possible to thwart it. Israel Auerbach, the local representative of the Hilfsverein who gave this information to Wangenheim, assured him, however, that 90 per cent of world Jewry spoke a German dialect, had natural inclinations towards Germany, and 'were therefore in a position to render her invaluable services as carriers of German *Kultur* and merchandise'. German protection of the Jews in Salonica had been widely appreciated and, if Berlin were to remind Romania appropriately of her obligations under the 1878 Treaty of Berlin, as well

---

[25] *The Memoirs of Raymond Poincaré* (London, 1926), p. 338. Owing to a misprint the date of the speech is given as 1913 instead of 1912.

[26] *Türkei* 195, K 176218–9, Stemmerlich to Marschall, 30 Nov. 1908; dis. no. 1885. A biographical note on Nahoum appears in *Modern Turkey*, ed. E. G. Mears (New York, 1924), p. 86; an obituary in the *Jewish Chronicle* and *The Times* (18 Nov. 1960); above, pp. 141, 144.   [27] *B.C.* ii, Lowther to Grey, 24 Apr. 1911, p. 577.

as induce the Porte to annul the restrictions on freedom of Jewish immigration to Turkey, it would have a most favourable effect on Jewish opinion.

Wangenheim was no stranger to Constantinople. At the turn of the century he had served in the Embassy as Secretary and Counsellor and, with a long experience in diplomacy behind him, he was well equipped for his new mission. Nor until the end of his life in October 1915 did he ever bypass the Jews. Auerbach's arguments could not fail to impress him. He wired Berlin: 'I am convinced that a certain amount of intervention on our part on behalf of the Jews would be economically, politically, and culturally advantageous to us.'[28] Several months later he wrote: 'If our civilizing work in Asiatic Turkey is not to be lost, we must exert ourselves more in the sphere of cultural propaganda . . . I am of the opinion that we ought to follow the French example.'[29] This advice did not necessarily relate to the Jews but it is worth citing here as an illustration of the working of Wangenheim's mind.

Rear-Admiral Trummler, Commander of the German naval unit in the Mediterranean, evaluated the importance of the Jews from a different angle. On a reconnaissance mission along the eastern shores of the Mediterranean, he wished not only to examine harbour and railway facilities, as well as development projects, but also to ascertain the political aspirations of the local population. The diligence, efficiency, and loyalty of the German colonists in Palestine impressed him. He was glad to note that the Turkish Government was determined to combat separatist propaganda in Syria but to his regret he found that, with the exception of one Arab party, the majority were working for independence. The strongest, the Decentralization party, with its seat in Cairo, advocated federation of Syria with Egypt under British protection. Other parties were striving for union with Egypt, with the Khedive as its head. Under these circumstances Trummler found that the distinct group of 100,000 Jews living in Palestine deserved 'special attention'. He attached particular significance to the Zionists who aspired to the renaissance

---

[28] *Türkei* 195, K 176393–4, Wangenheim to A.A., 4 Jan. 1913, tel. no. 5. Germany was one of the Powers that guaranteed the 1878 Treaty of Berlin. For rights accorded to Jews see Dubnow, *Die neueste Geschichte*, ii, pp. 488–91; Medlicott, *The Congress of Berlin and After*, pp. 31–2, 83, 91, 141, 358. On the Salonica episode see N. M. Gelber, 'An Attempt to Internationalize Salonica, 1912–1913', *Jewish Social Studies*, xvii (1955), no. 2.

[29] *Türkei* 189, Wangenheim to A.A., 19 June 1913, dis. no. 193.

of the Jewish people in Palestine. He singled out their loyalty to the Turkish Government which recently had become more favourably disposed to them—quite justly—because Turkey would 'undoubtedly profit from the Jewish element'. He envisaged that, 'thanks to their business talent and the large investments of the Zionists . . . in the not too distant future, the Jewish population will achieve a national coherence, which will give it a special weight and importance in Palestine'. These facts were also 'of special significance for Germany because of the Jews' strong pro-German leanings'. The majority of Palestinian Jews learned German as a foreign language; the projected Technical College in Haifa was to introduce German as its language of instruction, and the seat of the central office of the Zionist Organization was in Berlin. He thought it quite inevitable, therefore, that 'in case of a split amongst the population [Arabs versus Jews], the German Jewish element would certainly welcome German protection'. He concluded:

> Through the Jewish population in Palestine, Germany has undoubtedly the means to advance her interests, which in total would constitute such an important factor that any French claims to this rich and promising country should not come under discussion at all.[30]

Trummler's report was carefully studied at the Foreign Ministry. Zimmerman, as his marginal annotations testify, was impressed. The information was essentially correct. The assertion that the Turkish Government had modified its attitude towards the Zionists is corroborated by other sources. On 9 May 1913 Loytved-Hardegg wrote: 'there are individuals among the Young Turks who sympathize with Zionism. Some of them recognize the great economic and cultural value of their enterprises, responsible for the flourishing state of the country; others would like to exploit Zionism as a counterweight against the Arabs.'[31] The official Zionist report bears out this assessment: 'The Turks were far more vehemently opposed to the Arabs than to us—there was actually a disposition on the part of some of their leaders to play us off against the Arabs, and on that account to encourage our efforts.'[32] Reviewing the pre-war period,

---

[30] *Türkei* 177, *Der Libanon (Syrien)*, Bd. 9 (copy in *Türkei* 195, K 176427–32). The report (31 May 1913) was made to the Kaiser as Commander-in-Chief but was deposited in the files of the Foreign Ministry.

[31] *Türkei* 195, K 176407–14, Loytved-Hardegg to A.A., 9 May 1913, dis. J. no. 1280/ no. 58.

[32] *Palestine during the War*, p. 5.

Dr. Brode stated: 'the Turkish authorities, who had originally regarded Zionist activities with suspicion, subsequently treated them with goodwill'; particularly friendly was Talaat Bey, Minister of the Interior, who instructed the Ottoman authorities in Palestine to grant the Jews special privileges and extend the scope of their autonomy.[33] Restrictions on freedom of immigration (the notorious 'red ticket') were also abrogated and discriminatory ordinances with regard to the purchase of land largely modified.[34] As a result, in the period immediately before the war, over 6,000 Jews came into the country; colonization and urban development continued unhampered.[35]

Confronted with the rising tide of Arab nationalism, some Young Turk leaders discovered in the Jewish settlement in Palestine certain advantages for Turkey, provided the immigrants refrained from inviting the protection of foreign consuls and adopted Ottoman nationality. This appears from statements made by Mahdi Bey, the newly appointed Governor, an Albanian by origin. In the summer of 1912, soon after his arrival, he made an extensive tour of Jewish settlements and demonstrated an astonishingly obliging attitude. On one occasion he declared:

> Our Government has always shown friendship and hospitality towards your people, whenever they came to settle here. Your skill and knowledge are very beneficial to the country and its development. Our Government is aware that the Jews are not concerned with 'politics' but desire to live and work in peace . . . Like that of all other good Ottoman citizens, your work is appreciated, but you must become true sons of the Fatherland, not stepsons and nationals of foreign countries.

Should the Jews follow this advice, he would see to it that their autonomy was further extended, and the right of self-defence granted.[36] On another occasion he stated that although the Government rejected political Zionism it recognized the Jewish people and

[33] On Brode's memorandum of 26 Aug. 1915 see below, pp. 256–8.

[34] C.Z.A. Z 3/443, report by Tschlenow at the meeting of the Zionist Council, 23 Nov. 1913; Z 3/449, report by Jacobson to the same, 7 June 1914; Lichtheim, *She'ar Yashuv*, pp. 244–50; *Rückkehr*, pp. 222–6; Alsberg, loc. cit., pp. 160–1; Haim Nahoum, 'Jews', *Modern Turkey*, op. cit., p. 96.

[35] *Palestine during the War*, pp. 6–7.

[36] *Sefer Hayovel L'Rishon L'Zion [Jubliee Book of Rishon L'Zion]*, ed. D. Idelovitch (Rishon L'Zion, 1941), p. 405; Smilansky, *Zichronot*, iii, p. 132. Contemporary writers were puzzled by this sudden change of attitude and wondered whether it was a personal whim of an official or a deliberate strategem by the Porte to provoke the Jews.

their historical connection with Palestine. It would not hamper them in their cultural work and revival of Hebrew, provided they adopted Ottoman nationality. Arab protests later forced Mahdi to tone down his pronouncements and even issue contradictory ones. At the beginning of 1913 he was removed from his post, but Turkish policy remained on the whole consistent. Magid Shoukat Bey was more restrained than his predecessor, but by no means unfriendly. In one instance the editor of the Egyptian paper *Al-Ahram* sought to convince him of the dangers inherent in Zionism but Shoukat Bey replied that 'had the Central Government considered Zionist activities harmful, it would certainly have stopped them'. He thought it prudent for the Arabs to follow the example set by Tel Aviv and the Jewish settlements.[37]

With the Ottoman archives still largely unexplored these conclusions cannot be fully substantiated, but on the basis of the evidence adduced above it is safe to say that much of Turkey's earlier opposition to Jewish colonization had evaporated. Moreover, it seems that the Germans, and the Turks independently of them, discovered in Zionism certain advantages for their respective interests. That this new thinking did not lead to a *rapprochement* was largely the fault of the Palestinian Zionists. Ignorant of Germany's intentions, they launched in the winter of 1913–14 an anti-German language campaign, the *Sprachenkampf*. They also misjudged the seriousness of Mahdi Bey's appeal and evidently dissappointed the Turks by their delays in seeking naturalization.

Whatever course may have been suggested at the Wilhelmstrasse, in Palestine the Consulate reverted to its earlier position, insisting that after all it was safer to support the Hilfsverein. This was the burden of Loytved-Hardegg's dispatch dated 9 May 1913. It was true that the central seat of the Zionist movement was in Berlin, that the official language of Zionist congresses and of *Die Welt* was German, and that even the East European Zionists showed a notable interest in German philosophy and literature. All this created among foreign politicians and Press the erroneous impression that Zionism was a German organization, serving German interests in the East; but, politically, he pointed out, the Zionists were not particularly pro-German. They leaned more towards England because the Jews

---

[37] *S.T.H.* i, p. 184. On 28 November 1912 Albania proclaimed its independence, a fact which probably accounts for Mahdi's recall from his post.

there enjoyed equal civil rights. In Palestine they were disinclined to commit themselves to one Power exclusively and preferred to put themselves under the protection of their countries of origin. As most of them were Russian nationals they looked for protection to Russia which, although treating them badly at home, in Palestine served them in 'an exceedingly obliging manner, apparently because she wishes to support another separatist element in Turkey'. Some Young Turks sympathized with Zionism, but it should be noted that the Arabs regarded Zionism as an economic and a national danger. However, should the Reich Government favour an agreement with the Zionists, he thought the moment most propitious; German had not yet been completely displaced and the Zionists were still not in a position to behave too independently. He suggested that in return for German protection, scholarships, and assistance offered by German universities the Zionists should agree that German became the first compulsory language in their schools, 'with full respect for the particular needs of Hebrew'. However, upon learning that the Hilfsverein intended to introduce German as the language of instruction in the Grammar School affiliated to the Technikum, he changed his tune, suggesting that the Foreign Ministry should 'prevent the Zionists from increasing their influence over the Hilfs-verein', and tighten co-operation with those Jews who were loyal to Germany.[38]

Edmund Schmidt, the Consul-General in Jerusalem, went to greater lengths. Under the erroneous impression that the Hebrew Grammar School in Jerusalem had placed itself under French protection, he suggested that Berlin should declare that the Hilfsverein schools were under German protection. This, he hoped, would also restrain the 'radical Zionists from Hebraizing the Hilfsverein school. More disquieting was the news that the French Consulate had taken under its protection 7,000 Moroccan Jews in Palestine with a speed and zeal that astonished even the Jews themselves. Schmidt now suspected that the French desired to extend their sphere of interest from Syria to Palestine as well.[39]

[38] *Türkei* 195, K 176407–14, Loytved-Hardegg to A.A., 9 May 1913, dis. J. no. 1280/no. 58.

[39] Ibid. K 176437–9, Wangenheim to A.A., 30 June 1913, citing Schmid's dispatches of 15, 17 June. Denied recognition by the Ottoman Government (since the majority of teachers and students were foreign nationals) the Gymnasium decided to invite the protection of one of the European Powers. This would have entitled its graduates to enter universities abroad and by the same token would have made the Porte recognize

It is against this background that one can appreciate why the German Consulate attached such importance to the decision of the Board of the Technical College on the question of language of instruction. The issue was controversial. While the Hilfsverein representatives favoured German, ostensibly on pedagogical grounds, claiming that Hebrew was not yet sufficiently developed for teaching technology and science, the Zionists, who were in a minority, pointed to the successful experience in the Hebrew Grammar Schools of Jerusalem and Jaffa, and pressed that Hebrew be accepted in principle to replace German at some time in the future. To resolve the deadlock, they suggested a compromise: exclusive use of Hebrew in the preparatory Grammar School affiliated to the College, and in the College itself one scientific subject to be taught experimentally in Hebrew. The Hilfsverein rejected this proposal.

Loytved-Hardegg, fearing lest the Board's decision might have wider repercussions on the use of German in the East, advised the Foreign Ministry to support the Hilfsverein; should its position be adopted, all Jewish and non-Jewish Grammar Schools would be impelled to give greater scope to German in their curricula. On the other hand, once the Zionists were successful in conquering the Grammar School, they would easily win over the Technikum later; only humanistic subjects and religion should be taught in Hebrew. He believed that such a solution would be acceptable to the Board and advised that 'in the realm of science any political controversy between the national and non-national Jews should be avoided'.[40]

A copy of Loytved-Hardegg's dispatch, accompanied by Zimmermann's observation that it was 'worthy of serious consideration', stiffened the Hilfsverein's attitude.[41] At the opening of the Board's

it. It appears that the Quai d'Orsay was seriously interested in the deal, provided French was introduced as a compulsory subject; but this seemed to the Gymnasium too high a price and they did not proceed with the matter. (Israel Klausner, 'Episodes in the History of the Hebrew Gymnasium in Jerusalem', *Sefer Hayovel shel Hagimnasya Haivrit* (Hebrew) (Jerusalem, 1962), 49–55.) Unlike the Technikum, Hilfsverein schools were not under German protection.

[40] *Türkei* 195, K 176453–7, Loytved-Hardegg to A.A., 8 Aug. 1913, dis. J. no. 2026/ no. 100.

[41] This and the preceding material tend to contradict Dr. Ernest Feder's conclusion. Dr. Feder, the executor of Dr. Nathan's will and his biographer, stated that in all Dr. Nathan's letters, diaries, and notes there was 'not the slightest trace of any influence of the German authorities upon the school work of the Hilfsverein or in matters of the Technikum for purposes of intrigue or for other political or cultural-political motives' (quoted in Rabinowicz, *Fifty Years of Zionism*, pp. 90–1).

meeting on 26 October 1913 Dr. Nathan declared that he would regard rejection of his programme as a vote of no confidence and would resign. This rigid stand prejudiced the proceedings from the outset and excluded any possibility of discussion, let alone compromise. The Zionist members found themselves in an untenable position. They doubted Nathan's sincerity, suspecting that pedagogical arguments merely camouflaged his intention to establish German at the expense of Hebrew. After their counter-proposal was rejected, they consulted the Zionist Executive and subsequently resigned from the Board. The Russian members of the Board (representing the Wissotsky family), notwithstanding their sympathy for Hebrew, were reluctant to endanger the College's future and voted for Nathan's motion, which recommended that scientific and technical subjects be taught in German, but the humanistic ones in Hebrew, 'in accordance with the Jewish character of the Technikum'. In the absence of the American delegates, Nathan's motion gained a majority of 7 to 3[42] but, as events proved, it was a pyrrhic victory.

Loytved-Hardegg applauded the Board's resolution as an 'astute move'. It amounted to the unofficial introduction of German as 'the *de facto* language of instruction', thereby enhancing its standing in other schools as well. He rejoiced at the Zionists' failure,[43] but his jubilation was premature. Both the German Consulate and the Hilfsverein underestimated the depth of feeling and the vigour with which national Jewry in Palestine was prepared to fight for what it regarded as its cultural independence. To them the Board's decision was a menace to Hebrew. Stirring demonstrations were held all over the country which precipitated the bitter quarrel that went beyond cultural considerations. It led ultimately to the rift between the Hilfsverein and the Zionists and involved the German Consulate as well. Yet, contrary to the generally held view, the evidence shows that the Consulate was not inimical to Hebrew, but when the controversy came into the open, it could not remain indifferent and turned against the Zionists.

---

[42] C.Z.A. Z 3/443, Tschlenow's report of the meeting of the Zionist Executive, 23 Nov. 1913; Alsberg, loc. cit., p. 168.

[43] *Türkei* 195, K 176462–4, Loytved-Hardegg to A.A., 10 Nov. 1913, dis. J. no. 2758/no. 147.

10

The *Sprachenkampf*

T HOUGH at first it looked as if Franco-German rivalry in the Levant would benefit the Jews at large, and the Zionists in particular, as events proved it did more harm than good. Any French success prompted the Germans to a counter-move and in such an atmosphere it was only those who conformed who could be trusted. This explains the volte-face of the German Consulate, which in 1912 appeared to favour the Zionists. The irony of the latter's position was that while the French and British continued to regard them as subservient to German interests, the Germans now discovered in them tendencies in favour of the Entente and viewed their pro-Hebrew movement as tantamount to the suppression of German. In this competition among the European Powers for influence and prestige the Jews were made to feel like 'catspaws in this game'.[1] To resolve the paradox the Zionist Executive sought after its election in 1911 to explain that the aim of the movement was not to serve this or that Power, but solely Jewish interests. This was its *raison d'être*.[2] As members of an international organization, the Zionists were unwilling and unable to identify themselves with one bloc of Powers exclusively.[3]

The policy of non–identification was imperative to an even greater degree in Palestine. There the Jewish community felt itself torn apart by its benefactors and protectors,[4] and endeavoured to keep the schools free from the influence of the contending Powers. It was realized that 'any European language used as a vehicle for instruction must imprint on the school a one-sided political character to

---

[1] Weizmann, *Trial and Error*, p. 143.
[2] Stein, *The Balfour Declaration*, pp. 40–1.
[3] Lichtheim, *She'ar Yashuv*, pp. 259–62; *Rückkehr*, pp. 230–2; Alsberg, loc. cit., 'The Political Orientation of the Zionist Executive', p. 162.
[4] Weizmann, op. cit., p. 143.

the detriment of Palestinian Jewry'.[5] It was in these terms that Shmarya Levin appealed to Dr. Nathan before the crucial meeting of the Board on 26 October 1913, emphasizing that only Hebrew could provide the technical college with a semblance of neutrality. Nathan's reference to pedagogical considerations, which spoke in favour of German,[6] was hardly likely to convince the Palestinian Zionist who maintained that education was 'a national matter'.[7] Whatever the merits of this argument, it ignored the fact that the Zionist members on the Technikum Board were in a minority and could not claim an exclusive right to draft its programme. Moreover, the original agreement, to which all parties had committed themselves, stipulated that scientific subjects were to be taught in German. Ahad Ha'am, the prudent philosopher, repeatedly warned his fellow Zionists that, with the paucity of Hebrew textbooks and the inadequacy of Hebrew terminology, as well as the absence of experienced staff to teach scientific subjects in that language, a speedy conversion of the Technikum into a Hebrew institution was both impractical and unfair. The change amounted to a breach of the agreement with the Hilfsverein; it had never been discussed among the Zionists themselves; the claim was absolutely new. He was prepared to fight for the predominance of Hebrew in the affiliated Grammar School but, unlike the school, the Technical College was not an educational but a professional institution. It was concerned primarily with training skilled engineers and technicians. 'That was what *all* of us thought at that time . . . noisy propaganda in favour of Hebrew and "Hebrew only" smacks of demagogy, in which I shall not take part.'[8]

In an effort to bridge the gap Ahad Ha'am attempted to convince Dr. Nathan of the necessity of introducing Hebrew into the Technikum gradually. He pointed to the successful experiment of teaching scientific subjects in that language in the grammar schools of Jerusalem and Jaffa. That the University of Berlin accorded them recogni-

---

[5] *Im Kampf um die hebräische Sprache*, pp. 26–7.
[6] Cohn-Reiss: *M'Zichronoth Ish Yerushalaim*, ii, pp. 176–9; Alsberg, loc. cit., p. 167.
[7] *Im Kampf . . .*, p. 62.
[8] *Ig'groth Ahad Ha'am* [*Letters*] (Jerusalem–Berlin, 1924), v, Ahad Ha'am to Joseph Klausner, 25 May 1913 (p. 53); to Sh. Levin, 27 May, 10, 19 June (pp. 56–7, 62–8); to M. Ben-Hillel Hacohen, 15 June, 25 Nov., pp. 64–5, 119–20; to M. M. Ussishkin, 8 Aug. (pp. 75–6); to Druyanov, 23 Dec. 1913 (p. 136). Article 4 of the Agreement committed its signatories to maintain the Technikum merely as 'a Jewish institution'. As Ahad Ha'am rightly pointed out, no mention was made of its Hebrew, let alone Zionist, character, because the founders were eager to find a common denominator among all parties concerned.

tion showed that their standard was not adversely affected by the experiment. Moreover, it was politically desirable to refute the contention of the Entente that Jewish enterprises in Palestine were subordinated to German interests in the East. However, Nathan was unmoved. Ahad Ha'am gained the impression that his correspondent's counter-arguments merely camouflaged the real motives, the nature of which he was not in a position to divulge. He suspected that Nathan's inflexibility was determined by some secret agreement between the German Government and the Hilfsverein.[9]

In 1908, when the Hilfsverein–Zionist *rapprochement* took place, no serious difficulties were foreseen. Some German Zionist leaders such as Dr. Arthur Hantke, Kurt Blumenfeld, and Richard Lichtheim had grave misgivings about an association with anti-Zionist assimilationists, and even Ahad Ha'am urged caution before entering into an agreement with the Hilfsverein; but considerations of expediency prevailed. Attacked by other sections of Jewry, isolated politically, and lacking means to finance an independent school system, the Zionists were not in a position to renounce the partnership. The irony is that initially one of its greatest enthusiasts was Shmarya Levin. The Hilfsverein's splendid work enhanced Zionist confidence, but it was not long before a divergence of views made itself felt. A conversation between Lichtheim and Nathan in 1910 revealed the gulf between the two diametrically opposed schools of thought. Whilst Lichtheim adhered to his Zionist credo as the only solution of the Jewish question, Nathan regarded it as a mirage.[10] As the years went by Nathan feared lest partnership with the Zionists would prejudice the Hilfsverein's standing both with German Jewry and with the Turks. He lost no opportunity to stress that his Association was completely detached from Zionism and that its 'only purpose was the cultural and economic welfare of the Jews'.[11] The two organizations were thus drifting apart. Whereas the Zionists, as Weizmann put it, were struggling to weld the Jewish community in Palestine into 'one creative unit',[12] Nathan rejected Jewish exclusivism outright. All his life he had fought against

[9] *Ig'groth Ahad Ha'am* to Nathan, 28 Sept., 19 Oct. 1913 (pp. 81–2, 98–9); to Moshe Smilansky, 18 Nov. 1913 (pp. 113–16).

[10] Lichtheim, *She'ar Yashuv*, pp. 140, 181; *Rückkehr*, pp. 135, 170; *Ig'groth Ahad Ha'am*, to Schenkin, 11 Feb. 1908 (iv, p. 5); to Ben-Hillel Hacohen, 15 June, 25 Nov. 1913 (v, pp. 65, 121).

[11] *Osmanisches Lloyd* (29 Oct. 1910); Lichtheim, *She'ar Yashuv*, p. 137; *Rückkehr*, p. 132. [12] Weizmann, op. cit., p. 143; *Im Kampf . . .*, p. 62.

chauvinism, regarding it as 'a danger to peace and . . . humanity' and 'a crime against civilization'. Jews in particular, he insisted, should beware not to commit 'the greatest political stupidity'. Should they become infected by it, it would boomerang against themselves, would play into the hands of anti-Semitism, and in a country like Turkey would lead to 'a catastrophe', in which case the Zionist leaders would become the grave-diggers of their own idea.[13]

However disparate the two concepts, it would be wrong to assume that the conflict was inevitable. Neither the Hilfsverein nor the Zionist Organization desired it. Professor Otto Warburg, the Chairman of the Zionist Organization, continued to serve on the Hilfsverein Committee,[14] and Dr. Weizmann, at the Eleventh Zionist Congress held in Vienna in September 1913, publicly expressed his fears that the premature introduction of Hebrew into the Technical College might adversely affect the quality of teaching. The same doubts were felt by Dr. Yechiel Tschlenow, a Russian Zionist leader and a member of the College Board. In an appreciative reference to the Hilfsverein's work he went so far as to state that its educational programme was compatible with 'the national aim'. Shmarya Levin thought differently. At the same Congress he declared that upon the Zionist Organization lay 'an unconditional obligation to concentrate in its hands the total cultural work in Palestine', and to exclude those bodies 'which lacked that banner'.[15] Dr. Nathan took offence, all the more so since it was the Hilfsverein, as he had declared a year earlier at its general assembly, that had first grasped the importance of organizing the Jewish communities in the East, and especially of educating the youth. It was unthinkable to him that this primacy, gained by heavy investment and pioneering work, should now be lost. As he later confided to Loytved-Hardegg, the Zionist claims jeopardized the very independence of the Hilfsverein's activity, and he was determined to resist them.[16] Even so, he regarded the 'Palestinian *Exaltados*', the Teachers' Union, which the Zionist Executive in Berlin was 'too weak' to restrain, as chiefly

[13] Nathan, *Palästina und palästinensischer Zionismus*, pp. 51–2, 59–60.

[14] Lichtheim, *Geschichte*, p. 171.

[15] *Protokoll, XI. Kongress*, pp. 307–8; Nathan, op. cit., pp. 12–13, citing *Die Welt* (3 Sept. 1913). The discrepancy between the statement made by Weizmann at the Eleventh Congress and that referred to in *Trial and Error* was pointed out by Rabinowicz, *Fifty Years of Zionism*, pp. 85–97.

[16] *Türkei* 195, K 176357–62, Loytved-Hardegg to A.A., 10 July 1912, dis. no. 1707/89; K 176606–7, 29 Dec. 1913, dis. no. 3186/166.

responsible for the *Sprachenkampf*. But the teachers, too, had grievances; those in the Hilfsverein schools saw that since 1911 the progress of Hebrew had been held back in favour of German and for this, during the Teachers' Union conference in August 1913, they blamed chiefly Ephraim Cohn-Reiss, suspecting that he had submitted to 'secret pressure exercised by the German Government'.[17]

In his memoirs Cohn rejected the charge that he was a willing instrument in the 'germanization of the Yishuv'; in rural areas, where graduates of the Hilfsverein schools were not as a rule expected to pursue a higher education, German was excluded from the curriculum. Moreover, unlike France, Germany was interested in the dissemination of German only in so far as it enhanced her commercial prospects in the East, and for this very reason was inclined at first (i.e. in 1912–13) to come to terms with the Zionists.[18] In saying so Cohn was undoubtedly correct, and it was certainly due to him that Hebrew was introduced into the Hilfsverein's schools. But it was also true, as he had himself admitted, that in 1913 he rejected the teachers' proposal to accelerate the process of Hebraization in his schools. In Brode's opinion Cohn bore the prime responsibility for arousing Zionist suspicions, though indiscriminate condemnation of the Hilfsverein as 'betrayers of the national cause' was unjustifiable.[19] Had it not been for the tense atmosphere, the resignation of the Zionist representatives on the Board of the Technikum would have passed without any serious repercussions; but in the circumstances the episode served as the final fuse which sparked off the Teachers' Union struggle against 'the complete suppression of Hebrew'. Animated protest meetings were held all over the country and a strike was declared in the Hilfsverein schools. Yet, whatever the merits of the teachers' campaign and that of their followers, the form into which it degenerated brought no honour to their cause.

The German Consulate was incensed. Following the resolutions adopted at the Zionist mass meeting in Haifa,[20] Loytved-Hardegg noted:

The time will come when these doctrinaire and radical demonstrators will be grateful to [the Board] for having prudently considered in their

---

[17] Nathan, op. cit., pp. 54–5; *Im Kampf...*, pp. 16–18; Lichtheim, *She'ar Yashuv*, p. 138; *Rückkehr*, p. 133; Cohen, *The German Attack on the Hebrew Schools*, pp. 8–10.
[18] Cohn-Reiss, op. cit. ii, pp. 148, 168, 179, 208.
[19] *Türkei* 195, K 177336–7, memorandum by Brode, 26 Aug. 1915, on which see below pp. 256–8.   [20] *Im Kampf...*, pp. 26–30.

resolutions practical needs, having in mind, in the first place, efficient and well-educated Jews and not Hebrew-speaking chauvinists . . . So long as the Jews are not firmly rooted in Palestine, it will be short-sighted even from the Zionist point of view to press Hebrew into the foreground at the expense of the efficiency of Jewish education. Hebrew would in any case develop automatically, and those who protest overlook the fact that by excessive encouragement of a Jewish national language, they magnify the suspicions of the Arabs on the one hand, and weaken Jewry by this internal struggle on the other.[21]

Edmund Schmidt, the Consul-General, accused the Zionists of attempting to suppress German in order to impose Hebrew as the sole language of instruction in the Technikum and force the Hilfs-verein out of its schools. The fact that no comparable action had been taken against instruction in French in the schools of the Alliance Israélite Universelle was proof that the entire campaign was directed against Germany alone. It was satisfactory that Cohn-Reiss had not yielded to the teachers' demands, and Schmidt expected that Dr. Nathan, on his forthcoming visit to Palestine, would be able to stand up to his opponents.[22] But when Nathan arrived, accompanied by Dr. Bernhard Kahn, the Hilfsverein's Secretary-General, he failed 'to pacify excited public opinion'. He dismissed the agitation of the advocates of Hebrew as 'Zionist propaganda'; the fact that the Orthodox sympathized with the Hilfsverein gave him reason to believe that the strike lacked general support. This was not a sound conclusion for although the Orthodox viewed the revival of Hebrew as profanation of the holy language, they were equally opposed to the modern education in the Hilfs-verein schools. Nathan remained adamant, and when Dr. Mossin-sohn, Principal of the Tel Aviv Hebrew Grammar School, attempted to negotiate, he found him inaccessible. Influenced by Cohn-Reiss, the Hilfsverein leaders were determined not to yield an inch. Compromise solutions were rejected and it was decided to dismiss those teachers who declined to teach according to the syllabus.[23]

---

[21] *Türkei* 195, K 176485–7, Loytved-Hardegg to A.A., 17 Nov. 1913, dis. no. 2837/152.

[22] Ibid. K 176490–1, Schmidt to Wangenheim, 24 Nov. 1913. In fact the Teachers' Union intended to undertake a similar campaign in the Alliance schools but the Zionist Executive stopped them (Alsberg, loc. cit., p. 170).

[23] The above is based on the following sources: *Die Welt* (Jan. 1914); Cohen, *The German Attack . . .*, pp. 15–16; Nathan, op. cit., pp. 12, 34–51; Alsberg, op. cit., p. 168; *Türkei* 195, K 176592–602, Brode to A.A., 30 Dec. 1913, dis. no. 115/2010; K 176536,

This complicated matters still further. A demonstration was held on 10 December in front of the Laemel School in Jerusalem, and when certain unruly individuals smashed the windows, Cohn-Reiss called for the German Consul and the Ottoman police. Upon their arrival he dismissed those teachers who in any case had been scheduled for dismissal on that day. However, much to the consternation of Schmidt and Cohn the teachers were followed by their students. This was interpreted by the Zionist Press as evidence that it was the police who had expelled the teachers under Cohn's orders in the presence of the German Consul. In his report to the Foreign Ministry Schmidt vigorously denied this allegation. He had responded to Cohn's request reluctantly, and it was only because the disruption of the school seemed imminent that he felt obliged to be present and thereby indicate that it was under German protection. He dismissed Zionist Press reports as 'tendentious exaggerations' and 'systematic incitement'. The police had been called 'only to disperse the demonstrators'; the Zionist charge that in Hilfsverein's schools, Hebrew could no longer find a place was without foundation. Nor did the pro-Hebrew movement command general support; only the Zionist settlements and particularly the intelligentsia backed it. Yet, despite his annoyance Schmidt urged the Hilfsverein not to precipitate a complete rupture with its partners and considered that undue emphasis on the German character of its schools was undesirable.[24]

Brode described the Hebrew protagonists in Jaffa/Tel Aviv as 'anarchist agitators' and 'terrorists' imbued with revolutionary socialist doctrines; they were undermining the civilizing influence of German Jews and causing concern to the Orthodox. He had refrained from interfering in this internal Jewish conflict, lest it might 'add fuel to the fire unnecessarily'; but, in contrast to Schmidt, he realized that the Hebrew movement was 'not directed against *Deutschtum* as such', but only against the Hilfsverein. He hoped that the heated

Schmidt to Wangenheim, 16 Dec. 1913, dis. no. 2635. However, according to Cohn-Reiss, Nathan refused to negotiate with the teachers so long as they continued to strike (op. cit. ii, pp. 186–9).

[24] *Türkei* 195, K 176536–43, K 176584–6, Schmidt to Wangenheim, 16, 30 Dec. 1913; K 176548, same to A.A., 30 Dec., tel. no. 11. However, Schmidt was unable to explain the presence of the police outside the Girls School, although no demonstrations took place there. For Nathan's account see op. cit., pp. 18–19, and for the Zionist version *Die Welt* (Dec. 1913, Jan. 1914); *Im Kampf*. . ., pp. 37–46; Cohen, *The German Attack* . . ., pp. 15–16. That of Cohn-Reiss (op. cit. ii, pp. 190–4) is not very reliable.

controversy, 'staged with such characteristic Jewish ardour', would eventually subside. He noted that certain Zionist leaders disapproved of acts of violence and were resolved to curb excesses of any kind and that the interest of some of the people was slackening because of the considerable financial burden entailed in the maintenance of a competitive school system.[25]

Loytved-Hardegg was also annoyed. None the less, he appreciated that for Zionists the revival of Hebrew was 'one of the main prerequisites in the achievement of their aim. It serves them as a means for the unification of the Jewish people, separated by multilingualism, and as a manifestation of their distinct character. It represented their "national existential minimum".' But he disagreed with those who asserted that Hebrew was already sufficiently developed to provide the vocabulary for economic and scientific studies, and rejected the accusations levelled against the Hilfsverein of 'betrayal and suppression of Hebrew renaissance and culture'. Much as he wished the Hilfsverein to emerge victorious, he feared that in the last resort it would be the Zionists who would gain the upper hand. Should they succeed in winning over the non-German members of the Technikum's Board, the Hilfsverein would have to surrender. He also pointed to the difficulty of finding substitutes for the Zionist teachers, who as idealists worked enthusiastically for low salaries. Reconciliation was therefore the soundest solution, particularly as the controversy did not turn on matters of principle but only on the efficacy of Hebrew as a medium of instruction for scientific and technical subjects, and on this narrower question an agreement was likely to be reached. If the Zionists were made to realize that they were not likely to win, and if, on the other hand, their opponents were influenced in favour of Jewish national aims, a *rapprochement* would be possible. From the German point of view such an outcome was all the more desirable since both the Russian and the French Consulate had tried to use the conflict for its own ends. The former secretly encouraged the Zionists in the belief that it was in the Russian interest to support a separatist element to weaken Turkey internally, hoping simultaneously to gain Jewish sympathy; whereas the latter always did its best to counteract any enterprise that appeared to promote German influence in Palestine.

[25] *Türkei* 195, K 176478–94, K 176592–602, Brode to A.A., 24 Nov., 30 Dec. 1913, dis. nos. 100/1754, 115/2010; K 177307, Brode's memorandum, 26 Aug. 1915, on which see below, pp. 256–8.

Loytvedd-Hardegg assumed that, should the Zionists lose Otto-man goodwill, they would be more likely to come to terms with the Hilfsverein. He warned both the Turkish Governor and the Arab notables in Haifa that the introduction of Hebrew in the Technikum would, in fact, bar prospective non-Jewish students from admission to this 'unique' institution, and that its exclusive use by the Jews would give them a competitive advantage over the non-Jews. Later he prevailed upon the local Mufti and Cadi to appeal to Dr. Nathan to resist the Zionists' intention to exclude non-Jewish students. On his advice several Muslim notables cabled the Ministry of Education in Constantinople and the Press was also approached. On another occasion he urged the Turkish Governor to oppose Zionist exclusive-ness because their separatist aspirations were encouraged by the Russian Consul; only those Jewish enterprises which aimed to ottomanize the Jews deserved full support, since by and large Turkey would benefit from Jewish colonization. However, he had to admit that all his efforts were of no avail. Disappointingly, both the Otto-man officials and the indigenous Arab population 'lacked the fore-sight and proper understanding of the importance of cultural values'.[26] It had not occurred to him that the Zionists, by demons-trating their independence, had won the respect of the Turkish authorities and even of certain Arab notables.[27] Nor did he realize that Hebrew, because of its linguistic affinity to Arabic, was easier for the native student to master than German, and that the Turks might have had their own reasons for treating his advice with circumspection.

Events in Palestine took the Zionist Executive in Berlin entirely by surprise. The strike and particularly the teachers' exit *en masse* from the Hilfsverein schools, accompanied by their students, aroused general displeasure; the most outspoken critic was Ahad Ha'am.[28] But in spite of serious misgivings the Executive could not desert the militant teachers. As soon as their struggle assumed a more positive

[26] Ibid. K 176605–16, Loÿtved-Hardegg to A.A., 29 Dec. 1913, dis. no. 3186/166. That protection of Jewish institutions had become 'a factor in the political rivalry of foreign powers', was confirmed by P. J. C. Gregor, the British Consul in Jerusalem (*B.C.* ii, p. 584, Gregor to Mallet, 15 Mar. 1913).

[27] Lichtheim, *She'ar Yashuv*, p. 252; *Rückkehr*, p. 227.

[28] *Ig'groth*, v, pp. 123–5, 142–7, 160–1, 178–9. Statements by Chaim Nahman Bialik, Moshe Smilansky, Nahum Sokolow, Joseph Brenner, Max Nordau, and others are reproduced in Cohn-Reiss, op. cit. ii, pp. 184, 218–19, 227–32; *Jewish Chronicle*, 10 Apr. 1914.

character a widespread campaign was launched in Europe and in the United States to provide funds for the maintenance of independent Hebrew schools. Once involved, the Executive became a party to the conflict. It could not remain indifferent to the course pursued by the Hilfsverein and other sections of German Jewry, which endeavoured to implicate the Zionist Organization in responsibility for the teachers' strike. The German Press, both Jewish and non-Jewish, was practically unanimous in condemning the Zionists,[29] and even the non-party *Hamburger Israelitisches Familienblatt* (18 December 1913) argued that if German were displaced, the Palestinian Jews might fall under Russian influence.

With Nathan's return to Berlin the campaign intensified. In January 1914 his pamphlet *Palästina und palästinensischer Zionismus* appeared, and the influential *Frankfurter Zeitung*, which backed him consistently, opened its pages to him. In its issue of 4 February 1914 he complained bitterly of 'the scandalous terrorist scenes' in Palestine; the Hilfsverein's goal was to educate an élite which, while mastering Hebrew for daily use, would, through the medium of a European language, be brought into contact with modern trends in science and technology. Just as the Alliance Israélite Universelle and the Anglo-Jewish Association showed preference for French or English, it was natural for the Hilfsverein to favour German. However, the promising beginning had been disrupted by the Zionist political ambitions. In a country with such a diverse population as Palestine, 'it was particularly dangerous to kindle the torch of exaggerated chauvinism . . . it might destroy the cultural oasis, tended with such care'.

The Zionists replied in a pamphlet *Im Kampf um die hebräische Sprache*, and, judging from the generous response and the number of voluntary contributions for the Hebrew Schools Fund, it was clear that their arguments were gradually gaining ground. Shmarya Levin was particularly successful in enlisting the help of American Jewry. But it was not until the meeting of the Technikum's Board on 24 February 1914 that the Hilfsverein was decisively defeated. During that meeting the American and Russian members of the Board sided with the Zionists and it was decided to separate the Grammar School from the Technical College, thus removing the principal bone of contention. In the Grammar School Hebrew was to be

---

[29] *Palestine during the War*, p. 8; *Im Kampf . . .*, pp. 55–7; Lichtheim, *Geschichte*, pp. 171–3; Gruenbaum, *Hatnua Hatziyonit*, iii, pp. 244–6.

used immediately as the unchallengeable language of tuition while in the College it was to be introduced in the course of four years.[30] Thus the Zionist Executive emerged triumphant. Given the German Government's preference for the Hilfsverein, the Zionist victory on the political plane seems the more surprising. It was not immediate, but once won it endured and had far-reaching consequences. At the end of November, when Bodenheimer called on the Foreign Ministry, Zimmermann told him unequivocally that the Hilfsverein's policy suited German interests better than that of the Zionists. He promised, however, to look into the matter. In a subsequent memorandum Bodenheimer took pains to emphasize that the settlers in Palestine were by no means inimical to Germany. On the contrary, they showed marked preference for German goods; and German influence, despite the wishes of the Russian Consulate, was welcome; the German Zionists in particular would never support any enterprise inconsistent with the interests of their fatherland. Should the Palestinian Jews be convinced that Germany was positively disposed towards the revival of Hebrew, she would gain immensely in prestige. The Reich stood to profit from Jewish colonization since no cultural progress could be expected in the foreseeable future from the Arab population.[31]

However, it was the version put out by James Simon, not that of Bodenheimer, that was given publicity in the semi-official Wolff Telegraphic Bureau.[32] The head of the Eastern Department of the Ministry, Dr. Hans von Rosenberg, made no secret of his sympathies. Interviewed by Dr. Rosenbaum, editor of the *Hamburger Israelitisches Familienblatt* (1 January 1914 issue), he professed his

[30] *Jüdische Rundschau*, 28 Aug. 1914; *Im Kampf . . .*, pp. 70–2; Weizmann, op. cit., p. 144; Alsberg, loc. cit., p. 169; Rabinowicz, op. cit., p. 88; Gruenbaum, op. cit. iii, pp. 246–8. By January 1914 contributions totalled 300,000 marks. Before the war the Zionist Organization maintained about 140 schools, attended by 11,000 students (two-thirds of the total Jewish children), and employed over 500 teachers.

[31] *Türkei* 195, K 176472–3, Zimmermann's annotation on Mirbach's note dated 26 Nov. 1913; K 176503–14, Bodenheimer to Zimmerman, 12, 16 Dec. 1913. It appears that Bodenheimer submitted his memorandum after consultation with the Zionist Executive. This, in addition to the evidence adduced below (pp. 182–3), invalidates Dr. Alsberg's claim that the Zionist Executive used the *Sprachenkampf* as 'a political demonstration to refute the argument of the alleged German orientation of Zionist statesmanship', and that it fitted in well with the 'new political orientation towards Great Britain and France' (loc. cit. pp. 168, 170). This was perhaps true of individual Zionist leaders in the Entente countries (below, p. 185) but not of the Executive who aimed to win support from all Powers concerned (below, pp. 228–9, 236–40, 322–6).

[32] *Türkei* 195, K 176519–22, Simon to Zimmerman, 16 Dec. 1913; W.T.B. news paper clipping.

confidence in the leaders of the Hilfsverein, both as 'good Germans and good Jews'. He was convinced that their stand with regard to the language of tuition at the Technikum was dictated not by political motives but solely out of regard for Jewish interests. The German Government on its part had no desire to subordinate Jewish institutions of learning to political aims. The only purpose in cultivating German was to facilitate commercial and cultural relations consonant with the well-being of Palestine Jewry. With all due respect for its religious and historical importance, Hebrew 'can hardly be expected to serve as more than a language for internal communication'. Moreover, encouraging it disproportionately had certain risks, since Arabs resented the wider use of the Jewish national language and the Turkish Government might suspect that it was symptomatic of the development of 'a state within the state'. The policy of the Hilfsverein therefore made sense. None the less, as far as the *Sprachenkampf* was concerned, unless individual German nationals or institutions under German protection were attacked, his Ministry would remain strictly neutral.

However guarded Rosenberg's statement, it confirmed for the first time publicly the German Government's interest in the Jewish settlement in Palestine and its connection to Germany. The Hilfsverein was acknowledged as the favoured party, but the rebellious teachers were not condemned. The fact that strict neutrality was proclaimed so emphatically was of no little significance, but this fell short of satisfying the Zionists. Otto Warburg categorically denied the version released by the Wolff Telegraphic Bureau and blamed Paul Nathan for aggravating the conflict and so doing harm to German prestige in Palestine.

Die Welt (January 1914), a copy of which Warburg forwarded to Zimmermann, maintained that by its excessive zeal the Hilfsverein had achieved the opposite effect to that which it desired. By antagonizing the liberal sector of Jewry in Palestine it had 'artificially created an antipathy for the German language which had not existed before' and as a result the demand to replace German by French became more audible; the Hilfsverein had rendered a disservice to German interests. The semi-official *Bayerische Staatszeitung*, quoted by *Die Welt*, was also critical of the attempt to impose German on the nationalist Jews. 'If it was natural for the German Jews to press for German, then why should not the English and French Jews express similar wishes?' The *Bayerische*

Staatszeitung concluded that the Zionists were right in fostering Hebrew which, as a national language, was less likely to involve them in the rivalry among the Powers. Germany was likely to gain 'more sympathy by allowing things to develop quietly than by achieving hollow successes . . . which in reality do more harm than good'.[33]

The Palestinian Zionists were not idle either. Miss Vera Pinczower, headmistress of the Girls' School, endeavoured to impress upon Consul-General Schmidt that the teachers' strike had been misinterpreted as an anti-German move; even in the newly established Hebrew schools, she insisted, German was strongly encouraged though as a foreign language. Reassured, Schmidt authorized her to quote him that, had he been properly acquainted with the facts, he would not have visited the school in the presence of the police; the 'restrained and calm behaviour' of the teachers and their students had impressed him. This statement, published in the *Neue Jüdische Korrespondenz* (5 January 1914), coupled with the editorial comment that it robbed the Hilfsverein of 'the last shred of sympathy', enraged James Simon. 'The Consul has stabbed us in the back', he wrote to Zimmerman, adding that a 'life and death' struggle must now be waged against the Zionists, and requesting Zimmerman's support. Zimmermann received Simon on the same day but was unable to offer any practical assistance because it had become evident that Schmidt had composed his differences with the Zionists. He had been reassured early in January by two of their leaders (whose names were not given) that 'the *Sprachenkampf* was not directed against Germany'. Aware of their standing and keen to improve relations, he had replied that the pro-Hebrew movement 'did not affect German interests *directly*, but was an internal affair'. He disapproved of the methods used during the conflict but dismissed the contention that they had violated German interests '*intentionally*'.[34]

Whether the Consul-General had reconciled himself completely to the Zionist victory is another matter. The episode left a bitter memory and Brode, too, in his memorandum of 26 August 1915, pointed to 'the anti-German effect of the *Sprachenkampf*'; but in 1914 the Consulate appeared satisfied with Zionist assurances. In

[33] *Türkei* 195, K 176545-6, K 176561, K 176618-25, Warburg to Zimmermann, 29 Dec. 1913, 8 Jan. 1914.
[34] Ibid. K 176629-31, Simon to Zimmermann, 7 Jan. 1914; K 176626-7, Schmidt to A.A., 13 Jan. 1914.

fact, until the outbreak of war, the language question was never discussed again.

The German Embassy also modified its attitude. Since Herzl's death the Zionists had consistently been kept at arm's length. During the *Sprachenkampf* the Embassy's coolness became tinged with positive displeasure and on 29 December 1913, when Victor Jacobson called on Gerhard von Mutius, the First Counsellor, then acting as Chargé d'Affaires, he heard him refer to the Palestinian Zionists in uncomplimentary terms. Jacobson's arguments fell on deaf ears. A month later von Mutius still clung firmly to his conviction that German interests were far better served through the Hilfsverein than through the Zionists. It was Richard Lichtheim, Jacobson's newly appointed deputy, who succeeded in winning over the Embassy. Realizing how detrimental to the Zionist cause German hostility might be, he urged both Professor Warburg in Berlin and Dr. Ruppin in Jaffa to take the initiative in counteracting the Hilfsverein. Ruppin composed a strongly worded memorandum which, signed by twenty-seven German Zionists resident in Palestine, was submitted to the Embassy. It shook von Mutius's earlier convictions and even von Wangenheim, on his return from Berlin, was impressed, admitting that 'if in the signatories' opinion Hebrew enjoys a "natural superiority" over German and that, if this position "meets the requirements of Palestine Jewry", then further discussion of the controversial question is futile.' Aware also of the latest resolution adopted by the Board of the Technikum, he thought it was 'imperative to maintain the utmost reserve. The natural advantages of German', he wired Berlin, 'must be freely recognized.'[35]

The primacy of Hebrew was now fully conceded. In March 1915 Counsellor Richard von Kühlmann told Lichtheim officially that 'Germany would be sufficiently compensated if, besides Hebrew, German would also be cultivated'.[36] Külhmann's opinion was echoed in Brode's memorandum of 26 August 1915 and coincided with Dr. Paul Rohrbach's statement in the Reichstag on 3 March 1915. While expressing the hope that the Jews in Palestine would promote the German language and interests, Rohrbach was confident that the

[35] Lichtheim, *She'ar Yashuv*, pp. 270–2; *Rückkehr*, pp. 240–2; *Türkei* 195, K 176673–9, memorandum by Ruppin and others, 5 Mar. 1914; K 176672, Wangenheim to A.A., 5 Mar. 1914, tel. no. 809.
[36] C.Z.A., Z 3/52, Lichtheim to E.A.C., 13 Mar. 1915.

revival of a Hebrew culture and the creation of a Jewish economic entity in Palestine were no longer in doubt.[37] Major Franz Karl Endres, formerly General Staff Officer on von der Goltz's mission to Turkey and later military correspondent of the *Münchener Neueste Nachrichten* and the *Frankfurter Zeitung*, wrote in the *Jüdische Presse* (12 March 1915) that, if Germany wished to replace French cultural influence in the East, she should be careful not to offend the national feelings of the native populations. This applied particularly to the Palestinian Jews who saw in the revival of Hebrew 'the most important symbol of their renaissance in the land of their fathers'.

It appears that the British also took note of the episode. McGregor, the Consul in Jerusalem, was impressed by 'the nationalistic spirit . . . manifesting itself with increased vigour in the Zionist schools', and Sir Louis Mallet, when relaying this information to Sir Edward Grey, identified Zionism with 'a Jewish national revival'.[38] The matter was not important enough to produce any major shift in British policy, but it tended to take the edge off the deeply rooted belief that Zionism was a German instrument. It provided Dr. Weizmann with arguments to refute the accusation that the Zionists were 'catspaws of the Germans in Palestine. We are neither German nor French, but Hebrew, and those who would support our Hebrew culture would obtain our support in return.'[39] In France, too, Max Nordau, the veteran Zionist leader, seized upon the *Sprachenkampf* as an opportunity to protest to Stephen Pichon, the Foreign Minister, against 'the slander' that the Zionists were 'German agents'. He hinted that, should France take a positive interest, she would find in the Jews of Palestine 'ready and faithful friends'. However, they 'would not wish to remain French, but to be and remain Hebrew'. Nordau did not object to Pichon's suggestion that French be taught as a foreign language.[40]

The *Round Table*, a quarterly dealing with the political affairs of the British Empire, attributed the emergence of Zionism from 'comparative obscurity into the sunshine of popular acclamation' to, among other things, the pro-Hebrew revolt of 1913; it stimulated the development of 'a self-conscious and self-dependent national centre for Jewry . . . in Palestine'. *Syria and Palestine*, a Foreign

[37] *Die Jüdische Presse. Konservative Wochenschrift* (12 Mar. 1915), no. 11.
[38] *B.C.* ii, p. 583.   [39] Weizmann, op. cit., p. 145.
[40] C.Z.A. Z 3/1013, report by Nordau, dated 6 Dec. 1913; Nordau, *A Biography . . .*, pp. 205–6. For Pichon's letter to Sokolow of 14 Feb. 1918 see Stein, op. cit., p. 591.

Office Handbook, gave the following advice when referring to the Zionist struggle against the Hilfsverein: 'The whole secret of British popularity in Palestine depends on our willingness to give the people the freedom to develop their own national consciousness in their own way.'[41]

Recognition that a Jewish national renaissance was in the making, quite apart from the wider political implications that flowed from it, was, by the same token, a blow to the assimilationist school of thought. During his lengthy conversations with von Mutius, Lichtheim steadily hammered home the argument that assimilation would provide no solution to the Jewish problem. The German Jewish masses were neither willing nor able to integrate completely into Gentile society; nor was the type of a hybrid assimilated Jew, prone to radical socialism, desirable for Germany herself. Lichtheim found in von Mutius a receptive audience for he was not only 'an unusual scholar with a searching mind but also a personality with deep moral-religious convictions', for whom theoretical questions held a strong appeal. He was particularly interested in Jewish–Gentile relations. Eventually, he agreed that 'assimilation has no ideals behind it; it is opportunist and therefore corrupting'. However, when Lichtheim attempted to translate his discourse into political terms, he found the diplomat reserved. Von Mutius disclosed that the opposition of German Jews and regard for Turkey rendered public support of Zionism by Germany impractical. Lichtheim tried to dismiss the first item as 'unimportant . . . particularly if contrasted with the political benefits that Germany might derive from support of the colonization of Palestine'. As for Turkey, he pointed to a friendlier attitude developing at that time. All the same, von Mutius was unmoved. 'The Turks trusted Germany no more than any other Power', and, should she intercede for the Zionists, they would react 'with the greatest suspicion'. Lichtheim replied that he did not expect Germany to intervene officially; what he wanted was that 'her benevolent attitude be communicated occasionally to the Porte'. In von Mutius Lichtheim gained a staunch friend who opened the way to the Ambassador.[42]

---

[41] F.O. Handbook no. 60, *Syria and Palestine*, p. 63. The manuscript was circulated in 1917 for guidance of British statesmen. Its author was William Ormsby-Gore.

[42] The above and what follows is based on Lichtheim's letter to the Zionist Executive of 29 June 1914 (C.Z.A. Z 3/11) and on his account in *She'ar Yashuv*, pp. 272–7, *Rückkehr*, pp. 241–6, unless other interpolated sources are referred to.

If von Mutius represented the type of 'educated country gentle-man . . . von Wangenheim was a real *grand seigneur*'. Lichtheim was greatly impressed by his imposing stature, intelligence, and alertness of mind. In conversation, however, Wangenheim was unpredictable, sometimes tough and distant and on other occasions amiable, sarcastic, or congenial, according to his mood. Henry Morgenthau, the American Ambassador in Constantinople, was also struck by Wangenheim's personality. 'His huge solid frame . . . his bold defiant head, his piercing eyes, the whole physical structure, con-stantly pulsating with life and activity' symbolized to the American Ambassador the modern Germany of 'limitless ambitions'. Yet, despite the drive and ambition of the Prussian, Wangenheim had some of the milder characteristics of his native Thuringia; his most conspicuous quality was his tact. 'He dominated not so much by brute strength as by a mixture of force and amiability; he won by persuasiveness, not by the mailed fist.'[43]

Wangenheim's arrival in Constantinople did not signal a radical change of policy but his forceful personality and the altered condi-tions accelerated the pace of Germany's peaceful penetration of Turkey. This trend was reinforced by the sharpening rivalry with France. At this juncture Wangenheim did not bypass the Jews in the East, but it was not until the summer of 1914 that he came to regard the Zionists as a factor worthy of consideration. This may be deduced from the statement he made to Lichtheim on 29 June in his ambassadorial residence in Therapia; the tense political situation created by the murder of Archduke Franz-Ferdinand in Sarajevo did not prevent the Ambassador from keeping the appointment.

Wangenheim's frankness and straightforwardness during the conversation surprised Lichtheim. He reported to the Zionist Executive in Berlin:

Wangenheim declared himself to be in our favour. He told me that he had always felt great sympathy towards the Zionists and remembered Herzl. . . . He stated that Germany was in no position to commit herself politically, but within the limits of his capacity . . . and unofficially he would be prepared to support us. However, full-fledged activities on our behalf would be possible only after authorization from *Berlin*. In any case, he intends to discuss the matter with the Grand Vizier shortly.

[43] Morgenthau, *Secrets of the Bosphorus*, pp. 2, 4–5; cf. Poincaré, *Memoirs*, i, p. 105; Frank P. Chambers, *The War behind the War, 1914–1918*, p. 59.

He agreed with Lichtheim, however, that it would be more advisable to speak with Talaat Pasha, the Minister of the Interior, who was known to be favourably disposed towards the Zionists. He also showed understanding of Lichtheim's arguments in favour of Hebrew education and inquired whether the Zionists enjoyed the support of any other Power, particularly that of Russia. Lichtheim replied that Russia's friendly attitude was motivated by her interest in protecting Russian nationals, which, he remarked pointedly, was at variance with the Zionists' wish that the immigrants adopt Ottoman nationality. Wangenheim thereupon said: 'If the Zionists in Turkey suffer from persecution, I will do my best to protect them', adding that 'the idea of treating the Zionists benevolently emanated from Berlin'.

Lichtheim gained the impression that Wangenheim was animated by 'perfectly sincere sympathy', which stemmed from the conviction that the Zionists were able to do valuable work for Turkey and benefit Germany as well by spreading German cultural and economic influence in the East. Of his readiness to protect the Zionists, Lichtheim commented: 'this is not much, but still something'. The months following the outbreak of war gave Lichtheim ample opportunity to see how serious and sincere he was.

PART III

During the War
1914–1918

11

Germany Protects the Zionists in Palestine

WANGENHEIM's promise was not a hollow one. A fortnight later, on learning from Lichtheim that two hundred Jewish immigrants from Russia had been forbidden to disembark at Jaffa, he instructed the German Consulate General in Palestine to intercede with the local Ottoman authorities on their behalf.[1] Wangenheim's move was surprising, since it was unprecedented for a German Ambassador to plead for Russian nationals, especially as Russia was at war with Germany at that time. Wangenheim clearly overstepped his prerogatives; that he preferred to ignore the legalities shows at what he was aiming; protection of 50,000 Russian Jews in Palestine, in addition to German nationals and protégés, would have given him a paramount position there. For despite her professed interest in the integrity of the Ottoman Empire, Germany staunchly defended her treaty rights; Turkey's unilateral abrogation of the Capitulations on 9 September 1914 provoked a strong protest from Berlin.[2] However, with Turkey determined to emancipate herself from foreign protectorates, Wangenheim had to avoid arousing the suspicions of his ally that Germany was attempting to introduce 'a similar protectorate with regard to the Jews'.[3] It seemed therefore more prudent to agree with the Porte that Russian Jews should adopt Ottoman nationality, a solution which was welcome to the Zionists as well.

Naturalization of foreign Jews had been the goal of the Porte for decades. Early in 1914 far-reaching facilities had been granted in this respect but only twenty individuals had applied for naturalization. Talaat Bey, the Minister of the Interior, constantly drew the

---

[1] Lichtheim, *She'ar Yashuv*, p. 285; *Rückkehr*, pp. 251–2.
[2] Ahmed Emin, *Turkey in the World War* (Yale University Press, 1930), pp. 73, 163.　　　　　　　　　　　　　　　　[3] Below, pp. 241, 256.

Zionists' attention to this failure. Lichtheim in Constantinople, as well as his colleagues in Berlin, fully appreciated the importance of this problem and did their utmost to encourage Jewish settlers to embrace Ottoman nationality. Eliezer Ben-Yehuda untiringly propagated this idea in his paper *Haor*, as did a number of prominent Palestinian leaders. Yet only a few settlers accepted their advice; the notorious maladministration and miscarriage of justice at the hands of the Ottoman officials made any foreign resident think twice before jettisoning the advantages of consular protection.[4] However, with the outbreak of the war, all former reservations faded. Consular protection almost ceased to exist. It was widely feared that, should Turkey join the Central Powers and become involved in hostilities, especially against Russia, all Palestinian Jews of a belligerent nationality might be expelled, thereby bringing about most 'disastrous consequences' to the entire Zionist enterprise.[5] Ottomanization, however obnoxious, seemed to be the only course left to ensure the continuity of the Yishuv.

There were about 100,000 Jews in Palestine in 1914, of whom 15,000 lived in fifty agricultural settlements.[6] Half of the total lived in Jerusalem, where Jews formed the great majority of the population.[7] Next in importance were the communities of Safad (10,000 Jews out of a total of 19,000 inhabitants), Tiberias (8,000 Jews out of a total of 10,000), and Hebron (1,000 Jews out of a total of 20,000 inhabitants)—the 'holy cities'—in which the 'old' Yishuv was

---

[4] C.Z.A. Z 3/429, meeting of G.A.C., 4 Nov. 1914; Z 3/449, meeting of the same, 7 June 1914; Lichtheim, *She'ar Yashuv*, pp. 246–9, 285; *Rückkehr*, pp. 223–5; Elmaliyach, *Eretz-Israel V'Suria Bimey Milchemet Haolam* [*Palestine and Syria during the First World War*], ii. pp. 5–8; above, pp. 42–3.

[5] *Türkei* 195, K 176692–97, Ruppin to E.A.C., 5 Aug. 1914, encl. in Bodenheimer to A.A., 29 Aug. 1914.

[6] Ibid., Bodenheimer to A.A., 29 Aug. 1914. This is the standard figure which appears in Zionist, German, and British documentary sources. They cannot be reproduced here in full. Dr. Curt Nawratzki in his study *Die jüdische Kolonisation Palästinas* also quotes the figure of 100,000 for the year of 1912 as an estimate (p. 501). On pp. 395–6 he gives detailed statistics of the Palestine population, Jewish and non-Jewish, in urban centres in 1912/13. Ruppin's figure of 85,000 Jews in *The Jews in the Modern World* (London, 1934), pp. 55, 489, also in Bein, *The Return to the Soil*, p. 138, is underestimated. In a speech made on 27 Feb. 1908 Ruppin himself stated that there were 80,000 Jews in the country (*Building Israel*, pp. 1, 10), and in an address delivered before the Eleventh Zionist Congress in Sept. 1913 he quoted the figure of 100,000 Jews (ibid., p. 62). The total Arabic-speaking population in Palestine, Christian and Muslim, was estimated at between 600,000 to 700,000.

[7] 20,000 Christians, 15,000 Muslims, and 50,000 Jews making the total of 85,000 (Nawratzki, op. cit., p. 395; cf. Friedman, *The Question of Palestine*, p. 369 n. 48).

concentrated.[8] The centre of the Yishuv, however, was in Jaffa, where 10,000 Jews lived (out of a total of 50,000), particularly in its modern suburb, Tel Aviv. There was a more or less even numerical ratio between the 'old' and the 'new' Yishuv but in outlook, way of life, and aspirations they were worlds apart. The former was extremely orthodox and dedicated its life to prayer and learning; the latter, primarily secularist in thinking, aspired to build a new society and a home for its people. Neither community was economically viable. With the outbreak of the war the old Yishuv, which lived on charity, faced starvation. But the new Yishuv was also hard hit. Despite its remarkable progress in agriculture and industry it was still too vulnerable to weather a world conflict. Investment in business and colonization stopped, and so did the inflow of private money from relations abroad. A rush on the banks caused the Government to declare a moratorium on loans and consequently lack of credit paralysed all economic life. Maritime communications were disrupted and two basic export crops—wine and oranges—remained landlocked. Petroleum, needed as fuel for irrigation pumps, could not be imported, while fruit crops decayed on the trees. The colonists faced ruin. Moreover, the Turkish Government, though neutral (till 31 October 1914), began confiscating animals and food stocks. Consequently, the price of foodstuffs and other necessities rose sharply while wages fell as the result of mass unemployment. Flour disappeared from the market and famine threatened the country.

In contrast to the *Haluka* community, inactive and helpless, the new Yishuv displayed a remarkable degree of maturity and resourcefulness. Internal dissensions gave way to a new sense of solidarity and mutual help. A central emergency committee was elected which, headed by Meir Dizengoff, a dynamic leader and future mayor of Tel Aviv, set up a purchasing and selling agency to prevent speculation and combat the rise in the cost of living. It distributed work evenly among the unemployed and took care of the needy, old, and infirm. To meet the acute shortage of cash, the Anglo-Palestine Co. and the Tel Aviv council issued special banknotes. But, despite all these measures, it soon became apparent that without outside help the Yishuv would founder economically. Cables were therefore dispatched, particularly to the United States, asking for help.[9]

---

[8] On which see above, pp. 25, 29–31.

[9] As note 5; C.Z.A. L 6/38/I, Ruppin to E.A.C., 8 Sept., 4, 14 Oct. 1914; Elmaliyach, op. cit. i, pp. 101–56; Mordechai Ben-Hillel Hacohen, *Milchemet Ha-Amim* [*War*

The Palestine Jews were fortunate that Henry Morgenthau, the American Ambassador in Constantinople, was favourably disposed. In 1913, on his appointment, President Wilson had told him, 'Remember that anything you can do to improve the lot of your co-religionists is an act that will reflect credit upon America, and you may count on the full power of the Administration to back you up.'[10]

Morgenthau followed this advice faithfully, and not only out of regard for his chief, whom he deeply admired. Though a practical and self-made man, there was a streak of idealism in his character and an innate disposition to help human beings in distress. Morgenthau was not a Zionist, and Zionism as a theory interested him little. He became acquainted with its problems through Lichtheim, whose company he found congenial, and Lichtheim soon made him privy to all Jewish affairs. In April Morgenthau visited Palestine. Guided by Ruppin he was deeply impressed by what he saw: the pioneers appeared to him to be the very personification of a new type of Jew and he saw in their achievements an example of what could be done elsewhere. He vowed to do everything possible to aid them.[11]

Morgenthau's goodwill stood the Zionists in good stead during the war. As soon as he received Ruppin's call early in August, he cabled the Jewish relief organizations in the United States, and by the end of September 1914 he was able to inform Ruppin that M. Wertheim, his son-in-law, would shortly be arriving at Jaffa on the American warship *North Carolina* to hand over 250,000 francs in gold (25,000 dollars) for emergency purposes. Half of the money had been contributed by Jacob Schiff, the well-known American banker and philanthropist, and the other half by the Zionist Federation of America and the philanthropist Nathan Straus. The boat anchored at Jaffa port on 6 October 1914 and was welcomed by Palestine Jews with unbounded joy and relief; their prestige rose tremendously in the eyes of the Turkish authorities and among the Arabs. Morgenthau could congratulate himself on being so effective. Modestly he replied to Ruppin's letter of thanks:

I do not know whether you and your friends, or I have to be grateful for the fact that I am ambassador. It makes me feel that I have been the

---

Among the Nations] (Jerusalem, Tel Aviv, 1929–30), pp. 2–5, 11, 32–3; Bein, op. cit., pp. 138–53; *Ha-Achdut* (Hebrew weekly), 7 Aug. 1914; *Jüdische Rundschau*, reports from Palestine (1914), pp. 358, 380–2, 420; (1915), p. 17. (See above, p. 25.)

[10] Manuel, *The Realities of American Palestine Relations*, p. 116.

[11] Lichtheim, *She'ar Yashuv*, pp. 262–8; *Rückkehr*, pp. 233–8; Elmaliyach, op. cit. i, pp. 69–71.

chosen weapon to take up the defence of my co-religionists, and that I have been blessed with the opportunity to render them some service. So I really believe that I am the one who should be the most thankful and not the beneficiaries.

In conformity with the instructions from America, the distribution of money was placed in the hands of a committee, on which Ruppin served as chairman together with Aaron Aaronsohn, Director of the Agricultural Experimental Station at Atlit, near Haifa, and Ephraim Cohn-Reiss, the Director of the Hilfsverein schools.[12]

Concern for the Yishuv was not confined to a few philanthropists. On 30 August 1914 Louis D. (later Justice) Brandeis, jointly with Shmarya Levin, then in the U.S.A., established the Provisional Executive Committee for General Zionist Affairs. It was not merely a relief organization. It served as a political body, the influence of which on President Wilson proved highly beneficial to the Zionist cause later in the war, but its immediate objective was to avert an economic breakdown of the new settlement in Palestine. It undertook to maintain schools and a number of institutions; it advanced loans to the colonists and financed the Palestine Office and the Agency in Constantinople. As the war went on and conditions worsened, more warships and additional funds were sent. Once an entire ship, the S.S. *Vulcan*, arrived loaded with provisions. Thanks to this help the Jewish population remained alive.[13]

It was in deference to American Jewry and to the State Department that the British and French Governments conceded freedom of passage to United States warships carrying supplies for Palestine. Impressed by America's persistent efforts to assist the Jewish settlement, Whitehall consented also to the remittance of funds collected by British Jews.[14] Funds were raised in other European countries as well, notably in Russia; they were channelled through Egypt or through neutral countries like Holland.[15] Yet, however important

[12] Ruppin, *Memoirs*, pp. 151–2; Report of the Executive Committee of the American Jewish Committee, 8 Nov. 1914, cited also in the *Jüdische Rundschau* (1914), p. 460. On Schiff, see below, pp. 203, 205. On Aaronsohn see Friedman, op. cit., pp. 120–3 and *passim*.

[13] Lichtheim, *She'ar Yashuv*, pp. 283–4; *Rückkehr*, pp. 249–50; Elmaliyach, op. cit. i, pp. 173–80; *Palestine during the War*, pp. 14–17. Altogether there arrived thirteen American warships in Palestine. A total of 670,000 dollars was contributed apart from private donations to individuals and institutions.

[14] Friedman, op. cit., pp. 43, 344 n. 33.

[15] Lichtheim, *She'ar Yashuv*, p. 284; *Rückkehr*, p. 250.

materially all this help was, the security of the Palestine Jews, if not
their very physical survival, rested in the hands of the Ottoman
Government and its ally, Germany. It was therefore to them that
the Zionists had to look for protection.

Early in August Dr. Ruppin approached Zakey Bey, the Ottoman
Governor in Jerusalem, requesting that he garrison Jewish centres
with Ottoman military units 'should there be any excesses by the
[Arab] population' against the Jews; alternatively that he increase
the number of Jewish guards and recognize them officially. To
prevent speculation and ensure an equitable distribution of food,
Ruppin suggested that the Government sanction the establishment
of a Central Purchase Food Commission, but the most burning
problem was that of the naturalization of foreign Jews. Mahmoud
Mukhtar Pasha, the Turkish Ambassador in Berlin, to whom Dr.
Bodenheimer and Professor Warburg turned, showed understanding
and supported their plea to the Sublime Porte. The Zionist leaders
briefed the Auswärtiges Amt about their moves, and requested that,
should any difficulties arise on the question of naturalization, the
Reich grant the Palestinian Jews its benevolent protection.[16] Dr.
Zimmerman was responsive and, on the State Secretary's behalf,
advised von Wangenheim of Bodenheimer's concern that, should
Turkey be involved in a war with Russia, Russian Jews in Palestine
should not be driven out of the country, or be subject to assault from
the non-Jewish native population. 'It seems to us that in view of the
effect upon international Jewry, considerate treatment of the Russian Jews lies within Turkish interest.'[17]

The Porte, notably Talaat, shared this conviction and, with the
prospects for naturalization improving, the Zionists ventured to
take one further step. On 30 October they proposed the foundation
of a Jewish police force under the command of an Ottoman officer,
financed by the Jewish colonies. A nucleus of such a force did exist
—the Hashomer—the Jewish watchman organization. It contained
excellent human material, well-trained horsemen and riflemen,
familiar with Arab customs and language and well acquainted with
the conditions of the country. Before the war the Ottoman authorities
tolerated the Hashomer's existence, though they denied its members
licences for carrying arms. The Zionists asserted that if it were

---

[16] As note 5.
[17] *Türkei* 195, K 176701–2, State Secretary to Wangenheim, 30 Aug. 1914, tel.
no. 577.

expanded, properly equipped, and legalized, such a force would be able to repel any onslaught by Arab bands or marauders on Jewish colonies, and the Ottoman Government would be relieved of the burden of maintaining internal security.[18] The Porte viewed the project favourably and implementation seemed to be within reach, but the local authorities gave it eventually its *coup de grâce*.[19]

In Jerusalem Zakey Bey, who followed the Porte's instructions faithfully, evinced no objections to the proposal. Contemporary Jewish writers had nothing but praise for his probity of character and fairness. He preached tolerance and friendship among Muslims and non-Muslims. The Jews remained grateful and, led by the Haham Franco, the Chief Rabbi, demonstrated their loyalty to the Ottoman cause on a number of occasions.[20] But in Jaffa the atmosphere was totally different. Following the appointment of Beha-ed-Din to the position of *Caimakam* a reign of terror was instituted. He impressed his contemporaries as a 'clever, educated, incorruptible and self-reliant official',[21] but also 'repulsive in appearance, cunning and distrustful'.[22] Dr. Brode described him as 'a young ambitious man, who resented the increasing independence of the Jewish colonies'. On his arrival in Jaffa early in October he announced his intention of putting an end to the colonies which he, as a Turkish nationalist, regarded as 'separatist' in character and 'dangerous to the State'.[23] He particularly disliked the Russian Zionists, the Labour organization, and the Hashomer; the suburb of Tel Aviv was 'a state within a state'.[24]

Before coming to Palestine Beha-ed-Din had served in Macedonia where he witnessed how the intervention of the European Powers, coupled with native nationalism, paved the way towards Macedonia's secession. He moved thereafter to the Ministry of the Interior and headed the Department for Non-Turkish Nationalities. His

[18] Ibid. K 176705–8, Warburg to A.A., 30 Oct. 1914 and encl. memorandum by Loewy.
[19] Ibid. K 177025–6, Wangenheim to A.A., 6 Apr. 1915, dis. no. 214; below, pp. 198–9, 219.
[20] Elmaliyach, op. cit. i, pp. 94–7, 208–12; ii, pp. 8–9; Ben-Hillel Hacohen, op. cit. i, p. 58.
[21] *Kitvey Menahem Shenkin* [*Writings of . . .*], ed. A. Hermoni (Jerusalem 1936), i, pp. 51–2; Ben-Hillel Hacohen, op. cit. i, p. 15. The *Caimakam* was the administrative head of a sub-district.
[22] Smilansky: *Zichronot*, iii, p. 12: Meir Dizengoff, *Im Tel Aviv Bagola*, [*Tel Aviv Evacuated*] (Tel Aviv, 1931), p. 18.
[23] *Türkei* 195, K 177308–9, Brode to A.A., 26 Aug. 1915, dis. no. 76/1278.
[24] Ibid. K 176956, Ephraim Cohn-Reiss to Nathan, 18 Feb. 1915.

experiences intensified his chauvinism and made him receptive to the arguments of the Arab deputies to the Ottoman Parliament that Jewish immigration was detrimental to Ottoman interests; the Jews were 'a foreign element supported by foreign Powers'. Autonomous Jewish institutions, a Jewish national flag and anthem, and especially the traffic of American warships, which he saw on his arrival in Jaffa, reinforced his suspicion that there existed a well-organized separatist movement which, if unchecked, would follow Macedonia's example.[25] He took an early opportunity to declare to Rabbi Uziel, the Chief Rabbi of Jaffa, in the presence of a number of Jewish notables, that he was a determined opponent of those Jews who were named Zionists. Whilst in Constantinople he had devoted particular attention to this question. He also knew the Jewish prayer book, which was 'full of "Zion" . . . The Jews are acquiring land and founding "colonies", like the Romans, in order to form a state within a state.' He warned that he would deal rigorously with such a development.[26]

Unfettered by the Capitulations, Beha-ed-Din soon translated his threats into deeds. Sign-posts and street-plates in Hebrew were removed, immigration and purchase of land were prohibited, and the Hashomer was disbanded. On 5 November a meticulous house-to-house search was carried out in Tel Aviv and, although it failed to provide proof that the Zionists were pursuing separatist aims, several individuals were arrested and sentenced to exile. Following the search, the use of Jewish National Fund stamps was prohibited 'on pain of death', the Zionist flag and Zionist institutions were declared illegal, use of Hebrew was prohibited, and all branches of the Anglo-Palestine Company (which was registered in England) were closed. Moreover, Beha-ed-Din demanded that all illegal arms in the possession of Jews be given up, and he was not satisfied until large quantities were handed over; in fact the Jews in some cases were compelled to buy arms from Bedouins to fill the quota.[27] Alexander Aaronsohn vividly described what went on in his native colony of Zichron Yaakov:

. . . our people were in a state of great excitement because an order had recently come from the Turkish authorities bidding them surrender

[25] Shenkin, op. cit. i, pp. 51–2.   [26] *Palestine during the War*, pp. 19–20.
[27] Ibid., pp. 20–2; Ben-Hillel Hacohen, op. cit. i, pp. 34–8; Elmaliyach, op. cit. ii, pp. 26–36; Smilansky, op. cit. iii, pp. 15–21; Shenkin, op. cit., pp. 49–51; *Türkei* 195, K 177309, Brode to A.A., 26 Aug. 1915; C.Z.A., L 6/38/1, Ruppin to E.A.C., 15 Feb. 1915; Z 3/758, report by J. L[urie?], 15 Feb. 1915.

whatever firearms or weapons they had in their possession . . . we knew that similar measures had been taken before the terrible Armenian massacres, and we felt that some such fate might be in preparation for our people. With the arms gone, the head of the village knew that our last hold over the Arabs, our last chance for defense against sudden violence, would be gone, and they had refused to give them up. A house-to-house search had been made—fruitlessly, for our little arsenal was safely cached in a field.

A number of the young men were apprehended, but though tortured mercilessly in prison they did not reveal the secret. The Turks thereupon announced that, unless the arms cache was disclosed, a number of young girls would be carried off and handed over to the officers. This was an ordeal which the colonists could not withstand. They dug up the treasured arms and handed them over to the authorities only to learn that later they had been distributed among the native Arabs.[28]

Beha-ed-Din was assisted by Hassan Bey el Bassri, the District Military Governor. Described as 'the harshest and most cruel' of officials, 'the very type of Oriental satrap', he was, unlike the *Caimakam*, 'corrupt . . . and an ignorant fanatic'. Every Jewish institution was suspect in his eyes and each demand was accompanied by threats which threw the Jewish population into a state of terror. From his headquarters it had been announced that the Jewish colonists would be levelled to the state of *fellahin* and that Jewish property would be confiscated. Arab peasants were told that the country was dominated by a Muslim Government which would prevent the Jews from 'stealing the land' and that after the war Jewish land would be turned over to them.[29]

The entry of Turkey into the war on 31 October and the ensuing proclamation of *jehad*, the Holy War, had an inflammatory effect on the Muslim population. To mark the event Hassan Bey printed a pamphlet which included the statement that it was incumbent upon every devout Muslim to kill the infidels: Christians and Jews alike.[30] A tense atmosphere enveloped the country. Arabs grew restive

[28] Alexander Aaronsohn, *With the Turks in Palestine* (New York, 1916), pp. 29–35. Alexander was Aaron's brother, on whom see above, p. 195 and below, pp. 222–3, 354, 367. [29] As note 27.
[30] Shenkin, op. cit. i, p. 61. On *jehad* see Emin, op. cit., pp. 174–7; Morgenthau, *Secrets of the Bosphorus*, pp. 106–9; George Antonius, *The Arab Awakening* (New York, 1934), pp. 147–8.

and gossip was rampant that at long last 'an end had come to the Jews'.[31]

News from Palestine spread quickly throughout the United States, some of it in an exaggerated form. On 30 October Count Johan Heinrich Bernstorff, the German Ambassador to Washington, cabled Berlin: 'local Jewish circles are very much worried lest massacres of Jews in Turkey might take place, for which we would indirectly be held responsible'. Zimmermann relayed Bernstorff's cable to Wangenheim immediately and, whilst reminding him of his instruction of 30 August (no. 577), he requested that if it was still necessary, he should see to it that Jews, regardless of nationality, were unmolested. Wangenheim did not discount the possibility of individual attacks by the Muslim population against Jewish settlers in Palestine, but thought that anxiety regarding pogroms was unfounded. Talaat had promised him that Jews should remain unmolested and that naturalization of foreign Jews would be expedited, a course with which Chief Rabbi Nahoum fully concurred. Wangenheim added that he had instructed the consulates in Jerusalem, Jaffa, Haifa, and Beirut to emphasize to the local Turkish authorities the need for an accommodating attitude towards the Jewish inhabitants. Bernstorff was kept informed about all these moves.[32]

The Zionists were fortunate that right from the beginning of the war the German Government recognized their importance as a vehicle through which the sympathy of world Jewry could be won over. Early in August Baron Langwerth von Simmern, the Head of the Political Department of the High Command, received a long memorandum from Dr. Otto Sprenger of Bremen in which the Zionist movement was presented as the most powerful international organization in Eastern Europe. He claimed that the enrolled membership in Russia of 80,000 (out of a total membership of 140,000) did not reflect its true strength, since in Russia Zionism was prohibited. According to estimates four out of seven million Jews in Russia were Zionist sympathizers. They had an exceedingly well-spread

---

[31] Hillel Yaffe, *Dor Ma'apilim* [*Generation of Pioneers*] (Tel Aviv, 1939), p. 493, Yaffe to Ruppin, 3 Mar. 1915.

[32] *Türkei* 195, K 176709–18, Bernstorff to A.A., 30 Oct. 1914, tel. no. 262; Zimmermann to Wangenheim, 1 Nov. 1914, tel. no. 1096; same to Bernstorff, 1 Nov. 1914, tel. no. 212; Wangenheim to A.A., 5 Nov. 1914, tel. no. 1248; above, p. 196.

network. The movement was led by 'reliable and trustworthy' personalities who were subordinated to the headquarters in Berlin, which, in Springer's opinion, was German-oriented. Professor Otto Warburg, Dr. Arthur Hantke, Richard Lichtheim, and Dr. Arthur Ruppin were German nationals; Dr. Victor Jacobson and Dr. Yechiel Tschlenow were Russians but educated in German universities, and Nahum Sokolow of Warsaw had during his long sojourn in Germany acquired 'a German mentality'.

It is therefore superfluous to stress that such an organization, which is completely in German hands and scattered all over in enemy countries, represents a factor which can be utilized to Germany's advantage in a number of ways. First, it would be able to provide information on all political and military events in enemy countries and, should we avail ourselves of its useful intelligence and guidance, we might reduce substantially the heavy losses of our forces. Second, since trade in Russia is concentrated largely in Jewish hands, the Jews are familiar with local communications and are in the closest touch with the native population. They know precisely how to tap the resources of the country and how to deal with its inhabitants and Russian officials . . . Third, the Zionists might be used, though under a different cover, behind the Russian Army as carriers of revolutionary movements, to spread demoralization, and organize sabotage.[33]

Sprenger's conclusions were far fetched, if not illusory. Yet his findings were re-echoed in a memorandum by the Legation Secretary Friedrich von Prittwitz submitted two weeks later to the Political Department of the High Command. Comparing the Zionists to a Jesuit Order, which was pledged to 'absolute obedience' by its leaders, Prittwitz wrote:

In the Zionist Organization we have a tool of an immense value for our Information Service and propaganda activity abroad. This applies especially to Russia. Moreover, as all supplies of cereal and livestock for the Russian Army are delivered by Jewish middlemen, so we have in the Zionists an effective means to impede the catering and the operation of the Russian Army. Finally, we have come to an arrangement with two Zionist representatives in Constantinople and Jaffa about publishing authentic information on the events of the war. This will be done regularly through the good offices of the Wolff Telegraphic Bureau.[34]

---

[33] *Wk.*, Nr. 11, adh. 2, K 714/K 190219–25, Sprenger to von Simmern, 7 Aug. 1914 (a copy to A.A.).

[34] *Grosses Hauptquartier*, Nr. 23; *Revolutionäre Bewegungen*, Bd. 1, *Überblick über die in der islamitisch-israelitischen Welt eingeleitete Agitationstätigkeit, 11. Israelitische Welt*, Prittwitz to Simmern, 20 Aug. 1914.

It was of even greater significance to win over American Jewry. Propaganda, considered as the 'fifth weapon', played an important role in general warfare but in the United States, in contrast to the Entente Powers, Germany was at a great disadvantage. The English influence on the American daily Press was enormous and the Germans were not always successful in presenting their point of view. Bernstorff complained that Germany's enemies found very important allies in a number of leading American newspapers, which did all they could to spread anti-German feeling.[35] Although before the war there had been a certain tradition of amiable relations between the American and German governments, the two peoples had subsequently drifted apart. The existence of a large population in the United States of German origin and the fact that the most competent philosophers, historians, and scientists had been trained in Germany was of secondary importance, because the bulk of the population, as well as the authoritative political circles, relied on English sources.[36] As early as 8 August 1914 the German Embassy noted regretfully that the tide in the country was anti-German.[37]

Bernstorff realized that the most important diplomatic battle was taking place in Washington and that in the struggle for the soul of the American people a supreme effort had to be made to attract, in the first place, all the friends or the potential friends of the Central Powers;[38] among these were counted the Irish Americans, who were anti-British, the Germans, and the German Jews. As Sir Cecil Spring-Rice, the British Ambassador to Washington, attested, the influence of the last-named was very great and, in some parts of the country, supreme.[39] Emil Vietor, the German Consul in Richmond, Virginia, reported that the American Jews possessed 'great power. . . . On the whole they are inclined to sympathize with Germany. They do not wish to fall out with any [of the contending parties] . . .

[35] Johann Heinrich Bernstorff, *My Three Years in America*, trans. (New York, 1920), pp. 33, 43, 46; C. Hartley Grattan, *Why We Fought* (New York, 1929), p. 36; Lichtheim, *She'ar Yashuv*, p. 291; *Rückkehr*, p. 256.

[36] Grattan, op. cit., p. 81; Bernstorff, op. cit., pp. 45, 84; see also Clara E. Schieber, *The Transformation of American Sentiment towards Germany, 1870–1914* (New York, 1923).

[37] Ernest R. May, *The World War and American Isolation, 1914–1917* (Harvard University Press, Cambridge, 1959), p. 36.

[38] *The Memoirs of Count Bernstorff*, p. 106; *idem, My Three Years*, pp. 332–4; Charles Appun, 'L'ambassade de Bernstorff à Washington', *Revue historique de Guerre mondiale*, iii (1925), pp. 297–329.

[39] Spring-Rice, *The Letters and Friendships of Sir Cecil Spring-Rice*, ii, pp. 219, 238, 242–5, 270.

so, at least publicly, they avoid taking sides . . . Their influence over the editors of American newspapers is considerable.'[40] Horst Falcke, the German Consul-General in New York, was impressed with the vast circulation of the Jewish Press, which was only a fraction of the means through which Jewish influence in the States was exercised. He attached even greater importance to the fact that the great dailies, such as the *New York Times*, or the *New York World*, were either owned or published by Jews, themselves immigrants or descended from immigrants from Germany or Austria-Hungary.[41]

Jews were also influential in high finance, the most prominent personality being Jacob Schiff, a senior partner in the celebrated banking firm Kuhn & Loeb and one of the most powerful figures in American Jewish life. Erich Hossenfelder, Falcke's successor, referred to him as 'one of the ruling finance giants' and 'a power among the banking houses', who was in a commanding position to encourage or frustrate loans to any of the belligerents. Schiff came from Frankfurt-on-Main and, through a branch of his family, eminent in its own right, maintained close business relations with Germany. His sympathies lay with his country of origin, but his feelings towards his own people were even stronger. On these the Germans played well. 'If I ascribe so much importance to Jacob Schiff', wrote Hossenfelder, 'it is because he is accessible to representations, particularly when utilizing Russia's ignoble activities against her Jewish population.'[42] Germany's protection of the Jewish settlement in Palestine made an even stronger appeal to Schiff for, although he was not a Zionist, its welfare was close to his heart. This held true also in the case of Oscar Straus, the former United States Ambassador to Constantinople, whom Bernstorff sounded out early in September on the possibilities of American mediation for peace.[43] Diplomacy apart, the main target of German propaganda was the Jewish masses, particularly the immigrants or descendants

[40] *Wk.*, Nr. 11, adh. 2, K 191182, Vietor to A.A., 18 Sept. 1915.

[41] Horst P. Falcke, *Vor dem Eintritt Americas in den Weltkrieg. Deutsche Propaganda in den Vereinigten Staaten von America, 1914–1915* (Dresden, 1928), p. 95. In 1912 there were 113 dailies in Yiddish, 44 Jewish papers and periodicals in English, and four in Hebrew (ibid).

[42] *Wk.*, Nr. 11, adh. 2, K 191216–17, Hossenfelder to A.A., 12 Oct. 1914. On Jacob Schiff see Cyrus Adler, *Jacob Schiff. His Life and Letters* (London, 1929), 2 vols., and Paul Arnsberg, *Jacob H. Schiff: Von der Frankfurter Judengasse zur Wall Street* (Frankfurt-on-Main, 1972).

[43] Spring-Rice, op. cit. ii, pp. 221–2; May, op. cit., p. 74. On Straus's interest in the Yishuv see Manuel, op. cit., pp. 61–7, 75–87 and *passim*.

of families who had come from Eastern Europe. They formed about 90 per cent of the American Jewish community, three million strong. They had a deep-seated aversion towards Russia and this, as Falcke noted, made them more receptive to the German point of view.[44] It was also among this group that Jewish nationalism was at its strongest.

The person entrusted with the task of winning over American Jewry was Dr. Isaac Straus, a man of wealth and standing in his native city of Munich. Early in the war, upon the recommendation of the Komitee für den Osten, he was sent by the Admiralty to join the Information Service in the United States. With him went Meyrowitz of the North German Lloyd. Both men were Zionists, but unlike Meyrowitz who, owing to instability of character and failing health, had to withdraw from the mission, Straus proved to be a man of decision, intelligence, and political acumen. Like a true German patriot he discharged his duty conscientiously and won Bernstorff's unqualified confidence. He rendered simultaneously invaluable services to his people in Eastern Europe and in Palestine.[45]

On his arrival he was quick to detect that the East European Jews in America, although implacably anti-Russian, were 'neither anti-British nor anti-French, and still less pro-German'. England was regarded as 'a bulwark of liberalism' whereas Prussia was disliked and often compared to Russia, since naturalization there was restricted for Jewish immigrants and because it was on Prussian soil that theoretical anti-Semitism originated. Yet the desire for Russian defeat was unanimous and this by implication could only mean a German victory. Here was the *point d'appui*, Straus observed, from which the creation of a pro-German attitude could start. In contrast, Jews of German origin did not require much persuasion. They would, however, never forgive their former fatherland for letting equality remain a dead letter. Supported by his chief, Dr. Dernburg, formerly Colonial Minister and during the war in charge of German propaganda in the United States, Straus approached the American Jewish Committee and, at a meeting on 8 October 1914 under Schiff's chairmanship, he declared that:

[44] Falcke, op. cit., p. 95; Lichtheim, *She'ar Yashuv*, pp. 291–2; *Rückkehr*, pp. 256–7; Stein, *The Balfour Declaration*, Ch. 12; Friedman, op. cit., pp. 41–3.

[45] Falcke, op. cit., p. 95; Bodenheimer, *Memoirs*, p. 239; *Türkei* 195, K 177068–9, Straus to Bernstorff, 23 Apr. 1915. There is a biography written by his wife, Rahel Straus, *Wir lebten in Deutschland. Errinerungen einer deutschen Jüdin, 1880–1933* (Stuttgart, 1961). On K.f.d.O. see below, pp. 230–4.

Germany truly intended to remove a great number of historic social evils . . . and find a satisfactory solution . . . Her goodwill had already borne fruit in the benevolent treatment of the Jewish population in the Occupied Territories in Poland . . . and in protection of the interests of the foreign Jews, domiciled in Turkey.

This statement had been endorsed by Dernburg, by Consul-General Richard Kiliani, as well as by Ambassador Bernstorff. An official proclamation along these lines was mooted but the American Jewish Committee, fearing that it might irritate Russia unnecessarily, deemed it wiser to refrain from making any publication.[46] At any rate, so long as equality before the law in Germany remained on paper, there was little chance that such a proclamation would have inspired confidence. This was the point Jacob Schiff made in his letter to Zimmerman. He divulged that England and France had also made some overtures to the leaders of American Jewry, promising that they would try and prevail upon Russia to remove the disabilities of its Jewish citizens. To improve her credibility Germany ought therefore to put her own house in order first. The Kaiser's dictum at the outbreak of the war: 'I know Germans only, but no parties', should be reapplied to the Jews, in the sense: 'I know Germans, but no denominations.' Schiff reaffirmed to the Under-Secretary of State for Foreign Affairs that Germany's welfare was dear to his heart. 'It is the country of my birth, of my parents, and forefathers for hundreds of years.' The majority of Jews sympathized with her but it would be 'of greatest moral benefit' if Germany persuaded them that she was determined to bury old prejudices and make a tangible demonstration of goodwill.[47]

That demonstration was given during the war by a more liberal attitude to German Jews,[48] by the benevolent treatment of those in the Eastern Occupied Territories, and by numerous intercessions on behalf of the settlers in Palestine.

Contrary to general belief, Zimmermann was not anti-American. Colonel House, during his visit to Germany in June 1914, found him

---

[46] *Wk.*, Nr. 11, adh. 2, K 190829–40, Straus to K.f.d.O., Feb. 1915 (submitted thereafter to A.A., K 190828). This meeting gave rise to the suspicion at the British Embassy that the Jews 'show a strong preference for the Emperor and there must be some bargain' (Spring-Rice, op. cit. ii, p. 245).

[47] *Wk.*, Nr. 11, adh. 2, K 190465–9, Schiff to Zimmermann, 9 Nov. 1914.

[48] The influence and position achieved by personalities such as Max Warburg (in Finance), Walter Rathenau (in Industry), and Professor Fritz Haber (in Science) are only a few examples of the success of Jews, who were allowed to place their talents at the service of their country.

'responsive to . . . ideas concerning a sympathetic understanding between Great Britain, Germany and the United States'.[49] On account of his 'plain and hearty manners and democratic air' he became the favourite of James Gerard, the American Ambassador to Berlin[50]—a friendship which reflected Zimmermann's bias towards the United States. After the outbreak of the war he leaned heavily on the advice of Neoggarth, an American of German descent, who insisted that care for Germany's good name was as important as the battle fought by her armies. Her enemies 'must be prevented at any price . . . from supplying their "atrocity market" . . . They needed the "German atrocities", not only for propaganda abroad, but [also] to strengthen the morale of their peoples.'[51] Zimmermann's indefatigable efforts to prevent the Turks from maltreating the Jews in Palestine show that he well appreciated Neoggarth's doctrine. His reply to Schiff's letter has not so far come to light but, from his conduct, it would be safe to assume that Schiff's plea did not fall on deaf ears. Early in February 1916 he told Henry Morgenthau, during his visit to Berlin, how splendidly the German Jews had behaved during the war and how deeply obliged Germany felt towards them. He assured the American Ambassador that after the war the German Jews would be much better treated than they had been.[52]

Three days after Schiff had written to Zimmermann, Bernstorff issued a statement to the American Press that 'the war would do away with anti-Semitism in Germany completely'. Scorning it as 'folly', he expressed hope that with the democratization of the German people and decline in power of the nobility the problem would gradually disappear. He disclosed that the Kaiser had many Jewish friends, that in the German Army about 200 Jews had been promoted as officers, and that on the whole the social and economic status of Jews in Germany exceeded that of their co-religionists in England and in the United States.[53]

[49] *The Intimate Papers of Colonel House*, ed. Charles Seymour (London, 1926), i, p. 260.

[50] James W. Gerard, *My Four Years in Germany* (London, 1917), p. 17; *Papers of Col. House*, i, pp. 191, 352–3; below, pp. 298–303.

[51] *The Memoirs of Prince Max of Baden*, trans. W. M. Calder and S. W. H. Sutton (London, 1928), i, p. 22. Neoggarth supported Count Bernstorff in his desperate battle against the intensified submarine war and strengthened the Under-Secretary in his resistance to the demands of the navy (ibid).

[52] Morgenthau, *Secrets of the Bosphorus*, p. 265.

[53] Falcke, op. cit., p. 96. According to Falcke, Bernstorff's statement was made at the beginning of 1915, whereas Straus gives the date as 11/12 Nov. 1914, which seems to be more accurate.

Straus was not satisfied. Liberalization of domestic policy, however desirable, fell short of his expectations. If Germany wished to capture the sympathy of world Jewry, she must first accept the premiss that the Jewish problem was primarily 'a national problem . . . that of a nation living without a country of its own'. Unlike the Jews in the West, those in Eastern Europe had always been deeply interested in Zionism. This was also true of those who had emigrated to the United States. No longer oppressed, their national concept ripened on the free soil of the New World. Self-assertive and assiduously wooed during the American presidential and legislative elections, they used their power to the full whenever the fate of their co-religionists abroad was at stake. Abrogation of the economic treaty with Russia, following the anti-Jewish pogroms in 1905, as well as the active intervention of the American Embassy in Constantinople on behalf of Palestine Jews, demonstrated the extent to which they were able to influence American foreign policy. The emergence of a strong Zionist organization and voluntary contributions for relief on an unprecedented scale were a testimony to the feelings of solidarity and the awakening of Jewish national consciousness in America. Zionism had become 'a factor which could play a political role . . . a force to be reckoned with'. British statesmen had already begun to court it and Germany should not lag behind. American Jewry was aware that the German military occupation of Eastern Europe and Germany's alliance with Turkey brought large Jewish centres, including their ancient home in Palestine, into the German orbit. If Germany were to launch a bold policy and recognize Jewish nationality, she would undoubtedly emerge as their 'supreme champion' (*Vormacht*). She would be duly rewarded. In Eastern Europe, owing to the linguistic affinity of Yiddish, the Jews felt a closer attachment to German civilization than to any other. They might constitute 'a strong counterweight' to the predominant Slav element, which was anti-German, and in Palestine, through a large-scale colonization, they would be able to render valuable services to the German and Ottoman interests.[54]

Some of these points were elaborated on 3 November 1914 by Lichtheim when he called on Dr. Rosenberg before his return to

Constantinople. Lichtheim was the first Zionist to pay an official visit to the Auswärtiges Amt; until then Dr. Bodenheimer, the founder of the K.f.d.O., had acted as their spokesman. Lichtheim argued that, as it was in Germany's interest to consolidate the Ottoman Empire, so it equally lay in the German interest to support the Zionist aspirations. The colonization of Palestine would benefit Turkey both economically and politically. The Palestine Jews were a loyal pro-Turkish element which might 'counterbalance usefully the separatist aspirations of other sections of the population'. The Jews, particularly those in the United States, might play an important role in Turkey's economic regeneration, whilst for Germany a valuable market and new cultural vistas would be opened in the wake of large-scale Jewish immigration and colonization.[55]

Lichtheim's memorandum was closely studied and his appeal for the Government's 'mighty support and protection' was accepted in principle but with regard to his request 'to further Zionist interests' the Ministry had to go slow. Lichtheim was assured that 'as far as possible, and according to the merit of each case, the Ambassador in Constantinople would take an interest in the Zionist movement, although its international character as well as the known mistrust of the Turks imposed certain limitations' on Germany's goodwill. Wangenheim was advised of the meeting with Lichtheim and counselled that 'it would be very wise, especially at the present moment, if the Porte were to try to gain the sympathies of international Jewry, especially in America, by an accommodating treatment of Zionism'.[56] This instruction remained invariably the rule to follow. The interventions with the Porte on the Zionists' behalf were to bear an unofficial character, tempered by an appeal to Turkey's self-interest.

The Reich's Government, desirous of being helpful, exempted the Zionist representatives in Berlin, Constantinople, and Jaffa, and subsequently Copenhagen, from military service, thus enabling them to go ahead with their work.[57] Tschlenow and Sokolow, members of

[55] *Türkei* 195, K 176713–14, memorandum by Lichtheim, dated 3 Nov. 1914; Lichtheim, *She'ar Yashuv*, p. 297, *Rückkehr*, pp. 261–2. On Rosenberg see above, pp. 181–2. During the Weimar Republic he became Foreign Minister.

[56] *Türkei* 195, K 176716–17, pp. Sec. of State to Wangenheim, 3 Nov. 1914, dis. no. 704.

[57] This applied to Hantke, Lichtheim, Ruppin, and Rosenblüth. Warburg was not liable for military service. Technically the deferment had to be endorsed by the military every three months, and the Foreign Ministry had to give the reasons for renewal. (See, e.g., K 176704, K 178143, and below, pp. 251, 270–1, 303, 308–9, 338, 402.)

the Zionist Executive and both Russian nationals, were allowed to remain in Berlin unhampered until their departure for London in December 1914, and Jacobson, though not a German national, was allowed to travel freely between Berlin and Constantinople, as well as to neutral capitals, armed with German diplomatic documents. During the month of October the German Government had permitted the transfer of larger sums of money for relief of Palestinian Jews, and, at the request of the Zionist Executive, the Ambassador in Constantinople was instructed to intercede with the Porte on behalf of the Zionist financial institutions in Palestine, which had been closed by the Turkish authorities. He was also advised to cooperate in this matter with his American colleague, who was reported to have deposited large sums to the credit of Jewish institutions.[58] Wangenheim did not require much prodding. He replied that he had repeatedly intervened with the Turkish Government in the interest of the Jews, stressing the need to avoid any action that might cost it the sympathies of international Jewry. Wangenheim was gratified to learn that Talaat Bey had 'the fullest understanding' of the political importance of this question. The Porte had decided not to expel the Russian Jews; they were to be granted facilities to acquire Ottoman nationality and those liable to military service were to be given a further concession of deferment from conscription for one year. The consulates in Syria and Palestine had been informed of the directives from the Auswärtiges Amt.[59]

When Lichtheim returned to Constantinople he felt confident that, as far as the protection of the Jewish population in Palestine was concerned, they were in reliable hands. Morgenthau, with whom he was on the friendliest terms, 'did whatever he could and the German Embassy was prepared to help also'.[60] By then von Mutius,

---

[58] Lichtheim, *She'ar Yashuv*, pp. 304, 309; *Rückkehr*, pp. 266, 272; *Türkei* 195, K 176719–25, Warburg to A.A., 5 Nov. 1914; A.A. to Wangenheim, 10, 18 Nov. 1914, dis. nos. 720, 1280.

[59] *Türkei* 195, K 176718, Wangenheim to A.A., 5 Nov. 1914, tel. no. 1248; K 176741, same to same, 28 Nov. 1914, dis. no. 287.

[60] Lichtheim, *She'ar Yashuv*, pp. 308–9; *Rückkehr*, p. 271. Professor Manuel unjustly accuses Morgenthau of betraying 'a marked indifference to those Turkish measures of which he was aware' (op. cit., p. 125). Manuel thinks that Morgenthau deliberately toned down his reports in order to avoid giving the State Department the impression of being 'too zealous . . . on behalf of his co-religionists', and appearing as a 'special pleader for the Jews' (ibid., pp. 122, 136). Yet Manuel admits that during the economic blockade of Syria and Palestine Morgenthau helped his co-religionists 'diligently' (ibid., p. 144). Curiously, Morgenthau himself makes no mention in his memoirs of his persistent intercessions on behalf of the Palestinian Jews.

Lichtheim's staunch friend, had joined the colours, but his previous reports were studied carefully both by his successor Richard von Kühlmann and the newly appointed First Dragoman, Dr. Weber.[61] Kühlmann was Wangenheim's closest confidant. Industrious and remarkably well informed, he gave the impression that he was exerting a powerful influence in a quiet way. He was most eager to co-operate with Morgenthau in the matter of the reopening of the Anglo-Palestinian Bank, as well as in other matters concerning the Jews. This might partly be explained by Kühlmann's desire to become friendly with the American Embassy.[62] He took pains to acquaint himself more closely with Zionist problems and requested Lichtheim to elaborate a memorandum, assuring him that it would be used. 'Reichen Sie mir die Sache ein, ich werde dann dafür sorgen, dass sie nicht liegen bleibt.'

Kühlmann did not intend merely to please the Zionists. He was aware of the paramount influence of the Alliance Israélite among Oriental Jewry and, already during his first conversation with Lichtheim on 20 November, hinted broadly that he 'would have liked to see all Jewish aspirations centring on Germany'. With this in mind, Dr. Weber took an early opportunity of meeting Talaat to ventilate the German Embassy's displeasure at the Chief Rabbi's pro-French disposition, Talaat immediately grasped what Weber had in mind and advised the Rabbi to improve his relations with the Germans. The advice was effective and when Weber later met Nahoum Effendi the latter admitted that though he had been a Francophile, 'he never was a Germanophobe'. In support of his argument he pointed to his 'very good relations' with the official Zionist representatives in Constantinople. It was not only in this case that Weber's credentials as a diplomat were tested. He was practical, clever, persistent, and reliable. He possessed a tremendous capacity for work and a thorough knowledge of Turkey. Numerous discussions with Lichtheim deepened his understanding of Zionism and increased his eagerness to help. Wangenheim appreciated his

[61] Lichtheim, *She'ar Yashuv*, p. 309; *Rückkehr*, p. 272. On Mutius see above, pp. 186–7, and below, p. 282.

[62] Lichtheim, *She'ar Yashuv*, p. 305; *Rückkehr*, p. 267; Morgenthau, op. cit., p. 117. Kühlmann's and Wangenheim's ingratiating overtures did not escape Morgenthau's attention (op. cit., pp. 54–6, 86, 103; also *idem*, *All In a Life-time* (New York, 1922), pp. 174–81). Morgenthau noted that after the attack on the Marne had failed, German diplomats looked towards President Wilson as a potential peacemaker. Having no access to American ambassadors in other great European capitals, they turned naturally to him as the channel to the President (*Secrets of the Bosphorus*, pp. 96, 117).

qualities.[63] They stood the Zionists in good stead when conditions in Palestine became hazardous.

Until the middle of December the situation gave no reason for anxiety but, with the arrival of Djemal Pasha on the Syrian scene as the Supreme Commander of the Fourth Ottoman Army, the position became perilous. A former *Vali* (civil governor) of Adana (1909) and Baghdad (1911) and Military Governor of Constantinople (1913), he served as Minister of Public Works and later Marine. After the assassination of Shevket Pasha on 11 June 1913, he became a senior member of the triumvirate which ruled Turkey till the end of the war. The other members of the trio, Enver Bey, the Minister of War, and Talaat Bey, Minister of the Interior, were equally ruthless and possessed by an insatiable lust for power, but there were marked differences between them. Talaat, the most outstanding figure, was a real statesman. Gifted with a swift and penetrating intelligence, he understood people well. Though of humble origin, there was a streak of nobility in his character; among diplomats he behaved like a European. Resolute and with a will of iron, he also possessed great personal charm. Abraham Elmaliyach, a contemporary writer, who met him often in the office of *Le Jeune Turc*, admired him profoundly and thought that it was he who deserved the title of 'hero of the Revolution', not Enver. The latter rose to fame faster and at an earlier age but was no match for Talaat's abilities.[64]

Djemal was the least attractive personality of the three. At the beginning of the war Enver and Talaat removed him from the capital but to satisfy his *amour propre* gave him 'a geographical sphere of domination', a prerogative which he used, or misused, to the full. In addition to his ministerial rank and command of the Fourth Army, he became the virtual ruler of Syria and Palestine. In his memoirs Djemal claimed that he had obtained 'the full freedom of action', which the law conferred upon any army commander, but in fact he harboured a grudge against his colleagues for not consulting him on the most important issues before the outbreak of the war. He ruled independently and often disregarded the Central Government's instructions.[65] Liman von Sanders depicted him as a

[63] C.Z.A. Z 3/50, Lichtheim to E.A.C., 21 Nov., 2 Dec. 1914; *She'ar Yashuv*, pp. 305, 309, 314; *Rückkehr*, pp. 267, 271–2, 275.

[64] Elmaliyach, op. cit. i, pp. 225, 284–305.

[65] Emin, op. cit., pp. 100–1, 105–6; Morgenthau, *Secrets of the Bosphorus*, pp. 112–114, 149–50; Djemal Pasha, *Memoirs of a Turkish Statesman: 1913–1919* (London, 1922),

person who was 'unwilling to confide his ultimate thoughts and aims to another mortal'.[66] Mercurial and unpredictable in character, he always acted on the spur of the moment. He took decisions without consulting experts and issued orders without even briefing his colleagues. Though noted for his tremendous energy and flair for administration, he had little talent to grasp the deeper issues, particularly economic and social. Militarily his faculties were never tested.[67]

Formerly a Francophile, later in the war he became a bitter enemy of the Entente, but this did not make him any more pro-German. His relations with the Germans, as Ruppin noted, were 'very strained'. He resented their influence and denied the consuls the right to interfere. He lost no opportunity to remind them that the regime of Capitulations had come to an end and on one occasion was reported to have stated that at best 'all the Consuls were tolerated merely as "distinguished foreigners"'.[68] This was characteristic of his vanity and chauvinism for, though he professed to be a champion of Islam who was playing the *jihad* card for all it was worth,[69] he was first and foremost a Turkish nationalist, who endeavoured to ottomanize all the subject nationalities: the Arabs, the Jews, and the Armenians; he antagonized them all.

No documentary evidence has come to light to show how Djemal's hostility to Zionism originated. However, it would not be wrong to assume that his xenophobia, blended with Muslim fervour, provided fertile soil in which Beha-ed-Din's ideas could flourish. Their first encounter took place early in December in Damascus when, according to Brode, Beha-ed-Din found in the Commander of the Fourth Army 'a ready ear'.[70] Lichtheim, too, was of the opinion that it was Beha-ed-Din who was responsible for initiating the anti-Zionist campaigns (in which 'the Central Government had no hand'), and that it was he who had influenced Djemal.[71] Captain

pp. 108–9, 138; *Türkei* 195, K 177940–5, Ruppin to E.A.C., 12 Oct. 1916, encl. in E.A.C. to A.A., 20 Oct. 1916.

[66] Liman O. von Sanders, *Five Years in Turkey* (Annapolis, 1927), p. 5.

[67] *Palestine during the War*, p. 18; Aaronsohn, op. cit., p. 62; Smilansky, op. cit. iii, p. 125.

[68] Ruppin to E.A.C., 12 Oct. 1916 (source as note 65); Djemal, op. cit., p. 117 and *passim*; Morgenthau, op. cit., p. 114; Aaronsohn, op. cit., p. 62; von Sanders, op. cit., pp. 32, 43, 113–16.

[69] Antonius, op. cit., pp. 150–1, 200.

[70] *Türkei* 195, K 177308, Brode to A.A., 26 Aug. 1915, dis. no. 76/1278.

[71] C.Z.A. L 6/45, Lichtheim to Straus, 23 Apr. 1915.

Decker of the U.S.S. *Tennessee*, who made a thorough investigation, arrived at a similar conclusion.[72] So did Abraham Elmaliyach.[73] An assertion in the Zionist report that Beha-ed-Din acted under instructions from the Porte[74] is erroneous, for it is most unlikely that a policy of that nature would have emanated from Talaat, who was not hostile to the Palestine Jews and was known for his political maturity in the treatment of aliens.[75] That an executive official like Beha-ed-Din could have taken the law into his own hands may seem peculiar, but this was by no means an isolated incident in Turkish politics during the war. Powerful provincial governors habitually ignored the Porte's decrees. Thus Rahmi Bey, the Governor of Smyrna, implemented 'only such . . . measures as he saw fit',[76] and even Bedri Bey, the Prefect of Police in Constantinople, although an intimate friend of Talaat, frequently disregarded instructions when he found them to be lenient towards foreigners.[77]

Having secured Djemal's support, Beha-ed-Din issued an order, which Hassan Bey also signed, that all Jewish foreign nationals must leave the country on 17 December by the boat due to dock that day. The Zionist report and other contemporary accounts abound with descriptions of what happened.

Policemen and soldiers . . . beat and arrested men and women, old persons and children, and dragged them to the police buildings . . . The barbarity of the officials who carried out this expulsion passed all bounds. Before their eyes the boatmen dragged the exiles in the darkness of the evening out to sea. They threatened with knives and struck the people who refused to give them what they demanded. The ship could not take in all victims, and . . . many families were separated.

The Chief Rabbi of Jerusalem lodged a complaint against Beha-ed-Din's cruelty but in response Djemal Pasha threatened to remove the Rabbi from office 'if he dared to meddle with matters that did not concern him'.[78] Ruppin's plea was of no avail either: Djemal refused to receive him, although he had been recommended by the

---

[72] *F.R.U.S.*, Suppl. World War, 1914, p. 979; cited also in Straus to Warburg, 2 Mar. 1915 (*Türkei* 195, K 176877), and in Manuel, op. cit. pp. 127–8.
[73] Elmaliyach, op. cit. ii, p. 80.   [74] *Palestine during the War*, p. 19.
[75] Morgenthau, op. cit., p. 79.
[76] Emin, *Turkey in the World War*, pp. 105–6.
[77] Morgenthau, op. cit., pp. 87, 97.
[78] *Palestine during the War*, p. 23; Shenkin, op. cit., pp. 54–6; Smilansky, op. cit. iii, pp. 23–5; David Idelovitch, 'Gole Eretz-Israel B'Mitzraim' ['The Palestine Evacuees in Egypt'], *Miyamim Rishonim* (Tel Aviv, Dec. 1934), i, p. 215.

German Military Staff.[79] Brode was equally powerless and deprecated that the Turkish authorities lacked the political understanding to recognize the adverse effect of their harsh measures. The non-Ottomans, of whom 50,000 were Russians, were the backbone of Jewish colonization and their expulsion was tantamount to the 'entire break-up of Jewish economic and cultural life in Palestine'.[80]

When Lichtheim received Ruppin's telegram containing the news that the Ottoman authorities had ordered the immediate expulsion of all Russian Jews to Egypt, all equanimity in Constantinople disappeared. Wangenheim realized the gravity of the situation and lost no time in seeing Talaat Pasha. On the following day Lichtheim received a note from von Scharfenberg, the First Secretary to the German Embassy, that the Minister of the Interior, 'with Djemal Pasha's concurrence', had granted Russian Jewish nationals permission to remain in the country; the phrase 'with Djemal Pasha's concurrence' camouflaged the differences between the Porte and the Commander of the Fourth Army. Several days later Brode reassured the Embassy that the expulsions had been stopped and that no more were contemplated. Moreover, on the Porte's instructions, Beha-ed-Din was removed from his post. Yet, much to the surprise of the German Embassy, the Turkish authorities in the Jaffa district continued to make difficulties and, in Kühlmann's absence, Dr. Weber busied himself almost daily, working closely with Lichtheim, to alleviate the plight of Palestinian Jews.[81]

To forestall any new crises more effectively, Lichtheim was subsequently allowed to use the diplomatic courier service and code for direct communication with Ruppin in Jaffa and with the Zionist Executive in Berlin;[82] as later events showed, this proved to be very useful. To demonstrate his concern, Wangenheim readily received Lichtheim (6 January 1915) who, however, did not come as a supplicant.

I told him [Lichtheim advised his colleagues in Berlin] that expulsions from Palestine must stop . . . Such measures would be interpreted by the

---

[79] Arthur Ruppin, *Pirkey Chayai* [*Chapters from my Life*], ed. Bein (Tel Aviv, 1944, 1947), ii, p. 189; *idem, Memoirs*, pp. 153–4.

[80] *Türkei* 195, K 177308, K 177331, Brode to A.A., 26 Aug. 1915.

[81] C.Z.A. Z3/50, Lichtheim to E.A.C., 24, 30 Dec. 1914; Lichtheim, *She'ar Yashuv*, pp. 315–19; *Rückkehr*, pp. 277–81; *Palestine during the War*, p. 319.

[82] *Türkei* 195, K 176807, Wangenheim to A.A., 6 Feb. 1915, tel. no. 318; K 177006, same to same, 27 Mar. 1915, dis. no. 193; Lichtheim, *She'ar Yashuv*, p. 321; *Rückkehr*, p. 283.

Press, particularly in the U.S.A., as blatant anti-Semitism for which Germany will be held responsible. He agreed . . . and promised to do everything in his power to help us. Yesterday he cabled Djemal in Damascus and asked him to treat the Jews compassionately. Talaat also gave him firm assurances . . . Wangenheim was anxious that we give due publicity in America to the fact that the German Embassy supports . . . and protects us by all means at its disposal.[83]

The following day Wangenheim cabled Berlin that, as a result of his efforts and those of the American Embassy, the Porte had granted far-reaching facilities to all Jews who wished to become Ottoman subjects.[84] That the two Ambassadors should have been so successful is hardly surprising. After scoring the greatest of his diplomatic triumphs by smuggling the battleships *Goeben* and *Breslau* into the Sea of Marmora, Wangenheim's influence in the Ottoman capital was unrivalled. Morgenthau also occupied a strong position. As the American Ambassador he was much respected and even Djemal Pasha had told him that 'the Turks regarded the United States as their best friend'.[85]

However, the affair had far wider repercussions than Wangenheim could have foreseen. The expulsion from Jaffa on 17 December was given wide publicity in the United States, creating the impression that 'the Jewish settlement in Palestine was facing complete ruin'. At first, Dr. Straus tried to suppress publication of such items, particularly if authenticity could not be established. But he did not succeed, because 'the English Press gladly picked up news of this sort, using it to criticize the Germans and make them responsible for Turkish misdeeds'. To counter these charges Straus pointed out that Jewish interests were completely safeguarded by protection promised by the German Government, but the avalanche of reports coming from Egypt, where the expelled Jews found refuge, made his task difficult.[86]

Concerned Bernstorff cabled Berlin that according to the local Press 'a major massacre of Jews has taken place . . . Local Jewry is

[83] C.Z.A. Z3/51, Lichtheim to E.A.C., 6 Jan. 1915; Lichtheim, *She'ar Yashuv*, pp. 320–1; *Rückkehr*, pp. 282–3.

[84] *Türkei* 195, K 176762–4, Wangenheim to A.A., 7 Jan. 1915, tel. no. 61.

[85] Morgenthau, op. cit., pp. 33, 62, 98, 160, 167–72. On the *Goeben* and *Breslau* operation see ibid., pp. 46–53, 63–4; Emin. op. cit., pp. 69, 72–5; Gottlieb, *Studies in Secret Diplomacy during the First World War*, pp. 57, 60; Barbara Tuchman, *August 1914* (London, 1962), pp. 139–62.

[86] C.Z.A. Z3/52, Straus to Lichtheim, 10 Mar. 1915; *Wk.*, Nr. 11, K 190858–64, Straus to K.f.d.O., 20 Feb. 1915.

very agitated.' He was vexed by the unfavourable impression created by the Turkish conduct and complained: 'Wie immer zeiht man uns der Mitschuld.' The Foreign Ministry transmitted his cables to Wangenheim and reaffirmed the standing order that 'in principle it is desirable that the Porte displays an accommodating attitude towards the Russian Jews'.[87]

Wangenheim was alive to the harmful effect of Turkish behaviour on Germany's reputation and feared that she would be accused of anti-Semitism. He assured the Foreign Ministry that he had taken appropriate steps to help the Jews and was co-operating closely with Morgenthau to secure the smooth naturalization of Russian Jews. Moreover, the exorbitant fees of forty francs *per capita* had been drastically reduced, while poor applicants were exempt from payment altogether. The deportations had been stopped and even those who refused to change their nationality were permitted to remain in the country unmolested. Morgenthau and he had instructed their respective Consuls to support each other when encountering unjustified demands from the local Ottoman authorities.

Yet, by explaining away the expulsion as a measure to speed up or enforce ottomanization on reluctant individuals, Wangenheim showed that he had been misinformed. Satisfied with the Porte's co-operation and unaware of the divergence between the Porte and Djemal, he was puzzled by the mounting condemnation of the Turks abroad. He could not understand how Americans could be so mistaken as to describe the Turks as 'bloodthirsty haters' of Christians and Jews, when he knew that they were the most tolerant people in the world. He quoted Morgenthau, who had reported to the State Department that Turkey had behaved towards belligerent nationals in 'a far more humane way than England, France and Germany did'. It was England, bent on undermining German–Turkish friendship, that agitated most cunningly against Turkey. He learned also from Morgenthau about the 'sinister' activities of James Bryce, the former British Ambassador to Washington. Wangenheim suggested that it would be useful to remind the American Press of his repeated interventions on behalf of the Jews.[88]

---

[87] *Türkei* 195, K 176754, K 176772, Bernstorff to A.A., 23 Dec. 1914, 16 Jan. 1915, tel. nos. 645, 101; K 176784, State Secretary to Wangenheim, 23 Jan. 1915, tel. no. 67.

[88] Ibid. K 176763–78, Wangenheim to A.A., 7, 17, 21 Jan. 1915, tel. nos. 61, 157, 181; *Berliner Tageblatt*, 19 Jan. 1915. The Bryce Report was the chief document of British propaganda, which branded Germany with responsibility for precipitating the war and for committing a number of 'atrocities' (Grattan, op. cit., pp. 62–3, 68).

However, German assurances lost much of their credibility following the arrival at the State Department of an appeal from the refugees in Alexandria. It described the situation in Palestine as 'extremely dangerous'; the Turkish military authorities had embarked on a 'systematic destruction of . . . Jewish property . . . Arabs were being armed and Jewish defence groups disbanded . . . the Jewish colonies were to be suppressed . . . and Arabs were encouraged to take over their lands . . . famine had broken out.' When other telegrams confirmed the text of a Turkish proclamation 'to destroy Zionist institutions and organizations' Bernstorff immediately requested factual evidence from Berlin and demanded intervention. 'Public opinion holds Germany solely responsible for these conditions.' Straus also became alarmed, fearing a complete reversal of Jewish public opinion, which had so enthusiastically welcomed Germany's promises of protection. 'Ensure by every possible means, regular reports through diplomatic channels and an immediate intervention in Constantinople.' He suspected that the Embassy in Constantinople was completely misinformed.[89] Two days later Bernstorff learned that the State Department had instructed Morgenthau to intervene on behalf of Palestinian Jews and point out that 'the Zionists who have performed excellent pioneering work . . . were the most loyal subjects of Turkey'. Bernstorff expected Wangenheim to back Morgenthau's representations.[90]

Wangenheim felt that in view of his constant support of the Jewish cause there was no justification for accusing him of dereliction of duty. The reproach levelled against Germany was without foundation for he had repeatedly pointed out to the Turkish Government that, quite apart from other considerations, the moment was inopportune for launching an anti-Zionist policy. Wangenheim was satisfied that both the Grand Vizier and Talaat Bey were responsive to his arguments but regretted that so far they had failed to influence Djemal Pasha, who exercised supreme power in Palestine. Wangenheim dismissed the news circulating in the United States as 'enormous exaggeration'. However he was forced to admit that the local Turkish authorities in Palestine had intensified their hostility against

---

[89] *Türkei* 195, K 176794–7, Bernstorff to A.A., 30 Jan. 1915, tel. no. 182; Straus to A.A., same date, tel. no. 180.

[90] Ibid. K 176800, Bernstorff to A.A., 3 Feb. 1915, tel. no. 195. Bernstorff's version tallies with that reproduced in American official dispatches (see *F.R.U.S.*, Suppl. World War, 1914, p. 979).

Zionism and that the Jewish inhabitants had perhaps been treated 'more harshly' than he had originally assumed.[91]

The exaggerations were a product of the specific conditions of war. The Entente propaganda enjoyed not only a factual, but also a technical, advantage over the Central Powers. Control of the cables proved to be the most important cause of the astounding success the British had in manipulating the American mind. The German propagandists in America, for all their ability, energy, and funds, fought a battle which was already lost.[92] Moreover, lack of direct communication with Palestine and the influence of Allied propaganda made the reports of the Palestinian refugees in Egypt inaccurate.[93] Overtaken by emotion and anxious to rally support, the refugees were naturally prone to hyperbole. Yet, as Lichtheim was able to ascertain, the news concerning the persecution of the Zionists was 'essentially correct'.[94]

In Palestine the outlook remained dim. Although expulsions had been stopped there existed a considerable disparity between the Porte's orders to facilitate ottomanization of foreign Jews and their implementation. The local officials interpreted them as they wished and carried them out arbitrarily. The procedure varied according to the character and inclination of the officials. In Jerusalem, where Zakey Bey was still governor, matters proceeded smoothly. This was also the case in the Acre district, but in Jaffa the picture was different. Applicants for naturalization came in crowds, but the difficulties were great; the staff was inadequate to cope and the business 'dragged on for months'. Discouraged, very many individuals preferred to board the American warships and join the refugees in Alexandria.[95] During January about 7,000 Jews left for Egypt and by the end of 1915 the total figure of those expelled in December 1914 and those who had left of their own volition amounted to 11,277.[96]

An atmosphere of gloom engulfed the Yishuv when Djemal Pasha arrived in Jerusalem. The Chief Rabbi and a number of

[91] *Türkei* 195, K 176806–7, Wangenheim to A.A., 8 Feb. 1915, tel. no. 318.

[92] Grattan, op. cit., p. 41; Chambers, *The War behind the War*, p. 190.

[93] Lichtheim, *She'ar Yashuv*, p. 335; *Rückkehr*, p. 294.

[94] *Türkei* 195, K 176810, Lichtheim to Warburg, 8 Feb. 1915, tel. no. 323.

[95] *Palestine during the War*, p. 27; Elmaliyach, op. cit. ii, pp. 3–21, Ben-Hillel Hacohen, op. cit. i, pp. 66–7.

[96] Idelovitch, loc. cit., p. 215, where a table of statistics is reproduced.

notables who came to welcome him heard him say harshly that Palestinian Jews entertained 'separatist aspirations'; Zionism was a 'revolutionary and anti-Turkish movement, which must be eradicated'.[97] Several days later Zakey Bey was dismissed and Beha-ed-Din, previously removed by the Porte, was appointed by Djemal as his adjutant and political adviser. From this post Beha-ed-Din could launch an anti-Zionist campaign more vigorous than before. Orders, once imposed on the Jaffa district alone, were extended all over the country; Zionist flags were confiscated, the use of Hebrew in correspondence was forbidden, the Anglo-Palestine Bank was closed, possession of Jewish National Fund stamps could result in the death sentence, and several leading personalities were arrested. Moreover, arms which had been confiscated from the Jews were distributed freely among Arab hirelings. The project of a Jewish militia which had been considered at Zakey's office was rejected. Beha-ed-Din told Djemal that he did not trust the Arabs, but still less the Jews: 'should the latter be armed, they would side with the British and fight against the Turks'.[98] Such an argument did not sound odd. Hassan Bey, who had been obsessed by the fear of a British landing on the Palestinian coast, shared this suspicion.[99] It soon infected Djemal, who became even more persuaded following the publication of an article in *The Times* in London proposing 'to hand over Palestine to the Jews'.[100]

There was still an essential difference that characterized Beha-ed-Din's second phase of activity. While formerly it was directed against all foreign Jews, now it was concentrated solely against the Zionists, even those who were Ottoman subjects of long standing.[101] This distinction came crudely into the open in his proclamation published in the Hebrew paper *Hacherut* (25 January) in which he referred to the Jews as 'our allies' and 'the true sons of the Fatherland', in contrast to the Zionists who were branded as 'wicked revolutionary elements', who were trying to create in the Palestinian region of the Ottoman Empire 'a Jewish state . . . thus causing harm

[97] C.Z.A. Z 3/52, E.A.C. to the Provisional Zionist Executive Committee in New York (hereafter P.E.C.), Feb. 1915; *Neue Rotterdamsche Courant*, 23 Feb. 1915, evening edition (cutting in *Türkei* 195, K 176884-7); *Kölnische Zeitung*, 30 Feb. 1915.

[98] Elmaliyach, op. cit. ii, pp. 82-7; Smilansky, op. cit. iii, pp. 37-40, 47-9; Ben-Hillel Hacohen, op. cit. i, pp. 64-6; Manuel, op. cit., p. 129.

[99] Smilansky, op. cit. iii, pp. 67-8; Dizengoff, op. cit., p. 23.

[100] *Türkei* 195, K 176824-5, Wangenheim (citing Schmidt) to A.A., 12 Feb. 1915, tel. no. 364. The author was unsuccessful in tracing the article in *The Times*.

[101] *Türkei* 195, K 176810, Lichtheim to Warburg, 9 Feb. 1915, tel. no. 323.

to people of their own race'. This was why the Government had ordered the confiscation of Zionist flags, stamps, bank-notes of the Anglo-Palestine Company, and had decreed the dissolution of the 'secret' Zionist societies and organizations. Towards them, Beha-ed-Din concluded, 'we shall remain implacable enemies forever'.[102]

Beha-ed-Din overplayed his hand. His attempt to drive a wedge between one Jew and another elicited a strong protest from the Sephardi Chief Rabbi Moses Franco, which was published in *Hacherut*;[103] while in Constantinople powerful forces were set in motion against him. On 9 February Lichtheim wired to the Zionist Executive in Berlin: 'Chief culpability rests with Beha-ed-Din, Djemal's Secretary. Steps undertaken. The German and American Ambassadors promised support. Hope success . . .'[104] Lichtheim's hope was well founded. He noted how furious Wangenheim was on learning the source of the trouble. 'These two villains [Beha-ed-Din and Hassan Bey] must go . . . I shall not tolerate this swinish behaviour', he exclaimed. He got in touch with Morgenthau and they both exerted a concerted pressure on the Turkish Ministers. Normally Wangenheim won his case by diplomacy but on this occasion he did not hesitate to talk harshly with Talaat and reproach him forcefully.[105] Thereupon Talaat requested a report from Palestine and ordered that 'injustices should be rectified'. He promised Wangenheim that Beha-ed-Din would be recalled.[106] Talaat, at that time also Minister of Finance, had his own grievances against Djemal for not consulting him before closing the Anglo-Palestine Bank. He divulged to Morgenthau that measures implemented without his knowledge would be revoked.[107] Enver Pasha, who was also approached by Morgenthau, wired immediately to Hassan Bey that 'consideration must be shown to all Jews'.[108]

---

[102] Smilansky, op. cit. iii, pp. 58–9; Elmaliyach, op. cit. ii, pp. 87–8; Ben-Hillel Hacohen, op. cit. i, p. 70; Shenkin, op. cit. i, pp. 57–8. For the German translation see *Türkei*, 195, K 176934–5 and for the English see Israel Cohen, *The Turkish Persecution of the Jews* (London, 1918), App. 1, pp. 16–17; Manuel, op. cit., p. 129.

[103] The full text is reproduced in Cohen, op. cit., App. II, pp. 18–20. Ben-Hillel Hacohen (op. cit. i, pp. 77–8) revealed that it was he who had influenced Franco to protest publicly against Beha-ed-Din.

[104] *Türkei* 195, K 176810, Lichtheim to Warburg, 9 Feb. 1915, tel. no. 323.

[105] C.Z.A. Z 3/51, Lichtheim to E.A.C., 5, 8, 9 Feb. 1915; Lichtheim, *She'ar Yashuv*, pp. 336–7; *Rückkehr*, p. 295.

[106] *Türkei* 195, K 176814–15, Wangenheim to A.A., 10 Feb. 1915, tel. no. 339.

[107] C.Z.A. L 6/45 Lichtheim to Straus, 23 Apr. 1915.

[108] Lichtheim, *She'ar Yashuv*, p. 336; *Rückkehr*, p. 295; Manuel, op. cit., p. 126. Professor Manuel thinks that Enver, in making this statement, intended merely to

A few days later Lichtheim was able to inform his colleagues in Berlin that the Ottoman Ministerial Council had decided that the Anglo-Palestine Bank should be reopened, the majority of Zionist detainees released, and Beha-ed-Din recalled. On 16 February Dr. Weber advised Lichtheim that the Sublime Porte had issued additional instructions to the Palestine authorities 'to abstain from any oppressive measures against the Jews, because the moment was politically inopportune'.[109] Djemal consequently issued a proclamation, distributed by the thousand, asserting that all rumours insinuating that 'our [Jewish] Ottoman brothers living in Palestine are shirking their national duties . . . are contrary to the truth and harmful'. He warned that there would be severe punishments for those disseminating such rumours and gravely reproached Hassan Bey for doing so in the past. This seemed to herald a spectacular change of policy which was further demonstrated during his visit to Tel Aviv on 2 March. At an official reception given at the Herzliya High School he stated: 'I have full confidence in you and am sure that we shall be able to co-operate for our common fatherland. Place your trust in us, and the country, to which you are attached, will offer you refuge. We consider you as a good and faithful element.' The Tel Avivians, earlier filled with anxiety, were taken aback by this unexpected profession of cordiality.[110] Ruppin recorded in his diary:

I am still baffled by this sudden and blatant change in Jemal Pasha's attitude, but it has certainly raised the spirits of the Jews in Jaffa, who have been very pessimistic until now. The visit happened to have taken place on Purim and turned this day, which would otherwise have passed very sadly, into one of real rejoicing.[111]

Djemal delivered similar conciliatory speeches several weeks later at Mikve-Israel, an agricultural school near Jaffa, and at Rishon-le-Zion, implying that he was prepared to accept the Jewish *status quo*

soothe Morgenthau, 'while the local officials proceeded as usual [in their] time-worn technique' (ibid., also pp. 123, 128). However, failing to see the tug-of-war between the Porte and the local authorities, Manuel's charge of Turkish duplicity in this matter is untenable.

[109] *Türkei* 195, K 176819, Lichtheim to Warburg, 12 Feb. 1915; Lichtheim, *She'ar Yashuv*, pp. 338–9; *Rückkehr*, pp. 296–7.
[110] Elmaliyach, op. cit. ii, pp. 98–100; Ben-Hillel Hacohen, op. cit. i, p. 88. Dizengoff, op. cit., p. 45; Shenkin, op. cit., p. 62; *Türkei* 195, K 176882, Lichtheim to Warburg, 5 Mar. 1915; *Frankfurter Zeitung*, 10 Apr. 1915 (from a correspondent in Jaffa).   [111] Ruppin, *Memoirs*, p. 156.

in the country.[112] To demonstrate his good faith he announced that Jewish labourers employed by the army would be entitled to a rest on the Sabbath, Jewish soldiers would receive leave on Jewish festivals, poverty-stricken civilians, when ill, would be cared for free of charge in military hospitals and, in case of need, food would be sold more cheaply from Government stocks. Talaat was now in a good position to refute the accusations levelled against Turkey. He expressed satisfaction with the progress of naturalization of foreign Jews in Palestine and paid tribute to Turkish Jews for fulfilling their patriotic duties in 'an outstanding manner'. He was confident that their co-religionists in other states also entertained genuine sympathy for Turkey and were truly interested in her future welfare.[113]

It seems that the failure of the Suez expedition had a sobering effect on Djemal, and made him more amenable toward the Porte. For all his vanity and bluster, he was wily enough a politician to realize that a showdown with a united Ministerial Council would be self-defeating. Moreover, confronted with a restive Arab population after his defeat,[114] he had an added reason to refrain from antagonizing the Jewish population. The secret documents seized at the French consulates in Beirut and Damascus[115] opened his eyes to the inherent dangers of Arab nationalism. That he trusted the Jews more is evident from his administrative appointments during the summer of 1915. The most prominent appointee was Albert Antebi, an Ottoman Sephardi Jew who, on account of his political acumen and fluency in Turkish, Arabic, and French, had acted before the war as the Yishuv spokesman to Turkish officials. Djemal made him a member of the Political and Economic Advisory Committee and his special adviser. Another leading appointee was Moshe Wilbushewitz, who was asked to serve as Chief Civil Engineer and Head of the Development Department in Syria and Palestine. The most famous was Aaron Aaronsohn, an outstanding agronomist, who was charged with the task of combating the locust plague and advising

[112] Smilansky, op. cit. iii, p. 87; Elmaliyach, op. cit. ii, pp. 103–4; Ben-Hillel Hacohen, op. cit. i, pp. 147–8; Lichtheim, *She'ar Yashuv*, p. 347; *Rückkehr*, pp. 304–5.

[113] *Frankfurter Zeitung*, 10 Apr. 1915. The number of Jews who adopted Ottoman nationality amounted to 20,000 (*Türkei* 195, K 177536–9, Lichtheim to German Embassy, 22 Dec. 1915).

[114] Aaronsohn, op. cit., pp. 68–70. On the Suez campaign see Djemal, op. cit., pp. 156–9; Friedrich Freiherr Kress von Kressenstein, *Mit den Türken zum Suezkanal* (Berlin, 1938), pp. 85–122; Lt.-Gen. Archibald P. Wavell, *The Palestine Campaigns* (London, 1941), pp. 28–32.

[115] Antonius, op. cit., pp. 185–90.

on food production. Yet this still does not account for such demon-
strative expressions of cordiality towards the Yishuv. Was it merely
a stratagem, or was it a genuine change of heart? At all events, it
seems that Djemal's confidence in Beha-ed-Din was shaken.

It was Antebi who had undermined Beha-ed-Din's position. The
crucial encounter took place on 8 January 1915 when Antebi,
together with thirty other notables, was summoned before Djemal
and told that they would be deported to Brussa in Anatolia. They
were accused of maintaining autonomous institutions and of plotting
to found a separate state under the protection of an enemy Power.
Antebi, as the spokesman, was questioned alone for two hours and
managed to talk the Commander out of his misconceptions. As an
Ottoman and a descendant of a family which was distinguished for
its loyalty to the Ottoman cause, he strenuously protested against
these accusations. The Jews had always been grateful to Turkey
and remembered the hospitality given to the Spanish exiles during
the fifteenth and sixteenth centuries. The Zionists wished to revive
the Hebrew language, to return to the land of their ancestors, and
to make it into 'a veritable Jewish homeland under the Ottoman
flag'. Impressed, Djemal responded:

If this is so, I shall give you crown lands on which to build your
colonies, shall allow you religious and cultural autonomy, and will help
you to carry out the Zionist programme under Ottoman sovereignty.

To which Antebi wittily replied:

In this case, I shall proclaim Your Excellency President of the Zionist
Organization and shall be his faithful secretary.

During the interview Djemal intermittently interrogated Beha-
ed-Din and compared notes. When finally assured by Antebi that
the notables were innocent, he asked for the files which contained
the accusations and tore them up. Antebi thereupon returned to his
colleagues and with a serious expression on his face announced
solemnly that unfortunately he had failed to obtain a cancellation
of the deportation order. Once given by the Pasha it must remain in
force 'for ever'. Only a few minor points had been modified: 'You
will be deported not to Brussa, but to Tiberias; not for ever, but for
a fortnight, not all of you, but only some.'[116] Ruppin, who was

---

[116] Dizengoff, op. cit., pp. 31–5; Smilansky, op. cit. iii, pp. 37–40; Ben-Hillel Hacohen,
op. cit. i, pp. 67–8.

present, commented humorously: 'So a few of the notables took a holiday in Tiberias, and the Children of Israel were once more spared the decree.'[117]

On one occasion Djemal confided to Antebi that actually he had never expected any serious trouble from the Jews; his antagonism towards them was motivated by the need to appease the Arabs.[118] It would be wrong, however, to conclude that Djemal relented on Zionism completely. He restricted the persecutions to a relatively small number of persons who at some time, as Consul Brode put it gently, 'expressed themselves incautiously on the political aims of Zionism'.[119] On 9 February 1915 David Ben-Gurion and Itzhak Ben-Zvi, leaders of Poale Zion, were detained on charges of membership of a 'secret organization, detrimental to the interests of the State'. In vain did they protest that Poale Zion was an open organization, in no way inimical to Turkey. Both were former law students at the University of Constantinople and, following the outbreak of war, tried unsuccessfully to volunteer for the Turkish army. When the Capitulations were abrogated, they were among the first to adopt Ottoman nationality and actively encouraged their fellow Jews in Palestine to follow their example. On 15 March Djemal summoned them and in the presence of a number of Turkish officials declared:

> You are Poale Zionists and your motives are well known to me. Your aim is to build a Jewish State in Palestine, but your work is useless . . . We are giving you Mesopotamia and Anatolia, and in spite of this you want Palestine. It will not be.[120]

Then a deportation order was issued and their passports were confiscated so that they might 'never be permitted to return'.[120] Deported also were delegates to the Eleventh Zionist Congress such as: Ben-Zion Mossinsohn, Menahem Shenkin, Rabbi Yehuda Fishman, Yoseph Aaronowitz, Dr. Chaim Bugrashov, and Dr. Joseph Lurie. Other deportees were Israel Shohat, one of the founders of Hashomer, his wife Manya, and Yehoshua Hankin, a non-party man who devoted his life to the purchase of land in

---

[117] Ruppin, *Memoirs*, p. 153.   [118] Smilansky, op. cit. iii, p. 42; cf. below, p. 330.
[119] *Türkei* 195, K 177309, Brode to A.A., 26 Aug. 1915.
[120] Ibid. K 178006–10, Ben-Gurion and Ben-Zvi to Brandeis (New York), 31 Aug. 1916, encl. in Warburg to A.A., 1 Nov. 1916 (K 177994); I. Ben-Zvi: *Ktavim [Works]* (Hebrew), (Tel Aviv, 1936), i, p. 157; Elmaliyach, op. cit. ii, pp. 101–3. In 1948 Ben-Gurion became the Prime Minister of the State of Israel and in 1952 Ben-Zvi was elected its second President. On Poale Zion see above, p. 135.

Palestine. It was ironical that men like Mossinsohn and Lurie, who had been actively promoting the idea of naturalization and espousing the cause of the Central Powers, should have been thus condemned. No less astonishing was the banishing of Dr. Bugrashov, the headmaster of the Herzliya High School, who had welcomed Djemal at the official reception on 2 March. The organs of the Socialist-Zionist parties, the *Ahdut* and *Hapoel Hatzair*, were shut down, although they had consistently taken a pro-Turkish line in their editorials.[121]

Djemal disliked the Palestine Office and tried to intimidate Ruppin (in most cases through a third person) into leaving Palestine. At the beginning of March Djemal forwarded, through Loytved-Hardegg, a request to the German Embassy in Constantinople that Ruppin be recalled but, on Lichtheim's insistence, the Embassy rejected it. Lichtheim kept in constant touch with Weber and Kühlmann and on 7 April saw Wangenheim, who showed him the letter that had come from the Grand Vizier. According to this the Porte had decided not to do anything that might inflame public opinion abroad against Turkey; 'Dr. Ruppin will not be deported although he is one of the leading Zionists.'[122] A day earlier Wangenheim had cabled to Berlin that as a result of his intervention Djemal had declared that he did not insist on Ruppin's 'immediate' departure.[123]

Apart from these episodes the situation was calm till practically the end of the year. On 24 March Ruppin told Lichtheim that the local authorities were displaying on the whole a correct attitude and trying to avoid unnecessary vexation.[124] The newly appointed *Caimakam* of the Jaffa district was noted as 'being a decent and fair man' while Hassan Bey, its Military Commandant, was dismissed several months later.[125]

None the less, in the United States excitement did not abate. This was partly due to the late arrival of Captain Decker's report

---

[121] Ben-Hillel Hacohen, op. cit. i, pp. 89–90, 110–17; Smilansky, op. cit. iii, pp. 60–2, 84–5, 107; Shenkin, op. cit., pp. 61–3; *Türkei* 195, K 176929, K 176964, Lichtheim to Warburg, 16, 27 Mar. 1915; K 177129, Warburg to Lichtheim, 21 June 1915.

[122] C.Z.A. Z3/52, Lichtheim to E.A.C., 7 Apr. 1915; Lichtheim, *She'ar Yashuv*, pp. 343–5; *Rückkehr*, pp. 301–2; Ruppin, *Memoirs*, p. 159.

[123] *Türkei* 195, K 177026, Wangenheim to A.A., 6 Apr. 1915, dis. no. 214.

[124] C.Z.A. Z3/52, Ruppin to Lichtheim, 24 Mar. 1915; Lichtheim, *She'ar Yashuv*, p. 339; *Rückkehr*, p. 297.

[125] Ben-Hillel Hacohen, op. cit. i, pp. 72, 90. 159–60.

(prepared when Beha-ed-Din was still in office) which concluded that 'Zionism was in real danger' and that 'its destruction would be lamentable'.[126] On 16 March, after learning belatedly of the food requisitions, Bernstorff suggested that the German Consulate in Palestine be instructed to offer its good offices if necessary to the American warships which were supplying provisions to the Jewish colonies. On 3 April Straus cabled that 'Arabic pamphlets are being printed in Constantinople instigating massacres of the Jews'.[127] Even as late as June 1915, when the danger had disappeared, Bernstorff reported that there was an 'intense excitement of American and Jewish public opinion against Turkey'. He regretted 'the renewed doubt about the seriousness of German promises of protection for Jews'. He emphasized that it was necessary 'to enlighten the Ottoman Government about *principles* [of German policy] in order to stop definitely dangerous practices against Jews and Zionists'.[128]

Undue exaggerations in the foreign Press annoyed Wangenheim.[129] 'Is this the reward for my persistent interventions in favour of the Jews?' he kept asking Lichtheim.[130] The latter was undoubtedly grateful and did whatever he could to provide the news media in the United States with balanced and reliable reports. Thus in mid-February he advised Straus through the German diplomatic bag:

> The expulsions [of December 1914] took place without authorization from Constantinople . . . We are being continuously supported by the German and American Embassies. We have to thank them for the release of the detained Zionist notables and for the dismissal of the hostile Ottoman officials. German Consulate and German officers on Djemal Pasha's Staff were also helpful . . . Should the Porte's favourable attitude persist and diplomatic support continue, the situation will improve . . . Publish the above in Jewish and non-Jewish Press.[131]

[126] *Türkei* 195, K 176877, Straus to Warburg, 2 Mar. 1915, tel. no. 345; K 176892, Jacobson to Lichtheim, 5 Mar. 1915; Manuel, op. cit., pp. 127–31.

[127] *Türkei* 195, K 176937, Bernstorff to A.A., 16 Mar. 1915, tel. no. 453; K 177015 Straus to Warburg, 3 Apr. 1915.

[128] Ibid. K 177104, Bernstorff to A.A., 7 June 1915, tel. no. 126. As this cable was drafted in English, not as usual in cipher, it is possible to infer that the Ambassador intended to leak it to U.S. official circles. Secretary of State Bryan also instructed Morgenthau to 'urge Turkish Government to protect both Armenians and Zionists'. Morgenthau was the first diplomat to report about the Armenian atrocities. He suspected that it signalled a drive against all non-Turkish nationalities and that 'hostile action against the Zionists would follow' (Manuel, op. cit., p. 134).

[129] *Türkei* 195, K 177006, Wangenheim to A.A., 27 Mar. 1915, dis. no. 193.

[130] Lichtheim, *She'ar Yashuv*, pp. 331, 335; *Rückkehr*, pp. 290, 293.

[131] *Türkei* 195, K 176870-1, Lichtheim to Straus, (?) Feb. 1915.

Five weeks later in a confidential letter he explained that if the German Embassy did not always act as forcefully as one would have liked it was because it wished to avoid giving offence to its Turkish ally, but one should be pleased that 'the *worst* that might have happened was prevented.'[132]

On 24 March, when the storm seemed to be over, Ruppin asked Lichtheim to convey the Yishuv's heartfelt gratitude to Wangenheim and Morgenthau. Two days later he added: 'Had you not been successful in rallying the German and American Embassies to restrain Djemal our position would have been intolerable.'[133]

[132] C.Z.A. L 6/45, Lichtheim to Straus, 27 Mar. 1915 (confidential).
[133] Ibid. Z 3/52, Ruppin to Lichtheim, 24, 26 Mar. 1915; Lichtheim, *She'ar Yashuv*, pp. 339–40; *Rückkehr*, p. 297.

12

Formulation of Policy

WE have seen how sensitive the Wilhelmstrasse was about Germany's image, but propaganda apart German diplomats expected that, in return for protection of Palestinian Jewry, the Zionists would commit their movement to the side of the Central Powers. Kühlmann made no secret of this, nor did Zimmermann.[1] However, the Zionists steered clear of such a course, as it would have breached their self-imposed neutrality in the war. 'During my encounters with the German Embassy', Lichtheim told his colleagues in New York, 'I had always specifically emphasized that Zionism is not a German but *a general Jewish movement*.'[2] An identical stand was taken by Jacobson during his discussion with Zimmermann in July 1915.[3]

Zionist neutrality was conditioned by the international character of the movement. The problem which it aimed to solve was of international dimensions and it was therefore imperative to win the support of all the Powers concerned, not to rivet it to one Power exclusively. This policy, which originated with Herzl,[4] was followed by the 'practical' Zionists.[5] In June 1912, when Jacobson approached Ambassador Marschall and later von Mutius, Sokolow tried to rally support in London, while Nordau had a comprehensive discussion with Pichon at the Quai d'Orsay.[6] The overtures proved

[1] C.Z.A. Z 3/50, Lichtheim to E.A.C., 2 Dec. 1914.
[2] Ibid., same to P.E.C. (New York), 10 July 1916.
[3] *Türkei* 195, K 177177–80, Jacobson to Zimmermann, 30 July 1915.
[4] Above, pp. 59, 118.
[5] Following the Young Turk Revolution they refrained from active diplomacy in European capitals in the belief that a concerted effort in Constantinople would bring a *modus vivendi* with Turkey nearer but, meeting with little reciprocity, following the debate in the Ottoman Parliament in 1911, they decided to put out feelers to the Powers. (C.Z.A. Z 3/429 meetings of the G.A.C., 25 May, 4 Nov. 1911.)
[6] C.Z.A. Z 3/44, Jacobson to E.A.C., 1 June 1912; Z 3/402, Sokolow to E.A.C., 13 June 1912; Z 3/403, same to same, 14 Jan., 3 Mar. 1913; Alsberg, 'The Political Orienta-

fruitless but the Zionists managed at least to show that their policy was well balanced, not subordinated to this or any other Power. It was characteristic of Lichtheim to comment, following his crucial meeting with Wangenheim on 29 June 1914,[7]

the same ought to be achieved in England, where our arguments may carry even greater weight. England should welcome our civilizing work in Palestine, which lies astride the road from Egypt to India . . . She will not go out of her way to accommodate us, but what was possible to achieve in Germany, should not be ruled out in England. It would at least neutralize the ill-effects of the intrigues against us by [Fitzmaurice], the First Dragoman of the British Embassy.[8]

This thinking was consistent with the principle of neutrality declared at the Eleventh Congress in the summer of 1913 by Dr. Moses Gaster, the Chief Rabbi of the Spanish and Portuguese Congregation in Britain. He denied that Zionism was a German movement as had been described in the British Press. 'We are fighting everywhere to make it clear that we feel neither German nor English nor French nor Russian, but that our feelings and our thoughts are solely and exclusively Jewish.'[9]

The outbreak of the First World War put the Zionists in an unprecedented predicament. As individuals they discharged their duties in their respective countries of domicile as loyally as other citizens did, but the movement was in a quandary. It was split between two diametrically opposed schools of thought. Weizmann and his friends, who were convinced that England would win the war, endeavoured to unseat the Berlin-led Zionist Executive and transfer the headquarters to New York.[10] In contrast, Zionists in Germany thought that the *Blitzkrieg* pointed to Germany gaining the upper hand,[11] and did their best to maintain their leadership within the movement. There were, however, two inescapable factors which had to be taken into account: first, the fate of Jews in Russia, and second, the security of the Yishuv. This Otto Warburg did when outlining Zionist policy on 29 August 1914.

tion of the Zionist Executive on the Eve of the First World War' (Hebrew), *Zion* (1957), pp. 155–6, 171–6; above, p. 185.

[7] Above, pp. 187–8.

[8] C.Z.A. Z 3/11, Lichtheim to E.A.C., 29 June 1914.

[9] *Protokoll, XI. Kongress*, pp. 111–12; on Gaster see Stein, *The Balfour Declaration*, pp. 286–7.

[10] Weizmann, *Trial and Error*, p. 189; Stein, op. cit., pp. 99–100 and *passim*.

[11] Lichtheim, *She'ar Yashuv*, p. 289; *Rückkehr*, pp. 254–5.

The Executive should adopt a detached attitude [towards the war], because even if Germany and Austria-Hungary emerge victorious, Palestine's fate would still remain undecided . . . However, the German Zionists should be guided by the consideration that interests of Jewry at large coincide with those of Germany and Austria. If these two Powers are defeated, the position of Russian Jewry would be terrible. Only following a German–Austrian victory can we expect an improvement in their condition . . . Minor modifications in our attitude towards the Porte should also be made, but our basic policy will undoubtedly remain the same, i.e. an unconditional loyalty to the Ottoman Empire . . . Our people in Palestine should express attachment to Turkey in a quiet and dignified manner. It would in no way imply an irrevocable commitment to one side in the war since nothing is more natural for a population than to be loyal to a given government of the country.

Warburg urged Jacobson to accelerate the procedure of naturalization of foreign Jews and use whatever influence he had in Constantinople to ensure the Yishuv's security.[12] Cautious and pragmatic, Warburg had to strike a balance between the principle of neutrality and political realities but in taking his decision he was guided solely by Jewish interests.

Bodenheimer was less inhibited. In his memoirs he revealed how possessed he had become by the general feeling of euphoria following Germany's mobilization to stem the Russian 'steam roller', and by high expectations that Russian Jews might finally be delivered from the Tsarist yoke.[13] In November 1914 he wrote to Warburg:

I feel that in this war the interests of Russian Jews and those of the German Reich are identical . . . Although I am convinced that the Zionist Organization has a paramount interest in this question, I undertook my task simply as a German patriot and as a Jew, out of sympathy for my people and national solidarity.

So close an identification with Germany's war aims could have compromised the Zionist movement unnecessarily, and Bodenheimer therefore resigned from the chairmanship of the Board of Directors of the J.N.F.[14]

Bodenheimer's activity had begun four months earlier. On 4 August he got in touch with the Auswärtiges Amt and proposed the establishment in the aftermath of a German victory of an East

---

[12] C.Z.A. Z 3/49, Warburg to Jacobson (Constantinople), 29 Aug. 1914.
[13] Bodenheimer, *Memoirs*, pp. 231–3.
[14] C.Z.A. Z 3/472, Bodenheimer to E.A.C., 27 Nov. 1914.

European Federation ('ein osteuropäischer Staatenbund'), which was to extend from the Baltic to the Black Sea and be a *cordon sanitaire* between Germany and Russia. In this federation all ethnic groups were to enjoy national autonomy. The Poles, numerically the strongest element (8 millions), were to be balanced by the smaller nationalities, such as the Ukrainians (5 millions), the White Russians (4 millions), the Lithuanians, the Latvians, and the Estonians (3.5 millions), while the Jews (6 millions), jointly with the Germans (1.8 millions), were to tip the scales. Such a buffer state, Bodenheimer argued, would secure Germany's eastern borders, while the Jews would be liberated from the Russian knout.[15]

The memorandum aroused considerable interest at the Foreign Ministry and soon after Bodenheimer was invited by Count Hutten-Czapski, the Political Director of the General Staff, for a discussion. He was afterwards introduced to Diego von Bergen, the expert on Polish affairs at the Foreign Ministry. The latter was in the process of drafting an appeal for both the German and the Austrian High Command to be made to the Polish Jews and Bodenheimer's move seemed timely. Elated by his success, Bodenheimer revealed his plan to his friend, Dr. Franz Oppenheimer, a leading economist who had pioneered the idea of a co-operative settlement in Palestine. Oppenheimer welcomed it enthusiastically, and on 17 August, together with a number of Zionists, such as Dr. Alfred Klee, Dr. Adolf Friedemann, and Hermann Struck, founded the Komitee zur Befreiung der russischen Juden. Its name was its programme. It undertook the publication of an illustrated journal *Kol Mevasser* to which Sokolow contributed a leading article.[16] All this, coupled with the absence of any objection from Warburg, who appointed Hantke as a liaison officer, created the erroneous impression in German official circles that 'the whole of the Zionist movement was won over' to the German cause. But Bodenheimer had to correct this, emphasizing that the Zionist organization was an interterritorial one and could not be involved in the Committee's activities; the two bodies were not identical.[17] Several months later the Committee broadened its base and co-opted non- or even antiZionist personalities; they included Dr. Timendorfer, the President

---

[15] *Wk.*, Nr. 11, adh. 2, K 190239-48, 4, 14 Aug. 1914, Bodenheimer to Bergen and encls.

[16] Bodenheimer, op. cit., pp. 234-8.

[17] *Wk.*, Nr. 11, adh. 2, K 190276-80, 'Überblick . . .', 16 Aug. 1914; K 190291-6, Bodenheimer to Bergen, 19 Aug. 1914; K 190338-43, same to G.H.Q., 20 Aug. 1914.

of the Grand Lodge of the B'nai B'rith in Germany, Eugen Fuchs, Chairman of the Federation of German Jews, and the Orientalist, Professor Moritz Sobernheim. Connection was also established with the Jewish Socialists who delegated Dr. Oscar Cohn, a member of the Reichstag, to act as their representative.[18]

It soon transpired that Hutten-Czapski was interested more in short-term objectives; he intended to use the Jews as a disruptive element behind the enemy lines within the framework of his 'insurrection policy', rather than to assist Bodenheimer in laying the foundation of the East European Federation. Aided by Georg Cleinow, the editor of the *Grenzboten* and head of the East German Information Office, he drafted a leaflet which, after approval by both the German and the Austrian Foreign Ministry, was distributed both in German and in Yiddish to the Jewish population in Galicia. The text read in part:

> Jews of Russia! Rise! Take up arms! Leave all the quarrels aside, whether you are Nationalists, Zionists, or Socialists! Help to chase out the Muscovite from the Western territories, from Poland, Lithuania, White Russia and Podolia![19]

By comparison, leaflets dropped from aeroplanes to the Jews of Poland were more moderate in tone. The phrase 'take up arms' was deleted and their tenor was more of an appeal for collaboration than an overt call to rebellion. None the less, their contents were quite provocative.

> To the Jews in Poland! We, your friends, are approaching. The barbaric foreign rule is over!... It is your sacred duty to gather all your strength and co-operate in the liberation . . . We expect you to prove your sympathy by deeds.[20]

Bodenheimer had not been consulted and was deeply dismayed when he first read the leaflets. Not only had he been rebuffed—his proposed text had been completely disregarded—but incitement to open insurrection could gravely jeopardize the safety of his

[18] Bodenheimer, op. cit., p. 241. Documents on the foundation of the Committee and its activities are found also in C.Z.A., Z 3/204–6.

[19] *Wk.*, Nr. 11, adh. 2, K 190260; Graf Bogdan Hutten-Czapski, *Sechzig Jahre Politik und Gesellschaft* (Berlin, 1936), ii, p. 156; I. Friedman, 'The Austro-Hungarian Government and Zionism, 1897–1918', p. 154 n. 57 and App. I, p. 248, where the full text is reproduced.

[20] *Berliner Tageblatt*, 1 Sept. 1914, cutting in *Wk.*, Nr. 11, adh. 2, K 190332; first draft K 190258–9.

co-religionists in Russia, in the front-line area in particular. In the given circumstances to expect them to take up arms was completely unrealistic and the method employed by the German authorities was both frivolous and irresponsible. Bodenheimer's aim, as is evident from the text of his draft leaflets, was political, not military. Moreover, he complained, no reference whatsoever had been made to the civic status of Jews in Russia proper.[21]

Dissatisfied, Bodenheimer submitted yet another memorandum expanding on the merits of his plan.[22] He won his day when, with Oppenheimer, Chairman of the Committee, he was invited to call on the *Ober-Ost*, the headquarters of the eastern war-zone;[23] General Ludendorff received them with great affability and welcomed their project. He immediately grasped its significance: a federation of nationalities would be permanently dependent upon Germany; a Polish state spelled danger. He introduced the visitors to Field-Marshal Hindenburg who, after a dinner party, gave them a letter affirming that he was prepared to further the aims of their Committee.

The letter was signed in Radom on 15 October 1914. However, two weeks later the German troops had to retreat from the Congress Kingdom and the plan to establish the federation of nationalities had to be shelved. Subsequently, the Committee changed its name to Komitee für den Osten (K.f.d.O.), which was less provocative, and publication of the journal *Kol Mevasser* ceased. On 9 November 1914 State Secretary G. von Jagow advised Zimmermann that in view of the military situation a proclamation to the Russian Jews would be inopportune. After that Bodenheimer's project was never referred to again. Following reoccupation of Poland, the German military authorities advised him to negotiate with the Polish national leaders instead. As soon as discussions started Bodenheimer noted that the Poles were interested more in Jewish emigration to Palestine than in granting the Jewish minority in Poland the privilege of cultural autonomy.[24]

---

[21] *Wk.*, Nr. 11, adh. 2, K 190338–43, Bodenheimer to G.H.Q., 20 Aug. 1914.

[22] Ibid. K 190387–415, Bodenheimer to Hamann, 28 Sept. 1914, 'Richtlinien des D.K.B.R.J.' and encls.

[23] Ibid. K 190537, certificate, dated 19 Sept. 1914, valid till 31 Dec. 1914.

[24] Ibid. K 190638–59, K 190792–819, Oppenheimer and Bodenheimer to Bergen, 21 Jan., 23, 25 Mar. 1915; K 190454–60, Jagow to Zimmermann, 9 Nov. 1914; Bodenheimer, op. cit., pp. 248–50, 260; Franz Oppenheimer, *Erlebtes, Erstrebtes, Erreichtes: Erinnerungen* (Düsseldorf, 1964), pp. 227–35.

Throughout the war the German authorities treated the Jews in the Eastern Occupied Territories correctly. They abrogated the restrictions enforced under the Russian regime; elementary education was made compulsory without distinction of race or creed; secondary schools and universities were thrown open to Jewish students, whose admittance had previously been restricted by the notorious *numerus clausus*.[25] Jews were given fair representation in municipal councils (in Lodz a third of the city council consisted of Jewish deputies)[26] and, after the capture of Warsaw, Ludwig Haas, a member of the Reichstag, was appointed on the K.f.d.O.'s advice as head of the Jewish Department in the German civil administration of Poland, but the project of the East European Federation was dead. The Germans opted for the creation of a Polish state and Ludendorff lost interest in Bodenheimer's ideas.[27]

Early in the war members of the Zionist Executive in Berlin sympathized with the K.f.d.O. Amelioration of the position of Jews in Russia, let alone their liberation from Tsarist oppression, was something to which no Jew in the world could remain indifferent. It was therefore natural for Warburg to appoint Hantke as a liaison officer; Sokolow wrote an appeal to the Polish Jews; Lichtheim served for a short while as secretary to the K.f.d.O., and David Wolffsohn, before his death on 15 September 1914, gave it his personal blessing. But the Zionists soon sensed that they were drifting into dangerous waters. The first voice of dissent was raised during an informal meeting at Wolffsohn's home, after the funeral, by Jean Fischer of Belgium. He considered Bodenheimer's work useless, because in his opinion Germany could not win the war. As time wore on, criticism against Bodenheimer mounted. Exception was taken to his excessive zeal to integrate the Jews into Germany's *Ost-Politik* which could seriously compromise the Zionist movement.[28] Furthermore, however laudable his intention had been, the Committee's propaganda did more harm than good.

---

[25] *Jewish Chronicle*, 22 Oct. 1915. Interview with Boris Goldberg, a well-known Jewish leader in western Russia, who arrived in England in May 1915. See also below, pp. 322–4.

[26] *Wk.*, Nr. 11, adh. 2, K 190983–9, K.f.d.O. to Montgelas (A.A.) for Straus, 15 July 1915.

[27] Bodenheimer, op. cit., pp. 260, 262.

[28] Ibid., p. 240; Lichtheim, *She'ar Yashuv*, pp. 295–6; *Rückkehr*, p. 260. Bodenheimer admitted in his memoirs that he acted as 'a German patriot' and that his chief motive was to be 'of service to the Reich' (pp. 256, 274).

Leaflets distributed by both the German and the Austrian High Command (the K.f.d.O. did not draft them) heightened the suspicions of the Russian authorities and provided them with a ready excuse for mass deportations of Jews from the war-zone.[29] The propaganda tended also to undermine the credibility of professions of loyalty by Russian Jewish leaders to their country and triggered off unwarranted accusations of espionage.[30] Nor did the presentation of Jews as 'forerunners of *Deutschtum* in the East' endear them to the Poles.

Aware of these risks, the Zionist Executive on 27 October requested its officials to withdraw from the K.f.d.O.; the most outspoken critic was Victor Jacobson. He was followed by Tschlenow who, at the meeting of the Zionist General Council in Copenhagen on 3–6 December 1914, threw all the weight of his authority into a demand for a complete break with the K.f.d.O. It was incompatible with the principle of neutrality, it fed the suspicions of the Russian High Command, and it could antagonize the Russian officials who to a man sympathized with Zionist aspirations. The K.f.d.O.'s credit was not entirely overlooked, however, as other members of the Council praised its initiative in enlightening the German authorities on the pressing problems which beset East European Jewry.

Consequently, the Council resolved to welcome any activity which aimed at promoting equality of civic rights of Jews in countries where they were deprived of them but, in the same breath, condemned participation of leading Zionists in endeavours that could endanger the safety of the Jews living in one of the belligerent countries. Bodenheimer's resignation from the directorship of the J.N.F. was unanimously accepted but, as he was still a member of the General Zionist Council, his activities had to be watched with some care. Thus at a meeting of the General Council in The Hague, which took place on 23–4 March 1916, the publication of

---

[29] Friedman, *The Question of Palestine*, pp. 38–9; *idem*, 'The Austro-Hungarian Government and Zionism, 1897–1918', p. 154.

[30] Greenberg, *The Jews in Russia*, ii, pp. 96–101. The *Novyi Voskhod* (*New Sunrise*) wrote on 24 July 1914; 'We are ... inseparably allied with our mother country where we have been living for centuries and from which there is no power that can separate us— neither persecution nor oppression.' And the Deputy N. M. Friedman declared two days later in the Duma that the Jews were 'marching to the battlefield shoulder to shoulder with all the peoples of Russia' (Greenberg, op. cit., pp. 94–5). The Jewish population delivered its full quota of reservists and a large number volunteered, making the total of 400,000 Jewish soldiers in the Russian army.

the K.f.d.O.'s programme in the *Ostjudenheft*, a supplement to the *Süddeutsche Monatshefte*, was sharply criticized. The phrases that were particularly objectionable read: 'The K.f.d.O. has been founded . . . with the purpose of rendering a service to the Central Powers', and, if they were victorious, the K.f.d.O. would take care of the Jews in the East 'within the framework of the interests of the German fatherland'. The Zionists, as Hantke declared during that meeting, 'must take the utmost care not to be looked upon as agents for *Deutschtum*'. On 25 January 1917, when Bodenheimer suggested the revival of his committee, which had been defunct since Poland had been proclaimed independent, the Zionist Executive rejected his proposal on the grounds that the Committee's programme was inconsistent with Zionist neutrality.

The policy of neutrality had been decided by the General Council during its meeting on 3–6 December 1914 in Copenhagen, mentioned already. It was a result of much soul-searching and of intense discussion among local organizations (the Landes-Verbände). With the *Blitzkrieg* proving abortive, following the failure of the German offensive on the Marne, it became clear that the belligerents were set on a long struggle and that the Zionists could therefore no longer defer a decision on the direction of their movement. Jean Fischer, the delegate from Belgium who was in touch with the British Zionists, warned the Greater Council (during its meeting on 3 December 1914) of the risk involved in a pro-Turkish orientation; Turkey was both politically and otherwise insolvent. He demanded that the Zionist headquarters be moved to New York and that a branch be established in The Hague. The idea was rejected by Warburg on the grounds of both practicability and expediency. So long as Palestine was Turkish, Zionist policy should not change. Transfer of the office from Berlin would make an unfavourable impression on the German authorities and render ineffective the Zionists' *démarches* on behalf of the Yishuv. Tschlenow supported Warburg wholeheartedly but, in order to keep the balance, it was felt that a diplomatic effort should be mounted in the Entente and neutral countries which would parallel the activity in Berlin and Constantinople. In keeping with this principle it was decided that Sokolow should go to England where, it was noted, there was 'lack of suitable staff who could effectively help in the political work', while Jacobson was to go to France. Their activity was, however, to be strictly informative; it was expressly resolved that no negotiations should be conducted with 'any Government which was in a state of war with Turkey'. The seat of the Executive and of the Central Office was to remain in Berlin. A branch was to be opened in Copenhagen with Dr. Simon Bernstein from Russia and Dr. Martin Rosenblüth from Berlin acting as co-secretaries.

It was planned that Sokolow and Tschlenow would proceed from England to the United States but the former, finding himself fully occupied, remained throughout the war in London, while the latter was badly needed at home and returned to Russia. Nor did Jacobson's trip to Paris materialize. With Sokolow in London, Shmarya Levin in New York, and Tschlenow in Moscow, the conduct of the Executive's day-to-day affairs, and particularly contacts with the Auswärtiges Amt, remained in the hands of the trio of Warburg, Hantke, and Jacobson.

The dissenters were highly dissatisfied. Chaim Weizmann and Leopold Kessler, the two British members on the General Council, continued to boycott its meetings and severed relations with Berlin and Copenhagen. Other opponents, like Fischer and Jacobus Kann, the Dutch Zionist leader, did battle whenever they could. At the Council's meeting on 23-4 March 1916 in The Hague they delivered a scathing attack on the Executive, claiming that its very location in a capital of a belligerent Power constituted a breach of neutrality, and it confirmed the standard view held in the Entente countries that Zionism was German-oriented. Unless the seat of the Executive was transferred to New York the movement would be irretrievably compromised and its prospects at the future Peace Conference prejudiced; Kann went so far as to call for a complete change of leadership. They were countered by Dr. Louis Frank and Julius Simon, both from Germany, that absolute neutrality did not exist even in neutral countries and that at the future Peace Conference the attitude of the Entente Powers to Zionism would be motivated by their own interests, not by any wish to reward the Executive's centre of residence. The movement's centre of gravity lay in Europe and it would be unwise to shift it to America.

It was not until the members of the Executive themselves took the floor that its policy was explained authoritatively. Hantke pointed out that the factor which dominated its decision-making was concern for the preservation of the Yishuv; next to this was the need to maintain the movement's internal cohesion. Both tasks had so far been achieved. Zionism was the only international organization which had not been shaken by the war. The reproach that the Executive was one-sided was totally unfounded.

> We demand [diplomatic] work everywhere, in the neutral countries not the least. That achievements in England and France fell short of expectations was the fault of the Zionists in these countries . . . They also tend to overlook that Palestine is part of Turkey and that under no circumstances should we supply her with a weapon that could be used against ourselves. For this reason alone one should object to the proposed transfer of the Central Office elsewhere. The political informatory work must be carried out from Berlin.

Hantke was followed by Jacobson, who reminded the audience that Germany was the only Power which had some leverage on Turkey and that protection of the Palestine Jews could be afforded expeditiously only from Constantinople. Should pleas for intervention come from the United States, either through the German Embassy in Washington or the State Department, the Zionists would be running undue risks because the time element was vital. As past events showed, if disaster was to be averted, action had to be taken sometimes within twenty-four hours. It was largely thanks to Lichtheim's personal connections with the German and American embassies, as well as with the Chief Rabbi, that machinery guarding the welfare of the Yishuv was running so smoothly. And it was naïve to assume that American pressure alone on Turkey would ensure the safety of the Palestinian Jews. The fate that befell the Armenians illustrated its limitations. Jacobson declared:

> The course that we have hitherto pursued is the right one . . . One can live in a belligerent country and still be neutral and, just as one should not fall victim to the general war psychosis, so equally one's judgement should not be blurred by a neutralist psychosis . . . We reject complete passivity, as suggested by Dr. Nordau; nor can we allow complete autonomy in political work by the national constituent organizations as demanded by our colleagues from the other side . . . Should we accede to their demand, we shall be running the risk of perpetual violations of neutrality and of the disintegration of our movement.

At the end of the debate the Council gave the Executive an overwhelming vote of confidence and almost unanimously rejected Kann's motion.[31]

---

[31] C.Z.A. L 6/37, minutes of the G.A.C. meeting, 3–6 Dec. 1914; Z 3/450, report by Jean Fischer, dated 12 Dec. 1914; *Organisation Report.* From a Report presented to the

With the exception of the Zionists in Britain, who went their own way, and those in Belgium and Holland, who remained in opposition, all other constituent national organizations faithfully followed the Executive's lead; most important was the support from the two largest organizations in Russia and in the United States. The former played an active role in shaping Zionist policy, while the latter had little difficulty in accepting it, since it fitted well into the pattern of the American position in the war and President Wilson's Turcophil sentiments, as well as those of the State Department.

It has been noted that Jacobson disagreed with Nordau's concept of neutrality. Nordau insisted that 'the Jew as an individual should fulfil his duty as a citizen to his native country, but the Jewish people collectively, and the Zionists in particular, should wait with calm resignation for the end of the war, when they may present their claims for the consideration of the Powers'.[32] The Zionist Executive rejected this advice. Passive neutrality which bordered on inactivity led nowhere. It would have rendered the movement stagnant and left its claims unnoticed at a time when the question of nationalities engaged universal attention and was so central in the propaganda warfare of the contending Powers. International support, which the Zionists endeavoured to secure, in no way ran counter to their principle of neutrality, or reflected any proclivity for this or another Power. The war was not of their choosing and Jews as a people had little to gain from it. As late as 1918 *Der Jude*, a pro-Zionist bi-weekly, wrote: 'We have nothing to do with this war. Its origins, aims, and nature are totally alien to us. It lies completely outside our national sphere . . . Our neutrality is truly absolute, the only real and unconditional neutrality of a people in this war.'[33] It is indicative that as late as the end of November

---

Twelfth Zionist Congress, pp. 27–8; C.Z.A. Z 3/453, minutes of the G.A.C. meeting, 23–4 Mar. 1916; Z 3/539, minutes to the E.A.C. meeting, 25 Jan. 1917. There were 25 members on the General Council; 12 from Germany and Austria-Hungary, 7 from Russia, 2 from England, and 1 each from Belgium, France, Holland, and Romania. On Russia's attitude to Zionism see Friedman, op. cit., pp. 59, 113.

[32] *Le People Juif* (15 Jan. 1917); C.Z.A. Z 3/1014, Nordau to E.A.C., 4 Oct. 1915; Nordau, 'Die Pflicht der Stunde', *Menorah* (Vienna, Oct. 1915).

[33] *Der Jude* (1918/19), p. 197. Professor Egmont Zechlin, who quotes this statement also, maintains that neither the German Zionists, nor those in the Entente countries, adhered to their self-imposed principle of neutrality (*Die deutsche Politik und die Juden im Ersten Weltkrieg* (Göttingen, 1969), pp. 313–14, 445–6). This view, as our narrative shows, is untenable. The accusation is nearer the mark with regard to Weizmann and Bodenheimer, but Professor Zechlin ignores the fact that neither of them officially

1918, when Germany was beaten and the Balfour Declaration was already one year old, the Executive decided that the Zionist movement should preserve its international character.[34]

Jacobson's warm praise of Lichtheim during the meeting in The Hague was not misplaced. He could have had no more worthy successor to his post in Constantinople.[35] Lichtheim was a party ideologist who became a diplomat and a Zionist representative extraordinary. Comparatively young—he was then thirty years old—he displayed much maturity and balance in judgement. At times of crises he was tough, seldom an alarmist. Yet behind the veneer of his stern Prussian traits one could easily detect a highly sensitive and warm personality. A zealous practitioner of pragmatic diplomacy, his forte was analysis and logical persuasion. He had a unique talent to get on well with almost all successive ambassadors in Constantinople. At the German Embassy he was highly regarded for his geniality, intelligence, and tact, while Morgenthau found him so trustworthy that he soon became an intimate friend. Amicable and informal relations with Chief Rabbi Nahoum were also useful.

Though Lichtheim's primary concern was to ensure the preservation of the Yishuv, he never lost sight of the wider objective to elicit from the Powers, and from Germany in particular, a more definite commitment to the Zionist cause. However, in this pursuit he was less successful. 'I realize', Wangenheim told Lichtheim some time in December 1914, 'that Zionism aims to bring an end to Jewish wanderings', but on 6 January, following Weber's study of Zionist literature, Wangenheim concluded that a Zionist state was incompatible with Turkish interests. He complimented Lichtheim for his statesmanlike qualities in limiting his desiderata to immigration and colonization in Palestine, devoid of any political colouring,

---

represented the Zionist Organization. Zechlin did not use Zionist documentary sources. He also advances the view (ibid., p. 399) that in the late summer of 1917 Weizmann deliberately exaggerated the threat of a pro-Zionist declaration in order to spur the British Government to issue its declaration. This contention is groundless. Weizmann was genuinely concerned that the Germans might forestall the British. The latter had independent sources of information and were equally concerned. (See Friedman, *The Question of Palestine*, pp. 175–6, 213–14, 221–2, 244–6, 264, 275–7, 286–7.)

[34] C.Z.A. L 6/93, E.A.C. meeting, Copenhagen, 30 Nov.–2 Dec. 1918 (minutes).
[35] Early in the war Jacobson was commuting between Berlin and Constantinople but the Porte objected to his stay and late in April 1915 he returned to Germany.

but was not so naïve as to be misled by such innocuous wording. He realized the direction in which Zionism must eventually lead; it was diametrically opposed to Germany's proclaimed commitment to uphold the integrity of the Ottoman Empire. He therefore welcomed Lichtheim's later assurances that Zionism by no means entertained separatist aspirations. 'If so, we shall be complete allies.' Flattering as this may have sounded, Wangenheim did not mean it seriously. He was prepared to assist the Zionists in individual cases but not to conclude an alliance with them. During the war he was obliged to act with restraint so as not to offend Turkish susceptibilities but in its aftermath he confided to Lichtheim that 'should Germany assume the role of Turkey's protector, she will be able to do more for the Zionists'. In private he may have toasted their future but with the Turkish Ministers he had to be cautious.[36]

In March, when Lichtheim met Weber and subsequently Kühlmann, he again urged that German protection be put on a permanent basis. He went so far as to suggest that should the Zionists be offered 'something more serious, they will see to it that their movement will sail under a German flag'[37] but, as is evident from Wangenheim's reaction to Lichtheim's memorandum, nothing concrete emerged from these *pourparlers*. He wrote to Berlin:

As Your Excellency knows, I have repeatedly approached the Porte on behalf of the Zionists but have always avoided committing myself to a definite Zionist policy, as Lichtheim would have liked. I believe that, in view of the present political situation, I can best serve their interests by using my influence on behalf of the Jews in Turkey in general, but with regard to the Zionists' attempts to tighten their link with us, I think we should maintain every possible reserve. Turkey, being on the point of freeing herself from the various protectorates, would regard it as a hostile gesture on our part if we attempt to initiate a similar protectorate in relation to the Turkish Jews.

Zimmermann replied: 'I can only approve of the attitude which Your Excellency had hitherto adopted towards the Zionist movement and which Your Excellency intends to adopt in the future.'[38]

---

[36] Lichtheim, *She'ar Yashuv*, pp. 275, 310, 316, 345, 373; *Rückkehr*, pp. 244, 272–3, 278, 302, 322.

[37] C.Z.A. Z 3/52, Lichtheim to E.A.C., 9, 13 Mar. 1915.

[38] *Türkei* 195, K 176968–9, Wangenheim to Bethmann Hollweg, 24 Mar. 1915, dis. no. 185, encl. memorandum by Lichtheim of the same day (K 176971–96); K 177010, Zimmermann to Wangenheim, 4 Apr. 1915, dis. no. 1267.

The Germans had difficulties of their own with the Turks. Their diplomats and officers did not always get on well with their Turkish counterparts and even Enver, the celebrated Germanophil, displayed no particular friendliness. After the abolition of the Capitulations, the Turks, proud of their newly acquired independence, disliked any foreign interference. The Constantinople correspondent of the *Berliner Tageblatt* was expelled and that of the *Neue Freie Presse* deported to Angora merely because they expressed views which were not to the liking of the Ottoman Government. The defeat of the Allied fleet in the Dardanelles made the Turks even more self-assertive. They became 'absolutely contemptuous' not only of their Christian foes but even of their Christian allies.[39] But behind the façade of aggressive nationalism there lingered in all Turkish minds a very acute suspicion of Germany's post-war designs. Hence the Germans had to move warily.[40] As Pallavicini, the Austro-Hungarian Ambassador, told Morgenthau, 'Wangenheim would do nothing that would annoy the Turks'.[41]

Lichtheim harboured no illusions. 'Germany will not revoke her alliance with Turkey for our sake', he told Straus, 'Zionism is not her first priority . . . but on the whole we can be satisfied with what the German Embassy has done for us.'[42] Vigilance was still necessary because, though in Palestine the situation was calm, an upsurge of Turkish nationalism revived traditional antagonism against the non-Turkish elements. That Zionism became suspect was also largely due to Beha-ed-Din, who, on his return to Constantinople, brought with him incriminating material to prove that the Zionists entertained pro-Entente sympathies and wished to tear Palestine away from Turkey. 'We are surrounded by a sea of intrigues which we are unable to counter', Lichtheim complained. He thought it therefore useful to clarify the position with the Porte but, failing to cultivate relations with Turkish officials, he was at a disadvantage. However, as Jacobson happened to be in Constantinople at that time, Morgenthau prevailed upon Talaat to receive him. The meeting on 29 April 1915 was fruitless. A few days later Jacobson was requested by the Turkish authorities to leave the country, although he had earlier applied for Ottoman nationality.

[39] Morgenthau, *Secrets of the Bosphorus*, pp. 136, 146, 180–1; Lichtheim, *She'ar Yashuv*, p. 343; *Rückkehr*, p. 301; von Sanders, *Five Years in Turkey*, pp. 9, 209.
[40] Emin, *Turkey in the World War*, pp. 96–7.
[41] Morgenthau, op. cit., pp. 96–7.
[42] C.Z.A. L 6/45 Lichtheim to Straus, 6 July 1915.

Notwithstanding the fiasco, Wangenheim promised Jacobson to speak to the Grand Vizier, Enver, and Talaat. The last-mentioned had been approached by Morgenthau also and on 20 May received Lichtheim. Though gracious, Talaat did not conceal his opposition to Zionism; nor was he convinced that the J.N.F. stamps were an innocuous fund-raising device. Thereupon Lichtheim gave Talaat a memorandum in which he strenuously denied that the Zionists were creating 'a state within a state', let alone that they aspired to 'a Jewish kingdom'. They are 'not political adventurers, nor Utopian dreamers, but realistically minded people who are aware that the Empire is strong enough to crush any manifestation of separatism'. A settlement of 100,000 Jews in Palestine, half of whom were old, pauperized religiasts, constituted no danger to the integrity of the Empire. Even if the number of Jews were to increase to a million or more, they would always remain a small minority in the midst of neighbouring Arab countries, which *ipso facto* would make them gravitate towards the Central Government. He insisted that Herzl's pamphlet *Der Judenstaat* was in no way indicative of the nature of Zionist aspirations. It was written before the Zionist movement came into being and when the author was still unacquainted with the political realities in Turkey. Herzl himself had later modified it to *Heimstätte*. Following the Young Turk Revolution the Zionists abandoned the idea of the charter altogether and considered the new Ottoman Constitution an adequate safeguard for the security of the Jewish settlers in Palestine. The Zionist leaders had since repeatedly declared that they saw no incompatibility between their own interests and those of Turkey. The contention that the J.N.F. stamps and the blue-and-white flag were 'proof' of Zionists' separatist aspirations was preposterous; the internal taxation in the colonies was voluntary and not in lieu of state duties; bank-notes, issued early in the war, were designed to meet the shortage of currency; and it was equally absurd to consider the Hashomer as *gendarmerie* and as 'a danger to the security of the state . . . Zionism is an open, not conspiratorial organization', and the Ottoman Government should not be misled by reports based on ignorance or motivated by malicious intentions. Turkey could only profit from Jewish colonization. She should follow the Argentine's example and encourage immigration to her Asiatic provinces where the density of the population was very low. Thus in southern Palestine and east of the River Jordan there were no more than four people per one square kilometre. Jews would bring capital, culture, and technology to the country, from which the Arab population would benefit also. Lichtheim prefaced his memorandum with an outline of the origins of Zionism and endeavoured to show that it was a function of the Jewish historical association with Palestine and a genuine Jewish *Risorgimento*, not an instrument of foreign Powers.

Lichtheim did not leave the matter to chance and spoke also to Jambulat, the Chief of the Ottoman Police, whom he thought Talaat would consult. He gained the impression that his memorandum had somehow assuaged the Porte's suspicions, at least temporarily. Several weeks later he was advised by official circles as well as by the C.U.P. that after the war the Government would examine the question anew and would enter into negotiations with the Zionists.[43]

With the tragedy that befell the Armenians uppermost in their minds, the Zionist Executive had an additional reason to expect all the constituent bodies to adhere strictly to its policy. Shmarya Levin, who remained in New York throughout the war, was regularly apprised of the situation and took an early opportunity to state (*Das jüdische Volk*, 14 May 1915) that Jewish policy should be brought into line with the interests of Palestinian Jewry, whose future was tied to that of Turkey. He rejected the activities of individual Zionists in the United States which were not endorsed by the Zionist Executive.

Levin had primarily in mind Pinhas Rutenberg, a Russian Zionist of fiery temperament, who in 1915, soon after arriving in the States, embarked upon a noisy propaganda campaign in favour of the creation of a Jewish Legion, which would fight with the Allies on the Palestinian front and bring nearer the realization of the Jewish State. In Europe Vladimir Jabotinsky preached the same idea. Formerly a Turcophil and in 1909 a close collaborator of Jacobson, following Turkey's entry into the war Jabotinsky changed his mind and became convinced that the only hope of restoring Palestine lay in the dismemberment of the Ottoman Empire. Zionist leaders were aghast. As soon as they heard of Jabotinsky's project they denounced it as an unforgivable breach of neutrality. 'No Zionist should take

[43] C.Z.A. L 6/45, Lichtheim to Straus, 23 Apr. 1915; Z 3/52, same to E.A.C., 9 Mar., 27 Apr., 22 May 1915; Z 3/758, same to P.E.C., 30 Apr. 1915; Z 3/759, same to same, 25 Oct. 1915; Lichtheim, *She'ar Yashuv*, pp. 348–51; *Rückkehr*, pp. 305–7; *Türkei* 195, K 177541–65, 'Le Sionisme', memorandum by Lichtheim, (?) May 1915 (a copy).

part or support in any way such an enterprise', was the Council's decision. At the American end, Shmarya Levin launched a scathing attack on Rutenberg and accused him of irresponsibility.[44]

On 4 June 1915, when Straus called in Djelal Bey, the Turkish Consul-General in New York, he was able to gauge the extent of the damage done by the pronouncements made by Rutenberg and by other individuals, notably Richard Gottheil, a Professor at Columbia University and a prominent Zionist. Formerly pro-Turk, he switched his sympathies to the Entente. Djelal was exceptionally well informed and did not take the views of individuals to be the reflection of the Zionists as a whole; none the less it raised some serious questions in his mind about Zionist reliability. Straus hastened to warn the Provisional Executive Committee of the mounting Turkish distrust, which, if not mitigated, might assume ugly proportions. He insisted that the P.E.C. should dispel the erroneous impression created by British propaganda and by some 'irresponsible individuals . . . The Turkish Government must be persuaded that the Jews are their best and most trustworthy friends who are grateful for the tolerant Turkish attitude.' He composed a letter along these lines and prevailed upon prominent American Zionists and non-Zionists to sign it and send it to the Turkish Consulate-General. Jacobson, while complimenting Straus on his initiative, asserted: 'the work with Turkey . . . has always been the leitmotiv of our policy'. Lichtheim added: 'Our cause will not be fostered by demagogical noise and the fanciful plans of frivolous sham politicians.'[45]

That was why the idea of an American Jewish Congress was greeted with such mixed feelings by the Zionist leaders in Berlin and Constantinople. Its purpose was to elect a representative body of the American Jewish community and express its demands with regard to Jewish aspirations for Palestine and the according of internationally guaranteed minority rights to the Jewish people in Eastern Europe. However desirable such a move was, particularly as American Zionists were playing a leading role in it, the Executive

---

[44] C.Z.A. L 6/37, minutes of G.A.C. meeting, Copenhagen, 10–11 June 1915; Z 3/396, *Der Führer*, 22 June 1915, article by Levin. On Jabotinsky's activities see his *The Story of the Jewish Legion* (New York, 1945); Friedman, op. cit., pp. 43–7, 134–40, 260–1; Schechtman, *The Jabotinsky Story*, pp. 201–88.

[45] C.Z.A. L 6/45, Straus to Hantke, 3, 4 June 1915; same to P.E.C., 4 June 1915; same to Warburg, 2 July 1915; Hantke to Straus, 22 July 1915; Lichtheim to Straus, 6 July 1915. On Gottheil see Friedman, op. cit., p. 40.

was concerned lest the Congress debate should do more harm than good; the fact that Rutenberg was involved in the preparations added to their misgivings. It could, as Jacobson warned, open Pandora's box.

Lichtheim also thought that the moment was ill chosen. As propaganda the Congress might prove a palpable asset, but not politically. Russian Jews feared that premature presentation of claims on their behalf would antagonize St. Petersburg unnecessarily, without contributing substantially to the improvement of their position. The same consideration applied with regard to Turkey. Should the Congress and the American Jewish Press air demands for Jewish autonomy, let alone a Jewish state in Palestine, the position of the Zionists towards Constantinople would become intolerable. Turkey would regard it as a hostile gesture and a gross interference in her internal affairs. 'I am by no means a soft-pedaller', Lichtheim wrote to the P.E.C., 'but I do not think that the moment for an open battle is propitious.' Not until the war was over would the formulation of policy be feasible.

> Should Germany emerge victorious and Turkey remain unscathed, our policy here and in Berlin will prove more valuable than a thousand meetings in America. If, on the other hand, the Triple Entente wins, it is still doubtful if public opinion will be of any help. Assuming that Palestine is conquered by the British, are we certain that they will prefer us to the Arabs? . . . Quiet diplomacy is a more prudent course to follow than public demonstrations.

In his subsequent letter to the P.E.C. Lichtheim paid tribute to Morgenthau.

> He has rendered us great services in moments of crises and is always at our disposal whenever needed. Without his help transfer of money to Palestine would have been impossible, or telegraphic messages to America and elsewhere . . . Although he is not a party Zionist, he shows respect, understanding and sympathy for Zionism. I hope he will give us valuable help during peace negotiations and will support us *vis-à-vis* the American Government.

None the less, Lichtheim warned that military-political developments pointed to Germany occupying the position of paramount influence in Turkey and that it was therefore vital to create a favourable climate of opinion in Germany also. Had it not been for Germany's effective interventions, the Zionists would not have been able to maintain their positions in Palestine. That Morgenthau's lone efforts to save the Armenians from catastrophe proved unsuccessful, was a case in point. Lichtheim summed up: for the duration of the war connections with the Embassies in Constantinople would be cultivated as hitherto; anything that might irritate the Turks should be avoided; 'disloyal activities (e.g. the criminal agitation by Jabotinsky) should be suppressed'; if and when Congress met in the United States, claims with regard to Palestine should be phrased as moderately as possible and limited to freedom of immigration and purchase of land, as well as cultural autonomy; 'once we have achieved this we have achieved everything'; an appeal to the Powers should also be avoided; Zionists all over the world should organize and appear at the right moment as a united force; those in the United States should co-ordinate their policy with the Executive in Berlin and, jointly with other American Jewish organizations, continue supporting the Yishuv financially.[46]

Lichtheim's advice was well heeded. In November 1915 Louis Brandeis, Chairman of the Preparatory Committee for the Congress, declared that it maintained 'a strict neutrality towards the nations . . . at war', and the preliminary conference which was held in Philadelphia on 26–7 March 1916, issued a statement that the Congress 'considered the question of securing for the Jews full and equal rights—civil, political and religious—in all such countries where these rights are denied them'. Significantly, the word 'national' was omitted, as was 'Jewish Homeland in Palestine' from another section of the resolution which read: 'The Congress considered the problems of the Jewish development in Palestine in all its phases.'[47]

The German Embassy appreciated Lichtheim's activities but not Consul-General Schmidt. He did not forget the *Sprachenkampf* and did whatever he could to undermine the Zionists' position. He showed his hand first when objecting to the formation of a Relief

---

[46] C.Z.A. L 6/45, Jacobson to Straus, 1 Sept. 1915; Lichtheim to same 14 July 1915; Z 3/53, Lichtheim to P.E.C., 19 July 1915; Z 3/759, same to same, 25 Oct. 1915. Morgenthau later changed his attitude to Zionism (see his *All in a Life-time*, pp. 293–5, 349–50, 385–404; Friedman, op. cit., p. 299). Lichtheim ascribed the change to lack of proper appreciation by the American Zionist leaders (*She'ar Yashuv*, p. 264; *Rückkehr*, p. 234).

[47] *Jewish Chronicle*, 26 Nov. 1915, 14 Apr. 1916; Preliminary Conference of the American Jewish Congress, Report of Proceedings (New York, 1916), pp. 20–2. The Congress met finally on 17 Dec. 1918 in Philadelphia.

Committee for Palestine Jews on the grounds that it was 'inadvisable' for Germans to sponsor a Zionist body at a time when the local Turkish authorities were so hostile. He shared the Turkish view that the Zionists nourished 'separatist aspirations' and justified their objection to the foundation of a Jewish militia, although, he admitted, the Jewish colonies, scattered among the Arab population, required a certain degree of protection. Anxious to avoid the impression that Germany was supporting the Zionists, he urged that Ruppin be repatriated. Whatever his arguments, Schmidt's reports were coloured largely by emotion: 'If anybody had seen, as I did, the streets leading to the Hilfsverein school covered by German exercise books, torn to shreds by students at the Zionists' instigation during the *Sprachenkampf*, he could hardly be convinced by Mr. Lichtheim's theoretical assurances of the Zionists' pro-German feelings.'[48]

Schmidt's reports made some impact, but his principal recommendation that Germany should dissociate herself from Zionism was ignored. 'I will help the Zionists', Wangenheim told Morgenthau, 'but I can do nothing whatever for the Armenians.'[49] Nor did Wangenheim accept Schmidt's advice on Ruppin; Zimmermann justly complimented Wangenheim on the way he had handled Ruppin's case.[50] Zimmermann remained as friendly as ever. On 5 June, when Jacobson called on him, he reassured the Zionist leader of his continuous interest and that 'all possible steps would be taken to ensure the protection of the Jewish population in Palestine'.[51]

More baffling to German diplomats was the new Hilfsverein–Zionist controversy. Although it was eventually resolved in the

[48] *Türkei* 195, K 177027–34, K 177246–7, Schmidt to Wangenheim, 28 Feb., 29 May 1915, dis. nos. 20/541, 4/1151; K 176822–6, K 177025–6, Wangenheim to A.A., 12 Feb., 6 Apr. 1915, tel. no. 364 and dis. no. 214, where Schmidt's dispatches are quoted.

[49] Morgenthau, *Secrets of the Bosphorus*, p. 244. Talaat rejected Wangenheim's protests with regard to the treatment of the Armenians on grounds that it was a strictly internal Ottoman affair. To Wangenheim's plea that the Entente was using it as propaganda and accusing Germany with responsibility for Turkey's conduct, Talaat responded that if Germany was ashamed of her association with Turkey she 'could go her own way'. (G. A. Schreiner, *The Craft Sinister* (New York, 1920), p. 123; cf. Morgenthau, op. cit., pp. 218, 238.) The myth that Germany was indifferent to the massacres of the Armenians and did not try to prevent them was exploded by Johannes Lepsius in his *Deutschland und Armenia, 1914–1918* (Potsdam, 1919), where a substantial volume of documents is reproduced. Rich material is found in the official files *Türkei*, Nr. 183, *Armenien*. For the Turkish view see 'Posthumous Memoirs of Talaat Pasha', *Current History* (Nov. 1921), p. 228; Djemal, *Memoirs*, ch. IX; Emin, op. cit., pp. 212–13.

[50] *Türkei* 195, K 176943, Zimmermann to Wangenheim, 24 Mar. 1915, tel. no. 563; above, p. 225.   [51] C.Z.A. Z 3/53 Jacobson to Lichtheim, 17 June 1915.

Zionists' favour, the German Government could not define its policy until the autumn of 1915. Before the war the Hilfsverein had enjoyed almost exclusive access to official circles in all matters regarding the Jews in the Orient but, with the German–Zionist *rapprochement* becoming a reality, it feared that its monopoly would be broken. In the circumstances the Hilfsverein seemed to welcome Djemal Pasha's regime since this provided a unique opportunity to deliver a death blow to its opponents. The guiding spirit was Ephraim Cohn-Reiss. 'Seriously defamed by the Zionists during the *Sprachenkampf*, he found it convenient to take revenge against his opponents by denouncing them early in the war to Beha-ed-Din and Djemal Pasha.' He endeavoured also to convince the German Consulate that the Zionists were 'the worst enemies of *Deutschtum*'. Similarly, he attempted to influence the officers of the German Military Mission. Halberstadter, his subordinate, was even less discreet. When meeting Brode he 'ventured to insinuate tactlessly that one should drive the Zionists out of the country by "pinpricks"'. Brode had reason to think that it was Cohn-Reiss who had 'clearly and systematically encouraged the suspicions of the Turkish authorities against Zionism'.[52] Cohn-Reiss's cousin, who acted as Beha-ed-Din's secretary, busied himself collecting material 'to prove the Zionists' disloyalty'.[53]

Brode dissociated himself from this campaign and considered Cohn-Reiss's activities as 'disagreeable intrigues',[54] but Schmidt listened readily to him and concurred with his arguments.[55] Ignorant of Hebrew, he believed all the information Cohn-Reiss gave him.[56] So did James Simon who maintained that politically the Zionists were unreliable: whilst those in Berlin were endeavouring to solicit the support of the German Government, their colleagues in London and Paris counted on the possibility of Palestine being taken over by the Entente. He also claimed that the Zionists had provoked the Turkish Government to undertake countermeasures which endangered the safety of other Jews. Beha-ed-Din's

---

[52] *Türkei* 195, memorandum by Brode, 26 Aug. 1915, on which see below, note 89; Ben-Hillel Hacohen, *Milchemet Ha-Amim*, i. p. 69.

[53] Shenkin, *Kitvei Menahem Shenkin*, i, p. 57; Elmaliyach, *Eretz-Israel V'Suria . . .*, ii, p. 105.   [54] As note 52.

[55] In his letter of 29 May 1915 to Wangenheim, Schmidt remarked that it was only 'a pure coincidence' that he dealt with the same subject as did Cohn-Reiss. The latter revealed in his memoirs that he was 'on friendly terms with Consul-General Schmidt' (*M'Zichronoth Ish Yerushalaim*, ii, p. 270) but made no mention about his activities reported by Brode.   [56] C.Z.A. Z 3/52, Lichtheim to P.E.C., 30 Apr. 1915.

proclamation of 25 January showed that resentment was directed 'exclusively' against the Zionists and that the Turkish Government 'by no means wished to suppress Ottoman Jewry as a whole'.[57]

The onslaught left its mark on Wangenheim. Struck by its vehemence, he noted that the rift between the two Jewish parties was deeper than he had imagined at first,[58] and Weber did not conceal from Lichtheim his misgivings about the loyalty of the Palestinian Zionists.[59] Zimmermann too complained that the international character of Zionism was 'disturbing', to which Jacobson replied that an international movement could prove more advantageous to Germany than a parochial organization.[60] Lichtheim soon launched a counteroffensive. Anti-German sentiments among Palestinian Zionists, he told Weber, were rare. If Germany did not attain greater popularity it was because her interventions on their behalf with the Porte were not sufficiently known, whereas the German brand of anti-Semitism was a matter of common knowledge. 'The Reich Government must realize that it cannot expect Jewish sympathy for nothing.'[61] Ruppin's reply to Schmidt was also effective.[62] Owing to illness Schmid's influence was waning, while Brode's was in the ascendant. Brode thought that from the German point of view the campaign against the Zionists was 'highly undesirable';[63] an opinion that finally prevailed. On 10 January 1916 Zimmermann told Simon that he regarded Cohn-Reiss's suggestion to use the Hilfsverein 'as a means to fight Zionism . . . as doubtful' ('würde es sich für bedenklich halten . . .')[64] Both parties were urged by the German diplomats to compose their differences and by the end of 1916 the truce was concluded. Dr. Nathan strongly condemned Cohn-Reiss's 'vain insinuations and intrigues which misled James Simon'.[65] The Auswärtiges Amt for its part was careful from then on not to offend the Hilfsverein but political issues regarding Palestine were discussed solely with the Zionists.

---

[57] *Türkei* 195, K 176321–35, Simon to Zimmermann, 14, 17 Mar. 1915.

[58] Ibid. K 176968–9, Wangenheim to A.A., 24 Mar. 1915, dis. no. 185.

[59] As note 56.   [60] *Türkei* 195, K 177177–80, Jacobson to Zimmermann, 30 July 1915.

[61] C.Z.A. Z 3/52, Lichtheim to E.A.C., 14 Apr. 1915; Lichtheim: *She'ar Yashuv*, pp. 357–8; *Rückkehr*, p. 309; *Türkei* 195, K 177107–15, Lichtheim to Embassy (undated), encl. in Wangenheim to A.A., 6 June 1915.

[62] *Türkei* 195, K 177260–76, Ruppin to Schmidt, 21 July 1915, encl. in E.A.C. to A.A., 2 Sept. 1915.   [63] As note 52.

[64] *Türkei* 195, K 177515–16, Zimmermann to Simon, 10 Jan. 1916.

[65] Lichtheim, *She'ar Yashuv*, pp. 363–4; *Rückkehr*, pp. 314–15. Curiously, Dr. Nathan was not fully aware of the correspondence between Cohn-Reiss and Simon.

Lichtheim wondered why the Auswärtiges Amt sided with the Zionists when the most influential Jews in Germany, headed by James Simon, were implacably opposed to them.[66] Yet the Wilhelmstrasse had some cogent reasons for doing so, since it was the Zionists, not the Hilfsverein, who had exercised a considerable influence among their co-religionists outside Germany. In this respect the Zionist Bureau in Copenhagen proved its worth. It was established early in 1915, with the Foreign Ministry's knowledge and consent, to enable the Zionist Executive in Berlin to keep the policies of the national organizations in neutral and Entente countries in line with the German and Turkish interests.[67] It had a considerable influence on the formulation of Jewish opinion, especially in the United States, and as Leo Winz, the adviser on Jewish affairs to the German Legation in Copenhagen, affirmed, it had been successful on countless occasions in altering the attitudes of the American Jewish Press in Germany's favour. In view of its authoritative position Count Brockdorff-Rantzau, the Envoy to Copenhagen, considered it essential that nothing should interfere with the smooth running of the Bureau and therefore that the military service of Dr. Martin Rosenblüth, its co-Secretary, should be deferred.[68]

That Brockdorff-Rantzau should have attached such importance to a Zionist bureau looks perhaps strange but it is worth noting that the Germans rarely excelled as propagandists; they lacked the ability to grasp the point of view of any foreign people, of the Americans in particular.[69] Following the *Lusitania* incident Bernstorff was forced to acknowledge the complete collapse of German propaganda.[70] At this juncture it was thought that Jewish opinion might well prove useful. It was in this vein that Siegfried Bier, a German-American and a member of the Central Purchasing Mission, advised the Foreign Ministry:

If Germany could now secure certain rights from Turkey for the Jews and induce her to grant a home in Palestine for displaced Russian Jews, it would create a most profound impression upon American public opinion, from the President down to the simplest citizen.[71]

[66] *She'ar Yashuv*, p. 361; *Rückkehr*, p. 313.

[67] *Türkei* 195, K 178276-7, Zimmermann to Romberg (Berne), 24 Feb. 1917, dis. no. 178 (secret).

[68] Ibid. K 177235-42, Brockdorff-Rantzau to A.A., 21 Aug. 1915, dis. no. 4767.

[69] Bernstorff, *My Three Years*, p. 15; Ottokar Czernin, *In the World War* (London, 1919), p. 79; Grattan, *Why We Fought*, p. 84.

[70] Bernstorff, op. cit., p. 25; Ernest R. May, *The World War and American Isolation: 1914-1917*, p. 121.   [71] *Türkei* 195, K 177045-6, Bier to Johannes, 21 Apr. 1915.

Bier was not a Jew and had no connections with the Zionists. But apart from the short-term interests there were also long-term considerations. After the outbreak of the war Germany was for the first time confronted with a Jewish problem outside her own boundaries. Military conquests brought her directly into contact with the Jewish masses in Eastern Europe. Within a few months about two million and by the end of 1915 over five million out of a total of six and a half million Russian Jews came under German domination. The Germans realized that Polish antagonism made the future of so large a Jewish community very insecure. In addition, as a result of deliberate maltreatment and cruel expulsions by the Tsarist regime, over one and a half million Jews were completely uprooted from their homes. A very serious refugee problem emerged and it was feared, both in official and unofficial circles, that many of the refugees would migrate westwards. To spare Germany this problem it was suggested that if the Central Powers were victorious, the German Government should prevail upon her Turkish ally to remove all restrictions on freedom of immigration to Palestine. No forcible transfer was contemplated, but here Zionism offered itself to meet the need.

This was the line argued by Heinrich Class,[72] the leader of the Pan-Germans, as well as by the Ostmarken-Verein.[73] Friedrich von Schwerin, a leading annexationist, President of the Frankfurt-on-Oder district, and an influential personality, also expressed the hope that after the war the Polish Jews would move voluntarily eastwards to the Russian interior or, inspired by Zionism, to Palestine.[74] The idea was not novel; nor was it confined to anti-Semitic groups such as the Pan-Germans and members of the Ostmarken-Verein. As early as 1912 Professor Werner Sombart, the noted economist, had pointed to the Jewish problem in Eastern Europe. In his speeches and writings he went as far as to advise that all German Jews should become Zionists. Emancipation had failed

---

[72] *Denkschrift von Heinrich Class betreffend die national-, wirtschafts- und sozialpolitischen Ziele des deutschen Volkes im gegenwärtigen Kriege* (undated, but presumably autumn 1914), pp. 48–50. Found in the *Beseler Nachlass* papers, Bundesarchiv, Koblenz (referred to also briefly in Werner Conze's article: 'Nationalstaat oder Mitteleuropa?', *Deutschland und Europa*, ed. W. Conze (Düsseldorf, 1951), p. 209. I am grateful to Professor Conze of Heidelberg University for sending me a copy of this memorandum (letter to the author, 13 Mar. 1963).

[73] *Wk.*, Nr. 20c, Bd. 4, memorandum by Tiedemann-Seeheim, 22 Apr. 1916.

[74] Immanuel Geiss, *Der polnische Grenzstreifen, 1914–1918. Ein Beitrag zur deutschen Kriegszielpolitik im Ersten Weltkrieg* (Lübeck, 1960), p. 84.

and it brought about a result opposite to what was desired—anti-Semitism. Sombart insisted:

For the sake of humanity Jews must exert all their will-power to preserve their national entity [*Volksorganismus*], to be *Judenvolk*. Is it not Israel that, from the Prophets on, contributed its Ethics, to Civilization ... and Christianity? The mission that Israel is called upon to fulfil today is to provide a new set of values and a new model of life.

Sombart welcomed Jewish national regeneration in Palestine and pointed to it as an example to follow.[75] He was seconded by Professor Hartmann who, in a series of articles in the *Frankfurter Zeitung* in 1913, sought to prove the importance of the Jewish colonization of Palestine for German interests.[76]

Early in the war the theme caught on in *Mitteleuropa*[77] circles. Friedrich Naumann, their liberal minded and thoughtful leader, maintained that Germany could and should embrace Zionism within the framework of her Oriental policy.[78] Naumann edited a weekly *Die Hilfe* in which one of his followers noted that colonization of Palestine, which at first seemed Utopian, had, thanks to the Zionist creative endeavour, become a reality, worthy of support by Germany and Turkey.[79] Dr. Paul Rohrbach, Director of the Foreign Information Service, a noted writer, and a *Mitteleuropa* man, also urged that Germany make a compact with Zionism. In an address to the Prussian Parliament on 3 March 1915 he contended that it was the Zionist movement alone that could divert migration of Jewish masses from Europe to Asia, because the attraction of a 'free national life' in Palestine was the only factor that could outweigh any material inducements elsewhere. A national Jewish entity by no means clashed with Germany's *Weltpolitik* because, parallel with the development of Hebrew civilization, the Jews would be able to propagate German *Kultur* and commerce in the Orient. Rohrbach thought that interests of national Jewry

---

[75] Dubnow, *Die neueste Geschichte*, iii, pp. 464–5; Lichtheim, *She'ar Yashuv*, p. 227; *Rückkehr*, p. 210. Sombart's lectures were published later in *Die Zukunft der Juden* (Leipzig, 1912). He is also known for his treatise *Die Juden und das Wirtschaftsleben* (Leipzig, 1911), translated and abbreviated in English *The Jews and Modern Capitalism* (London, 1913). [76] Alsberg, loc. cit., p. 166.
[77] On which see Meyer, *Mitteleuropa in German Thought and Action, 1815–1945*.
[78] Friedrich Naumann, *Mitteleuropa* (Berlin, 1915), p. 72. On Naumann see Meyer, op. cit., pp. 201–16.
[79] Berthold Bürger, 'Die Zukunft Palästinas und die Judenfrage', *Die Hilfe* (15 Apr. 1915), 237–8.

coincided with German rather than with British aspirations for, in contrast to Germany, the British were bent on the destruction of the Ottoman Empire and were fostering Arab ambitions in preference to those of the Zionists.[80]

Rohrbach's address was the first in a series of weekly lectures on this subject in the Prussian Parliament. Other guest speakers were Dr. Martin Buber, the celebrated Zionist philosopher, Dr. Ernst Jäckh, a leading Turcophil and the founder of the German–Turkish Union, and Dr. Alfons Paquet, a learned writer and traveller. Buber spoke about peculiarities of Jewish nationalism, Jäckh showed that the Jews were the best link between the West and the East, while Paquet examined the potentialities and importance of Zionism to Germany.[81]

The subject-matter was discussed frequently in *Das grössere Deutschland*, a journal co-edited by Rohrbach and Jäckh,[82] and engaged the interest of a wide spectrum of politicians and writers, like Count Kuno von Westarp,[83] a leader of the Conservative party, Ludwig Quessel, a Social-Democratic deputy to the Reichstag,[84] Adolf Grabowsky,[85] and Major Karl Endres. The last-named, a military-political analyst for the *Münchener Neueste Nachrichten* and the *Frankfurter Zeitung* and an expert on Turkish affairs, emphasized the need to win over the Jews. Those in Russia were pinning their hopes on a German victory, while those in the Orient, in Palestine in particular, linked their future with Turkey. Germany would find in them 'most reliable friends' and, in her own interests and those of Turkey, should foster the systematic development of Jewish life in Palestine.[86] Davis Trietsch, a Zionist writer, argued that in a certain sense the Jews were a Near Eastern element in Germany and a German element in Turkey which qualified them for German protection.[87]

[80] *Die Jüdische Presse. Konservative Wochenschrift* (Mar. 1915) (cutting in *Türkei* 195, K 176917); *Jüdische Rundschau* (12 Mar. 1915), p. 87.

[81] *Jüdische Rundschau* (26 Mar., 9 Apr. 1915), pp. 105, 117. On Jäckh see Meyer, op. cit., pp. 219–21; on Paquet see above, p. 162.

[82] See, e.g., 'Die politische Bedeutung des Zionismus' (anonymous), *Das grössere Deutschland* (Jan.–June 1915), 290–8.

[83] *Türkei* 195, K 177165–8, Oppenheimer to Zimmermann, 27 July 1915.

[84] Ludwig Quessel, 'Deutsche und jüdische Orientinteressen', *Sozialistische Monatshefte*, Nr. 8 (Jan.–May 1915), 398–402.

[85] Adolf Grabowsky, 'Die Grundlagen der deutschen Orientpolitik', *Das neue Deutschland* (1915), cited in *Jüdische Rundschau* (11 June 1915), p. 192.

[86] *Die Jüdische Presse*, 12 Mar. 1915 (cutting in *Türkei* 195, K 176915–16).

[87] Davis Trietsch, *Die Juden der Türkei* (Leipzig, 1915).

More important was an essay by Kurt Blumenfeld 'Der Zionis-mus: Eine Frage der deutschen Orientpolitik' which appeared in the prestigious *Preussische Jahrbücher* (August/September 1915). Blu-menfeld expounded at length the thesis that from the political, economic, and cultural points of view, Germany would be well advised to co-operate with the Zionists. Turkey, too, stood to benefit. Her distrust of Zionism was ill founded and reflected her general domestic policy which was unsound. Turkey could never become a uniform national state and the system of centralization which she imported from France was ill suited to the particular con-ditions of the Ottoman Empire and in the long run self-defeating. Unless Turkey reached a *modus vivendi* with the non-Turkish minorities, their discontent would increase and accelerate the pro-cess of disintegration. Moreover, to check the centrifugal forces within the state, the Porte should cultivate trustworthy elements among whom the Jews should be counted. Provided their wishes in Palestine were met, they could visualize no better alternative to Turkey. For despite the friendly interest proffered by the British Press, they were aware that Britain was in no position to foster their national aspirations. British policy hinged on Egypt and should Palestine come under British control it would merely become the border province of an Anglo-Arab colonial empire. Blumenfeld endeavoured thus to show that a community of inter-ests between Germany, Turkey, and Zionism did exist and claimed that since Germany was interested in strengthening her ally she should exert her influence to bring about a better climate of opinion in Constantinople towards a Turco-Zionist understanding.

The Foreign Ministry took note of all these publications and the Zionist Executive made sure that Blumenfeld's essay reached the Under-Secretary of State. Zimmermann, as could be deduced from his later comments, was impressed but Turkey was still the perennial obstacle. On 21 June 1915, when Rabbi Jacobus of Magdeburg suggested that in order to win over the Jews in neutral countries Germany and Turkey should commit themselves to create an autonomous province in Palestine after the war, Zimmer-mann replied:

The Imperial Government is eager to use its influence with the Turk-ish Government to remove obstacles in the way of Jewish immigration to Turkey but the suggestion of the gradual creation of a Jewish province with an autonomous administration would encounter great difficulties.

Wangenheim remarked that for Turkey to allow such a scheme was 'entirely out of the question. The Porte was quite determined to set a limit to future immigration to Palestine, [though] settlement of Jewish colonists in other areas, e.g. in Asia Minor, would not be prohibited.'[88]

With so many views competing for the Government's attention a thorough review of the Zionist question was necessary. The task was left to Consul Brode who on 26 August 1915 submitted a comprehensive memorandum.[89] He recalled that, as early as 1912, he had pointed out the beneficial effects that Jewish colonization had on Palestine both economically and culturally, but the political importance of Zionism for Germany became evident only after the outbreak of the war. He therefore deprecated the repressive measures which the local Turkish authorities had adopted and for which Germany was made responsible. Yet, in view of Turkey's determination to assert her sovereignty and prevent the development of national majorities in various parts of the Empire, he appreciated why the Turks could not take the Zionists' declaration of loyalty too seriously; the Zionists themselves provided them with 'some justification for suspecting them of aspirations towards autonomy'. This inherent separatism was, in Brode's opinion, ingrained in the Basle Programme. The Zionists were divided between the 'politicals' and the 'practicals', but both schools of thought aspired to the same end. 'At the moment when things are going badly for them, all of them swear that their aims are solely economic.' This was correct, but it was equally true, as all colonial history had proved, that economic penetration was always a first step towards the actual occupation of any country where there was a political vacuum. On the other hand, since creation of an independent Jewish state was impracticable within the foreseeable future, the Zionists' desire for the continuation of Turkish sovereignty should not be dismissed as 'hypocritical'. On the contrary, he presumed that for the sake of Jewish national development in Palestine Turkish suzerainty was even preferable to that of any European Power, because the more inferior culturally the protecting Power was, the less risk there was of Jews being overwhelmed or assimilated.

---

[88] *Türkei* 195, K 177123–7, Jacobus to Zimmermann, 21 June; K 177130–1, Zimmermann to Jacobus, 26 June; K 177152, Wangenheim to Zimmermann, 11 July 1915, dis. no. 440. Rabbi Jacobus had no connection with the Zionists.

[89] Ibid. K 177300–46, 'Memorandum über den Zionismus und Weltkrieg' (confidential); and 'Geheime Bemerkungen zu dem Memorandum', encl. to dis. no. 76/1278. What follows is based on this memorandum.

Brode paid tribute to the German Zionists for their patriotism and for having fulfilled their military obligations faithfully. The position of the Russian Zionists in Palestine, to whom the German Government afforded protection, was more complex. Their most fervent desire was to see Moscow's downfall, an antipathy which the German Consulate did its utmost to intensify. Yet their aversion towards Russia and their gratitude for Germany's help fell short of outweighing pro-British and pro-French proclivities. He therefore warned the Ministry not to overestimate Zionist assurances of pro-German sympathies, because 'although cases of conscious hypocrisy were rare, there was undoubtedly an element of opportunism among those who had suddenly discovered their "German hearts"'. He thought it wiser for Germany not to tie her hands for the duration of the war and to postpone any commitment to the Zionists until the Peace Conference.

However, in spite of the 'undoubted sympathy' of many Jews for England and France, and in spite of America's attraction, there were overwhelming reasons, in Brode's opinion, for Germany to support the Zionist aspirations. First, the economic potential for German merchandise implicit in large-scale colonization was 'tremendous'. Second, Zionist influence upon international Jewry was out of all proportion to the actual numerical strength of the Zionists and, by protecting them in Palestine, Germany had done herself a considerable service, because she had thereby gained the goodwill of the whole of Jewry, particularly in the United States. 'This is one of the most important lessons that is to be learned from the war.'

To maintain the momentum, Brode thought Germany should display a more conciliatory attitude towards her Jewish citizens, but here he was caught in a dilemma. If Germany were to create too liberal conditions for the Jews, she might defeat her own purpose by attracting immigration from Eastern Europe. It was here that Zionism became relevant. Although it was unlikely that the German Jews would move to the Land of their Fathers, 'Zionism would ensure that at least the millions of Jews for whom things were getting "too hot" in Russia would not, as hitherto, flood to the West, but immigrate to Palestine.' However, in his 'Geheime Bemerkungen' ('Secret Observations') which, he stressed, did not contradict his earlier statements, Brode found that Zionism deserved consideration, because it could make 'a substantial contribution to the solution of the Jewish problem in Germany'. He concurred with General von Herbert who had stated in the Reichstag that the Jews were 'a foreign body in the German national entity', an opinion which though 'tactlessly' expressed was none the less 'to the point'.

The very idea that a Jew as a senior officer, or administrative official, might represent the authority of the State is somewhat repellent to our national feeling . . . As an homogeneous national state, our tendency is to encourage assimilation of foreign minority groups [but] . . . since Jewish characteristics have shown themselves extraordinarily dominant in inter-marriage, the question arises whether our *Volkstum* is able to digest such an increase without impairing its innate *Wesen*. From this point of view, Zionism must be welcomed by us almost as a deliverance. From the standpoint of a conscious anti-Semite one should even wish that, if possible, every Jew should deliberate on the consequences of Zionism in order to preserve our people from the excessive penetration of Oriental blood.

Brode speculated about the future. Assuming that the Central Powers emerged victorious, he envisaged two possible courses: first, that Turkey, freed from the system of Capitulations, would be capable of establishing herself as a sovereign and independent Power, and second, that Turkey, 'unable to function as a civilized state . . . will be forced to submit, to a certain degree, to German control . . . even in her domestic matters'. In the first case, he thought, the anti-Zionist policy, of the kind that had been demon-strated by Beha-ed-Din and Djemal Pasha, would continue with added momentum but even so, taking into account 'the toughness and perseverance with which the Jews pursue their aim to recon-quer . . . their home' which, in his opinion, was 'a justified historical necessity', he was confident that they would manage gradually to break down the resistance they encountered. In the second even-tuality, 'we shall play an important role in relation to the future of Zionism'. On economic and on cultural grounds Germany would do well to encourage Zionist colonization. Beyond that, he advised, their political ambitions should be carefully watched 'to ensure that the stability of the Turkish state is not endangered by any separatist movement'.

From the observation of an anonymous official at the Foreign Ministry that the memorandum did not reveal 'any important new material',[90] it may be inferred that Brode merely re-echoed estab-lished thinking in the Wilhelmstrasse. The licence that he took to

[90] *Türkei* 195, K 177299, A.A. note and an abstract.

voice anti-Semitic arguments in an official document is astonishing. Yet, it would be incorrect to deduce that German policy towards Zionism was largely motivated by anti-Semitism, though sentiments like those expressed by Brode and the Pan-Germans had to be taken into account.

Brode's memorandum told strongly in the Zionists' favour but there is no evidence to show that Schmidt's attitude changed as a result of it. Lichtheim was fully aware of his hostility and since May had endeavoured to prevail upon the Reich Government to clarify its stand on Zionism in a specially issued instruction to the Consulate in Jerusalem. Such a document, he hoped, would not only neutralize Schmidt but by implication commit the Government and put the protection of the Yishuv on a permanent basis. But, notwithstanding the friendship of both the Embassy and the Foreign Ministry, Lichtheim had still to travel a long way before his wishes were met. It was Paul Weitz who suggested how he could cut through the red tape. Weitz was the Constantinople correspondent of the *Frankfurter Zeitung*, an intelligence agent, and an old hand in diplomacy. His influence at the German Embassy was profound. He was fully informed about Zionism, and at their first meeting on 21 May 1915 Weitz told Lichtheim that Wangenheim held him in high esteem and thought that it would be more efficacious if the Zionists urged the Ministry to consult the Embassy about the instruction to the Consulate, rather than concentrate their efforts on the Ministry. This Lichtheim did after further consultation with Weber. A few days later he asked his colleagues in Berlin to get in touch with the Foreign Ministry and felt confident that the Embassy, if consulted, would respond favourably.[91]

When Warburg and Hantke approached Zimmerman and Rosenberg they found them ready to help. Several days later the Ministry received Brode's memorandum and on 6 September Zimmermann empowered the Embassy to comply with the Zionists' request, provided it was kept secret, adding that the treatment of the issue might be postponed.[92] Thus, while making his position known,

[91] Lichtheim, *She'ar Yashuv*, pp. 375–9; *Rückkehr*, pp. 324–7; C.Z.A. Z 3/52, Lichtheim to E.A.C., 24, 30 July 1915. In *She'ar Yashuv* the date of the meeting with Weitz (21 Dec. 1915) is wrong. (Lichtheim, letter to the author, Jerusalem, 1 Apr. 1962.)

[92] *Türkei* 195, K 177283, Zimmermann to Hohenlohe, 6 Sept. 1915, dis. no. 1680. On 19 Sept. the E.A.C. informed Lichtheim that Zimmermann approved of its request and wrote to the Embassy. (Lichtheim, *She'ar Yashuv*, p. 380; *Rückkehr*, p. 327.)

Zimmermann left the timing and, as events showed, also the wording of the instructions entirely to the discretion of the Embassy. Two and a half months passed, however, before the document saw the light of day. The delay was largely due to change of personnel at the Embassy which, owing to inexperience, became easily distracted by another scheme for Jewish immigration to Turkey. Wangenheim, the most qualified diplomat, was convalescing in Germany throughout the summer and Prince Ernst zu Hohenlohe-Langenburg, the Director of the Colonial Department at the Foreign Ministry, replaced him. Kühlmann had earlier been appointed Ambassador to The Hague and his post as Counsellor was filled by Constantin Freiherr von Neurath, a Swabian *Junker* of aristocratic lineage. Later Dr. Otto Göppert, a senior official at the Ministry, also joined the Embassy. Thus of the 'old guard' who had been acquainted with Zionist problems only Weber remained.

Soon after his arrival in Constantinople, Hohenlohe noted how zealously Lichtheim was trying to persuade the Embassy to issue instructions to the Consulate in Jerusalem, but wondered on what grounds Lichtheim assumed that, if consulted by the Ministry, the Embassy's reply would be favourable. 'The Zionist wishes always receive careful attention at the Embassy but as hitherto we have avoided giving the impression of committing ourselves to a definite policy.' On 4 August, when receiving Lichtheim, he was forthcoming and courteous but, as his subsequent dispatch shows, remained reserved towards Lichtheim's request. Several days later, after consulting the dossier which contained Schmidt's and Cohn-Reiss's correspondence, he cooled still further.[93] In the circumstances Lichtheim could rely only on Weber, but during August Weber's enthusiasm, too, diminished; he was affected by the trial of Arab nationalists which was taking place in Beirut. As one of the documents seized referred to Arab–Zionist negotiations in 1913–14, mentioning specifically Sokolow and Jacobson, there was room to suspect that there might be a joint Arab–Zionist plot against Turkey. Although Djemal Pasha did not make any use of this material against the Zionists, the German Consulate found it appropriate to draw the Embassy's attention to it. However, Lichtheim

[93] *Türkei* 195, K 177218–19, K 177226, K 177243–7, Hohenlohe to Bethmann Hollweg, 1, 14, 21 Aug. 1915, dis. nos. 480, 509, 525; Lichtheim, *She'ar Yashuv*, pp. 379–80; *Rückkehr*, p. 327.

explained to Weber that the purpose of the Zionist leaders in negotiations was to dampen Arab opposition to Zionism in the Ottoman
Parliament. Moreover, Lichtheim pointed to a letter in which
Hakki Bey, its author, expressed despair of the Zionists on the
grounds that they were too loyal to Turkey; Arab and Zionist
ambitions diverged, Hakki concluded.[94]

The arrival of Dr. Alfred Nossig in Constantinople early in
August posed a much graver threat to Lichtheim. Nossig was an
Austrian national but lived in Berlin where he was associated with
the board of the *Berliner Lokalanzeiger*. In 1902 he founded the
Jewish Statistical and Demographic Institute in which Dr. Ruppin
and Dr. Jacob Thon also worked. An active member of the Zionist
Organization, following the Young Turk Revolution, in 1909
Nossig established the General Jewish Colonization Organization,
whose aim was to encourage immigration to the Ottoman Empire
with no specific reference to Palestine. The Zionists regarded him
as an adventurer and were much irritated by his independent
exchanges with the Turks. At their Ninth Congress Wolffsohn
reprimanded and disowned him.

Nossig remained a free-lance politician and early in 1915 renewed
his activity. He approached both the German and the Austro-
Hungarian Foreign Ministry as well as the Ottoman Embassy in
Berlin. Encouraged by their interest, he founded a Preparatory
Committee for the Regulation of the Jews in the East (Vorbereiten-
des Komitee zur Regelung der Lage der Juden im Osten). Early in
August he travelled to Constantinople, bringing with him several
trucks of medical supplies as a gift for the Red Crescent, but the
real purpose of his mission was to persuade the Porte of the worth
of his plans. Through the good offices of the Austro-Hungarian
Embassy he was granted an audience with the Sultan and the heir
to the throne, Jussuf Izzedin. Enver Pasha, the Minister for War,
Talaat Bey, the Minister of the Interior, and Halil Bey, the Foreign
Minister, also received him and spoke appreciatively of the Jewish
population. Elated by their assurances, Nossig approached leading
Ottoman Jews, including deputy Emmanuel Carasso and, with the
Porte's agreement, established the Ottoman-Israélite Union. Its

[94] C.Z.A. Z 3/54, Lichtheim to E.A.C., 19 Sept. 1915; Ruppin to same, 16 Sept. 1915;
Lichtheim, *She'ar Yashuv*, pp. 381–2; *Rückkehr*, p. 328. On Arab–Zionist negotiations
see Neville Mandel, 'Attempts at an Arab–Zionist Entente, 1913–1914', *Middle Eastern
Studies* (Apr. 1946).

purpose was to foster an organized immigration of Jews from Eastern Europe to Turkey.[95]

Zimmermann considered Nossig 'a good person, but politically . . . a dreamer who should not be taken too seriously',[96] but Hohenlohe did take him seriously, perhaps even too seriously. This was due to Nossig's initial success and the recognition that his was perhaps the only plan that might be acceptable to the Turks. Hohenlohe noted:

I assume that the Turkish Government will be prepared to permit Jewish immigration to Anatolia and Mesopotamia [but] it seems certain that it will not allow free immigration to Palestine, at any rate during the next few years. The Jews will have to be satisfied if the Turkish Government did not declare that Palestine has to be closed for Jewish immigration altogether. That such a declaration has not taken place is rather important, because the religious attraction of the Holy Land will play an important role in the immigration propaganda and because, so long as no definite 'no' has been uttered, there is hope that ultimately immigration to Palestine, at any rate a limited one, will be possible . . . Under present conditions it would be impossible to wipe out the idea within the Turkish Government that the aim of the Zionists is to achieve political autonomy. Because of their incautious agitation in the past which aroused Turkish suspicion, non-Zionist Jews had to suffer also . . . From the German point of view it would be desirable if a number of Jews who have to leave their old homes in Poland will immigrate to Turkey. This is particularly desirable since, following the expulsion and extermination of the Armenians, connection with European commerce has been broken over a wide area.

Hohenlohe therefore thought that, as soon as the Turkish Government accepted Jewish immigration in principle, the German Government should advise German Jews, in conjunction with their co-religionists all over the world, to found an organization to facilitate it with 'the decisive rejection of the Zionist ideals'.[97]

[95] Friedman, 'The Austro-Hungarian Government and Zionism', 155–6; also below, notes 97 and 98.

[96] *Türkei* 195, K 177169–70, Zimmermann to Wangenheim, 31 July 1915, dis. no. 576. Zimmermann, however, erred in assuming that Nossig was pursuing Zionist aims also.

[97] Ibid. K 177284–7, Hohenlohe to Bethmann Hollweg, 1 Sept. 1915, dis. no. 542; K 177215, same to A.A., 7 Aug. 1915, tel. no. 1731. Morgenthau recalled that Wangenheim told him that after the war Germany would send some Polish Jews to the Armenian provinces if they promised to 'drop their Zionist schemes' (*Secrets of the Bosphorus*, p. 246). Such a statement was likely to be made by Hohenlohe, rather than by Wangenheim.

Baron Neurath who, following Hohenlohe's return to Berlin, acted as Chargé d'Affaires, also supported Nossig's plan. However, in order to ensure its success he suggested that the Ottoman-Israélite Union should embrace all the Jewish groups: neutrals and the Zionists, liberals and the Orthodox of all nationalities. There was as yet no certainty that the Turks would permit a large-scale immigration even under the banner of the O.I.U. When bidding farewell to Hohenlohe, Halil Bey remarked that Turkey had 'enough Jews and did not want any more of them', a comment which, Neurath noted, contradicted the decision that had been taken by the C.U.P. and statements made by Talaat and Halil himself. Neurath assumed that these might be just casual words to which no importance should be attached, but it was also possible that the Government and perhaps even the C.U.P. were 'only making a pretence of goodwill towards the Jews but in fact are determined to prevent the immigration plans being carried out'.[98]

It is worth noting that, unlike Hohenlohe, Neurath did not reject the Zionists completely and thought that they should be included in the O.I.U. with other Jewish groups. Still it is surprising that he supported Nossig at all, for by then Neurath was no longer unfamiliar with Zionism. He was impressed by Blumenfeld's article in the *Preussische Jahrbücher* as well as by Lichtheim's own memoranda and on 14 July assured him that the sympathy of the German Government 'had already been determined and fixed'. Lichtheim replied that the Consulate in Jerusalem was totally unaware of this, to which Neurath responded that appropriate instructions would be issued. He still feared that an excessively zealous application of such instructions might strain German–Turkish relations and thereby harm the Zionist cause; 'the Turks are perennially suspicious of foreign intervention'. None the less, he asserted, 'subject to local conditions and the general political situation, the instructions to the Consulate will be issued'.[99]

However, contrary to his promise, Neurath did not write to Berlin on the matter and, as may be inferred from his dispatches, he continued to support Nossig. Lichtheim attributed this inconsistency to the conflicting pressures under which Neurath was labouring.

---

[98] *Türkei* 195, K 177366–8, K 177375–9, Neurath to Bethmann Hollweg, 6, 21 Oct. 1915, dis. nos. 8376, 627 (and encls.).
[99] C.Z.A. Z 3/53, Lichtheim to E.A.C., 14 July 1915; Lichtheim, *She'ar Yashuv* pp. 377, 385–6; *Rückkehr*, pp. 326, 332.

On the one hand there was a standing order from Zimmerman which it was impossible for him to ignore. On the other hand Neurath had to take into account the position adopted by Hohenlohe, his immediate superior. Opinion at the Embassy was also divided. While Weber staunchly supported Lichtheim, Göppert sided with Nossig.[100] As Göppert was senior in rank, Weber could not overrride him, and on 21 October Lichtheim ventured finally to bring his case directly before Göppert. The debate was long and arduous. Lichtheim argued that Nossig's project was not feasible; it had no support among the Jews and it was illusory to expect that those from Eastern Europe would be willing to settle in Anatolia and Armenia. But to no avail. Göppert stubbornly clung to his view that Nossig's plan had a better chance of implementation than that of the Zionists.

Lichtheim went away more encouraged from his conversation with Wangenheim which took place on the same day. Wangenheim had just returned from Berlin but seemed well versed in the latest developments. He differed substantially from Göppert's assessment of Nossig's plan, and towards the end of the conversation made a remarkable statement that 'at the future Peace Conference Germany would stand by the Zionists and support their case'. Wangenheim seemed to be mortally ill and Lichtheim refrained from pressing for further clarification. Four days later he was dead.[101]

Sensing that Neurath had not written to Berlin as he had promised, Lichtheim visited him again on 1 November. He found him most forthcoming. Neurath revealed that Göppert's memorandum on Nossig would be 'changed' and that he had asked Weber to draft the instructions to the Consulate. Weber later assured Lichtheim that correspondence with Berlin was superfluous since the matter had been left entirely to the discretion of the Embassy. Neurath had therefore come down finally on the Zionists' side. Göppert was disregarded and Weber assumed the sole responsibility for drafting the document for which Lichtheim had fought so tenaciously.[102] However, since approval of it was left to Count Paul Wolff-Metternich, the newly appointed Ambassador who had not yet arrived in Constantinople, it was not issued until 22 November 1915.

[100] Letter to the author, Jerusalem, 18 Mar. 1962.

[101] Lichtheim, *She'ar Yashuv*, pp. 384–5; *Rückkehr*, pp. 331–2.

[102] C.Z.A. Z 3/55, Lichtheim to E.A.C., 1 Nov. 1915; Lichtheim, *She'ar Yashuv*, p. 386; *Rückkehr*, p. 332; letter to the author, 18 Mar. 1962, in which a very illuminating description of the tug-of-war which took place at the Embassy is given.

The Instructions were in two parts. The first concerned the Jews in general and was circulated to all German consular authorities in Turkey; the second was secret and addressed to the Consulate in Palestine alone. The first part read:

It has become evident that recent events make it advisable for the German Government to clarify its position towards the Jewish organizations and their aspirations in Turkey for the guidance of the Consular authorities.

With regard to Jewish organizations which from a legal point of view may be regarded as German in origin, there is no need to emphasize that they are always entitled to the full protection of the German Government. With regard to those Jewish organizations which are concerned with the furtherance of the cultural and economic well-being of their co-religionists in Turkey, or with the immigration and settlement of Jews from foreign countries who have no legal title to German protection, it can be stated, as a general principle, that the German Government is favourably inclined towards their aspirations and is prepared to act on this favourable attitude, in so far as this does not conflict with legitimate Turkish state interests, or with the interests of German nationals and German institutions.

The consular representatives were empowered 'to lend a friendly ear' to the wishes and demands of Jewish organizations and 'in case of need, to help them, as far as possible, by all practical means'. Both the timing and method of intervention with the Turkish authorities were left to the discretion of the consulates but, at all events, it had to be of a 'friendly and non-official nature'.

The second part explained that 'the instructions regarding the treatment of Jewish organizations and aspirations in Turkey, and particularly in Palestine, have arisen from the repeated steps taken by the leaders of the Zionist movement at the Foreign Ministry and by their local representative [in Constantinople] over a considerable period'. It went on:

It seems politically advisable to show a friendly attitude towards Zionism and its aims. Efforts should be made to respect as far as possible, the sensitivity, if any, of the German Jews, particularly those connected with the Hilfsverein who, without justification, behave as if interest in the Zionist movement implies a direct prejudice to their own position.

The Consul was requested to exert his 'calming influence' upon the Hilfsverein representative whenever the need might arise.[103]

---

[103] *Türkei* 195, K 177404–7, Metternich to Bethmann Hollweg, 22 Nov. 1915, dis. no. 693 and encls. For the full text in German see App. B.

Zimmermann endorsed the text of the Instructions, ordering that only the first part should be disclosed to the Zionists; the second part was to remain secret.[104] The documents were specific and worded with care. The first indicated that the German Government was determined not to relinquish its treaty rights, which entitled it to protect its nationals in the Ottoman Empire. That it was prepared to protect also those institutions and individuals who had no legal title to German protection shows that Wangenheim's recommendation, made on 4 January 1913, to intercede on behalf of all the Jews in the Orient, irrespective of their nationality,[105] was finally endorsed as a principle of German policy. It was circumscribed by the proviso that 'legitimate Turkish state interests' had to be taken into consideration. How far German interpretation of Turkish interests was compatible with that held by the Porte is another matter. Since her unilateral abrogation of the Capitulations, Turkey had denied the right of any Power, that of her ally not the least, to interfere in her domestic affairs. Such a specific wording as 'to show a friendly attitude towards Zionism and its aims', would in all probability have been regarded by the Turks as a flagrant violation of their prerogatives. However, if the German diplomats preferred to ignore the inherent implications of this directive, it shows that either they became convinced at last of the plausibility of the Zionist argument that there existed no incompatibility between Zionist and Turkish interests, or realized that promotion of Zionism was so important to Germany that in the event of a victory by the Central Powers Turkey would be forced to submit to Germany's control even in domestic affairs.[106] Whatever the case, for the Zionists, and

---

[104] Ibid. K 177420, Zimmermann to Metternich, 8 Dec. 1915, dis. no. 939. When the author brought the second part to Lichtheim's attention he commented: ' . . . it has indeed come as a surprise to me, and a very pleasant one, that this instruction went even further than I was told at that time. . . . With regard to the second decree the Germans as a matter of precaution did not wish to tell us about it . . . because it might have created the most serious trouble with the Turks, had it come to their knowledge. This does not imply that the Germans wanted to keep us in the dark about the seriousness of their pro-Zionist intentions.' (Letter to the author, 7 Jan. 1962.) Lichtheim was given the text of the first decree by Weber. It is reproduced in *She'ar Yashuv*, pp. 386–7; *Rückkehr*, pp. 332–3, and quoted in Stein, *The Balfour Declaration*, p. 213. However, the final text of the document was not brought for Bethmann Hollweg's approval, as erroneously stated by Stein (ibid., p. 214). The Chancellor was merely informed of the Instructions at a later stage. (Lichtheim's letter to the author, 18 Mar. 1962.)

[105] Above, p. 164; see also pp. 187–8, 191.

[106] Cf. Brode's argument above, p. 258.

for Lichtheim in particular, the Instructions heralded a signal victory.[107]

The German Government would not have troubled to issue these Instructions unless moved by serious political considerations. First, it wished to strengthen the hands of the German Zionist leaders within the Zionist movement and reap maximum propaganda benefit. This is evident from Zimmermann's statements to Warburg and Jacobson during their meeting on 29 December 1915. He allowed them to communicate the news to leading Zionist personalities, particularly in the United States where an American Jewish Congress was to convene, provided it was done with great caution and the news was not published in the Press. But the deeper motives for issuing the Instructions could be inferred from Zimmermann's reply to the question whether German interest in Jewish immigration to the Near East was related to the problem of emigration from the occupied territories in Eastern Europe. Zimmermann told Warburg and Jacobson that if Germany and Austria-Hungary annexed the Polish provinces considerable dissatisfaction among the Poles might be expected, in which case the Jews might be needed as 'a counterweight'. In such an eventuality large-scale Jewish emigration would not be desirable but, should Poland become an autonomous, or an independent, country, the position would be different. Yet 'in either case', Zimmermann concluded, 'life for the Jews would probably be easier in Palestine than in Poland'. He agreed with his visitors' assertion that official circles had begun to realize the importance of Zionism and agreed that no project of Jewish immigration to Turkey would be successful unless Palestine was made the corner-stone of it.[108]

---

[107] The Zionist Report confirmed that the German Consulate received instructions 'to promote Zionist interests. These instructions were, on the whole, punctually obeyed by all officials, no matter whether as individuals they sympathized with Jewish aspirations or not.' (*Palestine during the War*, p. 32.) The Zionists were ignorant, however, of the second part of the Instructions.

[108] C.Z.A. Z 3/13, note on a meeting in the A.A., dated 28 Dec. 1915.

13

The Political Climate in Berlin and Constantinople

THE Instructions to the Consulate in Palestine were a remarkable achievement for the Zionists and indirectly a rebuke to Schmidt. On 10 December 1915, when his views were re-echoed by Dr. Curt Prüfer, the liaison officer with the Fourth Ottoman Army, Zimmermann unhesitatingly dismissed them as 'inopportune'.[1] Schmidt subsequently kept silent till his death on 27 March 1916, when Brode succeeded him as Consul-General. The Hilfsverein's withdrawal, coupled with Nossig's fiasco, left the Zionists in an unchallenged position.

Nossig's failure was predictable. On 12 December 1915, following his return from Constantinople, he organized the German branch of the O.I.U., renaming it Deutsch-Israelitisch Osmanische Union (D.I.O.U.), but the Porte, apparently suspecting that this was the thin end of a German wedge, refused to sanction it. In desperation Nossig deleted the word 'Israelitisch' from the company's name, hoping that this would mollify the Turks, but all that his exercise in self-effacement achieved was to antagonize Carasso, who resigned from the board in protest and gave the project its *coup de grâce*.[2]

The attitude of the Porte notwithstanding, it was most unrealistic to expect that the Jewish masses, in Eastern Europe in particular, would follow Nossig's lead. A few months later Armado Moses, the Constantinople representative of the Information Bureau for German–Turkish Economic Affairs, tried in vain to induce leading

---

[1] *Türkei* 195, K 177480–7, Prüfer to Metternich, 10 Dec. 1915; K 177581, Zimmermann to Metternich, 4 Feb. 1916, dis. no. 83.

[2] Ibid. K 177451–63, Nossig to Zimmermann, 15 Dec. 1915 and encl.; 177575, Lichtheim to Warburg, 26 Jan. 1916; Lichtheim: *She'ar Yashuv*, pp. 366–7; *Rückkehr*, p. 317; Lichtheim to the author, letter dated 18 Mar. 1962.

Ottoman Jews to encourage their co-religionists to settle in Eastern Anatolia and replace the Armenians. Their apathy towards Moses's plan contrasted strongly with their enthusiasm and devotion for the colonization of Palestine. There the Jewish immigrants proved successful farmers, and enterprising industrialists and businessmen, which persuaded Moses that only through Jewish colonization in Palestine could a sound basis for German expansion in the East be created.[3] Moses's conclusion sounded all the more convincing since, though a Jew, he was not a Zionist and had no connection with the Zionist agency in Constantinople.[4]

The Berlin Executive rightly felt that the wind was blowing its way. The document of 22 November 1915 substantially enhanced its status. It had therefore little difficulty in scoring an overwhelming vote of confidence from the Greater Council during its meeting in The Hague on 23–4 March 1916. When criticized by Fischer and Kann for its 'one-sided policy', Shlomo Kaplansky, Secretary of the World Union of Poale Zion, retorted that the Zionists in London, Paris, and Rome had not achieved 'one-tenth' of what those in Berlin and Constantinople had. Jacobson was modest enough to remark that this was unfair to Sokolow who had successfully been enlightening public opinion in England; his diplomatic activity had been circumscribed by the Council's decision of 6 December 1914 not to negotiate with a government that was at war with Turkey.[5] Yet whatever criticism was raised against the Executive, there was no escaping the conclusion that it was Germany, not England or France, that was holding the most important cards. It was Germany's might alone that could ensure the liberation of East European Jews from the Tsarist yoke and it was thanks to Germany's persistent intercessions (jointly with those of the United States) that the Yishuv had survived. In 1916 Turkey was still a viable empire and the prospect of Britain's occupying Palestine seemed remote.

Zimmermann did his best to ensure the smooth running of the Zionist machinery and so steer the movement into the German orbit. On 10 February he told the Chief Recruiting Officer: 'it lay in our political interest to support the Zionist Executive in Berlin, in so far as it successfully manages to keep the Zionist Press and

---

[3] *Türkei* 195, K 177814–16, memorandum by Armado Moses, 1 Aug. 1916 (original in *Türkei* 134, Bd. 36).

[4] Lichtheim could not recall ever meeting Moses (letter to the author, 30 Jan. 1962).

[5] C.Z.A. Z 3/453, minutes, G.A.C. meeting, 23–4 Mar. 1916; above, pp. 237–8.

organizations in all countries under its leadership'.[6] Hantke and Jacobson were given every facility whenever they travelled abroad, and German envoys in allied and neutral countries were requested to assist them.[7] Jacobson, from the latter part of 1916, had to make frequent trips to Denmark and divide his time between the directorship of the Copenhagen Bureau and the Executive's office in Berlin. The Bureau had been formerly headed by Leo Motzkin, a Russian Zionist, and Jacobson's succession was welcome news to the Wilhelmstrasse. Moreover, those Zionist leaders who were liable to be called up were exempted from military service. This was not merely a routine administrative matter. The army increasingly interfered in foreign affairs and applications for deferment had to be fully justified. Zimmermann did it with consummate skill; his arguments provide us with an insight into the motivations of his policy. On one occasion he told the General Headquarters:

> In view of the influence of international Jewry on public opinion and Press in neutral countries, especially in the United States, it would be in Germany's political interest to show during the war an accommodating attitude towards Zionism which is the most widespread and best-organized international organization. It seems, therefore, desirable that the leadership of the Zionist Organization should centre in Germany, giving thus a greater guarantee that Jewish circles outside Germany are influenced in a pro-German direction. The Zionist Information Offices in Berlin, Copenhagen, and New York have been set up to furnish the Jewish Press with news from German and pro-German sources, which hitherto had been dependent on information from our enemies.
>
> Moreover, in view of our alliance with Turkey and the future developments in Russia and Poland, we have an interest that the political leadership of Zionism remains in German hands.[8]

Martin Rosenblüth's deferment was warmly recommended by Count Brockdorff-Rantzau, the Envoy in Copenhagen,[9] while Lichtheim's was advised by the Secretary of State, who on 5 January 1917 wrote to the Ministry of War:

'*Türkei* 195, K 177584, Zimmermann to Recruiting Officer, 10 Feb. 1916; K 177727–8, A.A. to Ministry of the Interior, 26 May 1916.

[7] Ibid., e.g., K 177387, A.A. to Bucharest, 2 Nov. 1915; K 177401, A.A. to Berne and The Hague, 2 Dec. 1915.

[8] Ibid. K 177743–6, Zimmermann to G.H.Q., 27 June 1916.

[9] Ibid. K 177800, K 177818, Brockdorff-Rantzau to A.A., 9 Aug., 6 Nov. 1916; K 177820–8, memorandum by Leo Winz, 31 Aug. 1916. For Rosenblüth's account of his activity in the Copenhagen Bureau see his memoirs *Go Forth and Serve* (New York. 1961), pp. 174–89.

Lichtheim is active in Constantinople on behalf of international Zionism, under difficult conditions which require tact . . . On a number of occasions he has successfully calmed American public opinion when it has been aroused against ourselves and our Allies by the events in Turkey. His removal from Constantinople would be detrimental to our cause.[10]

Interventions on the Yishuv's behalf were still necessary because the Turkish authorities in Palestine had reverted to their old practice of extortion and harassment. Hassan Bey for some time attempted to lay his hands on relief funds destined for the Jewish community. Early in November 1915, when a sum of £20,000 was brought to Palestine abroad the American warship S.S. *Des Moines*, he ordered that the money be placed under his control. The American Consul objected strongly because the Jewish Relief Committee had already generously offered (as in the past) to assign 45 per cent of the total for distribution among the Muslim and Christian population of Palestine, even though the donors were American Jews. It was not until Morgenthau personally intervened, at Lichtheim's instigation, that the crisis was resolved. Hassan satisfied himself with a token gift for 'development projects',[11] but the Jewish Relief Committee had to pay the price. Several months later it was dissolved and David Yellin, its Chairman, was deported to Damascus.[12]

In mid-September Djemal Pasha renewed his pressure on Ruppin to adopt Ottoman nationality or resign from his post, since 'such an important position could not be held by a foreigner'. Failure to comply would entail stern measures against the Zionist colonies, schools, and a number of institutions. Ruppin thereupon announced his decision to resign in favour of Dr. Jacob Thon, his deputy, who was willing to surrender his Austrian nationality and become an Ottoman subject. Djemal accepted the proposition, provided that the Palestine Office refrained from political activity. He agreed to let Ruppin stay in Jerusalem and engage in research on the economic conditions of Syria. He even gave Ruppin a letter of introduction to the Ottoman archives, but insisted that he should abandon his Zionist aspirations. Ruppin replied that he could not renounce his conviction that Zionism would benefit Turkey, to

---

[10] *Türkei* 195, K 178159, Jagow to Minister of War, 5 Jan. 1917.

[11] Ibid. K 177534–9, Lichtheim to Embassy, 22 Dec. 1915; Lichtheim: *She'ar Yashuv*, p. 393; *Rückkehr*, p. 336; Manuel, *The Realities of American-Palestine Relations*, pp. 145–6.

[12] *Palestine during the War*, pp. 25–6.

which Djemal commented wryly that 'perhaps in fifty years' the Government would agree with him.[13]

During the winter of 1915–16 Djemal stepped up his drive against Zionism. Early in December a number of arrests were made and individuals who decided to leave the country had to sign a humiliating declaration promising 'never to return'. Among those taken into custody were the editors and printers of the Hebrew papers *Ha-Achdut* and *Hapoel Hatzair*, Dr. Beham, Director of an American Health Institute, and a number of teachers. The alleged offences were trivial. Thus when Dr. Beham published an article in a scientific journal to enlighten the public on how to check the spread of epidemics which had been sweeping Turkish Asiatic provinces at that time, he was accused of improperly disclosing their existence and sentenced to prison for one year.[14] But it was the participation of the Zion Mule Corps (which had been recruited from amongst Palestine refugees in Egypt) in the Gallipoli campaign that aroused Djemal's wrath.[15] On 20 December Ruppin, Thon, and three other officials of the Palestine Office were summoned before a Turkish Court Martial in Jerusalem and accused of 'high treason' on grounds that the J.N.F. stamps in their possession were proof of separatist aspirations, inimical to the interests of the state. Ruppin did not lose his sense of humour and surprised the judges by disclosing that the Star of David, which they also suspected of being 'a secret sign', could be found on the wall of the Old City of Jerusalem near the Damascus Gate. When the prosecution failed to provide convincing evidence, the case was transferred to the Criminal Court of Justice, where the defendants were accused of forging Ottoman stamps, an indictment that compounded the absurdity of the proceedings since stamps bearing the images of Herzl or Nordau were circulated exclusively by the J.N.F.[16]

The comedy of the whole episode notwithstanding, the week-long legal procedure was menacing enough for the Zionists to feel the

[13] C.Z.A. Z 3/54, Ruppin to Lichtheim, 26 Sept. 1915; Z 3/759 Lichtheim to P.E.C., 25 Oct. 1915. Lichtheim doubted whether Ruppin had taken the right decision.

[14] As note 11.

[15] *Yoman Aaron Aaronsohn* [*Diary of . . .*] (Tel Aviv, 1970), 9 Jan. 1916, p. 20, and 20 Dec. 1915 (unpublished). On the Mule Corps see Lt.-Col. Henry J. Patterson, *With the Zionists in Gallipoli* (London, 1916); Jabotinsky, *The Story of the Jewish Legion*, pp. 30–43; Schechtman, *The Jabotinsky Story*, i, pp. 201–7.

[16] Lichtheim, *She'ar Yashuv*, pp. 396–7; *Rückkehr*, pp. 339–40; Ruppin, *Memoirs*, p. 157; *Palestine during the War*, pp. 24–6, where a translated official Turkish report is reproduced in full.

need for German intervention. Warburg in Berlin and Lichtheim in Constantinople found full understanding for their pleas. Count Metternich, though intensely preoccupied with the Armenian question, was always at Lichtheim's disposal and ready to assist. So was Baron Neurath; he was 'favourable and helpful . . . and never showed any sign of impatience or unfriendliness'.[17] His move was most effective. Rather than activate the Consulate, he ordered Colonel Kress von Kressenstein, Djemal's Chief of Staff, to ask the Turkish Commander to stop the trial. Djemal objected to German interference but renewed representations by Kressenstein, at Neurath's insistence, compelled him to comply. Soon after, Metternich was able to report that a favourable turn had taken place in the 'Stamp Trial' (*Markenprozess*) and that Djemal Pasha's mistrust of Ruppin 'had been overcome'. Instead of being deported Ruppin had been amiably received.[18] But in fact the German intervention made Djemal 'very angry . . . he banged on the table . . . though rapidly gave in',[19] only to postpone his attack to a more opportune moment.

So insecure did the Zionists feel that after the Stamp Trial had been suspended they thought it advisable to reaffirm their loyalty to Turkey.[20] The German officials never questioned it and Metternich himself tried on various occasions to reassure the Porte that there was 'no reason to be suspicious of the Zionist aspirations'; he thought that any additional statements to that effect were 'neither necessary nor useful'.[21] Metternich had his own difficulties with the Turks. Described as 'un grand seigneur, sans peur et sans reproche',[22] in Constantinople he was not at home. Unlike his predecessors he failed to win the confidence of his hosts, and his vigorous defence of the Armenians exacerbated his relations with the Turks still further.[23] In these circumstances over-zealous re-assurances about the Zionists would have been counterproductive.

Nor was there any pressing need to assuage the Porte's misgivings.

---

[17] Lichtheim to the author, 18 Mar. 1962; Lichtheim, *She'ar Yashuv*, pp. 376–7; *Rückkehr*, pp. 324–5.

[18] *Türkei* 195, K 177586, Metternich to Bethmann Hollweg, 7 Feb. 1916, dis. no. 51.

[19] C.Z.A. Z 3/58, Lichtheim to E.A.C., 10 Mar. 1916.

[20] *Türkei* 195, K 177595–609, E.A.C. to A.A., 5, 8 Mar. 1916 and encls.

[21] Ibid. K 177663, Metternich to Bethmann Hollweg, 27 Mar. 1916, dis. no. 133.

[22] Bernstorff, *Memoirs*, p. 50.

[23] Lichtheim, *She'ar Yashuv*, p. 397; *Rückkehr*, p. 340; letter to the author, 18 Mar. 1962; G. P. Gooch, *Recent Revelations of European Diplomacy* (London, 1930), p. xxx.

It seems that Lichtheim's memorandum of May 1915[24] had to a certain degree dispelled them already and, although later in the year Lichtheim himself had almost despaired of Turkey's ever countenancing the growth of Zionism on a larger scale,[25] in March 1916 he was able to detect a more favourable climate. A number of factors contributed to this change. The military setback on the Caucasian front dampened the inflated nationalistic spirit and gave rise to a more sober assessment. An opinion was gaining ground among some leading Young Turks that collaboration with Jewish financial circles might help Turkey to become more economically viable in the aftermath of the war and thereby also less dependent on her allies. Other Turkish politicians sensed that Palestine, inhabited predominantly by Arabs, might eventually be lost to Turkey unless it became populated by an element which was bound to lean on Constantinople. These calculations, however, applied to the more distant future. 'At the moment', Lichtheim noted, 'the Government attaches little importance to our question, as it has to deal with more urgent matters.' The Turks were also handicapped by their notorious inability to take decisions.

Unfortunately . . . the Government cannot bring itself to make any decision, even when Turkish interests are involved. The Turks . . . have no confidence in their own judgment and, when confronted by some far-reaching plans for the future, they have hundreds of scruples. Accustomed for decades to care only for the next moment, they shy away from any commitment; conscious of their weakness, they prefer to do nothing rather than risk opposition and difficulties such as any purposeful political action is bound to arouse.

He went on:

I have never found here any deep-rooted aversion from Zionism and, in spite of all scepticism, which one is bound to develop, I cannot give up hope that we can come to terms with the Turks when more propitious circumstances exist.

At any rate, Lichtheim was relieved to learn that the Porte was not responsible for the Stamp Trial. That at Jewish instigation it removed Hassan Bey from office and replaced him by a more sympathetic commandant was a good omen. Djemal Pasha, too, became

24 Above, pp. 243–4.
25 C.Z.A. Z 3/759, Lichtheim to P.E.C., 25 Oct. 1915.

friendlier and continued to employ Jewish engineers and agrono-
mists in his administration.[26] He found them so skilful and trustworthy that he felt justified in rejecting an offer from Berlin to
provide his army with German technicians and doctors.[27] On one
occasion he boasted in front of Enver that the achievements of the
armaments factory in Damascus were due to 'our man [Abraham
Krinitzi] not the result of German initiative'.[28]

Lichtheim was still in the process of assessing the new trends
in Constantinople, when Morgenthau's speech, made in Cincinnati
on 21 May 1916, came as a bombshell. According to the correspondent of *The Times* in London Morgenthau announced that he had
recently suggested to the Turkish Government that Turkey should
sell Palestine to the Zionists. He said that the proposal was well
received and the ensuing negotiations centred on the creation of a
Jewish republic. The encouragement of tourism, construction of
a major port at Jaffa, and other projects were also discussed. Moreover, the Turks were seriously considering the appointment of the
Chief Rabbi Nahoum as Ambassador to Washington.[29]

The speech was widely publicized in the belligerent and neutral
countries. The *Gazette de Lausanne* (17 July 1916) saw in it an
indication that the United States was bent on assuming a protectorate over an independent Jewish state in Palestine, whereas
Politiken (25, 26 July), the prestigious Copenhagen daily, although
sympathetic to the idea of Jewish statehood, suggested that Turkey
had succumbed to German pressure. On the other hand, the
Frankfurter Zeitung (25 July), as well as other German papers (e.g.
the *Berliner Allgemeine Zeitung* and the *Deutscher Kurier*, 27 July)
dismissed *The Times*'s report as 'tendentious bluff' and a deliberate
stratagem on the part of the Entente to drive a wedge between
Turkey and Ottoman Jewry.[30] The matter was discussed for weeks
by the Press and aroused considerable resentment in the Ottoman
capital. Talaat sought an immediate explanation from Nahoum, and
Halil Bey, the Foreign Minister, made no secret of his displeasure.

---

[26] Ibid. Z 3/58, Lichtheim to E.A.C., 10, 19 Mar. 1916; Z 3/60, same to P.E.C., 10
July 1916.   [27] Dizengoff, *Im Tel Aviv Bagola*, p. 91.
[28] Abraham Krinitzi, *B'Koah Hamaase* [*By Virtue of the Deed*] (Tel Aviv, 1940),
p. 42. In 1916–18 Krinitzi served as a technical director of a munitions factory at
Damascus. In 1922 he was one of the co-founders of Ramat Gan, near Tel Aviv,
and later became its first mayor, serving until his death in 1969.
[29] *The Times*, 22 May 1916; *Jewish Chronicle*, 26 May 1916.
[30] Cuttings in *Türkei* 195, K 177764–77; C.Z.A. L 6/12/VI, L 6/85.

He instructed the Ottoman diplomatic missions in the neutral countries to declare, without mentioning Morgenthau by name, that the news of the alleged sale of Palestine was 'ridiculous and senseless'.[31]

It is difficult to fathom the motives which prompted Morgenthau to make such an ill-advised statement, which was undoubtedly authentic. Early in the year he had been recalled to Washington by President Wilson to assist in the election campaign, but Palestine hardly played any role in it. Nor was it inspired by the Zionists as some papers suggested. One must seek the explanation rather in Morgenthau's own mental make-up. For all his merits, he was known to be sometimes careless in his utterances and was quite capable of making a statement which he would withdraw shortly afterwards; empirical in approach, he was somewhat superficial.[32] His negotiations with the Porte in 1913 for the purchase of tracts of land in the Adana district in northern Syria for the Jewish Colonization Association[33] might have contributed to the confusion in his mind. Whatever the reason, the Zionist leaders were greatly embarrassed. They hastened to remind the Auswärtiges Amt of Morgenthau's former association with Wangenheim and that, aware of the nature of the Zionist aspirations, he 'has not and could not have made the statement', which had been attributed to him.[34] Yet, not to leave the matter to chance, the Copenhagen Bureau cabled Brandeis, the P.E.C. in New York, and Morgenthau directly asking them to issue a categorical denial since the Press campaign was causing considerable harm to the Zionist Organization.[35]

Morgenthau replied that the State Department had already instructed the American Envoy in Copenhagen to deny the rumours that had been circulating of late,[36] and two weeks later Abram Elkus, Morgenthau's successor in Constantinople, declared that the story about the alleged sale of Palestine to the Zionists and creation of a Jewish republic was 'ridiculous and unworthy of serious consideration'.[37] Morgenthau wrote also to Nahoum and asked him to

[31] Lichtheim, *She'ar Yashuv*, pp. 401–2; *Rückkehr*, pp. 344–5.

[32] Lichtheim to the author, letter dated 7 Jan. 1962; cf. Friedman, *The Question of Palestine*, pp. 216–17.

[33] *Türkei* 195, K 176395, Wangenheim to Bethmann Hollweg, 10 Mar. 1913, dis. no. 1050.   [34] Ibid. K 177770–5, E.A.C. to A.A., 27 July 1916.

[35] C.Z.A. L 6/12/VI, L 6/85, cables dated 26 July, 8 Aug. 1916.

[36] Ibid. L 6/85, Morgenthau to Jacobson, 21 Aug. 1916.

[37] *Vossische Zeitung*, 5 Sept. 1916, evening edn. A *démenti* appeared also in *Politiken* (20 Aug.), *Journal de Genève* (23 Aug.), and in other papers.

reassure both Talaat and Enver. Urged on by Lichtheim, Nahoum fulfilled his mission admirably.[38]

That the Zionists felt so uneasy during the affair is not surprising. It coincided with rumours that the Allied Powers had adopted the partition of the Ottoman Empire as part of their war aims and Morgenthau's story inevitably invited the suspicion that the creation of the 'Jewish republic' might have been linked with the Entente's designs. The publicity given by the British Press to Jabotinsky's project tended to make the assumption more credible. Annoyed, Lichtheim wrote to his colleagues in Berlin:

> We must show . . . that we have nothing to do with Jabotinsky. Since we cannot form a pro-Turkish Mule Corps and, since we have not got a mule with a big mouth like him, we must come out against him, at least in the Press, and publish the resolution [of 11 June 1915 adopted by the Council] . . . but it would be better if Jabotinsky was disavowed by the English Zionists.[39]

Lichtheim did not wait for his colleagues to act and on 17 August submitted identical memoranda to Talaat and Halil explaining, among other things, the official Zionist attitude to Jabotinsky's propaganda. His exposition made a 'favourable impression'.[40] However, unlike Talaat and Halil, who were open to reason, Djemal's conduct was governed by emotion. The reports about Morgenthau's speech and Jabotinsky's plan to form a Jewish Legion for active service on the Palestinian front infuriated him. In a moment of pique he told Chaim Kalvarisky, Director of Galilean Settlements of the Jewish Colonization Association (I.C.A.): 'I could have hanged some Jews a long time ago, but I am tired of hanging.' On another occasion he told Dr. Itzhak Levy, Director of the Anglo-Palestine Bank in Jerusalem: 'Your Zionist friends have written a lot of nonsense in the foreign Press.' Levy was later deported. On 11 September Djemal summarily summoned Ruppin and requested that he leave Palestine within eight days, exclaiming that he had had 'enough of Zionism and wanted to get rid of it'. He warned

---

[38] C.Z.A. Z 3/60, Lichtheim to E.A.C., 24 Aug. 1916.

[39] C.Z.A. Z 3/60, Lichtheim to E.A.C., 7 Aug. 1916. For the G.A.C.'s resolution see above, pp. 244–5, and on the Jewish Legion controversy in Britain see Stein, *The Balfour Declaration*, pp. 484–96. Jabotinsky's letter to *The Times* appeared in its issue of 15 July 1916.

[40] *Türkei* 195, K 177837, Metternich to Bethmann Hollweg, 10 Sept. 1916, dis. no. 542; Lichtheim, *She'ar Yashuv*, p. 407; *Rückkehr*, p. 347.

Ruppin not to fight his decision; any foreign intervention would make matters worse. Ruppin realized that opposition on his part might invite serious retaliation against the Jewish settlement, for he had overheard Ottoman officials discussing plans for a wholesale evacuation of Jewish colonies on the coastal plains, and closure of schools and key institutions. He was also aware of Djemal's habitual disregard for the Government in Constantinople, let alone of the German Consulate. The latter confirmed that its relations with the Ottoman Commander had been worsening: 'Djemal was a hidden adversary of German influence.' In the circumstances Ruppin decided to go.[41] On 11 October, when he arrived in Constantinople, Lichtheim thought that he had been overcompliant; otherwise he found Ruppin's company congenial and useful.[42]

In Berlin Warburg complained that Ruppin's expulsion did not reflect favourably on the efficacy of Germany's protection. Thereupon Zimmermann asked the Embassy to examine the matter with Lichtheim, though he very much doubted if it would be in the Zionists' own interest to foist Ruppin's return on Djemal. He emphasized: 'Preservation of the *existing* [Jewish] settlements is undoubtedly in Turkish and German interests.' To which two weeks later he added: 'The Jewish settlement appears to be in no danger at present. If the situation changes . . . the Porte should be warned in a friendly way not to undertake measures, which would cost them the sympathies of international Jewry.'[43] Such an advance warning seemed to be necessary because Djemal was still in an ugly mood. With Ruppin's departure a number of other Jewish notables were deported, including Albert Antebi, formerly his trusted adviser.[44] Djemal also refused to grant permission to an American Zionist Medical unit to visit Palestine and only reluctantly consented to the import of medical supplies and the export of wine products, although the country was in a critical economic situation and threatened by epidemics.[45] Later he caused a diplomatic incident

[41] *Türkei* 195, K 177940–5, Ruppin to E.A.C., 10 Oct. 1916, encl. in E.A.C. to A.A., 20 Oct. 1916; K 177848, Lichtheim to Warburg, 21 Oct. 1916; Smilansky; *Zichronot*, iii, pp. 221–5; Ben-Hillel Hacohen, *Milchemet Ha-Amim*, ii, pp. 143–5.

[42] Lichtheim, *She'ar Yashuv*, pp. 407–8; *Rückkehr*, pp. 346–7.

[43] *Türkei* 195, K 177858–66, E.A.C. to A.A., 4 Oct., K 177949 Warburg to Lichtheim, 22 Oct.; K 177882–4, K 177963, Zimmermann to Radowitz (chargé d'affaires), 11, 26 Oct. 1916, dis. nos. 1146, 1155; also K 177971–3, Jacobson to Lichtheim, 26 Oct. 1916, reporting on a conversation with Rosenberg.

[44] Smilansky, op. cit. iii, p. 225; Ben-Hillel Hacohen, op. cit. ii, pp. 149–53.

[45] *Türkei* 195, K 177958, Zimmermann to Radowitz, 20 Oct. 1916, tel. no. 1204;

by trying to prevent some American Jews, resident in Palestine, from returning to the United States; the French Government had given the warship special permission to pass the blockade in order to collect them. Washington lodged a strong protest with Constantinople against such 'an extreme and unwarranted violation of American rights', and asked the German Government to use its influence with its ally to permit *Des Moines* to fulfil its task. The Germans had their own reasons for feeling embarrassed, since the incident coincided with Chancellor Bethmann Hollweg's peace initiative through American mediation. Renewed pressure on the Porte by Zimmermann 'to avoid unnecessary annoyance in the United States', made Djemal finally comply,[46] although it raised his temper to an even higher pitch. Late in December 1916 he declared that 'Zionism must be suppressed by all means'. He admitted that the Zionists were 'industrious and practical people but because of their ideology, Palestine might become a second Armenia'.[47]

Unaware of the full extent of the 22 November 1915 Instructions to the Palestine Consulate, the Zionist leaders continued throughout 1916 to press the German diplomats for a firmer commitment. Late in February Lichtheim broached the subject with Neurath.

He assured me once again [Lichtheim wrote to E.A.C.] that the Government is willing to support our plans. There is only one obstacle which prevents it from pursuing the matter according to our wishes, it is: their relationship with Turkey.

However, since the Porte appeared friendlier than expected, five weeks later Lichtheim ventured to approach Neurath again, suggesting that he urge the Turks to abolish restrictions against Jewish immigration and acquisition of land. But Neurath considered the moment inopportune. He revealed, nevertheless, that Germany would be willing to help the Zionists after the war. Should she

K 178126, Lichtheim to Warburg, 12 Dec. 1916; Lichtheim, *She'ar Yashuv*, p. 411; *Rückkehr*, p. 350. On the situation in Palestine in 1916 see Manuel, op. cit., pp. 146–9.

[46] *Türkei* 195; K 178127, Bernstorff to A.A., 13 Dec. K 178128–31, Montgelas to Rosenberg, 18 Dec.; K 178132–3, Zimmermann to Radowitz, 20 Dec. 1916; K 178139, Göppert to A.A., 21 Dec. 1916. On Bethmann Hollwegg's peace initiative see May, *The World War and American Isolation*, p. 387; Esther C. Brunauer, 'The Peace Proposals of December 1916–January 1917', *Journal of Modern History*, iv (Dec. 1932), no. 4, 544–71.

[47] C.Z.A. Z 3/62, Lichtheim to E.A.C., 2 Jan. 1917.

emerge as a dominant Power in the East and desire to promote Jewish immigration, current Ottoman restrictions would vanish.[48]

Berlin was more reserved. On 24 October Zimmermann told Jacobson that the main object of German policy was 'to preserve the Jewish settlement in Palestine unscarred until after the war. All the rest is *cura posterior*.' And two days later Rosenberg enlarged:

> The Reich Government will try, as hitherto, to extend its protection in individual cases, but it is neither able nor willing to identify itself with the [Zionist] affairs. The Zionists should not expect the Foreign Ministry to support them *officially* with the Turkish Government. It can only draw the latter's attention in a friendly way to the fact that the disturbance of the Jewish settlement in Palestine would be inadvisable and would create unnecessary . . . ill-will amongst international Jewry towards Turkey.

Rosenberg intimated that Germany herself was experiencing difficulties with the Turks and that it was undesirable to create new ones. At the same time, he assured Jacobson that, should Djemal Pasha initiate any new measures against Palestine Jews, Germany would take the necessary steps to foil them.[49]

These statements did not reflect the full depth of Germany's involvement. Early in March, when Jacobson met Zimmermann, he gained a strong impression that the Under-Secretary of State entertained 'unlimited sympathy' for the Zionist cause and 'intended to incorporate it into the framework of the political programme of the Central Powers' at the future Peace Conference.[50] Propaganda apart, Germany would not have gone to such lengths to protect the Yishuv unless she considered it to be the nucleus of a larger entity of some importance to German interests. What these interests were has been already mentioned;[51] that which loomed constantly in the background was the need to solve the problem of East European Jewry. It became increasingly relevant after 5 November 1916 when Poland was proclaimed independent.

The matter was debated in academic circles also. Professor Carl Ballod, Professor of Political Science and Economics at the University of Berlin, later a co-founder of the Pro-Palästina Komitee, made a detailed study of the socio-economic conditions of East

---

[48] C.Z.A. Z 3/58, Lichtheim to E.A.C., 2 Mar., 30 Apr. 1916; Lichtheim, *She'ar Yashuv*, pp. 409–10; *Rückkehr*, p. 348.

[49] Ibid. Z 3/61, Jacobson to Lichtheim, 24, 26 Oct. 1916, reports on meetings with Zimmermann and Rosenberg. (A copy of the second letter in *Türkei* 195, K 177967–73.)   [50] Ibid. Z 3/58, Jacobson to Lichtheim, 9 Mar. 1916.

[51] Above, pp. 200–4, 251–5, 257–9, 264–7, 270.

European Jewry, and reached the conclusion that their future was dim. Cooped up in the Pale of Settlement in the western provinces of Russia, nearly six million strong, they were primarily town dwellers. In Warsaw and Lodz they constituted 33–5 per cent of the total population, in Vilna and Kovno over 50 per cent, and in many other provincial towns about 80–90 per cent. Two-fifths were engaged in petty commerce and roughly three-fifths were artisans, factory workers, and professionals. Afflicted by 'terrible misery' and subsisting on an astonishingly low standard of living, they were imbued with deep piety and a rock-firm expectancy of deliverance from an unfriendly environment and of return to the Holy Land. Politically, they were divided between the Zionists and the Bundists (ideologically akin to the Russian Social Democrats), but both schools subscribed to the principle that territorial concentration offered their people the best solution to the problem.

Ballod thought that the programme of a territorial concentration in Eastern Europe, as propounded by the Bund, was impracticable, since it was unlikely that the native non-Jewish population would be willing to cede any territory for a Jewish province. The Poles, should they become independent, would increase their economic drive against the Jews and follow the example of the Russians. Nor did immigration to the United States provide the real answer. Ballod therefore strongly favoured the Zionist solution. It would give rise to 'an unprecedented cultural renaissance in the Land of Promise'. He estimated that, if irrigated and scientifically cultivated, Palestine could absorb about five to six million souls. The Hauran region north-east of the River Jordan could provide sufficient corn to feed the population, though it would be desirable if the native Palestinian *fellahin* were resettled elsewhere. Considering how degraded and exploited they were by the great Arab landowners and money-lenders, Ballod assumed that this would be advantageous to them, since fair compensation for their land would offer them an opportunity of becoming independent farmers elsewhere. Turkey, too, should welcome the plan, since after the war she would be in great need to strengthen her economy. The whole enterprise, Ballod calculated, would require an investment of 150 million marks.[52]

---

[52] Carl Ballod, 'Das Ostjuden Problem und die Frage seiner Lösung durch den Zionismus', *Europäische Staats- und Wirtschafts-Zeitung*, Nr. 10 (Berlin, 1916), a copy in *Türkei* 195, K 178225–31. On Germany's policy towards Poland see Werner Conze, *Polnische Nation und deutsche Politik* (Cologne, 1958).

Ludwig Haas shared Ballod's assessment. Before the war Haas was known to be an anti-Zionist, but his experience as Head of the Jewish Department in the German civil administration of Poland convinced him that a large-scale emigration of Polish Jews was the only way to blunt the edge of Polish antagonism: Polish independence boded ill for the Jews. As the subject of the Polish Legion was topical at that time, he proposed to establish Jewish Legions to fight against Russia and Romania under Ottoman command. He was convinced that a force of 25,000–30,000 volunteers of 'first-rate morale' could be raised, provided that after the war the ex-legionnaires and their families were given the right to immigrate freely and settle in Palestine. Furthermore, should Turkey be ready 'to meet the Zionist wishes half-way, she would create for herself boundless sympathy from Jews all over the world, in the United States in particular. This might prove no minor asset for her at the future Peace Conference.'[53]

The scheme won the support of von Mutius, the Head of the Political Department on the Ober-Ost and formerly Counsellor in the German Embassy in Constantinople, who considered it both 'attractive' and 'feasible'. Rosenberg at the Foreign Ministry doubted whether Turkey would be willing to make the concessions to the Zionists, but Zimmermann, who in the meantime had been promoted to Minister for Foreign Affairs, thought that it was worth trying. Although Hakki Pasha, the Ottoman Ambassador in Berlin, was not particularly encouraging,[54] Zimmermann had apparently reason to assume that the climate of opinion in Constantinople was now more congenial for the Zionists than ever before.

Zimmermann's optimism was well founded. In mid December 1916 Talaat sounded out Ambassador Elkus on the possibility of obtaining a loan from American financiers. Elkus replied that he might be able to interest American Jews to help Turkey financially after the war, provided restrictions on Jewish immigration to Palestine were removed; Talaat did not object to such a *quid pro quo*. Elkus corresponded with Jacob Schiff and felt confident that he

[53] *Türkei* 195, K 178173–80, Haas (Warsaw) to State Secretary, 23 Jan. 1917. On Haas see above, p. 234. During the Executive's meeting on 25 Jan. 1917 Hantke confirmed that the Jewish youth in Poland was quite enthusiastic about the idea of forming a Jewish Legion and that, in his estimate, about 10,000 young men would volunteer immediately (C.Z.A. Z 3/599).

[54] *Türkei* 195, K 178204–5, Zimmermann to Kühlmann, 7 Feb. 1917.

could count on his support to rally substantial funds, if there were serious negotiations. Schiff, though not a Zionist, was keenly interested in the well-being of his co-religionists in Palestine and was heartened by Elkus's reassurance that prospects for Jewish colonization were bright, if only there was a friendly administration in Palestine and personal safety was guaranteed to the immigrants.

Turco-American relations were warmer still at a dinner-party given by Chief Rabbi Nahoum, at which Talaat and Elkus were guests. Although 'nothing definite was arranged, it was', as Elkus told Lichtheim, ' "a Jewish dinner" '. Lichtheim, cautious as usual, did not overestimate the importance of these *pourparlers*. In December he still thought that it was premature to regard them as of any 'practical value', however useful they might have been in other respects, but by January he had become confident that, when American financial help to Turkey was discussed, the Jewish question would figure prominently. At the beginning of February his hopes soared higher still. Talaat had succeeded Prince Said Halim as Grand Vizier and Djavid Bey re-entered the Cabinet as Finance Minister. Together they formed a formidable combination. Talaat had risen to an almost unassailable position in the Cabinet, overshadowing his rivals Enver and Djemal. Djemal became even more isolated and Lichtheim hoped that this would have a restraining effect upon him.[55]

Zimmermann was in a good position to assess the situation because the German intelligence intercepted Lichtheim's correspondence with the Zionist Executive and he was privy to its contents.[56] He erred, however, in taking for granted the Embassy's goodwill towards the Zionists, for in the winter of 1916–17 the personnel had changed. Baron von Neurath, who sponsored the Instructions to the Consulate, vacated his post; Dr. Weber was appointed Consul-General in Smyrna, while Dr. Göppert and von Radowitz, who had consecutively taken charge of Jewish affairs, were recalled to Berlin. Count Josef Waldburg, the Embassy's new Counsellor, was a far less pleasant person to deal with. Of imperial lineage, he expected to be addressed as 'His Highness', although in

[55] C.Z.A. Z 3/62, Lichtheim to E.A.C., 21 Dec. 1916, 6, 12 Jan. 1917; Z 3/63, same to same, 13 Feb. 1917.

[56] *Türkei* 195, K 178155–8 (a copy); *Türkei*, Nr. 190, *Die Beziehungen der Türkei zu den Vereinigten Staaten von Nordamerika*, Kühlmann to Bethmann Hollweg, 20 Jan. 1917, dis. no. 46.

diplomacy he soon revealed himself to be 'a limited and ignorant person'. He also found it difficult to reconcile his social position with his duty to deal with the Jewish question.[57] Kühlmann, who succeeded Metternich (recalled on being declared *persona non grata* by the Porte), was no newcomer to Constantinople; nor was he ignorant of Zionist affairs, but his enthusiasm had somewhat waned. On 12 January 1917, when Lichtheim met him, he reiterated his view, made two years earlier, and promised that the policy of protection, which had been initiated by Wangenheim, 'would continue . . . I need hardly emphasize how desirable it is that the Zionist movement should remain concentrated in Germany.' But when Lichtheim suggested that he ask Djemal, during his forthcoming visit to the capital, to allow Ruppin to return to his post in Jaffa, Kühlmann thought it 'inadvisable to exert pressure that might convey the impression that a German interest was involved'.[58] Kühlmann's attitude towards the Zionists soured as time went on. It was General Otto von Lossow, the Military Attaché, who engendered this new antagonism; parallel with Ludendorff's domination of German politics, von Lossow emerged as the strongest man at the Embassy.

In the circumstances it was Elkus who proved a tower of strength to Lichtheim. A recommendation from Morgenthau as well as from the Zionist Provisional Executive in New York predisposed Elkus favourably, and on the very day of his arrival in Constantinople (11 September 1916), he invited Lichtheim for an interview, an unusual courtesy in diplomatic circles. Thereafter he assisted his co-religionists in Palestine to the best of his capacity. Lichtheim's relations with Elkus did not reach the same degree of intimacy that they had with Morgenthau, but over the next seven months a bond of mutual trust and respect eased their co-operation.

Elkus was of the same American-Jewish stock as Morgenthau. Both were self-made men who had moved from the world of business into politics. Both were enthusiastic supporters of President Wilson. Both were animated by a genuine spirit of philanthropy but whereas Morgenthau radiated greater warmth Elkus possessed a keener mind. Morgenthau was empiric, often even erratic in behaviour; Elkus was more methodical and rational in approach.[59]

[57] Lichtheim. *She'ar Yashuv*, pp. 410–11; *Rückkehr*, pp. 349–50.
[58] C.Z.A. Z 3/63, Lichtheim to E.A.C., 12 Feb. 1917.
[59] Lichtheim, *She'ar Yashuv*, p. 412; *Rückkehr*, p. 351.

That Elkus had a more refined personality than his predecessor was also the opinion of Kühlmann. Elkus had 'the gift of getting on well with people and was successful in establishing good personal relations with the omnipotent . . . Talaat'.[60] However, this fell short of preventing renewed deportations of the Armenians. Deeply distressed at 'the unchecked policy of extermination . . . and brutality' perpetrated by Turkish officials, he suggested that the State Department try to induce the German and Austrian Governments to intervene with the Turks on behalf of the Armenians. State Secretary Lansing took up the suggestion, but with no visible results.[61] Elkus, however, left no avenue unexplored and sounded out Lichtheim as to what Germany thought about the persecutions of the Armenians. Lichtheim replied, in his private capacity, that 'the German Embassy had always endeavoured to prevent the persecutions of the Armenians although without success'. Elkus apparently intended to use Lichtheim as an intermediary to convey his desire for collaboration with the German Embassy on Armenian and Jewish affairs. But Lichtheim was circumspect. No matter how desirable such collaboration might have been, 'to act as a political agent between the American and German Embassies, without being officially requested to do so', was to him unthinkable. Elkus kept pressing. He denied the current opinion that the American Embassy favoured the cause of the Entente and emphasized that personally he was by no means Germany's adversary. Questioned by Lichtheim on the aims of American policy in Turkey, he replied that, apart from the obligation to protect the life and property of American citizens, his Government 'has no other than humanitarian interests. . . . America is a peace-loving and strictly neutral country; least of all would she strive to embark upon a policy of conquests and territorial acquisitions which might lead to clashes with other Powers.' Lichtheim gained the impression that Elkus was sincere.[62] None the less, he refrained from undertaking the mission but, as he thought it desirable to bring the contents of his conversation to the attention of the German Embassy, he dispatched his letter to the Zionist Executive through the official courier.

Lichtheim's correct behaviour belies the charge levelled against him a few months later by the Naval and Military Attachés at the

---

[60] As note 56.
[61] *F.R.U.S.*, 1916 Suppl., pp. 857–8, Elkus to Lansing, 17 Oct. 1916; Lansing to Grew, 1 Nov. 1916. [62] C.Z.A. Z 3/61, Lichtheim to E.A.C., 17 Nov. 1916.

German Embassy that his close relationship with the American Ambassador constituted a security risk.[63] Bizarre as such a charge seemed to be, it was a product of the tense atmosphere which resulted from the severely strained German–American relations, coupled with the fear that Turkey might defect from the camp of the Central Powers. As Elkus observed, repeated Turkish threats to conclude a separate peace with the Entente made the Germans feel 'helpless'[64] and intensified their suspicions beyond a point that the case might have warranted.

German concern was not entirely unfounded as for some time the Turks had tried to steer an independent course. Turkey was no party to the unrestricted submarine warfare and did not feel obliged to break off diplomatic relations with the United States as Germany did. Not only did relations continue to be 'normal' but they even became 'more friendly than for some time past', a trend which reasserted itself after Talaat was made Grand Vizier. Elkus had little difficulty in convincing his hosts that it was in 'the mutual interests of both countries to avoid the suspension of friendly relations', in spite of the necessity to sever them with Germany.[65] At a dinner given in his honour by Elkus, Talaat declared in the presence of all foreign diplomats (except the German) that he wished the American Ambassador to stay in Constantinople 'for ever'.[66]

Djavid, Talaat's *alter ego*, was even more outspoken. At the outbreak of war he was one of the four ministers who had resigned in protest against Turkey's joining the Central Powers. He was the least pro-German of Turkish statesmen and from 1917 persistently endeavoured to win American friendship as 'a counter-balance to Germany, should she emerge victorious'.[67] Djavid agreed to accept the portfolio of finance on condition that Turkey modified her extreme nationalist policy and improved her treatment of non-Turkish and non-Muslim elements.[68] He made no attempt to conceal his views and early in March came out with a courageous speech in the Ottoman Parliament denouncing 'the spirit of nation-

---

[63] Below, pp. 303–4, 305–6, 308.

[64] *F.R.U.S.*, 1917, Suppl. 2, pp. 449–500, Elkus to Lansing, 23 Dec. 1916.

[65] Ibid., Suppl. 1, pp. 113, 134, 148–9, 191–2, Elkus to Lansing, 8, 11 Feb. 1917; Lansing to Elkus, 5 Feb., 31 Mar. 1917.

[66] C.Z.A. Z 3/63, Lichtheim to E.A.C., 17 Feb. 1917.

[67] *Türkei* 190, Bernstorff to Hertling, 1 Mar. 1918, dis. no. (?).

[68] *F.R.U.S.*, 1917, Suppl. 1, p. 134, Elkus to Lansing, 11 Feb. 1917.

alist maliciousness'. He maintained that Turkey's weakness and
financial predicament called for an early conclusion of peace to
enable her to enter into commercial intercourse with 'all countries,
especially the richest one in the world'. This oblique reference to
the United States was all the more telling since a day earlier Djavid
had invited Elkus to listen to his speech. Both Djavid and Talaat
courted Elkus assiduously, in the apparent hope that they might
secure America's backing in case of emergency.[69] On 2 April, when
America was about to declare war on Germany, Nessimy Bey told
Elkus that his country's attitude to the United States was friendlier
than ever and he saw no reason why it should not continue. In
return Elkus reassured the Porte that the American Government
'had no reason for any controversy with Turkey'.[70]

Djavid's demand for a more liberal policy towards non-Turkish
and non-Muslim minorities, coupled with Turkey's need for economic assistance, aroused Lichtheim's hope that perhaps a new era
was about to dawn upon the Turco-Zionist relationship also. He
subsequently established contact with Djavid and with another
minister (whose name he did not reveal) and felt confident that the
Turks, sensitive to American public opinion, would do their utmost
to avoid harsh treatment of Palestinian Jews. So sanguine did he
become that he thought the moment was ripe to initiate a diplomatic
move to extract from the Turks a moderate declaration in favour of the
Jewish establishment in Palestine. The new-born Turco-American
friendship seemed thus to have given an unexpected opportunity
to the Zionists but neither Lichtheim nor Jacobson counted on it
as the only way to further their ends. They were realistic enough to
appreciate that, no matter what flirtations Turkey might conduct
with America, on broader issues she was and would remain, at least
for the duration of the war, in Germany's orbit. America's inability
to guarantee to the Turks the retention of the most precious asset,
Constantinople and the Straits, inevitably imposed serious limitations on the scope of the Turco-American *rapprochement*. Moreover, Turkey, annoyed by the Entente's rejection of the Central
Powers' peace offer, and particularly by the offensive references
towards herself, had little choice but to rely on Germany and thereby
become 'more disposed than previously to follow the friendly

---

[69] C.Z.A. Z 3/63, Lichtheim to E.A.C., 17 Feb., 8 Mar. 1917.

[70] *F.R.U.S.*, 1917, Suppl. 1, p. 206, Elkus to Lansing, 2 Apr. 1917; ibid., Suppl. 11,
p. 18, same to same, 5 Apr. 1917.

advice' of her ally.[71] This double-barrelled policy, to effect a revolutionary change in Turkey's Zionist policy simultaneously through the United States and Germany, could perhaps have yielded a positive harvest if peace between Germany and America prevailed but, as it turned out, the rupture in American–German diplomatic relations was only a prelude to war. This could not but upset the Zionist calculations and inflicted a heavy blow on their standing.

[71] C.Z.A. Z 3/63, Lichtheim to E.A.C., 13 Feb., 17 Mar. 1917; Jacobson to Lichtheim, 18 Mar. 1917. For the text of the British note rejecting the peace offer made by the Central Powers see Erich Ludendorff. *The General Staff and its Problems* (London, 1920), i, pp. 310–14; Hans W. Gatzke, *Germany's Drive to the West* (Baltimore, 1950), p. 150. Lichtheim thought that had it not been for the Entente's Note, the Turks would have been more inclined to conclude a separate peace (*She'ar Yashuv*, p. 430; *Rückkehr*, p. 430).

14

The Zionists' Desideratum and its Frustration

THE need to elicit from Germany and Turkey a declaration of sympathy with Jewish aspirations in Palestine was first presented by Jacobson during the meeting of the Zionist Council in The Hague on 24 March 1916.[1] At the time the proposition was considered premature but following the peace offer made by the Central Powers on 12 December 1916[2] the time seemed ripe to launch a diplomatic drive which would further this aim. On 29 January 1917 Warburg and Jacobson told Zimmermann that the American-Jewish Congress would meet in May to discuss the whole gamut of Jewish claims to be presented at the future Peace Conference. These consisted of demands for:

(1) Complete equality of civil rights which had been denied to Jewish subjects in countries such as Russia, Romania, Morocco, and Persia.

(2) Rights of national cultural autonomy in countries where other minorities enjoyed or would enjoy them in the future.

(3) Creation of favourable conditions for unrestricted Jewish immigration and colonization in Palestine.

[1] C.Z.A. Z 3/453; above, p. 238.
[2] On which see: *Official German Documents Relating to the World War* (Oxford University Press, 1923), i, p. 158; *War Memoirs of Robert Lansing* (London, 1935), pp.181–2. A discussion is provided by Brunauer, 'The Peace Proposals of December 1916–January 1917', *Journal of Modern History* (1932), 544–71; May, *The World War and American Isolation*, pp. 387–8, 303–4; Gatzke, *Germany's Drive to the West*, pp. 162–4; Klaus Epstein, 'The Development of German–Austrian War Aims in the Spring of 1917', *Journal of Central European Affairs*, xvii (Apr. 1957), no. 1, 25–7.

They told Zimmermann that the majority of the Congress Committee, as well as Nathan Straus, its President, were Zionist-oriented, that Zionism in America had gained much strength, and that Justice Brandeis had been successful in enlisting the sympathy of the American Government. Other neutral countries, as well as the Entente Powers, would presumably take a greater interest in the Jewish question at the future Peace Conference and the Central Powers should make their voices heard too. Germany, in particular, should play a conspicuous role. She was one of the principal guarantors of equality of rights for Romanian Jews accorded by the Berlin Treaty of 1878, and in Poland, where her influence was supreme, she was in a position to ensure that the Jewish community, which constituted 15 per cent of the total population, be granted the right of proportionate representation, and its 'separate national-cultural entity' be recognized. This fully accorded with Germany's proclaimed principle of fostering the free development of nationalities and national minorities in the new Polish State.

However, Warburg and Jacobson were chiefly concerned with Palestine. They hoped that, consonant with her 'traditional understanding and friendship', Turkey would be willing to permit free Jewish immigration and colonization and would recognize Jewish cultural autonomy. This policy, they maintained, had been pursued during the last two years before the outbreak of the war and was in line with the *millet* system. The Jewish settlers for their part would embrace Ottoman nationality and willingly fulfil all the duties of citizenship. They could not, however, renounce their national aspirations, since this was the very life-blood of their pioneering enterprise. These aspirations were perfectly realizable within the framework of Ottoman sovereignty and it was preposterous to consider them 'dangerous'. The Zionist leaders had consistently rejected any separatist tendencies and declared that their interests were compatible with those of Turkey. Their loyalty was conditioned by hard geopolitical realities. The fact that the Jewish settlement was surrounded by an overwhelming and coherent Arab majority would make its very existence dependent on the protection of the Central Government and guarantee its loyalty. Moreover, should the Arabs give any trouble to Turkey, would it not be useful to have a strong Jewish settlement as a counterweight? Geographically Palestine might serve not only as a bridge that could unite but also that could divide the inhabited Arab territories. This did not mean the Zionists would be willing to become a permanent tool against the Arabs in return for Turkish friendship. This might be undesirable even for Turkey, and there was always a distinct possibility of a peaceful accommodation between Jews and Arabs. 'Jewish immigration would not necessarily involve the displacement of 500,000 Palestinian Arabs and should the land be scientifically cultivated it could absorb additional millions of immigrants.' The indigenous population would derive considerable economic benefit, as would the Ottoman Treasury.

Warburg and Jacobson pointed out the futility of the policy of 'turcification' of the non-Turkish inhabitants of the Empire and argued that it would be more prudent for Turkey to come to terms with the aspirations of the ethnic groups and foster their free national development, rather than suppress them. If Turkey was prepared in principle to show goodwill towards the furtherance of the Jewish settlement in Palestine, 'it lay in her own interest to decide as soon as possible, so that she might ensure that she remained in control of this question instead of allowing it to become the subject of international debate.' The forthcoming Jewish Congress in America added to the urgency and offered a good opportunity for Turkey to make a public declaration and thereby to retrieve her prestige. The German Government should influence the Porte and supplement an eventual Turkish declaration with her own.[3]

Attached to this memorandum were copies of articles in the *American Jewish Chronicle* (19 January 1917) and the New York Yiddish daily *Die Wahrheit* (24 January 1917) to show that the Zionist Executive was able to muster the Jewish Press in support of Turkey. The *Chronicle* emphasized Turkey's traditional hospitality to Jewish refugees and reasoned that 'had it not been for intrigues of the great powers in the past', Turkey would have been, perhaps, in a position to do 'much more' for the Jewish settlement in Palestine. It went on to argue that 'for the good of humanity and peace', as well as for the interests of the Jews, a kind of an equilibrium between Islam and Christianity should exist after the war. If the Ottoman Empire were dismembered, Palestine would become 'a prey to the European Powers, leaving little chance for the Jews to realize their thousand year old dream'. Having lost confidence in the Greeks and Armenians, and, recognizing how dangerous the Pan-Arab

[3] *Türkei* 195, K 178208, Warburg and Jacobson to Bussche-Haddenhausen, 4 Feb. 1917, and memorundum of the same date (K 178200-21).

movement would be for her, Turkey would surely acknowledge that 'the only [non-Turkish] people in the Empire who had proved their unimpeachable loyalty during the War ... were her Jewish subjects'.

C. M. Schenkin argued in *Die Wahrheit* that, despite Turkey's antagonism which, he maintained, was due to the frequent consular interferences, not a single Jew had been expelled from Palestine for the past twenty years. The native Jewish community was permitted to maintain its own institutions, appoint its own courts of arbitration, and introduce autonomous system of education and taxation. Turkish officials used to attend Jewish celebrations, where their national flag was displayed, and in fact, until the outbreak of the war, '*never* disturbed them ... If we have now in Palestine only forty colonies and not five hundred; one hundred thousand inhabitants, and not half a million ... it is only *our own fault* and not the result of Turkish ill-treatment.'[4]

In the Wilhelmstrasse the Zionist suggestion had a sympathetic hearing, but at the Embassy in Constantinople opinion hardened. Kühlmann's dispatch of 15 February in which he reported on his meeting with Chief Rabbi Nahoum signalled a sharp change. Kühlmann regarded Nahoum as an intelligent and articulate person, who possessed a wide knowledge of the Orient and who played an important role as a middleman between Talaat and Elkus. He therefore paid close attention to the Rabbi's views. According to Kühlmann, Nahoum told him that Ottoman Jews regarded Zionism as 'a foreign importation', which was chiefly supported by Germany and America.

The vocal and determined manner of the Zionist propaganda gave a false impression of their real influence among the Jews, but those in Turkey regarded it as an undesirable movement that endangered their interests ... The Jewish people, thousands of years after the destruction of their political existence, had no cause to revive a Jewish state. The Jews should unconditionally and with no ulterior motives consider themselves as nationals of the states in which they are domiciled and endeavour to identify themselves with their countries' interests. This was the basic principle of Ottoman-Jewish policy. The Jews had always been on good terms with their state and had no intention of sacrificing this good relationship to any fantastic foreign ideas.

Nahoum added that in past centuries the immigration of his co-religionists to Palestine had been free and unrestricted, and that it

---

[4] *Türkei* 195 (cuttings in K 178325–34). Schenkin was a prominent Palestinian Zionist. In 1915 he was deported by Djemal Pasha and during the war he lived in the U.S.A.

was 'only since the loud agitation of the Zionists in the European Press that the Turkish Government became suspicious'. In view of the numerous bitter experiences the Porte had had with foreign colonies, one could hardly blame it. The Porte feared that 'the existence of large and coherent Zionist colonies in Palestine might well lead to the diplomatic interference of foreign Powers'. Nahoum was well aware of the German Government's interest in Zionism and of her wish to gain popularity in the influential Jewish Press, but here he felt obliged to warn the Ambassador that Ottoman Jewry viewed Zionism as 'a danger rather than a benefit to herself'. At all events, he thought that Jewish cultural renaissance in Palestine was impractical.

Kühlmann was impressed. 'It seems to me', he told the Foreign Ministry, 'that the Chief Rabbi's views are worthy of a certain degree of consideration.' While the Turkish Government, both during the Hamidean absolute monarchy and under the Revolutionary Committee, had been unable to achieve a reasonable *modus vivendi* with the Armenian and Greek elements, the relationship between the Porte and the Ottoman Jews had on the whole been harmonious. This relationship, which he attributed to the skilful and extremely cautious policy of the official Jewish representatives, 'could serve as a source of strength for Turkey . . . and should not be endangered by excessive zeal in furthering the Zionist policy'. In addition, in view of the great military danger on the Palestinian front, he thought it imperative to be 'extremely cautious' before intervening on behalf of Zionist interests. He was therefore unable to follow the Berlin Ministry's suggestion to intercede for Ruppin's return to his post in Jaffa. 'Palestine is at present under a severe military threat and we should avoid annoying Djemal Pasha.'[5]

Nahoum's early education in France and his subsequent association with the Alliance Israélite Universelle had left a mark on him. His statement that 'the Jewish people, thousands of years after the destruction of the political existence, had no cause to revive a Jewish state' referred the doctrine enunciated by the Great Sanhedrin of Paris in 1807.[6] Yet whatever opinions he might have held it is strange that he should have voiced them to a German Ambassador. No document has so far come to light to corroborate Kühlmann's

---

[5] Ibid. K 178266–71, Kühlmann to Bethmann Hollweg, 15 Feb. 1917, dis. no. 108; same to A.A., 16 Feb. 1917, tel. no. 195.

[6] On which see Friedman, *The Question of Palestine*, pp. 27, 29.

report and it is almost certain that on no other occasion did Nahoum express similar sentiments on Zionism. On the contrary, in 1912 he used his influence with Talaat to abolish the notorious 'red ticket', and throughout the war stoutly aided the Zionist representatives in Constantinople; there is no evidence whatsoever to suggest that he regarded their activities as endangering the position of Ottoman Jewry. In October 1917, following Lichtheim's removal from Constantinople, he appealed personally to Kühlmann, then Foreign Minister, to reinstate him for the benefit of Ottoman Jews. Earlier he assured Nessimy Bey that Zionism was by no means incompatible with Turkish law and the interests of Jewry, a statement which contradicted that reported by Kühlmann on 15 February. Moreover, in the spring of 1918 Nahoum acted as one of the chief intermediaries with the Porte and a German-Jewish delegation, which included the Zionists; the negotiations centred on the creation of a national and religious Jewish centre in Palestine.[7] And a few years after the war, though under changed conditions, he published a remarkable statement:

> Jewish aspirations in Turkey center about the restoration of Palestine . . . Towards the year of 1860 newcomers from Russia began to devote themselves to agriculture . . . This back-to-the-land movement was the most important factor in the awakening of the desire for the repopulation of Palestine . . . [and] it was proved that the regeneration of Palestine was possible. It was at the time of . . . Herzl that Zionism gave to this aspiration a new vigour and a definite form . . . The Balfour Declaration became the basis for the settlement of the Jewish question and to-day the Jews of Turkey . . . do not fail to co-operate with all their might with the rest of the Jews in the intellectual, economic and commercial restoration of Palestine.[8]

Whatever impact Nahoum's views made on Kühlmann, the Auswärtiges Amt was still unimpressed. For Germany, regard for Ottoman Jewry was of secondary importance compared with the need to win the sympathy of other Jewish communities, in the United States in particular. This was why Zimmermann became concerned on learning of the formation of the British-Palestine Committee. The Committee, according to Konrad Romberg, the

---

[7] Below, pp. 335, 339, 386, 397–8, 405. The 'red ticket' was a popular name for *permis de séjour*, on which see above, p. 44.

[8] Haim Nahoum, 'Jews', *Modern Turkey*, ed. E. G. Mears, pp. 86–96.

Minister to Berne, propagated the idea of the Jewish establishment of a Zionist state in Palestine in order to create a buffer for Egypt and at the same time win world Jewry over to Britain's cause.[9] Apprehensive lest Britain should steal a march on Germany, Zimmermann hastened to instruct all the legations in neutral countries to keep a close watch on the local Zionists and report on their orientation.

Up till now the Zionist Executive in Berlin has been successful in keeping that Organization in line with the German and Turkish interests. Therefore, we and the Embassy in Constantinople have adopted an *ad hoc* benevolent attitude towards them, without pledging ourselves in principle.[10]

Romberg's subsequent dispatch was even more disquieting. On the basis of reliable sources he concluded that Germany could no longer remain indifferent. 'I am of the opinion that this question deserves investigation by our statesmen . . . England has always understood how to use the valuable Jewish sympathies although, in reality, she has made in return only very doubtful promises.' The British had been successful in winning over the House of Rothschild, as well as Morgan, and Kuhn & Loeb, a company whose financial assistance proved invaluable for the purchase of armaments in the United States. He warned the Ministry not to underrate the 'seriousness of the successful propaganda which the well-to-do Jews launched against Germany', and thought that the best means to counter it was to persuade the Porte to create in Palestine 'an autonomous Jewish reservation'. Should Germany be successful in this respect, she would score a point of great political importance, not only by making a strong appeal to millions of American Jews but also by creating a tangible solution for those in Eastern Europe; Poland, in whose resurrection Germany was interested, 'would be freed from a greater part of its *Lumpenproletariat*'. He assured his superiors that he came from a 'purely Christian stock' and was not speaking *pro domo*.[11]

Early in March Warburg and Jacobson approached the Foreign

---

[9] *Türkei* 195, K 178279–80, Romberg to Bethmann Hollweg, 21 Feb. 1917, dis. no. 501, encl. a cutting from the *Manchester Guardian* (14 Feb. 1917). On the British-Palestine Committee see Stein, *The Balfour Declaration*, pp. 301–4.

[10] *Türkei* 195, K 178275–8, Zimmermann to Berne (secret), 24 Feb. 1917, dis. no. 178; identical to other legations; a copy to Constantinople, dis. no. 199.

[11] Ibid. K 178292–6, Romberg to Bethmann Hollweg (secret), 2 Mar. 1917, dis. no. 594 and encl.

Ministry again. They told von dem Bussche Haddenhausen, the Under-Secretary of State, that the financial help that Talaat Pasha expected from Jewish circles in the United States would not be forthcoming unless the Turkish Government expressed its opposition to Djemal Pasha's policy. The latter's hostile measures had alienated Jewish opinion and might destroy the last shred of sympathy for the Central Powers. Germany, too, would be accused of moral complicity, since her influence over Turkey was common knowledge. If, however, Turkey were to change her policy and offer some tangible evidence of goodwill, the Zionists would use their entire world Press and organizational machinery to give it the widest possible publicity. Talaat was 'a man capable of giving due consideration to serious and authoritative arguments'; hence the moment was opportune for the German Embassy to sound out the Porte on making the desired declaration.[12]

For the Zionists the matter was one of urgent and 'absolute necessity'. The situation in Palestine was becoming 'intolerable' and Lichtheim's and Thon's dispatches were more alarming than ever. They feared that Djemal's irritability would increase with the advance of the British forces. 'What will cross his mind then cannot be foreseen . . . perhaps it is the greatest danger we have ever faced', Jacobson wrote to Lichtheim. From the beginning of the war the German Zionists did their best to play down the events in Palestine, fearing that too outspoken criticism might worsen the situation. Their efforts were not altogether in vain, since even the British Zionists showed restraint and subdued their feelings of revulsion. The same was true of the American Zionists. Articles like those which appeared in the *American Jewish Chronicle* and *Die Wahrheit* were 'achievements that surpassed all expectations'. But if the position were to become perilous, it would no longer be possible to contain Jewish anger. An anti-Turkish outburst would in turn increase Djemal's hostility and encourage 'his wild desire for destruction'. To forestall such an adverse development a friendly declaration by the Turkish Government was essential. To ease its birth, the Zionist leaders were prepared to content themselves with 'a general statement of principle', pointing to a more sympathetic attitude towards the Jewish work in Palestine. The formula, as

---

[12] *Türkei* 195, K 178300–5, memorandum by Warburg and Jacobson, 5 Mar. 1917; encl. also copies of Lichtheim's letters to E.A.C. (Dec. 1916–Feb. 1917) on which see above, pp. 282–3.

Jacobson told Lichtheim, was deliberately couched in mild terms in order to facilitate the task of the German diplomats to persuade the Porte. He thought that the Talaat–Djavid combination improved the atmosphere in Constantinople and hoped that, following the Entente Note, Turkey would become more receptive to the friendly suggestions of her ally.[13]

Jacobson also attempted to solicit the support of Dr. Rissoff, the Bulgarian Minister to Berlin, a personal friend of Talaat's, who was willing to expatiate on the advantages to be gained from a demonstration of sympathy. There is no evidence to show to what extent Rissoff did intervene. The deterioration in Turco-Bulgarian relations in the succeeding months presumably circumscribed his initiative. The support gained from Matthias Erzberger, the prominent leader of the Zentrum party and Director of the Intelligence and Propaganda Bureau, was of greater importance. Erzberger had intimate knowledge of Turkish affairs, acquired during his diplomatic missions to Constantinople, and was receptive to Zionist wishes. He shared Jacobson's conviction that 'moral victories' were an essential prerequisite for successful diplomacy at the future Peace Conference and, without hesitation, advised the Wilhelmstrasse that 'something should be done for the Zionist Organization, even if it is only a nice gesture'.[14] The influential *Berliner Tageblatt* (12 March 1917, evening edn.) made a similar recommendation.

Having had no comment from Kühlmann on the Zionist memorandum of 4 February, which the Ministry had forwarded to him, Zimmermann cabled the Ambassador on 16 March:

Dr. Jacobson handed over personally his second application [dated 5 March] and referred to his request once more. May I ask Your Excellency whether, and in which form, the desired declaration for the Zionists is obtainable in principle.

On the following day he cabled again:

In connection with the [previous] telegram no. 262, for your information and utilization: the severe measures taken by the Turkish Government against the Zionists in Palestine will create a very bad impression

---

[13] C.Z.A. Z 3/63, Jacobson to Lichtheim, 19 Mar. 1917; *Türkei* 195, K 178299, A.A. note on a conversation with Jacobson, signed by Rosenberg and Romberg, 7 Mar. 1917.

[14] C.Z.A. Z/63, Jacobson to Lichtheim, 19 Mar. 1917; *Türkei* 195, K 178342–7, Jacobson to Erzberger, 13 Mar. 1917; Erzberger to Rosenberg, same date. On Erzberger see Klaus Epstein, *Erzberger and the Dilemma of German Democracy* (Princeton University Press, 1959); idem, 'Erzberger's Political Operations', *Journal of Central European Affairs*, xix (1959–60).

not only on the . . . organized Zionists but also on the remainder of
Jewry. This appears to us at present inopportune.[15]

How serious Zimmermann was is evident from his reaction to
Lossow's dismissal of the idea of the Jewish Legion advocated by
Haas. Because of the unfortunate experience with the Georgian
Legion, the General did not place much hope in the success of a
Jewish one, a pessimism which Kühlmann fully shared. But, however doubtful the military usefulness of a Jewish Legion seemed to
be, what made the project so attractive to Zimmermann was its
political value: 'the very idea would make the Turkish Government
display a more favourable attitude towards Jewish colonization in
Palestine.' He instructed the Ambassador to sound out the Porte
along those lines.[16]

Zimmermann's motive was clear: in return for a demonstration
of Jewish goodwill he hoped to effect Turkey's change of heart
towards Zionism, an objective which, in the light of his record, is
quite understandable. What is at first sight surprising is Zimmermann's effort to bring about a Turkish declaration—directed principally to American Jewry—when he himself considered that the
rupture in American–German relations would in all likelihood lead
to war.[17]

Yet such a move did not necessarily conflict with his policy.[18]
Something has been said already about his pro-American proclivities and his desire to keep American-Jewish opinion on Germany's
side.[19] The last thing he wanted was a break with the United States.
Like Bethmann Hollweg, Zimmermann regarded an American

[15] *Türkei* 195, K 178356–9, Zimmermann to Kühlmann, 16, 17 Mar. 1917, tels. nos.
262, 269.
[16] Ibid. K 178298, Kühlmann to Bethmann Hollweg, 27 Feb. 1917, dis. no. 138;
K 178397, Zimmermann to Kühlmann, 19 Mar. 1917, dis. no. 274. On the failure of
the Georgian Legion see Fritz Fischer, *Griff nach der Weltmacht. Die Kriegszielpolitik
des kaiserlichen Deutschland: 1914–1918* (Düsseldorf, 1959), p. 154.
[17] On 7 Mar. 1917 Zimmermann cabled Eckhard, the German Minister in Mexico:
'In connection with my telegram of 16 January: emphasize that instructions were to be
carried out after Declaration of war by America . . .' (reproduced in Burton J. Hendrick:
The Life and Letters of Walter H. Page (London, 1926), iii, p. 352).
[18] Zimmermann's policies still await a worthy historian. No monograph has been
produced so far. Professor May's study, *The World War and American Isolation, 1914–
1917*, highlights Bethmann Hollweg's struggle with the military but overlooks the role
played by Zimmermann, whilst Professor Fischer in his chapter 'Deutschland und
Nordamerika' (op. cit., pp. 353–95) by no means exhausts the sources available on
Zimmermann's attitude. They are used here.
[19] Above, pp. 205–6, 270, below, pp. 302–3.

intervention as a calamity which Germany should avoid at all costs. Following Germany's Peace Note of 12 December 1916 he expressed his confidence to Ambassador Gerard that a frank and straightforward relationship with the United States would continue and he made a number of suggestions which, in Gerard's opinion, 'aided materially in the preservation of peace'.[20] But the Allied Powers' rejection of the peace offer made a negotiated peace 'difficult, if not impossible'. It caused the Chancellor a grave loss of prestige and paved the way for the Supreme Command's domination of German politics.[21] General Ludendorff in particular pressed for an unrestricted U-boat campaign to which Zimmermann strenuously objected, primarily 'on account of America'.[22] On 6 January, during a dinner given in Gerard's honour, he re-emphasized his sentiments on this matter, but as it turned out it was 'the last desperate attempt to preserve friendly relations'.[23] The issue was decided not at the German–American dinner, but in Pless on 9 January, when the Kaiser sided with the Supreme Command.[24]

Zimmermann had little choice but to concede defeat. None the less, he did try his best to diminish the danger of a break with the United States.[25] Even his ill-fated 'Mexico-telegram' of 16 January bore the stamp of an 'endeavour . . . to keep the United States neutral . . . in spite of . . . unrestricted submarine warfare'.[26] On

[20] Gerard, *My Four Years in Germany*, pp. 258-9.

[21] Gatzke, op. cit., pp. 150-1. May also obliquely concurs that 'the Allied reply killed all chances of immediate negotiations' (op. cit., pp. 412-13).

[22] Ludendorff, *The General Staff and its Problems*, i, p. 289, Ludendorff to Zimmermann, 20 Dec. 1916, Zimmermann to Lersner, 21 Dec. 1916.

[23] Gerard, op. cit., pp. 262-4, also p. 259. Gerard accused the Auswärtiges Amt of duplicity (ibid., pp. 260, 264-5), but contradicts himself stating that 'had the decision rested with the Chancellor and with the Foreign Ministry, the decision would have been against the resumption of this ruthless war, but Germany is not ruled . . . by a civilian power' (ibid., p. 260). Gerard was in no position to know the extent of the dramatic subterranean struggle which took place between the civilians and the military. Zimmermann, usually frank with Gerard, concealed from him Ludendorff's victory at Pless, fearing lest it would bring about a break in diplomatic relations with the U.S. (ibid., p. 273).

[24] For a full description see May, op. cit., pp. 414-15.

[25] Ludendorff, op. cit. i, p. 323, Zimmermann to Grünau, 22 Jan. 1917; Hans Peter Hanssen, *Diary of a Dying Empire* (Indiana University Press, 1955), pp. 161-3. Meeting of the Reichstag Finance Committee on 31 Jan. 1917.

[26] Ironically, it was this clumsy telegram that served as the last straw in bringing America into the war against Germany and subsequently ruined Zimmermann's career. For its full text see: *Official German Documents*, p. 1337; *F.R.U.S.*, 1917, Suppl. 1, pp. 147, 158; *Lansing Memoirs*, p. 310; R. B. Mowat, *History of European Diplomacy, 1914-1925* (London, 1928), p. 94; Hendrick, op. cit. iii, pp. 321, 324-5, 331-64. In

receiving Bernstorff's warning that war was 'unavoidable if we proceed as contemplated', Zimmermann made another desperate effort to induce Admiral von Holtzendorff, the Chief of the Admiralty Staff, to modify or postpone the U-boat campaign.[27] 'We will do all in our power to keep America out', he declared on 1 February to the Finance Committee in the Reichstag, and assured his audience that President Wilson would not come under the spell of the Anglo-Saxon Germanophobe section of the American population (which was concentrated in all the eastern states), because he was elected by the Western States, where the mood was pacifist.[28] Later, when the American Government expressed its desire to avoid war, he replied that he was ready for negotiations, provided the blockade against the Entente was not interrupted.[29] Even after the declaration of war by President Wilson, his attitude did not change and his critics in the Reichstag accused him of behaving as if Germany was not at war with the United States at all. He replied: 'We must distinguish between President Wilson, who is our enemy, and the American people, who are really not enthusiastic about the war. In order not to arouse them, we must avoid offensive transactions [*sic*].' It was also for this reason that he had permitted a number of American journalists of German descent to remain in Berlin, apparently to enable them to influence American opinion.[30]

However mistaken Zimmermann's judgement of President Wilson,[31] and however misplaced his hope of influencing the

contrast to Hendrick's conclusion that 'Germany was making preparations for war with the United States' (ibid., p. 331), Charles Seymour attributed Zimmermann's telegram to 'mistaken German diplomacy' (*American Diplomacy during the World War* (Baltimore, 1934), pp. 203–4). That Zimmermann was involved in a 'diplomatic blunder', rather than in a deliberate conspiracy against the United States, is also the view of Gatzke (op. cit., p. 222) and of Samuel Flagg Bemis, *A Diplomatic History of the United States* (New York, 1950), p. 613. An examination of its effect on President Wilson is made by Arthur Walworth, *Woodrow Wilson—World Prophet* (New York, London, 1958), pp. 89–90, 125. Barbara W. Tuchmann's book, *The Zimmermann Telegram* (New York, 1958), is not convincing.

[27] *Official German Documents*, p. 1108, Zimmermann to Holtzendorff, 22 Jan. 1917, encl. Bernstorff's dispatch of 19 Jan. 1917.

[28] Hanssen, op. cit., pp. 168, 171, 173; Gerard, op. cit., p. 274.

[29] *Official German Documents*, p. 1326, 8 Feb. 1917.

[30] Hanssen, op. cit., pp. 192, 198. The journalists, however, returned to the United States by order of the American Government.

[31] 'Wilson has never been our friend. He feels and thinks English . . .' (Zimmermann's statement in the Reichstag, 22 Feb. 1917, Hanssen, op. cit., p. 173). For Wilson's attitude to the belligerent Powers at that time, see May, op. cit., pp. 359–60, 368, 427, 437, who also describes admirably how Lloyd George managed to steer Wilson into the

American people over the head of their President, his tactics throw additional light on the importance which he attached to public opinion. They tend also to explain his eagerness to elicit from Turkey a declaration of sympathy such as the Zionists desired. The Jewish community in America, like that in Russia, was known to be largely pacifist and the impact that a Turkish declaration, followed in all probability by a German one, would have had on those Jews would have served Zimmermann's purpose well.

The Embassy in Constantinople held diametrically opposed views. Since his conversation with Nahoum, Kühlmann could find no identity between Zionism and Judaism and thought that, as relations between the Porte and Ottoman Jews, including those in Palestine, were good, no special declaration was needed. As for the Zionists, 'their ambition, in spite of all attempts to disguise the fact, is political in nature and aims at the creation of Jewish autonomy in Palestine'. In view of Turkey's lack of sympathy, and especially the critical military situation on the Palestinian front, he regarded furtherance of such aspirations as conflicting with German interests. Moreover, as a result of the severance of diplomatic relations with America, Germany's relationship with Zionism entered 'a new phase'.

> The very fact that we must pay particular attention at the present moment to Turkey's relations with the United States and that only recently we have expressed here our desire that in case of the outbreak of war between the United States and ourselves, the Turkish Government should voluntarily sever diplomatic relations with the United States, makes the fulfilment of the Zionist wishes very difficult at present.

The declaration, he maintained, would unduly encourage a close relationship between Turkey and America and was therefore from the German point of view undesirable.[32]

Kühlmann shared Lossow's suspicion that the American Embassy was indulging in anti-German propaganda and supported the General's recommendation that Lichtheim be called up. The American Embassy was 'the stronghold of Jewry' and its connection with

Allied camp (p. 382). 'What Germany and the United States lacked [was] . . . mutual comprehension and trust that allowed Britain and America to adjust their differences' (ibid., p. 435).

[32] *Türkei* 195, K 178451–2, Kühlmann to Bethmann Hollweg, 26 Mar. 1917, dis. no. 201.

Zionism was 'politically damaging' to German interests. Kühlmann had learned that Elkus had told the Swedish Ambassador that after a successful disengagement from Japan the United States would be in a position to withdraw 40,000 troops from the Philippines and place them at the disposal of the Entente on the Mesopotamian and Syrian fronts. On another occasion Elkus was reported to have stated that the United States Government would press for an autonomous Jewish settlement in Palestine and freedom of immigration, in order to satisfy the influential Jewish circles.[33] This information was based on hearsay and, as Kühlmann himself later discovered, was incorrect.[34]

It is of interest to note that it was Zimmermann who had first demanded that Talaat should adhere to his promise and sever relations with the United States if war between Germany and America were to break out. This he insisted was of the 'utmost importance . . . if only to prove to the enemy the undoubted solidarity of the Turco-German Alliance'.[35] That there was a certain contradiction between this objective and his wish to bring about a pro-Zionist declaration, which presumably would have improved American–Turkish relations, did not strike him. By pointing out this inconsistency Kühlmann put his finger on the weakest spot of Zimmermann's arguments and thereby frustrated the Zionists' move.

The declaration was shelved;[36] even so, Zimmermann did not accept Kühlmann's conclusion *in toto*. In spite of altered conditions Zionism still had some value, if only negative. Zimmermann explained his policy:

In consideration of the mood of international Jewry in enemy and neutral countries, especially in America, we have since the beginning of the war shown our willingness to meet Zionism half-way, on an *ad hoc* basis, without committing ourselves to it. We have thereby been able to keep it within a framework, which was compatible with our own and Turkey's interests. Even now if it is only of a minor benefit to us, it would

---

[33] *Türkei* 195, K 178441, K 178454-5, Kühlmann to A.A., 27, 28 Mar. 1917, tels. nos. 400, 411.   [34] Below, p. 305.

[35] Zimmermann to Kühlmann, 1 Apr. 1917, *A.A.A., Deutschland,* Nr. 128, no. 5 secr. *Verhandlungen mit der Türkei über die Erweiterung des Bündnisvertrages,* Bd. 7. There must have been an earlier instruction to this effect, as Kühlmann refers to this matter in his dispatch of 26 Mar. 1917.

[36] Göppert, who was in charge of the Zionist matters at the Ministry, conveyed its decision to Jacobson verbally (*Türkei* 195, K 178453, note by Göppert).

nevertheless be undesirable to drive Zionism into the ranks of the enemy, as it could harm us and the Turks with its skilful propaganda. We shall, therefore, at any rate, till the end of the war, not alter our attitude towards Zionism. The call-up of Lichtheim would undoubtedly be interpreted by the Zionists as an unfriendly act.

Zimmermann thought it advisable, therefore, that the Military Attaché should revise his decision, especially since he himself had previously recommended to the War Office the further deferment of Lichtheim's call-up.

Against Lichtheim's tact and carefulness there have hitherto been no complaints. Should Lichtheim make himself unpopular through his contact with the American Embassy, a hint from the local Zionist Central Bureau will suffice to make him more reserved.[37]

But Kühlmann would not hear of it. 'Lichtheim's intimacy with Elkus was previously *justified*, but now that Elkus is working more and more openly against us, it is becoming increasingly embarrassing.'[38] Many years later, when in retirement, Kühlmann reflected:

the diplomat abroad is merely the instrument of a policy decided at home. The diplomatic representative abroad can give advice and offer suggestions; but in every instance he must obediently carry out his instructions from the authorities at home, even to the exclusion of his own personal opinion and convictions.[39]

But in fact, as his biographer admitted, 'Kühlmann never was on good terms with the leading men of the Berlin Foreign Office.'[40] This, however, was not the only reason why he found it so 'hard to eradicate . . . the error of confusing diplomacy [with] the direction of foreign policy'.[41] Aware of the military's control of German politics, and that perhaps his own career was very much in the soldiers' hands, he deemed if safer to identify himself more closely with their representatives at the Embassy. The line he advocated is

[37] *Türkei* 195, K 178442–3, (?) Apr. 1917 (no number); cf. Thomas Massaryk's statement: 'In America, as in Europe, the Jews have great influence in the field of journalism; it was highly advantageous to us not to have this Great Power against us' (quoted in Stein, *The Balfour Declaration*, p. 227). For Zimmermann's recommendation for Lichtheim's deferment from military service see K 178476.

[38] *Türkei* 195, K 178463, Kühlmann to A.A., 2 Apr. 1917, tel. no. 423.

[39] Richard von Kühlmann, *Thoughts on Germany*, trans. E. Sutton (London, 1932), p. 69.

[40] Thomas Rhodes, *The Real Kühlmann* (London, 1925), p. 18.

[41] As note 39.

strikingly similar to theirs. At the end of March Hans Humann, the Naval Attaché, reported that Elkus had informed Lichtheim confidentially of the United States determination 'to enforce an autonomy in the Holy Land coupled with freedom of entry of Jews to the Orient'.[42] Humann also learned of Elkus's representations to the Turkish Government to prevent the forcible evacuation of the Jews from Palestine and the destruction of their property, should the British continue to advance, adding that, 'above all Djavid Bey, the Jewish [*sic!*] Finance Minister is urging a moderate attitude towards the Americans'. These data made Humann conclude:

I am of the opinion that the local German Zionist representatives constitute at present a political perhaps even a military danger because they work in closest possible contact and intimacy with the American Embassy . . . On the one hand the international cohesion of Jewry, on the other hand the interests of the United States, influenced by Jewish high finance and directed to the interests of the Jewish element in Palestine are coming out crudely into the open . . . The activities of the German Zionist representatives are likely to compromise the direction and aims of our policy here in the eyes of the Turks.[43]

General von Lossow forwarded an identical report to the General Headquarters. It prompted General Ludendorff to inquire of the Foreign Ministry what action had been taken to combat 'the military danger' to which the Military Attaché had referred.[44] It was at this moment that Kühlmann chose to kill the idea of the Jewish Legion. He wrote:

The political aspect of Dr. Haas's plan perpetuated the Zionist wishes to gain concessions in Palestine. The Jewish Legions are to fight [there] on condition that they and their families would be allowed free immigration, acquisition of land and the Jewish settlements granted autonomy . . . The Turkish Government is actively suspicious of this idea and is unwilling to make any concessions to Zionist wishes. In view of the military situation in Palestine the moment is most unfavourable for the implementation of this idea.[45]

[42] *Türkei* 195, K 178466, Humann to Admiralty; to Chief of Naval Staff; to Foreign Minister, 31 Mar. 1917, tel. no. 573 (very secret).
[43] Ibid. K 178469–70, Humann to Chief of Admiralty; to Foreign Secretary, 2 Apr. 1917, tel. no. 610 (very secret).
[44] Ibid. K 178471, Lersner to A.A., 7 Apr. 1917, tel. no. 442. Lersner was the liaison officer of the Foreign Ministry with the Supreme Command.
[45] Ibid. K 178475, Kühlmann to Bethmann Hollweg, 6 Apr. 1917, dis. no. 236.

Zimmermann was taken aback. Although independent, he could not afford to antagonize the military and, following Ludendorff's intervention, decided to drop his recommendation for Lichtheim's deferment. The Zionist Executive was told that 'in spite of complete understanding . . . for the loss incurred', in view of the shortage of manpower, only those individuals whose service was indispensable to the interests of the state could be exempted from the service. Dr. Haas was also notified that the Embassy did not think it advisable to pursue his project.[46]

The Embassy triumphed over the Foreign Ministry. Yet the premiss on which its arguments rested was faulty. It is strange that a sagacious and able diplomat like Kühlmann could have believed the rumours that the United States intended to launch a military offensive in Syria and Mesopotamia, when Turco-American friendship was reaching its zenith. Of this Kühlmann was undoubtedly aware. On 13 February Talaat himself told him that Elkus had been instructed 'to maintain diplomatic relations with Turkey'.[47] Several weeks later Kühlmann concluded that the United States did not intend to declare war on Turkey just because the latter had broken off diplomatic relations. To resolve the contradiction between this and two earlier dispatches Kühlmann shifted the blame to the American Embassy. 'All that Elkus and his helpmates have spread about this is plain bluff.'[48]

Kühlmann's contention that Elkus engaged in anti-German propaganda is not supported by any available evidence. Quite the contrary. From his arrival in Constantinople, Elkus, like his predecessor, was most eager to co-operate with the German Embassy, and on 13 February Kühlmann himself reported that Elkus was 'exerting his entire influence to avoid any German–American conflict, which would also result in a breaking off of relations with Turkey'.[49]

More peculiar are Lossow's and Humann's suspicions that Lichtheim's presence in Constantinople constituted 'a political,

---

[46] Ibid. K 178478, Zimmermann to Lersner, 14 Apr. 1917, tel. no. 625; K 178477, same to E.A.C., 12 Apr. 1917; K 178498, same to Haas, 23 Apr. 1917.

[47] *Official German Documents*, ii, 13 Feb. 1917, tel. no. 183; above, pp. 282–3, 285–6.

[48] *Türkei* 190, Kühlmann to A.A., 20 May 1917, tel. no. (?). The Kaiser scrawled the following marginalia: 'Typically Anglo-Saxon . . .'.

[49] *Official German Documents*, ii, p. 1330, Kühlmann to A.A., tel. no. 183. That America did not desire war with Germany was confirmed also by Bernstorff (Washington, 10 Feb.), Rosen (The Hague, 14 Feb.), and Romberg (Berne, 21 Feb. 1917) (ibid., pp. 1330–1).

perhaps even a military danger'. Lichtheim never made any secret of his contacts with the American Embassy and, following the rupture of German–American relations, he took great pains to acquaint the German Embassy of the nature of his dealings with the Americans. Significantly, the Germans raised no specific objections to this. At the end of March, when he appealed to Count Waldburg for German intervention to forestall the possibility of the evacuation of Jews from Palestine, Waldburg appeared reluctant to take any steps and advised him to turn to the United States Embassy instead. Lichtheim replied that the Americans had always supported Jewish interests but, in view of the situation, he thought it inadvisable to do so, as they 'reckoned almost with certainty on the outbreak of war with Germany'.[50] Ironically, the interview took place two or three days after Humann's report had been written.

There is no evidence from any available source to confirm Humann's contention that the United States Government was 'determined to enforce an autonomy in the Holy Land'. His suspicion of 'Jewish high finance' was equally unwarranted. Jacob Schiff was avowedly pro-German and if subsequently he cooled towards Germany it was primarily on account of the unrestricted submarine warfare.[51]

Unlike the Wilhelmstrasse the High Command was seldom guided by political considerations. It had long regarded the United States as a potential enemy. As early as 1 January 1917 General Hindenburg said he was ready 'to meet all eventualities from America',[52] and a week later he told Holtzendorff that he counted on the possibility of war with the United States and had made 'all preparations to meet it'.[53] At the end of March some German officers who had arrived in Constantinople stated that if the United States declared war on Germany, Turkey as Germany's ally would

---

[50] C.Z.A. Z 3/63, Lichtheim to E.A.C., 30 Mar., 2 Apr. 1917 (copies in *Türkei* 195, K 179723-4). On 31 Mar. 1917, following Wilson's address to Congress, Lansing advised Elkus: 'it is possible that a state of war will be declared between the United States and Germany'. (*F.R.U.S.*, 1917, Suppl. 1, p. 191.)

[51] Above, p. 203; Adler, *Jacob Schiff*, ii, pp. 192, 201.

[52] Ludendorff, op. cit. i, pp. 304-6.

[53] Quoted in May, op. cit., p. 414; Walter Görlitz, *The German General Staff*, trans. (London, 1953), p. 186. A characteristic statement was made by von Capelle, the Minister of the Marine, before the Finance Committee of the Reichstag that from the military point of view the effect of America's entering the war was 'practically nil' (Hanssen, op. cit., p. 184, 26 Apr. 1917).

have to declare war against America also.[54] This was why Turco-American flirtations made Humann and Lossow so nervous. They suspected that it was a prelude to Turkey's defection from the camp of the Central Powers, which they were determined to prevent at all costs. Regarding Djavid Bey as 'Jewish'[55] and, aware of his influence over the Grand Vizier, the picture which in the given atmosphere must have emerged in their minds about the Talaat–Elkus–Schiff negotiations[56] was that of a world-Jewish conspiracy designed to wrest Turkey from Germany's hands using Zionism as a lever. Otherwise it is inconceivable that they would have made such a serious charge against Lichtheim. As our narrative shows, there was no substance in their suspicion. Whatever designs might have been simmering in the minds of some Turkish ministers about the possibility of Turkish defection, no Jew was a party to such a scheme. On broader political grounds, both Lichtheim and Jacobson discounted the possibility.[57]

In contrast to the Embassy, the Foreign Ministry never lost confidence in Lichtheim, but, although convinced of his innocence, it was powerless to prevent his removal from Constantinople, on which the attachés were so strenuously insisting. Constitutionally the attachés were under the jurisdiction of the Supreme Command, not of the Ministry, and the former was responsible to the Kaiser alone. This system resulted in a peculiar diarchy which ultimately led to the complete military domination of German politics.[58] In Constantinople General von Lossow must have felt particularly favoured as it was through him that in the spring of 1917 Ludendorff conducted negotiations with the Turks over the head of the Wilhelmstrasse.[59] This was possibly an additional factor accounting for

[54] *F.R.U.S.*, 1917, Suppl. 1, pp. 81–2, 206–7, Elkus to Lansing, 8 Jan., 2 Apr. 1917.

[55] Above, p. 304; Djavid was Dönmeh, see above, p. 151 n. 67.

[56] Above, pp. 282–3.

[57] Above, pp. 287–8. When I was writing this chapter Mr. Lichtheim was ill and not available for comment. He died in Jerusalem on 29 Apr. 1963.

[58] See: Görlitz, op. cit.; Wheeler-Bennett, *The Nemesis of Power: The German Army in Politics 1918–1945* (London, 1953); Gerhard Ritter, *Deutsche Militär-Attachés und das Auswärtige Amt* (Heidelberg, 1959); *idem*, 'The Military and Politics in Germany', *Journal of Central European Affairs*, xvii (Oct. 1957), no. 3; *idem*, 'The Political Attitude of the German Army, 1900–1944', *Studies in Diplomatic History and Historiography in Honour of G. P. Gooch*, ed. A. O. Sarkissan (London, 1961), 331–47; Gordon A. Craig, 'Military Diplomats in the Prussian Army', *Political Science Quarterly*, lxiv (Mar. 1949), 65–94.

[59] Epstein, 'Development of German-Austrian War Aims', 39–40.

Lossow's intractability to the wishes of the Auswärtiges Amt on matters pertaining to Zionism. When Lichtheim returned to Berlin, Göppert reassured him that the Foreign Ministry had always considered his conduct to be 'honest and loyal' but that it was beyond its powers to reinstate him in Constantinople: 'the Supreme Command was omnipotent . . . and Mars held the field.'[60]

Lichtheim was completely unaware of the charges levelled against him. The refusal to extend his deferment from military service dealt a severe blow to the Zionists and late in May, when the news of the evacuation of the Jewish population from Jaffa reached Berlin, the Executive made yet another effort to bring about both his return and that of Ruppin. Zimmermann did not require much persuasion. The Entente was using the evacuation not only to denounce the Turks but also to create 'violent antagonism' against Germany, thereby damaging her standing in neutral countries and in Russia. Zimmermann insisted that 'immediate and determined counter-measures [were] urgently needed' and that a relief service for the evacuees was essential; Lichtheim's presence in Constantinople was indispensable because 'he alone possessed the required understanding of the prevailing conditions and enjoyed the necessary authority among international Jewry'. The War Ministry acceded to the Foreign Minister's appeal to defer Lichtheim's call-up to the army, but the Embassy's objections to his return to Constantinople and that of Ruppin's to Jaffa could not be overcome. To the acting Military Attaché Lichtheim was a security risk, while Ruppin's presence in Palestine was unnecessary: the work of colonization had come to a standstill and the Turks would permit no Zionist activities in the theatre of war.

. . . they have every right to do this . . . I regard it as more important that at the present time, when Germany's military manpower is stretched to the utmost, that Ruppin fulfil his military duty than administer the relief finance. . . . For this purpose the Zionists can find another co-religionist who is not liable for military service.[61]

Earlier Karl von Schabinger, the newly appointed Consul in Jaffa, had warmly recommended Ruppin's further deferment from army service[62] but, like Ludendorff, the acting Attaché was unable

---

[60] Lichtheim, *She'ar Yashuv*, p. 434; *Rückkehr*, p. 369.

[61] *Türkei* 195, K 178708–11, Warburg to A.A., 25 May 1917; K 178713–15, Zimmermann to War Ministry, same date; K 178783, Kühlmann to Bethmann Hollweg, 25 May 1917, dis. no. 2732. On evacuation from Jaffa see below, Ch. 16.

[62] *Türkei* 195, K 178784–5, Schabinger to Kühlmann, 15 Apr. 1917, dis. no. 43/880.

to think except in terms of power. The military leaders in Germany failed to understand the psychology of war.[63] Their zeal to conscript a person like Ruppin demonstrated how ignorant they were that one of the most powerful instruments in modern warfare was propaganda[64] and that in this sphere Germany's adversaries held the upper hand. Zimmermann appreciated this. Following Djemal Pasha's gesture in agreeing to admit a Jewish fact-finding commission to Palestine,[65] he thought that it would be an adroit move if Ruppin were included as the Zionist representative. He wired Kühlmann:

Dr. Ruppin is a renowned expert, who enjoys the confidence of his co-religionists in the enemy and neutral countries. The very fact of his participation would suffice to calm Jewish opinion perturbed by exaggerated reports from Palestine. . . . The evacuation is exploited in the enemy and neutral countries in a violent campaign against us . . . and energetic counter-measures are urgently required. . . . It would be in our interest if Lichtheim also returns to Constantinople. . . . While Ruppin, if permitted by Djemal Pasha, would administer relief work, Lichtheim would supervise the transfer of the relief funds and gold expected from Denmark; his reports, if made from Turkey, would enjoy even greater authority in foreign countries. . . . Report in detail what are the *positive* suspicions against him. . . . Here the military authorities have postponed his call-up. . . . Unless there are very strong reasons . . . I intend to recommend his continued deferment.[66]

Zimmermann found backing at the War Ministry, but Kühlmann stuck to his guns:

The Zionist representative should not be a too prominent personality because, in view of increasing evidence of English and American Zionists' intentions to sever Palestine from Turkey, the Porte has become very suspicious. . . . Any attempt to force Djemal Pasha's hand to accept Ruppin at the present moment would prejudice the chances for his return at a later date.

Zimmermann was not deceived. He felt obliged to lecture the recalcitrant Ambassador that 'as the propaganda campaign abroad

---

[63] Görlitz, op. cit., p. 186; Matthias Erzberger, *Erlebnisse im Weltkrieg* (Berlin, 1919), p. 7. The Deputy Military Attaché's name is not mentioned.
[64] Harold D. Lasswell, *Propaganda Technique in the World War* (New York, 1927), p. 220.   [65] Below, p. 360.
[66] *Türkei* 195, K 178773–5, Zimmermann to Kühlmann, 29 May 1917, tel. no. 527. Since the entry of the United States into the war, the transfer of relief money was made through Denmark and Holland. Owing to depreciation of Ottoman currency, in Palestine in particular, the transactions were made in gold.

continued unabated, Ruppin's participation in the Investigation Committee . . . would have a calming effect', and asked him to sound out Djemal Pasha. But Kühlmann did not give in and rallied General von Lossow to his support. Von Lossow considered Lichtheim's return to Constantinople 'undesirable for reasons of espionage' and thought that 'his anti-Turkish agitation, as a Zionist, caused more damage to Palestinian Jews than profit'. 'Under no circumstances' would he consent to Lichtheim's return.[67] Von dem Bussche-Haddenhausen was not convinced. He feared that, should Ruppin be called up, the Zionist Agency in Constantinople would be closed, and that this would be exploited by the Entente to show that Germany was inimical towards Jewish interests. He insisted that Ruppin was 'irreplaceable'. None the less, Ruppin's chances of returning to Jaffa did not improve. Djemal, as Kühlmann learned later from Brode, had no intention of permitting a team of observers to come to Palestine.[68]

The Zionists were dissatisfied. Warburg pointed out that Lichtheim's removal from his post did a disservice to German interests. Had the cable from Palestine describing the evacuation not been suppressed by the Embassy,[69] he would have been able to invoke Germany's intervention in good time; at least to learn the facts and be in a position to rebut the exaggerated reports published in the foreign Press. Lichtheim had not overstepped his terms of reference; his relationship with Elkus, Warburg maintained, was confined principally to matters of relief, on which he had briefed the German Embassy 'regularly and with precision'. Failure to effect Lichtheim's and Ruppin's return would undermine confidence in Germany's goodwill and weaken the influence of the German Zionists. Moreover, Chief Rabbi Nahoum demonstrated that the welfare of the Palestinian Jews did not concern the Zionists alone. He had authorized Lichtheim to administer the relief funds on account of his experience and standing in the Jewish world, and

[67] *Türkei* 195, K 178831, Zimmermann to W.O., 1 June 1917; K 178858–9, Kühlmann to A.A., 1 July 1917, tel. no. 675; K 178869, Zimmermann to Kühlmann, 3 June 1917, tel. no. 551; K 178952, Kühlmann to Bethmann Hollweg, 7 June 1917, dis. no. 323 (secret).

[68] Ibid. K 178971–2, Bussche to Kühlmann, 16 June 1917, tel. no. 596; K 178966–7, K 178982, Kühlmann to A.A., 13, 17 June 1917, tel. nos. 708, 726.

[69] It appears that not only Dr. Thon's telegrams were suppressed but also transfer of the consular reports to Berlin was greatly delayed. It was only when the Entente Press reported the evacuation that the Auswärtiges Amt became aware of it (below, pp. 353–4, 360).

also because he was badly needed in Constantinople for political reasons. Here Warburg disclosed that shortly before his departure Lichtheim had been successful in getting into close touch with Djavid Bey and another influential member of the Ottoman Government. So keen was Djavid for Lichtheim's return that he had invited him officially to discuss financial matters which were only a cover for political negotiations with leading Turkish statesmen on Zionist affairs. This, Warburg stressed, 'might prove to be of extraordinary importance for the shaping of our political future'.[70]

As if to prove Warburg right, on 13 July the Ottoman Embassy in Berlin requested the Auswärtiges Amt to enable Lichtheim to travel speedily to Constantinople, where he was expected for 'an important mission'. Two days later Edham Bey, the Turkish Ambassador, himself repeated the request on Djavid's behalf to secure Lichtheim's immediate departure.[71] Such an unprecedented move gave the matter a new complexion. How highly the Turkish Note was valued may be judged from the fact that the Chancellor endorsed it. The Ministry lost no time in briefing the Embassy on Djavid's wishes to discuss 'questions of Jewish immigration' with Lichtheim, adding that the Military Attaché's suspicions were dubious since Lichtheim's visits to the American Embassy were presumably misunderstood by officials who were 'insufficiently acquainted with the matter'.[72] But Kühlmann evaded the issue and instead forwarded a copy of Ephraim Cohn-Reiss's letter of 16 May 1915, considering it be to 'still valid'. In this letter, written at the height of the Hilfsverein's controversy with the Zionists, Cohn-Reiss referred to his opponents as 'internationalists', who had 'an extraordinary arrogance to pretend that they would further German *Kultur*'. However, Kühlmann's attempt to revive the arguments which had been long buried by his predecessors made no impact in Berlin. The Under-Secretary of State reiterated the urgency of Lichtheim's journey and pointed to the Turkish Embassy's *démarche*. All the same, the acting Military Attaché refused 'categorically' to grant the necessary travel permit.[73]

---

[70] *Türkei* 195, K 179096–100, K 179143–5, Warburg to A.A., 29 June, 12 July 1917.
[71] Ibid. K 179162, *Note verbale* (French), 13 July 1917; K 179168, Menemenlizade Edhem to Zimmermann, 15 July 1917.
[72] Ibid. K 179159–61, Bussche to Kühlmann, 13 July 1917, dis. no. 636 (*immediately*).
[73] Ibid. K 179172, Kühlmann to Bethmann Hollweg, 10 July, dis. no. 374; K 179180, Bussche to Kühlmann, 18 July, tel. no. 749; Kühlmann to A.A., 20 July 1917, tel. no. 862.

A few days later Kühlmann was recalled to Berlin to become Foreign Secretary, but did not take up office before mid August. Waldburg's position as Chargé d'Affaires was relatively weaker than Kühlmann's and consequently, at the Foreign Ministry's request, he approached Djavid Bey. Djavid told Waldburg that unless overriding military doubts existed he would have liked to see his wish realized, and that Ottoman Jews and the Chief Rabbi had expressed a similar desire. Zimmermann reacted unequivocally:

> The Zionist Executive expects that Lichtheim's return to Constantinople would strengthen pro-German and pro-Turkish influence within international Zionism. They hope that discussions with Djavid Bey might become a turning-point in Turkish policy towards the Zionist movement.

Dissatisfied with the Embassy's procrastination, he reiterated his request to report 'in detail' about the actual reasons for suspecting Lichtheim since he 'must be given an opportunity to refute them'. The acting Military Attaché, however, contented himself with the stereotype statement that because of Lichtheim's intimacy with the American Embassy after the severance of German–American relations and 'in view of the widespread American espionage, the entry permit cannot be given'.[74] The Ministry had little choice but to concede its inability to overrule the Attaché and the Zionists had to content themselves with permission for Lichtheim to continue his political work in Berlin, while Ruppin administered the Agency in Constantinople.

The Wilhelmstrasse remained sensitive to Jewish opinion. 'In view of the inflammatory propaganda spread by the Entente, a counter-propaganda among Jews in the neutral countries is necessary', reads its instruction to Hellmuth von Lucius, the German Envoy in Stockholm. The Legation reported regularly on the mood in the Jewish community in Sweden and Norway and kept a close watch over events in Russia. That the All-Zionist Conference, which took place on 6 June in Petrograd, avoided any anti-German resolution was good news, particularly since the forthcoming Zionist conference in Stockholm coincided with the meeting of the Socialist

---

[74] *Türkei* 195, K 179259, K 179274, Waldburg to A.A., 27, 31 July 1917, tel. nos. 885, 888; K 179263–4, Zimmermann to Waldburg, 29 July 1917, tel. no. 810.

International Conference.[75] The latter had been called at the initiative of the Russian Social Democrats in the hope of finding common ground for peace among the belligerents. It was widely believed that its proceedings would have some repercussions on public opinion in Russia and in Germany.[76] Delegates of the international Zionist Labour party, the Poale Zion, as well as Dr. Tschlenow, the Russian Zionist leader, were to attend both conferences and Zimmermann hoped that Hantke, when in Stockholm, would be able to influence them to support Germany's cause. Zimmermann advised von Lucius that Nissim Matzliach, a member of the Turkish delegation, was a Jew, a fact 'worth keeping in mind should the question of Jewish autonomy in Palestine be discussed'.[77]

Zimmermann's expectations of Hantke were too sanguine. The Zionist Executive was committed to the principle of neutrality, and from the spring of 1917 its influence within the movement declined. Its authority stood in direct relation to Germany's ability to back its cause. America's entry into the war, and the emancipation of Russian Jews following the February/March Revolution, were contributory factors that swayed the Jewish masses towards the Entente. An adviser on Jewish affairs at the German Embassy in Vienna warned that Germany was losing the propaganda battle. Whilst the Provisional Government in Russia was becoming favourably disposed towards the Zionists, the Austrian Government remained indifferent.[78] Romberg, from his vantage-point in Berne, noted 'increasingly daily indications' that the Entente was seeking to win over world Jewry. Their policy was 'very concrete: Jerusalem is to be conquered . . . the Jews are to be given a state under American sovereignty which, linked with the Kingdom of Arabia under

[75] *Gesandtschaft Stockholm. Politisches, 1914–1917, Krieg. Tätigkeit der Zionisten*, HO48405–13, Radowitz to Lucius, 17 May 1917; Kienlin to the Chancellor, 25 July 1917, dis. no. 3008/889. On the Zionist Conference in Petrograd see Friedman, *The Question of Palestine*, pp. 195–6, notes 77, 81, and 84.

[76] Rosenberg, *The Birth of the German Republic*, p. 184; *F.R.U.S.*, 1917, Suppl. 2, i, 738–9, Morris to Lansing, 14 May 1917. On the proposal to hold the International Socialist Conference in Stockholm see Arno J. Mayer, *Political Origins of the New Diplomacy, 1917–1918* (New Haven, Conn., 1959), pp. 125–7, 192–208, 214–41; Julius Braunthal, *History of the International* (New York, 1967), ii, pp. 70–2, 84–7, 91–4.

[77] *Türkei* 195, K 178973, Zimmermann's marginalia on Lucius's dispatch of 15 June 1917; K 179114, A.A. note, 3 July 1917; K 179124–5, A.A. to Chief of Police, 6 July 1917. On Matzliach, see above, pp. 143–4, 148, and on Tschlenow's attitude above, pp. 236–7, and Friedman, op. cit., pp. 195–9, 272, 292.

[78] *Türkei* 195, K 178521–6, Wedel to Bethmann Hollweg, 26 Apr. 1917, dis. no. 128 and encl.; Friedman, 'The Austro-Hungarian Government and Zionism', 153–5.

British auspices, would constitute a defensive barrier for Egypt.' He learned also that Rothschilds, Kuhn & Loeb and Co., and other magnates in the New York Stock Exchange had agreed to large-scale transactions in the Entente's favour, after being categorically assured of support for Jewish claims after the war. An article in the *Retsch* from the pen of the Russian Foreign Minister Miliukov provided additional proof for Romberg that 'by offering the Jewish people a republic in Palestine, the Entente is undoubtedly seeking to achieve a diplomatic success of the first order . . . '. He urged Berlin:

it would be a good thing if Germany too were able to show her goodwill in solving the Zionist problem on a large scale . . . I appreciate the resistance of the Turkish Government to such a radical solution but, should it be possible to reassure the Jews officially of the creation of a Jewish reservation in Palestine under Turkish sovereignty . . . the harmful impression made by the Entente moves will be neutralized . . . the land itself will greatly benefit, Poland would rid itself of her [Jewish] proletariat and we shall regain valuable sympathies everywhere, particularly in America.[79]

Dr. Friedrich Rosen, the Minister to The Hague, thought differently. In his opinion the Jewish national movement had 'very little inherent impetus'. Essentially it was an Entente enterprise, and Britain in particular was making very skilful use of the Russian Revolution and of Zionism to win new international allies. He added:

Experience of many years has shown that the Jewish [national] movement abroad does not serve the German cause but that of our enemies. The Dutch Jews in particular are overwhelmingly opposed to Germany and if the Zionists [in Holland] are adopting an attitude of strict neutrality, their only purpose is to win over Germany to their plans at the future Peace Conference. Their main concern, however, is the foundation of a Jewish State in Palestine. Such a state could be carved out only from the flesh of our Turkish allies and, if founded, would certainly come under the protection of one or several Powers unfriendly to Turkey and ourselves. Quite apart from the political undesirability of the consequences of such a situation, it would be a matter of shame for the whole of Christendom if the Holy Places . . . were to come under Jewish sovereignty.[80]

---

[79] *Türkei* 195, K 178532–4, Romberg to Bethmann Hollweg, 28 Apr. 1917, dis. no. 1251 and encl.

[80] Ibid. K 178539–45, Rosen to Bethmann Hollweg, 3 May 1917, dis. no. A 1756. In 1899–1900 Rosen served as consul in Jerusalem.

In spite of their diametrically opposed conclusions Romberg and Rosen were alike victims of British propaganda. Though it is true that the British regarded the Jewish National Home as a stepping-stone towards a Jewish state,[81] it was erroneous to assume that they intended to offer the Jews a ready-made 'republic' immediately after the war. Nor did the Jews entertain any aspirations to sovereignty over the Christian and Muslim Holy Places,[82] as Rosen suspected. Whether the Jewish national movement had 'very little inherent impetus' was a matter of opinion, but certainly it was not a product of the Entente or of Britain. Zionism was an international movement which aimed to solve an international problem and sought support from all the Powers. That Weizmann and his friends were British-orientated did not reflect on the Executive; till the end of the war it remained internationally minded and neutral.

A week had hardly elapsed when Rosen modified his views. Reviewing the Press he realized that Britain was 'not entirely in favour of . . . an extreme Zionism in the form of a Jewish National State', and that, to avoid a clash with France, and perhaps to sweeten the pill for the Turks, the British had suggested an American protectorate over a neutral Palestine. Excluding the possibility of a German protectorate, Rosen now hit upon the idea of declaring Palestine to be neutral which, he thought, might win international support.[83]

While the debate among German diplomats raged, Zionism was making rapid strides in the Entente countries. David Weinbaum, a Swiss Zionist, told Hermann von Simson, the Legation Secretary, about Weizmann's statement (of 16 May) that the British Government was ready to support the Zionist plans, that Sokolow had been well received in Paris and Rome, and that Lord Rothschild and Jacob Schiff had come down on the Zionist side. Since the question of Palestine was bound to come before the future Peace Conference, Weinbaum thought it desirable that the Central Powers, especially Germany, issue a general non-binding declaration to the effect that they were prepared to allow the Jews free access to Palestine, to build a cultural-autonomous entity there as an integral part of the Turkish State. He was convinced that such a gesture would gain for

---

[81] Friedman, op. cit., ch. 18.

[82] Above, pp. 69, 79, 112.

[83] *Türkei* 195, K 178584–7, Rosen to Bethmann Hollweg, 10 May 1917, dis. no. A 1857.

the Central Powers the sympathies of Jews throughout the world, whereas failure to make it would turn them to whichever side would promise them the fulfilment of their hopes.[84]

Much perturbed by this report, Göppert invited Lichtheim to the Foreign Ministry and told him how damaging for Germany's cause Weizmann's and Sokolow's moves were. Lichtheim, who in the meantime had taken charge of the Political and Propaganda Department of the Zionist Executive in Berlin, replied that the activities of his colleagues in London could not be stopped and that, if the Central Powers wished to counter the Entente, the only suitable means was to further Zionism as their adversaries did. He added that the Executive was about to submit a memorandum: this Göppert wished to obtain urgently, as on the following day he intended to present a comprehensive report to the State Secretary.[85]

In this memorandum the Zionists argued that the Turks were slow to realize that their policy was both contrary to the spirit of the times and in the long run self-defeating. The Ottoman Empire was by no means homogeneous, either ethnically or socially. And it was furthermore inconceivable that the seven million Anatolian peasants would, in the foreseeable future, be able to supersede the non-Turkish elements which were both culturally and economically superior. The failure of the Turkish Government to revitalize the moribund Empire, to accumulate capital, and, above all, to win the confidence of non-Turkish minorities, made the interference of foreign Powers in Turkey's internal affairs all the easier, but worst of all was the regime of oppression. It invited Turkey's own destruction. Because the Young Turks had brought upon themselves the hatred of the majority of the population they could not survive indefinitely. If Germany was interested in the viability of Turkey, she must see to it that 'valuable elements such as the Armenians, Arabs, Greeks, and Jews be not sacrificed to the chauvinism of the Young Turks'.

As for Jewish colonization in Palestine, was it not ludicrous to suppress civilizing activities in a country inhabited by no more than 600,000 Arabs, where not a single Turk was living, and which by

[84] *Türkei* 195, K 179007–8, Bethmann Hollweg (Legation Counsellor and the Chancellor's cousin) to Bethmann Hollweg, 19 May 1917, dis. no. 1891. For Weizmann's statement see Stein, op. cit., pp. 450–1 (reproduced also in *Bulletin Juif* (Berne, 6 July 1917), and for Sokolow's moves in Paris and Rome, Stein, ch. 27; Friedman, op. cit., ch. 9.

[85] C.Z.A. Z 3/13, minutes of Lichtheim's meeting with Geheimrat Göppert in the Auswärtiges Amt on 23 June 1917.

intensive cultivation could support an additional three million inhabitants? Should not the creation of such 'a cultural oasis in the midst of deserts be welcomed by any government of foresight, on both political and economic grounds?' Did not the fact of being surrounded by an overwhelming majority of Arabs in the neighbour- ing countries guarantee inviolably the inherent loyalty of the Jewish settlement to the Central Government? The Jews were always pro-Turkish but the ill-treatment meted out to their people in Palestine and the dangerous measures of evacuation had gravely undermined their confidence. The Zionist movement struck deep roots among Jewish communities in the United States, Britain, Russia, and elsewhere and colonization of Palestine was not the concern of 'a party'. It was:

a religious and national expression of the cravings of a vast majority of Jewish people . . . The Turkish Government is not in a position to strangle this mighty movement . . . whereas the Jews cannot and will not renounce their peaceful and civilized work. . . . To live and work in their ancient homeland . . . is a right that the civilized world cannot deny them. . . . Nor should Turkey ignore it. Jewish colonization in no way endan- gered Turkish interests; the Zionists had always protested that their ambitions could be realized within the framework of Turkish law and sovereignty.

It was essential that the evacuees from Jaffa should be speedily repatriated, that regulations forbidding freedom of immigration and colonization be rescinded, and that local authorities be instructed to display a friendlier attitude. Should Turkey revise her policy, Jewish public opinion would be mollified and the campaign waged in the Entente countries for the dismemberment of the Ottoman Empire greatly weakened. It lay therefore in Germany's interests as well that Turkey should alter her policy.[86]

Zionist criticism of Turkey's internal policy re-echoed that of Djavid Bey, aired in the Turkish Parliament three months before.[87] It also foreshadowed President Wilson's speech on 8 January 1918 in which he advocated that the non-Turkish nationalities 'under Turkish rule *should* be assured an undoubted security of life and an absolutely unmolested opportunity of autonomous development . . .'.[88]

[86] *Türkei* 195, K 179059–68, E.A.C. to A.A., memorandum, dated 24 June 1917, signed by Hantke. On the role played by non-Turkish minorities in the Ottoman Empire see Mears (ed.), *Modern Turkey*, pp. 60–97.   [87] Above, pp. 286–7.
[88] Point 12 of the celebrated fourteen points made by President Wilson in his speech on 8 Jan. 1918 (Bemis, op. cit., p. 626).

But these ideas were far too advanced for Turkish statesmen and attempts to implant them through Germany's mediation were doomed to failure; not because the diagnosis of Turkey's ills was faulty, or the medicine prescribed wrong. Had the Young Turks been gifted with foresight, they would have realized that in order to deprive the Entente of its trump card and prevent partition concessions to non-Turkish nationalities were needed.

By contrast, Germany showed greater flexibility towards the people in the German-occupied territories of Belgium, Poland, Lithuania, and Kurland. With the principle of self-determination asserting itself, she modified her policy of annexation into a more elastic method of 'combination' (*Angliederung*), although this was merely a convenient stratagem to exercise power indirectly.[89] But the Turks, who were not noted for their flexibility, did not follow this pattern. The Porte's principal concern was to secure, with German–Austrian guarantees, the territorial integrity of the Empire and the abolition of the Capitulations. Relaxation of the centralized system of government never came under serious consideration. Autonomy was repugnant; in the past it had constituted a perennial cause for intervention by foreign Powers and ran completely counter to Turkish policy. Germany could not demur for since America's entry into the war she was anxious, both for 'considerations of prestige' and the necessity 'to keep the Quadruple Alliance intact', to prevent Turkey's defection 'at all costs'. This basic fact underlined the Wilhelmstrasse's weakness *vis-à-vis* the Porte. Hence the inclination to accede to 'all Turkish demands in the hope that when peace came to be negotiated, the Ottoman Government would voluntarily forego them', realizing that insistence on their fulfilment would involve a continuation of the war.[90] 'The Turks are used to promises made by European Powers being unfulfilled' was Kühlmann's[91] comment on the eve of Talaat's negotiations in Berlin, a statement which does not speak for its author's honesty, and suggests that Germany had perhaps no option but to follow the line of least resistance. In these circumstances to assume the role of Turkey's mentor, as the Zionists desired, was for Germany unthinkable. Had the desired negotiations between Djavid Bey and Lichtheim[92] reached a favourable

---

[89] Fischer, op. cit., p. 577.   [90] Bernstorff, *Memoirs*, p. 154.
[91] *Deutschland* 128, no. 5, Bd. 7, Kühlmann to A.A., 20 Apr. 1917.
[92] Above, p. 311.

conclusion, Germany would perhaps have been able to follow suit. As nothing materialized, Germany's goodwill remained sterile.

This explains Jacobson's failure to obtain the desired German–Turkish declaration. Zimmermann's cryptic note to Count Brock-dorff-Rantzau, the Minister to Copenhagen, to whom Jacobson had intended to turn for support, is indicative. The Minister was instructed to tell the Zionist leader, 'in a friendly way', that his plan was for the time being 'not practicable'.[93] Nor was Romberg more successful. He pressed Berlin that 'in view of the Entente's increasing endeavours to win over the Zionist movement completely' Germany should pay 'greater attention and, in all circumstances, prevent this exceedingly influential body from going over to the enemy camp'.[94]

This apprehension was, to a lesser extent, shared by the German Zionists. In February 1917 the Executive was powerful enough to oust Dr. Pincus from his chairmanship of the Swiss Zionist Organization because of his indiscretions in making some pro-Entente statements,[95] but during the later months of the year its influence seemed to be waning. Although encouraged by news that their colleagues in the Entente countries were making headway, the German Zionists feared that unless the Central Powers strengthened their hands their leadership would eventually be forfeited. The forthcoming conference in Copenhagen with delegates from neutral and allied countries[96] presented a serious challenge, while rumours about the possibility of peace[97] added an element of urgency. As the Foreign Ministry did not respond to its memorandum of 24 June the Executive wrote to the Ministry again warning that 'the Entente Governments were prepared to a considerable degree to meet Jewish wishes'. The British Government, Warburg pointed out, was aiming at the establishment of a British Protectorate over Palestine

[93] *Türkei* 195, K 179131, Zimmermann to Brockdorff-Rantzau, 10 July 1917, tel. no. 526. Jacobson could not meet the Count. However, see below, p. 336.

[94] Ibid. K 179226–9, Romberg to the Chancellor, 17 July 1917, dis. no. 2174. Bethmann Hollweg resigned on 13 July 1917.

[95] Ibid. K 178288–9, A.A. note on Jacobson's oral report. Pincus's statement was published in the *Israelitisches Wochenblatt für die Schweiz* (5 Jan. 1917).

[96] Below, pp. 322–6.

[97] 'I gather from the . . . press and reports . . . that there is a widespread opinion at home that the war will end this autumn at the latest.' (Hindenburg to the Chancellor, 19 June 1917, Ludendorff, op. cit. ii, p. 446.) For the text of the Peace Resolution adopted by the Reichstag on 19 July 1917, see ibid., pp. 475–6; also *F.R.U.S.*, 1917, Suppl. 2, i, pp. 139–40; Gatzke, op. cit., p. 199. On Erzberger's role see Gatzke, p. 166, and Epstein, op. cit., pp. 182–213.

but, encountering French opposition, it was making use of Zionism to outmanœuvre it. Britain's motives were political, idealistic, and economic; through a large-scale Jewish colonization she hoped to be able to create a self-supporting British-dominated Palestine. The French Government, initially ill-informed on Zionism and generally reserved towards it, 'has declared herself recently prepared to recognize Jewish aspirations'. In Italy and in official Catholic circles a radical change had also taken place. The Provisional Government in Russia was favourably disposed, and the Government of the United States 'extremely friendly'. However, Warburg assured the Auswärtiges Amt that in spite of the Entente's efforts to win over the sympathies and material resources of Jewry

the Zionist adherents throughout the world, neither in the past, nor at present have been willing to place their Movement at the service of one Power or group of Powers. Nor did they wish to take sides in the world conflict.

This was inconsistent with the international character of Zionism, whose sole aim was to create a secure and legal basis for an unimpeded colonization of Palestine.

The nature of the administration, to which Palestine would be subject in the future, could not be foreseen. Jewish nationals of the Central Powers were taking the view that it was an integral part of Turkey and formulated their programme solely on that premiss. That British Jews prefer a British-protected Palestine 'is understandable'. None the less, if the British Zionists refrained from advancing 'exaggerated claims' it was only because they too had to reckon with a possibility of Palestine remaining under Turkish sovereignty. The same applied to the American and Russian Zionists. Warburg recalled the principle that had been laid down by Tschlenow, that 'Jews all over the world ought to preserve the strictest loyalty to their Governments and . . . that the Zionists must take heed of the fact that Palestine is Turkish territory'. The Zionist question, he concluded, had assumed world-wide political dimensions and in the circumstances the Central Powers, in their own interests, should break the Entente's monopoly.[98]

Warburg wrote with his characteristic candour and insight. The information contained in his memorandum was essentially accurate but he was unaware how deeply the British Zionists were involved

---

[98] *Türkei* 195, K 179201–21, E.A.C. to Göppert, 22 July 1917, encl. Warburg's memorandum of the same date.

at that time, and that already in April Weizmann was 'anchored firmly' to Great Britain.[99] How ignorant the German Zionists were might be deduced from the fact that Weizmann's election as President of the British Zionist Federation was welcomed by Jacobson as 'victory for the Berlin Executive', an opinion that tallied with that held in Swiss Zionist circles.[100] It is worth mentioning that shortly before the outbreak of the war Weizmann had been half inclined to accept a pressing invitation to join the Zionist Central Office in Berlin,[101] a fact that might have accounted for the misapprehension. Yet no matter how plausibly Warburg might have argued his case the German Government would not go beyond passive benevolence. When Hantke called on the Foreign Ministry he was told that 'in principle, there was no change in the Imperial Government's attitude towards Zionism' and that, 'so far as the general political conditions will permit, the interests of the Jews in Turkey [i.e. Palestine] will be supported' as hitherto.[102] But the issue of the declaration was not discussed.

With this general statement the members of the Executive had to be content before departing for their conference in Copenhagen.

[99] Stein, op. cit., pp. 336–7.

[100] *Türkei* 195, K 178288–9, A.A. note on Jacobson's oral report (undated); K 179226–9, Romberg to the Chancellor, 17 July 1917, dis. no. 2174.

[101] Stein, op. cit., p. 117.

[102] *Türkei* 195, K 179290–1, A.A. note on a conversation with Hantke (undated, presumably end of July).

15

The Renewed Effort Fails

THE meeting of the Zionist Executive took place in Copenhagen from 29 to 31 July 1917.[1] It was attended by Warburg, Hantke, Tschlenow, and Goldberg.[2] Tschlenow represented the Russian Zionists, whilst Goldberg, although himself a Russian, was empowered to speak on behalf of the British. The latter avoided direct relations with their colleagues in Berlin and Copenhagen and used Goldberg in various missions as their roving ambassador. Goldberg's intention was to secure the Executive's approval for the policy initiated in London. At a public meeting in Copenhagen on 10 July he made the challenging statement that unlike the German Zionists, who were bound to limit their programme to relatively modest claims, Zionists in England were negotiating with their Government on an 'equal footing'.[3] But it was at the confidential meeting of the Executive that he showed his hand when requesting that the Russian and American Zionists support Weizmann's and Sokolow's programme, euphemistically termed 'the demands'.[4] Although there was nothing specific in these 'demands' pointing to any preference in respect of the future ruler of Palestine, the inference drawn was that it would be Britain. Goldberg was at pains not to mention the Executive by name, thereby obliquely questioning

[1] The following section is based on the minutes of this meeting, C.Z.A. L 6/64/I, unless quoted otherwise.

[2] Warburg's and Hantke's trip to Copenhagen had been approved by the Auswärtiges Amt (*Türkei* 195, K 179253, 25 July 1917). Jacobson was ill, Shmarya Levin remained in the United States for the duration of the war, and Sokolow would not attend. Lichtheim did not go to Copenhagen, as erroneously stated by Stein, *The Balfour Declaration*, p. 440.

[3] *Jüdische Korrespondenz*, Nr. 7 (Aug. 1917), cutting in *Türkei* 195, K 179307.

[4] For the draft of these 'demands' see Stein, op. cit., p. 369. It was in this document that the term 'Jewish National Home' was first introduced into British political vocabulary.

its authority, but when Tschlenow made his consent conditional on the approval of that body, it became evident that the approval of Warburg and Hantke was necessary to give official sanction to Sokolow's and Weizmann's activities.

When Hantke took the floor it became clear that Goldberg's mission would have a rough passage. Though unable to point to any diplomatic achievement comparable to that of the London Bureau, he freely criticized their 'demands'; they were too moderate and approached the British orbit too closely. Nor did they offer any guarantee that the Jews would have a decisive voice in the shaping of Palestine's future. Weizmann's statements aroused vain hopes and bore no relation to the factual achievements. 'All in all', Hantke complained, 'Weizmann and Sokolow have acted too independently and consulted neither the Executive nor the Committee in The Hague.'

The divergence was resolved when Tschlenow declared that in principle he accepted the 'demands' on the understanding that to correct the balance parallel assurances must be elicited from the Central Powers as well. This would conform to the Basle Programme, which aimed to solve the Jewish problem openly and with the support of all Powers concerned. Tschlenow dismissed the Dutch Zionists' formula of a Jewish state as impractical. Such a state, under the prevailing conditions, he maintained, even if under the protection of a foreign Power, would violate the principle of democracy and would provoke opposition from the Arabs. The Russian Zionists were anxious that the right of the Jewish people to a national home in Palestine should be recognized at the future Peace Conference, and that unrestricted colonization should be internationally guaranteed 'irrespective of the Arab majority'. If Palestine remained under Turkish sovereignty, they wanted one Power or a group of Powers to be appointed as Trustees of the Jewish National Home. The Russian Government could be relied on to give its support. Prince Lwow, when Prime Minister, his Foreign Minister Miliukov, and other Ministers were ready to issue a declaration of sympathy similar to that given to Sokolow by both the French and the Italian Government; if he had not rushed to accept it, this was because he hoped to obtain a better formula, expressed in more concrete terms. He felt justified in temporizing because he had received positive assurances that when the question of Palestine was discussed at the forthcoming Inter-Allied War Aims Conference in Petrograd, Zionist representatives would be consulted. The Provisional Government under Kerensky was no less favourably disposed to the Zionist cause than its predecessor, and the strongly worded protest of the Entente Powers lodged at Tereshchenko's suggestion against the Turkish policy of evacuation was encouraging.

The Zionists' influence made itself felt on the domestic scene, too. It was thanks to their energetic intercession that the Edict of Emancipation of 21 March 1917 was not shelved. However, the Edict did not do away with anti-Semitism altogether. Virulent anti-Jewish propaganda was still much in evidence, especially in military circles and among the landlords who resented the increasing Jewish participation in the ranks of the Maximalists, known later as the Bolsheviks. Thus in spite of the liberal regime the nightmare of pogroms still hovered over Russian Jewry. This was an extra spur to the spectacular expansion of the Zionist movement. Even the extreme assimilationists, Tschlenow continued, had not found the courage to oppose Jewish national demands. The attitude of the Jewish masses 'surpassed all expectations'. The youth, in particular, was gripped by the Zionist idea. The number of the *shekel* payers rose from 25,000 in 1916 to 140,000 after the March Revolution.[5]

The reports of Goldberg and Tschlenow were reassuring. The declared principle of the belligerent Powers to meet the aspirations of the small nationalities was a contributory factor that inspired optimism. The Zionist leaders felt that for the first time since the outbreak of the war conditions were ripe for the realization of the Basle Programme. To keep the balance it was unanimously decided that parallel to the political work in the Entente countries, a similar effort should be made in Berlin, Vienna, Sofia, and Constantinople in order to solicit the support of the Central Powers. The diplomatic offensive was to be accompanied by a campaign of enlightenment. To effect this it was decided that a committee comparable with the British Palestine Committee[6] should be formed in Germany by Warburg and Hantke. Names of staunch Zionist friends, such as Professor Ballod, Professor Auhagen, Dr. Paquet, Major Endres, Ludwig Quessel, and even that of State Secretary Zimmermann were mentioned. The committee was to publish a periodical and

---

[5] Cf. statistics: Stein, op. cit., p. 339; Friedman, *The Question of Palestine*, p. 178. On the *shekel* see above, p. 127 n. 15.

[6] On which see Stein, op. cit., pp. 299, 301, 303, 376–7, 539.

keep public opinion informed on Zionist and Jewish affairs. Hantke was entrusted with the task of revitalizing the sister organization in Austria-Hungary, which had been inactive since the outbreak of the war. The representation of the Poale Zion at the forthcoming Socialist Conference in Stockholm was also discussed. Their delegates were to be advised to demand 'recognition of the right of the Jewish people to a national concentration in Palestine' and 'recognition of Palestine as an independent Jewish territory'.[7]

The phrasing conspicuously skirted the question of the future sovereignty of Palestine but the addenda to the resolutions shed some light on the Executive's thinking. They provided that the Jewish settlement 'should not be a part of the Arab self-administered territory' or its well-being placed at the Arabs' 'mercy'. From this it could be inferred that the Zionist leaders were under the impression that an Arab state, or semi-state, might replace Ottoman sovereignty in the Asiatic provinces after the war. Hence the demand for recognition of Palestine as 'an independent Jewish territory'. This wording runs counter to the proclaimed Zionist policy of realizing their aspirations within the bounds of the Ottoman Empire, but the contradiction is only superficial. With a cloud of uncertainty enveloping Turkey's future, the Executive had to consider an alternative solution. This was why British-oriented Zionism was tacitly allowed to plough its own furrow, even though the movement as a whole had to steer clear of any involvement in power politics, let alone subordination to one of the warring camps. For the German Zionists in particular the programme of a British Protectorate over Palestine was tantamount to political suicide and had to be turned down. Warburg was quite honest when he told the Auswärtiges Amt on his return to Berlin that the international character of the Zionist movement remained essentially unaltered. Not only had it not become subservient to Entente

---

[7] In a statement to the Dutch–Scandinavian Socialist Committee (26 July 1917) the leaders of the Poale Zion demanded, amongst other things, creation of conditions to enable the foundation of a Jewish National Homeland in Palestine. This, they maintained, was 'compatible with the principle of democracy . . . and with the interests of the country which was sparsely populated . . . There is a fundamental difference between the Jewish colonization in Palestine and the policy of colonial exploitation and expansion. . . . The Jews are no bearers of colonial policy . . . their aims in Palestine are consistent with the rights of self-determination.' *Jewish Labour Correspondence*, no. 1 (Oct. 1917); also *Jüdische Korrespondenz*, Nr. 11 (Aug. 1917); *Die Judenfrage der Gegenwart, Dokumentensammlung*, hrsg. von Leon Chasanowitsch und Leo Motzkin (Stockholm, 1919), pp. 14–19.

interests, but Germany's continued friendship would be highly valued. The Auswärtiges Amt, he maintained, should secure German interests in the future Jewish colonization in Palestine and foster the influence of the German-led Executive. Hitherto, on the basis of promises made on various occasions, as well as of effective intercessions with the Porte, it had been widely assumed that the German Government was in earnest in its support of Zionist aspirations, but Lichtheim's removal from his post in Constantinople coupled with the failure to reinstate Ruppin in Jaffa had created a certain amount of uneasiness among the Zionists abroad and undermined their confidence in the Berlin leadership.[8]

Warburg's move coincided with Romberg's dispatch warning of the Entente's increasing efforts to win over the Zionists. He thought that the March Revolution in Russia had deprived Germany of her trump card. Jacob Klatzkin, a celebrated Zionist writer and philosopher, had resigned from the editorship of the *Bulletin juif*, which hitherto had taken an anti-Russian line, and the *Jüdische Korrespondenz* had also changed its policy.[9] However, neither Warburg nor Romberg made any impression on the Wilhelmstrasse.

In contrast to official circles, the German Press began to awaken to the importance of the problem. In the 2 May 1917 issue of the *Reichsbote*, a *Junker* weekly, von Dobbeler pointed to the strategic importance of Palestine as a bridge between Asia and Africa. 'By the creation of a Jewish republic England is about to carry out the cleverest of political moves'; it would protect Egypt from the north and form a link with India. England was using Zionism to entrench herself in this vital area, and the Central Powers should appropriate the same weapon. '*The establishment of a Jewish state under Turkish supremacy would be for us a measure of defence, just as the U-boat is the only possible reply to the English blockade.*' Turkey would benefit considerably. 'The Jew is a born colonist and his industry would infuse . . . fresh blood into the enfeebled Ottoman body.' This suited German interests well. Moroever, a Jewish state was desirable out of domestic considerations for, although German Jews were extremely devoted to the fatherland, because of their characteristics they constituted a 'troublesome' problem and were essentially

---

[8] *Türkei* 195, K 179288, Warburg to Göppert, 5 Aug. 1917. A copy, found at the C.Z.A. Z 3/22, is signed by Lichtheim, who apparently had prepared the draft for Warburg.

[9] Ibid. K 179300–2, Romberg to the Chancellor, 7 Aug. 1917, dis. no. 2456.

unassimilable. 'The Jew never ceases to be a Jew, even when he becomes a Christian. The racial element in him can never be eradicated. . . . The establishment of a Jewish state would give these restless people a fresh cohesion and a positive, no longer disintegrating strength.' If successful, the Jews might become intermediaries *par excellence* between Europe, Asia, and Africa.

Von Dobbeler by no means ploughed a lonely furrow. His thesis was re-echoed by the liberal *Vossische Zeitung*. C. A. Bratter, in an article entitled 'The Fight for Palestine' (1 August 1917), agreed that the Zionist movement had assumed 'world-wide political importance' and therefore deserved serious attention. If the Central Powers wished to foil British plans, they should back the German Zionists, who 'have no desire to tear Palestine away from the Turkish Empire'. The *Chemnitzer Volksstimme* (8 August) seconded the *Vossische Zeitung* as did the *Deutsche Warte*, the *Düsseldorfer Generalanzeiger*, and the *Leipziger Neueste Nachrichten*.[10]

Encouraged by this support, von Dobbeler embarked on a more vigorous campaign insisting (*Der Reichsbote*, 13 August) that Zionism should be implemented under the aegis of the Central Powers. It would ensure that Palestine remained Turkish. He was motivated primarily by German interests, not by anti-Semitism, though 'if at the same time something beneficial would result from Zionism to the Jews also, so much the better'. The *Allgemeine Anzeiger* (27 August) asserted that the Palestine question had become an integral part of the *Weltpolitik*; by meeting the Jewish demands, the Central Powers would render the Entente propaganda ineffective. Turkey would benefit economically and Germany would gain 'a strong outpost' in the Near East. In the *Münchener Neueste Nachrichten* (28 August) Major Endres repeated his warning that Germany was slow to realize the danger that England was about to become 'the protector of the Jews' and criticized Turkey for her short-sightedness.

The German Press was studied carefully in German and British official circles.[11] But it appears that it made an incomparably greater impact on the latter than on the former. In London it was assumed that if articles in the German Press of almost every political shade were speaking with the same voice then those articles must have been inspired and stimulated by the German Government and

---

[10] Quoted in *Jüdische Rundschau*, Nr. 34 (24 Aug. 1917).
[11] Stein, op. cit., pp. 516–17; Friedman, op. cit., pp. 244–5, 275–7, 286–7.

reflected its thinking. The British were under the firm impression that the Germans were courting the Zionists and might at any moment publicly identify themselves with the Zionist cause. How deep rooted was this belief is shown by the fact that Balfour felt obliged to warn the War Cabinet that 'the German Government were making great efforts to capture the sympathy of the Zionist Movement'. But, as documentary evidence shows, the British Government's concern lest they might be forestalled by the Germans was unfounded. During the late summer and autumn of 1917 the Wilhelmstrasse remained completely uninterested in suggestions made in various quarters that it come out openly in support of the Zionists.

Opinion was by no means unanimous. Von Kaufmann, Head of the Information Department (*Nachrichten-Abteilung*), was, it seems, influenced by Romberg's dispatches and agreed with Dr. Nahum Goldmann, at that time on the staff of his Department, that it was imperative to counter the Entente but Göppert, Head of the Political Department (*politische Abteilung*), wavered. He feared that the risk of offending Turkey was too great. The matter was thereupon brought before Zimmermann, who was reluctant to take any decision because he was about to resign. When Kühlmann became Foreign Minister, all prospects of a public declaration in favour of Zionism were dimmed. He pointed to the mounting chauvinism in Turkey and deemed it wiser to defer the discussion to 'a more opportune moment'.[12]

The assessment made by Prüfer, who in the meantime had been appointed Head of the Information Department of the Embassy in Constantinople, contrasted starkly with Kühlmann's. On the 15 August Prüfer told Ruppin how sorry he was that the Central Powers 'had missed a splendid opportunity' to counteract the manœuvres of the Entente. He hoped that it was still not too late to induce the Turkish Government to issue a declaration favourable to the Zionists, provided they declared unswerving loyalty. Ruppin recalled that numerous pronouncements had been made to this effect in the past but Prüfer thought that in consequence of the widespread propaganda in the foreign Press this had been forgotten and

[12] C.Z.A. Z 3/22, two notes by Lichtheim to E.A.C., 10 Aug. 1917. Dr. Goldmann's memorandum to von Kaufmann could not be traced in the A.A. archives. Dr. Goldmann, however, recollects that he submitted it. His private papers were destroyed by the Nazis. (Letter to author, 14 Mar. 1963.)

that a new *démarche* was needed. Ruppin promised to report on the matter to his colleagues in Berlin but, in view of Djemal's unabated hostility, he was still dubious.[13]

In all probability Prüfer would not have advised Ruppin as he did unless he considered his source of information reliable. No evidence can be found among the files of the German Foreign Ministry to support it, and with the Ottoman archives unexplored, the mystery cannot be resolved, but it tends to confirm our earlier information that certain Turkish statesmen expected Lichtheim's return to Constantinople in order to negotiate with him on important political matters.[14] Yet whatever might have been mooted in the Sublime Porte it was Djemal Pasha's attitude that counted most. Not only was he an important member of the Triumvirate and the Supreme Commander of the Fourth Ottoman Army, but with increasing frictions between Talaat and Enver, Talaat was forced to lean on Djemal[15] whose antagonism to Zionism was as deep as ever. In an interview given to Ernst Jäckh in May 1917 Djemal said that he would not allow any further Jewish immigration to Palestine; Zionism was 'extremely injurious' to the Ottoman Empire.[16] If any doubts lingered about Djemal's attitude, his statements made in Constantinople and Berlin dispelled them completely. On meeting Waldburg in Constantinople *en route* to Germany Djemal declared himself to be 'not an anti-Semite, but an enemy of Zionism'. He strongly objected to the repatriation of the Jaffa evacuees, which made Ruppin concede that all endeavours to effect a change of heart in the Turkish Government had failed.[17]

The Wilhelmstrasse was not so pessimistic and Göppert thought that a meeting between Djemal and the Zionist leaders might be useful. Djemal was indeed polite and amiable when he met Lichtheim and Hantke (28 August) and assured them 'on his honour' that the Palestinian Jews would be well treated. Lichtheim remarked that such an attitude would accord with Turkey's traditional benevolence and wondered why Zionism could not be treated in the

---

[13] Ibid. Z 3/1484, Ruppin to E.A.C., 17 Aug. 1917. On Prüfer see above, p. 268.

[14] Above, pp. 311–12.

[15] C.Z.A. Z 3/63, Lichtheim to E.A.C., 2 Apr. 1917.

[16] *Deutsche Politik. Wochenschrift für Welt- und Kulturpolitik*, hrsg. von Ernst Jäckh und Paul Rohrbach, Nr. 23 (8 June 1917), pp. 721–5; reproduced also in *Palestine. The Organ of the British Palestine Committee*, ii, no. 3, p. 24. On Jäckh see above, p. 254.

[17] *Türkei* 195, K 179417, Waldburg (not signed) to A.A., 21 Aug. 1917, tel. no. 998; C.Z.A. Z 3/1485, Ruppin to E.A.C., 28 Aug. 1917.

same spirit. Djemal blamed the anti-Turkish propaganda in the Entente countries, to which Lichtheim replied that in 'all certainty, the German Government would not have tolerated a movement nourishing pro-Entente tendencies . . . Zionism is purely a Jewish affair.' Djemal insisted that creation of a nationality problem was repugnant to Turkey; nor did Turkey wish 'further Zionization of Jews. . . . The immigrants are welcome to any part of the Empire, except Palestine.' Lichtheim did not give ground and emphasized the special relationship of the Jews to Palestine. Moreover, the Ottoman Government should not remain indifferent to the financial benefits that would accrue from the Jewish enterprise. Djemal showed interest in the last point and, on learning of the Zionists' desire to support the evacuees, observed smilingly: 'money, as much as possible, this is always welcome', but on political grounds he had to take a negative stand since the Arabs were bitterly opposed to Zionism and he, as Governor, was obliged to take heed of the majority of the population. He added that his successor, or perhaps he himself, would alter the policy in the future, but for the duration of the war, out of regard for the Arabs, his anti-Zionist stand must be clearly pronounced. Lichtheim and Hantke went away with the grain of comfort that the Palestine Jews would not be ill treated. Djemal refused to reinstate Ruppin in his post in Jaffa, but had no objection to Dr. Thon representing the Zionist Office.[18]

However self-assured Djemal Pasha seemed to be, his arguments were by no means infallible. How far Zionism could benefit Turkey was a matter of opinion but to hold the Palestine and German Zionists responsible for the Entente propaganda was folly. Djemal was confusing cause with effect, overlooking the fact that it was his policy of evacuation that provided the Entente with gratuitous ammunition against Turkey. Djemal's wish to escape the Arabs' odium might have suggested that their welfare was close to his heart, but this was not the case. Both Kühlmann, when Ambassador in Constantinople, and Count Trautmansdorff, the Austro-Hungarian Chargé d'Affaires, were extremely critical of his Arab policy. His notorious treason trials, executed with 'draconian severity'; his failure to alleviate the hardships caused by the war; his 'foolish

[18] C.Z.A. Z 3/83, minutes on a meeting with Djemal Pasha on 28 Aug. 1917; *Türkei* 195, K 179435, A.A. note, signed by Göppert; K 179486, Bussche to Waldburg, 14 Sept. 1917, dis. no. 787. Earlier Brode also suggested that Djemal's stay in Germany be utilized to dispel his mistrust of Zionism and ask him to repatriate the evacuees (K 179454–5, cited in Waldburg to A.A., 31 Aug. 1917).

attempts to Ottomanize the Arab people . . . suppression of the Arab language; discrimination against Arab officials . . . and above all the manifest arrogance of his subordinates, made the Turks so unpopular . . . in Arab countries, that the English would be welcomed with open arms.'[19] Yet whatever the rights or wrongs of his policy, the Germans would in no circumstances take it upon themselves to be his mentors. It was apparently as a result of this meeting with Lichtheim and Hantke that the Foreign Ministry finally adopted the attitude of *non possumus*.

There was yet one additional factor that made the Ministry reserved. News filtering through from abroad tended to confirm its suspicion that the Entente Powers were bent on the establishment of a Jewish state, and from such a scheme it had to steer clear. Most of this information was exaggerated, but here the Germans made the same blunder as the British by taking Press reports as the reflection of their adversaries' official policy. Thus the Legation in Stockholm learned from an informant that during the Balfour–Brandeis meeting in the United States it had been agreed that 'Palestine should become an independent state under an American Protectorate', a scheme to which President Wilson had given his prior consent.[20] The information was inaccurate.[21] The United States Government was disinclined to assume the protection of any territory, particularly in Turkey with which America was not at war. However, the Auswärtiges Amt had good reason to rely on the Legation in Stockholm since other sources tended to confirm its information. The *Jüdische Korrespondenz*, quoting the *American Jewish Chronicle*, reported that Leo Motzkin, a Russian Zionist leader, was bringing a personal letter from President Wilson to the Provisional Government in St. Petersburg urging that the two Governments undertake common action on Zionism. The Foreign Ministry took note of the paper's affirmation that President Wilson

[19] *Türkei* 177, K 197061–4, Kühlmann to Bethmann Hollweg, 25 Apr. 1917, dis. no. 261; Haus-, Hof- und Staatsarchiv, Vienna, Politisches Archiv XII (quoted thereafter H.H.S. Pol. Arch.), Karton 212, Nr. 3𝑟 B.
                                    p

[20] *Türkei* 195, K 179452, Lucius to Michaelis, 29 Aug. 1917, dis. no. 3842/1062. The informant was George Sokolowski, formerly Secretary of the Jewish Association in New York.

[21] On the Balfour–Brandeis meetings in Apr. 1917 see Stein, op. cit., pp. 426–8; Friedman, op. cit., pp. 200–2. However, on 30 Apr. Weizmann wrote to Brandeis: 'Press here reports American Administration favours Jewish Republic in Palestine.' (Stein, op. cit., p. 425.)

would support its realization.[22] Dr. U. W. F. Treub, the Dutch Minister of Finance, welcomed the idea of the formation of a Jewish state in Palestine: 'the rejuvenation of the Jewish nation in their ancient homeland is a commendable ideal, to which every humanitarian must subscribe'.[23] Camille Huysmans, the Belgian Socialist leader, expressed himself in a similar vein and hoped that, with Germany's mediation, Turkey would grant the Jewish community in Palestine self-government.[24]

It was this very impression that Germany took pains to avoid. With the Turco-German Treaty of Mutual Alliance being re-negotiated at that time, the Germans had to tread warily. Turkey's main ambition was to secure from Germany the abrogation of the system of Capitulations and a guarantee of her territorial integrity and sovereignty.[25] During the meeting which took place in Constantinople on 17 October 1917 it became evident that the Turkish statesmen were greatly concerned about the future of their Asiatic provinces. From the speeches of British Ministers and Press reports they deduced that Britain was intent on securing a certain measure of autonomy for Arabia, Mesopotamia, and Palestine, or even detaching them entirely from Ottoman rule. The Pope's Note, declaring that Armenia's well-being was irreconcilable with Turkish domination, was another source of anxiety. The Porte apparently distrusted Germany also, fearing a German arrangement with the Entente Powers at Turkey's expense. Kühlmann was aware that, unless Germany dispelled these suspicions, 'the pro-German regime in Turkey would be faced with great difficulties'. He therefore acceded to all Turkish demands to sign a Supplementary Treaty for a 'mutual guarantee' of territorial integrity.[26] Arab,

---

[22] *Jüdische Korrespondenz*, Nr. 11 (Aug. 1917); 'Wilson und der Zionismus' (cutting in *Türkei* 195, K 179461, underlined by the A.A. reader). No document has come to light to support this information.

[23] *Vossische Zeitung*, 20 Oct. 1917 (cutting in *Türkei* 195, K 179514). The *V.Z.* editor pointedly commented that the Dutch Minister's reference to the Jewish State did not reflect the aspirations of the German Zionists. It was only the Entente Powers that aimed at the destruction of the Ottoman realm.

[24] *Jüdische Korrespondenz*, Nr. 13 (Sept. 1917), copy in K 179490–1; *Jüdische Rundschau*, Nr. 34 (24 Aug. 1917).

[25] *Deutschland* 128, Nr. 5, Bd. 7, note on Talaat Pasha's visit to Berlin. The original treaty and its revision are found in Carl Mühlmann, *Deutschland und die Türkei 1913–1914* (Berlin, 1929), pp. 94–8; see also Gerard E. Silberstein, 'The Central Powers and the Second Turkish Alliance, 1915', *Slavic Review*, xxiv (1965), 77–89.

[26] *Deutschland* 128, Nr. 5, Bd. 7, *Aide-Mémoire*, 23 Oct. 1917; also Kühlmann to Grünau (G.H.Q.), 17 Nov. 1917. The German delegation was represented by State

Armenian, and Zionist affairs were not brought up at this meeting. The Turks were reluctant to seek German advice on issues which they considered to be strictly within their own competence, and the German delegation, conscious of their ally's susceptibilities, would not broach them.

Against this background it seems odd that an expert like Paul Weitz, the Constantinople correspondent of the *Frankfurter Zeitung*, should have attempted at his paper's behest to solicit a pro-Zionist declaration. The matter is all the more surprising because the *Frankfurter Zeitung* took the initiative entirely without the Zionists' knowledge. Moreover, with the exception of Heinrich Simon, its entire body of political editors were never known to be in sympathy with Zionism.[27] It was not until the spring of 1917 that the *Frankfurter Zeitung* began to show some positive interest. In its issues of 24 and 25 May it criticized Djemal Pasha's evacuation policy and argued that 'in view of the very promising commercial prospects' the Reich authorities 'should have a tangible interest in Zionism'.

Weitz's proposals put Göppert in a dilemma. With Rosenberg's imminent departure for negotiations in Constantinople, no decision could be taken but as soon as the report on Djemal's conversation with the Zionist leaders reached him Göppert told Weitz unequivocally that official publication of 'the Zionist letter' was 'inopportune'; an editorial by the *Frankfurter Zeitung* was more appropriate, though 'in view of Turkish suspicions, the German attitude should be discussed with the greatest reserve, or preferably not at all. Stress should be laid on the good relations between Ottoman Jewry and the Porte . . . and on the fact that all *sensible* Zionists in all countries pay no attention to the seductions of the Entente Powers.'[28]

Weitz's move coincided with that made by Professor Hubert Auhagen, a well-known Middle-East economist and the author of a study entitled *Beiträge zur Kenntnis der Landesnatur und der*

Secretary Kühlmann, Ambassador Count Bernstorff, and Geheimrat von Rosenberg, and the Turkish by Talaat Pasha, the Grand Vizier, Nessimy Bey, the Foreign Minister, and Hakki Pasha, the Ottoman Ambassador in Berlin.

[27] Ernest Kahn, 'The Frankfurter Zeitung', *Leo Baeck Institute Year Book*, ii (1957), 231. The paper was held in high esteem and exercised a tremendous influence on its readers.

[28] *Türkei* 195, K 179465-9, Weitz to Rosenberg, 5 Oct.; Göppert to Weitz, 7 Sept. 1917 (confidential). The exact wording of the proposed declaration is not known, since on Weitz's request it was returned to him and no copy of it remained in the A.A. files. On Weitz see above, p. 259.

Landwirtschaft Syriens. Impressed by the Zionist colonization, he established in 1913 the International Union of Christian Friends of Zionism, headed by Count Beiland, Chamberlain to Queen Wilhelmina of Holland. Its activities were suspended at the outbreak of the war but following the German occupation of Poland Auhagen concluded that the three million poverty-stricken Jews were facing a very insecure future and that to avert a catastrophe they should be resettled in Palestine. Its soil was fertile and might yield the very produce that Germany needed. Subject to the Government's permission, he proposed the foundation of a German-Christian Union of Friends of Zionism which would undertake the preparatory steps for a large-scale Jewish emigration to Turkey. The Ministry replied cryptically that, under prevailing political conditions, the foundation of such a Union was 'not feasible'.[29]

In compliance with the Zionist Executive's decision at its meeting on 31 July 1917 in Copenhagen, Lichtheim approached Göppert on 20 September and tried to gain his approval for the creation of a German-Zionist Committee but found him very reserved. 'Our attitude towards you remains as friendly as before', he told Lichtheim, 'but out of regard for Turkey, the Foreign Ministry is wary of any open demonstration.' The Pope's Note, in which the liberation of the Armenians was mentioned, had made the Turks even more touchy. He hinted that there was some opposition among German Jews and objected to Zionist propaganda being launched even by a private body. He thought that the national character of Zionism prejudiced its cause with the Turks but was forced to admit that nationalism was the very source that inspired the colonists in their pioneering efforts. The discussion thereafter assumed a theoretical nature from which Lichtheim inferred that, although potential goodwill still existed in the Wilhelmstrasse, no practical results could be expected.[30]

It seems that Göppert was over-cautious. The Porte was not as antagonistic to Zionism as he imagined. Nor was it indifferent. This

---

[29] *Türkei* 195, K 179397–9, Auhagen to A.A., 15 Aug.; K 179504–5, A.A. to Auhagen, 21 Sept. 1917 (confidential).

[30] C.Z.A. Z 3/13, minutes on a discussion with Göppert on 20 Sept. 1917. For the Pope's Note of 1 Aug. see *F.R.U.S.*, 1917, Suppl. 2, i, pp. 161–2. Talaat replied that Turkey had been 'forced to fight for the maintenance of [her] existence and . . . independence . . . which consists of guaranteeing the rights of her entire and limitless sovereignty over all the territory of [her] national frontiers.' (Ibid., pp. 221–2.) He referred to the Pope's Note again on 24 September during his speech at the C.U.P. Congress (*Norddeutsche Allgemeine Zeitung*, 29 Sept. 1917).

is evident from a meeting that took place early in September between Nessimy Bey and Nahoum Effendi at the former's invitation. The Rabbi reassured the Minister that the Zionist movement was in no way directed against Turkey's interests; it aimed to create 'a cultural centre in Palestine' and not an autonomous realm. The 'centre' was to provide Jews with an ambience for 'spiritual and physical regeneration in a Jewish milieu', which was compatible with Turkish law. On the basis of his close personal acquaintance with Zionist leaders and his reading of the resolutions adopted by the Zionist congresses, Nahoum was confident that there was no risk of violation of Ottoman integrity. It is not clear what was the purpose of Nessimy's inquiry but it seems that he was satisfied with the Rabbi's explanation and asked him to submit a comprehensive memorandum.[31]

The encounter instilled in the Zionist Executive new hope that a more favourable judgement might be forthcoming from Constantinople, and Hantke hastened to brief Kühlmann about it.[32] Yet the only concession that the State Secretary was prepared to make was to lift the embargo on Zionist propaganda, though with a proviso that it was done on the sole responsibility of its initiators. Major Endres, formerly careful not to come into conflict with official policy, now accepted Lichtheim's invitation to edit a periodical.[33] He continued to write for the *Münchener Neueste Nachrichten*, whereas Lichtheim, in addition to the *Jüdische Rundschau*, made use of the *Vossische Zeitung*. In its 18 October 1917 issue he published a long article[34] explaining why support of the Central Powers was important for the Jews. 'While the Entente can only make promises, Turkey, being in virtual possession of Palestine', was in a position to offer them more tangible concessions. The article, as the editorial comment suggests, was evidently written for official consumption in Berlin, but it appears that the only impact that Endres's and Lichtheim's arguments made, was on *The Times* of London. Alarmed at the 'insidious German propaganda', its leader (26 October 1917) warned Whitehall that the German Government had

---

[31] C.Z.A. Z 3/66, Ruppin to E.A.C., 13 Sept. 1917.
[32] *Türkei* 195, K 179522–3, Hantke to A.A., 24 Sept. 1917.
[33] C.Z.A. Z 3/20, Endres to Lichtheim, 26 Sept.; Lichtheim to Endres, 28 Sept. 1917.
[34] Cutting in *Türkei* 195, K 179604–6. The article was written anonymously but the editor pointed out that it came from the pen of a Zionist leader intimately acquainted with conditions in Turkey and Palestine, who obviously was Lichtheim.

'not been idle in attempting to forestall' them. That this was not the case is evident from the failure of Count Brockdorff-Rantzau to convince the Foreign Ministry of the urgency of a German–Turkish pro-Zionist declaration. Impressed by Jacobson's memoranda and conscious of the wide repercussions that such a proclamation might have, he pressed his point hard, only to be told by his superiors that the proposed move did not accord with German interests.[35]

Pressure was exerted also in the opposite direction. It was Max Warburg whom Göppert apparently had in mind when hinting to Lichtheim, during their meeting on 20 September, that there was some opposition to Zionism among German Jews. Warburg was a leading banker in Hamburg and during the war became a pillar of German finance.[36] In October 1915 he supported the foundation of the Deutsche Vereinigung für die Interessen der Osteuropäischen Juden,[37] and soon after came into conflict with the Komitee für den Osten. Assuming that the K.f.d.O. was Zionist inspired, he blamed the Zionist movement *in toto* for exacerbating Polish anti-Semitism by showing an excessive zeal for bringing the Polish Jews into the German fold.[38] He considered the Zionist aspirations Utopian and, like most of his contemporary co-religionists in Western Europe, feared that the recognition of Jews as a nation would jeopardize their civic status. Although he represented no Jewish organization, he felt free to speak on their behalf. Early in September 1917, learning from the *Lemberger Tageblatt* of Leo Motzkin's mission on behalf of President Wilson to the Provisional Government in Russia, he concluded that the Entente Powers were contemplating the 'foundation of a Jewish State under their Protectorate' and soon after urged Kühlmann to come out openly against Zionism. This, he insisted, was imperative because, should Palestine secede from Turkey, her attitude towards her Jewish subjects, hitherto

[35] C.Z.A. Z 3/11, minutes on Martin Rosenblüth's conversation with Count Brockdorff-Rantzau on 23 Oct. 1917.

[36] Not to be confused with another branch of the family of which Professor Otto Warburg, Chairman of the Zionist Executive, was a member. On Max Warburg see: E. Rosenbaum, 'Max M. Warburg and Company. Merchant Bankers of Hamburg', *Leo Baeck Institute Year Book*, vii (1961), 121–41; for his contacts with the German Government see *The Memoirs of Prince Max of Baden*, i, pp. 266, 271; ii, pp. 13, 27, 40, 202.

[37] The co-founders of this philanthropic organization were Dr. James Simon, Dr. Paul Nathan, Gen. Justizrat O. Cassel, and Dr. Bernhard Kahn.

[38] *Wk.*, Nr. 11, adh. 2, K 714/K 191102–13, K 191305–7, Warburg to Zimmermann, 22 Oct. 1915, 5 Feb. 1916.

benevolent, might change. Moreover, the German Jews, who were sharing the war effort equally with their Christian compatriots, would abhor the idea of 'giving up their fatherland. . . . Had Zionism been energetically countered in good time, their movement, now well entrenched, would not have been successful in winning control of such primitive and politically naïve minds.' He thought that if each country were to absorb its own Jewish minority and treat it decently, the creation of a refuge in Palestine for the unfortunate ones would not be necessary. Here Warburg took the opportunity to air his complaints on discriminatory practices against Jews in the German Diplomatic Service and pleaded for a greater degree of tolerance.[39]

Warburg obviously wished Kühlmann to deliver the *coup de grâce* to the Zionists but Kühlmann would not go so far. Although Warburg's exposé appeared to him to be 'worthy of consideration', he deemed it wiser to leave this proposition to the discretion of those Jews who, like Warburg, opposed Zionism. Should it become known that the Reich Government had instigated such a campaign, the Entente and the neutral countries would not be slow to exploit the fact and blacken Germany's record. Kühlmann dismissed outright Warburg's complaint of discrimination against Jews as unjustified, at least as far as the Foreign Ministry was concerned, and assured him that in future he would 'not allow any religious prejudices to prevent the appointment of the right man to the right job'.[40]

Warburg had miscalculated badly. It did not occur to him that his own contention that 'anti-Semitism found its "scientific motivation" in Germany'[41] was one of the mainsprings that kept Zionism alive. He was also unaware that the Hilfsverein had in the meantime composed its differences with the Zionists and that although the Orthodox Jews were still in sharp conflict with the Zionists on policy in the Eastern Occupied Territories, the divergence narrowed

---

[39] *E.G.*, Nr. 79, *Akten betreffend die polnische Frage*, Bd. 12, K 693/K 181629–36, 'Polen und Juden', memorandum by Max Warburg, Jan. 1917; *Türkei* 195, K 179475–7, Warburg to Kühlmann, 7 Sept. 1917. The original issue of the *Lemberger Tageblatt* could not be traced. However, cf. above, pp. 331–2.

[40] *Türkei* 195, K 179515–16, Kühlmann to Warburg, 22 Sept. 1917 (personal). To refute Warburg Kühlmann quoted a few instances: e.g. Hugo Meyer had been appointed to the Turkish War Ministry to deal with food-supply matters, Oscar Wassermann served as co-director of the Deutsche Bank and participated in the Reich's Financial Delegation to Turkey, and Köbner was the Financial Counsellor of the Embassy in Constantinople.

[41] Ibid. K 179478–84, Warburg to A.A., memorandum dated Nov. 1916.

on Palestine. This became evident early in November when Rabbi Jacob Rosenheim, the celebrated leader of the Orthodox Agudat Israel, urged the German Government to persuade Turkey 'to foster free Jewish immigration and settlement in Palestine', and issue a declaration of her own in this vein. 'Such a realistic formula will make a far greater impression on informed public opinion, than the Entente's exaggerated promises of a Utopian Jewish state.'[42] Rosenheim's move coincided with one by Wolf Jacobson of Hamburg, a leader of the religious youth organization, who assured the Foreign Ministry that, should a religious-national centre for the Jews be established in Palestine, it would not conflict with their loyalty to the countries of their domicile.[43] Unable to rally support, Warburg revised his views five months later.[44]

Kühlmann might have shared Warburg's sentiments but he was enough of a statesman to realize that on broader lines of policy the Zionist boat should not be rocked. He certainly would not play the enemy's game. This was why he felt so strongly about recommending continued deferment of the Zionist leaders from military service. The War Ministry, more out of administrative routine than from ill will, insisted on the call-up of Ruppin, Lichtheim, and Hantke, but Kühlmann advised them that should this take place the Zionist Headquarters would probably move to a neutral country where, 'deprived of German influence, they would fall under that of the enemy'. The fact that no material change had taken place in the orientation of the Zionist Executive justified in his eyes deferment of these three men for the duration of the war.[45]

But this was the only relic of Zimmermann's legacy. Otherwise Kühlmann did little to help the Zionists. When Ruppin learned from Count Bernstorff, the newly appointed Ambassador in Constantinople, that it was Lossow who was responsible for Lichtheim's removal, the Executive protested vigorously against the unwarranted misrepresentation of Lichtheim's connection with the American Embassy and demanded his reinstatement:[46] but to no

[42] *Türkei* 195, K 180025–31, Rosenheim to Ludwig Haas, Frankfurt, 3 Nov. 1917 (copy, original in *Wk.*, Nr. 14 a).

[43] Ibid. K 179661–3, Jacobson to A.A., 29 Oct. 1917.   [44] Below, pp. 382, 394–5.

[45] *Türkei* 195, K 179614–27, E.A.C. (Warburg) to A.A., 18 Oct. ; K 179833, Göppert to Warburg, 19 Oct.; K 179629–31, W.O. to A.A. 18 Oct.; Kühlmann to W.O., 22 Oct.; K 179801, W.O. to A.A., 22 Oct. 1917.

[46] C.Z.A. Z 3/1485, Ruppin to E.A.C., 22 Oct. 1917; *Türkei* 195, K 179713–17, Warburg to Kühlmann, 5 Nov. 1917. Excerpts from Lichtheim's correspondence during

avail. The Executive was heartened when Chief Rabbi Nahoum interceded personally with Kühlmann on Lichtheim's behalf, declaring that his presence in Constantinople was necessary for relief work among the native Jewish communities; among the poor families of the Jewish servicemen in particular. But Kühlmann, though admittedly placed in 'a difficult position', replied that the military authorities would not concede that another person equally qualified to carry out that philanthropic work could not be found in Constantinople.[47] Kühlmann was well informed of the nature of Lichtheim's expected sphere of activity in Constantinople, as some time earlier he had dismissed Djavid Bey's repeated plea for Lichtheim's return on the ground that he was 'indispensable for Zionist [political] work in Berlin'. Such disingenuous tactics left the Zionists in no doubt as to the limits of the Foreign Minister's goodwill.[48] Lichtheim sensed correctly during his conversation with Göppert that since Kühlmann had become Foreign Minister the Zionists' prospects had worsened.[49] But the bitterest pill they still had to swallow was his refusal to grant Warburg and Jacobson an interview, an unprecedented act of discourtesy.

It was the publication of the Balfour Declaration that had impelled the Zionist leaders to seek this urgent interview. They asserted that the document was of 'extraordinary political importance'. It was the first time that the Zionist movement had been recognized officially by a great Power; the United States, the French, and the Italian Governments were to follow suit. They were told, however, that the Foreign Minister would not be able to receive them 'in the foreseeable future'.[50] Thus at the very crest of victory in the Entente countries the Zionists in Germany suffered their worst setback, although their disillusionment was tempered by the exhilarating news from London. The Balfour Declaration gave the Zionists

the winter of 1916/17 and the following spring were included (K 179718–24). Cf. above, pp. 285–7.

[47] *Türkei* 195, K 179725–6, Nahoum to Kühlmann, 29 Oct. 1917; K 179775–8, Kühlmann to Nahoum, 13 Nov. 1917 (confidential and personal. For Kühlmann's earlier encounter with Rabbi Nahoum see above, pp. 292–3.

[48] Lichtheim, *She'ar Yashuv*, p. 435; *Rückkehr*, p. 370.

[49] C.Z.A. Z 3/13, Minutes on a meeting with Göppert on 20 Sept. 1917. Referred to above, pp. 334.

[50] *Türkei* 195, K 179794–5, Warburg and Jacobson to A.A., 12 Nov. 1917; K 179796, A.A. note, undated. The Balfour Declaration was published on 9 Nov. 1917.

everywhere a sense of having a place in the world. They could no longer be looked upon as dreamers divorced from life. Their recognition by the Entente helped even those in Germany to hold their heads higher, though an exclusive victory in one camp of the belligerent Powers spelt patent dangers. Should their jubilation force them off balance, the German Zionists would make themselves vulnerable to a charge of joining hands with the enemy's cause. The need for a change in the policy of the Central Powers now became more compelling than ever. The Executive lost neither its tenacity nor its good sense in striving to bring this about.

The first note was struck in two successive articles by Lichtheim in the *Jüdische Rundschau* (16 and 23 November 1917).[51] He saluted the British declaration as 'an event of world historical importance'; it was 'for the first time that demands of the Jewish people were officially recognized by a European Power. . . . To dismiss England's assurances as mere bluff . . . was both preposterous and petty.' England undertook a firm commitment which would not be evaded so easily. From the point of view of international law Palestine was Turkish, but its future sovereignty would be decided at the Peace Conference. Hence, to fortify their position, the Central Powers would be well advised to take a leaf out of the British Government's book. The Zionists, on their part, would not embroil themselves in power politics. They pledged strictest loyalty to the factual suzerain of the country, and no pressing world events would detach them from the line adopted since the First Zionist Congress to realize their aspirations 'in an accord with the whole civilized world'. Lichtheim dismissed as unfounded the fears of the anti-Zionists that recognition of the Jews as a nation would undermine their civic status. The relevant proviso in the text of the Balfour Declaration, that 'nothing shall be done which may prejudice . . . the rights and political status enjoyed by Jews in any other country', constituted a sufficient guarantee. 'Let the Jews learn their lesson themselves and shake off their ghetto-fear complex.' With Zionism taken seriously on the international scene, the German Jews would do a disservice to themselves by continuing to disregard it. They should rise to the occasion and overcome their inhibitions; otherwise they would lose their influence among their fellow Jews for good and find themselves 'overrun by the wheels of history'.

[51] The articles were published anonymously. A cutting of the latter issue in *Türkei* 195, K 179959–60.

Major Endres warmly supported Lichtheim. Lecturing in Munich[52] he said that the Balfour Declaration placed the Zionist question on the agenda of the future Peace Conference, 'not to be removed from it'. For England Palestine constituted an essential link in the chain of her grand Oriental design. Her support of the aspirations of the indigenous population was a mere stratagem to destroy the Ottoman Empire from within and replace Turkish influence by her own. But it was primarily her role as the Zionists' patron that enhanced her reputation so much all over the world— 'an ingenious move' to which Germany could not remain indifferent. Turkey should realize that the question of nationalities was not an obstacle to her survival; a tolerant treatment would be a source of strength.

Emil Ludwig, too, was critical of Turkish policy, especially that of Djemal Pasha. In an article in the *Vossische Zeitung* (20 November 1917, evening edn.) he dismissed the Turkish fears of a 'Jewish invasion' as impolitic; the Empire had much to gain from Jewish settlement in a highly underpopulated country.[53] Dr. Manfred Georg in an article 'Um den jüdischen Staat' in the *Deutsche Montags-Zeitung* (26 November 1917) complained that the Central Powers 'missed another opportunity of gaining the support of world Jewry'.

Zionism has become a factor in the *Weltpolitik* and the Jewish masses in the United States and Russia, who formerly had harboured friendly sentiments towards Germany have, as a result of the Balfour Declaration, turned to the Entente. Only prompt action can reverse this trend. . . . For Turkey there is an infinite number of reasons to encourage a flourishing and loyal province, whereas for Germany, it was essential to regain the Jews' sympathy and to fortify her diplomatic position at the future Peace Conference.

The *Berliner Volkszeitung*, the *Deutsche Levantzeitung*, and the *Fränkischer Kurier* insisted that it would be 'a great pity if Germany fails to make use of the great force of Zionism . . . allowing England to gain an easy moral victory'. The Berlin *Welt am Montag* too

[52] 'Zionismus und Weltpolitik', quoted in the *Jüdische Rundschau*, Nr. 47 (23 Nov. 1917), cutting in K 17996304 from the *Münchener Neueste Nachrichten*; also in *Palestine*, ii, no. 24, pp. 223–4. Selected quotations in *The Times* of London (25 Nov. 1917).

[53] According to Ludwig the average density of population in Palestine was 27 persons per 1 km²; in the territory east of the River Jordan and south of Beersheba 4 persons per 1 km² only. By contrast, in Egypt approximately 10,000 persons lived on 1 km².

urged the Central Powers to make their position clear on this 'important world problem'.[54]

In Stockholm von Lucius was reasonably satisfied with the stand taken by the local Zionists. From a statement made by one of their leaders he deduced that, however gratified they were by Balfour's letter, they would not depart from their neutrality. In The Hague Friedrich Rosen remained reticent but in Berne the Legation grew alarmed by the stir caused by the news from London. Romberg deprecated the fact that the Swiss Zionists, despite their professed neutrality, had hastened to congratulate the British Government officially.[55] The *Züricher Zeitung* (23 November 1917) and other papers described at length the tremendous impact the Balfour Declaration had made upon Jewish people all over the world, which bore out Romberg's warnings that in propaganda warfare Germany was losing the battle. He struck a more hopeful note when reporting on a conversation between Legation Counsellor von Schubert and Dr. Jacob Klatzkin. The latter admitted that the British declaration, in favour of 'Jewish statehood' (*Staatswesen*) was 'an exceedingly astute move . . . of far-reaching consequences', but believed that Germany could still recover a good deal of lost ground. 'Zionism was inherently an international movement . . . It would not become uncritically subservient to the Entente propaganda machinery and would not depart from its original aim of neutrality.' Should Germany fail to persuade her ally, a unilateral non-binding statement in favour of the Zionist programme might also have a good effect. There was still a great store of confidence in Germany's *Realpolitik* and the sooner she made such a declaration the better. Romberg, apprehensive lest the number of pro-German Jews in Switzerland and elsewhere would dwindle drastically, supported Klatzkin's proposition wholeheartedly. The report was studied carefully at the highest administrative echelons in Berlin but the responses were negative. Count von Hertling, the newly appointed Chancellor, discarded Romberg's recommendations with a bold *NEIN*, whereas Baron von Richthofen, deputizing for Kühlmann, surpassed the Chancellor by commenting *UNSINN* ('nonsense'). He found that Germany was in no position to make a unilateral declara-

[54] For a summary of the reaction of the German Press to the Balfour Declaration see the *Jüdische Rundschau*, Nr. 52 (28 Dec. 1917); *Palestine*, ii, pp. 199, 239–40.

[55] *Türkei* 195, K 179887, Lucius to Hertling, 22 Nov., dis. no. 5181/1488. Chancellor Michaelis resigned on 31 Oct. and was succeeded by Hertling on 1 Nov.; K 179797, K 179889, Romberg to A.A., 12, 19 Nov. 1917, tel. nos. 1819, 1851.

tion 'without *full* consideration for Turkey' and thought that the effect of such a declaration on Jews would be minimal since Judaism was 'not identical with Zionism'.[56] It did not occur to him that in six weeks' time the Wilhelmstrasse would have to revise its policy radically.

The Auswärtiges Amt remained unsympathetic towards the Zionists even after they had managed to placate Hakki Pasha, the Turkish Ambassador to Berlin, whose wrath had been aroused by the *Jüdische Rundschau* and the *Vossische Zeitung* (28 November) for publishing the full text of the Balfour Declaration. Hakki was certain that the British intended to wrest Palestine from Turkey and to found a Jewish state there under their own protection. When Jacobson and Lichtheim called on him they found him very agitated, accusing these papers of lending themselves to enemy propaganda. The Zionist leaders adroitly pointed out that neither a Jewish state nor the question of sovereignty was mentioned in the text of the British declaration. 'The realization of Zionism did not lie within the exclusive competence of England, but depended largely on agreement of all the Powers concerned, especially that of Turkey.' The English declaration had been published in the German national Press, even in the semi-official *Kölnische Zeitung*, and the Zionists would make a laughing-stock of themselves by suppressing it, or minimizing its importance. Had the German Zionists sacrificed their independence they would have lost for good their influence with international Jewry, of whom four-fifths were domiciled in the countries outside the Central Powers. Only by taking the British declaration seriously on the one hand, whilst emphasizing their wish to realize their aspirations under Ottoman suzerainty on the other, could the Zionists improve Turkey's prospects of retaining Palestine. Jacobson and Lichtheim warned the Ambassador that Turkey could no longer enjoy an exclusive say in its future —that issue was bound to figure on the agenda of the Peace Conference. Had Turkey shown greater understanding in the past, the matter would not have gone so far, although it was still not too late, they implied, to reach some sort of accommodation.[57]

Lichtheim and Jacobson left with the impression that they had mollified the Ambassador and briefed Ruppin about the meeting

[56] Ibid. K 179917–23, Romberg to Hertling, 24 Nov. 1917, dis. no. 3611, and marginalia by Hertling, Richthofen, and others.

[57] Ibid. K 179965–8, E.A.C. to Ruppin, 3 Dec. 1917 (a copy in C.Z.A. Z 3/1485).

through the official German courier. Even so, Warburg found it necessary to reassure Hakki the next day of the Zionists' 'complete and undoubted loyalty' and to reiterate his colleagues' contention that had the Executive ignored the British declaration its own voice within the councils of international Jewry would have been irretrievably silenced, whereas by accepting it, the Executive added weight to its demand that 'Palestine was and will remain Turkish territory'. He showed that the Ambassador had overlooked a statement in the articles in question that 'no events of the war would deflect the Zionists from their original intentions . . . of fulfilling their aspirations *within the framework of the Ottoman Empire*'.[58] But whatever opinion Hakki might have formed the Auswärtiges Amt was unconvinced. 'Clearer proof that the Zionists consider themselves internationalists—does not exist', runs Richthofen's marginalia; and on the suggestion of Zionism being realized under Turkish protection the annotation reads: 'but the Turks do not wish that'. These comments show how firmly established was the Kühlmann–Rosen school.

For the Zionists, however, *rapprochement* with the Central Powers was becoming increasingly pressing. As Ruppin put it, 'should Turkey be persuaded to issue a favourable declaration, our friends in Germany, Austria, Hungary and those in occupied territories would be relieved from an embarrassing dependence on England'. A Turkish declaration, if followed by one from Turkey's allies, would check the inevitable drift into the Entente camp, invalidate possible accusations, and give substance to 'our proclaimed principle of strict neutrality'. Germany should persuade the Turkish Government that 'the victorious march of the nationalist principle cannot be stopped'. To improve its image, Constantinople should grant the non-Turkish nationalities their well-deserved rights and thereby undermine the English pretence of being the protector of small nationalities. No longer a target for criticism, and armed with a constructive policy, Turkey would speak with a more effective voice at the future conference and her prospects of retaining her Empire, if not of recovering the provinces lost during the war, would be greatly improved. Would it not be in Turkey's best interests to review her policy earlier, and not be overtaken by events? The concession of national rights for the Jews in Palestine would mark a fine start for such a liberal policy. It would also be a timely

[58] *Türkei*, 195 K 179953–8, Warburg to Hakki Pasha, 4 Dec. 1917 (a copy to A.A.).

reply to the British declaration and prove that Turkey was determined to make a definite break with her ignominious past. Ruppin
considered the moment opportune for the German Government to
approach the Porte. In the past months, when the evacuation from
Jaffa was in full swing, a Turkish declaration would have made no
impression. Now, with this problem partly solved by military
events, the acceptance of such a decision would be greatly eased.[59]

Save for his lucid exposition, there was nothing essentially new
in Ruppin's thinking; his colleagues in Berlin had been acting on
these very premises for some time. Lichtheim fully subscribed to
Ruppin's thesis and replied that, despite unfavourable political
conditions, the Executive had two weeks earlier made a strong
representation to the Foreign Ministry.[60] Moreover, on 30 November, at Jacobson's instigation, Erzberger wrote to Kühlmann and
advised him to grant Jacobson an interview and express 'a few
friendly words about the Zionists' aspirations'. Erzberger enclosed
the draft of a declaration, which 'took full consideration of Turkish
interests'. It read:

> The Imperial Government is favourably disposed to the aspirations of
> the Zionist Organization to create a Jewish National Home for the Jewish
> people in Palestine and is willing to promote this aim energetically.
> In recognition of the great economic and cultural benefits which would
> accrue to the Ottoman Empire from a Jewish settlement of Palestine, the
> Imperial Government is prepared to intercede with the friendly Turkish
> Government, so that a basis may be created for the unhindered develop-
> ment of a Jewish settlement in Palestine.[61]

However, Richthofen had different views. His cryptic annotations
on Erzberger's Note, advising Göppert to consult his earlier
observations on Romberg's dispatch,[62] show that nothing had
materially changed in official thinking. Warburg might well have
warned the Foreign Ministry that the Zionist movement had
become 'a factor of political importance', and that Jews everywhere
had embarked on large-scale preparations for an appearance at

---

[59] C.Z.A. Z 3/1485, Ruppin to E.A.C., 5 Dec. 1917. The British occupation of Jaffa
(15 Nov. 1917) enabled the evacuees, encamped in the neighbourhood of Petach-Tikva
and Kfar-Saba to return to their homes. Those staying in Galilee remained in the
Turkish zone.

[60] Ibid. Z 3/1486, Lichtheim to Ruppin, 16 Dec. 1917.

[61] *Türkei* 195, K 179939–41, Erzberger to Kühlmann, 30 Nov. 1917. It seems that
the author of the draft declaration was Jacobson. For the text in German see
Appendix C. [62] Above, pp. 342–3.

the future Peace Conference,[63] but the Ministry remained as cool as ever.

On 17 November 1917 Count Czernin, the Austro-Hungarian Foreign Minister, received Hantke and pledged the support of his Government to the realization of the Zionist aspirations in Turkey. The statement, which was made public, took the Wilhelmstrasse entirely by surprise, Later, however, Count Wedel, the German Ambassador in Vienna, reassured Berlin that Czernin's statement was not as far-reaching as had been reported in the Press. He told Hantke that the Austro-Hungarian Government, 'although favourably disposed towards the Zionist aspirations, could not possibly interfere in the [internal] affairs of the Turkish state'. Moreover, a *démenti* had been forwarded to the Austro-Hungarian Embassy in Constantinople confirming that Czernin's conversation with Hantke had been published incorrectly. But Wedel would not rest at that. On 23 December he found it expedient to tell Czernin that the current friendly attitude which the British Government was displaying towards the Zionists 'should not be taken too seriously'— a transparent hint that it was unnecessary for the Central Powers to emulate the Entente.[64]

[63] *Türkei* 195, K 179927–33, Warburg to A.A., 30 Nov. 1917.
[64] I. Friedman, 'The Austro-Hungarian Government and Zionism, 1897–1918', 160–4.

16

The Evacuation from Jaffa and its Repercussions[1]

SENSITIVE to Turkish susceptibilities, the German Government was unable, and from August 1917 unwilling, to rival the British. Yet it cannot be denied that it was chiefly owing to Germany's forceful intervention that the danger which hovered over the Palestinian Jews in 1917 was averted. The chief credit for this must go to Zimmermann. Had it not been for his singular determination nothing would have stopped Djemal Pasha from delivering a crippling blow to the Yishuv. Kühlmann, at that time Ambassador in Constantinople, proved in this respect unhelpful. The Palestine Jews were, however, fortunate that both Dr. Brode, the Consul-General in Jerusalem, and Colonel Kress von Kressenstein,[2] were vigilant enough to expose the true motives behind Djemal's action.

On 27 March 1917, following the British defeat at Gaza on the previous day,[3] Izzet Bey, *Mutassarif* of Jerusalem, arrived unexpectedly in Jaffa. He summoned the notables of all denominations and warned them that in consequence of the enemy's advance the civilian population of Jaffa and its environs would have to be evacuated. Only the farmers could remain until after the harvest. Save for the Sanjak of Jerusalem and the coastal towns of Haifa, Acre, and Beirut the evacuees could go anywhere; those without means would be transported to the Syrian hinterland and be looked after by the Ottoman Government. The Muslim orange-grove owners made it

---

[1] This chapter was published in the Jan. 1971 issue of *Jewish Social Studies*, xxxiii, no. 1, 23–43 under the title 'German Intervention on Behalf of the Yishuv, 1917'.

[2] On whom see above, p. 273, below, pp. 351–3.

[3] On the battles of Gaza see: George MacMunn and Cyril Falls (eds.), *Military Operations in Egypt and Palestine* (London, 1928–30), i, pp. 279–320, 326–49; Wavell, *The Palestine Campaign*, pp. 67–88.

clear that they would not leave their property and the *Mutassarif* seems to have shown them some consideration, but when their Jewish neighbours resorted to an identical argument they were threatened with immediate expulsion. This, together with the fact that German and Austrian non-Jewish nationals were allowed to stay 'at their own risk', was interpreted by the Jewish population as an act directed primarily against themselves. With the memory of the Armenian atrocities fresh in their minds, the Jews feared the worst.[4]

That same day the Military Governor of Jaffa broke the news of the impending evacuation to the newly appointed German Consul, Karl Freiherr von Schabinger. From the Governor's disclosures Schabinger learnt that the evacuees would be likely to face hunger and death, and that the chief sufferers would be the Jews. On the next two days, accompanied by the Austro-Hungarian Consul, Schabinger made an urgent call on the *Mutassarif*. By then the news of the British defeat at Gaza had become public and the military justification for the evacuation became invalid. Nevertheless, the order remained unaffected. The exemption of the Christian Germans reinforced Schabinger's suspicion that the only objective of the Turks was to annihilate the Jews, irrespective of citizenship. Terror-stricken, they were storming the German Consulate in Jaffa appealing for help. On the last day of March Schabinger approached the *Mutassarif* for the third time, drawing his attention to the adverse effect the evacuation would have on public opinion abroad. Schabinger asserted that discrimination against the Jews was inexcusable and held that the military case for evacuation was unconvincing. The German Jews, in particular, he insisted, were 'loyally devoted to Turkey' and he was bound to protect them. The *Mutassarif* remained indifferent. 'Ce ne me regarde pas!' was his stereotyped reply. Schabinger thereupon warned him that, should the German Jews be forcibly evicted, he, as their consular representative, would go with them; the evacuation would be interpreted as deliberate persecution for which not only Turkey but also Germany would be held responsible. Heretofore the anti-Jewish pogroms in Tsarist Russia had been the strongest propaganda card of the Central Powers; now the tables would be turned on them.[5]

[4] C.Z.A. L 6/2/I, Thon (Jerusalem) to E.A.C., 18 Apr. 1917; Ben Hillel Hacohen, *Milchemet Ha-Amim*, iii, pp. 103–7; Smilansky, *Zichronot*, iii, pp. 271–5.

[5] *Türkei* 195, K 179239–46, Schabinger (Jaffa) to Brode (Jerusalem), 14 May 1917 (secret), dis. no. 74, encl. in Brode to A.A., 30 June 1917, dis. no. 137/1966.

The encounter was evidently reported to Djemal Pasha in Jerusalem. On the following day, 1 April, Palm Sunday, Brode was summoned to Djemal's office to receive a stern warning against unwarranted interference in Ottoman internal affairs. Djemal complained that Schabinger had equated the order of evacuation with Russian pogroms and threatened to obstruct its application to German Jews. For such an affront Schabinger would be denied diplomatic privileges, his correspondence would be liable to censorship, and he would be made to apologize before an Ottoman Military Court.

Brode had been unaware of the incident, but he was quick to sense that Schabinger had overstepped his authority and had protested to the wrong quarter. Yet that a Turkish Commander should have threatened a German Consul with court martial and interfered with his diplomatic immunity was intolerable. However, as an experienced diplomat aware of Turkey's excessive pride, he trod warily. Rather than precipitate a head-on collision with the powerful Commander, Brode elected to appeal to his self-interest. He advised Djemal not to present the enemy with gratituous propaganda and waived the privilege of exemption from evacuation for Gentile German nationals. 'Discrimination on religious grounds', Brode emphasized, 'is unknown to us. Such preferential treatment would not be acceptable in Germany and would make a very bad impression upon the Jews.'[6]

The remonstrance made some impact on Djemal, but it affected his tactics more than his purpose. Two days later, when visiting Jaffa, he assumed the air of a gracious ruler. He spoke agreeably to Schabinger and, to the latter's surprise, withdrew his demand for an apology.[7] The order for evacuation was now presented as humanely as possible and explained away as an unavoidable military necessity. Out of consideration for the Jewish Passover the date of evacuation, originally set for 31 March, was postponed to 9 April. The farmers were allowed to stay and the evacuees were promised free transport facilities. Representatives of the Jewish community were told that the measure was not directed exclusively against

[6] Ibid. K 179232–8. Brode to A.A., 30 June 1917, dis. no. 137/1965 (original in *Türkei* 177). Zimmermann later agreed with Brode that Schabinger did not follow the right method. None the less, his conduct warranted no reproach. Overzealous and young, he was inexperienced in dealing with Turkish officials. (*Türkei* 195, K 179271–2, Zimmermann to Brode, 1 Aug. 1917 (secret).)

[7] *Türkei* 195, K 179232–8, Brode to A.A., 30 June 1917, dis. no. 137/1965.

their people. It concerned '*all* the inhabitants'. It was meant to ensure their own safety. Had he acted otherwise, Djemal declared, he would have been guilty of dereliction of duty. 'I am not an anti-Semite, I am only an anti-Zionist!'[8]

But the Jews were not deceived. 'The purpose of Djemal's visit', Jacob Thon commented, 'was reminiscent of that made in December 1914, on the eve of mass expulsion ordered by Beha-ed-Din'.[9] Brode strongly suspected that the Turkish Commander was using the abortive British attack on Gaza as a pretext for accomplishing his own political designs; the evacuation of Jaffa would serve merely as a prelude to that of Jerusalem.[10] The Austrian Consulate fully shared Brode's suspicions; Captain Moro, an Austrian Staff Officer, had been the first to realize that Djemal intended to deliver a death-blow to the Jewish enterprise in Palestine.[11]

Contemporary records of the evacuation of Jaffa abound with moving descriptions. 'We shall never forget this gruesome spectacle, nor shall we forgive,' wrote one of the evacuees.[12] 'By general consensus', Thon told his colleagues, 'this was the hardest blow we have ever experienced.'[13] About 9,000 Jews were deported. Jaffa, or rather Tel Aviv, its Jewish quarter, remained a dead city. No transport facilities were arranged and, without horses (which had been requisitioned by the Ottoman army), the evacuees had to travel on foot. Thefts and extortions by Turkish officials were rife. No shelter or food was provided and there were some deaths from exposure. About 6,000 of the evacuees concentrated in the neighbourhood of Petach-Tikva, others moved northwards to Samaria and Galilee. Their position was unenviable. But in times of adversity Jewish solidarity is at its strongest. The colonists not affected by the order responded magnificently. People living as far away as Galilee rushed to rescue the afflicted. Their condition was ameliorated but nothing could assuage their bitterness against the Turkish authorities. Despite assurances to the contrary, the Jews found

---

[8] *Türkei* 195, K 179503–8, Brode to Kühlmann, 5 Apr. 1917, dis. no. 33/908; C.Z.A. L 6/2/I, Thon to E.A.C., 18 Apr. 1917; Dizengoff, *Im Tel Aviv Bagola*, pp. 45–52; Ben Hillel Hacohen, op. cit. iii, pp. 124–5.

[9] C.Z.A. L 6/2/I, Thon to E.A.C., 18 Apr. 1917. In Apr. 1917 the Palestine Office was transferred from Jaffa to Jerusalem.

[10] As note 8.

[11] Friedman, 'The Austro-Hungarian Government and Zionism, 1897–1918', 157–9.

[12] Ben Hillel Hacohen, op. cit. iii, p. 133.   [13] See note 9.

themselves to be the principal victims. Muslim inhabitants of Jaffa were treated with conspicuous indulgence; they were allowed to seek shelter among the surrounding orange groves, whence they filtered back to their homes. The only concession granted to the Jews was permission to appoint a dozen or so watchmen to guard the property left behind.[14]

Brode's forecast proved right. Ten days after Jaffa's evacuation Djemal summoned all the consuls and told them that in spite of the successes on the Gaza front he had to evacuate Jerusalem's civilian population within twenty-four hours. The enemy might advance faster than expected and he urged the consuls to advise their respective nationals to leave as soon as possible. Brode, supported by other consuls, challenged Djemal's premiss, since according to competent authority there was no military danger threatening Jerusalem.[15] The authority to which Brode referred was the Bavarian Colonel (later General) Friedrich Freiherr Kress von Kressenstein, Chief of Staff of the Eighth Corps of the Fourth Ottoman Army. Described as its 'guiding military brain, Kress was 'a gallant, resolute and able soldier [who] always commanded the respect of his British opponents'.[16] Rafael de Nogales, the Ottoman Military Governor of Sinai, who knew Kress closely, testified that he was 'the idol of his officers', to whom the credit of repelling the British on the Gaza front was mainly due.[17] In Kress's opinion Djemal's intention of transferring the entire population of Jerusalem to the east of the River Jordan and the Syrian interior bordered

[14] C.Z.A. L 6/2/I, Thon to E.A.C., 18, 22, 26 Apr.; Dizengoff, Lev, and Yoffe (Petach-Tikva) to Thon (Jerusalem), 24 Apr. 1917; ibid., Vilkansky (Rosh-Pina) to Thon, 14 May 1917; 'Die Leiden der jüdischen Bevölkerung in Palästina . . ., Bericht Nr. 1 (by Thon, an undated copy); circular letter by Hantke, 1 June 1917 (confidential) (a copy in Z 3/82); Dizengoff, op. cit., pp. 51–63; Ben Hillel Hacohen, op. cit. iii, pp. 125–40; Smilansky, op. cit. iii, pp. 276–7, 284–9; *Sefer Hayovel shel Petach Tikva*, pp. 40–4; *Türkei* 195, K 179187–91, Cohn-Reiss to Nathan, 15 May 1917, encl. in Kühlmann to A.A., 14 July 1917, dis. no. 377. Christian Germans, advised by their Consulate, moved from Jaffa to the adjacent village of Wilhelma and to Jerusalem.

[15] *Türkei* 177, *Der Libanon (Syrien)*, Brode to Kühlmann, 23 Apr. 1917, cited in Kühlmann to A.A., 25 Apr., tel. no. 524 (copy in *Grosses Hauptquartier, Türkei, Nr. 41, Allgemeine Politik*, Bd. 3/4, cited in Zimmermann to Grünau (Gr. Hq.) 26 Apr. dis. no. 744). As to reaction of the Austrian Consulate see Friedman, 'The Austro-Hungarian Government and Zionism', 158–9.

[16] Wavell, op. cit., p. 28.

[17] Rafael de Nogales, *Four Years beneath the Crescent*, trans. M. Lee (London, 1926), pp. 181, 334. Djemal never acknowledged Kress's achievements. On the former's intrigues against Kress see ibid., p. 317.

on the insane. The position on the Egyptian front seemed to have been stabilized and even had the High Command intended to defend Jerusalem, German and Ottoman forces would hardly have been allowed to fight within the confines of the Holy City. This disposed of any necessity of evacuating the civilian population. Kress strongly suspected that Djemal nourished 'hidden political designs' of ridding Jerusalem of its alien inhabitants and converting it into a purely Muslim city and a Turkish stronghold. However wild the idea, it was not entirely out of keeping with Djemal's mental make-up, for though fond of displaying a certain tolerance, he was nevertheless a Muslim fanatic and a Turkish chauvinist. Kress could offer no other explanation. 'The evacuation of Jerusalem', he tells us in his memoirs, 'would have been a great tactical error' and would have involved those concerned in terrifying hazards.

Dislocation of so large a population would have led to unimaginable consequences. The terrible incidents of the Armenian exodus would have been repeated . . . Thousands would have died of starvation . . . and epidemics . . . and we Germans would have again been made scapegoats for this senseless measure. Thank God, the danger was averted in good time. The German Consul-General cabled to the Embassy and I . . . appealed to our Military Attaché at Constantinople, with the result that Enver Pasha instructed Djemal that evacuation of Jerusalem was not practical.[18]

This account is fully borne out by contemporary records. On 26 April(?) Kress warned the German Embassy at Constantinople that despite the favourable situation at the front Djemal was preparing the evacuation of Jerusalem, using the shortage of food as a pretext. The city had no military value and its evacuation was unnecessary.

The evacuation of a town in Turkey is tantamount to its complete annihilation . . . that of Jerusalem is aimed at the total ruin of its populace and of all Jewish and Christian institutions. History will burden Turkey's allies with the responsibility for this act . . .

I consider it our inescapable duty to resist it energetically and reject Djemal's assurances as worthless . . . If necessary, a warning should be given that all Christian officers and troops stationed in Palestine would be withdrawn.

---

[18] Kress von Kressenstein, *Mit den Türken zum Suezkanal*, 248–50. According to Carl Baedeker, *Handbuch: Palästina und Syrien*, there were before 1914 about 70,000 inhabitants in Jerusalem, 45,000 Jews, 15,000 Christians, and 10,000 Muslims. (See English edition 1918, i, p. 46.)

These were bold words; coming from such a competent officer as Kress, they could not remain unheeded. Kühlmann promised to raise the matter with Talaat Pasha, the Grand Vizier, though not in such drastic terms.[19]

Zimmermann was more effective. On 26 April, when he took the matter up with the High Command,[20] he knew what he was doing. The military authorities had little use for diplomatic niceties and on their explicit instructions Enver Pasha ordered Djemal to cancel the evacuation.[21] Kress was delighted at the defeat of his arch-enemy;[22] even more gratifying was the fact that Jerusalem, at least for the time being, was saved.

Richard Lichtheim, who at the time was still in Constantinople, was unaware of the events at Jaffa. Always sensitive to adverse currents, his instinct warned him of danger. As early as 13 March he had aired his fears to Count Waldburg, the Chargé d'Affaires. He approached Waldburg again on 7 April, pointing out that world opinion would react sharply to Jaffa's evacuation. By then Djemal Pasha's order was known at the Embassy, but Waldburg showed a peculiar indifference. It was discovered later that all Thon's cables to Lichtheim, dispatched through the official German cipher, had been suppressed. The Zionist Executive in Berlin later complained that had it not been for the Embassy's obstructive attitude they could have alerted the Auswärtiges Amt in good time to prevent Jaffa's evacuation.[23]

Nor did the Embassy inform the Foreign Ministry independently of the situation; Brode's dispatch of 5 April[24] had been forwarded after considerable delay. On 22 April the Hilfsverein leaders received a strange telegram from Ephraim Cohn-Reiss requesting urgent relief for 7,000 evacuees.[25] A few days later Zimmermann asked Kühlmann for information,[26] but no response was forthcoming. On 3 May an intercepted letter of Lichtheim, dated 27

[19] *Türkei* 177, Kühlmann to A.A., 27 Apr. 1917, tel. no. 537, where Kress's cable to the Embassy is cited.

[20] *Türkei* 41, Zimmermann to Grünau, 26 Apr. 1917, dis. no. 744.

[21] Ibid. Zimmermann to Lersner, 28 Apr. 1917, tel. no. 774; *Türkei* 177, Kühlmann to A.A., 28 Apr. 1917, tel. no. 537.   [22] Kressenstein, op. cit., p. 250.

[23] C.Z.A. L 6/2/I, circular letter by Hantke, 1 June 1917 (confidential) (a copy in Z 3/82); *Türkei* 195, K 179143–52, E.A.C., to A.A., 12 July 1917, and encl.

[24] On which see above, note 8.

[25] *Türkei* 195, K 178497, cited in Brode to A.A., 20 Apr. 1917, tel. no. 11.

[26] Ibid. K 178535, Zimmermann to Kühlmann, 3 May 1917, tel. no. 430.

April, was brought to the attention of the Foreign Ministry. It made grim reading: Jaffa had been completely evacuated and the evacuation of Jerusalem ordered. 'What the fate of the thousands of deportees would be nobody can imagine. For alleged military reasons they would be driven into misery and starvation. It is said that General von Kressenstein objected to the evacuation. But Djemal is omnipotent.'[27] However, as Djemal had in the meantime been overruled, Lichtheim's letter was outdated. It was not until 7 May, when a cable from the Zionist Bureau in Copenhagen reached Berlin, that the Wilhelmstrasse first learned about the events that had taken place.[28]

The news was alarming. According to sources in Egypt considered to be reliable, 'Tel Aviv had been sacked, ten thousand had been made homeless, Djemal Pasha had declared that Armenian policy would be applied to Jews . . . the whole Yishuv threatened with destruction.'[29] How did this information leak out? The Turkish authorities in Palestine exercised a strict censorship and the German Embassy at Constantinople was excessively secretive. It was the Aaronsohn group, a small but efficient spy-ring in Palestine, which was responsible for giving the news to the world.[30] Its leader, Aaron Aaronsohn, was working at the time for British Military Intelligence in Egypt. The group furnished him with information, mostly on military matters, and from 28 April Aaronsohn, availing himself of the British cipher, was able to inform the Zionist Bureau in London and a great number of Jewish organizations in allied and neutral countries about Jaffa's evacuation.[31] The news that the Yishuv was threatened with destruction spread quickly among the Jewish communities all over the world. The Press was alerted and governments in belligerent and neutral countries were approached. The London *Jewish Chronicle*[32] was the first paper to give warn-

---

[27] *Türkei* 195, K 178536, excerpts of Lichtheim letter to E.A.C., 27 Apr. 1917.

[28] Ibid. K 178552, A.A. note (undated); C.Z.A. L 6/2/I, circular letter by Hantke, 1 June 1917 (confidential).

[29] *Türkei* 195, K 178517, legation in Copenhagen to A.A., 5 May 1917, citing a letter dated 5 May from the Zionist Bureau in London (signed by Boris Goldberg) to Copenhagen.

[30] *Nili* (Hebrew), ed. Eliezer Livneh (Jerusalem, Tel Aviv, 1961), pp. 148–50. Far less scholarly is Anita Engle, *The Nili Spies* (London, 1959).

[31] P.R.O., F.O. 371/3055/87895, Turkey (War) Pol. 1917, cited in Wingate to F.O., 28 Apr. 1917, tel. no. 474; also ibid., same to same, 11 May 1917, tel. nos. 505, 507; C.Z.A. L 6/2/I.

[32] The issue of 4 May 1917. Cuttings of various newspapers found in P.R.O., F.O. 371/3055/87895; C.Z.A. L 6/2/II, and in the files of the German Foreign Ministry.

ing that should Djemal Pasha's proclaimed intention be carried out not only tens of thousands of Jews 'will be put to the sword . . . but the whole work of Palestinian resettlement will be utterly destroyed'. The *Manchester Guardian* (8 and 9 May) condemned the maltreatment of Jews in Palestine in the strongest terms: 'Djemal Pasha is too cunning to order cold-blooded massacres. His method is to drive the population to starvation and to death by thirst and epidemics.' *The Times* in London, the *Daily Telegraph*, the *Morning Post* (9 May), *Le Temps* (10 May) and other leading papers in the Entente and neutral countries expressed themselves in a similar vein. Reuter's message from Cairo was given the widest publicity. Some items were grossly exaggerated and subsequently Aaronsohn reproached his agents for not sticking to a strictly factual account.[33] But for Entente propaganda accuracy was not a primary concern; lurid stories suited their purpose admirably.[34] The Zionist Bureau in Copenhagen also did its best to give the reports the widest publicity, though for entirely different reasons.[35]

Sympathy in the Entente and neutral countries was encouraging, but only Germany could influence Turkey, and it was to her that Jews all over the world (some of them reluctantly) appealed. Cables from London, New York, Stockholm, Madrid, and elsewhere poured into the Zionist Bureau in Copenhagen[36] and were instantly forwarded by Hantke to Zimmermann.[37] Independently, Leo Winz contacted Erzberger, who wrote twice within a week to von Rosenberg, and separately to Zimmermann.[38] The Hilfsverein approached the Foreign Ministry,[39] and Oscar Cohn, Social Democratic Reichstag Deputy, prompted by Hantke, raised the question in the Reichstag.[40]

[33] *Nili*, op. cit., p. 149.
[34] P.R.O., F.O. 395/109/96621, News (Russia), 1917, Wingate to F.O., 11 May 1917, tel. no. 505, and Lord Robert Cecil's marginal annotation.
[35] *Türkei* 195, K 178570, Military Censorship to A.A., 8 May 1917; C.Z.A. L 6/2/I, Bernstein to Weizmann, 6 May 1917.
[36] C.Z.A. L 6/2/I.
[37] *Türkei* 195, K 178576–7, Hantke to Zimmermann, 6 May 1917.
[38] *Türkei* 195, K 178556, K 178559, letters dated 8 May 1917, and K 178604–5, 13 May 1917; also C.Z.A. L 6/2/I, Winz to Erzberger, 17 May 1917. Winz was editor of the magazine *Ost und West*. During the war he served in German Intelligence in Copenhagen. On Erzberger see above, pp. 297, 345.
[39] *Türkei* 195, K 178581–3, Nathan to Langwerth von Simmern (undated).
[40] Ibid. K 178550–1, König (Assessor-in-Chief) to A.A., 7 May 1917. Cohn's inquiry was widely reported in the German Press on the following day.

The next day, 8 May, Zimmermann appeared before the Budget Committee (Ausschuss für den Reichshaushalt). He denied the rumours that Jerusalem had been evacuated and attested that the necessity of evacuating Jaffa 'had not yet arisen'. Nor did he believe that Djemal Pasha had made such foolish statements about the Jews. On his recent visit to Berlin Talaat Pasha had specifically promised that there would be no repetition of the atrocities against the Armenians for which Germany had been unjustly blamed. Zimmermann concluded that Entente reports about Jewish persecution were tendentious; their transparent objective was to incite American Jewry to bring pressure to bear on President Wilson to declare war on Turkey and dispatch American troops to Palestine.[41]

Zimmermann believed what he said. The following day he informed all German diplomatic missions that the Reuter message was war propaganda.[42] He did not rest there. On 7 May, and again on the following day, he asked Kühlmann to make urgent inquiries about the truth of the reports which had so deeply alarmed the Jews and public opinion generally. 'The alertness of the Jewish Press all over the world would make more capital out of the excesses against their co-religionists in Palestine than [the Entente] did out of the Armenian atrocities. Accusations would be levelled principally against Turkey, but we should also be made responsible indirectly.'[43] He also requested that Thon in Jerusalem should be allowed to re-establish contact with his colleagues in Constantinople and Berlin, as statements emanating from Zionist quarters would win more credence than those inspired officially.[44]

But Kühlmann continued to maintain a sphinx-like attitude. In the meantime the clamour all over the world was gathering momentum. There was hardly any important paper outside the Central Powers[45] which failed to give prominence to the news from Palestine. All of them carried the same story of the Turkish intention to bring starvation and death to their helpless victims. In Madrid Professor Abraham Yahuda[46] and Dr. Max Nordau received letters

---

[41] *Türkei* 195, K 178553–5, minutes of the meeting, no. 155, 8 May 1917. (Original in *Deutschland* 122, Nr. 2 m.i.)

[42] Ibid. K 178568, Zimmermann to legation in Copenhagen, 9 May 1917, tel. no. 343, copies to Vienna, Berne, The Hague, Stockholm, and Kristiana.

[43] Ibid. K 178548–9, K 178562–3, Zimmermann to Kühlmann, 7, 8 May 1917, tel. nos. 448, 450.   [44] Ibid. K 178582, same to same, 12 May 1917, tel. no. 466.

[45] e.g. *The Times, Daily Telegraph, Manchester Guardian, Petit Parisien, Journal de Genève, La Suisse Genève, Berlinske Tidende* (of 14 May 1917).

[46] On whom see below, p. 363.

from Jerusalem indicating that the evacuation of Jaffa was worse than the notorious expulsions from Tsarist Russia.[47] The German legations in neutral countries watched helplessly the rise of public indignation.[48] In the Reichstag Oscar Cohn challenged the Chancellor, asking him whether the German Government was prepared to intervene with Turkey.[49]

Zimmermann became impatient. Suspected of complicity in the maltreatment of Palestine Jews, Germany's standing, particularly in Russia and America, was adversely affected. Kühlmann's persistent reticence deprived Berlin of the information needed to rebut the enemy's charges.[50] It was not until 17 May, on receipt of Brode's cable (of 15 May), that the Wilhelmstrasse at last could assess the situation. Brode's report contained two versions, one designed for the general public, but the second one, for official consideration, was nearer the truth. There Brode reiterated his belief that Djemal had used the military situation as a pretext to destroy Jewish colonization. Though reports on pillage and massacres were 'blatant lies', the plight of the evacuees was none the less grave. Lack of transport, food, and shelter exposed them to exhaustion and disease, and they had no protection against the excesses of individual Ottoman officials.[51]

Zimmermann urged Kühlmann to persuade the Turkish Government that it was in its own as well as its allies' interest to make it unambiguously clear that it harboured no sinister intentions against the Jews. If possible—and here Zimmermann followed the advice given to him by the Zionist and non-Zionist Jewish organizations in Germany—the evacuees should be allowed to return to their homes; alternatively measures should be taken to alleviate their plight.[52]

It was not without good reason that Zimmermann was so deeply concerned. Reports and comment in the Entente and neutral Press

[47] *Türkei* 195, K 178611, E.A.C. to A.A., 14 May 1917, encl. Yahuda and Nordau to the Zionist Bureau in Copenhagen, 13 May 1917.

[48] Ibid. K 178613, legation in Copenhagen to A.A., 13 May 1917; K 178591, Rosen (The Hague) to A.A., 11 May 1917; K 178607, Romberg (Berne) to A.A., 14 May 1917.

[49] Ibid. K 178595–7, Kaempf to President of the Reichstag, 14 May 1917; K 180424, Kühlmann to same, 25 Aug. 1917. (Cohn's question no. 156.)

[50] Ibid. K 178606, Zimmermann to Kühlmann, 15 May 1917, tel. no. 477.

[51] Ibid. K 178628–30, cited in Kühlmann to A.A., 16 May 1917, tel. no. 617.

[52] Ibid. K 178640–1, Zimmermann to Kühlmann, 19 May 1917, tel. no. 500; K 178651, Hantke to Göppert, 20 May (résumé of an interview on the previous day).

presented the bleakest picture. The New York *Sun* (16 May) alleged that even the massacres of the Armenians paled before the 'outrages in the Holy Land . . . whenever the Jews have attempted to defend their homes . . . they have been hanged . . . their homes pillaged and all property confiscated and burned'. *The Times* in New York (20 May), the New York *Journal* (21 May), and other American papers also described the events in Palestine in gruesome terms. *The Times* of London (19 May) pointed to the 'thousands of Jews wandering helplessly on the roads . . . starving . . . The evacuation of colonies', the paper predicted, 'is imminent.' This was also the view of the *Manchester Guardian* and the *Daily Telegraph* (21 May). The *Jewish Chronicle* (24 May) alleged that the Turkish Government appeared to have entered upon a course of 'calculated brutal ruthlessness'; Djemal's intention was 'to wipe out mercilessly the Jewish population of Palestine'; whilst the Italian papers such as *Corriere della Sera*, *Il Cittadino*, and *L'Unità Cattolica* (21 May), amongst others, conveyed the impression that Palestine had already been devastated.

With the Havas Agency joining Reuter, the French and Swiss Press[53] followed suit. The *Journal de Genève* (22 May) alleged that Germany bore part of the responsibility for the 'inhuman measures' adopted by the Turkish authorities. The Turco-German alliance 'wished to revive the Tsarist practices repudiated by the new regime in Russia'. The Scandinavian papers pursued the same theme; in *Politiken* (22 May) George Brandes, a leading Danish journalist, was most scathing. In vain did the German and Austrian Press[54] endeavour to deny, or at least correct, the exaggerated reports. With few exceptions[55] the version put out by the Wolf Telegraphic Bureau gained little credence.[56]

In Berne Romberg was chagrined to see how skilfully the Entente had exploited the situation. He insisted that something must be done immediately to counteract the unfavourable impression. 'It is a matter of concern that influential Zionist circles have also been

[53] e.g. *Petite République*, *Agence Républicaine* (23 May), *Neue Züricher Zeitung*, *Le Genevois*, *Journal de Genève*, and *Gazette de Lausanne* (21 May), *Tribune de Lausanne* (24 May).

[54] e.g. *Berliner Tageblatt* (15 May), *Deutsche Warte*, *Arbeiter Zeitung*, *Neues Wiener Tageblatt* (20 May), *Münchener Neueste Nachrichten* (23 May), *Frankfurter Zeitung* (24 May, evening edn.).

[55] Such as *Züricher Post* and *De Maasbode Rotterdam* (20 May).

[56] *Türkei* 195, K 178675–6, Winz to A.A., Copenhagen, 22 May 1917; C.Z.A. Z 6/2/I, the same to E.A.C., 23 May (citing *Berlinske Tidende*).

provoked . . . It is [universally] believed that Djemal Pasha wanted to put an end to the Jewish enterprise in Palestine.'[57] The question was raised in the British[58] and Swedish parliaments.[59] In Germany too there was much frustration and anger. No less a person than Gustav Stresemann approached the Foreign Ministry.[60] So did the leader of the Social Democratic party;[61] the Deutsch-Israelitisch Osmanische Union warned that the Entente would not miss the opportunity of using Turkey's misdemeanour to compromise Germany's position at the future Peace Conference.[62]

With such manifold pressures building up, Zimmermann dispatched another cable to Constantinople:

We hear from [various] sources that the expulsions from Jaffa are being systematically utilized to stir up feelings against us, especially in Russia, where the influence of the Jewish element is growing. Reports provoke great excitement and bitterness. German Jewry is also seriously alarmed by the discriminatory nature of the Turkish anti-Jewish measures. Your Excellency is requested urgently and emphatically to influence the Porte to follow our suggestions without delay.[63]

Kühlmann consequently spoke with all leading Turkish statesmen: Talaat Pasha, Nessimy Bey, and Enver Pasha; against all expectations he met complete understanding. The Turkish Government, he was told, intended to issue categorical denials and undertake full-scale relief work to meet Jewish grievances. Kühlmann now revealed that originally all the Jewish colonies were to be evacuated, but later the order had been restricted to Jaffa alone.[64]

---

[57] Ibid. K 178677, Romberg to A.A., 22 May 1917, tel. no. 903 (very urgent); K 178700-1, same to same, 22 May, dis. no. 1569.

[58] *Hansard* (House of Commons), 1917, Cols. 1333-4. On 14 May Lord Robert Cecil stated that 'the Allied Governments would do all in their power to avert such a calamity' (i.e. expropriation or massacre of Jews in Palestine) but added, 'it is difficult to see what effective measures are open to them'.

[59] On 22 May; C.Z.A. L 6/2/I, Zionist Bureau (Copenhagen) to E.A.C., 24 May 1917.

[60] *Türkei* 195, K 178780-2, note dated 24 May, 1917. In the following month Stresemann was elected leader of the National Liberal Group in the Reichstag and in November 1917 leader of the National Liberal party.

[61] Ibid. K 178770, note by Zimmermann, dated 29 May 1917.

[62] Ibid. K 178667-72, D.I.O.U. (signed Nossig and Professor Israel) to Zimmermann, 22 May 1917. On the Deutsch-Israelitisch Osmanische Union see above, p. 268, and below, pp. 386, 388.

[63] Ibid. K 178681, Zimmermann to Kühlmann, 24 May 1917, tel. no. 575. This was a follow-up to the telegram of 19 May, no. 500 (on which see above, note 52).

[64] Ibid. K 178688-9, Kühlmann to A.A., 23 May 1917, tel. no. 642.

All the same, he could not explain his earlier silence at so crucial a time. When asked by von dem Bussche-Hadenhausen, the Under-Secretary of State, why, since the end of March, Thon's telegrams had failed to reach Lichtheim,[65] he could only reply that 'all except one' of Thon's telegrams had been passed on;[66] the one referred to was that of 28 March warning Lichtheim of the impending evacuation. In fact none of Thon's telegrams reached its destination. Even more puzzling was the suppression of Ephraim Cohn's letter to Paul Nathan. Cohn had written that the position of the evacuees was becoming 'desperate... The mortality, in consequence of epidemics, is great.'[67] The letter, dated 15 May (and forwarded through official channels), was not released by the Embassy until two months later.[68]

On 27 May Kühlmann finally gave his qualified approval for Thon to use the official cipher to re-establish contact with his friends in Constantinople and Berlin.[69] But on the whole his attitude to the Zionists remained antagonistic. It was General Lossow, the Military Attaché, who was Kühlmann's mentor, not the Foreign Minister, and for Lossow the overriding concern was to keep relations with Djemal smooth. Lossow disliked Kress's independence of mind intensely; he thought his statements[70] might have undermined Djemal's trust and considered them to be 'extremely dangerous and damaging'. Djemal had the undisputed right to order Jaffa's evacuation;[71] he had to protect the lives of the population in case of bombardment by British warships; he was perfectly willing to invite a German-Jewish Commission of Inquiry and thought that the calumnies spread by the Entente were meant merely to cover up the British defeats at Gaza.[72]

Kühlmann could now triumphantly tell Berlin that, in view of all the evidence, '*no one* could ... continue to believe that the Turks

---

[65] *Türkei* 195, K 178707, Bussche to Kühlmann, 25 May 1917, tel. no. 519 (on Hantke's verbal request).

[66] Ibid. K 178744, Kühlmann to A.A., 27 May 1917, tel. no. 656.

[67] Ibid. K 178835, same to same, 31 May 1917, tel. no. 671.

[68] Ibid. K 179187–91, Cohn-Reiss (Jerusalem) to Nathan (Berlin), 15 May 1917, encl. in Kühlmann to A.A., 14 July 1917, dis. no. 377.

[69] Ibid. K 178743, Kühlmann to A.A., 27 May 1917, tel. no. 655.

[70] On which see above, pp. 351–3.

[71] *Türkei* 195, K 178694–5, cited in Kühlmann to A.A., 23 May 1917, tel. no. 641. The War Ministry eventually agreed with Lossow that Colonel von Kress should not interfere in political measures undertaken by Djemal (K 178933, to A.A., 2 June 1917).

[72] Ibid. K 178741–2, cited in Kühlmann to A.A., 26 May 1917, tel. no. 650 (copy in C.Z.A. L 6/2/I); Lossow's report was carefully leaked to the German Press.

are pursuing a policy of systematic persecution', and added sarcastically: 'those without bona fides will never let themselves be convinced'.[73] A week later, still angry, he noted:

> *The Turks will never forget* that the entire diplomatic machinery has been set in motion against them over the Jaffa case . . . even the Pope . . . and the Spanish Government made representations . . . Such exaggerations create the danger that the Turks will revenge themselves against Ottoman Jewry as a whole . . . The Turkish Government . . . feels itself blameless and is angered by excessive pressure.[74]

Kühlmann's statement reflected his own state of mind rather than that in Constantinople. The Porte fully realized the damage done to Turkey's image, and in Berlin Ambassador Hakki Pasha did his best to explain away Jaffa's evacuation as an unavoidable military necessity; Turkey's traditional benevolence towards her Jewish subjects, he took pains to emphasize, was as strong as ever.[75] Hakki's declaration was eagerly taken up by the German Press[76] but its effect was limited. The Zionists were certainly not lulled into a false sense of security. Well informed about the situation,[77] they could distinguish between propaganda and the truth.

Of greater consequence were the declarations made in Palestine. These Djemal Pasha managed to extract by summoning some prominent Jewish leaders[78] to a meeting on 28 May at which he was demonstratively friendly. Pointing to the papers where the Havas Agency reports made prominent headlines, he said that the sole purpose of this campaign was to prejudice Turkey's position at the Peace Conference. Since the matter concerned vital state interests he asked all those present to communicate with their friends abroad and refute the Havas and Reuter allegations. He attached particular importance to Zionist influence and, in an unexpected gesture,

---

[73] Ibid. K 178858–9, Kühlmann to A.A., 1 June 1917, tel. no. 675.

[74] Ibid. K 178930–1, same to same, 8 June 1917, tel. no. 694.

[75] Ibid. K 178724, encl. in D.I.O.U. to Göppert, 24 May 1917 (K 178722–3). Published by the Wolf Telegraphic Bureau on the following day (K 178730 and C.Z.A. L 6/2/II).

[76] e.g. *Frankfurter Zeitung, Der Tag, Vossische Zeitung, Kölnische Zeitung* (25 May), *Berliner Tageblatt* (26 May).

[77] *Türkei* 195, K 178745, Ruppin to Warburg, 26 May 1917, tel. no. 656 (copy in C.Z.A. L 6/2/I).

[78] They included Chief Rabbi Danon, Rabbi Horowitz, Meir Dizengoff, Ephraim Cohn-Reiss, Eliyahu Krause, Yechiel Brill, Aaron Eisenberg, Menase Meyerowitz, and Dr. Jacob Thon.

charged Meir Dizengoff, the Mayor of Tel Aviv, with the task of forming a relief committee.[79] He contributed for this purpose 3,000 Turkish pounds. Rabbis Marcus Horowitz and Nissim Danon were given 1,000 Turkish pounds each for the needy in Jerusalem. Moreover, he promised to release from the army three physicians to care for the evacuees and to provide the necessary medicines free of charge.[80]

The Jewish leaders had no alternative but to comply. Chief Rabbi Danon telegraphed his counterparts in Constantinople, Sweden, Holland, Denmark, and Switzerland that the Jews had to leave Jaffa for their own safety; that transport facilities had been procured and the poor assisted; that Djemal Pasha, both by word and deed, had shown his 'benevolence and magnanimity'; and that stories of massacres and plunderings, let alone of a total evacuation, were 'slanders'.[81] Thon, on behalf of the Palestine Office, also cabled thirteen Zionist papers, though in a less ingratiating tone *vis-à-vis* Djemal than Rabbi Danon. None the less, he felt tormented: 'With our own hands', he confided to Warburg, 'we had to act against our own convictions and render a disservice to our cause.'[82]

The Press campaign had a restraining effect on Djemal, and it seemed that he had relented. But appearances were deceptive. With the statements extracted from the Chief Rabbi and other Jewish leaders the proposal to invite a fact-finding commission was soon dropped. Brode was contemptuous of Djemal's duplicity. The evacuation had nothing to do with the military situation (an opinion which he requested the Foreign Ministry not to disclose to the Zionists, nor utilize against the Porte) and the evacuees, he advised Berlin, should be allowed to return without further delay.[83]

---

[79] This had existed unofficially under Dizengoff's chairmanship since the early days of evacuation.

[80] *Türkei* 195, K 178804-5, Thon to Warburg, 29 May 1917, cited in Brode to A.A., 29 May, tel. no. 17; C.Z.A. L 6/2/I, Thon to Warburg, 29 May, 1 June 1917; ibid., Hantke's circular letter, 1 June 1917; Dizengoff, op. cit., pp. 64-7; Ben Hillel Hacohen, op. cit. iii, pp. 194-7; Cohn-Reiss, *M'Zichronoth Ish Yerushalaim*, ii, pp. 276-8. Djemal had a separate meeting with representatives of the Christian community in Palestine. One Turkish pound was equal to 1 pound sterling, 25 French francs, 5 U.S. dollars.

[81] *Türkei* 195, K 178947-8, Danon to Rabbi Littmann (Zürich), 28 May 1917; to Nahoum, 3 June (K 178877-8); to Nathan, 29 May (K 178844-8); to Ehrenpreis (Stockholm), 3 June (K 178886); to Professor Simonsen (Denmark), 29 May (C.Z.A. L 6/2/I).

[82] C.Z.A. L 6/2/I, Thon to Warburg, 1 June 1917.

[83] *Türkei* 195, K 178870, cited in Kühlmann to A.A., 2 June 1917, tel. no. 678, and K 178898, cited in same to same, 5 June 1917, tel. no. 685.

The German Press made the most of the Danon–Thon statements. 'Persecution of Jews in Palestine', the *Frankfurter Zeitung* wrote, 'is a fiction . . . a product of Anglo-French imagination.'[84] This stereotyped message emanating from the Wolf Telegraphic Agency made little impact in Jewish circles. The Zionists, aware that it was fabricated, took the statement with an extra grain of salt. The *Jüdische Rundschau*[85] had to walk a tightrope between factual accuracy and the imperative need not to offend Turkish susceptibilities. But to the German propaganda machine denials from the mouth of competent Jewish leaders in Palestine came as a godsend. Not only public opinion but even foreign envoys, such as the Spanish, could be told that reports emanating from allied sources were false.[86]

Among neutral countries Spain took the leading role in interceding for the Palestinian Jews. The young King, Alfonso XIII, was said to be a man of quick intellect, conscious of his duties and prerogatives; he was the 'real seat of political power',[87] and it was to him that Professor Yahuda (Professor of Hebrew Literature and Semitic Languages at the University of Madrid) appealed for help. Yahuda was effectively seconded by Señor Eduardo Dato, ex-Premier and leader of the Conservative party, and the Marquis of Alhucemas, the Prime Minister. They soon won over the King, who ordered his Ambassadors in Berlin, Vienna, and Constantinople to protest against the maltreatment of Jews.[88] Alfonso's response was in keeping both with his own ambition to appear as a champion of humane causes in general and with the renewed interest Spain was showing in the welfare of the Spanish-speaking Jews in Morocco and the Near East, descendants of the fifteenth-century exiles.[89]

It was also through Spain that the governments of Britain, France, Italy, and Russia—the last initiated the move—lodged their protests against Turkey. As co-signatories of the treaties of Paris

[84] The issue of 1 June 1917; also of 29 May. For this version given by the W.T.A. on 29 May to the Press see K 178798 and K 178800-1.

[85] In its issue of 1 June; *Türkei* 195, K 178953-4, Leo Heimann (editor of the *J.R.*) to Hantke, 10 June 1917; also Hantke's circular letter, 1 June 1917 (C.Z.A. Z 3/82).

[86] *Türkei* 195, K 178795-6, Zimmermann to Spanish Embassy, 29 May 1917.

[87] Salvador de Madariaga, *Spain* (London, 1942), p. 107.

[88] *Jewish Chronicle*, 9 May 1919, p. 17. Statement by Yahuda.

[89] P.R.O., F.O. 371/3055/87895, Hardinge (Madrid) to Cecil (London), 15 May 1917, dis. no. 261.

(1856) and Berlin (1878) the Entente Powers were fully within their rights to make such representations, which in time of war had to be channelled through a neutral Power. The Dutch Government was the second instrument chosen for that purpose. To a move of this nature Germany was sensitive. Both in Spain and in the Netherlands sympathy for the belligerents was divided and German Envoys kept a constant watch for any adverse tilt against the Reich. However, when the Spanish and Dutch Governments approached Berlin and Constantinople early in June the latter was in the comfortable position of being able to point to the recent denials by the Jewish leaders in Jerusalem. Djemal Pasha could also be quoted as having promised to invite the Spanish Consul (this in addition to an independent Jewish fact-finding commission) to investigate the position on the spot, and the Porte had issued specific orders to the authorities in Palestine to allow the Jews 'to return to their homes as soon as possible'.[90]

Yet the gap between these assurances and their implementation remained wide. This was not necessarily because the German and Turkish Governments were insincere. It was Djemal Pasha who proved the chief stumbling-block. In vain did Zimmermann press for an early dispatch of the commission.[91] The effect of the *démenti* soon wore off and the neutral Press met it with growing distrust.[92] Zimmermann was well aware that until the evacuees were allowed to return to their homes the Central Powers would remain dangerously vulnerable.[93] The Ministry of War fully concurred with this opinion,[94] and it seemed that there was hardly any need for Zimmermann to convince the Turkish Ambassador in Berlin of the dangers of alienating international Jewry.[95] Hakki, of his own accord, had earlier suggested that a German-Jewish commission of inquiry should visit Palestine and promised that it would be given extensive

---

[90] P.R.O., F.O. 371/3055/87895, same to same, 11 June 1917, dis. no. 316 and encl. Alvaro to Hardinge, 8 June; ibid., Townley (The Hague) to Balfour, 10, 11 June 1917; dis. no. 144 and tel. no. 1610; *Türkei* 195, K 179041, Winz to E.A.C., 21 June 1917, citing Yahuda of 20 June, and K 179053, Rosen (The Hague) to A.A., 21 June 1917, dis. no. 2495; *Nationaltidende* (22 June 1917), quoting the Russian paper *Ryech*.

[91] *Türkei* 195, K 178773–5, Zimmermann to Kühlmann, 29 May 1917, dis. no. 527.

[92] Ibid. K 178895–7, same to same, 6 June 1917, tel. no. 562; see, e.g., *Algemen Handelsblad* (Amsterdam, 17 June), cutting in K 178986, and for a German translation K 178987–91.

[93] Ibid. K 178962–3, same to same, 14 June 1917, tel. no. 590.

[94] Ibid. K 178977, War Ministry to A.A., 13 June 1917.

[95] Ibid. K 179074, A.A. note, dated 26 June 1917.

facilities.[96] He reiterated his assurances a month later,[97] but Djemal considered the question closed and was reluctant to admit any team of observers to Palestine.[98] The suggestion that the Spanish Consul in Jerusalem should make a separate inquiry was also shelved.[99]

The Sublime Porte was frustrated. Talaat urged Djemal ceaselessly to repatriate the evacuees, insisting on the need to counteract Entente propaganda. But Djemal was evasive.[100] He played the military card for all it was worth but at heart he was deeply xenophobic. In an interview with a correspondent of *Deutsche Politik* he stated that after the war he would root out every vestige of Entente influence in Syria and Palestine. Nor would he allow Jewish colonization. This he regarded as injurious to Ottoman interests.[101]

Any lingering doubts about Djemal's intentions were dispelled, but the Zionists could still take comfort from the powerful support they were receiving. By early August the Zionist Executive was assured that no further evacuation was expected in the foreseeable future.[102] Relief funds were permitted to flow without interference,[103] and the evacuees showed enough ingenuity to overcome the odds.[104] Periodically, with an eye on the Press, Djemal continued to make gestures of goodwill, but on the question of repatriation he was adamant.[105] Jaffa was to remain *judenrein*. Whilst Arabic-speaking inhabitants were allowed to stay and the German colonists could return to the nearby colony of Sarona, the Jews languished in their camps. Relief was a palliative and there was no new British attack in sight to justify their displacement. This was an anomalous

[96] Ibid. K 178955–6, D.I.O.U. (Nossing and Simon) to A.A., 14 June 1917.

[97] Ibid. K 179138–9, same to same, 10 July 1917; K 179193, Bussche to Kühlmann, 21 July 1917, tel. no. 769.

[98] Ibid. K 178966–7, Kühlmann (citing Brode) to A.A., 13 June 1917, tel. no. 708.

[99] Ibid. K 179267–8, Waldburg to A.A., 27 July 1917, tel. no. 393.

[100] Ibid. K 178944, K 179058, Kühlmann to A.A., 11, 26 June 1917, tel. nos. 703, 759.

[101] The issue of 8 June cited in the *New York Times* of 30 June (cutting in K 179281); also in E.A.C. to A.A., 24 June 1917 (K 179059–72).

[102] *Türkei* 195, K 179297, Ruppin to Warburg, 9 Aug. 1917 (copy in C.Z.A. L 6/2/I) and K 179330–7, E.A.C. to A.A., 17 Aug. (copy in C.Z.A. Z 3/1484).

[103] A sum equivalent to 2,459,815 francs was contributed by the Jewish communities in Russia, Germany, and Holland. American Jewry contributed the equivalent of 1,359,946 francs. The funds were channelled through the Zionist Bureau in Constantinople (*Palestine during the War*, pp. 70–1). For the sum transferred through Egypt see below, note 115.

[104] For the position of the evacuees see: *Türkei* 195, K 179039, Thon to Warburg, 20 June 1917; C.Z.A. L 6/2/I, Thon to Ruppin, 22 June, 6 Aug.; ibid., same to Hantke, 11 July 1917 (a copy in K 179081).

[105] *Türkei* 195, K 178966–7, Kühlmann to A.A. (citing Brode), 13 June 1917, tel. no. 708.

position which Dizengoff was brave enough to point out, but only to invite Djemal's wrath: 'I shall hang you in your Tel Aviv. The return of your people would imply that my original order was incorrect!' Subsequently, Djemal requested Dizengoff to modify his report. He offered him 13,500 Turkish pounds as a subsidy for the evacuees and an equivalent sum in the form of loans. He also promised to supply grain from army stores.[106]

Following such ostentatious generosity Brode hoped that Djemal's visit to Berlin would soften him still further. He thought it advisable for the Foreign Ministry to use the opportunity to discuss with Djemal the question of Jewish colonization and to press for an early repatriation of the evacuees, 'by the end of October at the latest, as by then, with the stormy season approaching, an enemy landing could be safely discounted'.[107] Zimmermann hardly required this advice. Two weeks earlier, before Brode's cable arrived in Berlin, he suggested that Talaat's good offices should be used to influence Djemal.[108] But all overtures were in vain. When approached by Waldburg at Constantinople, Djemal stated that his objection was motivated not by personal pique but by overriding military necessity; he was not a Jew-baiter but only 'an opponent of Zionism'.[109] Again, in Berlin, when meeting the Zionist leaders Hantke and Lichtheim at the suggestion of the Auswärtiges Amt, Djemal was amiable and courteous. He assured his visitors that the Jews in Palestine would be treated well.[110] The weakness of his argument was exposed when set against Kress's assessment, made known to Thon. Kress discounted the likelihood of a British landing along the Gaza–Jaffa seaboard and thought there was no justification for keeping Jaffa's population away from their homes.[111] But with Djemal remaining as obdurate as ever the Zionists had to resign themselves to the situation in the hope that it would not deteriorate any further.

[106] Dizengoff, op. cit., pp. 76-80; C.Z.A. L 6/2/I, Dizengoff, 'Rapport sur les émigrés de Jaffa', 1 July 1917 (submitted to Djemal Pasha); ibid., Thon to Ruppin, 6, 9 July; same to Hantke, 11 July; K 179122, same to Warburg, 4 July 1917; Ben Hillel Hacohen, op. cit. iv, pp. 5, 30-3, 65, 76.

[107] *Türkei* 195, K 179454-5, Brode to Zimmermann, 31 Aug. 1917, tel. no. 1048.

[108] Ibid. K 179325-6, Zimmermann to Chargé d'Affaires, 16 Aug. 1917, tel. no. 901.

[109] Ibid. K 179417, Waldburg (not signed) to A.A., 21 Aug. 1917, tel. no. 998; C.Z.A. Z 3/1485, Ruppin to E.A.C., 28 Aug. 1917.

[110] C.Z.A. Z 3/83, minutes of a meeting with Djemal Pasha on 28 Aug. 1917; also K 179435, A.A. note signed by Göppert; above, pp. 329-30.

[111] C.Z.A. Z 3/1485, Ruppin to E.A.C., 28 Aug. 1917, citing Thon.

During August and September there seemed to be no reason for anxiety. The Committee of Inquiry, headed by Dr. Julius Becker,[112] was about to depart; in Palestine the Jews were left unmolested and there were no disturbing omens. However, by October the position had changed drastically for the worse. The very survival of the Yishuv now seemed in question. It was the discovery of the Nili spy-ring[113] that aroused the anger of the Turks. The ring was transmitting military information to Egypt in the hope that it would accelerate the British invasion and facilitate recognition of the Jewish claim to Palestine. However, it had to pay a heavy price. On 1 October the Turkish troops surrounded Zichron-Yaakov, the Nili's headquarters, and its members were brutally tortured. The Aaronsohn family, in particular, became the target for Turkish cruelty. Sara, who after her brother Aaron's departure, had assumed command of the activities, committed suicide. Others were thrown into the dungeons of Nazareth and Damascus.[114]

Nearly all Palestinian Jews had steered clear of any association with Nili; they felt instinctively that any act of disloyalty to the regime, let alone active assistance to the enemy, was bound to imperil the well-being of the whole community; however bitter they were against their Turkish overlord, no pretext was to be given which could be used against them. The lesson of the Armenian tragedy was well appreciated. Thon was reported to have called the Aaronsohn group 'a calamity for the Yishuv', and even when some contact had to be established with Nili during the summer of 1917, when funds were transmitted through them for the evacuees, it

---

[112] A Zionist correspondent of the *Vossische Zeitung*.

[113] On 4 Sept. 1917 a carrier pigeon with a message in a peculiar script fell into Turkish hands. The message could not be deciphered but two weeks later, when two Arab spies from Nazareth in the pay of British Intelligence were arrested, the Turks finally came on the track of the Nili headquarters at Atlith and Zichron-Yaakov. (*Türkei* 195, K 179658–60, Bernstorff to A.A., 29 Oct. 1917, tel. no. 1343; K 18004–9, Schulenburg to Bernstorff, 22 Nov. 1917, dis. no. 74/1779; *Nili*, op. cit., pp. 245–9, 316. Not all the information reported by the Consulate in Damascus was accurate.) About ten days later Naaman Belkind, a Nili member, was captured by beduoin when attempting to cross to the British lines south of Beer-Sheeba. He was handed over to the Turkish army; a notebook found among his belongings, containing a list of names of some of his friends and their plans, betrayed his own identity and the purpose of his mission. According to Dr. Moshe Neumann, who later shared a cell in the Damascus prison with him, Belkind refused to give any details about Nili to his interrogators. However, the Turkish Intelligence outwitted him. One of its officers feigned friendship for Belkind and, after plying him with drink, extracted information from him (*Nili*, op. cit., pp. 250–8, reproducing also an extract from Neumann's memoirs).

[114] *Nili*, op. cit., pp. 271–85; C.Z.A. Z 3/80, Daniel Oster to E.A.C., 13 Oct. 1917.

was done with great reluctance. In September all relations were severed,[115] and espionage was repeatedly and openly condemned.[116] But this was of little avail. Several days after the raid on Zichron-Yaakov the Turkish authorities carried out extensive searches all over the country. Hundreds of individuals, including most of the communal leaders, were arrested and received harsh treatment. Djemal Pasha now suspected all Jews of being enemy agents. Evidence was collated in the courts to 'prove' that a plot had been hatched to foment a general rebellion. Jaffa evacuees who had found temporary shelter in the neighbourhood of Petach-Tikva, Kefar-Saba, Haifa, or Tiberias were ordered to move northwards to the Syrian interior or east to the River Jordan. The Governor of Haifa, noted for his cruelty, accused the Jews of treachery. 'The mass arrests', he admitted, 'were meant to outlaw them and deliver them to the rage of the [Muslim] population as had been done in the case of the Armenians.'[117] On 19 October Izzet Bey, the *Mutassarif* of Jerusalem, called two hundred Arab notables and sheikhs and six Jewish representatives to the mosque of Ramleh. His speech was calculated to incite the Arabs against the Jews. From the latter he demanded the capture of a wanted spy, still in hiding. Failing that, he warned, 'all Jewish colonies will be turned into a heap of ruins'. Although Joseph Lishansky, the suspected Nili ringleader, was caught the next day by bedouin among the Nabi Rubin dunes incitement against the Jews continued unabated; there was little doubt in their minds of what the Turks intended. The mood of despair can be recaptured from an appeal sent urgently to Ruppin: 'All the Jews are accused of espionage . . . *Something must be done, a strong power must intervene . . . Otherwise . . . the whole population will be destroyed.*'[118]

The Zionist Executive in Berlin first learned about these events on 15 October. Warburg feared the worst.[119] Von dem Bussche-

---

[115] *Nili*, op. cit., pp. 171–92, 339; Smilansky, op. cit. iii, pp. 311, 324–48; *Sefer Toldoth Ha'aganna*, ed. Dinur, i, Pt. I, pp. 369–70, 381; Pt. II, App. 35, p. 862. It was estimated that up to Feb. 1918 a relief committee in Egypt transferred £25,000 in gold to Palestine through the Aaronsohn group (*Nili*, op. cit., p. 158).

[116] *Türkei* 195, K 179640–1, Thon to Warburg, 26 Oct. 1917, tel. no. 1326.

[117] C.Z.A. Z 3/80, Daniel Oster to E.A.C., 13 Oct. 1917.

[118] *Türkei* 195, K 179786–93, Ruppin to Bernstorff, Constantinople, 7 Nov. [mistyped Oct.] 1917, and encls. dated 19, 28 Oct. 1917; Dizengoff, op. cit., pp. 83, 100, 105; Smilansky, op. cit. iii, pp. 312–13, 316–17; Ben Hillel Hacohen, op. cit. iv, pp. 91–107.

[119] Ibid. K 179596–8, Warburg to A.A., 15 Oct. 1917.

Hadenhausen, to whom Warburg appealed for support, was equally shocked by the news. That the Turks had resumed such a brutal course was bound to produce a wave of revulsion around the world, and the coincidence of the Kaiser's visit to Constantinople might give added substance to the suspicions of German complicity. Edhern Bey, the Turkish Chargé d'Affaires, was summoned immediately to the Foreign Ministry[120] and Count Johan Heinrich Bernstorff, newly appointed Ambassador to Constantinople, was advised accordingly.[121] Bernstorff replied that during the conferences in Constantinople State Secretary Kühlmann himself had raised the matter.[122]

Since assuming office as Foreign Minister, Kühlmann must have done some drastic rethinking about the Zionists. He did not go so far as to show towards them the positive sympathy of his predecessor, but, briefed about the damage caused to Germany's reputation following Jaffa's evacuation, he was sensible enough to realize the harm that a similar episode would do. Not only would Germany become the object of world-wide condemnation but the Turks would also defeat their own purpose. Their primary concern, which re-emerged during the Conference of 17 October, was to safeguard the territorial integrity of the Ottoman Empire and ensure the abrogation of the system of Capitulations. But with her ally's record so stained, how could Germany stand by her at the future Peace Conference?

The Turkish Ministers did not dispute this thinking but seemed unaware of what was going on in Palestine. However, steps had been taken to prevent any new evacuation. Arthur Ruppin could go away from his meeting with Bernstorff with a lighter heart. He found him well informed and was confident that the Zionists could reckon on his support.[123] But the news from Palestine continued to be disquieting. Thon's report about the *Mutassarif*'s speech in the mosque

[120] Ibid. K 179600–2, A.A. note, dated 17 Oct. 1917.

[121] Ibid. K 179562, Bussche to Bernstorff, 15 Oct. 1917, tel. no. 1230; K 179607–8, same to State Secretary (Constantinople), 17 Oct., tel. no. 1241, *immediate*: 'Hiernach ist zu befürchten, dass die öffentliche Meinung der ganzen Welt wieder in Aufruhr gerät, wobei das Zusammentreffen . . . mit Kaiserbesuch natürlich als Beweis unserer Mitschuld oder Urheberschaft gedeutet werden wird.'

[122] Ibid. K 179611, Bernstorff to A.A., 18 Oct. 1917, tel. no. 1283. On 17 Oct. 1917 representatives of the Reich Government met their Turkish opposite numbers in Constantinople to discuss the extension of the German–Ottoman treaty.

[123] Ibid. K 179684–5, Ruppin to E.A.C., 23 Oct. 1917 (a copy submitted by Lichtheim to A.A.)

of Ramleh on 19 October was particularly disturbing. 'It had the evident intention of arousing hatred against the Jews . . . [Ottoman] authorities seek to involve wide circles . . . We need protection . . . in order to stop . . . persecution of innocent people and prevent excessive punishment of the guilty.'[124] Bernstorff found the report hard to believe; suspecting gross exaggeration, he advised the imposition of a stricter surveillance over the cables dispatched through the official cipher. All the same, he warned Talaat not to let a single case of espionage give rise to indiscriminate persecution.[125]

Three days later Brode confirmed that Izzet's speech was unwise. He himself had advised the *Mutassarif* to refrain from any activities against the Jewish population which would furnish the enemy with material for further propaganda. The impending arrival in Jerusalem of General von Falkenhayn, Head of the German Military Mission to the Orient, gave Brode some hope that the Governor's new evacuation project would be abandoned. In the meantime he advised Bernstorff to intervene with the Grand Vizier for as mild a treatment of the Jews (*für tunlichst milde Behandlung*) as was practicable.[126] No longer sceptical, the Ambassador lost no time in approaching Nessimy Bey and Talaat once more. The latter gave him unequivocal assurances: 'We have done much harm to the Armenians but we shall do nothing to the Jews.' The Porte had decided to leave the question of the spy case to von Falkenhayn in order, as Nessimy Bey confided, 'to share the responsibility'. Yet there was no getting over the fact that a number of Zionist Jews in Palestine made 'common cause with the enemy', and that in this respect Entente propaganda 'has borne fruit'.[127] Ruppin, considerably embarrassed, assured Bernstorff that the Yishuv at large had nothing to do with the few 'adventurous' and 'irresponsible individuals'. He was greatly comforted to learn about Talaat's statement and that the investigation would be conducted by von Falkenhayn.[128]

Reports from Palestine made grim reading at the Wilhelmstrasse. Some of them sounded so incredible that Kühlmann thought it

---

[124] *Türkei* 195, K 179640–1, Thon to Warburg 26 Oct. 1917, tel. no. 1326.
[125] Ibid. K 179639, Bernstorff to A.A., 26 Oct. 1917, tel. no. 1327.
[126] Ibid. K 179767–9, Brode, cited in Bernstorff to A.A., 29 Oct. 1917, tel. no. 1342.
[127] Ibid. K 179664, Bernstorff to A.A., 30 Oct. 1917, tel. no. 1345. A few days later Bernstorff spoke to Talaat and Nessimy Bey again (K 179701, same to same, 3 Nov. 1917). Cf. Bernstorff: *Memoirs*, p. 172, Bernstorff to Bernhard, 3 Nov. 1917.
[128] C.Z.A. Z 3/1485, Ruppin to E.A.C., 2 Nov. 1917: K 179698, Ruppin to Warburg, 1 Nov., tel. no. 1365.

inadvisable to transmit them to the Zionist Executive.[129] But the matter now concerned him too closely to be left in abeyance. Suspecting that Talaat had failed to impose his will on subordinate Ottoman authorities in Palestine, he took a leaf out of Zimmermann's book and got in touch with the High Command.[130] No document has come to light to show the military's reaction. We have only circumstantial evidence from Ephraim Cohn-Reiss's memoirs that, before leaving for the East, von Falkenhayn was summoned by the Kaiser and instructed to prevail upon Djemal Pasha to treat the Jews considerately.[131] On this point von Falkenhayn discharged his mission admirably, particularly after he found that the mass of the Jews were innocent.[132]

Von Falkenhayn arrived in Jerusalem on 5 November at the right moment. The Turks had reverted to their old practices[133] and Djemal was in an ugly mood. On 8 November he summoned Jewish representatives to tell them that he considered all their people guilty of espionage. He was particularly bitter against Aaron Aaronsohn. None the less, Dizengoff, who recorded this dramatic meeting, gained the impression that Djemal was powerless to translate his anger into deeds.[134] With von Falkenhayn's appearance Djemal's days as Commander of the Fourth Ottoman Army were numbered. The Porte also vigorously asserted its authority and gave instructions that all individuals who had been unlawfully arrested were to be released.[135] Talaat made a point of sharply condemning the anti-Jewish excesses and warning that the officials who failed to comply with his orders would be punished or dismissed.[136] On 17 November the Ottoman Embassy in Berlin finally assured the German Government that no new evacuation was contemplated.[137]

However, the Palestinian Jews were still anxious[138] and in Berlin

[129] *Türkei* 195, K 179687-8, Kühlmann to Bernstorff, 1 Nov. 1917, tel. no. 1300 (urgent).

[130] Ibid. K 179688-9, Kühlmann to Gr.Hq., 31 Oct. 1917, tel. no. 1728.

[131] Cohn-Reiss, op. cit. ii, p. 275. Cohn-Reiss was staying in Berlin at that time.

[132] *Türkei* 195, K 179755, cited in Bernstorff to A.A., 9 Nov. 1917, tel. no. 1408.

[133] Ibid. K 179728, same to same (citing Brode), 7 Nov. 1917, tel. no. 1383; K 179748, Ruppin to Warburg, 8 Nov., tel. no. 1391; also K 179824-6, Cohn-Reiss to A.A., 14 Nov. 1917.

[134] Dizengoff, op. cit., pp. 102-4; C.Z.A. Z 3/80, Oster to E.A.C., 8 Nov. 1917.

[135] As note 132.

[136] *Türkei* 195, K 179945-7, Kühlmann to Bernstorff, 3 Dec. 1917, tel. no. 1035.

[137] Ibid. K 179868, *Aide-Mémoire*; K 179875, A.A. to Warburg, 23 Nov. 1917.

[138] Ibid. K 180004-9, Schulenburg (Damascus) to Bernstorff, 22 Nov. 1917, dis. no. 74/1779.

Oscar Cohn insisted that the investigation of the espionage case be left to the exclusive competence of the German military authorities.[139] The Entente had just begun another propaganda campaign[140] and Kühlmann thought it politically important for the Turkish Government to avoid any appearance of anti-Jewish sentiments.[141] But Talaat kept his word and von Falkenhayn handled the matter skilfully. Djemal Pasha 'the Small', Commander of the Eighth Ottoman Corps, was appointed to supervise the proceedings of the Military Court at Damascus. He was known to be more humane and more friendly to the Jews than his namesake, the Commander of the Fourth Ottoman Army. The trial proceedings were carefully conducted and only the actual members of the Nili group were sentenced: two principal leaders, Joseph Lishansky and Naaman Belkind, were executed (16 December), and others were imprisoned for various periods. But all those against whom no evidence could be produced were acquitted and released.[142]

The main objective was thus achieved. The Jewish community was exculpated and Djemal (though for different reasons) was deprived of his army command. But his long shadow was still cast over Palestine; he was by no means rendered harmless. He was reported to have made a vow that, should the Turks be forced to retreat, the Jews would not survive to welcome the British.[143] Only forty American Jews and an unspecified number of Zionists of Ottoman nationality were expelled from Jerusalem. They were driven away, in Curt Ziemke's words, 'like criminals and beaten up'. Thereafter they had to travel on foot to Jericho and east of the River Jordan, In addition, some prominent Zionist leaders, amongst them Dr. Thon, against whom Izzet nourished a particular grudge, were also arrested. They were marked for deportation on 9 December. It was their good fortune that Count Don Antonio Ballobar,

---

[139] *Türkei* 195, K 179913, Cohn to Kühlmann, 26 Nov. 1917. For Cohn's account of the situation in Palestine see K 180056–61. On Cohn see also above, p. 355.

[140] According to Reuter's Agency the Turks, in co-operation with the Germans, were committing fearful atrocities in Palestine. 'All the leading men . . . were accused of espionage and [thereafter] on confessions extorted by torture were convicted by a German court-martial and hanged with many members of their families in the presence of German officers.' (P.R.O., F.O. 371/3055/87895, p. no. 217597.) Reuter's statement was approved for publication by the British Foreign Office (ibid., to Paget (Copenhagen), 18 Nov. 1917, tel. no. 4746).

[141] *Türkei* 195, K 179945–7, Kühlmann to Bernstorff, 3 Dec. 1917, tel. no. 1035.

[142] Ibid. K 18004–9, Schulenburg to Bernstorff, 22 Nov. 1917, dis. no. 74/1779; K 180039–40, Bernstorff to A.A., 22 Dec. 1917, tel. no. 1701 (citing Consul of Damascus of 17 Dec.). [143] C.Z.A. Z/1486, Thon to E.A.C., 24 Dec. 1917.

the Spanish Consul, succeeded in getting their release on bail and on 8 December, when the Turks vacated the city in haste, they failed to collect their detainees. Sheer vindictiveness and the extraordinary severity with which the *Mutassarif* treated his victims[144] marked the last chapter of Ottoman rule in Jerusalem.

Bernstorff was disgusted. He wrote to von Papen:

> This continued policy of expulsion is merely stupid; it does no good from a military point of view, it damages the reputation of Turkey and in the last resort we shall have to bear the blame. Armenians, Jews or Greeks, the folly is the same. The country will be depopulated, partly from nationalist and selfish motives. I constantly discuss these matters . . . but the Turks are incorrigible . . . I am convinced that the conquest of Jerusalem was hailed with joy by almost the entire population of the city.[145]

Jerusalem was captured by the British on 9 December. To their surprise they found that with the exception of Jaffa the Jewish colonies had on the whole survived unscathed.[146] Nor had the population in Jerusalem been bled white as might have been expected.[147] The Zionist leaders duly expressed their deep appreciation of, and gratitude for, the German Government's energetic protection. Particularly moving was Thon's acknowledgement:

> . . . We would have suffered irreparable harm had the mighty hand of the German Government not protected us in the hour of danger. Altered circumstances will not make us forget this.
>
> . . . It was particularly fortunate that in the last critical days the supreme command was in the hands of General Falkenhayn. Had Djemal been responsible, he would, as he had so often threatened, have driven out the population . . . and turned the country into a ruin. We, and the rest of the population . . . must hold Falkenhayn in deep gratitude for having prevented the projected total evacuation and thus preserved the civil population from destruction.[148]

---

[144] *Türkei* 195, K 180093–7, Ziemke (Damascus) to A.A., 17 Dec. 1917, dis. no. 227/3660 (original in *Türkei* 177); also as note 143. Dr. Ziemke was on the staff of the German Consulate in Jerusalem. Early in December he was transferred to Damascus.

[145] *Memoirs*, p. 177, letter dated 10 Dec. 1917.

[146] P.R.O., F.O. 371/3055/87895, Wingate to F.O., 21 Nov. 1917, tel. nos. 1244, 1245; also K 180089 citing Reuter's telegram of 12 Jan. 1918.

[147] C.Z.A. Z 3/1468, Thon to Jacobson, 24 Dec. 1917.

[148] *Türkei* 195, K 180161, Thon to E.A.C., 15 Nov. 1917, forwarded by the latter to A.A., 1 Feb. 1918; cited also in K 180072–3, Ruppin to Bernstorff, 1 Jan. 1918.

17

The Volte-Face

KÜHLMANN's frigidity towards the Zionists was conditioned, *inter alia*, by the belief that their aspirations were not shared by the majority of their co-religionists. The enthusiastic response of the Jewish masses all over the world, in Eastern Europe in particular,[1] showed that he was wrong. It was Ludwig Haas[2] who opened his eyes to his error. Haas was not a Zionist. For political reasons he had consistently refused to give in to the demands of the K.f.d.O. that the Jews in the Occupied Territories be recognized as a separate nationality and granted cultural autonomy. The Poles harboured intense prejudices against their Jewish neighbours and suspected them of being German stooges. In this context promotion of Jewish nationalism was risky. Haas had also to consider the opinion of the majority of Polish Jews, who were strictly orthodox, apolitical, and lacking a 'national will'. On the other hand it was the Zionists who exercised both political and economic influence. Their movement was in the ascendant and attracted youth. Though initially reserved, Haas was converted to the idea of large-scale emigration to Palestine by the virulent anti-Semitism in Poland and the economic backwardness of the Jewish masses. His interest intensified following the publication of the Balfour Declaration. From his vantage-point in Warsaw he was in a position to assess the depth of its influence. 'The Entente courts the Jews in neutral countries and those in Eastern Europe, in a striking manner', he

---

[1] On which see Stein, *The Balfour Declaration*, Ch. 38; Friedman, *The Question of Palestine*, pp. 291–308. For Kühlmann's views see above, pp. 292–3; cf. pp. 342–3.

[2] Deutsches Zentralarchiv, Potsdam. *Reichsamt des Innern*, Nr. 19802–4, *Die jüdische Frage in besetzten Gebieten Russisch-Polens, 1915–1919*, Bd. 3 (cited thereafter D.Z., Potsdam, *Die jüdische Frage*), Haas to A.A. (through the Ministry of the Interior), 23 Nov. 1917. What follows is based on this memorandum. On Haas see above, pp. 234, 282.

warned Berlin and wondered whether the time was ripe for the Central Powers to formulate 'a clear programme' on the Jewish question; his own was moderate, and in his opinion sufficient to win over the Jews, especially those in Eastern Europe. Their sympathy, in view of the Central Powers' future relationship with Russia, was of particular importance. Haas's programme envisaged:

(a) A declaration by Turkey in favour of unrestricted immigration and colonization of Palestine, on the understanding that the immigrants would comply with Ottoman law[3] and disclaim any separatist aspirations.

(b) An international guarantee and the establishment of an international authority to supervise the implementation of equality of rights for the Jews in Romania as provided in the 1878 Treaty of Berlin, which so far the Romanian Government had failed to carry through.

(c) Equality of civic rights for Jews in all East European countries; recognition of their Religionsgesellschaft as a public body; support of Jewish clergy and rabbinical seminaries.

(d) Modernization of the Religionsgesellschaft and reform of the school system; Jewish schools to be autonomous but their curriculum brought into line with that prevailing in the country in question.[4]

Gerhard von Mutius, who until the outbreak of the war had served as Counsellor to the Embassy in Constantinople and in 1917 was appointed Political Adviser to the Administration in Warsaw, supported Haas wholeheartedly. He advised Kühlmann, his old friend: 'If we do not take the Jewish question into our hands, the Entente . . . will . . . at or after the conclusion of peace.' Von Mutius thought that it would be both useful and practical, alone or with Turkey, to draw up a minimum programme for Jewish immigration and settlement in Palestine.[5]

Kühlmann was impressed. Whatever his personal views, he was enough of a diplomat to appreciate the value of Jewish opinion and its possible effect on Germany's relations with Russia. The Bolshevik

---

[3] The term used in the original is *Staatsidee*.

[4] Commenting on the educational reform Haas wrote: 'The Jewish question cannot be solved by political theories but by shift of occupations from trade to more productive ones. . . . For the physically degenerated Jewish population, manual work and gymnastics are more important than exaggerated scholarship.'

[5] *Türkei* 195, K 179976–8, von Mutius to Kühlmann, 3 Dec. 1917.

Revolution had brought many Jews to positions of power, and it was reasonable to expect that a gesture of goodwill would ease the negotiations at the forthcoming conference at Brest-Litovsk.[6] Kühlmann did not go so far as to embrace Haas's recommendation on Palestine but, save for this, he unreservedly endorsed his programme. Repeating it almost verbatim, he solicited the approval of General Ludendorff before approaching the Austro-Hungarian Government. Ludendorff, with a few reservations, concurred with the proposed policy, assuring Kühlmann that the *Ober-Ost* had treated the Jewish population in the Eastern Occupied Territories with the 'greatest kindness'. He welcomed the idea of modernizing Jewish schools as well as granting official recognition to the Religionsgesellschaft. But, given the deeply rooted aversion to Jews in Romania, he doubted whether it would be wise to force Bucharest's hand.[7] Thus the new *Judenpolitik* taking shape was still circumscribed by the desire not to offend Polish and Romanian susceptibilities on the one hand, and those of the Turks on the other.

Early in December 1917 the German Foreign Ministry sent Adolf Friedemann, a member of the K.f.d.O., to Switzerland to assess the effect of the Balfour Declaration upon world Jewry and to devise some countermeasures. On his arrival in Berne he suggested that the Reich Government should declare Jerusalem an open city in order to safeguard the Holy Places and ensure that Palestinian Jews in the war-zone remained unmolested. He thought that this would create a most favourable impression, which would be enhanced still further if the Kaiser undertook a personal *démarche* with the Sultan. The impact of the Balfour Declaration would thus be diminished.[8]

Friedmann found leading Swiss-Jewish personalities responsive. Boneff, chairman of the Jewish community, and Dr. Messinger, Vice-President of the Swiss Zionist Organization, approached both

---

[6] The Jewish question was not put on the agenda of this conference. Trotski, like other Jewish Bolshevik leaders, dissociated himself from the Jewish masses and was not interested in their problems. Cf. W. Wheeler-Bennett, *Brest-Litovsk. The Forgotten Peace. March 1918* (London, 1956); Solomon M. Schwarz, *The Jews in Soviet Russia* (Syracuse University Press, 1951), p. 93.

[7] D.Z., Potsdam, *Die jüdische Frage*, Kühlmann to Berckheim (for Ludendorff), 12 Dec. 1917; Lersner (on Ludendorff's behalf) to A.A., 19 Dec. 1917 (original found in *Gr. Hq.*); *Türkei* 195, K 179994, A.A. note, dated 12 Dec. 1917.

[8] D.Z., Potsdam, *Die jüdische Frage*, Friedemann to K.f.d.O., 17 Dec. 1917, encl. in K.f.d.O. to Hertling, 19 Dec. 1917; *Türkei* 195, K 179797–9, Romberg to A.A., 12 Nov. 1917, tel. no. 1819; K 179915–16, same to same, 24 Nov. 1917, dis. no. 3610.

the German and British Legations at Berne to express their anxiety about the fate of their co-religionists in Palestine. Romberg, who showed consistent interest in the Zionist cause, supported them wholeheartedly and hoped to redress the balance as local Jewish opinion was now drifting towards the Entente. The British Legation was also sympathetic. Its Military Attaché told Boneff and Messinger that as soon as Palestine was conquered the British would found there an 'independent [Jewish] state'. But the most enthusiastic response came from the Vatican. Mgr. Marchetti, its representative in Switzerland, assured the delegation of the Holy See's interest, and soon after, on the instruction of Pope Benedictus XV, Eugen Pacelli, Archbishop of Sardi and the Apostolic Nuncio in Bavaria, approached the German Government. He was assured that the Turkish authorities would not adopt repressive measures against the Jewish population and that both the Christian and Jewish Holy Places would be protected, as far as military requirements would permit. But as pressure mounted, on 21 November 1917 Berlin issued a special communiqué that Jerusalem would not be turned into a battleground and its Holy Places would be safeguarded.[9]

Its publication coincided with a move made by von Papen, the Chief of Staff of the Fourth Ottoman Army. 'Enver is . . . insistent that Jerusalem should be held to the last—for political effect', he wrote to Bernstorff, his former chief in Washington. 'This would be wrong from the military point of view, as this disorganized army could only be rallied by being entirely disengaged from the enemy, and it would take months before it is reconstituted with new divisions.' Djemal Pasha, before leaving for Constantinople, also declared in his farewell speech at Beirut that 'Jerusalem would not be abandoned . . . as it is the key to Syria'. But the German High Command disregarded both Enver and Djemal and on 7 December 1917 ordered the Ottoman troops to withdraw from the city.[10] General Allenby took it two days later without a fight and its population was spared the horrors of war.

[9] *Türkei* 195, K 179797–8, K 179829, Romberg to A.A., 12, 16 Nov. 1917, tel. nos. 1619, 1888; K 179834, same to same, 16 Nov. 1917, dis. no. 3519; K 179868, 179902, Pacelli to von Dandl, Munich, 16 Nov. 1917; K 179799–800, K 179879–81, A.A. to Romberg, 14, 21 Nov. 1917, tel. no. 1309, dis. no. 3578; K 179900–1, A.A. note, dated 28 Nov. 1917. For the text of the communiqué see Appendix E.

[10] *Türkei* 41, Bd. 5, von Papen (Nablus) to Bernstorff, 21 Nov. 1917; cf. Bernstorff, *Memoirs*, p. 174; *Türkei* 177, von Mutius (Beirut) to A.A., 7 Dec. 1917, dis. no. 2533; Franz von Papen, *Memoirs* (London, 1952), p. 76.

In mid December Friedemann returned from Switzerland and the German policy-makers were able to learn about the tactics employed by their adversaries. The British Legation in Berne employed two Swiss Jews and put ample sums at their disposal for propaganda. So potent had been the response following the declaration in favour of the creation of a 'Jewish state in Palestine', that the British were now bent on capturing the sympathies of all Jews, including those in the countries of the Central Powers. Like Romberg, Friedemann deprecated Germany's failure to meet the challenge, all the more regrettable since Jews in neutral countries had formerly been pro-German. In Eastern Europe the trade in provisions and raw materials, so essential for the Reich's war machine, was concentrated in Jewish hands, and since the November Revolution in Russia 'very gifted' Jewish political leaders had risen to positions of power. Friedemann thought that German statesmen should keep these facts in mind, not only to meet current exigencies but even more so in consideration of long-term post-war objectives.[11]

There was no disagreement with Friedemann's analysis, but against the slogan of the Jewish State in Palestine, which intoxicated the Jewish masses, the Auswärtiges Amt stood completely helpless. It was at this point that the Havas Agency in Switzerland released a sensational report that 'in response to pressure from important German-Jewish quarters, the Reich Government would not oppose the establishment of an independent Jewish State in Palestine'. The news aroused lively interest in Swiss-Zionist circles and Romberg urgently requested Berlin for instructions. The State Secretary replied:

> Havas's message is an invention. We are, of course, in no position to declare ourselves in agreement with plans which would deprive Turkey of a province. A report will shortly be made public of a discussion between Talaat Pasha and a German Zionist, which should satisfy the Zionists. We associate ourselves with the Turkish viewpoint as expressed therein.[12]

Whatever the source of the Havas message it acted like a litmus test on the Foreign Ministry. The British propaganda machine had

---

[11] D.Z., Potsdam, *Die jüdische Frage*, Friedemann to K.f.d.O., 17 Dec. 1917, memorandum, forwarded to Hertling, 19 Dec.; cf. *Türkei* 195, K 180410–21, Friedemann to Radowitz (Under-Secretary at the Chancellery), 3 May 1918.

[12] *Türkei* 195, K 180051, Romberg to A.A., 30 Dec. 1917, tel. no. 2081; K 180052, Kühlmann to Romberg, 31 Dec. 1917, tel. no. 1540, and annotation on K 180051.

scored by allowing the term 'National Home' to be read universally as 'Jewish State'. Not only the English Press and public men[13] but even Lansing, the American Secretary of State, understood it in this sense.[14] It was this image of Zionism that scared the Turks and determined Germany's attitude. Now, with Talaat Pasha readjusting his policy, Kühlmann dropped his reservation. From then on the Wilhelmstrasse's policy followed the line long advocated by the German Zionists, but coming belatedly and pursued hesitantly, at a time when Jerusalem was already in British hands, it could hardly rival London's.

The Zionist to whom Kühlmann referred was Dr. Julius Becker, correspondent of the *Vossische Zeitung*. He had gone to Constantinople at the invitation of the Turkish Government as a member of a fact-finding commission to investigate the position of the Jewish evacuees in Palestine. The military situation prevented him from proceeding further, and during his stay in Constantinople he met some leading Turkish statesmen and senior officials. Bernstorff received him warmly, describing the Zionist cause as a 'historic necessity, bound to triumph despite numerous adversities'. It was on Bernstorff's recommendation that Talaat granted Becker an audience. The interview took place on 12 December and was made public in the *Vossische Zeitung* on 31 December.

Talaat dismissed the Balfour Declaration as 'une blague', equating its credibility with the promises made by the British Government to Sharif Hussein. Turkey did not need to justify her attitude towards the Jews since this had always been proper; anti-Semitism had never struck root in her soil; had it not been for Turkish tolerance, colonization of Palestine would never have been possible. If the Porte was subsequently compelled to enforce certain restrictions it was because Jewish immigrants were obliged by their respective governments, especially Russia, to retain their original citizenship. This gave rise to the growth of a privileged class which evaded Ottoman jurisdiction; the consuls had become more powerful, and the lawful Government had consequently lost its authority—an anomaly that could not be tolerated. However, with the abrogation of the system of Capitulations, Turkey could afford to dispense with

[13] Sokolow, *History of Zionism*, ii, p. 88; Stein, op. cit., pp. 560, 562–3; Friedman, op. cit., pp. 312–14.

[14] 'Investigate discreetly and report . . . to Department reasons for Balfour's recent statement relative Jewish State in Palestine' (*F.R.U.S.*, 1917, Suppl. 2, i, p. 473, Lansing to Page, 15 Dec. 1917).

former restrictions, though on the understanding that the immigrants adopted Ottoman nationality and fulfilled their civic duties. As before the war, they would be entitled to complete religious, cultural, and economic freedom, but their migration to Palestine, the Grand Vizier concluded, would be regulated by its economic absorptive capacity. Nor would they be given any special privileges over those of other citizens.

On 1 January 1918 Becker met Djemal Pasha, who had returned to Constantinople a week earlier and was his usual self—jocular and amiable but, on matters of principle, as adamant as ever. His opposition to Zionism was absolute. 'In Djemal', Becker commented, 'we have an enemy who could never be persuaded.' He took some comfort in Bernstorff's assessment that Djemal's star was declining, but all in all his conclusion was pessimistic, as most of the Turkish leaders whom he met shared Djemal's sentiments in varying degrees. Arguments about the economic benefits accruing from Jewish colonization carried little weight. Having failed to solve the problem of nationalities they were obsessed by the fear that Palestine would also be lost like other Asiatic provinces. Nor did Becker place much hope in the efficacy of the advice given by their German mentors; the Turks plainly resented 'interference by foreigners' in their internal affairs. Yet, for all his gloomy analysis, which Bernstorff endorsed, Becker hoped that at the end of the war Turkey, pressed by international opinion, might concede certain privileges to the Jews.[15]

Whatever the undercurrents in Turkish politics, those concerned with foreign affairs, like Nessimy Bey, did their best to improve Turkey's image. He hotly denied rumours about desecration of the Holy Places in Jerusalem and assured the world of Turkey's traditional friendship towards the Jews. For centuries they had found in Turkey a refuge and after the war further Jewish immigration would be welcome. All civil rights would be granted to them.[16]

The reaction to Talaat's statement differed from country to country. In The Hague Jacobus Kann appreciated the Grand Vizier's goodwill though he regretted his derogatory reference to the Balfour Declaration and the qualification about the volume of

---

[15] C.Z.A. Z 3/11, Becker's report to the E.A.C. (? undated, presumably early in Jan. 1918). Reference to Becker is made in Bernstorff, *Memoirs*, pp. 172–3.

[16] *Der Tag*, 22 Dec. 1917 (cutting in K 180049). On Becker's meeting with Nessimy Bey see also *Türkei* 195, K 180035–6, Waldburg to A.A., 15 Dec. 1917, tel. no. 6972.

immigration. Administrative provisions alone were insufficient. The Zionists could not be expected to invest capital and human resources without legally binding guarantees. The Jews had an 'inviolable historic right' to their ancient homeland and the Turkish Government should join other civilized countries in acknowledging the justice of their claim.[17] Swiss-Jewish opinion was not over-impressed, while the Zionist Bureau in London dismissed Talaat's declaration as 'insincere'. By contrast, in Germany, and German-occupied territories the Zionist Press, though deprecating the omission of any reference to Jewish 'historical rights', welcomed it as an important step forward.[18]

Talaat's motive was to salvage Turkey's reputation. But it was not so much the wording of his statement, so different in tone and intent from that of Djemal Pasha, that encouraged the Zionists in Germany, as the stimulus it provided to the Reich Government to rid itself of its former inhibitions. However welcome the Balfour Declaration was to German Zionists, it imposed a strain on their civic loyalty. It tended to invalidate their neutrality and undermine their authority among their friends in Russia and in neutral countries. To balance the British declaration, a German one was essential.

This theme was the keynote of Hantke's address to the meeting of the Central Committee of the German Zionist Organization on 23–4 December. He was at pains to show that in the text of the Balfour Declaration there was no reference to the future sovereignty of Palestine which could have cast doubt on the neutrality of the Zionist movement. The question of Palestine was bound to be tabled at the future Peace Conference, and Germany would be well advised to make her voice heard. The Zionist principle remained unaltered: Jews, wherever they lived, were obliged as individual citizens to discharge their patriotic duties, but as a people they had no part in the war. They possessed an identity of their own and were entitled to submit their case to the comity of nations. Foremost in their mind was their imprescriptible claim to unhindered cultural and economic activity in Palestine. 'The Jewish people had been wandering in the world for centuries, but in their minds they lived in their [ancient] homeland.' With the rights of small

[17] *Jüdisches Korrespondenzbureau*, 9 Jan. 1918, encl. in Bethmann Hollweg (Berne) to A.A., 12 Jan. (*Türkei* 195, K 180101–2).
[18] C.Z.A. Z 4/1176, annotation on a cable from Copenhagen, dated 7 Jan. 1918; *Jüdische Rundschau*, *Jüdische Presse* (4 Jan.), *Lemberger Tageblatt* (31 Jan. 1918).

nationalities gaining universal recognition they expected the world
to appreciate their problem as well. The meeting agreed that in
accordance with the principles laid down in the Basle Programme
the Zionist movement should endeavour to win the support of all the
Powers concerned. 'Zionism is neither subservient nor hostile to
any of the warring camps. Its sole purpose is peaceful colonization
of Palestine.' Thanks were conveyed to the British, Austrian, and
Turkish Governments for their public expressions of support and
the hope was expressed that the Reich Government would soon
follow suit.[19]

So deep was the impact of the Balfour Declaration that even Max
Warburg, an old enemy of the Zionists, thought it important for the
Central Powers to announce their policy on the Jewish question.
The Entente was reaping the fruits of its initiative: President
Wilson by winning Jewish votes and England by establishing her
position in Palestine at the crossroads between Egypt and India. It
was therefore imperative, he told Baron Langwerth, that Germany
should follow the example set by Czernin and Talaat.[20]

Kühlmann was on the point of leaving for the conference at
Brest-Litovsk and von dem Bussche-Haddenhausen, the Under-
Secretary of State, acted for him. An adherent of the Zimmermann
school of thought, Bussche needed little prodding. On 5 January he
called to the Ministry Otto Warburg and Hantke, as representatives
of the Zionist Executive, and Oppenheimer, Friedemann, and
Sobernheim of the Komitee für den Osten, and made the following
statement:

We appreciate the desire of the Jewish minority in countries where
they have a strongly developed culture of their own, to pursue their
own way of life and we are willing to give benevolent support to these
aspirations.

This section referred to the Jews in Eastern Europe, particularly
Poland. The statement went on:

With regard to the aspirations of Jewry, especially of the Zionists,
towards Palestine, we welcome the recent statement of Talaat Pasha, the
Grand Vizier, as well as the intentions of the Ottoman Government, made
in accordance with its traditional friendship towards the Jews in general,
to promote a flourishing Jewish settlement in Palestine, in particular by
means of unrestricted immigration and settlement within the absorptive

[19] C.Z.A. Z 3/801; also *Jüdische Rundschau*, 28 Dec. 1917.
[20] *Türkei* 195, K 180076-7, Warburg to Langwerth, 9 Jan. 1918.

capacity of the country; local self-government in accordance with the country's laws, and the free development of their civilization.[21]

The declaration was widely publicized in the Press and attracted lively comment. The *Jüdische Rundschau* (11 January 1918) saw it as an acknowledgement of the demand that the Jewish minority in Eastern Europe should be recognized as a separate national cultural entity, and official confirmation that Zionist aspirations were viewed sympathetically: 'The German Government will not only continue to protect and assist . . . but also, as a matter of principle, foster the Zionist work in Palestine, so far as respect for Turkish prerogatives permits.' The *Jüdische Presse* (of the same date) felt relieved that the strain on Zionist neutrality had been removed. Germany had a long-standing regard for Zionism but it was up to Turkey to take the first step. The *Frankfurter Israelitisches Familienblatt* (11 January) was satisfied with the inauguration of the new Jewish policy, while *Der Israelit* (10 January) affirmed that Orthodox Jewry would exert their influence in favour of retaining the Holy Land within the jurisdiction of the Ottoman Empire. The anti-Zionist *Israelitisches Familienblatt* (Hamburg) pointed out that in contrast to the British declaration, which was concerned exclusively with the Zionist programme, the German referrred to wider aspects of the Jewish question. The Zionist-oriented *Hamburger Jüdische Nachrichten* regretted the delay but welcomed Turkey's decision to revert to her traditional hospitality, and what was a good omen for the unhindered development of a 'truly autonomous settlement in Palestine'. In the *Neue Jüdische Monatshefte*, the organ of the K.f.d.O., Professor Oppenheimer greeted Bussche's declaration with 'great joy'. The principle laid down there would prove of more lasting benefit than the dubious *Realpolitik* motivated by greed.

Jewish papers outside Germany were more critical. The *Hatzefira* (10 January), the Hebrew-language paper of the Polish Zionists, wondered whether the reservation on the volume of immigration did not tend to annul the value of Talaat's statement. It was up to the Zionists themselves to regulate it and assess the country's absorptive capacity. *Das Jüdische Volk* (10 January), another organ of the Polish Zionists, took an identical stand. It regarded the declarations as 'a step in the right direction . . . but rendered useless by omission of the term "national"'. The sympathies of the

---

[21] *Norddeutsche Allgemeine Zeitung*, 6 Jan. 1918; *Jüdische Rundschau, Jüdische Presse* (11 Jan.).

Auswärtiges Amt were beyond doubt but the outline drawn by the Grand Vizier was still 'far removed from the legal basis necessary to make possible the realization of the Zionist programme'. The Yiddish *Wochenblatt* (25 January), appearing in Copenhagen, and the Dutch *Joodsche Wachter* (31 January), both local Zionist organs, deplored the inadequacy of the Grand Vizier's assurances, while the *Lemberger Tageblatt* (31 January) in Austrian Galicia noted that 'in contrast to the decisive words of Balfour . . . the declarations issued by the statesmen of the Central Powers are . . . non-committal and reserved'. The forecast made by the *Jüdische Zeitung* in Vienna (11 January) that they would fail to have the desired effect upon world Jewry proved correct. The Zionist Organization in Scandinavia was the only one (apart from the Berlin Executive) to congratulate the German Government officially; those in other neutral and Entente countries kept a remarkable silence.

Reactions in the German Press were mixed. That of the semi-official *Norddeutsche Allgemeine Zeitung* (13 January) was analogous to the view expressed by the *Jüdische Rundschau*. In the *Deutsche Zeitung* (15 January) Georg Fritz, a Privy Councillor, welcomed the new development and thought that 'Germany could now work for the creation of a Jewish homeland under Turkish sovereignty', naturally after the southern part of Palestine had been reconquered. Maximilian Harden, the celebrated journalist, hitherto aloof from Judaism, became an enthusiastic supporter of Zionism. He was sceptical about Turkey's credibility, but in the article in *Zukunft* (12 January) he wrote that 'Germany has the power and the duty to support the revival of the spirit of Zion'. The *Chemnitzer Volksstimme* organ of the Social Democratic party, was gratified that the Central Powers were gradually beginning to recognize the importance of Zionism. Its editors were convinced that it lay in Turkey's 'true interests' to co-operate with the Zionists and regretted that the moves in Constantinople, Vienna, and Berlin had been made so belatedly; the *Deutsche Levantzeitung* (1 February) aired similar sentiments. The most outspoken critic was Major Endres. In a long article in the *Münchener Neueste Nachrichten* (17 January) he found Bussche's statement 'disappointing. . . . It is a dialectic masterpiece [*ein diplomatisch-dialektisches Meisterstück*].' What was needed was 'a short, binding, and unequivocal' document.[22]

[22] Cuttings and abstracts of the Press in *Türkei* 195, K 180166-86, K 180192-6; cited also in *Jüdische Rundschau* (18, 25 Jan. and 22 Feb. 1918).

Bussche's inhibited language did not reflect the extent of his interest. Familiar with Turkish obduracy under pressure, he was unwilling to go beyond the wording of the Grand Vizier, and that might have done the Zionists more harm than good. But it was significant that a few days later Jacobson was told by the Foreign Ministry that it was inadvisable for the German Jews to lag behind their co-religionists in the Entente countries in promoting their enterprise in Palestine. Bussche took one step further by strongly recommending that Lichtheim should go to Constantinople to negotiate with the Turkish Government. The purpose of this mission, as Bussche put it, was to obtain a 'practical expression of Turkey's goodwill towards Zionist aims'.[23] However, as General Lossow continued to veto Lichtheim's return, Bernstorff had to comply. Moreover, he thought, Talaat's statement to Becker offered only a shaky basis for negotiations. The Grand Vizier, like other leading Turkish statesmen, especially Djemal Pasha, was 'friendly towards the Jews but definitely hostile to Zionism'. Nor did Bernstorff consider the timing of the negotiations opportune. Since the capture of Jerusalem by the British the main area of Zionist activity was no longer under Turkish control and, with the strong probability that further areas would be lost, any overtures to the Porte would only cause annoyance. However, he added, 'should our troops return victoriously to Jerusalem, or should we regain [southern] Palestine for Turkey by diplomacy, I would be glad to revise my view. We shall then be able to approach Turkey with terms favourable to the Jews.'[24]

This seemed sound reasoning, but all the same Bernstorff misjudged the situation. For it was the fall of Jerusalem, more than any other factor, that made Talaat realize that diplomacy was the only means open to retrieve the lost territory of Palestine and that to this end a supreme effort should be made to rally Jewish support. With Djemal Pasha bowing out of the picture, the Turkish Premier was able to move more freely; the interview given to Becker was only the first step. But Bernstorff was still feeling the impact of Becker's pessimistic report, compounded a month later by the gloomy assessment of Kress von Kressenstein of the 'hopeless' military situation

---

[23] *Türkei* 195, K 180086, note by Göppert, 15 Jan. 1918, and annotation on K 180085; K 180081-2, Warburg and Hantke to A.A., 9 Jan. 1918; K 180105-6, Bussche to Bernstorff, 17 Jan. 1918, tel. no. 47.

[24] Ibid. K 180128-30, Bernstorff to Hertling, 25 Jan. 1917, dis. no. 29.

in Palestine.[25] Nor was Bernstorff fully informed of Talaat's subsequent moves.

Talaat was perceptibly more cordial when he arrived in Berlin *en route* to the conference at Brest-Litovsk. On 5 January 1918 he told Dr. Alfred Nossig that Turkey's attitude towards its Jewish subjects was one of the 'utmost goodwill'. The Ottoman Government fully appreciated their unquestionable loyalty. He had numerous Jewish friends and, whatever machinations might be attempted, the friendship between Ottomans and Jews would not be impaired. As to Palestine, Talaat recalled that when Minister of the Interior he had removed a number of administrative restrictions, a process interrupted by the war. But as soon as Jerusalem and southern Palestine reverted to Turkish sovereignty the Porte would regulate the situation to the full satisfaction of the Jewish population and meet 'all their wishes'. 'Even the Pope', he went on, 'will eventually come to recognize that from the Christian point of view the sovereignty of a neutral power . . . is more desirable than the frictions among the various Christian sects themselves.'[26]

Talaat's assurances gave Nossig an opportunity to suggest that the time was propitious to continue the work begun in 1915 under the auspices of Emmanuel Carasso, Midhat Shukri Bey, and himself on the question of Jewish immigration and colonization, and that for this purpose it would be advisable to resuscitate the defunct Ottoman-Israélite Union. Talaat agreed and authorized Nossig to summon Carasso to Berlin. Bernstorff considered him 'one of Germany's best friends' and facilitated his journey. Before departing, Carasso was advised by Chief Rabbi Nahoum that if the Deutsch-Israelitisch Osmanische Union was to be revived, it should embrace all Jewish parties including the Zionists. Carasso and Nossig had hardly started their preparations when a breakdown in the Brest-Litovsk negotiations brought the Grand Vizier back to Berlin much sooner than expected. After hearing the report of Carasso and Nossig he summoned the representatives of the Deutsch-Israelitisch Osmanische Union and the Allgemeine Jüdische Kolonisations-Organisation to a meeting on the next day, 23 January. They included Professor James Israel, Alois Marcus,

---

[25] *Türkei* 41, Bd. 5, Bernstorff to A.A., 22 Jan. 1918, tel. no. 110.
[26] *Berliner Lokalanzeiger*, 5 Jan. 1918, reprinted in *Der Orient. Zeitschrift für die wirtschaftliche Erschliessung des Orientes*, Berlin, Feb. 1918 (cutting in K 180235–6). On Nossig see above, pp. 261–2, 268.

Dr. Alfred Nossig, Gerson Simon, and Professor Ludwig Stein. Insufficient time prevented other interested Jewish organizations from being invited.

Carasso stated that the desiderata of the Jewish groups had formerly not been clear to him but after studying them intensively he realized that they all converged on the creation of a Jewish centre under Ottoman sovereignty. This, he considered, would be very advantageous to Turkey and both by reason of his Jewish national feelings ('auf Grund seiner eigenen jüdischen Nationalgefühle') and as a Turkish patriot he had recommended it to his Government. Nossig explained that the forthcoming negotiations aimed at the creation of a *modus vivendi* between Turkey and the Jews, especially with regard to Palestine; that would give Turkey an opportunity to see for herself that no Jewish group entertained separatist aspirations. In any case a consensus had recently been reached among German Jewry; the Jews now formed a united front. If the Turkish Government was rightly concerned about the integrity of its Empire, the Jews for their part felt justified in expecting some guarantees that their immigration to Palestine would be free and the development of their centre undisturbed. Talaat replied that he shared the views of the delegation; he himself wanted Turkey to accept a large number of Jewish immigrants. However, considerable obstacles had still to be overcome, especially with regard to Palestine, as the Arabs might be annoyed. Yet if carefully handled the difficulty was not insuperable. Turkey had always recognized Palestine as 'the religious centre of the Jews' and the only problem was how to enlarge it. For this purpose the O.I.U. must be given greater authority and act as a mediator between the Porte and Jewry. Moreover, a special company ought to be established to deal with economic problems. He delegated the matter to Carasso, who enjoyed his confidence, and invited the delegation to Constantinople to work out the details and bring the negotiations to a successful conclusion.[27]

Talaat played his cards skilfully. While making the point that Turkey had long recognized Palestine as the 'Jewish religious centre', he left no doubt that the term 'religious' was not necessarily

---

[27] *Türkei* 195, K 180148–50, *Verhandlungen des Grossveziers Talaat Pascha mit der Abordnung jüdischer Organisationen am 23. Januar 1918 in Berlin*. Copy received at the A.A. on 31 Jan. For the Press communiqué by the W.T.B. see K 180237; also *Vossische Zeitung*, 24 Jan. (cutting in K 180123); K 180087–8, Bernstorff to A.A., 11 Jan. 1918, tel. no. 59; K 180099, Ruppin to Warburg, 14 Jan. 1918; C.Z.A. Z 3/1486, same to Hantke, 15 Jan. 1918.

synonymous with spiritual. The delegation got the distinct impression that though the word 'national' was not used, it was none the less implied. At any rate they could point out with confidence that the 'most important Jewish national demands were not rejected'. To forestall any risks and make the idea of a Jewish colonization company more palatable to Turkish opinion and the C.U.P. in particular, Talaat was anxious that all dealings should be conducted through the O.I.U. and the D.I.O.U., its German counterpart; it was only within this framework that an understanding with the Zionists was possible. Compared with the obduracy, if not hostility, displayed in former years, these concessions were quite substantial. They were calculated to reduce the impact of the Balfour Declaration, to invalidate Britain's claim to occupy Palestine, and to reinforce Turkey's own standing at the Peace Conference.[28] That her prospects were not too promising was a matter of common knowledge, since not only the British Prime Minister[29] but even the neutral Vatican had made known its objection to the perpetuation of Turkey's sovereignty over Palestine and Armenia. In this context the opinion of world Jewry might make some difference.

Talaat did not rely solely on information received in Berlin. On 28 January Faud Bey, the Ottoman Envoy to Berne, approached Alfons Sondheimer, a Zionist, and inquired about the objectives of British policy. Faud also wished to find out what steps would be welcome to the Jews. Sondheimer had no official standing in the Zionist organization and could reply only in his private capacity. He thought that the Balfour Declaration was a logical consequence of the allies' principle of protecting the rights of small nations, strengthened by strategic and political considerations. He was, however, quick to remark that there was no mention in the letter to Lord Rothschild of Palestine's future sovereignty and that Turkey's traditional hospitality to the Jews was always borne in mind. He recommended that Turkey should abrogate all restrictions on Jewish immigration and acquisition of land in Palestine; sanction the establishment of a Jewish colonization company; recognize

---

[28] *Türkei* 195, K 180143–7, D.I.O.U. to the Chancellor, 21 Jan. 1918 (copy received at the A.A. 31 Jan.).

[29] In his speech to the Trade Unions on 5 Jan. Lloyd George said: 'While we do not challenge the maintenance of the Turkish Empire in the homeland of the Turkish race . . . Arabia, Armenia, Mesopotamia, Syria and Palestine are in our judgment entitled to recognition of their separate national conditions.' (David Lloyd George, *War Memoirs* (London, 1935?), ii, pp. 150–7.)

Hebrew as one of the official languages of the country; and agree to Jewish self-administration, sanctioned by international law on the pattern of the Lebanon.[30]

Talaat was briefed by Faud about Sondheimer's recommendations but his ability to follow them depended in great measure on his success in overcoming internal opposition. For not only had Arab reactions to be taken into account but also those of his rival, Djemal Pasha. Although no longer the omnipotent commander of the Fourth Army, Djemal was far from being the 'dead man' Bernstorff had depicted to Becker. Formally the Minister of Marine, Djemal made himself the rallying point for all discontented elements, nourishing an ambition to become Grand Vizier. One of Djemal's favourite weapons in his subterranean struggle against Talaat was Zionism. The uncovering of the Aaronsohn spy-ring fortified his belief that Palestine Jews were all pro-Entente minded. Ruppin totally rejected this thesis; it was Djemal's own repressive measures, culminating in the Jaffa evacuation, that had made the Jews despair of Turkey.[31] Talaat was aware of the damage caused to Turkey by Djemal's short-sightedness, and it was largely to undo its effects that he now directed his efforts.

The report of the D.I.O.U. about its meetings with the Grand Vizier was studied at the Auswärtiges Amt and duly transmitted to the Embassy in Constantinople. Particular note was taken of Talaat's suggestion that Turkey would accept a 'large number of Jews'.[32] The prospect that after the war Germany would retain its predominant position in Eastern Europe was becoming real and the thinning-out of such a large concentration of Jews (five to six millions) had to be considered. There was an additional reason for Berlin to applaud Talaat's initiative. Once the Turks realized that they had to come to terms with reality, the door was open for further concessions, and this, in view of the Vatican's stand on the future of Palestine, was becoming increasingly important.

According to the *Osservatore Romano* (13 December 1917) and

[30] C.Z.A. L 6/49/II/2, Klatzkin and Olswanger (Basle) to Zionist Bureau at Copenhagen, 28 Jan. 1918; also Z 4/128, Kann and others (The Hague) to Zionist Bureau in London, 14 Feb. 1918.

[31] Becker's report, on which see above, pp. 379–80. *Türkei* 41, Bd. 6, Bernstorff to A.A., 4 Apr. 1918, tel. no. 512; *Türkei* 195, K 180373–4, Ruppin to E.A.C., 13 Jan. 1918 (copy).

[32] See above, notes 27 (*Verhandlungen* . . .) and 28; K 180151–2, Bussche to Bernstorff, 1 Feb. 1918, dis. no. 86.

La Sera, the Milan daily, Cardinal Gasparri, the State Secretary, expressed himself in favour of the British occupation of the Holy Land; the Papal Curia, he added, was also in sympathy with the creation of a legally based homeland for the Jews. This statement, coming from such an authority, placed the German Government in a quandary, and no less a person than Chancellor Hertling went into the matter. He told Eugen Pacelli, the Apostolic Nuncio, that the objectives of the British were quite different from those of the Crusaders, and the capture of Jerusalem could not be separated from its political context. The Vatican appeared to be favouring the Entente Powers, an attitude of which Germany could not approve. Pacelli replied that the Vatican's concern was of an 'exclusively religious character' and that the statement published in the *Osservatore Romano* had originated with Cardinal Basilius Pompili and not with State Secretary Gasparri. In spite of these assurances[33] Berlin was not satisfied. On 28 February von dem Bussche, the acting Foreign Minister, advised Bernstorff:

> We have committed ourselves to support Turkey with all the means at our disposal in her claim to retain her possessions . . . and to prevent any curtailment of her sovereign rights over individual territories. But we cannot disguise from ourselves that this will present great difficulties, especially in the case of Palestine, as the return of the Holy Places to the unrestricted sovereignty of Turkey will arouse the most violent opposition throughout the Christian world.

Bussche wondered therefore whether a solution could be devised which, whilst having regard for Christian sensibilities, would at the same time not unduly restrict Turkish prerogatives. He suggested leaving the sovereignty and protection of the Holy Places to the Sultan, but entrusting their administration to a board of custodians on which all religious denominations would be represented.[34]

It now fell to Dr. Brode (at that time in Constantinople) to work out a detailed scheme. He suggested the foundation of a tiny king-

---

[33] *Türkei* 177, Radowitz (for the Chancellor) to Pacelli, 22 Dec. 1917; A.A. note, dated 23 Dec. 1917; Pacelli to Hertling, 26 Dec. 1917. The Kaiser's reaction was quite characteristic. On the margin of the *Münchener Neueste Nachrichten*, 17 Jan. 1918 (cutting in *Türkei* 195, K 180116) he noted: 'To the joy of the Pope, who is the representative of Christ on earth, Jerusalem is taken away from the Mohammedans by the heathen [British] Indians in order to hand it over to the Jews who have crucified Christ! And about this Benedict XV is enthusiastic! . . . In such an incomprehensible muddle I shall not take part!'

[34] *Türkei*, Nr. 175e, *Die heiligen Stätten*, Bd. 2, Bussche to Bernstorff, 28 Feb. 1918, dis. no. 163 (secret).

dom of Jerusalem, encompassing Bethlehem in the south, stretching to the River Jordan and the Dead Sea in the east, the village of Ramallah in the north, and the ridge of the mountains near Abu Gosh in the west. The Kingdom, to be administered by a German Catholic prince, was to remain under the nominal suzerainty of the Sultan, who would be paid an annual tribute of one million pounds sterling by interested Christian Powers. Christian, Muslim, and Jewish custodians were to take care of their respective Holy Places; Jews in particular would have to be treated tolerantly. The Reich Government would also have to 'ensure that the Porte granted concessions for Jewish colonization and autonomy [presumably outside the territory of the Kingdom] and see to it that these are adhered to.'

Bernstorff was in agreement with Brode's proposal. If Jerusalem was recaptured Germany should have no qualms of 'Christian conscience', since Turkey's administration of the Holy Places had always been better than the conduct of the Christian sects amongst themselves. However, if Jerusalem had to be retaken by diplomacy, the Turkish Government would be very reluctant to swallow the medicine which 'we shall be obliged to give her in the form of Arab autonomy [in Syria and Mesopotamia], Zionism [in Palestine] and the Christianization (*Christianisierung*] of the Holy Places [in Jerusalem]. . . . Care must be taken to avoid any arrangement which will enable the Turks to make their usual mental reservations, promising much and afterwards doing nothing . . . The Turks in any case will blame their allies for letting them down.' Bernstorff hoped that such a solution would also be welcomed by the Jews. The Sultan's formal suzerainty and the annual tribute would pacify the Muslims but on the whole 'the Kingdom of Jerusalem would awaken quite different historical associations from Mr. Balfour's Anglo-American Jewish State, which after all could never attain the glory of the kingdoms of David or Solomon'.[35]

This scheme was apparently a tentative blueprint to neutralize any moves by the Entente and the Vatican at the future Peace Conference. Such a master plan, designed to appeal simultaneously to Christians, the Arab Decentralization party, and Zionists while leaving the Sultan with nominal sovereignty over Turkey-in-Asia, involved far-reaching reform. Whether the Turks would willingly have acceded to it is doubtful.

[35] Ibid., Bernstorff to Hertling, 30 Mar. 1918, dis. no. 93, and encl. memorandum by Brode, 28 Mar. 1918 (secret).

18

Abortive Negotiations

IT will be recalled that on 23 January 1918, when in Berlin, Talaat invited a Jewish delegation to Constantinople to work out with the Porte details of the foundation of an immigration and colonization company in Palestine. But before discussing the ensuing Turco-Jewish negotiations we must first trace the evolution of Jewish policy and examine how the formulation of a unified Jewish programme was possible. The fact that former opponents, at loggerheads with one another for decades, composed their differences, was largely due to the electrifying effect of the Balfour Declaration. As in the Entente and neutral countries so also in Germany it greatly strengthened the Zionist position and made it respectable. Zionism suddenly became a factor in world politics and a topical subject for debate. It engendered a radical change in Jewish opinion. Thus the *Jüdische Presse* (16 November 1917), a conservative paper, called for a revision in attitude to Zionism and its recognition by the Central Powers, primarily by Turkey. The *Israelit* (16 December), the organ of the Orthodox, consistently hostile to Zionism, also came out in favour of a moderate Palestinian programme. Even more surprising was the process of self-discovery that took place in assimilated circles. Theodor Wolff, editor of the *Berliner Tageblatt*, Georg Bernhard, editor-in-chief of the *Vossische Zeitung*, and Maximillian Harden, star writer and editor of *Zukunft*, fell under Lichtheim's spell and lent their columns to the Zionist cause; Harden himself wrote a brilliant article in the *Zukunft* of 12 December.[1] The conversion of such eminent Press lords and journalists reflected the transformation in the climate of opinion. German Jewry—and this was even more typical of the anti-Zionists—watched uneasily as the Entente reaped the rewards of the Balfour Declaration and they

---

[1] Lichtheim, *She'ar Yashuv*, pp. 440–1; *Rückkehr*, pp. 374–5.

considered it their patriotic duty to see that the imbalance was righted. The plight of Jews in Eastern Europe, now within the German sphere of interest, was a complementary factor calling for greater unity.

The idea of founding a unified body to represent the interests of German Jews at the peace negotiations originated with James Simon, the head of the Hilfsverein der deutschen Juden. On 30 November 1917 he invited together a number of notable German Jews but excluded the Zionists under the pretext that they were an international, not a German, organization. However, the notables refused to proceed without the Zionists and the latter made it known that, unless their programme was accepted, they would not join. It consisted of three points: civil equality (e.g. in Romania); national-cultural autonomy in countries with large Jewish populations; demands relating to Palestine.[2] There was little chance that such a programme would be rejected. But in his address to the Zionist Conference on 24 December Hantke went a step further, complaining that the orthodox and liberal German Jews were slow to recognize the 'national character' of the Jewish problem. In Russia, the United States, and elsewhere the Jewish masses proclaimed their identity as a people, but in Germany they still lagged behind. The fight for civil emancipation, he declared, was nearly over, the struggle for recognition of the Jews as a people still continued.[3]

The declarations of Talaat and Bussche removed a serious obstacle to agreement. That a man like Ludwig Quessel should have so suddenly adopted the Zionist concept[4] indicated how much the gap had narrowed. Eugen Fuchs, chairman of the Zentralverein deutscher Staatsbürger jüdischen Glaubens, struck a patriotic note. He greeted the declarations as a 'happy combination' (*eine glückliche Synthese*) of German, Turkish, and Jewish interests. He admitted that German Jewry had erred in opposing Zionism and suggested the formulation of a common approach to all questions that might arise at the Peace Conference.[5] In the February 1918 issue of *Im Deutschen Reich*, the organ of the Zentralverein, he wrote that the

---

[2] C.Z.A. Z 3/801, circular letter, 16 Dec. 1917, signed by Hantke; Fuchs, *Um Deutschtum und Judentum*, p. 304.

[3] C.Z.A. Z 3/801, minutes of the conference.

[4] Ludwig Quessel, 'Die Judenfrage als nationales Problem', *Neue Jüdische Monatshefte*, no. 2 (1917–18), 299–306.

[5] Fuchs, op. cit., pp. 303–4.

British were utilizing the Jewish national movement for their own interests and Germany could not afford to let them pose as the sole protectors of the Jews. 'Germany can and must take the wind out of their sails.'

Fuchs was one of the moving spirits behind the agreement with the Zionists. On 20 January 1918 a joint meeting drafted the following programme:

(a) Equality (both in law and in practice) in civic rights and duties.
(b) Religious freedom.
(c) The right to an independent Jewish culture.
(d) The right to free immigration and economic activities in all parts of the Ottoman Empire.
(e) The right to free immigration to Palestine and to cultural autonomy there.

The first three items were intended primarily for the territories in Eastern Europe; the last two were the standard claims of the Zionists to which the other parties now subscribed. With a common programme thrashed out, the foundation of the Vereinigung jüdischer Organisationen Deutschlands zur Wahrung der Rechte der Juden des Osten (V.J.O.D.) was possible. It was an umbrella organization for all sections of German Jewry. James Simon was elected President, Oscar Cassel and Franz Oppenheimer Vice-Presidents, Arthur Hantke and Paul Nathan Honorary Secretaries. The ultra-orthodox Agudat Israel and the Freie Vereinigung appointed a committee to negotiate affiliation to the new body.[6]

Fuchs paid a warm tribute to the foundation of the V.J.O.D., while stressing that the need to frame a common Jewish foreign policy did not obscure ideological differences.[7] The *Jüdische Rundschau* (15 February) also pinpointed the significance of the event and expressed satisfaction that the Zionist idea was incorporated into the programme of the new body. By contrast, Max Warburg

---

[6] C.Z.A. Z 3/1486, E.A.C. to Ruppin, 28 Jan. 1918; *Jüdische Rundschau*, Nr. 7 (15 Feb. 1918), 49–50. The member organizations were: Zentralverein deutscher Staatsbürger jüdischen Glaubens; Deutsche Vereinigung für die Interessen der europäischen Juden; Deutsch-Israelitischer Geimeindebund; B'nai B'rith Grosslodge für Deutschland; Hilfskomitee für die notleidenden osteuropäischen Juden (Frankfurt a. M.); Hilfsverein der deutschen Juden; Komitee für den Osten; Verband der deutschen Juden; Vereinigung für das liberale Judentum in Deutschland; Zionistische Vereinigung für Deutschland.   [7] Fuchs, op. cit., p. 305.

argued that it was the Zionists who had modified their position.[8]
Whatever the truth, the fact remained that a compromise had been
achieved. The Orthodox, too, were adjusting themselves to the new
situation. On 29–30 January 1918 they held a conference in Frankfurt-on-Main attended by delegates from Germany, Austria, and
the Occupied Territories. Unable to decide between rival concepts
of the Jews as a nation or a religious community, the conference
adopted a compromise definition, that of a *Volksgemeinschaft*. Its
most revolutionary resolution concerned Palestine. It read *inter
alia*: 'The Agudat Israel regards the settlement of Jews in the Holy
Land as the fulfilment of a sacred religious duty based on religious
law. It is incumbent upon the entire Jewish people to secure its full
realization.' Another resolution appealed to the Turkish Government to permit unrestricted immigration and land settlement,
religious freedom, and self-administration to a degree compatible
with Ottoman sovereignty. Save for the emphasis on the religious
aspect there was not much difference in substance between this
programme and that of the Zionists.[9] When the Jewish community
in the Habsburg Empire joined the V.J.O.D. and links with the
O.I.U. were forged, Jewry in the countries of the Central Powers
was united as never before.[10]

The Zionists were confident that the tide was now flowing in
their direction. Turkey's new policy, as defined by Talaat, had been
reported to the V.J.O.D. leaders in Carasso's presence by Professor
Ludwig Stein on 24 January. The next day Carasso met the Zionist
representatives separately.[11] With the Jewish scene radically
changed and negotiations with the Porte imminent, the Zionists had
to take stock of the situation. To plan their strategy, Ruppin was
called to Berlin for consultations which took place from 1 to 8
March. The Arab question loomed heavily in the background and
most of the thinking was conditioned by the need to bring the
Yishuv from minority to majority status during the transitional
period. The suggestion that Palestine should become a unified self-
governing *vilayet* was rejected as premature. A limited programme

[8] *Türkei* 195, K 180225, Warburg to A.A., 18 Feb. 1918.
[9] Friedman, 'The Austro-Hungarian Government and Zionism', 238–9; Friedman,
The Question of Palestine, pp. 307–8. On relations between the Orthodox and the
Zionists see also *Jüdische Rundschau*, Nr. 5, 8 (1, 22 Feb. 1918), 33, 57–8.
[10] In view of the strained relations between Turkey and Bulgaria, Bulgarian Jews had
to be discounted.
[11] C.Z.A. Z 3/95, minutes, dated 24 Jan. 1918.

of internal autonomy in matters of education, culture, and law and the establishment of a colonization company were considered more prudent. It was estimated that fifty million francs would be needed as basic investment capital. The Colonization Company, in the administration of which the Zionists were to have a decisive voice, was to be registered in Turkey, but its shareholders and board of directors did not have to be of Ottoman nationality. The Company was to obtain concessions to construct railways and ports, develop natural resources, and acquire land. On the last item discrimination was essential. Only waste lands and sparsely populated areas were to be earmarked for colonization. Among the regions specifically mentioned were the dunes stretching southwards of the Gaza–Beersheba line, the marshes in the Hula and Esdraelon valleys, the Crown (*Jiftlik*) lands in the Jericho–Beisan section of the Jordan Valley, and the Haifa–Gaza seaboard. With regard to Arab-owned land a distinction was drawn between the small holders (*fellahin*) and the absentee landlords (*effendis*). It was presumed that the *effendis* would be ready to sell at least part of their property, but it was agreed that on no account should the *fellahin* be asked to sell, since a landless proletariat would present serious social problems. The Zionist leaders took great care to ensure that the indigenous population should not be dispossessed or their rights ignored. But this was not to bar the Jews from becoming in due course the majority—an idea almost axiomatic in Zionist thinking. Ruppin estimated that within thirty years their number would pass the one million mark. The scheme was applicable, *mutatis mutandis*, should Palestine come under British rule. If it remained under Turkish jurisdiction it was essential that international guarantees, on the model of the Lebanese constitution, should be drawn up at the future Peace Conference.[12]

Significantly, no preference regarding the future sovereignty of Palestine was aired at the meeting but, till that issue was resolved, the Zionist Executive had to assume that it would be Turkish. A few days after the meeting, a copy of the *American Jewish Chronicle* (11 January 1918) arrived at the Berlin Bureau. It reproduced President Wilson's celebrated fourteen points, expounded in his address of 8 January. Point twelve advocated that the non-Turkish

---

[12] C.Z.A. Z 3/359, minutes of the meetings on 1–8 Mar. 1918, signed by Lichtheim. Present: Warburg, Hantke, Jacobson, Lichtheim, and Ruppin; secretaries: Hermann and Löwenstein.

nationalities in the Ottoman Empire 'should be assured . . . an absolutely unmolested opportunity of autonomous development'. The Zionists considered that this also applied to those of Jewish nationality. It was proof that Washington was by no means intent on the dismemberment of the Ottoman Empire and as confirmation of their own contention that by meeting Jewish wishes half-way, Turkey would improve her prospects of regaining Palestine during the peace negotiations.[13]

After his return to Constantinople Talaat gave Carasso full authority to proceed with the preparations begun in Berlin, and he himself energetically popularized the Palestine scheme among men of influence in Turkish politics. Carasso soon defined the framework for the V.J.O.D.–Porte negotiations on the creation of a 'Jewish Centre' in Palestine, as well as on the foundation of a colonization company. The company was to be given the right to acquire land, administer concessions, regulate Jewish immigration and colonization, and grant local autonomy to individual settlements. Looking even further ahead, Carasso asked Ruppin, who in the meantime had returned to Constantinople, whether this scheme, if endorsed by the Turkish Government, would also satisfy the American, British, and Russian Jews. Ruppin thought that it would, 'provided the Government did not take away with one hand what it gave with the other; the agreement must allow for a large-scale Jewish immigration to Palestine so that the Jews could ultimately form the majority.' Carasso concurred with this objective and was pleased that he could 'reconcile his duty as a Turkish patriot with that of a nationalist Jew'. In his opinion—and so he had told the Grand Vizier—the fear that the Jews would ultimately go their own way had little substance. Should Turkey remain weak she would lose Palestine to the Arabs anyhow, whereas Jewish help in making Turkey a viable state was worthy of consideration. Once Turco-Jewish co-operation was established a relationship of trust and friendship was likely to develop, and any separatist tendencies would die out.[14]

In mid-April Talaat reiterated his assurances both to Nossig (who made a flying visit to Constantinople) and to Nahoum, the Chief

---

[13] *Türkei* 195, K 180269, E.A.C. (Lichtheim) to A.A., 11 Mar. 1918, and enclosed copy of *A.J.C.* Cf. above, p. 317.

[14] *Türkei* 195, K 180328–31, Ruppin to E.A.C., 26 Mar. 1918 (a copy) encl. in Bernstorff to A.A., 2 Apr. 1918, dis. no. 97 (copy in C.Z.A. Z 3/1486).

Rabbi, that he intended to reach an accommodation with the Jews. He agreed to the colonization of Palestine and was ready to grant the Jews all the facilities necessary for immigration, purchase of land, and development of cultural institutions, including the foundation of a university.[15] However, Talaat was not omnipotent. A week later an embarrassed Carasso told Ruppin and Nossig that he thought it inadvisable for the Jewish delegation to present demands which would require special legislation, since once the matter was brought before Parliament the negotiations would 'never reach an end'. It was more prudent to concentrate on items which the Government was able to grant in its executive capacity and within the compass of existing laws.[16]

Carasso's advice was well founded. In December 1917 a motion to decentralize government within the Empire had been laid before Parliament[17] but not ratified. Nevertheless, Ruppin thought that negotiations might be worth trying, because on that same day he had learned that the Government had taken some preparatory steps. Izzet Bey, the former *Mutassarif* of Jerusalem, now serving as the Vali of Constantinople, had consulted Albert Antebi and, more important, had invited Said Husseini and Ragheb Nashashibi, two leading Palestine Arab deputies to the Ottoman Parliament, to take part in the discussions. Having informed them of the Porte's intention to negotiate with the Jews, Izzet asked the deputies for their opinion. They replied that they had 'always got on well with the Jews. . . . They did not mind if the Jews bought land, immigrated and received trading concessions, provided that the Arabs remained unmolested on their own land, and that they too profited from the economic development.' Antebi gathered that Izzet was well acquainted with the subject and that his soundings were inspired by a higher authority.[18]

With Turkey's opposition to Zionism evaporating, the German Press launched a vigorous propaganda campaign. The Constantinople correspondent of the *Frankfurter Zeitung* (2 April 1918)

[15] C.Z.A. Z 3/1486, Ruppin to E.A.C., 13 Apr. 1918; *Türkei* 195, K 180352, Bernstorff to A.A., 13 Apr. 1918, tel. no. 526.

[16] C.Z.A. Z 3/95, Ruppin to E.A.C., 21 Apr. 1918.

[17] Ibid. Z 3/11, Becker's report to E.A.C., (?) Jan. 1918; *Frankfurter Zeitung*, 2 Apr. 1918 (cutting in *Türkei* 195, K 180324); *Kölnische Volkszeitung*, 23 June 1918 (cutting in *Türkei* 195, K 180639).

[18] As note 16; C.Z.A. Z 3/95, Ruppin to E.A.C., 21 Apr. 1918; ibid. Z 3/1487, same to same, 21 Apr. 1918. The Husseini and Nashashibi families were the most influential among Palestinian Arabs.

expressed satisfaction that at last Turkey had recognized the achievements of the Jewish colonists in Palestine and wished to harness
them to its own economic advantage. He suggested that Germany
should not hesitate to abandon her former restraint. In the same
issue the editor argued that by making skilful use of 'an autonomous
Jewish state', the British were endeavouring to buttress politically
their military exploits in Palestine—tactics that should be resolutely
checked. Ottoman sovereignty over Palestine must be a precondi-
tion to peace, and the Zionists could be relied upon to steer their
course in that direction. The *Vossische Zeitung* (1 May 1918) and
the *Reichsbote* (2 May) urged Germany to put herself at the head of
the movement of those Zionists who had no desire to detach Palestine from the Turkish Empire; whilst Otto Hoetzsch, Professor of
Russian History at the University of Berlin and editor of *Osteuropa*,
contended in the *Neue Preussische Kreuzzeitung* (20 March 1918)
that Zionism was of importance to Germany not merely to counter
England's political ambitions but also as a means of solving the
Eastern Jewish question, which had been accentuated by the war.

It is undeniable that Palestine can be developed by means of Jewish
labour and enthusiasm . . . Turkey is in need of capital, and still more of
human material . . . Zionism has become a factor in world politics. . . .
It is therefore in Germany's interest to pay more attention to this
problem.

The most outspoken advocate of this policy was Major Endres.
His booklet *Zionismus und Weltpolitik* appeared at the end of
February 1918. It was an elaboration of his ideas, expounded earlier
in his articles in the *Münchener Neueste Nachrichten*, that intoler-
ance towards non-Turkish nationalities was prejudicial to Turkey's
national interests and that repression was bound to provoke resistance that would cripple the machinery of state. It was unfortunate
that in Turkey reforms had never gone beyond theory, and the
prospect of reaching a *modus vivendi* with non-Turkish nationalities
had become even more remote with the spread of a Pan-Turkish
ideology. The idea of converting the Empire into a Turkish entity
was not practical. Nor were Turkish fears with regard to Zionist
aspirations warranted. If, before the war, Jewish settlers had become the instruments of their respective consuls, it was largely due
to the incompetence and hostility of the Ottoman officials. They
failed to see the specific '*Jewish* character' of Zionism; if treated

tolerantly, 'the Jew is always willing to submit to the *de facto* government of the country'. In the final analysis the risk of intervention by a hostile Power behind Zionism was conditioned by Turkey's own conduct. On all counts Turkey stood to gain from Jewish colonization of Palestine; so too would the *fellahin*. If separatist ideas were to spread, the Porte should open its eyes to 'the very dangerous young Arab movement', and for this reason alone it 'should prefer a Jewish Palestine to an Arab Syria'.

Endres then dealt with the importance of Palestine to Germany's Eastern policy. Had Germany been able, while remaining Turkey's friend, to take Zionism under her protection, as England had, then a threefold problem could have been solved: the Zionists would not feel that they had been used as pawns in imperial politics; Turkey would in a short time own a flourishing province; and Germany would acquire a promising market in the Orient. Moreover, for internal political reasons Berlin should not feel displeased if East European Jews migrated to Palestine rather than to Germany. This point of view, Endres asserted, was not motivated by anti-Semitism, which he personally regarded as an irrational doctrine. Germany was already an overpopulated country which would have to carry a heavy economic burden in the aftermath of war, and a substantial influx of Jews was bound to foment ill will. He concluded by expressing the hope that a 'victorious Germany would create the best preconditions for the realization of the Zionist programme'.

The foundation of the Pro-Palästina Komitee[19] on 25 April 1918 highlighted the pro-Zionist trend. This committee was the brainchild of Victor Jacobson[20] and the culmination of efforts begun in August 1917, when the Zionist Executive (at its meeting in Copenhagen) decided that a body comparable to the British Palestine Committee should be formed in Germany.[21] Born belatedly, it far excelled its British rival in composition. The board included such pillars of respectability as Professor Carl Ballod, who was elected chairman, Professor Hans Delbrück, Konstantin Fehrenbach, President of the Reichstag (Centre party), Georg Gotheim (Liberal), Johannes Junck (National Liberal), Gustav Noske (Social Democrat), Ludwig Raschdau, former Ambassador and member of the Reichstag, and Major Endres. The council covered the political spectrum: Count Kuno Westarp, leader of the Conservative party,

---

[19] On which see: C.Z.A. Z 3/26–8; *Jüdische Rundschau*, Nr. 18 (3 May 1918), 133–4.
[20] Lichtheim, *She'ar Yashuv*, p. 440, *Rückkehr*, p. 374.   [21] Above, pp. 294–5, 324.

Matthias Erzberger, leader of the Centre party, Philipp Scheide-mann, Ludwig Quessel, and Oskar Cohen-Reiss, leading members of the Social Democratic party; also included were distinguished academicians and writers like Professors Max Weber, Werner Sombart, Karl Meinhoff, Otto Auhagen, Gottfried Zoepfl, and Otto Hoetzsch, and Dr. Adolf Grabowsky and Dr. Ernst Jäckh. Such a broad coalition was an unusual phenomenon in German politics. The *Israelitisches Wochenblatt* noted that if personalities from such diverse backgrounds, Jews and Gentiles, both philosemites and anti-Semites, found a common denominator, it was because an important German interest was involved. For a leading assimila-tionist like Georg Gotheim to speak of a 'national community' in Palestine was indicative of a radical transformation in German policy. 'We are witnessing, for the first time, the emergence of an outspoken and unequivocal Jewish and Zionist *Realpolitik*.'[22]

The aims of the Committee were formulated as follows:

to support the aspirations of Zionism for the free development of a Jewish culture in the ancient home of the Jewish people . . . The regeneration of Palestine will be a great help to our ally Turkey, and thereby further German culture and influence in the Near East.

Moreover, as Ludwig Raschdau pointed out, Palestine offered 'the soundest solution for millions of Jews living in miserable conditions in Eastern Europe'. He praised the German Zionist policy of neutrality and advised world Jewry not to be hoodwinked by the British promise of a 'Jewish state', since this was motivated merely by expediency.[23] Georg Gotheim went further by suggesting that East European and German Jews should be interested in the failure of the English plan. The British looked upon Palestine as a strategic asset and in these circumstances 'the so-called Jewish State would become merely a British colony'. Germany, on the other hand, had a tangible interest in solving the problem of East European Jewry. Although socially degraded and permanently insecure, East European Jews possessed a strong sense of identity. Even if eman-cipated, they would not easily assimilate. Hence the rationale of their emigration to Palestine, all the more commendable since they

---

[22] *Israelitisches Wochenblatt*, 24 May 1918, signed 'Spectator' (cutting in *Türkei* 195, K 180600–1).

[23] Ludwig Raschdau, 'Palästina und der Zionismus', *Der Tag*, 7 May 1918 (cutting in K 180404–7).

might simultaneously act as agents of German political and cultural interests in the Orient.[24] The idea of a 'return to the homeland' was now seen as an insurance policy against an excessive influx of East European Jews. As the *Kölnische Volkszeitung*,[25] organ of the Centre party, rather crudely put it: 'we do not want Germany to be flooded with Jews as happened in the case of Austria. . . . On the other hand, the Jew is the most suitable settler for Palestine—a land which in spite of its present neglect holds a promising future.'

The aims of the Pro-Palästina Komitee commended themselves to Wilhelm II. He regretted that Germany had been forestalled by England in winning the sympathy of the Jews—'we as usual trail behind'—and, as his copious marginal annotations attest, he approved unreservedly of the ideas of Raschdau and Gotheim. But the Auswärtiges Amt, for which the Kaiser marked these articles 'important', refrained from showing its hand. It neither encouraged nor discouraged Pro-Palästina activities. General von Eisenhart, the Commander of the Field Army, who asked General Ludendorff whether his membership of the board of the Committee might be interpreted as an official endorsement of its aims, was told by the Foreign Ministry that it neither objected to nor recommended membership.[26]

This response did not indicate indifference. The War Ministry was told that the Entente Zionists must be prevented from snatching the leadership of the movement from the Berlin Bureau. It should be given every assistance to keep international Zionism in line with German and Turkish interests. Exemption from military service for Lichtheim, Hantke, and Ruppin was extended; Jacobson was allowed to commute freely between Berlin and Copenhagen, as well as other neutral capitals; and steps were taken to ensure that Jews in central and northern Palestine remained unmolested.[27] Goodwill was also shown on a number of other issues, but on matters affecting Turkish domestic affairs the German Government had to consider

[24] Georg Gotheim, 'Pro-Palästina', *Berliner Tageblatt*, 12 May 1918 (cutting in *Türkei* 195, K 180435–7).

[25] The issue of 23 June 1918, 'Deutschland und der Zionismus' (cutting in *Türkei* 195, K 180639).

[26] *Türkei* 195, K 180757–8, Eisenhart to A.A., 17 Aug. 1918; K 180768, Von Stumm to Eisenhart, 27 Aug. 1918.

[27] Ibid. K 180247, K 180451–2, Under-Secretary of State to War Ministry, 1 Mar., 21 May 1918; K 180348–9, same to General Staff, 15 Apr. 1918; K 180325–6, same to Bernstorff, 6 Apr. 1918, tel. no. 494; K 180335, Bernstorff to A.A., 7 Apr. 1918, tel. no. 486.

whether intervention might not produce an effect contrary to that desired. On 3 April 1918 a meeting was held at the Ministry of the Interior and it was decided to issue a declaration on the Jewish question but without mentioning immigration to Palestine.[28] As Bernstorff put it three months later: 'If we press the Turks politically, they will take refuge in passive resistance and everything will go wrong.'[29] This was as true of Turco-German relations as it was of the Palestine problem.

A Turco-Jewish *rapprochement* on other and broader questions was also desirable. Berlin, jointly with Vienna, was committed to maintaining the integrity of the Ottoman Empire. Palestine was of particular importance, as even from a purely German point of view it was imperative to deny it to the British. 'Should the English succeed in conquering this land-route to India', Bernstorff wrote in November 1917, 'they would have achieved their main war aim.'[30] On 9 April 1918 General Ludendorff suggested to Chancellor Hertling that an interdepartmental meeting be convened to consider which of Turkey's territories could be regained by force of arms and which should await the Peace Conference. Although faithful to the alliance with Turkey, Ludendorff began to doubt its advantage.

So long as we adhere to our Oriental policy, we need a viable Turkey. However, she has already lost so many of her possessions . . . that her viability and usefulness have become rather questionable. Moreover, without assistance Turkey cannot prevent her further decline. We must support her internally and reconquer her lost territories, without which she cannot remain a strong Great Power. If we fail in this the Entente will block our route to the East with Turkey's ruins.[31]

No document has come to light to show whether any decision was taken, but the restoration of Palestine to Turkey by military means was becoming less and less certain.[32]

[28] *Wk.*, Nr. 20c, K 200716–18, note dated 1 June 1918. The publication of this declaration was delayed, and eventually was rendered obsolete.

[29] *Memoirs*, p. 197.

[30] *Türkei* 41, Bd. 5, Kühlmann to G.H.Q., 10 Nov. 1917, tel. no. 522, citing Bernstorff's cable dated 9 Nov. 1917.

[31] Ibid., tel. no. 791, signed by Lersner (copy in *Deutschland*, Nr. 128, Bd. 7).

[32] *Memoirs of Prince Max of Baden*, i, memorandum dated 20 Mar. 1918, p. 276; Bernstorff, *Memoirs*, pp. 162–3, letter to Gwinner, 23 Mar. 1916. On 27 April 1918 Bernstorff told Chancellor Hertling that 'only by a miracle' would the Turks be able to reconquer Jerusalem (*Türkei* 41, Bd. 6, dis. no. 134), and by June 1918 Kühlmann no longer believed in a decisive German victory even on the Western front (Rosenberg, *The Birth of the German Republic*, p. 227).

Diplomacy remained now the only option and on 10 June Kühlmann gave his blessing to the V.J.O.D.–Porte negotiations, hoping for a satisfactory result. Jacobson was to head the delegation and Bernstorff was asked to report on its progress.[33] Bernstorff too was of the opinion that negotiations should start as soon as possible.

> The Turkish Government would not be able to avoid giving the Jewish delegation promises in writing. . . . This would be useful to us at the Peace Conference. If these promises are incorporated in the peace terms, Turkey will be forced to keep some of them. This country has become so underpopulated that every kind of immigration is to be welcomed.[34]

The date for starting the negotiations was fixed for 18 June, and the Grand Vizier appointed a special committee for this purpose. Much to Constantinople's disappointment the V.J.O.D. delegation did not arrive on time. The delay was caused partly by the wrangling over its composition, but more especially by the obstruction of the Military Attaché. It took von dem Bussche seven weeks (from 2 May till 21 June) to make him grant the necessary travel facilities.[35]

Jacobson had arrived earlier and on 28 June was received by the Grand Vizier, who explained the reason for his invitation: 'Les Juifs sont une force, je ne veux pas quil's soient contre l'Empire.' He promised to do 'everything possible, taking into consideration the situation of the Turks and the *rebellion* of the Arabs'.[36] Talaat seems to have realized that something more substantial was needed than the declaration made to Becker and Nossig but refrained from commenting on the proposed draft. The deeper Jacobson delved into the labyrinth of Turkish politics the clearer it became to him that the Grand Vizier was not the absolute master. Yet one thing seemed certain: 'the Grand Vizier wishes to do something . . . to satisfy the Jews'.[37]

---

[33] *Türkei* 195, K 180558, Kühlmann to E.A.C. and to Bernstorff, 10 June 1918 (copy in C.Z.A. Z 3/23).

[34] *Türkei* 195, K 180563–4, Bernstorff to A.A., 10 June 1918, tel. no. 881.

[35] Ibid. K 180499, K 180566, K 180598, Bernstorff to A.A., 5, 11, 21 June 1918, tel. nos. 862, 894, 996; K 180508, Kühlmann to Bernstorff, 9 June 1918, tel. no. 930; K 180381, K 180583, K 180593–4, Bussche to Bernstorff, 2 May, 19, 21 June 1918, tel. nos. 682, 996, 1006; K 180498, K 180567–8, Nathan and V.J.O.D. to A.A., 5, 18 June 1918.

[36] Ibid. K 180624, Jacobson (Constantinople) to Warburg, 28 June 1918, tel. no. 1024 (copy in C.Z.A. Z 3/95).

[37] C.Z.A. Z 3/95, Jacobson to E.A.C., 2 July 1918 (strictly confidential) (not sent through official German cipher).

Jacobson met Bernstorff and Carasso and showed them the Palestine programme, sent earlier to Kühlmann. Bernstorff advised him to tone down the Zionist terminology and, if possible, to omit the word 'national' from the phrase 'Jewish national centre'; otherwise the programme seemed to him unobjectionable. Carasso on the other hand, versed in Oriental tradition, thought it advisable for the V.J.O.D. to make maximum demands. Nor was he unduly disturbed that Parliament was not to be consulted. All his hopes were pinned on Talaat's goodwill and on the Commission, of which he, Deputy Matzliach, and the Chief Rabbi were members. The non-Jewish members were Midhat Shukri Bey, Sia Bey, and Dr. Niazim Bey. Ruppin considered Midhat 'friendly'; Sia and Niazim were extreme nationalists, but the former was known as 'a Talaat man' and the latter showed little interest in territories uninhabited by the Turks.[38]

A few days later Jacobson was invited to dinner by Aziz Bey, Director of the Press Department, formerly Chief of Public Security, and his successor, Essed Bey. They urged him to start a propaganda campaign in favour of a Turkish Palestine and of Turkey's cause in general. Jacobson replied that this was his objective and that of his friends in Berlin, but that the key was in Turkish hands. The more impressive the declaration the greater the success of the campaign. However, diplomatic preparations for the Peace Conference was more important. 'Turkey should earn her moral right to Palestine by conceding justified Jewish demands.' Aziz and Essed appear to have agreed with Jacobson's statements and promised to relay them to Talaat.[39]

Jacobson's meeting with Talaat was welcomed in Berlin. Intelligence reports suggested that the British were making considerable propaganda capital of the plan to set up a 'Zionist Republic'; that a Zionist Commission headed by Dr. Weizmann had arrived in Jerusalem; that funds had been raised to found a university; and that members of the Jewish battalions were to settle on the land after the war, and large immigration would follow.[40] Bussche lost no time in urging the War Ministry to permit the departure of

---

[38] Ibid., same to same, 19 June, 2 July 1918; Z 3/1488, Ruppin to E.A.C., 21 June 1918. On the programme submitted by the Zionist Executive to Kühlmann see K 180517–50, encl. in Jacobson to Göppert, 9 June 1917.

[39] As note 37.

[40] *Türkei* 195, K 180617, K 180620, K 180629, Intelligence reports to the Admiralty, 17, 18, 21 June 1918; also K 180665, K 180669, Intelligence reports to G.H.Q., 8, 11 July 1918.

the Jewish delegation for Constantinople, since it was 'politically
desirable that their negotiations with the Turkish Government
should lead to a satisfactory conclusion'.[41]

Public pressure was mounting. The *Kölnische Volkszeitung*[42]
wrote that since the conquest of Jerusalem the British had behaved
as if they were going to stay there 'for ever'. It was imperative for
the Central Powers to take 'a definite stand in this matter'. Two
weeks later the Pro-Palästina Committee officially approached the
Foreign Ministry:

> It is our conviction that the settlement of Palestine by the Jews is an
> event of historical importance which should be of outstanding interest to
> German policy. . . . Current British policy is to make use of Zionism to
> gain the sympathy of Jews for themselves and their allies, and to secure
> their position in the Near East . . . Germany, in view of her great interest
> in Turkey's economic and political future, should undermine the British
> plans and seize for Turkey and herself the advantages which England
> expects to gain from furtherance of Zionism.

The Committee reached the conclusion that, given adequate political, economic, and legal conditions, Palestine could absorb millions
of Jews whose talents, emotional attachment, and command of
financial resources would make the country flourish in a relatively
short period. Turkey would derive an enormous benefit and Germany would gain the sympathy of the Jewish people and expand
her influence in the Orient.[43]

The memorandum (accompanied by bulky enclosures) was studied
at the Ministry and Bernstorff was consulted,[44] but by the time the
report reached its destination it was clear that the results expected
from the negotiations would not be satisfactory. The late arrival
of the V.J.O.D. delegation coincided with the hottest season in the
year and the Muslim feast of Ramadan. Midhat Shukri Bey and
the Chief Rabbi were on holiday and Matzliach was not yet back.
Turkey was preoccupied by a border dispute with Bulgaria and by
a serious disagreement with Germany over the Caucasus. Moreover,
strong Arab opposition to all Zionist plans had surfaced, which,
Bernstorff understood, had forced the Grand Vizier to conclude

---

[41] *Türkei* 195, K 180615, A.A. to War Ministry, 28 June 1918.
[42] Dated 23 June 1918, 'Deutschland und der Zionismus' (cutting in K 180639–40).
[43] *Türkei* 195, K 180648–53, Pro-Palästina to A.A., 7 July 1918; and enclosures
K 180713–29.
[44] Ibid. K 180668, Kühlmann to Bernstorff, 15 July 1918, dis. no. 587.

that by satisfying Jewish wishes Turkey had 'little to gain because if the Arabs were to be expelled from their homes by the Jews, England would emerge as protector of the Arabs'.[45]

Bernstorff was over-pessimistic since, despite obstacles, Talaat was still interested in reaching an accommodation with the Jews. He met the V.J.O.D. delegation on 14 July 1918. It was represented by Victor Jacobson, Arthur Ruppin (Zionists), Bernhard Kahn (Hilfsverein), Max Grünwald (Austrian Jewry); Moses Auerbach, Isaac Breuer, Rabbi Marcus Horovitz, and Rabbi Perlmutter represented the Orthodox. Jacobson said that the purpose of the negotiations was 'the creation of a Jewish centre in Palestine by means of orderly immigration and colonization'. Talaat would not be drawn into a discussion of details and restated his views which had been made known in Berlin. He desired to win over the Jews, whom he believed to be a power to be reckoned with, and he assured the delegates that he would stick to his position in spite of opposition. But, in view of certain unspecified political difficulties, he could not at present make an official declaration. He was willing to concede every demand, especially with regard to maintenance of schools and development of a Jewish national culture. Local autonomy too would be extended, as stipulated in a special law for non-Turkish provinces and communities about to be promulgated by the Chamber. Jacobson insisted that cultural autonomy alone would not suffice; the centre in Palestine required a solid economic basis. The Grand Vizier replied that he would always be prepared to meet Jewish wishes with regard to economic and social matters; he approved of the concession for the Colonization Company and did not rule out administrative reforms. However, details would have to be worked out by the mixed V.J.O.D.–Ottoman Commission. Jacobson gained the impression that Talaat's desire to satisfy the Jews was 'sincere', though Talaat, fearful of a possible negative reaction from his opponents, was chary of issuing a declaration, or even a communiqué, about the meeting. That it had taken place at all was a promising sign, but the practical outcome still hung in the balance.[46]

---

[45] Ibid. K 180681–2, Bernstorff to A.A., 17 July 1918, dis. no. 1145. For the Turco-German dispute over Transcaucasia in 1918 see Ulrich Trumpener, *Germany and the Ottoman Empire, 1914–1918* (Princeton University Press, 1968), Ch. VI.

[46] C.Z.A. Z 3/95, Jacobson to E.A.C., 23 July 1918; Z 3/378, Ruppin to Hantke, 5 Aug. 1918; Z 3/517, Lichtheim to Simon (Holland), 19 Aug. 1918; *Jüdische Rundschau*, no. 33 (16 Aug. 1918), 253; *Die Post*, 5 Aug. 1918 (cutting in *Türkei* 195, K 180755).

The Auswärtiges Amt blamed the Embassy (or rather its Military Attaché) for the belated arrival of the V.J.O.D. delegation and implicitly for the disappointing result.[47] Bernstorff, too, seems to have been annoyed and took the memorandum of the Pro-Palästina Committee almost as a personal affront.

Had I not repeatedly discussed the question with the Grand Vizier, as well as with other influential personalities . . . we should never have got as far as the present negotiations. . . . Their outcome was not very favourable, but everyone familiar with Turkey knows that political fruits ripen here only if they are cultivated with great care and patience. If the expected statements of the Grand Vizier still sound somewhat unsatisfactory, they do at any rate hold open the door for future negotiations, which is always the most important thing here.

He went on:

The memorandum of the Pro-Palästina Committee gives the impression that 'Zionism', 'Jewish aims in Palestine', 'Jewish colonization of Palestine', all involve the same concept, which is by no means the case. Zionism sees the Jewish problem as a national problem and therefore aims to recreate a home for the Jewish nation. But every nation which has a home will soon want to found a State. This is why Zionism meets with active opposition here, because the Turks and the Arabs foresee that if Zionism is successful, they will ultimately be driven out of Palestine. . . . The case is quite different with regard to the orthodox Jews, who consider themselves to be a religious community and see the return to Palestine largely as a religious question. They do not demand a State, but primarily want to follow Jewish religious laws. . . . This is why the orthodox Jews are not seen as a danger to Turkish or future Arab sovereignty in Palestine.

Bernstorff assumed that the Turks would try to appease both Arabs and Jews; if that were not possible, they would have to choose the party which seemed politically the more useful to them. 'There is no doubt that the economic benefit which Turkey would gain from a Jewish settlement in Palestine would be very great.' But, he continued:

There is absolutely no understanding here for State economic advantage. There is no interest in anything but gain for the individual. Apart from this they simply indulge in politics. As a result, the idea that Palestine may be politically lost through Zionism weighs far more heavily than

---

[47] *Türkei* 195, annotation on Bernstorff's cable of 17 July 1918 (signature undecipherable).

the prospects of higher tax returns or of tribute from an autonomous Jewish entity. The memorandum of the Pro-Palästina Committee would alarm official circles here. The 'settlement of several million Jews' no doubt sounds very attractive to Zionist ears, but damages the Zionist case by exaggeration. It seems to me very questionable whether a quarter of all the Jews of the world would really go to Palestine. But if this should happen, there would certainly be no room there for any other nationality. Such a plan may perhaps be acceptable to Mr. Wilson, because his first concern is to gain the votes of the three million American Jews at the next election. . . . But England cannot really want to carry through such a plan, because she intends to found an Anglo-Arab Empire, and Turkey can want it still less. This is why I have always advised the Zionists here to deal with the situation step by step, and to keep nationalist and political aspects in the background. The problem cannot be solved in the simple manner fondly imagined by one of the Zionists here, who told me that the Arabs would have no cause for complaint, but on the contrary would be able to command very high prices for their land. If matters should be carried through as quickly as this, the Jews would have to found a national army, to protect themselves from pogroms. The Arabs will not leave their homes without protest, although they do love gold so much. Jewish immigration without a political background should and, no doubt, would be very welcome to Turkey, particularly in Palestine, because that devastated country above all needs people.

Bernstorff added that Germany's interest was indirect in that the colonization of Palestine would protect her from an influx of East European Jews and strengthen Turkey's economy. Apart from this the question was primarily one of propaganda at the Peace Conference. 'If we cannot regain Palestine by force of arms, we shall have to achieve it by diplomatic means. To this end, it will be necessary to make concessions to Christians regarding the Holy Places, as well as to Jews and Arabs. But here too Germany should beware of giving the impression of being partisan.

If the Jews succeed in getting the Turks to allow them free immigration and good treatment after the war, the rest will follow in any case, provided they themselves have the inner strength. If they don't have this, then even the greatest Turkish concessions will not succeed in reviving the glories of the kingdom of David and Solomon.[48]

This was a very able memorandum, but there were flaws in it. There was not such a distinct polarization between the Orthodox

---

[48] Ibid. K 180708–12, Bernstorff to Hertling, 20 July 1918, dis. no. 195.

and the Zionists as Bernstorff implied. Following the establishment of the V.J.O.D. the gap between Jewish parties had narrowed and a common policy towards Palestine had evolved. Bernstorff must have been projecting the ultra-Orthodox concepts on to the Orthodox; not all religious parties considered Judaism and Zionism mutually incompatible, and those which did, like the ultra-Orthodox, carried too little weight within Jewry to constitute a viable political alternative to the Zionists. Bernstorff also overstated Zionist objectives. Three weeks earlier, with the exception of the word 'national', he had accepted the proposed Zionist programme for negotiations with the Turks which Jacobson had shown him.[49] The reference to 'millions of Jewish immigrants' in the Pro-Palästina memorandum was meant merely to illustrate the absorptive capacity of Palestine which, if scientifically cultivated, could well have accommodated the newcomers and simultaneously raised the standard of living of the indigenous population. The plans of the Zionists and the Pro-Palästina Committee stipulated that the Arabic-speaking inhabitants would not be dispossessed. Only the waste lands and sparsely populated regions were marked for colonization, and if the estates of absentee Arab landlords were bought, the interests of their tenants would be respected.[50]

In his memoirs Bernstorff recollected that Talaat was ready to promise him 'all that [he] wanted, provided Palestine remained Turkish after the war, but he took every opportunity of saying: "I will gladly establish a national home for the Jews to please you, but mark my words, the Arabs will destroy the Jews" '.[51]

Bernstorff was frustrated. He had arrived in Constantinople hoping that Germany would be able to cure the 'Sick man of

---

[49] Above, p. 405.

[50] See particularly K 160725, enclosure no. 2 to Pro-Palästina memorandum dated 7 July 1918; also above, p. 396.

[51] *Memoirs*, p. 171. In a speech in Hamburg in 1930 Bernstorff, then President of the Pro-Palästina Committee, recollected this episode: 'I discussed these matters for weeks together with the Grand Vizier, and he always answered: "I am quite ready to do what you want. But I warn you in advance that there will be difficulties with the Arabs." ' (Ibid., p. 287). However, William Yale, the American Intelligence Officer in Cairo, had some evidence that the Turks, while conciliating the Jews with fine promises, were at the same time using the Balfour Declaration to stir up the Arabs against the Jews and make them suspicious of the purposes of the Entente. They were pointing out to the Arabs that 'the first move the Allies after conquering southern Palestine was to give it, an Arab country, to the Jews'. (Report no. 17, p. 3. General Records of the Department of State. Record Group 59. State Decimal File 1910–29. File 763 72/13450. National Archives, Washington.)

Europe', only to realize that Turkey had become a 'political, financial, economic, and moral burden'. Yet for good or ill she was bound to Germany who had guaranteed her territorial integrity. It was no longer practicable in the spring of 1918 to reconquer the lost territories, of southern Palestine in particular; the only means left was diplomacy. However, the amount of support Turkey was likely to marshal at the conference table depended primarily on her ability to reform herself. In this respect, Bernstorff noted, 'if any statesman could have succeeded in reforming the old Ottoman Empire it would have been Talaat Pasha, provided he had been able to consolidate his power and influence'. He was the only man whom Bernstorff, during his service in Constantinople, learned to like and respect. 'A statesman . . . in the truest sense of the word. There was not a sign of the parvenu in his behaviour or ideas . . . and his political conceptions were unencumbered by any pettiness.'[52] However, by mid summer 1918, Talaat's position had weakened. A new factor had emerged to challenge his authority. On 3 July Sultan Mehemed V died and his successor Mehemed VI nourished high ambitions. Known to be 'an enemy of the Union and Progress group and an associate of those who opposed them', he endeavoured to revive Pan-Islamic ideas and enjoyed great popularity among the Arabs.[53] This fact helps to explain the sudden intensification of Arab opposition to 'all Zionist plans'. Formerly the Arab deputies in the Ottoman Chamber supported Talaat so as to keep Djemal Pasha out of power,[54] but with the accession of Mehemed VI their loyalty turned away from Talaat and back to Djemal.

Talaat was not discouraged and it took him less than two weeks to approve the text of a communiqué about his meeting with the V.J.O.D. delegation. It referred to:

the creation of a Jewish centre in Palestine by means of a well-organized immigration and colonization. . . . Being convinced of the importance and usefulness that the settlement of Jews in Palestine would have for the Ottoman Empire, His Highness is desirous of placing it under the protection of the Ottoman Government and encouraging it by every means compatible with the sovereign rights of the Ottoman Empire, and without prejudicing the rights of the non-Jewish population.

[52] *Memoirs*, pp. 144–5, 156, 162.
[53] Emin, *Turkey in the World War*, p. 99; Friedman, 'The Austro-Hungarian Government and Zionism, 242.
[54] *Türkei* 41, Bd. 5, Bernstorff to A.A., 11 Feb. 1918 (a copy).

The text specified that the Grand Vizier would issue 'categorical orders to abrogate all the restrictions on immigration and the settlement of Jews in Palestine' and 'in conformity with Ottoman tradition, he would accord the Jewish population in Palestine benevolent treatment on a basis of complete equality with other elements' in the country, and would name a 'special commission to elaborate without delay a detailed project relating to this enterprise.'[55]

This wording went a long way to satisfy the Jewish delegation. Had it been published in the proposed form it might have been a good omen, particularly as a few days later all restrictive decrees concerning immigration and colonization in Palestine were abrogated by the Council of Ministers. Curiously, Bernstorff regarded the text as unsatisfactory and merely as 'a foundation stone'. Yet against all expectations and at the last minute the key words 'Jewish centre' were deleted and the Jewish delegates refused to agree to the publication of the revised text. Jacobson immediately called on Talaat who assured him that he was determined to satisfy his requests but, in view of the prevailing mood among the Arabs, was unable to sponsor a suitable declaration. Jacobson took this as a pretext and left for Berlin.[56]

Talaat must have had second thoughts, and when Perlmutter, one of the Orthodox members of the delegation, called on him on 11 August, Talaat explained that he had misunderstood the meaning of 'Jewish centre'. To Perlmutter's delight, Talaat agreed to insert in the communiqué the phrase 'national and religious Jewish centre'. Bernstorff informed Berlin of the modification, only to be told by Ruppin the next day that in the meantime the Grand Vizier had decided in favour of 'a religious Jewish centre' and that the word 'national' had been deleted. Bernstorff advised Talaat to limit himself to the shorter phrase 'Jewish centre', or better still to preface it by both attributes, 'national and religious'. Ruppin hoped that additional pressure from Carasso and Matzliach would persuade Talaat to accept Bernstorff's advice, but is seems that the Ottoman Premier had made up his mind. The published communiqué spoke about 'the creation of a religious Jewish centre in Palestine'. The delegates (most of whom had already left Constantinople) considered

[55] *Türkei* 195, K 180737–8, copy of a draft communiqué, encl. in Bernstorff to Hertling, 27 July 1918, dis. no. 4695. See Appendix F.

[56] Ibid. K 180736, Bernstorff to Hertling, 27 July 1918; K 180745, Rosenheim to Perlmuter (no date); C.Z.A. Z 3/378, Jacobson to Hantke, 7 Aug. 1918; Z 3/378, Ruppin to same, 5 Aug. 1918.

the deliberate omission of the word 'national' as proof that the negotiations had failed. The only positive result was the expression of sympathy for the Jewish enterprise in Palestine and the abrogation of all former restrictive decrees.[57]

The German Embassy saw no point in continuing the negotiations.[58] Baron Szilassy, the Austrian Ambassador in Constantinople, also regretted that the Jewish delegation had failed to secure the desired formula and attributed its dilution to the objections raised by the Arabs and the adverse influence of the Sultan.[59] However, this was only partly correct for, had it been the case, the communiqué would have been substantially altered or not published at all. Talaat's principal difficulty concerned the word 'national', which suggests that there must have been additional considerations. Foremost was the chronic distaste in Young Turk circles for the idea of national autonomy, whereas the term 'religious' could bring the Jewish centre within the existing *millet* system. Moreover, public approval of a Jewish national entity in Palestine could have set a dangerous precedent for other provinces and weakened the Porte's hand in its *pourparlers* with Emir Feisal, the standard-bearer of Arab nationalism. The Turks hoped to detach him from the British but in this they failed. Feisal's demand for the reorganization of the Empire on a federal basis was too radical for the central-minded politicians in Constantinople. Neither the Porte nor the Sultan could entertain such a scheme. Thus, even at her last gasp, Turkey, much to Germany's dismay, failed to reach a *modus vivendi* with any of her non-Turkish nationalities. On 23 September 1918 Haifa was captured by the British forces and a week later Damascus was taken. On 31 October an armistice with Turkey was concluded. The Imperial Ottoman era in Asia had come to a close.

With negotiations for peace well in sight, the Zionists lost no time in making their position known. On 25 October 1918 the Copenhagen Bureau issued a manifesto stating that a permanent and just peace could be built only when the legitimate demands of

[57] C.Z.A. Z 3/1488, Ruppin to E.A.C., 12, 15, 26 Aug. 1918; Z 3/517, Lichtheim to Simon, 19 Aug. 1918; *Jüdische Rundschau*, no. 33 (16 Aug. 1918), 253; *Türkei* 195, K 180742, Bernstorff to A.A., 13 Aug. 1918, tel. no. 1298; K 180772, A.A. to Bernstorff, 5 Sept. 1918, tel. no. 168. For the text of the communiqué see Friedman, 'The Austro-Hungarian Government and Zionism', 249, App. III.

[58] *Türkei* 195, K 180790, Waldburg to Hertling, 17 Sept. 1918, dis. no. II, 5789.

[59] Friedman, 'The Austro-Hungarian Government and Zionism', 242.

both the big and small nations were recognized. In line with this the Jewish people should also be given a fair hearing at the Peace Conference. The manifesto demanded that:

(1) Palestine should be reconstituted as the National Home for the Jewish people; to facilitate its unrestricted growth its boundaries should be delineated in conformity with [Jewish] history, as well as with its political and economic requirements.

(2) Civic equality should be granted to Jews in countries which so far had failed to do so.

(3) Right of national, cultural, social, and political autonomy should be accorded to the Jews in countries where they live in large numbers.[60]

Apart from the question of the boundaries of the Jewish National Home, the origin of the first time could be traced to the formula presented by Lord Rothschild to Balfour on 18 July 1917,[61] whereas the last item derived from the idea propounded by Simon Dubnow, the celebrated Jewish historian. Applying his concept of history to contemporary Jewish life, Dubnow published at the turn of the nineteenth century a series of articles in which he laid the foundation of Diaspora nationalism. He claimed that, although the Jews had lost their political independence, they did not cease to exist as a national entity. Despite their dispersion, they were held together by historical, cultural, and religious ties. But even though they existed as a spiritual nation, the Jews needed some structural framework in order to preserve their distinct identity. Dubnow thought that they ought to claim a large measure of autonomy in matters relating to their internal affairs, particularly in the countries where they lived in large numbers. The idea was taken up during the war by the K.f.d.O. and later by Leo Motzkin who, as head of the Comité des Délégations Juives, advocated it at the Peace Conference in Paris in 1919 and subsequently at the League of Nations.[62]

The Copenhagen Manifesto went further than the Basle Programme. It related also to countries other than Palestine and it

[60] C.ZA. Z 3/665, draft of the Copenhagen Manifesto, 24 Oct. 1918; Böhm: *Die zionistische Bewegung*, i, pp. 689–90.

[61] Stein, *The Balfour Declaration*, p. 470.

[62] On this issue see Koppel S. Pinson, 'The National theories of Simon Dubnow', *Jewish Social Studies*, x (Oct. 1948), no. 4, 335–58; Oscar Janowsky, *The Jews and Minority Rights, 1898–1919* (New York, 1933), pp. 57–62, 107–13, 287–319.

seems that the Zionists assumed the role of trustees for the Jewish people. Such a move would have been unthinkable before the war; that they ventured to do so in October 1918 testified both to their newly won status and their sense of confidence. The Manifesto evoked no opposition from German Jews. So deep was the shock following Germany's defeat and so high the prestige of the Zionists in the wake of the declarations made by all belligerent Powers that former controversies were rendered irrelevant. Co-operation within the V.J.O.D. enhanced mutual trust and after the war German Jewry was united as never before. This was clearly demonstrated early in March 1919, during a meeting with Count Bernstorff, now in charge of Jewish affairs at the Foreign Ministry, when representatives of the Hilfsverein, the Zentralverein, and of other German-Jewish organizations expressed their unanimous support of the Copenhagen Manifesto and allowed Lichtheim to speak for them. Bernstorff thereafter invited him to serve as adviser.[63] Other leaders who joined the advisory committee to the German delegation at the Peace Conference were Dr. Eugen Fuchs, head of the Zentralverein, representing the non-Zionists, and Rabbi Pinchas Cohn of Ansbach representing the Orthodox. Subsequently, the programme was expanded and the clause on Palestine changed. It demanded:

... creation of such political, administrative, and economic conditions in Palestine so that its development into an autonomous Commonwealth [*Gemeinwesen*], supported by the whole of Jewry, be secured.[64]

This wording was a modified version of that submitted by the World Zionist Organization to the Peace Conference in Paris.[65] Brockdorff-Rantzau, who succeeded Kühlmann as Foreign Minister, expressed some reservations about the demand for Jewish autonomy in East European states, as it was bound to raise similar demands from other national minorities, but as far as all other items were concerned he declared himself to be in 'fundamental agreement'.[66]

---

[63] Lichtheim, *She'ar Yashuv*, pp. 448–9; *Rückkehr*, p. 380. The meeting with Bernstorff at the A.A. could not have taken place in April as erroneously stated by Lichtheim.

[64] *A.A.A., Geschäftsstelle für die Friedensverhandlungen. Judenfrage, 1919*. L 381517, Bergen to the Office for Peace Negotiations, 22 Mar. 1919; L 381507, note, dated Mar. 1919 (confidential).

[65] See Friedman, op. cit., p. 318.

[66] As note 64. L 381482–3, State Secretary to the Minister of the Interior, 25 Apr. 1919.

This was a marked departure from the past. No longer inhibited by the need to pay heed to Turkey's susceptibilities, the German Government could unreservedly support a programme for a 'Jewish Commonwealth'. In an explanation that followed it was stated that the new Government saw nothing objectionable in a 'Jewish Palestine' and 'in colonizing a country which is sparsely populated'.[67]

During the period of the Weimar Republic interest remained undiminished and the Pro-Palästina Committee experienced an unprecedented growth. Leading members of all parties joined and it commanded the support both of the Government and of public opinion. In 1926, at the express wish of the Foreign Ministry, Bernstorff became its chairman. In a speech at Hamburg in 1930 he said that, having become a member of the League of Nations and with a seat on the Mandates Commission, Germany ought to help in reconstruction, not merely where German interests were concerned, but 'in every case where cultural work is needed. And of such work, the reconstruction of Palestine . . . is a pre-eminent example.' He added that the idea of the constitution of a national home for the Jews in Palestine did not suddenly emerge at the end of the war with the Balfour Declaration. The idea had already existed for some time; it had been actively encouraged by the German Government and negotiations to this effect were in fact conducted by himself when Ambassador in Constantinople. 'It had been our purpose to promote it had the war ended otherwise.'[68]

Ruling out the possibility of a total German victory, it would be tempting to speculate what would have been Germany's plans had the war ended in a negotiated peace. Speculation is no part of history, and to speculate would be risky. Yet if one reads aright the signs of the times one can discern certain probabilities. It might be recalled that on 30 March 1918 Bernstorff suggested that, in order to retake Jerusalem and southern Palestine by diplomacy, the German Government should propose a comprehensive plan at the Peace Conference, of which one element was implementation of Zionist aspirations within the ambit of Ottoman sovereignty.[69] Bernstorff's suggestion was motivated by concern not only for Turkish but also for German interests. In April 1918 a secret order was issued by the

---

[67] *Deutsche Allgemeine Zeitung*, 1 Apr. 1919 (morning edn.); *Jewish Chronicle*, 15 Aug. 1919, 13–14.
[68] *Memoirs*, pp. 286–8.   [69] Above, p. 391.

Ministry of the Interior forbidding admission of Polish Jewish labourers. But the Foreign Ministry feared lest such a step would damage Germany's reputation and the order was subsequently rescinded.[70] Hence the importance of Zionism, which alone could attract East European Jews and divert them from Germany. Against this background it would be safe to assume that, had the terms of peace been negotiated and had German influence in Eastern Europe remained as paramount as it had been in the spring of 1918, Germany would in all probability have pressed for the creation of such political and economic conditions in Palestine as would facilitate large-scale Jewish immigration. There is no reason to believe that in the period immediately after the Balfour Declaration Britain would have objected to this proposition but she would have opposed most emphatically the perpetuation of Turkish sovereignty. With British and German claims cancelling each other out, Palestine would inevitably have had to be placed under a neutral or an international trusteeship as the only feasible compromise. The wisdom of the de Bunsen Committee would have been useful. It was a special interdepartmental Committee appointed by Prime Minister Asquith in 1915 to consider British desiderata in Turkey-in-Asia when British policy was still non-annexationist. With regard to Palestine the Committee recommended that it 'must be recognized as a country whose destiny must be the subject of special negotiations, in which both belligerents and neutrals are alike interested'.[71] This suggestion would not have conflicted with the Basle Programme and in all probability would have been welcome to the Zionist Executive.

However, events took a different turn. Britain emerged as the chief beneficiary, while Germany was denied a say. Germany should nevertheless be given due credit. She was the first European Power to assist the Zionists and protect their enterprise in Palestine; the Instructions to the Consulate of 22 November 1915 were a remarkable document. Public opinion proved a tremendously effective weapon and Germany was highly sensitive to it but, once the United States had entered the war, Zionism became less attractive. The decline of German enthusiasm was accentuated by Zimmermann's resignation and Kühlmann's succession as Foreign Minister in August 1917. All the same, the policy of protection did not

---

[70] *Politische Jüdische Nachrichten*, 25 Nov. 1918 (cutting in *Türkei* 195, K 180850).
[71] Friedman, op. cit., p. 21.

change. This was the most singular service that Germany had rendered Palestine Jews during the war. Had it not been for her persistent interventions (as well as those of the United States till April 1917) the Yishuv would not have survived. Particularly perilous was the position late in 1917 when Djemal was determined to deliver a death-blow to the Jewish population. Dr. Thon commented: 'We may thank God that we have here so warmhearted and energetic a representative of Germany [as General von Falkenhayn].'[72]

Events thus fully vindicated the policy of the Zionist Executive. Passive neutrality, let alone a one-sided pro-Entente orientation, as advocated by its opponents, could have proved fatal to the settlement in Palestine. If the German Government was helpful it was largely owing to the persuasiveness of Warburg, Hantke, Jacobson, and Lichtheim and in response to their suggestions. Lichtheim in particular distinguished himself as a superb diplomat. During his stay in Constantinople he cultivated warm friendships with successive German and American ambassadors whose goodwill proved of inestimable value. He had to contend with Djemal, the perplexingly capricious and hostile ruler in Palestine, and with a frigid and suspicious Government in Constantinople. The Turks based their policy on the mistaken assumption that, once the non-Turkish minorities were granted a certain degree of autonomy, territorial separation would inevitably follow. This had been the case with the Balkan provinces, but it did not apply to Palestine. Loyalty to Turkey was the leitmotiv of Zionist policy and they had no intention whatsoever of tearing Palestine away from the Ottoman Empire, provided they were well treated and accorded the right of free immigration and colonization coupled with cultural autonomy. Talaat eventually acknowledged this, but by then it was too late to make any difference.

In handling their world image the Turks were their own worst enemies. They were completely unaware that events were running against them and, ironically, in their ineptitude they brought upon themselves what they most feared. With the notable exception of perhaps Talaat and Djavid, the Porte was dominated by second-rate politicians who were short-sighted, indecisive, and prone to

[72] C.Z.A. Z 4/1176, cited in Bernstein and Rosenblüth (Copenhagen) to the Zionist Bureau in London, 26 Feb. 1918 (confidential); cf. above, p. 373.

intrigue. Common to all was an instinctive distrust of foreigners. Uppermost in Turkish minds was the desire to rid themselves of European interference and this did not exclude Germany. The Germans had to tread warily and not alienate a sensitive and unenthusiastic ally. This was why Berlin could not act as the Zionists' spokesman *vis-à-vis* the Porte. However, when the climate of opinion in Constantinople improved and a favourable opportunity for *pourparlers* between Djavid and Lichtheim presented itself, German diplomatic machinery became paralysed by an insubordinate Ambassador and an obdurate Military Attaché. It is a matter of opinion whether Foreign Minister Kühlmann served his country's interests well by rejecting repeated suggestions to issue a declaration of sympathy with Zionism, at a time when the British were about to release theirs. But the German Zionist leaders, though unsuccessful in their demands at home, paradoxically as it may seem, had some influence on the publication both of Jules Cambon's statement to Sokolow and of Balfour's letter to Lord Rothschild. Though primarily concerned with safeguarding the Yishuv, by maintaining good relations with German officials and Press, they inadvertently created an atmosphere of competition among the Powers thus indirectly accelerating the decision-making process in Paris and London.[73] Subsequently, the limelight turned on the Zionist leaders in Britain, but the achievements of those in Germany were of no less momentous importance, for in a *judenrein* Palestine the later development of a National Home would have been very unlikely.

[73] Friedman, op. cit., pp. 145, 244–5, 275–7, 283, 286–7.

APPENDIX A

Letter and a postscript from Count zu Eulenburg to Dr. Herzl, 27 and 28 September 1898

Nachlass Eulenburg, Nr. 52. Bundesarchiv, Koblenz.

Rominten, 27. September 1898.

An Dr. Theodor Herzl

Sehr geehrter Herr Doktor! Ich habe mit grösstem Interesse und bestem Dank Ihr Schreiben aus Paris vom 24. d. Mts. soeben erhalten. Wenn ich nicht durch Arbeit überlastet gewesen wäre, hätten Sie eher schon einen Brief von mir erhalten.

Ich habe Ihnen nur *Gutes* zu melden — wenn auch vielleicht nicht in der Richtung, wie Sie es *momentan* wünschten.

Se. Majestät der Kaiser hat — wie ich es erwartete — ein volles und tiefes Verständnis für die Bewegung gezeigt, an deren Spitze Sie stehen. Ich bin ein eifriger Fürsprecher gewesen, da ich durch Sie von der Bedeutung der zionistischen Bewegung vollkommen überzeugt wurde. — In gleicher Weise denkt mein Freund Bülow und das ist für Ihre Sache von grosser Bedeutung.

Nach meinem Vortrag hat Se. Majestät sich bereit erklärt, in sehr eingehender und — so weit dieses möglich sein wird — *dringender* Weise bei dem Sultan für Ihre Interessen einzutreten. Der Kaiser wird dabei durch den ihn begleitenden Staatssekretär von Bülow unterstützt werden.

Da ich in der Lage war, Sr. Majestät von dem Entgegenkommen Meldung zu erstatten, das der Sultan gegenüber der Anregung durch Herrn von Marschall gezeigt hatte, sah der Kaiser keinen hindernden Grund, um seinerseits weitere Schritte zu tun.

Die Lebhaftigkeit seines Geistes wird ihn zu einem geschickten Interpreten machen — daran zweifle ich nicht.

Wertvoll ist mir Ihre Aufzeichnung in dem Briefe vom 24., da dieselbe als aide Memoire figurieren kann.

Einer Audienz Ihrerseits wollte Se. Majestät (da dieselbe unmöglich geheim gehalten werden könnte) *jetzt* nicht gern zustimmen. Der Kaiser fürchtete zu allen lästigen Commentaren, die seine Reise nach Palästina erfahren hat, noch neue Erörterungen unbequemer Art.

Aber Se. Majestät haben sich gern bereit erklärt, eine Deputation der Zionisten in Palästina zu empfangen. Ich habe bereits meinen Vetter, den Oberhofmarschall Grafen August Eulenburg im Geheimen davon verständigt.

Würden Sie diese Deputation führen, so würden Sie die allerbeste Gelegenheit haben, Sr. Majestät persönlich Ihre Wünsche vorzutragen. — Ich lege einen kleinen Zettel mit den Daten der Anwesenheit in Palästina bei.

Schliesslich muss ich Sie, geehrter Herr Doktor, auf das *Dringendeste bitten*, diese Zeilen und ihren Inhalt absolut geheim zu halten.

Mit der Versicherung, Ihrer Sache stets gern und aufrichtig förderlich sein zu wollen, verbleibe ich ehrfurchtsvoll Ihr ganz ergebener

(gez.) Philipp Eulenburg.

Nachschrift 28. September 1898.

Ich habe soeben wiederum mit Sr. Majestät gesprochen — in eingehender Weise an der Hand Ihres Briefes.

Se. Majestät beauftragt mich Ihnen zu sagen, dass Sie sich nicht getäuscht hätten, wenn Sie Vertrauen zu seinem Interesse, die Förderung Ihres Werkes und den darin liegenden Schutz armer und unterdrückter Juden betreffend, gehabt hätten. Se. Majestät würden in nachdrücklichster Weise die Angelegenheit mit dem Sultan besprechen, und werden sich freuen, von Ihnen in Jerusalem Näheres zu hören.

Der Kaiser hat bereits Ordre gegeben, dass diesem Empfang der Deputation kein Hindernis in den Weg gelegt werde.

Schliesslich lassen Se. Majestät Ihnen sagen, dass allerhöchstderselbe *bereit sei*, das eventuell in Frage kommende Protektorat zu übernehmen. — Se. Majestät rechneten natürlich bei dieser Mitteilung auf Ihre Diskretion.

(gez.) Eulenburg.

APPENDIX B

Instruction of the German Embassy in Constantinople to the Consulate in Jerusalem

(*Türkei* 195, Bd. 7, K 177404–7, copy encl. in Metternich to Bethmann Hollweg, 22 Nov. 1915, dis. no. 693)

Kaiserlich Deutsche Botschaft   Pera, den 22. November 1915.
A.Nr.5328.

     an das Kaiserliche Konsulat.

Vertraulich!

Es hat sich nach den Wahrnehmungen der letzten Zeit als zweckmässig erwiesen, zur einheitlichen Regelung des ferneren Verhaltens der Konsularbehörden die Stellung der Reichsregierung gegenüber den Einrichtungen und Bestrebungen des Judentums in der Türkei in ihren Hauptrichtlinien zu kennzeichnen.

Soweit es sich um solche jüdische Einrichtungen handelt, die vom rechlichen Standpunkte aus als deutsche Schöpfungen angesprochen werden können, so bedarf es nicht besonderer Betonung, dass der Schutz des Reiches ihnen im vollen Umfange nach wie vor zusteht.

Hinsichtlich derjenigen Bestrebungen des Judentums, welche auf die Hebung des geistigen und wirtschaftlichen Niveaus der in der Türkei lebenden Juden oder auf die Förderung der Einwanderung und Ansiedelung ausländischer Juden gerichtet sind und welche auf die Gewährung des deutschen Schutzes keinen Rechtsanspruch besitzen, so kann im Allgemeinen als Grundsatz aufgestellt werden, dass die Kaiserliche Regierung den gedachten Bestrebungen des Judentums freundlich gegenübersteht und ihre wohlwollende Haltung auch zu betätigen bereit ist, sofern dem nicht als gerechtfertigt zu betrachtende türkisch-staatliche Interessen oder solche deutscher Reichsangehöriger und Einrichtungen entgegenstehen.

Die Kaiserlichen Konsularvertreter sind demnach ermächtigt, Wünschen und Anliegen der in Frage kommenden jüdischen Kreise freundliches Gehör zu schenken und ihnen vorkommenfalls nach Möglichkeit auch durch tätiges Eingreifen zur Erfüllung zu verhelfen.

Ob im einzelnen Falle eine persönliche Verwendung des Konsuls bei den türkischen Stellen überhaupt angezeigt, oder in welche Form ein derartiger Schritt am besten zu kleiden ist, bleibt zweckmässigerweise dem Ermessen des Kaiserlichen Konsularvorstehers überlassen. Es liegt jedoch auf der Hand, dass der türkischen Behörde gegenüber der rein freundschaftliche, nicht-amtliche Charakter der Verwendung stets nachdrücklich zu betonen ist. Ueber vorkommende Fälle des konsularischen Eingreifens zugunsten der jüdischen Interessen bitte ich der Kaiserlichen Botschaft umgehend Meldung erstatten zu wollen.

Kaiserlich Deutsche Botschaft   Pera, den 22. November 1915.
B.Nr. 5328.
Im Anschluss an den Erlass vom
   heutigen Tage.

Geheim.

Die im nebenstehenden bezeichneten Erlasse enthaltenen Weisungen betreffend die Behandlung der jüdischen Einrichtungen und Bestrebungen in der Türkei und insbesondere in Palästina sind durch Schritte veranlasst worden, die die Leitung der zionistischen Bewegung im Auswärtigen Amt, sowie der hiesige Vertreter der Zionisten bei der Kaiserlichen Botschaft bereits seit geraumer Zeit wiederholt unternommen haben.

Die Zusicherung einer freundlichen Haltung gegenüber dem Zionismus und seinen Bestrebungen erschien aus politischen Gründen angezeigt. Etwaigen Empfindlichkeiten der deutschen Juden, insbesondere der dem Hilfsverein nahestehenden Kreise, die sich zu Unrecht so gebärden, als bedeute die Bekundung eines Interesses für die zionistische Bewegung eine unmittelbare Schädigung ihrer eigenen Stellung, ist nach Möglichkeit vorgebeugt worden.

Euer Hochwohlgeboren bitte ich ergebenst, nach dieser Richtung erforderlichenfalls auch Ihrerseits beruhigend wirken zu wollen.

APPENDIX C

A draft for a declaration as proposed by the Zionists and recommended by Matthias Erzberger to Richard von Kühlmann, Minister for Foreign Affairs

(Türkei 195, Bd. 17, K 179939–41, encl. in Erzberger to Kühlmann, 30 Nov. 1917)

Die Kaiserliche Regierung steht dem Bestreben der Zionistischen Organisation, in Palästina eine nationale Heimstätte für das jüdische Volk zu schaffen, mit Wohlwollen gegenüber und ist gewillt, diesem Bestreben ihre tatkräftige Förderung angedeihen zu lassen.

In der Anerkennung der grossen wirtschaftlichen und kulturellen Bedeutung, die eine jüdische Siedlung in Palästina für das mit Deutschland verbündete türkische Reich besitzt, ist die Kaiserliche Regierung bereit, bei befreundeten türkischen Regierung dafür einzutreten, dass die Grundlagen für die unbehinderte Weiterentwicklung der jüdischen Siedlung in Palästina geschaffen werden.

APPENDIX D

An excerpt from Dr. Thon's letter (Jerusalem) to the Zionist Central Bureau (Berlin), 15 November 1917

(*Türkei* 195, Bd. 18, K 180161, encl. in E.A.C. to A.A., 1 Feb. 1918)

Da dies wahrscheinlich die letzte Gelegenheit ist für ein direktes Schreiben an Sie, möchte ich Sie nun im Namen aller Palästinenser, die unseren Jdeen Folge leisten, bitten, der deutschen Botschaft und dem Auswärtigen Amt für den energischen Schutz, der uns während der ganzen Kriegszeit gewährt wurde, unseren aufrichtigsten tiefen Dank auszusprechen. Wir haben wunschgemäss unsere Beziehungen zu den deutschen Behörden stets vertraulich behandelt, doch ist es allgemein bekannt, dass uns nicht wiedergutzumachendes Unheil angetan worden wäre, wenn nicht die mächtige Hand der deutschen Regierung in Stunden der Bedrängnis uns geschützt hätte. Wir werden dies auch unter veränderten Umständen nicht vergessen. —

Herrn Generalkonsul Brode habe ich hier zusammen mit Herrn Hoofien den Dank der Organisation ausgedrückt.

Eine besonders glückliche Fügung war es, dass in den letzten kritischen Tagen Falkenhayn den Oberbefehl hatte. Djemal hätte in diesem Falle — wie er es oft in Aussicht gestellt hatte — die Bevölkerung des ganzen Gebietes verjagt und das Land in eine Ruine verwandelt. Wir und die gesamte übrige Bevölkerung, die christliche und mohammedanische, müssen mit tiefer Dankbarkeit an Falkenhayn denken, der durch Verhinderung einer geplanten vollständigen Evakuierung dieses Gebietes die Zivilbevölkerung vor Untergang bewahrt hat.

APPENDIX E

Preservation of the Holy Places in Palestine

(*Türkei* 195, Bd. 17, K 179881–2, encl. in Romberg to Chancellor
Hertling, 21 Nov. 1917, dis. no. 3578, encl. no. 1 (copy))

Kaiserlich Deutsche Gesandtschaft.   Bern, den 21. November 1917.
Nr. 3578.

Auf Ansuchen der beiden Vizepräsidenten des schweizerischen Israeliti-
schen Gemeindebundes und des schweizerischen Zionistenverbandes um
Schonung der heiligen Stätten in Palästina und um Schutz für die dort
lebende jüdische Bevölkerung ist von amtlicher deutscher Stelle folgende
Zusicherung eingegangen:

'Nach den vorliegenden Nachrichten von türkischer Seite ist bereits auf
die Schonung der heiligen Stätten in Jerusalem, die auch bei den Moha-
medanern Verehrung geniessen, Bedacht genommen worden, und soweit
es die militärischen Interessen nur irgendwie gestatten, wird man der
Bevölkerung jede Rücksicht angedeihen lassen. Selbstverständlich haben
die Juden dabei keinerlei Ausnahmemaßregeln zu befürchten.'

Ein gleicher Schritt ist auch bei der englischen Regierung unternommen
worden.

APPENDIX F

Copy of a draft communiqué about Talaat's meeting with the V.J.O.D. delegation in Constantinople on 14 July 1918

(*Türkei* 195, Bd. 21, K 180737–8, encl. in Bernstorff to Hertling, 27 July 1918, dis. no. 4695 (copy))

Anlage zum Bericht der Kaiserl. Botschaft, Konstantinopel, Nr. 4695 vom 27. Juli 1918.

Copie.

S. A. le Grand Vésir Talaat Pacha a reçu les délégués des différentes sociétés juives venus à Constantinople sur l'invitation de S. A. pour prendre part aux pourparlers concernant la création d'un centre juif en Palestine par la voie d'une immigration et d'une colonisation bien organisées.

Au cours de la réception S. A. a bien voulu exprimer aux délégués ses sympaties pour cette œuvre. Etant convaincu de l'importance et de l'utilité que l'installation des juifs en Palestine pourra avoir pour l'Empire Ottoman, S. A. est désireux de prendre l'œuvre de la protection du Gouvernement Ottoman et de l'encourager par tous les moyens compatibles avec les droits souverains de l'Empire Ottoman et sans léser les droits de la population non-juive. S. A. donnera des ordres catégoriques pour abolir définitivement toutes les mesures restrictives concernant l'immigration et l'installation des juifs en Palestine et pour assurer à la nation juive en Palestine en conformité avec les traditions ottomanes un traitement bienveillant et sur la base d'une complète égalité avec les autres éléments. S. A. nommera une commission spéciale pour élaborer dans le plus court délai un projet détaillé concernant cette œuvre.

Les délégués ont salué vivement la décision de S. A. d'abolir toutes les mesures restrictives et de mettre fin aux difficultés créés à la population juive en Palestine. Ils ont exprimé leur satisfaction d'apprendre que le Gouvernement ottoman désireux d'encourager et de faciliter la création d'un centre juif en Palestine constituera une commission spéciale pour continuer les pourparlers avec les représentants autorisés des différentes sociétés juives. Les délégués exprimèrent en même temps leur ferme espoir que le travail de la commission aboutira à l'élaboration d'un projet pouvant donner satisfaction aux aspirations juives qui sont bien réalisables sous la souveraineté ottomane et dans le cadre de l'Empire Ottoman, en complète compatibilité avec les intérêts de l'Etat et les droits de la population arabe.

Bibliography

I. UNPUBLISHED SOURCES

1. *Auswärtiges Amt Akten*, Bonn (Documents of the German Ministry for Foreign Affairs. Some are microfilmed and deposited at the Public Record Office, London).

Türkei, Nr. 195, *Die Juden in Türkei*. K 692/K 175834–K 180790, 21 Bände, covering the period 1890–1918 (Public Record Office, boxes G.F.M. 3/284–G.F.M. 3/288).

Türkei, Nr. 158, *Die Beziehungen zwischen der Türkei und Deutschland* (P.R.O., Box G.F.M. 11/29).

Türkei, Nr. 175 e, *Die heiligen Stätten*, Bd. 2.

Türkei, Nr. 177, *Der Libanon (Syrien)*—contains material on Palestine. 19 Bände (P.R.O., G.F.M. 10/405 and G.F.M. 10/406).

Türkei, Nr. 189, *Plan deutscher Ansiedelungen in Kleinasien, 1891–1913* (P.R.O., G.F.M. 10/472).

Türkei, Nr. 190, *Die Beziehungen der Türkei zu den Vereinigten Staaten von Nordamerika*.

Grosses Hauptquartier, Nr. 23; *Revolutionäre Bewegungen*, Bd. 1.

Grosses Hauptquartier, Türkei, Nr. 41, *Allgemeine Politik*.

Deutschland, Nr. 128. Nos. 4–7 secr. *Verhandlungen mit der Türkei über die Erweiterung des Bündnisvertrages* (P.R.O., G.F.M. 10/14, 10/15).

Gesandtschaft Stockholm. *Politisches, 1914–17, Krieg, Tätigkeit der Zionisten* (P.R.O., box G.F.M. 2/6238).

Weltkrieg, Nr. 11, adh. 2, K 714/K 190217–191410 (P.R.O., G.F.M. 3/301).

Weltkrieg, Nr. 20c, Bd. 4.

Geschäftsstelle für die Friedensverhandlungen. Judenfrage, 1919.

Europa Generalia, Nr. 79, *Akten betreffend die polnische Frage.*

Europa Generalia, Nr. 84, *Akten betreffend Alliance Israélite Universelle* (P.R.O., G.F.M. 3/289).

2. Bundesarchiv, Koblenz.

Nachlass Eulenburg, Bände Nr. 52–8.

Denkschrift von Heinrich Class betreffend die national-, wirtschafts- und sozialpolitischen Ziele des deutschen Volkes im gegenwärtigen Kriege, undated but presumably autumn 1914. (Found among the *Beseler Nachlass* papers.)

3. Deutsches Zentralarchiv, Potsdam, East Germany.

Reichsamt des Innern, Nr. 19802–4, *Die jüdische Frage in besetzten Gebieten Russisch-Polens, 1915–1919*, Bände 1–3.

4. Österreichisches Staatsarchiv, Abt. Haus-, Hof- und Staatsarchiv, Vienna, Politisches Archiv XII, Karton 212.

5. Public Record Office, London, Foreign Office Files.

F.O. 195/604 (1859); F.O. 371/3055/87895 (1917); F.O. 800/79 (1911); F.O. 395/109/96621 (1917).

6. General Records of the Department of State, National Archives, Washington. Record Group 59. State Decimal File 1910–29. File 763 72/13450.

7. The Central Zionist Archives, Jerusalem, Israel.

Files of the Central Zionist Office, Cologne, 1905–11: Z 2

Z 2/6–12 *Schriftwechsel zwischen dem E.A.C. und dem politischen Vertreter der Zion. Organisation in Konstantinopel, Dr. Victor Jacobson, 1908–1911.*

Z 2/31 *Beziehungen zur Alliance Israélite Universelle, 1911.*

Z 2/223–6 *Protokolle der Sitzungen des Engeren Aktions-Comitees (E.A.C.), 1905–1911.*

Z 2/237–49 *Protokolle der Sitzungen des Grossen Aktions-Comitees (G.A.C.), 1907–1911.*

Files of the Central Zionist Office, Berlin, 1911–20: Z 3

Z 3/2–13 *Allgemeine politische Korrespondenz des E.A.C.; Politische Memoranden des oder an das E.A.C.; Protokolle von Unterredungen zionistischer Führer mit Politikern und Staatsmännern, 1912–1919.*

Z 3/14–17 *Beeinflussung der Presse; Presseäusserungen über den Zionismus, 1914–1920.*

Z 3/19–21 *Politische Beeinflussung von Politikern, Journalisten und Gelehrten in Deutschland, 1914–1919.*

Z 3/22–3 *Schriftwechsel mit dem Auswärtigen Amt, Botschaften, Konsulaten, etc., 1914–1920.*

Z 3/26–8 *Deutsches Komitee Pro-Palästina, 1917–1919.*

Z 3/38–64 *Politische Tätigkeit in Konstantinopel und Palästina, 1911–1917.*

Z 3/66–70 *Zionistische Politik in Konstantinopel, etc., 1913–1918.*

Z 3/72–4 *Stellung der Türkei zum Zionismus und zum Jischuw Palästinas, 1914–1918.*

Z 3/76 *Deutsche Regierung und die Schutze der Zionismus in Palästina, 1915–1917.*

Z 3/78–84 *Judenfeindliche Verordnungen der türkischen Behörden in Palästina, 1914–1918.*

Z 3/89–93 *Pressestimmen, etc., 1914–1919.*

Z 3/95 *Verhandlungen von Vertretern der VJOD mit der türkischen Regierung in Konstantinopel, 1918.*

Z 3/354–64 *Protokolle der Sitzungen des Engeren Aktions-Comitees (E.A.C.), 1911–1918.*

Z 3/428–54 *Protokolle der Sitzungen des Grossen Aktions-Comitees (G.A.C.), 1911–1919.*

Z 3/592–601 *Besondere Aktionen des Zentralbüros im ersten Weltkrieg, 1914–1918.*

Z 3/616–80 *Das Kopenhagener Zionistische Büro (Schriftswechsel), 1915–1919.*

Z 3/758–63 *Provisional Executive Committee for General Zionist Affairs, New York, 1914–1919.*

Z 3/796–802 *Zionistische Vereinigung für Deutschland, 1911–1919.*

Z 3/1031–50 *Propaganda: mündliche und schriftliche, 1911–1918.*

Z 3/1150–74 *Nachrichtendienst für die Presse, 1911–1919.*

Z 3/1484–9 *Schriftwechsel mit Dr. A. Ruppin während seines Aufenthaltes in Konstantinopel, 1917–1918.*

Z 3/1569–97 *Der Kampf mit dem Hilfsverein der deutschen Juden um die Unterrichtssprache am Technikum in Haifa (Sprachenkampf), 1913–1914.*

Files of the Copenhagen Bureau, 1915–1919
    L 6/2/I and II; L 6/12/VI; L 6/37; L 6/38/I and II; L 6/45; L 6/49/II/2; L 6/64/I; L 6/68; L 6/79/I and II; L 6/80; L 6/81; L 6/85; L 6/88; L 6/89; L 6/90; L 6/93.

Files of the Executive of the Zionist Organization, 1917–1918
Z 4/128; Z 4/1176
Theodor Herzl Papers (1896–1904)
    H IV B/3; H IV B/5; H VI B/5; H VI E I
Max Bodenheimer Papers (1898–1918)
A 15/IV/17; Z 3/471–3
David Wolffsohn Papers (1904–11)
W 16; W 35/3; W 61/II
Max Nordau Papers (1911–18)
Z 3/1012–14
Shmarya Levin Papers (1911–17)
Z 3/394–7
Arthur Hantke Papers (1911–19)
Z 3/373–9
Julius Simon Papers (1918)
Z 3/517

II. PUBLISHED SOURCES

(a) Official Publications and Collections of Official Documents

Die Grosse Politik der Europäischen Kabinette 1871–1914 (Berlin, 1922–7), Bände. x, xii, and xviii.

Official German Documents Relating to the World War. Translated under the supervision of the Carnegie Endowment for International Peace (Oxford University Press, 1923), 2 vols.

Ludendorff, Erich, General, *The General Staff and its Problems. The History of the Relations between the High Command and the German Imperial Government as revealed by Official Documents*, trans. F. A. Holt (London, 1920), 2 vols.

The British Consulate in Jerusalem in relation to the Jews of Palestine, 1838–1914. Documents ed. by A. M. Hyamson (London, 1941), 2 vols.

British Documents on the Origins of the War, 1898–1914, ed. G. P. Gooch and H. W. V. Temperley, *The Near East*, v, x (London, 1934).

Handbooks prepared under the Direction of the Historical Section of the Foreign Office, x, No. 60, *Syria and Palestine* (London, H.M.S.O., 1920).

Handbooks prepared under the Direction of the Historical Section of the Foreign Office, No. 155, *German Opinion on National Policy prior to July 1914* (London, H.M.S.O., 1920).

Handbooks prepared under the Direction of the Historical Section of the Foreign Office, x, No. 162, *Zionism* (London, H.M.S.O., 1920).

Hansard (House of Commons), 1917.

United States Foreign Affairs. Vols. 1864–5, 1865–6.

Papers relating to the Foreign Relations of the United States. Vols.: 1886, 1879, 1881, 1882, 1885, 1888, 1893, 1894, 1898, 1901.

Papers Relating to the Foreign Relations of the United States. Supplement to the World War, 1914, 1915, 1916, 1917 (Washington, 1928).

(b) Official Zionist Publications and Collections of Documents on Jewish Affairs

Stenographische Protokolle der Verhandlungen des Zionisten Kongresses: I (Basle, 29–31 Aug. 1897); VI (Basle, 23–8 Aug. 1903); VII (Cologne, 27 July–2 Aug. 1905); VIII (The Hague, 14–21 Aug. 1907); IX (Hamburg, 26–30 Dec. 1909); X (Basle, 9–15 Aug. 1911); XI (Vienna, 2–9 Sept. 1913).

Bericht des Aktion-Komitees der Zionistischen Organisation an den XI. Zionisten Kongress (Berlin, 1913).

Im Kampf um die hebräische Sprache, herausgegeben vom Zionistischen Actions-Comité (Berlin, 1914).

Organisation Report; Palestine during the War; Financial Report. From a Report presented to the Twelfth Zionist Congress at Carlsbad, September 1921 (Zionist Organisation, London, 1921).

Ellern, Hermann and Bessie, *Herzl, Hechler, the Grand Duke of Baden and the German Emperor, 1896–1904*, with an introduction by Alex Bein and a foreword by Hermann Ellern (Tel Aviv, 1962). Contains forty-eight documents in facsimile.

Tama, Diogène, *Collection des actes du Grand Sanhédrin* (Paris, 1807).

—— *Collection des procès-verbaux et décisions du Grand Sanhédrin* (Paris, 1807).

Druyanov, Alter (ed.), *Ktavim L'Toledoth Hibbath Zion V'Yishuv Eretz-Israel* [*Letters regarding the History of Hibbath-Zion and the Settlement in Palestine* (Odessa, 1919), 3 vols.

Galante, Abraham, *Documents officiels turcs concernant les Juifs de Turquie* (Stamboul, 1931).

Die Judenfrage der Gegenwart. Dokumentensammlung, herausgegeben von Leon Chasanowitsch und Leo Motzkin (Stockholm, 1919).

Die Juden im Kriege. Denkschrift des Jüdischen Sozialistischen Arbeiterverbandes Poale Zion an das internationale Sozialistische Bureau, 2 Aufl. (The Hague, 1917).

Herzberg, Arthur, *The Zionist Idea*. A Historical Analysis and Reader (New York, 1959).

Preliminary Conference of the American Jewish Congress, *Report of Proceedings* (New York, 1916).

(c) Letters, Diaries, Memoirs, Contemporary Statements

Aaronsohn, Alexander, *With the Turks in Palestine* (New York, 1916).

Ahad Ha'am, 'Summa Summarum', *Ten Essays on Zionism and Judaism*, trans. Leon Simon (London, 1922).

Ballod, Carl, *Palästina als jüdisches Ansiedlungsgebiet. Die Schriften des Deutschen Komitees Pro-Palästina* (Berlin, 1918).

Bartlett, W. H., *Jerusalem Revisited* (London, 1855).

Bauer, Bruno, *Die Judenfrage* (Brunswick, 1843).

Bernstorff, Johann Heinrich, Count, *My Three Years in America*, trans. (London, 1920).

—— *The Memoirs of Count Bernstorff*, trans. (London, 1936).

Bethmann Hollweg, Theobald von, *Reflections on the World War*, trans. (London, 1936).

Blumenfeld, Kurt, 'Der Zionismus, eine Frage der deutschen Orientpolitik', *Preussische Jahrbücher* (Berlin, 1915).

—— *Zionistische Betrachtungen* (Berlin, 1916).

—— *Erlebte Judenfrage. Ein Vierteljahrhundert deutscher Zionismus* (Stuttgart, 1962).

Bodenheimer, Max, 'Theodor Herzl', *Theodor Herzl—A Memorial*, ed. M. W. W. Weisgal (New York, 1929).

—— *So wurde Israel. Erinnerungen von Dr. Max T. Bodenheimer*, herausgegeben von Henriette Hannah Bodenheimer (Frankfurt am Main, 1958), trans. into English: *The Memoirs of Max I. Bodenheimer: Prelude to Israel* (New York, London, 1963).

Bülow, Bernhard, Prince, *Memoirs*, trans. (London, 1931), 4 vols.

Bürger, Berthold, 'Die Zukunft Palästinas und die Judenfrage', *Die Hilfe* (15 Apr. 1915).

Cohen, Israel, *The German Attack on the Hebrew Schools in Palestine* (London, 1918).

Cohen, Israel (*cont.*), *The Turkish Persecution of the Jews* (London, 1918).

—— *Travels in Jewry* (London, 1952).

Cohen-Reuss, Max, *Die politische Bedeutung des Zionismus. Die Schriften des Deutschen Komitees Pro-Palästina* (Berlin, 1918).

Czernin, Ottokar, *In the World War* (London, 1919).

Dernburg, Bernhard, *Von beiden Ufern* (Berlin, 1917).

Djemal, Ahmed, Pasha, *Memoirs of a Turkish Statesman: 1913–1919* (London, 1922).

Dumba, Constantin, *Memoirs of a Diplomat* (London, 1933).

Einstein, Lewis, *Inside Constantinople* (London, 1917).

Endres, Franz Carl, *Die wirtschaftliche Bedeutung Palästinas als Teil der Türkei. Die Schriften des Deutschen Komitees Pro-Palästina* (Berlin, 1918).

—— *Zionismus und Weltpolitik* (Munich, 1918).

Erzberger, Matthias, *Erlebnisse im Weltkrieg* (Berlin, 1919).

Falcke, Horst P., *Vor dem Eintritt Americas in den Weltkrieg. Deutsche Propaganda in den Vereinigten Staaten von America, 1914–1915* (Dresden, 1928).

Finn, James, *Stirring Times or Records from Jerusalem Consular Chronicles* (London, 1878), 2 vols.

Fuchs, Eugen, *Um Deutschtum und Judentum* (speeches and essays), ed. Leo Hirschfeld (Frankfurt-on-Main, 1919).

Geiger, Ludwig (ed.), *Abraham Geigers' Leben in Briefen* (Berlin, 1878).

Gerard, James W., *My Four Years in Germany* (London, 1917).

Goldmann, Nachum, 'Zum Polnisch-Jüdischen Problem. Eine Erwiderung', *Preussische Jahrbücher*, Nr. 162 (1915), 457–67.

Grobba, Fritz, 'Palästina in Weltkrieg', *Preussische Jahrbücher*, Nr. 163 (1916), 465–78.

Hanssen, Hans Peter, *Diary of a Dying Empire* (Indiana University Press, 1955).

Herzl, Theodor, *Gesammelte Zionistische Werke* (Berlin, 1934), 5 vols.

—— *The Jewish State*, trans. (New York, 1946).

—— *The Complete Diaries of Theodor Herzl*, ed. Raphael Patai, trans. Harry Zohn (London, 1960), 5 vols.

Hess, Moses, *Rome und Jerusalem* (Cologne, 1862), trans. into English by M. Waxman (New York, 1945).

Hohenlohe-Schillingsfuerst, Prince, *Memoirs of Prince Chlodwig of Hohenlohe-Schillingsfuerst*, ed. Friedrich Curtius (London, 1907), 2 vols.

House, Edward M. *The Intimate Papers of Colonel House*, ed. Charles Seymour (London, 1926), 2 vols.

Hutten-Czapski, Bogdan, Graf, *Sechzig Jahre Politik und Gesellschaft* (Berlin, 1936), 2 vols.

Jabotinsky, Vladimir, *Turkey and the War* (London, 1917).

—— *The Story of the Jewish Legion* (New York, 1945).

Jäckh, Ernst, *The Rising Crescent* (New York, 1944).

—— *Der Goldene Pflug, Lebensernte eines Weltbürgers* (Stuttgart, 1954).

Jessup, H. H., *Fifty-three Years in Syria* (New York, 1910), 2 vols.

Kressenstein, Friedrich Kress von, Freiherr, *Mit den Türken zum Suezkanal* (Berlin, 1938).

Kühlmann, Richard von, *Thoughts on Germany*, trans. E. Sutton (London, 1932).

—— *Erinnerungen* (Heidelberg, 1948).

Lagarde, Paul de, *Deutsche Schriften* (Göttingen, 1903).

Lansing, Robert, *War Memoirs of Robert Lansing* (London, 1935).

Lawrence, T. E., *T. E. Lawrence to his Biographers, Liddel Hart and Robert Graves* (London, 1938).

Lichnowsky, Karl M., Prince, *Heading the Abyss. Reminiscences* (London, 1928).

Lichtheim, Richard, *Das Programm des Zionismus* (Berlin, 1911).

—— *Rückkehr. Lebenserinnerungen aus der Frühzeit des deutschen Zionismus* (Stuttgart, 1970).

Lipsky, Louis, *A Gallery of Zionist Profiles* (New York, 1966).

Lloyd George, David, *War Memoirs* (London, 1935?), 2 vols.

—— *The Truth about the Peace Treaties* (London, 1938), ii.

Maximilian, Alexander F., *The Memoirs of Prince Max of Baden*, trans. W. M. Calder and S. W. H. Sutton (London, 1928), 2 vols.

McCaul-Finn, Elizabeth Anne, *Reminiscences of . . .* (London, 1929).

Moltke, Helmuth von, *Essays, Speeches and Memoirs*, Engl. trans. (London, 1893), i.

Montefiore, Sir Moses and Lady, *Diaries of . . .*, ed. L. Loewe (London, 1890), 2 vols.

Morgenthau, Henry, *All in a Life-time* (New York, 1922).

—— *Secrets of the Bosphorus, Constantinople, 1913–1916* (London, 1928).

Nahoum, Haim, 'Jews', *Modern Turkey*, ed. E. G. Mears (New York, 1924).

Nathan, Paul, *Palästina und palästinensischer Zionismus* (Berlin, 1914).

Naumann, Friedrich, *Mitteleuropa* (Berlin, 1915).

Neumann, Bernhard, *Die heilige Stadt* (Hamburg, 1877).

Nogales, Rafael de, *Four Years beneath the Crescent*, trans. M. Lee (London, 1926).

Nordau, Max, 'Die Pflicht der Stunde', *Menorah* (Vienna, Oct. 1915).

Oppenheimer, Franz, *Erlebtes, Erstrebtes, Erreichtes, Erinnerungen* (Düsseldorf, 1964).

Papen, Franz von, *Memoirs* (London, 1952).

Patterson, Henry J., Lt.-Col., *With the Zionists in Gallipoli* (London, 1916).

Poincaré, Raymond, *The Memoirs of Raymond Poincaré*, trans. (London, 1926), 2 vols.

Pomiankowski, Joseph, *Der Zusammenbruch des Ottomanischen Reiches* (Vienna, 1928).

Quessel, Ludwig, 'Die Judenfrage als nationales Problem; *Neue Jüdische Monatshefte*, no. 2 (1917/18), 299–306.

Rhodes, Thomas, *The Real Kühlmann* (London, 1925).

Rosen, Baron, *Forty Years of Diplomacy* (London, 1922), 2 vols.

Rosen, Friedrich, *Aus einem diplomatischen Wanderleben* (Berlin, 1931).

Rosenblüth, Martin, *Go Forth and Serve* (New York, 1961).

Ruppin, Arthur, *Building Israel. Selected Essays: 1907–1935* (New York. 1949).

—— *Memoirs, Diaries, Letters*, ed. Alex Bein (New York, 1971).

Sacher, Harry (ed.), *Zionism and the Jewish Future* (London, 1916).

—— *Zionist Portraits and other Essays* (London, 1959).

Sanders, Liman O. von, *Five Years in Turkey* (Annapolis, 1927).

Seetzen, Ulrich J., *Reisen durch Syrien, Palästina* . . . (Berlin, 1854), 2 Bände.

Spring-Rice, Cecil, Sir, *The Letters and Friendships of Sir Cecil Spring-Rice*, ed. Stethen Gwynn (London, 1929), 2 vols.

Stein, Ludwig, 'They Have Prevailed. A Tribute to Herzl and Nordau', *Theodor Herzl—A Memorial*, ed. M. W. W. Weisgal (New York, 1929).

Straus, Oscar S., *Under Four Administrations* (New York, 1923).

Straus, Rahel, *Wir lebten in Deutschland. Erinnerungen einer deutschen Jüdin, 1880–1933* (Stuttgart, 1961).

Talaat Pasha, 'Posthumous Memoirs of Talaat Pasha', *Current History* (Nov. 1921).

Weizmann, Chaim, *Trial and Error* (London, 1949).

Wilhelm II., *Briefe Wilhelms II. an den Zaren, 1894–1914*, ed. Walter Goetz (Berlin, 1920).

Wischnitzer, Mark, *To Dwell in Safety* (Philadelphia, 1948).

Witte, S., Count, *The Memoirs of* . . ., ed. A. Yarmolinsky (New York, 1921).

Wolff, Theodor, *The Eve of 1914*, trans. (London, 1935).

(d) Studies

Adler, Cyrus, *Jacob Schiff. His Life and Letters* (London, 1929), 2 vols.

Ahmad, Feroz, *The Young Turks* (Oxford University Press, 1969).

Albertini, Luigi, *The Origins of the War of 1914* (Oxford University Press, 1952), 3 vols.

Altman, Alexander, *Studies in Nineteenth Century Jewish Intellectual History* (Harvard University Press, 1964).

Antonius, George, *The Arab Awakening* (New York, 1934).

Arnsberg, Paul, *Jacob H. Schiff: Von der Frankfurter Judengasse zur Wall Street* (Frankfurt-on-Main, 1972).

Auhagen, Hubert, *Beiträge zur Kenntnis der Landesnatur und der Landwirtschaft Syriens* (Berlin, 1913).

Becker, Joseph, *Paul de Lagarde* (Lübeck, 1935).

Bein, Alex, *The Return to the Soil* (Jerusalem, 1952).

—— *Theodore Herzl: A Biography* (London, 1957).

Bemis, Samuel Flagg, *A Diplomatic History of the United States* (New York, 1950).

Ben-Horin, Meir, *Max Nordau: Philosopher of Human Solidarity* (New York, 1956).

Berlin, Isaiah, *The Life and Opinions of Moses Hess* (Cambridge University Press, 1959).

Bodenheimer, Henriette Hannah (ed.), *Im Anfang der zionistischen Bewegung* (Frankfurt-on-Main, 1965).

—— *Die Zionisten und das kaiserliche Deutschland* (Bensberg, 1972).

Böhm, Adolf, *Die zionistische Bewegung*, 2nd enlarged edn. (Tel Aviv, 1935), 2 vols.

Braunthal, Julius, *History of the International* (New York, 1967), ii.

Bruntz, George G., *Allied Propaganda and the Collapse of the German Empire in 1918* (Stamford University Press, 1938).

Chambers, Frank P., *The War behind the War, 1914–1918* (London, 1939).

Chirol, Valentine, *Fifty Years in a Changing World* (London, 1927).

Chouragi, André, *Theodor Herzl* (Paris, 1960).

Cohen, Israel, *The Zionist Movement* (London, 1945).

—— *A Short History of Zionism* (London, 1951).

—— *Theodor Herzl: His Life and Times* (London, 1953).

—— *Theodor Herzl, Founder of Political Zionism* (London, 1959).

Cohn, Emile Bernhard, *David Wolffsohn: Herzls Nachfolger* (Amsterdam, 1939).

Conder, Claude Reignier, *Tent Work in Palestine*. Palestine Exploration Fund (London, 1878), ii.

Conze, Werner, *Polnische Nation und deutsche Politik* (Cologne, 1958).

Cumming, Henry H., *Franco-British Rivalry in the Post-war Near-East* (London, 1938).

Dahlin, Ebba, *French and German Public Opinion on Declared War Aims, 1914–1918* (Stamford University Press, 1933).

Davison, Roderic H., *Reform in the Ottoman Empire, 1856–1876* (Princeton University Press, 1963).

Dawson, William Harbutt, *The German Empire, 1867–1914* (London, 1919), 2 vols.

De Novo, John A., *American Interests and Policies in the Middle East, 1900–1939* (Minneapolis, 1963).

Dill, Marshall, *Germany: a Modern History* (University of Michigan, 1961).

Dillon, E. J., *The Eclipse of Russia* (London, 1918).

Druck, David, *Baron Edmund Rothschild. The Story of Practical Idealism* (London, 1928).

Dubnow, Simon M., *History of the Jews in Russia and Poland*, trans. (Philadelphia, 1916), 3 vols.

—— *Die neueste Geschichte des jüdischen Volkes, 1789–1914* (Berlin, 1923), 3 vols.

—— *Die Weltgeschichte des jüdischen Volkes* (Berlin, 1929), 10 vols.

Earle, Edward Mead, *Turkey, the Great Powers and the Bagdad Railway. A Study in Imperialism* (London, 1923).

Elbogen, Ismar, *A Century of Jewish Life* (Philadelphia, 1946).

Emin, Ahmed, *Turkey in the World War* (Yale University Press, 1930).

Engle, Anita, *The Nili Spies* (London, 1959).

Epstein, Klaus, *Erzberger and the Dilemma of German Democracy* (Princeton University Press, 1959).

Evans, Laurence, *United States Policy and the Partition of Turkey, 1914–1924* (Baltimore, 1965).

Eversley, Lord, *The Turkish Empire* (London, 1923).

Eyck, Erich, *Das persönliche Regiment Wilhelm II. Politische Geschichte des deutschen Kaiserreiches von 1890–1914* (Zürich, 1948).

Fay, Sidney B., *The Origins of the World War*, 2nd edn. (New York, 1934), 2 vols.

Feder, Ernst, *Politik und Humanität, Paul Nathan. Ein Lebensbild* (Berlin, 1929).

Fischer, Fritz, *Griff nach der Weltmacht. Die Kriegszielpolitik des kaiserlichen Deutschland: 1914–1918* (Düsseldorf, 1961).

Flenley, Ralph, *Modern German History* (London, 1959).

Florinsky, Michael T., *Russia. A History and an Interpretation* (London, 1960), 2 vols.

Franco, Moïse, *Essai sur l'histoire des Israélites de l'Empire ottoman* (Paris, 1897).

Friedman, Isaiah, *The Question of Palestine, 1914–1918: British–Jewish–Arab Relations* (London, 1973).

Galante, Abraham, *Turcs et Juifs* (Stamboul, 1932).

—— *Don Solomon Aben Jaech* (Stamboul, 1936).

—— *Histoire des Juifs d'Istamboul* (Stamboul, 1941).

Gatzke, Hans W., *Germany's Drive to the West* (Baltimore, 1950).

Geiss, Immanuel, *Der polnische Grenzstreifen, 1914–1918. Ein Beitrag zur deutschen Kriegszielpolitik im Ersten Weltkrieg* (Lübeck, 1960),

Gooch, George P., *Recent Revelations of European Diplomacy* (London, 1930, also 1940 edn.).

—— *Before the War. Studies in Diplomacy* (London, 1936), 2 vols.

Goodman, Paul, *Zionism in England* (London, 1949).

Görlitz, Walter, *The German General Staff. Its History and Structure, 1657–1945*, trans. (London, 1953).

Gottlieb, Wolfram W., *Studies in Secret Diplomacy during the First World War* (London, 1957).

Graetz, Heinrich, *History of the Jews* (Philadelphia, 1894), 5 vols.

Grattan, C. Hartley, *Why We Fought* (New York, 1929).

Greenberg, Louis, *The Jews in Russia: The Struggle for Emancipation, 1881–1917* (Yale University Press, 1951), 2 vols.

Gunter, Plant W., *The Rise of Reform Judaism* (New York, 1963).

Haas, Jacob de, *Louis Brandeis* (New York, 1929).

—— *History of Palestine* (New York, London, 1934).

Hall, Edward, *A Treatise on International Law*, 8th edn. (Oxford University Press, 1924).

Haller, Johannes, *Philip Eulenburg: The Kaiser's Friend*, trans. E. C. Mayne (London, 1930), 2 vols.

Halpern, Ben, *The Idea of the Jewish State* (Cambridge, Mass., 1961).

Headlam-Morley, James W., *Studies in Diplomatic History* (London, 1930).

Helfferisch, Karl, *Die deutsche Türkenpolitik* (Berlin, 1929).

Helfritz, Hans, *Wilhelm II. als Kaiser und König. Eine historische Studie* (Zürich, 1954).

Henderson, Philip, *The Life of Laurence Oliphant* (London, 1956).

Hendrick, Burton J., *The Life and Letters of Walter M. Page* (London, 1926), iii.

Heyd, Uriel, *Foundations of Turkish Nationalism* (London, 1950).

Howard, Harry, *The Partition of Turkey, 1913–1923* (Norman, Oklahoma, 1931).

Hyamson, Albert, *British Projects for the Restoration of the Jews* (London, 1917).

Holdheim, Samuel, *Geschichte der Entstehung und Entwickelung der jüdischen Reformgemeinde in Berlin* (Berlin, 1857).

Janowsky, Oscar, *The Jews and Minority Rights, 1898–1919* (New York, 1933).

Jöhlinger, Otto, *Bismarck und die Juden* (Berlin, 1921).

Johnpoll, Bernard J., *The Politics of Futility: The General Jewish Workers Bund of Poland, 1917–43* (Oxford University Press, 1961).

Kohn, Hans, *The Mind of Germany. The Education of a Nation* (New York, 1960).

Kohut, Adolph, *Judenfreunde* (Berlin, 1913).

Kreppel, Jonas, *Der Weltkrieg und die Judenfrage* (Vienna, 1915).

Kruck, Alfred, *Geschichte des Alldeutschen Verbandes, 1890–1939* (Wiesbaden, 1954).

Kühlmann, Richard von, *Die Diplomaten* (Berlin, 1939).

Langer, William L., *The Diplomacy of Imperialism, 1890–1902* (New York, London, 1935), 2 vols.

Laqueur, Walter, *A History of Zionism* (London, 1972).

Lasswell, Harold D., *Propaganda Technique in the World War* (New York, 1927).

Lepsius, Johannes, *Deutschland und Armenien, 1914–1918* (Potsdam, 1919).

Levy, J., *Fichte und die Juden* (Berlin, 1935).

Lewin, Percy Evans, *The German Road to the East* (London, 1916).

Lewinsohn, Ludwig, *Theodor Herzl: A Portrait for this Age* (New York, 1955).

Lewis, Bernard, *The Emergence of Modern Turkey* (London, 1961).

Lichtheim, Richard, *Die Geschichte des deutschen Zionismus* (Jerusalem, 1954).

Löwenthal, Marvin, *The Jews of Germany* (Philadelphia, 1944).

Luke, Harry C. and Keith-Roach, Edward, *The Handbook of Palestine and Transjordan* (London, 1930).

MacMunn, George and Falls, Cyril (eds.), *History of the Great War. Military Operations in Egypt and Palestine* (London, 1928–30), 3 vols.

Madariaga, Salvador de, *Spain* (London, 1942).

Manuel, Frank, *The Realities of American–Palestine Relations* (Washington, 1949).

Margalith, Israel, *Le Baron Edmond de Rothschild et la colonisation juive en Palestine: 1882–1899* (Paris, 1957).

May, Ernest R., *The World War and American Isolation, 1914–1917* (Harvard University Press, Cambridge, 1959).

Mayer, Arno J., *Political Origins of the New Diplomacy, 1917–1918* (New Haven, Conn., 1959).

Mears, E. G. (ed.), *Modern Turkey* (New York, 1924).

Medlicott, W. N., *The Congress of Berlin and After. A Diplomatic History of the Near Eastern Settlement, 1878–1880* (London, 1938).

Meisner, Otto H., *Militärattachés und Militärbevollmächtigte in Preussen und im Deutschen Reich* (Berlin, 1957).

Meyer, Henry Cord, *Mitteleuropa in German Thought and Action, 1815–1845* (The Hague, 1955).

Miller, William, *The Ottoman Empire and its Successors, 1801–1927*, 4th edn. (Cambridge University Press, 1936).

Mowat, Robert B., *History of European Diplomacy, 1914–1925* (London, 1928).

Mühlmann, Carl, *Deutschland und die Türkei, 1913–1914* (Berlin, 1929).

—— *Das deutsch-türkische Waffenbündnis im Weltkriege* (Leipzig, 1940).

Münz, Sigmund, *Prince Bülow: The Statesman and Man*, trans. A. Chambers (London, 1935).

Nawratski, Curt, *Die jüdische Kolonisation Palästinas* (Munich, 1914, Berlin, 1919).

Nielsen, Frederick, *Das moderne Judentum, seine Emanzipation und Reform* (Flensburg, 1880).

Nordau, Anna and Maxa, *Max Nordau: A Biography*, trans. (New York, 1943).

Paquet, Alfons, *Die jüdischen Kolonien in Palästina*. Deutsche Orientbücherei, hrsg. von Ernst Jäckh (Weimar, 1915).

Parkes, James, *A History of Palestine from 135 A.D. to Modern Times* (London, 1949).

Philipson, David, *The Reform Movement in Judaism* (London, 1931).

Pietri, François, *Napoléon et les Israélites* (Paris, 1966).

Pinson, Koppel, *Modern Germany: Its History and Civilization* (London, 1954).

Poliak, A. N., *Feudalism in Egypt, Syria, Palestine and the Lebanon, 1250–1900* (London, 1939).

Posener, S., *Adolphe Crémieux* (Paris, 1933), i.

Prothero, George W., *German Policy before the War* (London, 1916).

Pulzer, Peter C. J., *The Rise of Political Anti-Semitism in Germany and Austria* (London, New York, 1964).

Rabinowicz, Oscar K., *Fifty Years of Zionism* (London, 1952).

—— *Herzl, Architect of the Balfour Declaration* (New York, 1958).

Ramsaur, Ernst Edmondson, *The Young Turks, Prelude to the Revolution of 1908* (Princeton University Press, 1957).

Reichman, Eva G., *Hostages of Civilisation. A Study of the Social Courses of Anti-Semitism* (London, 1950).

Revusky, Abraham, *Jews in Palestine* (London, 1938).

Ritter, Gerhard, *Staatskunst und Kriegshandwerk. Das Problem des 'Militarismus' in Deutschland* (Munich, 1954).

—— *Der Schlieffen Plan* (Munich–Oldenburg, 1956). Also trans. into English (London, 1958).

—— *Deutsche Militär-Attachés und das Auswärtige Amt* (Heidelberg, 1959).

Rohrbach, Paul, *Deutschland unter den Weltvölkern. Materialien zur auswärtigen Politik, 1899–1918* (Berlin, 1908).

—— *Die Bagdadbahn* (Berlin, 1912).

Roloff, Gustav, *Die Orientpolitik Napoleons* (Weimar, 1916).

Rosenberg, Arthur, *The Birth of the German Republic, 1871–1918* (London, 1931).

Roth, Cecil, *A Short History of the Jewish People* (London, 1948).

—— *The House of Nasi. The Duke of Naxos* (Philadelphia, 1948).

Ruppin, Arthur, *The Jews of Today*, English trans. (London, 1913).

—— *Syrien als Wirtschaftsgebiet*, 2nd edn. (Berlin, 1920).

—— *The Jews in the Modern World* (London, 1934).

Rustam, As'ad Jibrail, *Materials for a corpus of Arab Documents relating to the History of Syria under Mehemet Ali Pasha* (Beirut, 1930–4), 5 vols.

Schechtman, Joseph B., *The Jabotinsky Story, 1880–1923* (New York, 1956), 2 vols.

Schieber, Clara E., *The Transformation of American Sentiment towards Germany, 1870–1914* (New York, 1923).

Schorsch, Ismar, *Jewish Reactions to German Anti-Semitism, 1870–1914* (New York, 1972).

Schreiber, Emanuel, *Abraham Geiger als Reformator des Judentums* (Loebau, 1879).

Schreiner, G. A., *The Craft Sinister* (New York, 1920).

Schwarz, Solomon M., *The Jews in Soviet Russia* (Syracuse University Press, 1951).

Seligman, Caesar, *Geschichte der jüdischen Reformbewegung von Mendelsohn bis zur Gegenwart* (Frankfurt-on-Main, 1922).

Seton-Watson, Robert William, *The Rise of Nationality in the Balkans* (London, 1917).

Seymour, Charles, *American Diplomacy during the World War* (Baltimore, 1934).

Sibner, Edmund, *Moses Hess* (Leiden, 1966).

Simon, Leon, *Ahad Ha'am. A Biography* (London, 1960).

Snyder, Louis L., *From Bismarck to Hitler* (University of Pennsylvania Press, 1935).

Sokolow, Nahum, *History of Zionism* (London, 1919), 2 vols.

Sombart, Werner, *Die Zukunft der Juden* (Leipzig, 1912).

Sontag, Raymond J., *Germany and England. Background to Conflict, 1848–1894* (New York, London, 1938).

Sousa, Nasim, *The Capitulatory Regime of Turkey* (London, Baltimore, 1933).

Spectator, *Prince Bülow and the Kaiser* (London, n.d.).

Stein, Leo, *The Racial Thinking of Richard Wagner* (New York, 1950).

Stein, Leonard, *Zionism* (London, 1932).

—— *The Balfour Declaration* (London, 1961).

Stern-Rubarth, Edgar, *Edgar Graf Brockdorff-Rantzau. Wanderer zwischen zwei Welten. Ein Lebensbild* (Berlin, 1929).

Temperley, H. D. V., *England and the Near East: The Crimea* (London, 1936).

Tibawi, A. L., *British Interests in Palestine: 1800–1901* (London, 1961).

Toynbee, Arnold J., *Turkey. A Past and a Future* (New York, 1917).

—— and Kirkwood, K. P., *Turkey* (London, 1926).

Trietsch, Davis, *Die Juden der Türkei* (Leipzig, 1915).

Trumpener, Ulrich, *Germany and the Ottoman Empire, 1914–1918* (Princeton University Press, 1968).

Tuchman, Barbara, *August 1914* (London, 1962).

Valentin, Veit, *The German People*, trans. (New York, 1946).

Walworth, Arthur, *Woodrow Wilson—World Prophet* (New York, London, 1958).

Wavell, Archibald P., Lt.-Gen., *The Palestine Campaign* (London, 1941).

Webster, Charles K., *The Foreign Policy of Palmerston* (London, 1951), i.

Wertheimer, Mildred S., *The Pan-German League, 1880–1914* (New York, 1924).

Wheeler-Bennett, John, Sir, *The Nemesis of Power: The German Army in Politics, 1918–1945* (London, 1953).

—— *Brest-Litovsk. The Forgotten Peace. March 1918* (London, 1956).

Wiener, Max, *Abraham Geiger and Liberal Judaism* (English trans. Philadelphia, 1962).

Wriston, Henry Merriott, *Executive Agents in American Foreign Relations* (London, 1929).

Zechlin, Egmont, *Die deutsche Politik und die Juden im Ersten Weltkrieg* (Göttingen, 1969).

Zeine, Zeine N., *Arab–Turkish Relations and the Emergence of Arab Nationalism* (Beirut, 1958).

Zeman, Zbynck, A. B., *The Break-up of the Hapsburg Empire, 1914–1918* (Oxford University Press, 1961).

Zlocisti, Theodor, *Moses Hess* (Berlin, 1921).

(e) Articles and Pamphlets

Adler, Saul, 'The Palestine Question in the Wilson Era', *Jewish Social Studies*, x (Oct. 1948), no. 4.

Angell, James, B., 'The Turkish Capitulations', *American Historical Review*, vi (Jan. 1901), 254–9.

Anstett, Jean-Jacques, 'Paul de Lagarde', *The Third Reich* (London, 1955).

Appun, Charles, 'L'ambassade de Bernstorff à Washington', *Revue historique de Guerre mondiale*, iii (1925), 297–329.

Ballod, Carl, 'Das Ostjuden Problem und die Frage seiner Lösung durch den Zionismus', *Europäische Staats- und Wirtschafts-Zeitung*, Nr. 10 (Berlin, 1916).

Barker, J. E., 'The Future of Asiatic Turkey', *XIX Century and After* (June 1916), no. 472.

Bodenheimer, Max, 'Theodor Herzl', *Theodor Herzl—A Memorial*, ed. M. W. W. Weisgal (New York, 1929).

Brodetsky, Selig, 'Cultural Work in Palestine', *Zionism and the Jewish Future*, ed. Harry Sacher (London, 1916).

Brunauer, Esther C., 'The Peace Proposals of December 1916–January 1917', *Journal of Modern History*, iv (Dec. 1932), no. 4, 544–71.

Cahnman, Werner, J., 'Munich and the First Zionist Congress', *Historia Judaica*, iii (1941), 7–23.

Chapman, Maybelle K., 'Great Britain and the Bagdad Railway, 1888–1914', *Smith College Studies in History*, xxxi (1948).

Christoph, Paulus 'Die Tempel Colonien in Palästina', *Zeitschrift des Deutschen Palästina-Vereins*, vi (Leipzig, 1883), 31–42.

Conze, Werner, 'Nationalstaat oder Mitteleuropa?: Die Deutschen des Reiches und die Nationalitätenfrage Ostmitteleuropas im Ersten Weltkrieg', *Deutschland und Europa*, ed. W. Conze (Düsseldorf, 1951).

Craig, Gordon A., 'Military Diplomats in the Prussian Army', *Political Science Quarterly*, lxiv (Mar. 1949), 65–94.

Earle, Edward Meade, 'The Secret Anglo-German Convention of 1914 regarding Asiatic Turkey', *Political Science Quarterly*, xxxviii, (1923).

Epstein, Klaus, 'The Development of German-Austrian War Aims in the Spring of 1917', *Journal of Central European Affairs*, xvii (Apr. 1957), no. 1.

—— 'Erzberger's Political Operations', *Journal of Central European Affairs*, xix (1959–60).

Esh, Saul, 'Kurt Blumenfeld on the Modern Jew and Zionism', *Jewish Journal of Sociology*, vi (1964), 232–42.

Feder, Ernest, 'Paul Nathan and His Work for East-European and Palestinian Jewry', *Historia Judaica. A Journal of Studies in Jewish History, Especially in the Legal and Social History of the Jews*, xiv (New York, 1952).

—— 'Paul Nathan: The Man and his Work', *The Leo Baeck Institute Year Book*, iii (London, 1958).

Fischer, Fritz, 'Deutsche Kriegsziele, Revolutionierung und Separatfrieden im Osten, 1914–1918', *Historische Zeitschrift*, lxxxviii (1959), 249–310.

Fraenkel, Josef, *The History of the Shekel* (London, 1952).

—— 'Lucien Wolf and Theodor Herzl', *Transactions of the Jewish Historical Society of England* (London, 1960).

Friedman, Isaiah, 'The Austro-Hungarian Government and Zionism, 1897–1918', *Jewish Social Studies* (July, October 1965), 147–67, 236–49.

—— 'Lord Palmerston and the Protection of Jews in Palestine, 1839–1851', *Jewish Social Studies*, xxx (Jan. 1968), no. 1, 23–41.

—— 'German Intervention on Behalf of the Yishuv, 1917', *Jewish Social Studies* (Jan. 1971), 23–43.

Gelber, Nathan M., 'The Palestine Question and the Congress of Berlin', *Historia Judaica*, ii (Apr. 1940) (New York).

—— 'An Attempt to Internationalize Salonica: 1912–13', *Jewish Social Studies*, xvii (1955), no. 2, 105–20.

Graupe, Heinz M., 'Kant und das Judentum', *Zeitschrift für Religions- und Geistesgeschichte*, 4 (Cologne, 1961), pp. 308–33.

Gross, Walter, 'The Zionist Students' Movement', *Leo Baeck Institute Year Book*, iv (London, 1959), 143–64.

Hoffman, J., 'Die wirtschaftliche Arbeit der Templer in Palästina', *Deutsches Orientjahrbuch* (Prien a. Chimsee, 1913), 46–50.

Kahn, Ernst, 'The Frankfurter Zeitung', *Leo Baeck Institute Year Book*, ii (1957), 228–35.

Katz, Jacob, 'The German-Jewish Utopia of Social Emancipation', *Studies of the Leo Baeck Institute*, ed. Max Kreutzberger (New York, 1967).

Kedourie, Elie, 'Young Turks, Freemasons and Jews', *Middle Eastern Studies* (Jan. 1971).

Kobler, Franz, 'Napoleon and the Restoration of the Jews to Palestine: Discovery of an Historic Document', *New Judea*, xvi, no. 12, xvii, nos. 1–2, 3, 5.

Kurat, Y. T., 'How Turkey Drifted into World War I', *Studies in International History*, ed. K. Bourne and D. C. Watt (London, 1967).

Laqueur, Walter, 'The German Youth Movement and the Jewish Question', *Leo Baeck Institute Year Book*, vi (1961), 193–204.

Lorch, Fritz, 'Die deutschen Tempelkolonien in Palästina', *Mitteilungen und Nachrichten des Deutschen Palästina-Vereins* (Leipzig, 1909).

Mandel, Neville, 'Attempts at an Arab–Zionist Entente, 1913–1914', *Middle Eastern Studies* (Apr. 1946).

—— 'Turks, Arabs and Jewish Immigration into Palestine, 1882–1914', *St. Antony's Papers*, no. 17, *Middle Eastern Affairs*, no. 4, ed. Hourani (Oxford, 1965).

Meyer, Gustav, 'Early German Socialism and Jewish Emancipation', *Jewish Social Studies*, i, no. 4, (New York, 1939).

Meyer, Michael, 'Great Debate on Antisemitism. Jewish Reaction to New Hostility in Germany, 1879–80', *Leo Baeck Institute Year Book*, ii (1966), 137–70.

Mutius, Gerhard von, 'Die Türkei, 1911–1914', *Preussische Jahrbücher*, ccxxxvi (1934), 212–20.

Namier, Louis B., 'Introduction to Arthur Ruppin', *The Jews in the Modern World* (London, 1934).

Pinson, Koppel S., 'The National Theories of Simon Dubnow', *Jewish Social Studies*, x (Oct. 1948), no. 4, 335–58.

Rabinowicz, Oscar K., 'Herzl and England', *Jewish Social Studies*, xiii (Jan. 1951), 25–46.

—— 'New Light on the East Africa Scheme', *The Rebirth of Israel*, ed. Israel Cohen (London, 1952).

Ravdal, G. B., 'Capitulations', *Modern Turkey*, ed. E. G. Mears (New York, 1924).

Reichmann, Hans, 'Der Centralverein deutscher Staatsbürger jüdischen Glaubens', *Festschrift zum 80. Geburtstag von Leo Baeck* (London, 1953).

Reichmann-Jungmann, Eva, 'Der Centralverein deutscher Staatsbürger jüdischen Glaubens', Sonderabdruck aus dem Septemberheft 1930 der *Süddeutschen Monatshefte: Die Judenfrage*, 818–24.

Reinharz, Jehuda, '*Deutschtum* und *Judentum* in the Ideology of the Centralverein deutscher Staatsbürger jüdischen Glaubens, 1893–1914', *Jewish Social Studies* (Jan. 1974), 19–39.

Ritter, Gerhard, 'The Military and Politics in Germany', *Journal of Central European Affairs*, xvii (Oct. 1957), no. 3.

—— 'The Political Attitude of the German Army, 1900–1944', *Studies in Diplomatic History and Historiography in Honour of G. P. Gooch*, ed. A. O. Sarkissan (London, 1961), 331–47.

Rosenbaum, E., 'Max M. Warburg and Company. Merchant Bankers of Hamburg', *Leo Baeck Institute Year Book*, vii (1961), 121–41.

Rosenberg, Arthur, 'Treitschke und die Juden', *Die Gesellschaft* (Berlin, 1930), 78–83.

Roth, Cecil, 'The Jews of Jerusalem in the Seventeenth Century', *Miscellanies of the Jewish Historical Society of England* (1935).

Sauzin, Louis, 'The Political Thought of Constantin Frantz', *The Third Reich* (London, 1955).

Schmidt, Bernadotte, E., 'The Relation of Public Opinion and Foreign Affairs before and during the First World War', *Studies in Diplomatic History and Historiography in Honour of G.P. Gooch*, ed. Sarkissian (London, 1961), 322–30.

—— 'The Origins of the First World War', *From Metternich to Hitler, Aspects of British and Foreign History, 1814–1939*, ed. W. N. Medlicott (London, 1963).

Schmidt, H. D., 'The Terms of Emancipation, 1871–1812', *Leo Baeck Institute Year Book*, i (1956), pp. 28–47.

Seton-Watson, Robert, 'Pan-German Aspirations in the Near East', *Journal of the Royal Society of Arts*, 64 (31 Mar. 1916), no. 3306.

Silberstein, Gerard E., 'The Central Powers and the Second Turkish Alliance, 1915', *Slavic Review*, xxiv (1965), 77–89.

Steed, Wickham, 'A non-Jewish view of Zionism', *Chaim Weizmann. A Tribute on his 70th birthday*, ed. Paul Goodman (London, 1945), Pt. I, sect. xiii, pp. 69–77.

Thayer, Lucius E., 'The Capitulations of the Ottoman Empire and the Question of Their Abrogation as it Affects the United States', *American Journal of International Law*, xvii (Apr. 1923), 207–33.

Thimme, Friedrich, 'Fürst Bülow und Kaiser Wilhelm II.', *Front wider Bülow. Staatsmänner, Diplomaten und Forscher zu seinen Denkwürdigkeiten* (Munich, 1931).

Thon, Jacob, 'Jewish Schools in Palestine', *Zionist Work in Palestine*, ed. Israel Cohen (New York, 1912)—a translation of a special issue of *Die Welt*, 1912.

Toury, Jacob, 'Organizational Problems of German Jewry', *Leo Baeck Institute Year Book*, xiii (1968), 57–90.

Trumpener, Ulrich, 'German Military Aid to Turkey in 1914: An Historical Reevaluation', *Journal of Modern History*, xxxii (June 1960), 145–9.

—— 'Liman von Sanders and the German–Ottoman Alliance', *Journal of Contemporary History*, i (1966), 179–92.

Vermeil, Edmund, 'The Origin, Nature and Development of German Nationalist Ideology in the 19th and 20th Centuries', *The Third Reich* (London, 1955).

Walson, C. M., 'Bonaparte's Expedition to Palestine in 1799', *Palestine Exploration Fund* (Jan. 1917).

Weisbord, Robert G., 'Israel Zangwill's Jewish Territorial Organization and the East African Zion', *Jewish Social Studies* (April 1968), 89–108.

Weltsch, Robert, 'Deutscher Zionismus in der Rückschau', *In zwei Welten*, ed. Hans Tramer (Tel Aviv, 1962), pp. 27–42.

Wilhelm, Kurt, 'The Jewish Community in the Post-emancipation Period', *Leo Baeck Institute Year Book*, ii (1957), 47–75.

Wolf, John B., 'The Diplomatic History of the Bagdad Railroad', *University of Missouri Studies*, xi, no. 2 (April 1936) (Columbia).

Zechlin, Egmont, 'Friedensbestrebungen und Revolutionierungsversuche im Ersten Weltkrieg', *Aus Politik und Zeitgeschichte*. Beilage zur Wochenzeitung. *Das Parlament* (21 June, 1961).

III. PUBLISHED SOURCES IN HEBREW

(a) Letters, Diaries, Memoirs, Contemporary Statements, etc.

Aaronsohn, Aaron, *Yoman . . . [Diary of . . .]* (Tel Aviv, 1970).

Ahad Ha'am, *Ig'groth Ahad Ha'am [Letters]* (Jerusalem, Berlin, 1924), iv–v.

—— 'Emeth Me'Eretz-Israel' ['The Truth from Eretz-Israel'] *Al Parashat Derachim [At the Crossroads]* (Berlin, 1924), i.

Ben-Yehuda, Eliezer, *Kol Kitvey . . . [Works of . . .]* (Jerusalem, 1941), v.

Ben-Zvi, Itzhak, *Ktavim [Works]* (Tel Aviv, 1936), i.

Bodenheimer, Max, *Darki L'Zion [My Road to Zion]* (Jerusalem, 1953).

Cohn-Reiss, Ephraim, *M'Zichronoth Ish Yerushalaim [Memoirs]* (Jerusalem, 1933, 1936), 2 vols.

Dizengoff, Meir, *Im Tel Aviv Bagola [Tel Aviv Evacuated]* (Tel Aviv, 1931).

Elmaliyach, Abraham, *Eretz-Israel V'Suria Bimey Milchemet Haolam [Palestine and Syria during the First World War]* (Jerusalem, 1928–9), 2 vols.

Gordon, David, *Ktavim [Works]* (Tel Aviv, 1925–9), 5 vols.

Hacohen, Mordechai Ben-Hillel, *Milchemet Ha-Amin* Jerusalem, [*War among the Nations*] (Tel Aviv, 1929–30), 2 vols.

Herzl, Theodor, *Michtavim [Letters]* (Tel Aviv, 1937).

Idelovitch, David, 'Gole Eretz-Israel B'Mitzraim' ['The Palestine Evacuees in Egypt'], *Miyamim Rishonim*, monthly (Tel Aviv, Dec. 1934), i.

Kalisher, Zvi Hirsch, *Mivhar Ktavim [Selected Writings]* (Tel Aviv, 1943).

Krinitzi, Abraham, *B'Koah Ha-Ma'ase [By Virtue of the Deed]* (Tel Aviv, 1940).

Lichtheim, Richard, *Toldoth Haziyonut B'Germania* [Hebrew edition of *Die Geschichte des deutschen Zionismus*] (Jerusalem, 1951).

—— *She'ar Yashuv—Zichronot Ziyoni M'Germania [A Remnant will Return. Memoirs]* (Tel Aviv, 1953).

Motzkin, Leo, *Ktavim U'Neumim Nivcharim [Essays and Selected Speeches]*, edited and accompanied by a biographical essay by Dr. A. Bein (Jerusalem, 1939).

Ruppin, Arthur, *Pirkey Chayai [Chapters from my Life]*, ed. Dr. A. Bein (Tel Aviv, 1944, 1947), 2 vols.

Sefer Ha'aliya Hashniya [The Book of the Second Aliya], ed. E. Schochat (Tel Aviv, 1947).

Sefer Hashomer [*The Book of the Hashomer*], ed. I. Ben-Zvi, I. Schohat, and others (Tel Aviv, 1957).

Sefer Hayovel shel Petach Tikva [*Jubilee Book of Petach-Tikva*], ed. Yaari Poleskin (Petach–Tikva, 1929).

Sefer Hayovel L'Rishon L'Zion [*Jubillee Book of Rishon L'Zion*], ed. David Idelovitch (Rishon L'Zion, 1941).

Shenkin, Menachen, *Kitvei Menahem Shenkin* [*Writings of Menahem Shenkin*], ed. A. Hermoni (Jerusalem, 1936), i.

Smilansky, Moshe, *Zichronot* [*Memoirs*] (Tel Aviv, 1929), 3 vols.

Tschlenow, Yechiel, *Pirkey Hayav U'Peulato, Zichronot, Ketavim, Neumim, V'Michtavim* [*His Life, Activities, Memoirs, Letters, and Speeches*] ed. S. Eisenstadt (Tel Aviv, 1937).

Warburg, Otto, *Michtavim, Ne'umim, Uma'amarim* [*Letters, Speeches, and Articles*], ed. Jacob Thon and accompanied by a biographical essay (Tel Aviv, 1948).

Yaffe, Hillel, *Dor Ma'apilim* [*Generation of Pioneers*] (Tel Aviv, 1939).

(b) Studies and Articles in Hebrew

Alsberg, Paul Abraham, 'The Political Orientation of the Zionist Executive on the Eve of the First World War', *Zion. A Quarterly for Research in Jewish History*, xxii (1957), nos. 2–3.

Ben-Zvi, Itzhak, 'Le'Yishuvenu B'Eretz-Israel B'Mea XVII' ['Palestine Settlement in the Seventeenth Century'] *Zion* (Apr.–July 1942).

—— *Eretz-Israel Ve'Yeshuva* [*Palestine under Ottoman Rule. Four Centuries of History*] (Jerusalem, 1955).

—— and Benayahu, M. (eds.), *Sefer Tsfat* [*Safad Volume. Studies and Texts on the History of the Jewish Community in Safad*] (Jerusalem, 1962).

Bodenheimer, Henriette Hannah (ed.), *Toldot Tohnit Basel* [*The History of the Basle Programme*] (Jerusalem, 1947).

Braslavsky, Moshe, *Tnuat Hapoalim Ha-Eretz-Israelit* [*The Palestine Labour Movement*] (Tel Aviv, 1955), 2 vols.

Braslawski, Joseph, 'Jewish Settlement in Tiberias from Don Joseph Nasi to Ibn Yaish', *Zion* (Oct. 1939).

Dinaburg, Ben-Zion, 'Ideological Background of Palestine Immigration: 1740–1840', *Zion* (Apr. 1937).

—— 'The Beginnings of Hassidism and its Social and Messianic Elements', *Zion* (Apr.–July 1945).

Dinur, Ben-Zion (ed.), *Sefer Toldoth Ha-Hagana* [*History of Self-Defence*] (Tel Aviv, 1955), i.

Dubnow, Simon M., 'Ha-Chassidim Ha-Rishonim B'Eretz-Israel' ['The First Hassidim in Palestine'] *Pardess*, ii (Odessa, 1893).

—— *Divré-Yemey-Israel B'Dorot Ha-Achronim* [*History of the Jews during the Recent Generations*] (Berlin, 1924), 3 vols.

Feinberg, Nathan, 'The Basle Programme—its Legal Meaning', *Shivat Zion. Year Book of Research in Zionism and the State of Israel* (Jerusalem, 1950), i.

Gath, Ben-Zion, *Ha'Yishuv ha-Yehudi B'Eretz-Israel B'Shnot: 1840–1881* [*The Jewish Settlement in Palestine: 1840-1881*] (Jerusalem, 1963).

Gelber, Nahum M., *Hazharat Balfour V'Toldotea* [*History of the Balfour Declaration*] (Jerusalem, 1939).

—— *Napoleon* (Jerusalem, 1950).

Gruenbaum, Itzhak, *Hatnua Hatziyonit* [*The Zionist Movement*] (Jerusalem, 1949), 3 vols.

Halpern, Israel, *Ha-Aliyot Ha-Rishonot shel ha-Chassidim b'Eretz-Israel* [*The First Waves of Immigration of the Hassidim to Palestine*] (Jerusalem, 1940).

Horodetzki, Shlomo A., *Ha-Chassidut Ve'Hachassidim* [*Hassidism and the Hassidim*] (Jerusalem, 1923), iv.

Katznelson, Berl, *Prakim l'Toldoth Tnuat Ha-Poalim, Kitvei . . .* [*Chapters in the History of the Labour Movement*] (Tel Aviv, 1949).

Klausner, Israel, *Hibbath-Zion b'Rumania* (Jerusalem, 1958).

—— *B'Ithorer Am* [*Awakening of a People*] (Jerusalem, 1962).

—— 'Episodes in the History of the Hebrew Gymnasium in Jerusalem', *Sefer Ha-Yovel shel Ha-Gimnasya Ha-Ivrith* (Jerusalem, 1962).

Kressel, Getzel, *Moshe Hess* (Tel Aviv, 1961).

Marmor, D. I., 'The Diplomatic Negotiations of the Jewish Territorial Association and the Reasons for their Failure', *Zion* (Jerusalem; Sept. 1945–Apr. 1946 and July 1946).

Medzini, Moshe; *Ha-Mediniyuth Ha-Tziyonith* [*The Zionist Policy*] (Jerusalem, 1936).

Nili, eds. E. Livneh, J. Nedava, Y. Ephrati (Jerusalem, Tel Aviv, 1961).

Rozanes, Shlomo Abraham, *Divre-Y'me Israel b'Turgma* [*History of Jews in Turkey*] (Tel Aviv, 1930; Sofia, 1938), 5 vols.

Shochet, A., 'Yehudey Yerushalaim B'Mea XVIII' ['The Jews in Jerusalem in the Eighteenth Century'] *Zion*, i, no. 4 (1936).

Smilansky, Moshe, *Prakim B'Toledoth Ha-Yishuv* [*Chapters in the History of the Jewish Settlement in Palestine*] (Tel Aviv, 1945), 3 vols.

Szajkowski, Zosa, 'Alilath Damesek' ['The Damascus Affair'] *Zion* (Jerusalem, 1954).

Weinryb, Dov, 'Problems of Research on the History of the Jews in Palestine and their Economic Life since the Turkish Conquest', *Zion* (Jerusalem; July, Oct. 1937).

Yaari, Abraham, 'The Vicissitudes of the Ashkenazi Jews in Jerusalem at the Beginning of the Nineteenth Century' (reprint from *Sinai*) (Jerusalem, 1940).

Yavnieli, Shmuel, *Tkufat Hibbath-Zion* [*The Period of Hibbath-Zion*] (Jerusalem, 1961), 2 vols.

IV. NEWSPAPERS AND JOURNALS: DAILIES, WEEKLIES,
AND MONTHLIES

(Selected newspaper cuttings are found among the files of the German Foreign
Ministry and those of the Central Zionist Archives, Jerusalem.)

Agence Républicaine
Allgemeiner Anzeiger
Allgemen Handelsblad
American Jewish Chronicle
Berliner Lokalanzeiger
Berliner Tageblatt
Berlinske Tidende
Bulletin juif
Chemnitzer Volksstimme
Daily Telegraph
Das Grössere Deutschland
Das Jüdische Volk
Das Neue Deutschland
Davar (Hebrew daily), *Herzl Centenary Supplement* (6 May 1960)
De Maasbode Rotterdam
Der Jude
Der Orient
Der Tag
Deutsche Allgemeine Zeitung
Deutsche Levantzeitung
Deutsche Montags-Zeitung
Deutsche Politik. Wochenschrift für Welt- und Kulturpolitik
Deutsche Warte
Deutsche Zeitung
Deutsches Handelsarchiv (Oct. 1913)
Die Hilfe
Die Jüdische Presse. Konservative Wochenschrift
Die Wahrheit (Yiddish daily in New York)
Die Welt
Frankfurter Israelitisches Familienblatt
Frankfurter Zeitung
Gazette de Lausanne
Ha-Achdut
Hamburger Israelitisches Familienblatt
Hamburger Jüdische Nachrichten
Hatzefira (Hebrew weekly in Warsaw)
Israelitisches Familienblatt
Israelitisches Wochenblatt für die Schweiz
Jerusalem Post, Herzl Centenary Supplement (6 May 1960)
Jewish Chronicle
Jewish Labour Correspondence
Joodische Wachter
Journal de Genève

Jüdische Arbeits-Korrespondenz
Jüdische Korrespondenz
Jüdische Nachrichten
Jüdische Presse
Jüdische Rundschau
Jüdische Zeitung
Le Genevois
La Suisse (Geneva)
Le Peuple Juif
Kölnische Volkszeitung
Kölnische Zeitung
Lemberger Tageblatt
Manchester Guardian
Menora
Münchener Neueste Nachrichten
National Tidende
Neue Jüdische Monatshefte
Neue Preussische Kreuzzeitung
Neue Züricher Zeitung
New York Times
Norddeutsche Allgemeine Zeitung
Osmanisches Lloyd
Palestine. The Organ of the British Palestine Committee (4 vols.)
Petit Parisien
Petite République
Politische Jüdische Nachrichten
Reichsbote
Round Table
Sozialistische Monatshefte
The Times
Tribune de Genève
Tribune de Lausanne
Wochenblatt (Yiddish weekly in Copenhagen)
Zukunft
Züricher Post
Züricher Zeitung

V. REFERENCE BOOKS

Annual Register (London, 1898).
Cambridge Modern History, x (Cambridge, 1960).
Encyclopædia Britannica, iv (London, 1963).
Encyclopædia Ivrit, vi (Jerusalem, 1957).
Encyclopædia Judaica (Berlin, 1928).
Encyclopedia of Zionism and Israel, ed. Raphael Patai (Herzl Press, McGraw Hill, New York, 1971).
Jüdisches Lexicon (Berlin, 1928).
Wer ist Wer (Leipzig, 1922).
Zionistisches A-B-C Buch (Berlin, 1908).

Index